CELLULAR AUTOMATA - INNOVATIVE MODELLING FOR SCIENCE AND ENGINEERING

Edited by **Alejandro Salcido**

Cellular Automata - Innovative Modelling for Science and Engineering
Edited by Alejandro Salcido

Published by InTech
Janeza Trdine 9, 51000 Rijeka, Croatia

Publishing Process Manager Iva Lipovic

Technical Editor Teodora Smiljanic

Cover Designer InTech Design Team

Additional hard copies can be obtained from orders@intechopen.com

Cellular Automata - Innovative Modelling for Science and Engineering,
Edited by Alejandro Salcido
p. cm.
ISBN 978-953-307-172-5

For EU product safety concerns:
IN TECH d.o.o., Prolaz Marije Krucifikse Kozulić 3, 51000 Rijeka, Croatia,
info@intechopen.com or visit our website at intechopen.com.

Meet the editor

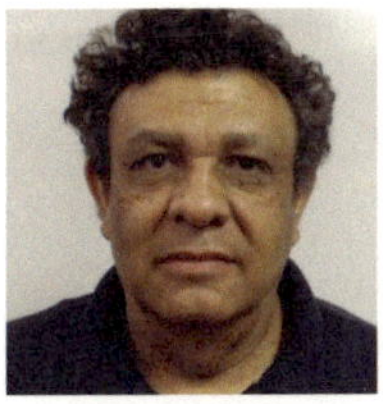

Alejandro Salcido is currently Lead Scientist in the Alternative Energy Division (División de Energías Alternas) at the Institute of Electrical Research (Instituto de Investigaciones Eléctricas) in Cuernavaca, Mexico. Dr. Salcido received his Ph.D. in Physics from the Physics Department of the Faculty of Sciences at the National University of Mexico (Universidad Nacional Autónoma de México, UNAM) in 1992. From 1979 up to 1991 Dr. Salcido was Staff Scientist (Statistical Physics and Lattice Gas Models) and Faculty Professor (Thermodynamics, Fluid Mechanics and Electrodynamics) at the Physics Department of UNAM. Dr. Salcido has published close to a hundred scholarly articles in international journals, proceedings of conferences and book chapters. His main research topics include micrometeorology, air pollution modelling, wind taxonomy, lattice gas dynamics, cellular automata fluids, traffic cellular automata, non-equilibrium thermodynamics, thermodynamic and phonon properties of high Tc superconductors, and mathematical modelling.

Contents

Preface

Modelling and simulation are disciplines of major importance for science and engineering. There is no science without models, and simulation has nowdays become a very useful tool, sometimes unavoidable, for development of both science and engineering. The numerical solution of differential equations has for many years been a paradigm of the computational approaches for simulation. Nevertheless, some conceptually different strategies for modelling and simulation of complex behaviour systems have been developed from the introduction of the innovative concept of cellular automata by Stanislaw Ulam and John Von Neumann in the early 1950s. Cellular automata are dynamical systems which consist of a finite-dimensional lattice, each site of which can have a finite number of states, and evolves in discrete time steps obeying a set of homogeneous local rules which define the system's dynamics. These rules are defined in such a way that the relevant laws of the phenomena of interest are fulfilled. Typically, only the nearest neighbours are involved in the updating of the lattice sites.

The main attractive feature of cellular automata is that, in spite of their conceptual simplicity which allows an easiness of implementation for computer simulation, such as a detailed and complete mathematical analysis in principle, they are able to exhibit a wide variety of amazingly complex behaviour. This feature of cellular automata has attracted the researchers' attention from a wide variety of divergent fields of the exact disciplines of science and engineering, but also of social sciences, and sometimes beyond. The collective complex behaviour of numerous systems, which emerge from the interaction of a multitude of simple individuals, is being conveniently modelled and simulated with cellular automata for very different purposes.

In this book, a number of innovative applications of cellular automata models in the fields of *Quantum Computing, Materials Science, Cryptography and Coding,* and *Robotics and Image Processing* are presented. Brief descriptions of these outstanding contributions are provided in the next paragraphs.

Quantum Computing. Chapter 1 presents an information-theoretic framework to investigate the relationship between stochastic behaviors and achievable reliable performance in quantum cellular automata technology. The central idea is that quantum cellular automata devices can be modelled as a network of unreliable information processing channels. In Chapter 2, cellular automata with graphane structured molecules and graphane nanoribbons to propagate and process digital information are proposed. The cells that make up the architecture of the automata correspond to the molecules and to sections of the nanoribbon. It is also intended to verify theoretically that the proposed system is scalable, and binary information can be stored, propagated and processed at room temperature. Chapter 3 describes a magnetic quantum dot cellular automata approach for twisting computation and its technological implementation. The fundamental technological hypothesis (the snake-clock implementation) is explained, and an example of circuit description is given, followed by a specific architectural solution adopted with the low-level details. The contribution presented in Chapter 4 extends and implements several of the reversible and quantum computing concepts to the context of elementary cellular automata, and this includes a new method for modelling and processing via the reversibility property in the existence of noise. The main contribution is the creation of a new algorithm that can be used in noisy discrete systems modelling using conservative reversible elementary cellular automata and the corresponding quantum modelling of such discrete systems. This approach considers the important modelling and processing case which uses Swap-based operations to represent reversible elementary cellular automata even in the presence of noise. Chapter 5 reviews self-assembly of InAs quantum dot molecules with different features fabricated by the combination of conventional Stranski-Krastanow growth mode and modified molecular beam epitaxy technique using thin or partial capping as well as droplet epitaxy. InGaAs quantum rings with square shaped nano-holes are realized by droplet epitaxy, which are utilized as nano-templates for quadra quantum dot molecules where four InAs quantum dots are situated at the four corners of a square. This quadra quantum dot set is a basic quantum cellular automata cell for future quantum computation. Chapter 6 provides a brief overview of the basic properties of quantum information processing and analyzes the quantum versions of classical cellular automata models. Then it examines an application of quantum cellular automata, which uses quantum computing to realize real-life based truly random network organization. This abstract machine is called a quantum cellular machine, and it is designed for controlling a truly random biologically-inspired network, and to integrate quantum learning algorithms and quantum searching into a controlled, self-organizing system. Chapter 7 proposes a new and simple approach for designing high-performance molecular quantum cellular automata. It reviews two approaches for the theoretical study on the two-site molecular quantum cellular automata and discusses the influence of complex charge n on the signal transmission through molecular quantum cellular automata.

Materials Science. Chapter 8 of this section discusses a combined approach of a three-dimensional frontal cellular automata model with a finite element model which has been developed for modelling the macrostructure formation during the solidification in the continuous casting line. This joint has allowed improving accuracy of modelling. Calculated distribution of the temperature gives a basis for the simulation of macrostructure formation close to the real one. In Chapter 9, a novel point automata method is developed and applied to model the dendritic growth process. The main advantages of this method are: no need for mesh generation or polygonisation; the governing equations are solved with respect to the location of points (not polygons) on the computational domain; it allows rotating dendrites in any direction since it has a limited anisotropy of the node arrangements; it offers a simple and powerful approach of cellular automata type simulations; it offers straightforward node refinement possibility, and straightforward extension to 3D. Chapter 10 proposes a model based upon the coupling of a modified cellular automaton model with the growth calculation of a nucleus in a given nucleation cell, to simulate the evolution of the dendritic structure in solidification of alloys. For a free dendritic growth in the undercooled melt, it is found that the proposed model can quantitatively describe the evolution of dendritic growth features, including the growing and coarsening of the primary trunks, the branching of the secondary and tertiary dendrite arms, as well as the solute segregation patterns. Moreover, the directional solidification with the columnar and equiaxed grains is simulated by the proposed method and the evolution from nucleation to impingement between grains is observed. Chapter 11 underlines that modelling at a mesoscopic scale using cellular automata appears as an interesting tool to understand general properties of corrosion processes. One part of the chapter focuses on the diffusion and the feedback effect of the layer on the corrosion rate, but no explicit reactions are taken into account. The model developed gives a simple description of a phenomenon of passivation. In other part the models are improved by introducing more explicitly some basic chemical and electrochemical processes. This was illustrated by considering a heterogeneous process in which a metal recovered by an insulating film is put in contact with an aggressive medium due to a local rupture in the film.

Cryptography and Coding. Chapter 12 describes the variable-length encryption method. It is a cryptographic model based on the backward interaction of cellular automata toggle rules. This method alternates during the ciphering process the employment of the original reverse algorithm with a variation inspired in Gutowitz's model, which adds extra bits when a preimage is calculated. Using the variable-length encryption method it is guaranteed that ciphering is possible even if an unexpected Garden-of-Eden state occurs. A short length ciphertext depends, however, on the secret key specification. The proper specification of the rules/key was deeply investigated in this chapter. In Chapter 13, as an application of quantum cellular automata technology, the Serpent block cipher (a finalist candidate of Advanced Encryption Standard) was implemented. This cryptographic algorithm has 32 rounds with a 128-bit block size and a 256-bit key size, and it consists of an initial permutation, 32 rounds, and a final permutation. Each round involves a key mixing operation, a pass through S-boxes, and a linear transformation. In the last round, the linear transformation is replaced by an additional key mixing operation. Simulation results were obtained from QCADesigner v2.0.3 software. Chapter 14 proposes a multi-dimensional and multi-rank pseudorandom generator for applied cryptography, which combines the 3D cellular automata algorithm and the linear feedback shift register architecture. The feasibility and efficiency of the algorithm were studied by using several tests. The final result showed they also can provide better pseudorandom key stream and pass the FIPS 140-1 standard tests. In Chapter 15, an efficient pseudorandom number generator based on hybrid between one-dimension and two-dimension cellular automata is proposed. The proposed algorithm is compared with previous works to check the quality of randomness. It could generate a good quality of randomness and pass by the ENT Walker and DIEHARD Marsaglia test suite. In Chapter 16, from a series of definitions, propositions and theorems, a solid foundation of variant logic framework has been constructed. Under selected sample images and operational matrices, a set of typical results is illustrated. This construction can be observed from different view-points under locally and globally symmetric considerations, in addition to detect emerging patterns from each recursively operations and a functional space viewpoint, further global transforming patterns can be identified. The mechanism can be developed further to establish foundations for logical construction of applications for computational models and structural optimisation requirements.

Robotics and Image Processing. Chapter 17 presents a problem of human and robot interaction called the Human State Problem and it shows how it can be partially analyzed and solved using deterministic hardware based approach using a Cellular Automaton as well as probabilistic Bayesian Network. This robotic processor is illustrated using cellular automata for adaptive resources selection and it is shown, in particular, how it can be used for machine learning of robot behavior by modifying the local state-transition function of the cellular automaton in real time. The aim of Chapter 18 is to apply a robust self-assembly strategy to the design of self-assembling robotics. It describes various models for morphogenesis and existing techniques for designing self-assembling robotics. Then, it introduces a cellular automata model for morphogenesis and determines the necessary conditions for its robust self-assembly and self-assembly to a pre-defined shape. Finally, it demonstrates the model coordinating the self-assembly of 55,000 cell virtual robot. Chapter 19 presents a number of cellular automata-based algorithms for medical image processing. It starts by introducing cellular automata fundamentals necessary for understanding the proposed algorithms. Then, a number of cellular automata algorithms for medical image edge detection, noise filtering, spot detection, pectoral muscle identification and segmentation were presented. In this regard, 2D mammogram images for the breast cancer diagnosis were investigated. Chapter 20 explores the possibility of using General Purpose Graphic Processing Unit in the context of integrative biology. The proposed approach is explained and presented with the implementation of two cellular automata algorithms to compare different memory usage. The performances showed significant speedup even when compared to the latest CPU processors. The results obtained were compared in particular with an Nvidia Tesla C1060 board to a sequential implementation on 2 kinds of CPU (Xeon Core 2 and Nehalem).

We hope that after reading the contributions presented in this book we will have succeeded in bringing across what engineers and scientists are doing about the application of the cellular automata techniques for modelling systems and processes in diverse disciplines, so as to produce innovative simulation tools and methods to support the development of science and engineering. We also hope that the readers will find this book interesting and useful.

Lastly, we would like to thank all the authors for their excellent contributions in different areas covered by this book.

Alejandro Salcido
Instituto de Investigaciones Eléctricas
Cuernavaca,
Mexico

Part 1

Quantum Computing

1

Information-Theoretic Modeling and Analysis of Stochastic Behaviors in Quantum-Dot Cellular Automata

Lei Wang[1], Faquir Jain[2] and Fabrizio Lombardi[3]
[1,2]*University of Connecticut*
[3]*Northeastern University*
USA

1. Introduction

Over the last two decades , quantum-dot cellular automata (QCA) has received significant attention as an emerging computing technology (Lent et al., 1993). The basic elements in this technology are the QCA cells, as shown in Fig. 1. Each cell contains two mobile electrons and four quantum dots located in the corners. As per the occupancy of the electrons in the dots, a QCA cell can take different states. A null state (polarization 0) occurs when the electrons are not settled. The other two states are referred to as polarization +1 and −1, denoted as $P = +1$ and $P = -1$ respectively. In these states due to Coulombic interactions, the electrons occupy the two diagonal configurations as shown in Fig. 1(b) and (c). These two states are identified with the so-called ground (stable) states. Any intermediate polarization between +1 and −1 is defined as a combination of states $P = +1$ and $P = -1$. By encoding the polarizations −1 and +1 into binary logic 0 and logic 1, QCA operation can be mapped into binary functions. For clocking and to allow QCA cells to reach a ground state, an adiabatic four-phased switching scheme has been introduced (Lent & Tougaw, 1997). By modulating the tunneling energy between the dots in a cell, this clocking scheme drives each cell through a depolarized state, a latching state, a hold phase, and then back to the depolarized state, such that the information flow is controlled through the QCA devices.

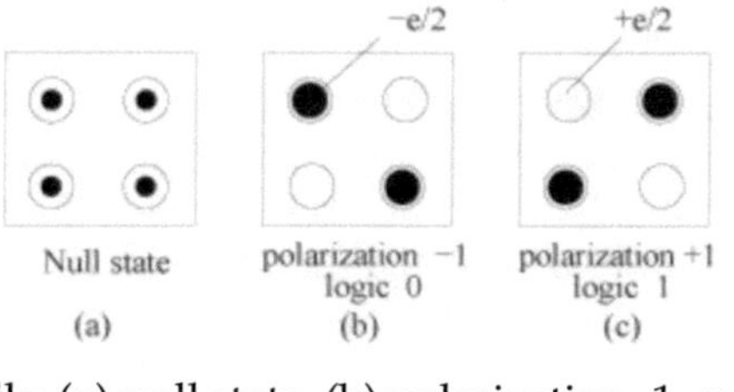

Fig. 1. Schematic of QCA cells: (a) null state, (b) polarization -1, and (c) polarization +1.

Different fabrication technologies (Amlani et al., 1998)–(Jiao et al., 2003) have been proposed to implement QCA devices; QCA logic circuits have also been extensively reported in the literature (Ottavi et al., 2006)–(Tougaw & Lent, 1994). As a common challenge spanning all emerging technologies, the stochastic behaviors of QCA devices impose a significant hurdle to reliable system integration for high performance and scalability. These stochastic behaviors stem from the nondeterministic quantum mechanisms in combination with the large number of defects and variations from fabrication. In particular, it is anticipated that the defect rates of emerging technologies could be several orders of magnitude higher than today's CMOS. Defect characterization of different QCA implementations has been discussed in (Momenzadeh et al., 2005)–(Niemier et al., 2006).

To achieve reliable operation, defect tolerance is a significant concern. Among many possible alternatives, redundancy-based defect tolerance is one of the most effective approaches. By using shorter QCA lines and exploiting the self-latching property of clocked QCA devices, a triple modular redundancy (TMR) with shifted operands has been proposed in (Wei et al., 2005) to design a 1-bit full adder with the same level of fault/defect tolerance as a conventional TMR. In (Fijany & Toomarian, 2001), a defect-tolerant block majority gate has been proposed for the design of various QCA devices. In (Huang et al., 2006)–(Dysart, 2005), tile-based designs were proposed to improve the reliability of QCA devices. All of these techniques employ spatial redundancy for achieving an improvement in reliability.

While effort has been directed towards the improvement of reliability for emerging technologies, current literature has also shown that it is very difficult to deal with defects/variations at device and circuit levels alone. For QCA devices, analysis of reliability is usually performed on a probabilistic basis. A study in (Liu, 2006) has analyzed the robustness with respect to defects and temperature of clocked metallic and molecular QCA circuits. Methods based on statistical mechanics have been proposed in (Wang & Lieberman, 2004) to investigate the total number of QCA cells that could correctly operate together in a molecular QCA device prior to thermal fluctuations (as causing errors at the output). In (Niemier et al., 2006), the probability of a correct output in molecular QCA devices has been established with respect to spacing and cell size by utilizing a statistical quantum mechanical analysis. In (Dysart & Kogge, 2007), probabilistic transfer matrices were employed to study the effectiveness of TMR on the reliability improvement for a 1-bit full adder. A probabilistic model based on Bayesian networks has been proposed in (Bhanja & Sarkar, 2006), (Srivastava & Bhanja, 2007) to model the cell state probabilities of QCA devices for input polarizations. The reliability of QCA devices subject to variations in temperature has been also assessed in (Bhanja et al., 2006), (Ungarelli et al., 2000).

Few results exist in determining the fundamental limit on achievable reliability given the stochastic nature of emerging technologies. In the past, this problem was investigated for conventional logic gates. In (von Neumann, 1955), a multiplexing technique was proposed to obtain reliable synthesis from unreliable components. Since then, several approaches have been reported in deriving the error bounds for individual gates. It was theoretically proved in (Pippenger, 1985), (Pippenger, 1989) that with constant multiplicative redundancy, a variety of Boolean functions built upon unreliable components may be operated reliably. The error bounds were derived for three-input majority gates (Hajek & Weller, 1991), arbitrary-input majority gates (Evans & Schulman, 1999), and two-input NAND gates (Evans & Pippenger, 1998). A nonlinear mapping and bifurcation approach was proposed in (Gao et al., 2005) to provide a new solution to this problem. In (Bhaduri & Shukla, 2005), entropy was used to describe the energy of noisy logic states thereby reflecting the uncertainty inherent in thermodynamics. It should be pointed out that most of these studies were based on the general von Neumann model of basic gate errors, which is more suitable to describe transient errors caused by signal noise in conventional digital logic. The information storage capacity of a crossbar switching network was derived in (Sotiriadis, 2006). This work, however, does not consider the defects in molecular devices explicitly.

In this chapter, we present an information-theoretic framework to investigate the relationship between stochastic behaviors and achievable reliable performance in QCA technology. The central idea is that QCA devices can be modeled as a network of unreliable information processing channels. In contrast to probabilistic measures at device/circuit levels, this model allows us to employ information-theoretic concepts (Shannon, 1948) and study some fundamental issues associated with the QCA technology. Specifically, we employ an information-theoretic analysis to QCA devices by explicitly considering the quantum mechanisms of this technology. By employing statistical channel models, we derive information-theoretic measures to quantify various nano/molecular effects such as cell displacement and misalignment. We determine the information transfer capacity that, from the information-theoretic viewpoint, can be interpreted as the achievable bound on the reliability for QCA devices. One key problem that we will address is what level of redundancy is needed to achieve reliable operation out of unreliable QCA devices. The proposed method provides us with a common framework to evaluate the effectiveness of redundancy-based defect tolerance in a quantitative manner.

We will review the relevant information-theoretic concepts that provide the basis of this work. We will then discuss various stochastic behaviors in QCA devices and develop an information-theoretic framework for the analysis of reliable operation in the presence of defects and variations. By applying the proposed method, we determine the achievable bound on the reliability of QCA devices.

2. Preliminaries

Emerging technologies such as QCA present a large degree of uncertainty in operation due to the underlying quantum mechanisms; these mechanisms inevitably lead to a large number of defects and variations in the implementation and operation of QCA devices and circuits. Therefore, it is necessary to develop a common framework for evaluating these non-ideal effects and their impact on system-level performance. In this work, we model QCA devices as defect-prone information processing media and employ information-theoretic measures to investigate the reliability problems associated with them. This section will review the information-theoretic concepts relevant to the proposed analysis.

Consider a discrete variable X with alphabet $\mathcal{X}$ and probability distribution function $p(x) \triangleq Pr\{X = x\}$, where $x \in \mathcal{X}$. From Shannon's joint source-channel coding theory (Shannon, 1948), the entropy $H(X)$ of this variable is defined as

$$H(X) \triangleq - \sum_{x \in \mathcal{X}} p(x) \log_2(p(x)), \tag{1}$$

where $H(X)$ is expressed in bits.

The entropy $H(X)$ is a measure of the information content in the variable X. A higher entropy implies a greater uncertainty in this variable and thus, the larger information content it carries. Assume that the variable X is passed through a transformation $\mathcal{F} : X \rightarrow Y$, where $\mathcal{F}$ is a non-ideal (e.g., error-prone) mapping function from $X \in \mathcal{X}$ to $Y \in \mathcal{Y}$. The mutual information $I(X;Y)$ between X and Y is defined as

$$\begin{aligned} I(X;Y) &= H(X) - H(X|Y) \\ &= H(Y) - H(Y|X), \end{aligned} \tag{2}$$

where $H(Y|X)$ is the conditional entropy of Y conditioned on X, and it is expressed as

$$\begin{aligned} H(Y|X) &= -\sum_{x\in\mathcal{X}}\sum_{y\in\mathcal{Y}} p(x,y)\log_2(p(y|x)) \\ &= -\sum_{x\in\mathcal{X}}\sum_{y\in\mathcal{Y}} p(x)p(y|x)\log_2(p(y|x)), \end{aligned} \tag{3}$$

where $p(x,y)$ and $p(y|x)$ are the joint probability and conditional probability, respectively, of variables X and Y. For a given $\mathcal{F}$, the values of $p(x,y)$ and $p(y|x)$ are determined by the distribution of the input X.

The conditional entropy $H(Y|X)$ can be viewed as the residual uncertainty in Y given the knowledge of X. Thus, the mutual information $I(X;Y)$ measures the reduction in uncertainty in Y (by an amount $H(Y|X)$) due to the information transferred through $\mathcal{F}$.

The maximum information content that can be transferred through the transformation $\mathcal{F}$ with an arbitrarily low error probability, is given by its capacity as

$$C_u = \max_{\forall p(x)} I(X;Y), \tag{4}$$

where C_u is the information transfer capacity per use obtained by maximizing over all possible distributions of the input X.

The information transfer capacity C_u represents the achievable bound on the reliable operation in a non-ideal information processing medium. The following example illustrates these information-theoretic measures as applied to a conventional CMOS gate.

Example 1: Consider a 2-input NAND gate in conventional CMOS technology. Assume that the implementation of this gate is non-ideal such that the output will generate errors (e.g., due to variations of process parameters, voltage and temperature) at a probability $\varepsilon = 10^{-6}$. By employing (1)- (3), the information transfer capacity of this error-prone gate can be obtained as

$$\begin{aligned} C_u &= \max_{\forall p(x)}\{H(Y) - H(Y|X)\} \\ &= 1 + \varepsilon\log_2\varepsilon + (1-\varepsilon)\log_2(1-\varepsilon) \\ &= 0.99997 \text{ bits/use}. \end{aligned} \tag{5}$$

As indicated, the information transfer capacity is very close to 1 bit per use. Note that an ideal error-free NAND gate is able to transfer at most 1 bit of information per use; thus for an error rate as low as 10^{-6}, this gate is quite reliable.

Figure 2 compares the information transfer capacity under different error rates. The information transfer capacity of the NAND gate is symmetric around an error rate of 0.5. This indicates that from an information-theoretic viewpoint, the NAND gate is able to achieve the same level of reliability under a pair of error rates ε_1 and $\varepsilon_2 = 1 - \varepsilon_1$. This is not surprising because for an error rate larger than 0.5, we can deliberately interpret the output by its complement as the gate actually produces more errors than correct results.

Note that the above example concerns transient output errors, of which the error rate is typically obtained by averaging over time (Wang & Shanbhag, 2003). In emerging technologies, defects from fabrication have become a critical problem. The defect rate p_d reflects the spatial variations over different fabricated samples. Thus, although defects are permanent in a given sample, the nature of randomness stands when considering a large number of samples. In other words, the occurrence and location of defects vary with great uncertainty across these samples. Without conducting an exhaustive test, one can only say

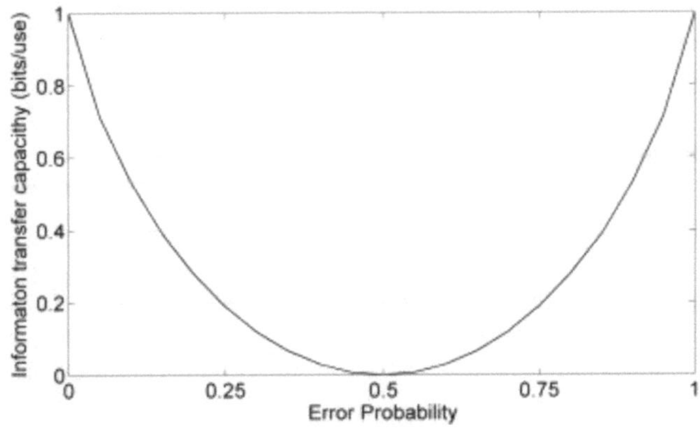

Fig. 2. Information transfer capacity of a NAND gate under different error rates.

that a circuit may be defective with a probability of p_d. The following example illustrates the information-theoretic measures for nanowire crossbars under this scenario.

Example 2: Consider a 2-input AND gate implemented by two different nanowire crossbar columns, one with 2 crosspoints and the other providing 3 crosspoints where one crosspoint is redundant. In both cases the defect rate is assumed to be $p_d = 0.1$.

Case 1: In this case, a 2-crosspoint column is employed to implement the 2-input AND gate. Note that this implementation does not provide any redundancy. It can be shown (Dai et al., 2009) that the conditional probability of the output Y conditioned on the input X is

$$\begin{aligned} &P(Y = 1|X = 00) = 0.01, \\ &P(Y = 1|X = 01) = 0.09, \\ &P(Y = 1|X = 10) = 0.09, \\ &P(Y = 1|X = 11) = 1, \\ &P(Y = 0|X) = 1 - P(Y = 1|X). \end{aligned} \tag{6}$$

Substituting these values into (1)–(3), we obtain $C_u = 0.959$ bits/use. Comparing this result with the Example 1, the achievable bound on reliability as measured by C_u is reduced due to the high defect rate in nanowire crossbars.

Case 2: The second case introduces one redundant crosspoint in implementing the 2-input AND gate. Applying the method in (Dai et al., 2009), we get

$$\begin{aligned} &P(Y = 1|X = 00) = 0.001, \\ &P(Y = 1|X = 01) = 0.0145, \\ &P(Y = 1|X = 10) = 0.0145, \\ &P(Y = 1|X = 11) = 1, \\ &P(Y = 0|X) = 1 - P(Y = 1|X), \end{aligned} \tag{7}$$

and proceeding in the same way, we obtain $C_u = 0.994$ bits/use.

Apparently, the bound on reliability is improved by exploiting the redundancy in nanowire crossbars. Information-theoretic measures enable us to quantify this improvement and thus evaluate the effectiveness of redundancy-based defect tolerance in an analytical manner. Questions arise on how much redundancy is needed in order to obtain a desired level of reliable performance. Naturally, we would also like to compare the achievable reliability of QCA devices with conventional CMOS technology. These problems will be addressed in the following sections.

3. Information-theoretic analysis of QCA

In this section, we will show that the stochastic behaviors of QCA enable us to model these devices as unreliable information processing channels. While different QCA implementations (Amlani et al., 1998)–(Jiao et al., 2003) have been proposed, we will focus on lithographically made QCA devices which are electrostatic based. We will first discuss the possible defects in QCA technology and then develop statistical channel models for various QCA devices. Based on these models, we will derive the information-theoretic measures to quantify the uncertainties in the operation of QCA devices.

3.1 Defects in QCA

Under their manufacturing process, lithographically made QCA devices are likely to have defects. It has been reported that defects can occur in both the synthesis and the deposition phases (Momenzadeh et al., 2005), (Taboori et al., 2004) of QCA devices. In the synthesis phase, a cell may have missing or extra (additional) dots and/or electrons, while in the deposition phase cell misplacement may occur. It has been projected that defects caused by cell misplacement will be dominant in QCA devices due to the difficulty in precise control of the cell location at nanoscale ranges. The various types of cell misplacement that may occur, are as follows:

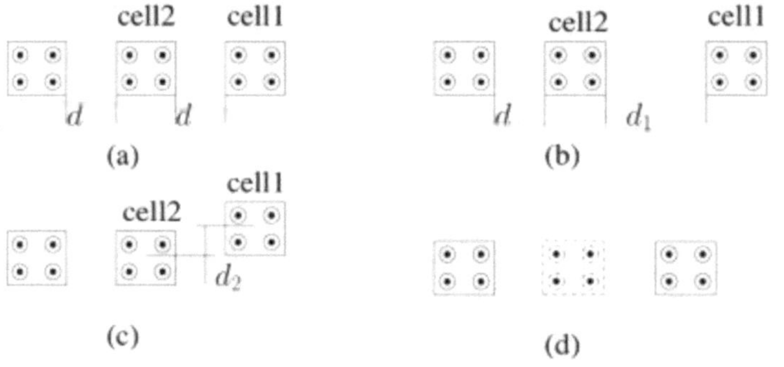

Fig. 3. Three types of misplacement: (a) defect-free, (b) displacement, (c) misalignment, and (d) omission.

1.) *Cell displacement* represents a type of defect in which the distance between cells does not match the nominal value. As shown in Fig. 3(b), the distance between cell1 and cell2 should be equal to d in the correct (ideal) design. Due to displacement, the distance becomes d_1 in the fabricated device.
2.) *Cell misalignment* indicates the deviation in cell location along certain directions. As shown in Fig. 3(c), cell1 has a vertical misalignment equal to d_2, whereas in the ideal case this value should be zero.
3.) *Cell omission* occurs when a particular cell is missing from its pre-specified location in the layout. This is shown in Fig. 3(d). Cell omission may not be a dominant type of defects in lithographically made QCA devices.

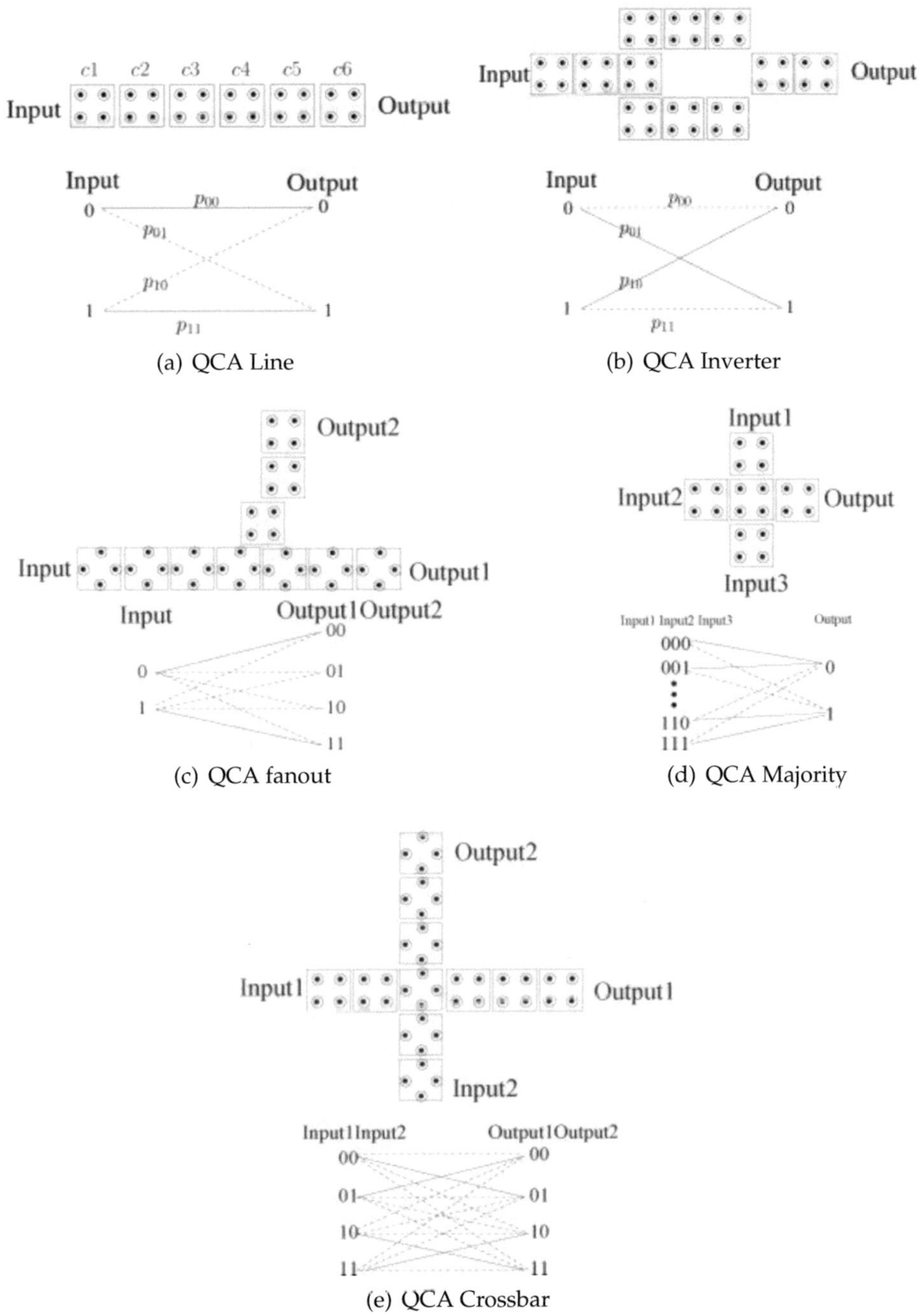

Fig. 4. Statistical channel models for different QCA devices.

In addition to the above defects, device size and temperature will also affect the operation of QCA devices. As shown in the following section, these factors affect the density matrices and thus the values of statistical mapping p_{ij} in the channel model (refer to Fig. 4). This in turn will affect the values of the information-theoretic measures such as channel capacity.

3.2 Statistical channel models of QCA devices

For an error-free logic function, the mapping between the input and output is well-defined, i.e., $P(Y = y_o|X = x_i) \equiv 1$, where $X = x_i$ is the input and $Y = y_o$ is the corresponding output determined by the logic function. However, QCA devices are nondeterministic because each input will only generate an output with certain probability. This phenomenon is further complicated by the presence of defects as discussed previously in section 3.1. Therefore, mappings between the input and output of QCA devices may not follow predefined functions. These uncertainties can be modeled by employing statistical information processing channels, as illustrated in Fig. 4 for QCA devices. In these models, the unreliable logic operation is quantified by the probability $p_{ij} = p(Y_j|X_i)$, i.e., the probability of the output $Y = Y_j$ conditioned on the input $X = X_i$. The solid lines in these models indicate the desired mappings (e.g., the correct output determined by the logic function), whereas the dotted lines represent the erroneous mappings induced by defects and variations.

For QCA, the desired output is generated with certain probability even when the implementation is perfect. Therefore, the p_{ij}'s of the desired mappings are not equal to 1 in the general case. For erroneous mappings the p_{ij}'s are also a function of defects and variations. By employing the statistical channel models, we can assess the impact of these stochastic behaviors using information-theoretic measures, as discussed in the next subsection.

The proposed statistical channel models can also be applied to assess other features of QCA. Different QCA implementations are affected by different types of defects and fabrication variations. This diversity may result in changes of topology (e.g., when the entire parts of a circuit are missing) or numerical values of the mapping p_{ij} (e.g., when defects/variations have different statistics) in the corresponding channel model in Fig. 4. However, the information-theoretic measures and the relationship between defects/variations and performance can be determined in the same manner using the proposed method, thus showing its flexibility in various applications.

3.3 Information transfer capacity of QCA devices

We now derive the information-theoretic measures for investigating the uncertainties in the computing process performed by unreliable QCA devices. As clocking schemes for QCA are typically implemented in a relatively reliable technology such as CMOS (Momenzadeh et al., 2005), (Hennessy & Lent, 2001), (Niemier et al., 2007), we assume these schemes to be highly reliable relative to QCA; thus only defects/variations related to QCA devices and circuits (which operate under an adiabatic four-phased clocking scheme) are considered in the following analysis.

From section 2, to derive information-theoretic measures such as entropy and information transfer capacity, the conditional probabilities p_{ij}'s between the input and output of QCA devices (modeled by the statistical channels in Fig. 4) must be established. These conditional probabilities can be determined by examining the underlying quantum mechanisms of QCA. Unlike conventional CMOS in which computation is performed by voltage/current levels, QCA operates through Coulombic interactions among neighboring cells by affecting their polarizations. The Coulombic interaction between any two cells can be characterized by the so-called kink energy E_k. Let $E^{i,j}_{opposite}$ and $E^{i,j}_{same}$ denote the energy between two cells i and j with opposite polarization and with same polarization, respectively. The kink energy between these two cells can be expressed as

$$E^{i,j}_k = E^{i,j}_{opposite} - E^{i,j}_{same}, \tag{8}$$

and $E^{i,j}_{opposite}$ and $E^{i,j}_{same}$ can be calculated from

$$E^{i,j} = \frac{1}{4\pi\varepsilon_0\varepsilon_r}\sum_{n=1}^{4}\sum_{m=1}^{4}\frac{q^i_n q^j_m}{|r^i_n - r^j_m|}, \tag{9}$$

where ε_0 is the permittivity of free space, ε_r is the dielectric constant, q^i_n and q^j_m are the charges in dot n of cell i and dot m of cell j, respectively. The positions of dot n of cell i and dot m of cell j are denoted by r^i_n and r^j_m, respectively. From (9), the kink energy between cells i and j depends on their relative locations.

By employing the kink energy, the matrix representation of the Hamiltonian using the Hartree-Fock approximation is given by (Timler & Lent, 2002)

$$H = \begin{bmatrix} -\frac{1}{2}\sum_{j\in\Omega_i} E^{i,j}_k P_j & -\gamma_i \\ -\gamma_i & \frac{1}{2}\sum_{j\in\Omega_i} E^{i,j}_k P_j \end{bmatrix}, \tag{10}$$

where $E^{i,j}_k$ is given by (8), Ω_i represents the set of neighboring cells of cell i within the so-called "radius of effect", P_j indicates the polarization of the jth neighboring cell, and γ_i is the tunneling energy between the two states of cell i.

From (Timler & Lent, 1996), (Mahler & Weberrruss, 1998), QCA cells tend to settle to the ground states due to inelastic dissipative heat bath coupling. When QCA cells achieve thermal equilibrium, the steady-state density matrix can be derived from (10) as

$$\rho^{ss} = \frac{e^{-H/KT}}{\mathrm{Tr}[e^{-H/KT}]}, \tag{11}$$

where H is defined in (10), K is Boltzmann constant, and T is the operating temperature. Using the diagonal entries ρ^{ss}_{11} and ρ^{ss}_{00} of this density matrix, we can get the steady-state polarization of cell i as

$$P^{ss}_i = \rho^{ss}_{11} - \rho^{ss}_{00} = \frac{E}{\Lambda}\tanh(\Delta), \tag{12}$$

where

$$E = \frac{1}{2}\sum_{j\in\Omega_i} E^{i,j}_k P_j, \tag{13}$$

$$\Lambda = \sqrt{E^2/4 + \gamma_i^2}, \tag{14}$$

$$\Delta = \frac{\Lambda}{KT}. \tag{15}$$

Applying a self-consistent approximation by factorizing the joint wave function over all cells into a product of individual cell wave functions, the polarization of the output cells can be determined under a specific polarization (as applied to the input cells). Let P_{ij}^{ss} denote the polarization of the ith output cell under the given polarization of a set (indexed by j) of neighboring cells (e.g., cells in Ω_i as in (10)). These neighboring cells can be considered as the inputs of the ith output cell, so the conditional probabilities with respect to the logic value corresponding to the polarization between the set of input cells $\{x_j\}$ and the output cell y_i can be obtained as (Bhanja & Sarkar, 2006)

$$P(y_i = 1|\{x_j\}) = 0.5(1 + P_{ij}^{ss}), \tag{16}$$

$$P(y_i = 0|\{x_j\}) = 0.5(1 - P_{ij}^{ss}), \tag{17}$$

where P_{ij}^{ss} is given by (12) with the set of input cells $\{x_j\}$ expressed explicitly. The above expressions on conditional probabilities can also be applied to the case in which the input cells themselves are out of the radius of effect of the output cells, however they are connected to the output cells via some intermediate cells. In this case, the polarization of the primary input cells will affect their neighboring cells which in turn will affect the final output cells. Thus, the value of P_{ij}^{ss} is determined iteratively from the primary input cells to the final output cell. In section 4, a design tool QCADesigner (Walus et al., 2004) is employed to compute P_{ij}^{ss} for various QCA devices. Note that we do not make any assumption on the polarization of neighboring cells when deriving (16) and (17).

Based on the conditional probabilities in (16) and (17), the information-theoretic measures (such as output entropy and mutual information for a generic QCA circuit) can be derived as

$$H(Y) = -\sum_{Y_i \in \mathcal{Y}} \Big(\sum_{X_j \in \mathcal{X}} 0.5^L \prod_{\substack{y_m \in Y_i \\ y_m = 1}} \prod_{\substack{y_n \in Y_i \\ y_n = 0}} (1 + P_{mp,X_j}^{ss})(1 - P_{nr,X_j}^{ss})\Big)$$
$$\times \log_2\Big(\sum_{X_j \in \mathcal{X}} 0.5^L \prod_{\substack{y_m \in Y_i \\ y_m = 1}} \prod_{\substack{y_n \in Y_i \\ y_n = 0}} (1 + P_{mp,X_j}^{ss})(1 - P_{nr,X_j}^{ss})\Big), \tag{18}$$

$$H(Y|X) =$$
$$- \sum_{X_j \in \mathcal{X}} \sum_{Y_i \in \mathcal{Y}} p(X = X_j) \times 0.5^L \prod_{\substack{y_m \in Y_i \\ y_m = 1}} \prod_{\substack{y_n \in Y_i \\ y_n = 0}} (1 + P_{mp,X_j}^{ss})$$
$$(1 - P_{nr,X_j}^{ss}) \times \log_2(0.5^L \prod_{\substack{y_m \in Y_i \\ y_m = 1}} \prod_{\substack{y_n \in Y_i \\ y_n = 0}} (1 + P_{mp,X_j}^{ss})(1 - P_{nr,X_j}^{ss})), \tag{19}$$

where $X_j \in \mathcal{X}$ is the primary input, $Y_i \in \mathcal{Y}$ is the final output, y_m and y_n are the 1-value and 0-value bits, respectively, of Y_i, P_{mp,X_j}^{ss} and P_{nr,X_j}^{ss} are the polarizations of the output cells y_m and y_n with neighboring cells x_p and x_r, respectively, under a specific input X_j.

The information transfer capacity of the QCA circuit can be determined accordingly as

$$C_u = \max_{\forall p(x)} (H(Y) - H(Y|X)), \tag{20}$$

where the maximization is taken over all possible inputs under the assumption that independent defects and variations are applicable. This assumption reflects the worst case scenario (i.e. it is pessimistic) because independent defects/variations incur the largest information loss (Shannon, 1948). Thus, the resulting information transfer capacity will be lower than for correlated defects/variations. Moreover, the information transfer capacity represents the upper bound on reliability that a QCA circuit can achieve.

Using information-theoretic measures, uncertainties in the operation of QCA devices can be studied based on the polarizations provided at the input cells and the topological structure of the QCA devices. A QCA line is used next as an example to illustrate this process.

Example 3: Consider a QCA line as shown in Fig. 4(a), where cells $c1$ and $c6$ are the input and output, respectively. The size of these cells is 20nm, the cell-to-cell pitch is $d = 20$nm, and the radius of effect is assumed to be 80nm. The clocking scheme is not shown as it won't affect our analysis (i.e., it is much more reliable than the QCA line). Initially the polarization of all six cells is in the -1 state. After the polarization $+1$ is applied at the input cell, a multiple iterative process (Walus et al., 2004) is carried out to determine the polarization of all cells in the QCA line, including the output cell $c6$. Initially, $c2$ is taken as the target cell under the new input polarization. Based on the radius of effect, the polarization of $c2$ is calculated under the influence of neighboring cells $c1$, $c3$, $c4$, and $c5$, as indicated by $\Omega_2 = \{c1, c3, c4, c5\}$ in (10) for cell $c2$. Using the relative distances between the dots in $c2$ and the dots in other cells (e.g., $|r_n^i - r_m^j|$ in (9)), the charges q_n^i, q_m^j of each dot in these cells are determined. Substituting these values into (9) and (10), we can determine the values of the kink energy between $c2$ and its neighboring cells $c1$, $c3$, $c4$, and $c5$. From these kink energies and the initial polarizations of the neighboring cells, the matrix representation of the Hamiltonian H can be formed and a new polarization of $c2$ will be determined by solving (11) and (12). This procedure is repeated iteratively for all cells in the QCA line. Once all cells have settled in the stable states, the polarization of the output cell can be obtained for the given input polarization. For this example, the polarization of the output cell $c6$ is found to be 0.95425 when the input $c1$ is $+1$.

Similarly, it is possible to determine the polarization of the output cell under other values of input polarization. Therefore, from (16)–(19) we get

$$H(Y) = \\ -\sum_{Y_i \in \{0,1\}} \Big(\sum_{X_j \in \{0,1\}} 0.5 \times S \Big) \times \log_2 \Big(\sum_{X_j \in \{0,1\}} (0.5 \times S) \Big), \tag{21}$$

$$H(Y|X) = \\ -\sum_{X_j \in \{0,1\}} \sum_{Y_i \in \{0,1\}} p(X = X_j) \times 0.5 \times S \times \log_2(0.5 \times S), \tag{22}$$

where

$$S = \begin{cases} (1 + P_{1p,X_j}^{ss}) \text{ for } Y_i = 1,\ X = X_j, \\ \\ (1 - P_{1p,X_j}^{ss}) \text{ for } Y_i = 0,\ X = X_j. \end{cases}$$

Finally, the information transfer capacity of this QCA line can be determined as $C_u = 0.8427$ bits/use. Note that this result is obtained for a defect-free implementation. Compared with the CMOS gate in Example 1 (in which an ideal implementation achieves $C_u = 1$ bit/use), the achievable bound on reliable operation (as measured by the information transfer capacity) is significantly lower in QCA devices. This is not surprising because QCA devices are inherently nondeterministic.

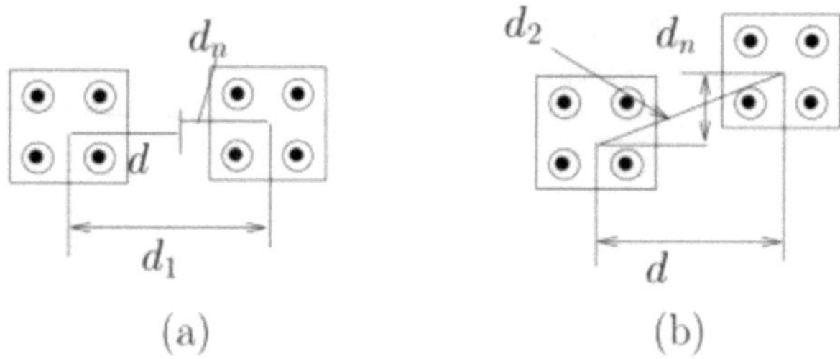

Fig. 5. Defects due to (a) displacement and (b) misalignment.

3.4 Effects of Defects on Information-Theoretic Measures

QCA devices also suffer from a large number of defects and variations in manufacturing and design. Defects can affect the information-theoretic measures as derived previously. Consider a pair of cells such that cell i is defect-free, but cell j is misplaced by an offset η_j from its desired location. The difference in polarization energy between the defect-free and defective implementations can be derived from (9) as follows

$$\begin{aligned}\sigma^{i,j} &= E_f^{i,j} - E_d^{i,j} \\ &= \frac{1}{4\pi\varepsilon_0\varepsilon_r}\sum_{n=1}^{4}\sum_{m=1}^{4} q_n^i q_m^j \left(\frac{1}{|r_n^i - r_m^j|} - \frac{1}{|r_n^i - (r_m^j + \eta^j)|}\right),\end{aligned} \tag{23}$$

where $E_d^{i,j}$ and $E_f^{i,j}$ represent the $E^{i,j}$ for the defective and defect-free cases, respectively.

The presence of $\sigma^{i,j}$ will lead to a different kink energy between the two cells. Let $E_{k,d}^{i,j}$ and $E_{k,f}^{i,j}$ denote the kink energy for the defective and defect-free cases, respectively. Thus,

$$E_{k,d}^{i,j} = E_{k,f}^{i,j} + \delta^{i,j}, \tag{24}$$

where $\delta^{i,j}$ can be obtained from (23) and (8). Substituting $E_{k,d}^{i,j}$ into (10) and (11), the matrix representation of the Hamiltonian can be obtained for cell i. The difference in matrix representation compared to a defect-free device is given by

$$\Delta_H = \begin{bmatrix} -\frac{1}{2}\sum_{j\in\Omega_i}\delta^{i,j}P_j & 0 \\ 0 & \frac{1}{2}\sum_{j\in\Omega_i}\delta^{i,j}P_j \end{bmatrix}. \tag{25}$$

Due to this difference, the steady state matrix ρ^{ss} in (11) and the steady state polarization P_i^{ss} in (12) of cell i are changed by the misplacement in cell j. According to (16) and (17), the conditional probabilities between cells i and j will also be affected which in turn will affect the information-theoretic measures of this QCA circuit.

Figure 5 illustrates two examples of cell misalignment and displacement defects. Assume d is the cell-to-cell pitch in the defect-free case and d_n is the defective misplacement. The actual distances between the two cells are therefore

$$d_1 = d + d_n, \tag{26}$$

$$d_2 = \sqrt{d^2 + d_n^2}. \tag{27}$$

The cell misalignment and displacement defects will have a different impact on the information-theoretic measures of QCA devices. In the next section, we will show the application of the proposed method when analyzing these defects.

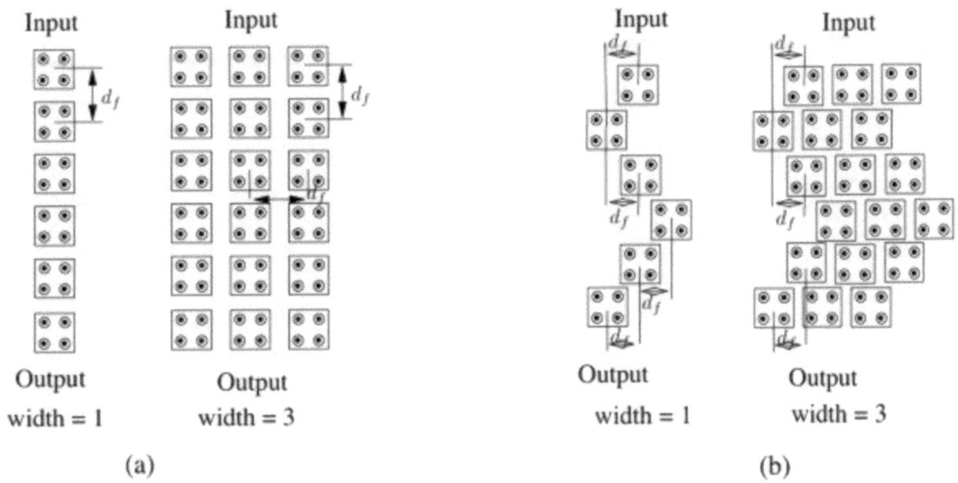

Fig. 6. Tile-based design of a QCA line under (a) displacement (b) misalignment defects.

4. Evaluation and discussion

Tile-based QCA design employs spatial redundancy to overcome various defects and variations in QCA devices (Huang et al., 2006)–(Dysart, 2005). It is a modular approach based on elementary building blocks to construct QCA circuits. The building blocks are referred to as tiles. The width of a tile can be adjusted to achieve different levels of reliability. In this section, we will study the effectiveness of this technique by using the proposed information-theoretic measures. We will consider cell displacement and misalignment defects. The coherence vector simulation engine QCADesigner v2.0.3 (Walus et al., 2004) is utilized to obtain an accurate result on the polarization. The parameters used in the simulation are as follows: cell dimension 18nm, cell-to-cell pitch 20nm, radius of effect 80nm, relative permittivity 12.9. Lithographically made QCA devices require a very low temperature (few degrees Kelvin). Therefore in the simulation, a temperature of 1K is chosen; this is consistent with many existing works (Srivastava & Bhanja, 2007), (Schulhof et al., 2007). An adiabatic four-phased clocking scheme is employed in the QCA circuits.

The QCA devices in Fig. 4 are evaluated under cell displacement defects first. QCA lines with widths of 1 and 3 (shown in Fig. 6(a)) are utilized for the simulation setup. For each simulation run, the same cell displacement d_f is applied to all cell-to-cell pitches. As discussed in section 3.4, cell displacements affect the inter-cell quantum mechanisms and the P_{ij}^{ss} in (16) and (17), thus changing the information transfer capacity.

Figure 7 shows the information transfer capacity of different QCA devices implemented by different widths (e.g., levels of spatial redundancy) subject to displacements from 0% to 30% of the size of the QCA cells. As reported in (Timler & Lent, 1996), a displacement of 30% of cell size is sufficient to affect the correct operation of a QCA device. For QCA crossbars, only the width of horizontal lines is increased (as proposed in (Bhanja et al., 2006)). Some important phenomena are observed from the simulation results. The information transfer capacity of

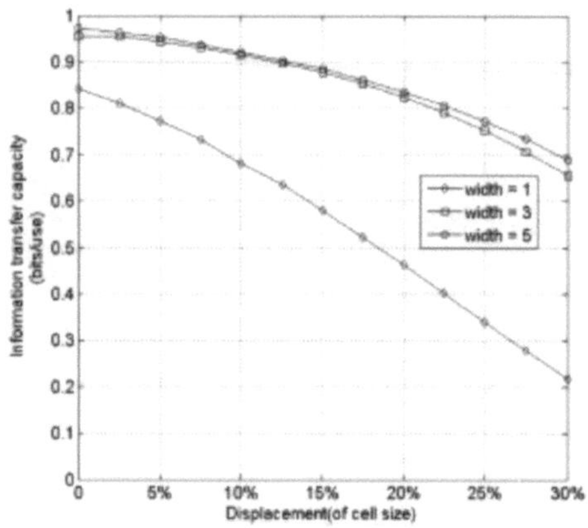

(a) QCA Line

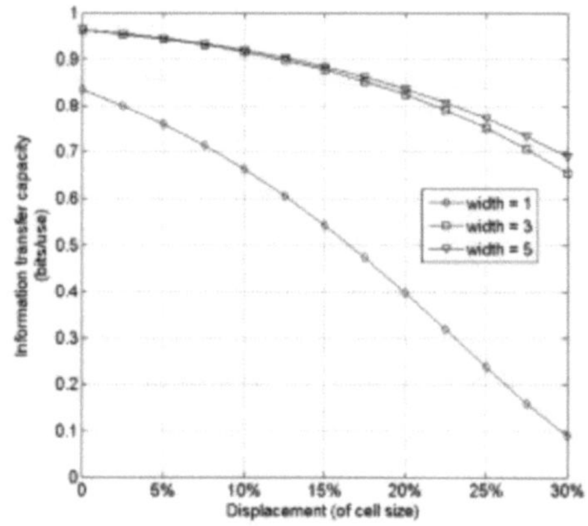

(b) QCA Inverter

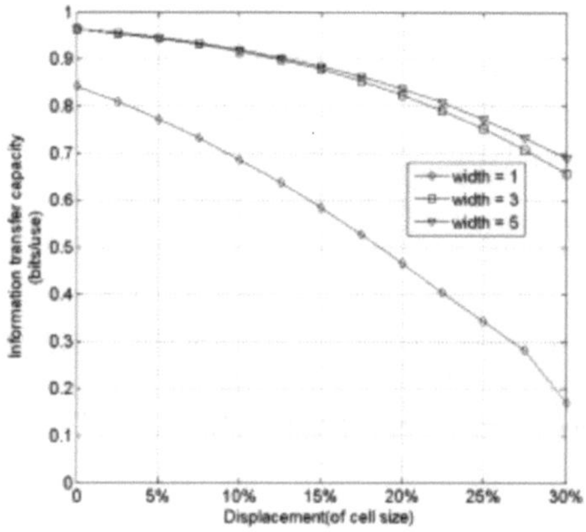

(c) QCA Majority

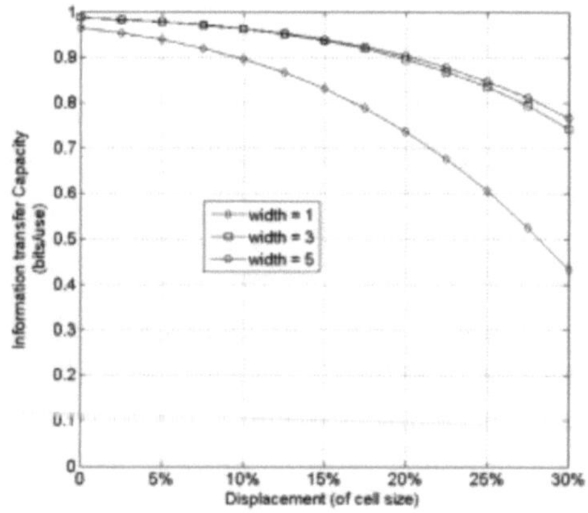

(d) QCA Crossbar

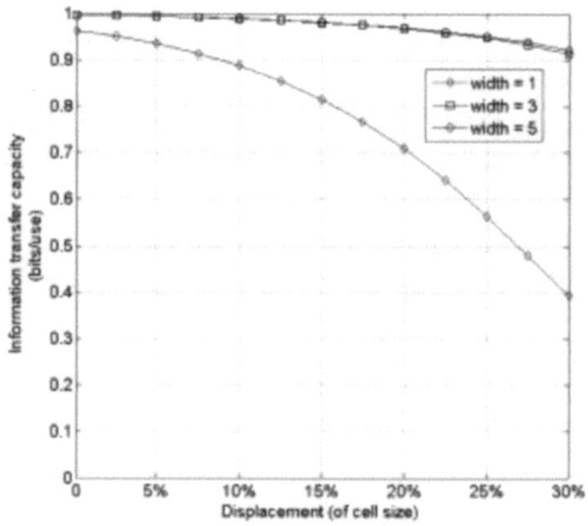

(e) QCA Fanout

Fig. 7. Information transfer capacity of QCA devices under cell displacement defects.

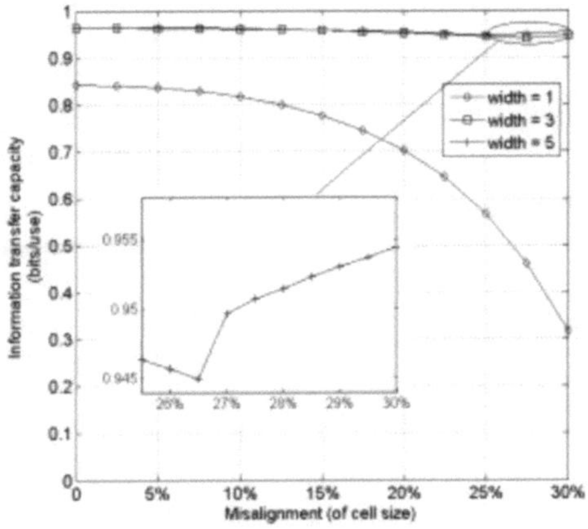

(a) QCA Line

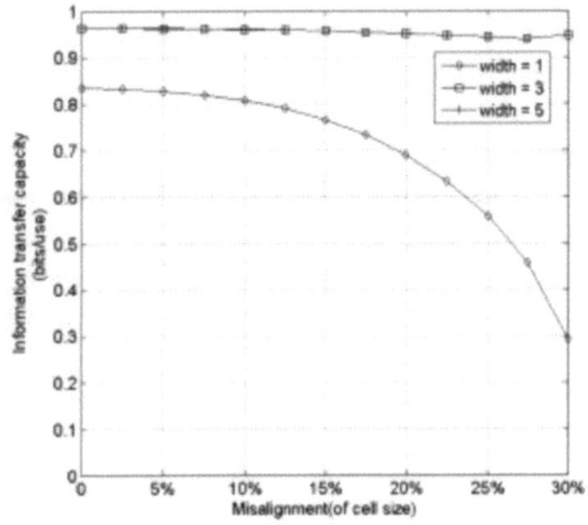

(b) QCA Inverter

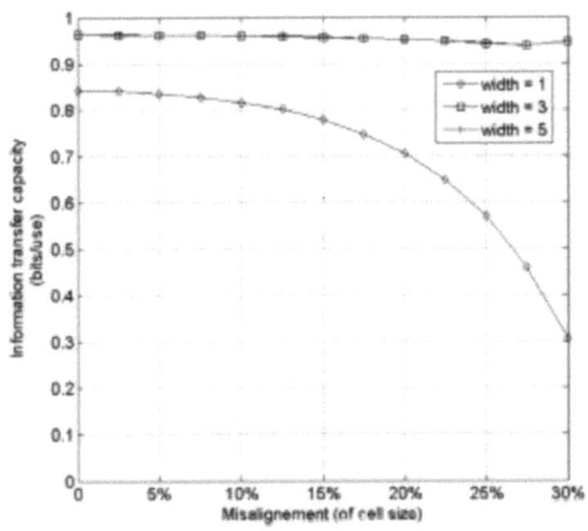

(c) QCA Majority

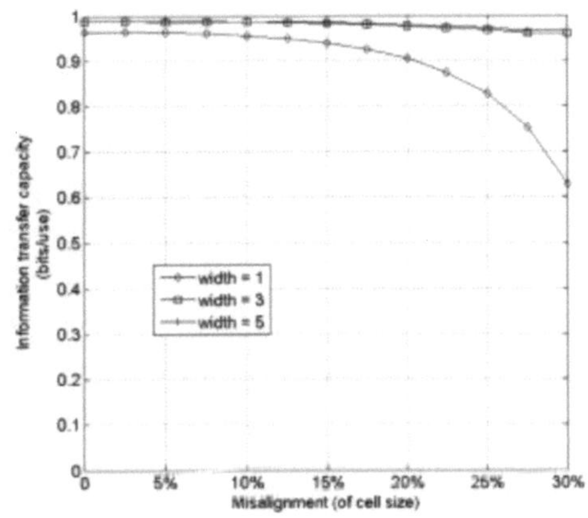

(d) QCA Crossbar

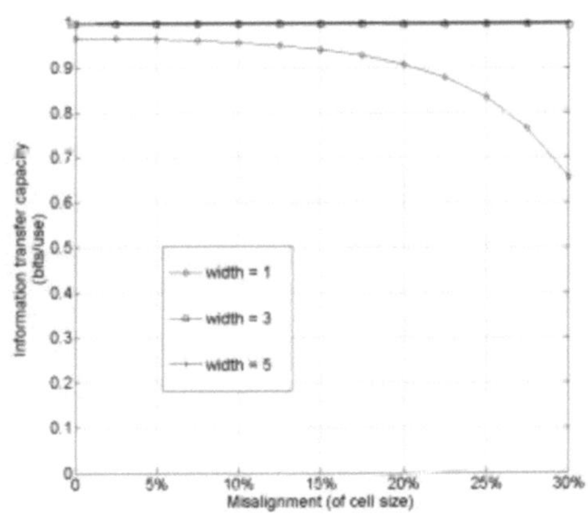

(e) QCA Fanout

Fig. 8. Information transfer capacity of QCA devices under cell misalignment defects.

QCA devices degrades quickly due to the probabilistic nature of their operation. This may be a significant issue for robust nanocomputing. Also, to achieve the same level of reliability, a higher level of spatial redundancy is needed if the displacement is large. For the example of the QCA line shown in Fig. 7(a) with a displacement of 30% of cell size, a width = 5 is needed to achieve an information transfer capacity of 0.69 bits/use (a width = 3 achieves the same information transfer capacity at a displacement of 27.5%). Finally, although tile-based design can improve the reliability of QCA devices, the effectiveness of this approach saturates quickly with an increase in width. This shows that it is difficult to further improve the reliability of QCA devices beyond a certain level of spatial redundancy. The simulated QCA devices are single output gates. Under the ideal (error- and variation-free) operation, the information transfer capacity will be equal to 1 bit/use while it will be less than 1 bit/use in the presence of defects and variations.

The effect of cell misalignment on the reliability of QCA devices has also been studied. A scenario of cell misalignment defects is shown in Fig. 6(b) for QCA lines; each pair of neighboring cells has the same offset d_f from the center line. This corresponds to the worst case scenario, e.g., the largest difference in kink energy (refer to (23) and (24)).

Figure 8 shows the information transfer capacity of QCA devices under cell misalignment defects ranging from 0% to 30% of cell size. The relationship of information transfer capacity, defects, and level of spatial redundancy follows a similar trend as for the QCA devices under cell displacement defects. Compared to the results in Fig. 7, the information transfer capacity of QCA devices under cell misalignment is larger than under cell displacement. This is consistent with the observation that QCA technology is relatively less sensitive to cell misalignment defects.

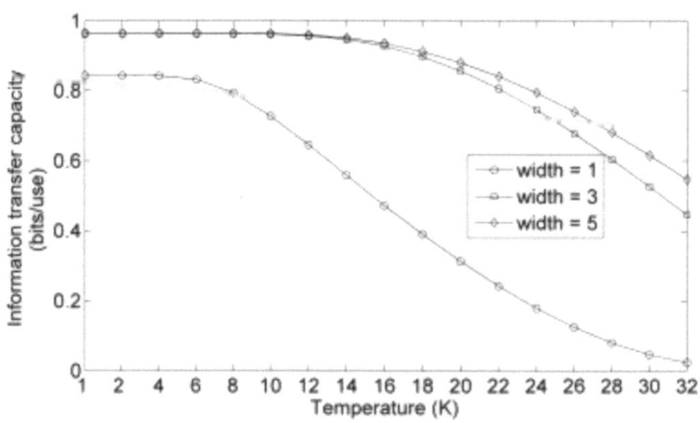

Fig. 9. Information transfer capacity of QCA lines under different temperatures.

Another interesting observation drawn from Fig. 8 is that for some QCA devices, the information transfer capacity does not monotonously decrease with an increase in misalignment among QCA cells. For example in Fig. 8(a), the information transfer capacity of the QCA line with a width of 5 increases slightly at a misalignment of 26.5% of cell size. This seems to counter the well-prevalent intuition; however, a careful examination of this result reveals that when the misalignment is nearly 26.5% of the cell size, the QCA line actually acts like a QCA inverter due to entanglement among misaligned QCA cells, i.e., the QCA line generates more flipped outputs. According to the discussion related to Fig. 2, the output can be interpreted by its complement to get more correct results. While the QCA function is fixed, this interpretation is by default reflected in the information-theoretic measures (as shown in Fig. 2). From these results, we can see that the proposed information-theoretic analysis can effectively quantify the impact of various defects on reliable operation, e.g., cell displacement will reduce the reliability monotonically, while cell misalignment may cause a sudden change of device functionality.

Finally, we apply the proposed method to study the impact of temperature on QCA operation. Figure 9 shows the information transfer capacity of QCA lines implemented with different widths subject to variations in temperature from $1K$ to $32K$; QCA lines become less reliable for all implementations as temperature increases, but a high level of spatial redundancy utilization achieves a better reliability.

5. Conclusion

An information-theoretic framework has been developed for the analysis of stochastic behaviors in QCA devices. The proposed method establishes a direct correspondence between spatial redundancy and the reliability of this technology in the presence of defects and variations, thereby allowing to evaluate the capabilities and limitations of QCA-based nanocomputing systems. We have conducted a comprehensive set of simulations on different QCA devices. These results show that the proposed method can be used to address the evaluation of the reliability as achieved under a specified level of spatial redundancy; also the proposed method allows to quantitatively evaluate the uncertainties in the operation of QCA devices.

From an information-theoretic perspective, reliability measured by the information transfer capacity can be interpreted as an upper bound (of which the numerical values are determined by specific design techniques) that QCA devices can achieve. The proposed method does not specify a design technique that would achieve this bound because the proposed method is derived from (Shannon, 1948), i.e., to establish an achievable bound on the information transfer capacity but not the method for achieving such a bound. In the absence of a general theory, the method proposed in this paper focuses on determining the information transfer capacity. The ability to determine this achievable bound has substantial implications on the design optimization of QCA devices and circuits.

6. References

Lent, C. S., Tougaw, P. D., Porod, W. and Bernstein, G. H. (1993). Quantum cellular automata, *Nanotechnology*, pp.49-57, vol. 4.

Lent, C. S. and Tougaw, P. D. (1997). A device architecture for computing with quantum dots, *Proceeding of the IEEE*, 541-557.

Amlani, I., Orlov, A., Snider, G. and Lent, C. (1998). Demonstration of a functional. quantum-dot cellular automata cell, *J. Vac. Sci. Tech. B.*, vol. 16, 3795-3799.

Cowburn, R. and Welland, M. (2000). Room temperature Magnetic Quantum Cellular Automata, *Science*, 1466-1468.

Smith, C., Gardelis, S., Rushforth, A., Crook, R., Cooper, J., Ritchie, D., Lineld, E., Jin, Y. and Pepper, M. (2003). Realization of quantum-dot cellular automata using semiconductor quantum dots, *Super lattices and Microstructures*, vol. 34, 195-203.

Jiao, J., Long, G., Grandjean, F., Beatty, A. and Fehlner, T. (2003). Building blocks for the molecular expression of Quantum Cellular Automata. Isolation and characterization of a covalently bonded square array of two ferrocenium and two ferrocene complexes, *J. Am. Chem. Soc.*, vol. 125, 1522-1523.

Momenzadeh, M., Huang, J. and Lombardi, F. (2005). Defect characterization and tolerance of QCA sequential devices and circuits, *Defect and Fault Tolerance in VLSI Systems*, 199-207.

Tahoori, M. B., Momenzadeh, M., Huang, J. and Lombardi, F. (2004). Defects and faults in quantum cellular automata at nano scale, *VLSI Test Symposium*, 291-296.

Niemier, M., Crocker, M., Hu, X. S. and Lieberman, M. (2006). Using CAD to shape experiments in molecular QCA, *Int. Conf. on Comp. Aided Design*, 907-914.

Ottavi, M., Pontarelli, S., Vankamamidi, V., Salsano, A. and Lombardi, F. (2006). QCA memory with parallel read/serial write: design and analysis, *IEE proceeding circuit, devices, and systems*, vol. 153, 199-206.

Frost, S., Rodrigues, A. F., Janiszewski, A. W., Raush, R. T. and Kogge, P. M. (2002). Memory in motion: A study of storage structures in QCA, *First Workshop on Non-Silicon Computing*.

Vankamamidi, V., Ottavi, M. and Lombardi, F. (2005). Tile Based Design of a Serial Memory in QCA, *Proceedings of ACM Great Lakes Symposium on VLSI*, 201-206.

Niemier, M. T. and Kogge, P. M. (1999). Logic in wire: using quantum dots to implement a microprocessor, *IEE proceeding circuit, devices, and systems*, 118-121.

Dutta, M. and Stroscio, M. A. (2000). Quantum-based electronic devices and systems, *World scientific publishing company*.

Niemier, M. T. (2004). Designing digital systems in quantum cellular automata, *Master's thesis, University of Notre Dame*.

Walus, K. and Jullien, G. A. (2006). Design tools for an emerging SoC technology: quantum-dot cellular automata, *Proceedings of IEEE*, vol. 94, 1225-1244.

Tougaw, P. D. and Lent, C. S. (1994). Logical devices implemented using quantum cellular-automata, *Journal of Applied Physics*, vol. 75, 1818-1825.

Wei, T., Wu, K., Karri, R. and Orailoglu, A. (2005). Fault tolerant quantum cellular array (QCA) design using Triple Modular Redundancy with shifted operands, *2005 conference on Asia South Pacific design automation* , 1192-1195.

Fijany, A. and Toomarian, B. N. (2001). New design for quantum dots celluar automata to obtain fault tolerant logic gates, *Journal of Nanoparticle Research*, 27-37.

Huang, J., Momenzadeh, M. and Lombardi, F. (2006). On the tolerance to manufacturing defects in molecular QCA tiles for processing-by-wire, *Journal of Electronic Testing: Theory and Applications*, 163-174.

Huang, J., Momenzadeh, M. and Lombardi, F. (2006). Defect tolerance of QCA tiles, *Design, Automation and Test in Europe*, 1-6.

Dysart, T. J. (2005). Defect properties and design tools for quantum dot cellular automata, *Master's thesis, University of Notre Dame*.

Liu, M. (2006). Robustness and power dissipation in quantum-dot cellular automata, *Ph.D. Dissertation, University of Notre Dame*.

Ungarelli, C., Francaviglia, S., Macucci, M. and Iannaconne, G. (2000). Thermal behavior of quantum cellular automaton wires, *J. Appl. Phys.*, 7320-7325.

Wang, Y. and Lieberman, M. (2004). Thermodynamic behavior of molecular-scale quantum-dot automata (QCA) wires and logic devices, *IEEE Trans. on Nano.*, 368-376.

Dysart, T. J. and Kogge, P. M. (2007). Probabilistic analysis of a molecular quantum-dot cellular automata adder, *IEEE International Symposium on Defect and Fault Tolerance in VLSI Systems*, 478-486.

Bhanja, S., Ottavi, M., Lombardi, F. and Pontarelli, S. (2006). Novel designs for thermally robust coplanar crossing in QCA, *Design Automation and Test in Europe*, 786-791.

Bhanja, S. and Sarkar, S. (2006). Probabilistic modeling of QCA circuits using bayesian networks, *IEEE Transactions on Nanotechnology*, 657-670.

Srivastava, S. and Bhanja, S. (2007). Hierarchical probabilistic macromodeling for QCA circuits, *IEEE Transactions on Computers*, 174-190.

von Neumann, J. (1955). Probabilistic logics and the synthesis of reliable organisms from unreliable components, *Automata Studies, Shannon C.E.and McCarthy J., eds.*, Princeton University Press, Princeton N.J., pp. 43-98.

Pippenger, N. (1985). On networks of noisy gates, *Proc. 26th Annu. Symp. on Foundations Comput. Sci.*, pp. 30-36.

Pippenger, N. (1989). Invariance of complexity measures for networks with unreliable gates, *Journal of the ACM.*, vol. 36, pp. 531-539.

Hajek, B. and Weller, T. (1991). On the maximum tolerable noise for reliable computation by formulas, *IEEE Trans. Inf. Theory*, vol. 37, no. 2, pp. 388-391.

Evans, W. and Schulman, L. J. (1999). Signal propagation and noisy circuits, *IEEE Trans. Inf. Theory*, vol. 45, no. 7, pp. 2367-2373.

Evans, W. and Pippenger, N. (1998). On the maximum tolerable noise for reliable computation by formulas, *IEEE Trans. Inf. Theory*, vol. 44, no. 3, pp. 1299-1305.

Gao, J. B., Qi, L., and Fortes, J. A. B. (2005). Bifurcations and fundamental error bounds for fault-tolerant computations, *IEEE Trans. on Nanotechnology*, pp. 395-402.

Bhaduri, D. and Shukla, S. (2005). NANOLAB – A tool for evaluating reliability of defect-tolerant nanoarchitectures, *IEEE Trans. on Nanotechnology*, vol. 4, pp. 381-394.

Sotiriadis, P. P. (2006). Information capacity of nanowire crossbar switching networks, *IEEE Trans. on Information Theory*, vol. 52, pp. 3019- 3032.

Wang, L. and Shanbhag, N. (2003). Energy-efficiency bounds for deep submicron VLSI systems in the presence of noise, *IEEE Transactions on VLSI Systems*, vol. 11, 254-269.

Dai, J., Wang, L. and Jain, F. (2009). Analysis of defect tolerance in molecular crossbar electronics, *IEEE Transactions on VLSI Systems*, vol. 17, 529-540.

Shannon, C. E. (1948). A mathematical theory of communication, *Bell Syst. Tech. J.*, vol. 27, part I, 379-423, part II, 623-656.

Timler, J. and Lent, C. S. (2002). Power gain and dissipation in quantum-dot cellular automata, *Journal of applied physics*, vol. 91, 823-831.

Timler, J. and Lent, C. S. (1996). Dynamic behavior of quantum cellular automata, *Joural of applied physics*, vol. 80, 4722-4736.

Mahler, G. and Weberruss, V. A. (1998). Quantum networks: dynamics of open nanostructures, *New York: Springer-Verlag*.

Hennessy K. and Lent, C. S. (2001). Clocking of molecular quantum-dot cellular automata, *Journal of Vacuum Science and Technology*, 1752-1755.

Niemier, M., Alam, M., Hu, X. S., Bernstein, G., Porod, W., Putney, M. and DeAngelis, J. (2007). Clocking structures and power analysis for nanomagnet-based logic devices, *Proc. of international symposium on Low power electronics and design* , 26-31.

Walus, K., Dysart, T. J., Jullien, G. A. and Budiman, R. A. (2004). QCADesigner: a rapid design and simulation tool for quantum-dot cellular automata, *IEEE transcation on Nanotechnology*, 26-29.

Schulhof, G., Walus, K. and Jullien, G. A. (2007). Simulation of random cell displacements in QCA, *ACM Journal on Emerging Technologies in Computing Systems*, Vol. 3, Issue 1, Artical No. 2.

2

Architectural Design of Quantum Cellular Automata to Implement Logical Computation

Alejandro León
Facultad de Ingeniería, Universidad Diego Portales Ejército 441, Santiago Chile

1. Introduction

The limits to miniaturization of electronic devices are reached with sizes where quantum mechanics rules over the dynamics of the system. Because of this, enormous efforts are being made in search of new technologies to store and process information that can efficiently replace classic electronics. The proposal for quantum systems for carrying out computation represents an attempt to create a new generation of information processors (Nielsen & Chuang, 2003). The major advantage of quantum computation is that it can resolve numeric problems that cannot be resolved by classical computation. However, there remains the unresolved problem of the coherence of the proposed systems. Some significant advances have been made in addressing these problems using dislocated qubits with global control protocols (Fitzsimons et al., 2007), with small molecular systems.

On the other hand, a completely different solution to quantum computation has been attempted using cellular automata architecture to develop classical computational processes with quantum entities. Important advances have been made with automata based on quantum dot arrays (QCA), the idea for which was proposed by C. Lent and collaborators (Lent et al., 1993). The original idea was introduced as a system of quantum corrals with

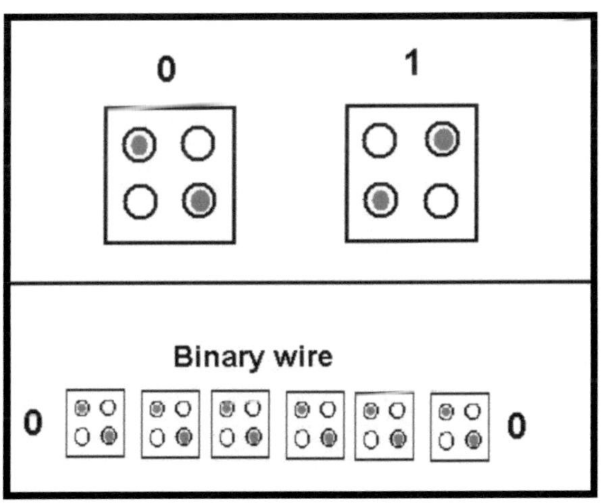

Fig. 1. Quantum dot scheme proposed by the Lent group.

four quantum dots inside it and doped with two electrons. The electrons can tunnel through the quantum dots, but cannot get out of the corrals that form the cells of the automata. This architecture can propagate and process binary information with adequate control protocols (Csurgay et al., 2000). Figure 1 shows a scheme of the original idea of the Notre Dame group.

We can appreciate from Figure 1 that the cell that makes up the cellular automata is composed of four quantum dots and that the two extra electrons in the cell can locate themselves in any of the four quantum dots. Owing to Coulomb interaction between the electrons, the minimum energy configurations of the cell correspond to the diagonals of a square. This allows for defining a 0 logic state and another state that corresponds to 1 logic (the two diagonals). Figure 2 shows the implementation of two important classical logic gates using this architecture.

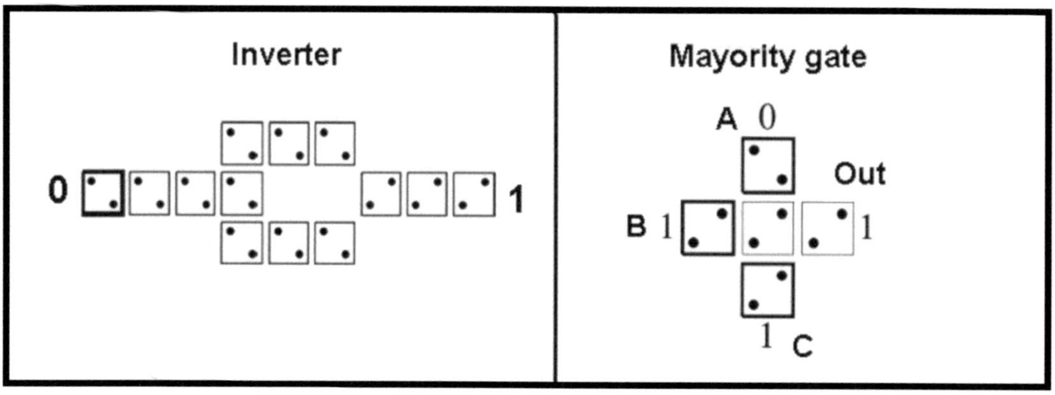

Fig. 2. Scheme of the implementation of the inverter gate and the majority gate with the architecture proposed by the Lent group.

The first experimental demonstration of the implementation of a QCA was published in 1997 (Orlov et al., 1997). A subsequent work also demonstrated an experimental method for the implementation of a logic gate (Amlani et al., 1999), and a shift register was also reported (Kummamuru et al., 2003). These results provide good agreement between theoretical predictions and experimental outcomes at low temperatures. Implementation at room temperature requires working at the molecular level, and in the context of molecular cellular automata; there are also important contributions at the experimental level (Jiao et al., 2003). In the molecular case, the quantum dots correspond to oxide reduction centers, and as in the case of metallic quantum dots or semiconductors are operated with electrical polarization. The implementation of this cellular automata architecture is achieved with complex molecules, supported in a chemically inert substrate. The implementation is achieved in an extremely small chain of molecules (Jiao et al., 2003). Another implementation at room temperature corresponds to an array of magnetic quantum dots that can propagate magnetic excitations to process digital information (Macucci, 2006). These systems use the magnetic dipolar interaction among particles whose size is at the submicrometer scale. A theoretical study was recently published about the behavior of cellular automata composed of an array of polycyclic aromatic molecules (León et al., 2009), using the polarization of electronic spin. In this work it is established that by increasing molecules in one of the directions of the plane, forming graphene nanoribbons, binary

information can be transmitted at room temperature. The disadvantage of the proposed system is that the nanoribbons will reach sizes on the order of micrometers and consequently the miniaturization of the circuits will be only partial.
In this work we propose a cellular automata with graphane structured molecules and graphane nanoribbons to propagate and process digital information. The cells that make up the architecture of the automata correspond to the molecules and to sections of the nanoribbon. We intend to verify theoretically that the proposed system is scalable and binary information can be stored, propagated and processed at room temperature.

2. Graphene and Graphane

2.1 Graphene and Graphene Nanoribbons

Graphene is a simple bidimensional structure of carbon atoms. In 2004 the group of Kostya Novoselov (Nonoselov et al, 2004) succeeded in isolating a simple layer of graphene using a technique by mechanical exfoliation of graphite. This work represented the beginning of many theoretical and experimental studies and their potential applications to systems derived from graphene (Geim, 2009; Castro Neto et al., 2009). A schematic view of the graphene is shown in figure 3.
Recent studies have shown than the electronic structure of graphene nanoribbons (GNRs) exhibits remarkable geometric-dependent properties: it can have metallic or semiconductor behavior depending on the ribbon width and on the arrangement of the atoms on its side edges. It has been demonstrated that the transport and optical properties of GNRs are strongly affected by the edge shape, in particular in the case of ribbons with zigzag edges due to the existence of localized edge states which gives a sharp peak in the density of states at the Fermi level (Nakada et al., 1996; Wakabayashi, 2001). Different device junctions based on patterned GNRs have been proposed (Wang et al., 2007; Ren et al., 2007; Silvestrov & Efetov, 2007) and constructed which can confines electronic states realizing quantum-dot like structures. The electronic states of these confined GNRs structures can be manipulated by chemical edge modifications or impurities addition. A schematic view of the GNRs is shown in figure 4.

Fig. 3. Scheme of the graphene.

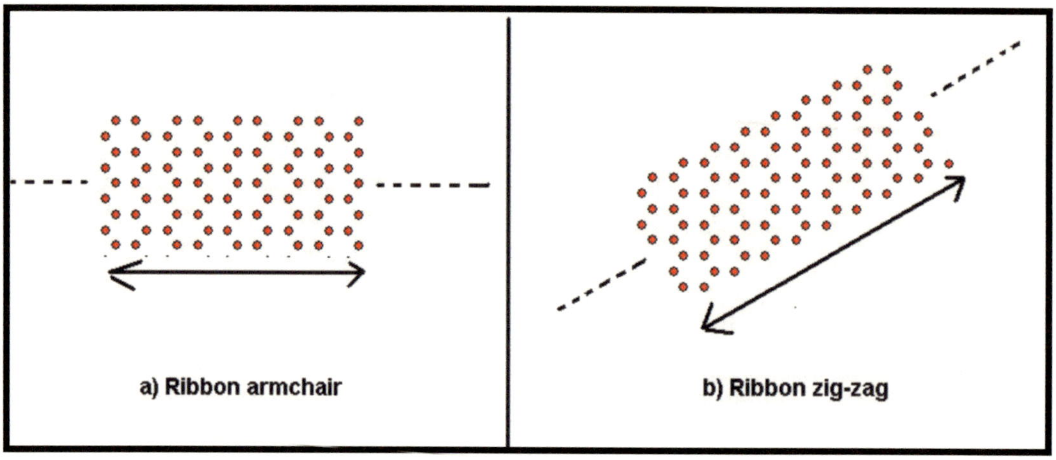

Fig. 4. Scheme of the graphene nanoribbons with armchair and zig-zag edges.

2.2 Graphane

A theoretical investigation in 2007 (Sofo et al.,2007) predicted a new form of graphene totally saturated with hydrogen. The authors of this paper give the name "graphane" to this new form derived from the graphene. The shape of this new structure is similar to graphene, with the carbon atoms in a hexagonal lattice and alternately hydrogenated on each side of the lattice. Figure 5 shows a scheme of this structure.

Fig. 5. Scheme of graphane. The gray spheres represent carbon atoms and the white spheres represent hydrogen atoms.

In January 2009, the same group that isolated graphene in 2004 published a paper in Science magazine reporting the hydrogenation of graphene and the possible synthesis of graphane (Elias et al., 2009). Since then there has been growing scientific interest in the study of hybrid graphene-graphane systems and their potential applications (Singh & Yakobson, 2009; Li et al., 2009; Lu & Feng, 2009; Balog, 2010). In this chapter we will discuss graphene nanoribbons and hydrogenated graphene nanoribbons according to the graphane structure. We can imagine these structures as a ribbon-like bidimensional graphane structure. The atoms of the edges of the ribbon are connected to hydrogen atoms to passivate the free bond. The other system studied in this research is polycyclic aromatic molecules (León, 2009), and polycyclic aromatic molecules but with hydrogen atoms alternately bonded to carbon atoms such that they can be considered as a section of rectangular graphane.

3. Graphene Nanoribbon array in a cellular automata architecture with spin polarization

In this work we propose the implementation of a cellular automaton with cells containing graphene nanoribbons (GNRCA). This kind of carbon-based nanostructures can be obtained by different experimental techniques (Berger et al., 2006; Han et al., 2007; Heersche et al., 2007). In our study we will consider our GNRCA with cells composing by finite GNRs passivated with hydrogen atoms, these structures are also known as polycyclic aromatic hydrocarbons. In Fig. 6 we have displayed two $C_{44}H_{18}$ finite GNRs. The electronic and magnetic properties of the systems are obtained by means of first principles calculations based on the pseudo-potentials method and by using the generalized gradient approximation Perdew–Burke–Ernzerhof with spin polarization (Perdew et al., 1996). All structures are relaxed using the Direct Inversion Iterative Subspace method (Csaszar & Pulay, 1984) with a residual force criteria less than 10^{-4} (Hartree / bohr). Calculations were performed using the OPENMX Code (Openmx, 2007). We found that the minimum energy state of this GNR presents spin polarization along the zigzag-type edges, corresponding to the edges containing more carbon atoms (Son et al., 2006; Jiang et al., 2007; Wang et al., 2008; Fernandez-Rossier & Palacios, 2007). This state is degenerate as it is shown in Fig. 7, therefore we can define the 0 or 1 logical states for the automata.

Fig. 6. Molecule $C_{44}H_{18}$

By considering a cluster formed by two interacting finite ribbons we found the distance for which the total energy of the cluster is minimum (figure 8). This energy minimum occurs when the nearer edges of the ribbons have opposite total density spin polarization, i.e., energy states with configurations 00 or 11, we call it the "antiferromagnetic state" (AS). Furthermore, this system also presents a metastable state with spin polarizations of 01 or 10 for neighbor edges with the same type of spin polarization, we call it "ferromagnetic state" (FS). These are the two kinds of states represented in Fig. 7. For this cluster the energy separation between the states FS and AS is ΔE(FS−AS) = 0.0629 meV. This difference in energy is very little as compared with the energy separation between the FS (or AS) state and the paramagnetic state calculated without spin polarization (corresponding to 278 meV for the molecule of C44H18). This energy difference is shown in Figure 9.

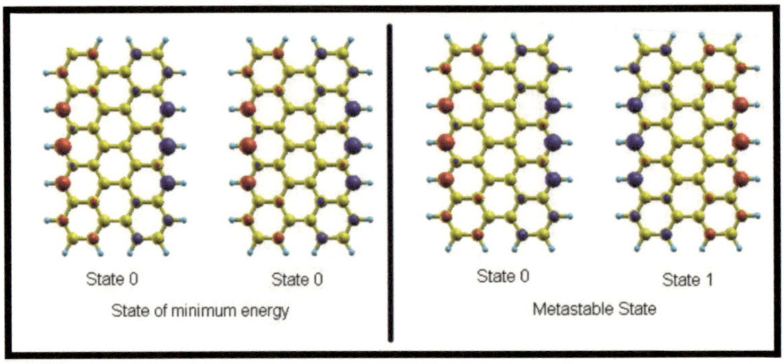

Fig. 7. Minimum energy state (left panel) and metastable state (right panel) for a system of two $C_{44}H_{18}$ molecules. Red balls represent the spin up total density and blue balls represent the spin down total density.

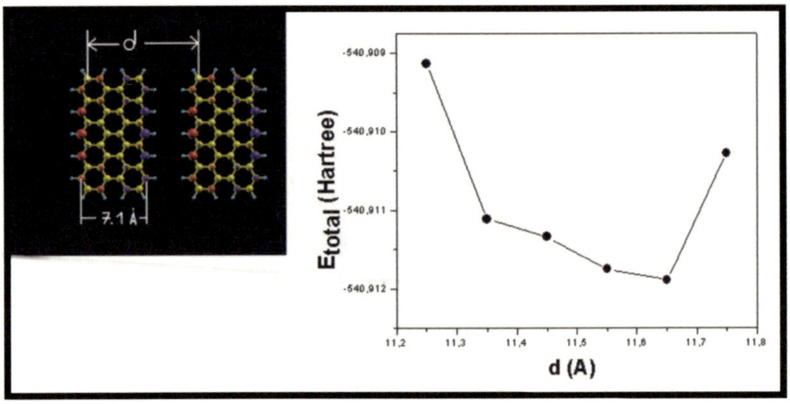

Fig. 8. Study to get the distance that minimizes the energy of the cluster.

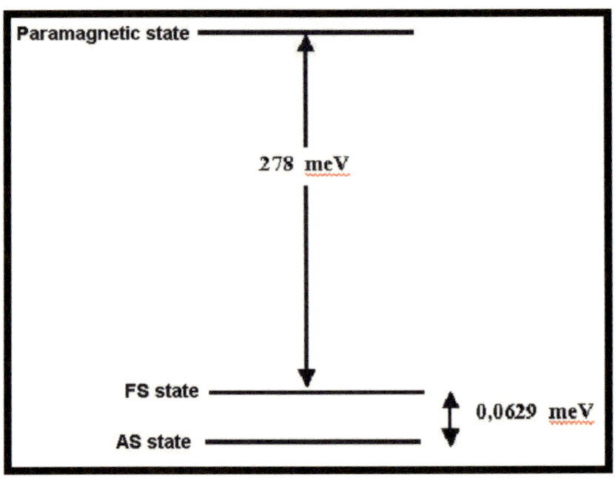

Fig. 9. Energy separation between FS state and the paramagnetic state.

The energy separation between the states AS and FS is usually referred in the cellular automata literature as "kink energy" E_K. In the context of magnetic properties we call it the parameter of "superexchange" between cells $J = E_K$. To postulate these systems as room-temperature binary information processors we have to study the feasibility of this superexchange effect, which we have found for small structures as not limited in scaling. We have performed the same study for longer nanoribbons with more atoms along its zigzag edges. Our results are displayed in Fig. 10 and they indicate that effectively this effect can be scaled to greater size systems. To verify that the scaling works linearly for very long ribbons we have performed first principles calculations for two infinitely long GNRs. To do this we built a tridimensional (3D) crystal but considering only interaction between the two GNRs. Figure 11 shows a scheme in the *X-Y* plane, in the *Z* direction the ribbon separation was 15 Å. We consider three unitary cells with a different number of atoms along the zigzag edges N_Z = 9,10,11. Our results show that independent of the size of the unitary cell the normalized *J* parameter is J(meV) / N_Z = 0.022 which corresponds to the slope obtained in the case of the finite nanoribbons in Fig. 10.

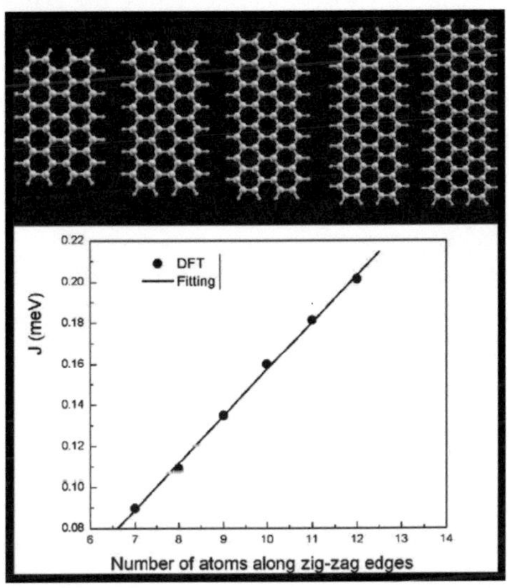

Fig. 10. Superexchange energy parameter of in meV as a function of the number of carbon atoms along the zigzag edges.

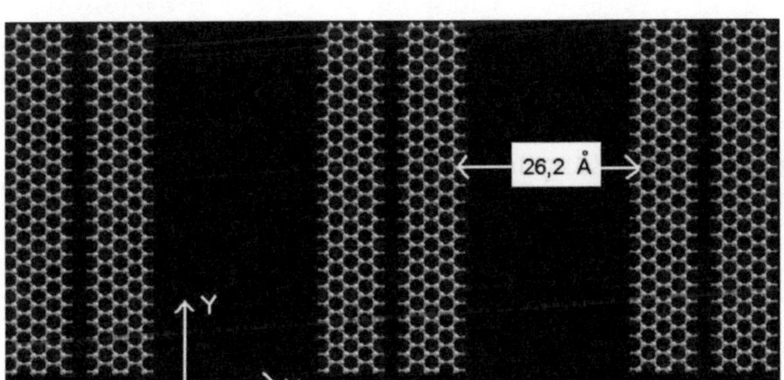

Fig. 11. Scheme in the X-Y plane of the 3D crystal used to perform the calculation of the *J* value for two infinite ribbons in the Z direction the ribbon separation was 15 Å.

The dynamic response of the GNRCA is studied by implementing an "accelerated algorithm for discrete systems" (Krauth, 2006) based in the Glauber dynamics (Glauber, 1963). To perform this study we must define a unit of time for doing the simulation. Due to the phenomenon of spin polarization has a completely quantum origin, we will use the evolution propagator to estimate the time for the signal transmission. The system consisting of two finite GNRs, such as the one shown in Fig. 7, can be seen as a two-level system so a general state of the system can be written as $|\Psi\rangle = ae^{-i\omega t}|0\rangle + be^{i\omega t}|1\rangle$ with $\omega = \Delta E/\hbar$ where $\Delta E = J$. With this frequency and a threshold J value of 150 meV, we define the time unit adopted in modeling the dynamic behavior of the automaton as $T = \hbar/\pi J \approx 10^{-15}$ s.

We intend to study the form in the binary information is propagated through a molecular wire formed by N cells. To do this we must have one or more control cells that trigger the change in the state of the GNRCA. By defining nc as the number of control cells that change simultaneously its polarization spin state under an external excitation, then the input parameters for the GNRCA dynamic simulation will be N, nc, J, and the system temperature T. The results indicate the existence of a threshold value for the superexchange parameter J for a given temperature, above that value the automaton state can be changed and it will remain in that state, meanwhile the control cell cannot be changed. The threshold value of J is obtained by the following procedure: (1) for an automaton of N cells (GNRs) and with nc control cells, it is defined as an initial configuration with all cells having the same polarization state (+1 or -1). The magnetization will be given by: $M = (1/N)\sum_{j=1}^{N} m_j$, where m_j is the polarization of each cell. (2) For a temperature T and a given value of J, the control cell polarization is reversed and an average value for the magnetization of the whole automaton is calculated for a sufficiently long time (infinite time compared with the automaton operation time). The top panel of Fig. 12 shows the study for automata with 3, 4, 5, and 6 cells, and one control cell ($n_C = 1$). All cells are in an initial configuration -1. The polarization of the first cell is changed to +1 and then it is waited for t =30 ps. We can see that for all values of the parameter J, the average magnetization is always positive because the polarization of the control cell remains fixed in +1, and the rest oscillates between -1 and +1. For the molecular automaton that works as a cable, it is expected that once the polarization of the control cell changes, the other cells also change and they remain in the new state of polarization (meanwhile the polarization of the cell control does not change). In the study illustrated in the Fig. 12 it is observed that for T=300 K the J value for which that state is reached is close to J =150 meV for all automata. This value increases with the number of cells in the automaton, as shown in the bottom panel of Fig. 12 for automata with nc =1 and N = 7, 8, 9, and 10, respectively. To obtain this value for J the former study of scaling shows that it would be required ribbons of an approximated length of 2.1 μm along the zigzag edges.

Figure 13 shows a simulation for an automaton with a variable number of control cells. The figure displays the time (in picosecond) that the signal takes to go from one end to the other as a function of the number N of cells for T =300 K, J=150 meV, and nc from 1 to 4. It can be observed that the time increases exponentially with the number of cells N and it decreases linearly with the number of control cells. In this way we can postulate a molecular cable to transmit digital information. Figure 14 shows a diagram of the molecular wire.

This study shows that it is possible to propagate binary information through cellular automata based on carbon based nanostructures. We have analyzed other types of shaped

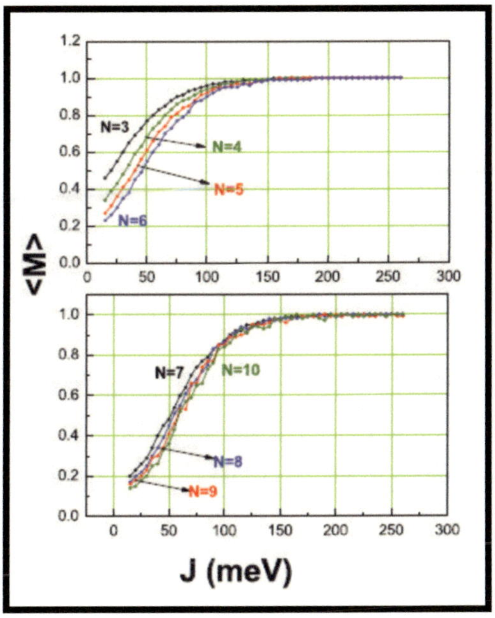

Fig. 12. Upper panel shows the average of the magnetization as a function of J for automata with one control cell and N = 3, 4, 5 and 6 cells, respectively. Lower panel the same study for automata with N = 7, 8, 9 and 10 cells.

graphene fragments, for instance triangular structures (figure 15) that have the advantages of having an even number of them in the automaton, an inverter logic gate could be automatically implemented. Other structures studied are Z-shaped (figure 16) ribbons (León et al., 2008) and antidot lattices formed by holes with zigzag edges on a graphene nanoribbon (Rosales et al., 2009). The disadvantage of these types of clusters arises from the difficulty in the synthesis process and scaling. The systems of graphene nanoribbons

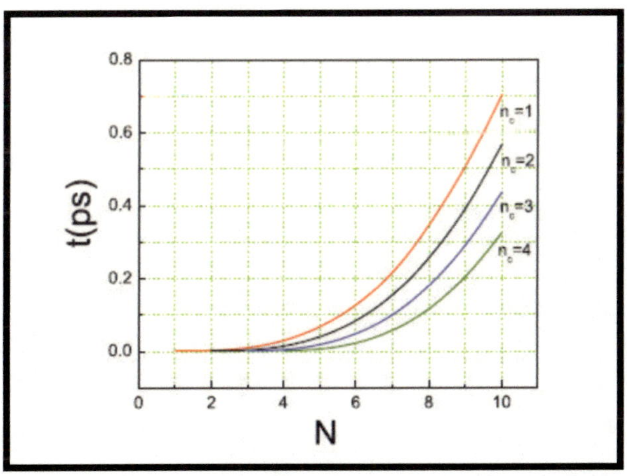

Fig. 13. Time taken by the signal to travel from one end to the other of the automaton as a function of the total number of cells The simulation was performed for J = 150 meV and T = 300 K. Different curves represent simulations with distinct number of control cells.

proposed in this work are scalable for working at room temperature. Besides, standard lithographic techniques and other controlled cutting processes (Ci et al., 2008) can be used for creating graphene nanoribbons with zigzag edges and length desired.

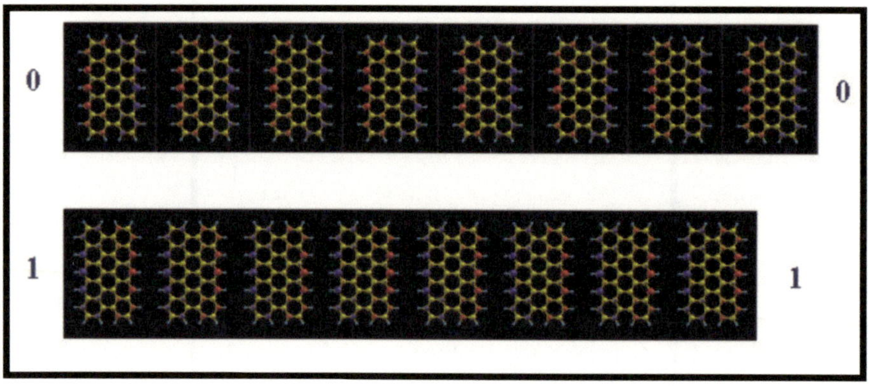

Fig. 14. Molecular wire.

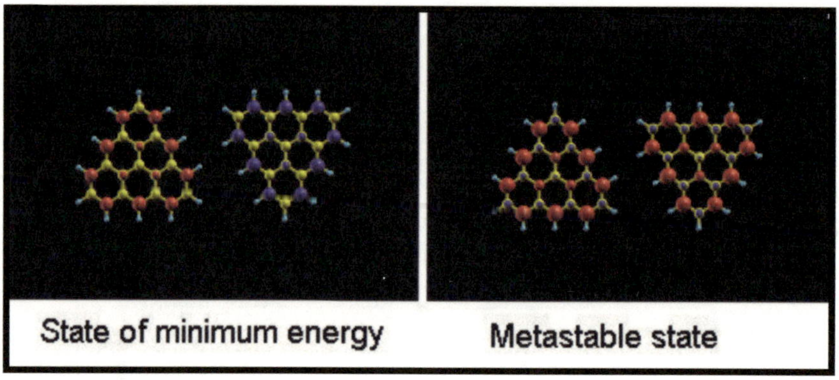

Fig. 15. Triangular structures.

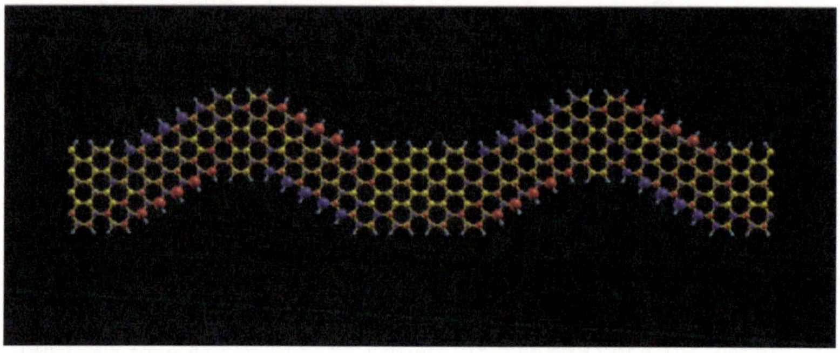

Fig. 16. Structures Z-shaped ribbons.

4. Graphane Nanoribbon array in a cellular automata architecture with electric polarization

4.1 Quantum dots in graphane nanostructures

The role of quantum dots in the studied nanostructures will be played by oxide reduction centers. These centers will be obtained by leaving two regions, on opposite edges, with three unhydrogenated carbon atoms. As a result of this, the free electrons will locate themselves in one of the quantum dots if they are confined with an external electrical field. To verify the feasibility of our research we made calculations of the stability of these nanosytems. The results show that these structures are stable at room temperature. Figure 17 shows the scheme of a $C_{28}H_{36}$ molecule with two quantum dots of the type previously described. In this figure, we can appreciate the isosurface of the HOMO for a determined value, when the molecule is in an electrical field of 1.0 GV/m according to the direction in the figure.

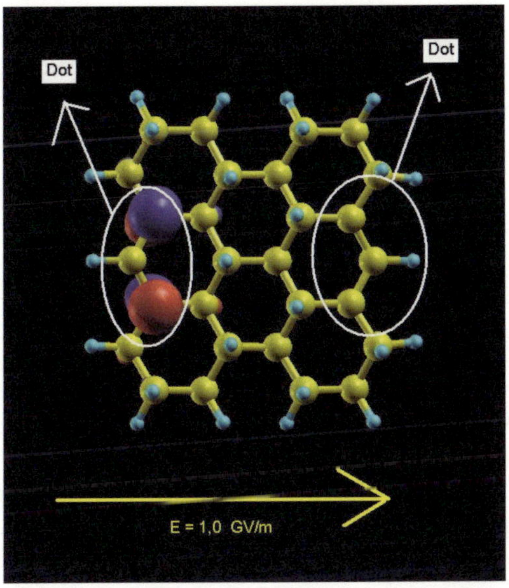

Fig. 17. Scheme of a hydrogenated aromatic molecule, except in the regions where quantum dots are located.

In the case of the graphane nanoribbon, the regions with two quantum dots will be separated by a region sufficient to create an infinite barrier for the electrons compared to the barrier between the quantum dots (figure 18). This distance should allow for the electrostatic interaction among neighboring cells. The value of this parameter in function of the width of the ribbon, the temperature and the type of substrate that supports the structure are determined in this investigation. In the case of molecular arrays, this distance represents the separation among the mass centers of the molecules. Figure 19 shows a scheme of the quantum dots in the nanoribbons and in the molecular array. The manner of arranging the quantum dots in the ribbon and molecular array allows for propagating information, that is, this structures represent molecular wires to join the different devices that process and store information. The quantum dot arrays in both structures are designed in this investigation to develop universal logic operations and the form of the arrays are designed so that they function as data storing devices.

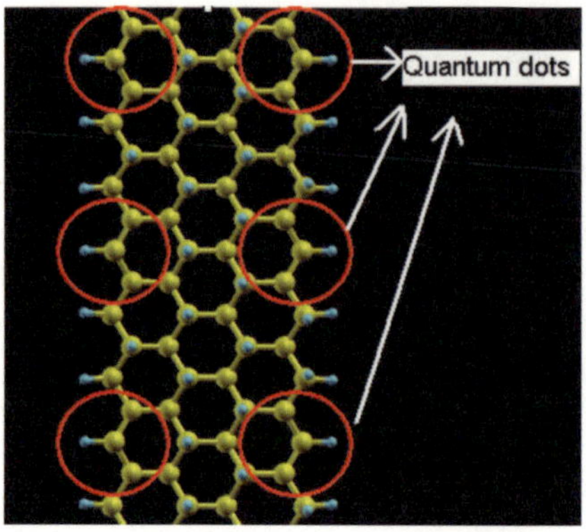

Fig. 18. Scheme of quantum dots in the graphane nanoribbons.

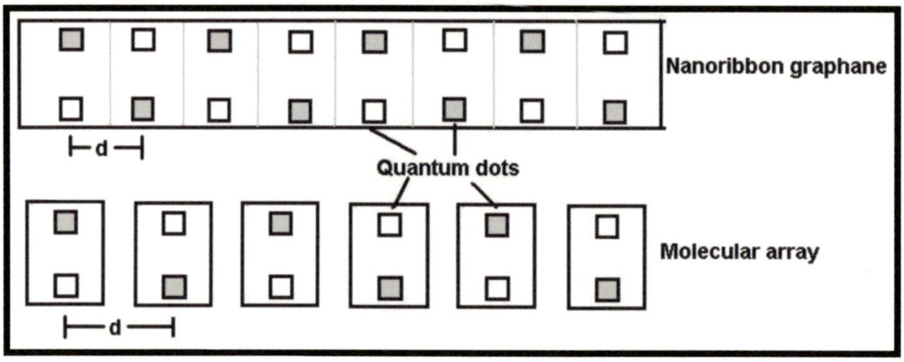

Fig. 19. Scheme of quantum dots in the studied structures

4.2 Electronic and magnetic properties of the Nanoribbons Graphene

The electronic and magnetic properties of the systems are obtained by means of first principles calculations based on the pseudo-potentials method and by using the generalized gradient approximation Perdew-Burke-Ernzerhof with spin polarization (Perdew et al., 1996). All structures are relaxed using the Direct Inversion Iterative Subspace method (Csaszar & Pulay, 1984) with a residual force criteria less than 10^{-4} (Hartree / bohr). Calculations were performed using the OPENMX Code (Openmx, 2007). Figure 20 shows the result of the calculation for a neutral nanoribbon. The zero energy corresponds to the Fermi level. We can see that the electrons with energy near the Fermi level, are located on both sides of the nanoribbon. Analyzing Figure 21, we see that the ground state of the system is degenerated to the value of spin. This means that if we remove an electron from the unit cell, we have a system with two quantum dots and an electron tunneling between quantum dots.

The calculations of the electronic properties of a cell (molecule) show that in the presence of an electric field (polarization of the neighboring cell), electric charge is located, as shown in Figure 22.

The calculation of the interaction energy between two consecutive cells for the nanoribbons and the molecular arrangement is about 540 meV. This implies that we can spread information through the cellular automata at room temperature.

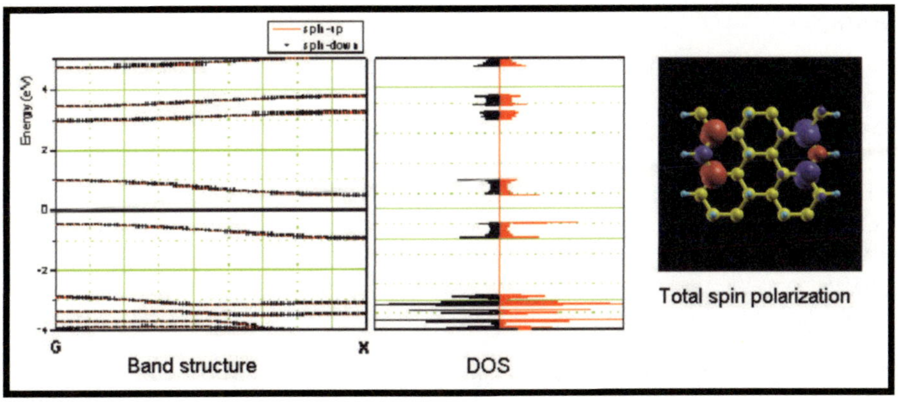

Fig. 20. Band structure, density of states and total spin polarization of the unitary cell.

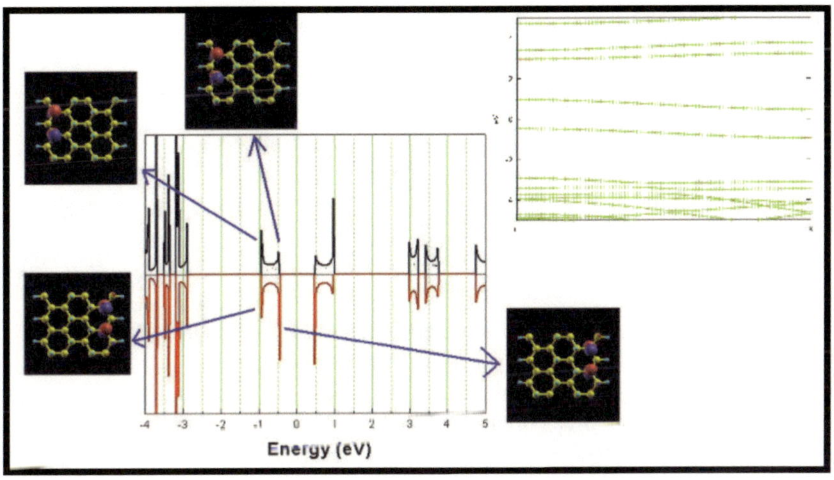

Fig. 21. Real part of the wave function, density of states and band structure for neutral nanoribbon.

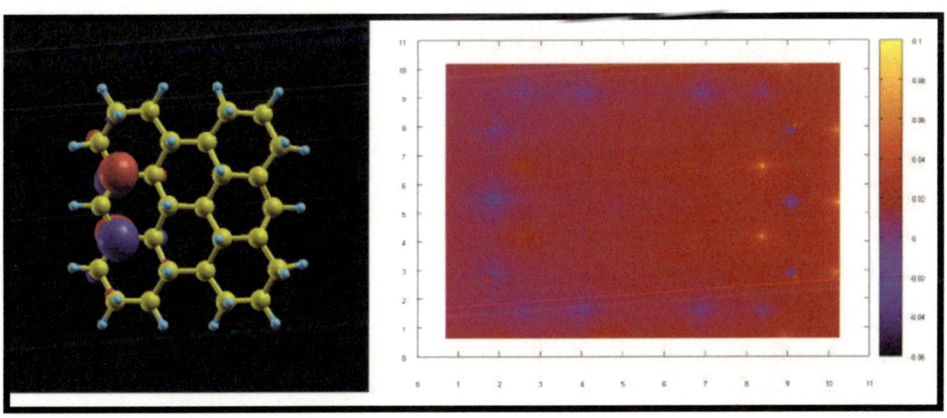

Fig. 22. HOMO and excess of electrical charge in the molecule E = 1,0 GV/m Q = + 1

5. References

Amlani, I.; Orlov, A. O.; Toth, G.; Bernstein, G. H.; Lent, C. S. & Snider, G. L. (1999). *Science* 284, 289.

Balog, R.; Jørgensen, B.; Nilsson, L.; Andersen, M.; Rienks, E.; Bianchi, M.; Fanetti, M.; Lægsgaard, E.; Baraldi, A.; Lizzit, S.; Sljivancanin, Z.; Besenbacher, F.; Hammer, B.; Pedersen, T. G.; Hofmann, P. & Hornekær, L. (2010). *Nature Materials* 9, 315.

Berger, C.; Song, Z.; Li, X.; Wu, X.; Brown, N.; Naud, C.; Mayou, D.; Li, T.; Hass, J.; Marchenkov, A. N.; Conrad, E. H.; First, P. N. & de Heer, W. A. (2006). *Science* 312, 1191.

Castro Neto, A. H.; Guinea, F.; Peres, N. M. R.; Novoselov, K. S. & Geim, A. K. (2009). *Rev. Mod. Phys.* 81, 109.

Ci, L.; Xu, Z; Wang, L.; Gao, W.; Ding, F.; Kelly, K. F.; Yakobson, B. I. & Ajayan, P. M. (2008). *Nano Res.* 1, 116.

Csurgay, A. I.; Porod, W. & Lent, C. S. (2000). *IEEE Trans. On Circuits and Systems* I 47, 1212.

Elias, D. C.; Nair, R. R.; Mohiuddin, T. M. G.; Morozov, S. V.; Blake, P.; Halsall, M. P.; Ferrari, A. C.; Boukhvalov, D. W.; Katsnelson, M. I.; Geim, A. K. & Novoselov K. S. (2009). *Science* 323, 610.

Fitzsimons, Xiao, L.; Benjamin, S. C. & Jones J. A. (2007) *Phys. Rev. Lett.* 99, 030501.

Geim, A. K. (2009). *Sience* 324, 1530.

Glauber, R. J. (1963). *J. Math. Phys.* (Cambridge, Mass.) 4, 294.

Han, M. Y.; Özyilmaz, B.; Zhang, Y. & Kim, P. (2007). *Phys. Rev. Lett.* 98, 206805.

Heersche, H. B.; Jarillo-Herrero, P.; Oostinga, J. B.; Vandersypen, L. M. K. & Morpurgo, A. F. (2007), *Nature* 446, 56.

Jiao, J.; Long, G. J.; Grandjean, F.; Beatty, A. M. & Fehlner, T. P. (2003). *J. Am. Chem. Soc.* 125, 7522.

Krauth, W. (2006). *Statistical Mechanics: Algorithms and Computations* (Oxford University Press, New York).

Kummamuru, R. K.; Orlov, A. O.; Ramasubramaniam, R.; Lent, C. S.; Bernstein, G. H. & Snider, G. L. (2003). *IEEE Trans. On Electron Devices* 50, 1906).

Lent, C. S.; Tougaw, P. D.; Porod, W. & Bernstein, G. H. (1993). *Nanotechnology* 4, 49.

León, A.; Barticevic, Z. & Pacheco, M. (2009). *Appl. Phys. Lett.* 94, 173111.

León, A.; Barticevic, Z. & Pacheco, M. (2008). *Microelectron. J.* 39, 1239.

Li, Y.; Zhou, Z.; Shen, P. & Chen, Z. (2009). *J. Phys. Chem C* 113, 15043.

Lu, Y. H. & Feng, Y. P. (2009). *J. Phys. Chem C* 113, 20841.

Macucci, M. (2006). *Quantum Cellular Automata*, Imperial College Press, ISBN 1-86094-632-1, London, United Kingdom.

Nielsen, M. A. & Chuang, I. L. (2003). *Quantum Computation and Quantum Information*, Cambridge University Press, ISBN 0-521-63503-9, Cambridge, United Kingdom.

Nakada, K.; Fujita, M.; Dresselhaus, G. & Dresselhaus M. S. (1996). *Phys. Rev. B* 54, 17954.

Nonoselov, K. S.; Geim, A. K.; Morozov, S. V.; Jiang, D.; Zhang, Y.; Dubonos, S. V.; Grigorieva, I. V. & Firsov, A. A. (2004) *Science* 306, 666.

OPENMX (2007). http://www.openmx-square.org.

Orlov, A. O.; Amlani, I.; Bernstein, G. H.; Lent, C. S. & Snider, G. L. (1997). *Science* 277, 928.

Rosales, L.; Pacheco, M.; León, A.; Barticevic, Z.; Latgé, A. & Orellana, P. (2009). *Phys. Rev. B* 80, 073402.

Singh, A. K. & Yakobson, B. I. (2009). *Nano Letters* 9, 1540.

Sofo, J. O.; Chaudhari, A. S. & Barber, G. D. (2007). *Phys. Rev. B 75*, 153401.

Wakabayashi K. (2001). *Phys. Rev. B* 64, 125428.

3

Magnetic QCA Design: Modeling, Simulation and Circuits

Mariagrazia Graziano, Marco Vacca and Maurizio Zamboni
Electronics Department, Politecnico di Torino
Italy

1. Introduction

QCA, in their general meaning, are bistable cells coupled through electrostatic forces. There are two main implementations of this principle: molecular and magnetic QCA. In molecular QCA the base cell is represented using complex molecules with many oxide-reduction centres. They have a great potential, mainly for the high speed reachable, but they are not expected to be feasible with current and near term technology. On the contrary, magnetic QCA, where the base cells are single-domain nanometer pills-shaped magnets, are feasible right now, using high end electron beam lithography (EBL). Single domain nanomagnets exhibit two stable magnetic states, "up" and "down", carrying thus a binary information thanks to their reciprocal influence based on a "domino" effect. Even thought their perspective frequency is not high, they are interesting because they represent the real possibility to build a full magnetic electronic circuit, with all the inherent advantages that this implies: extreme low power consumption and intrinsic memory ability, i.e. the possibility to implement circuits with mixed computational and memory abilities.
Many works have been proposed in recent years either on circuits and architectures (see for all (1),(2),(3)) or on detailed physical nanomagnets behavior analysis (see for an example (4)). In the former case it is shown that, should technology be of support, computation would be feasible, and many of the traditional CMOS based digital implementations could be adopted. In the latter case, experiments are carried on to demonstrate the feasibility of the MQCA idea adopting to date production phases. Anyway, the two aspects are seldom integrated, thus the design approach is splitted in two averted points of view, while, as we have experienced especially in the recent CMOS technology success story, the strength of a design methodology is based on the ability of linking them as much as possible. We believe thus that the current scientific MQCA scenario requires to entangle circuit design with technology when the aim is demonstrating the feasibility of the MQCA computation paradigm.
In this chapter we show our approach for twisting computation and implementation. The idea is to assess a practicable and not theoretical technological implementation for MQCA; to constraint the circuit design to such a base; to solve at the architectural level, when possible, the critical limitations due to it; to describe the circuit behavior so that real implementation details can be taken into account, thus circuit performance can be estimated and feedbacks to technologists suggested; to step progressively to the physical implementation and to enrich the circuit description with on the field data. Here we show the preliminary results of such approach. In section 2 the base theory of quantum dot cellular automata is explained,

while in section 3 the magnetic implementation is described. In section 4 the fundamental technological hypotesis, the so-called "snake-clock" implementation, is explained. In section 5 an example of circuit description is given, followed (section 6) by a specific architectural solution adopted and with the "low-level" details added to it. In section 7 the preliminary technological implementation are described. In section 8 the conclusion and the direction of our future research are summarized.

2. Quantum dot Cellular Automata (QCA)

Quantum dot Cellular Automata (QCA) are a recent (5),(6),(7),(8) specific application to microelectronics of the original cellular automata principle (9). The logic values 0 and 1 are represented using bistable charge configurations of many identical square shape cells (10). The base cell, shown in figure 1.A, is constituted by four quantum dots, one for each corner. Each dot can be occupied by electrons, however, if two are the available electrons and since they tend to repel each others, at the equilibrium only the two dots on the diagonal will be filled. Square cells have only two diagonals, therefore only two are the possible states, which represent the two logic values 0 and 1.

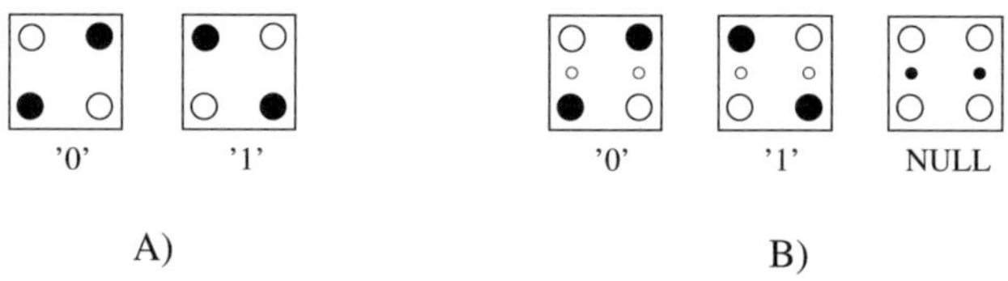

Fig. 1. Quantum dot Cellular Automata (QCA) cells. A) Four dots cells. B) Six dots cells.

Circuits can be built placing many cascaded cells (11), and using electrostatic interaction among them to drive the information through the circuit. An example of a simple circuit, a wire, is shown in figure 2. Starting from the initial status indicated in figure 2.A, if the first cell is forced from 0 to 1 using an external electric field (figure 2.B), the second cell will switch due to the electrostatic interaction between adjacent electrons (figure 2.C). This process will continue until the end of the wire (figure 2.D).

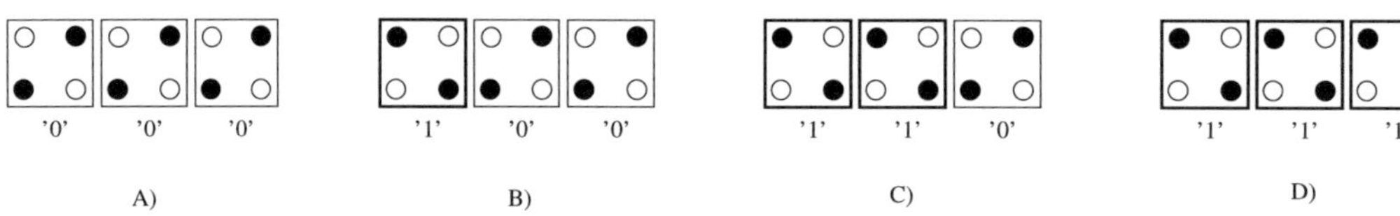

Fig. 2. Quantum dot Cellular Automata (QCA) wire. A) Starting condition, each cell is 0. B) First cell is forced to 1. C) Second cell switches to 1, due to the electrostatic interaction. D) Third switches to 1.

Following this principle many types of circuits can be built. In particular, four are the blocks which perform the basic logic operations (figure 3): the wire (figure 3.A), the inverter (figure 3.B), the majority gate (figure 3.C) and the crosswire (figure 3.D). The inverter and the majority gate are the two blocks which enables the logic computation, but, while the inverter performs a simple signal inversion, the logic equation of the second one is uncommon: the value of the output is equal to the value of the majority of the inputs. The last fundamental block, the crosswire, represents a special feature of this technology: it allows the crossing of two different signals on the same plane without interferences.

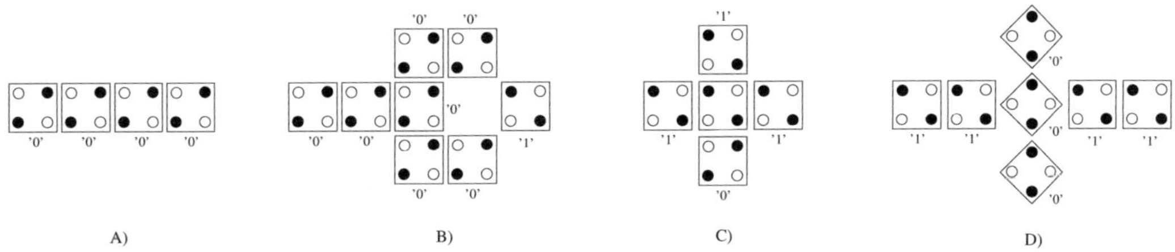

Fig. 3. Quantum dot Cellular Automata (QCA) basic blocks. A) Wire. B) Inverter. C) Majority gate. D) Crosswire.

The limitations of this theoretical principle are two: the energy barrier between different states is high, while the electrostatic interaction between neighbour cells is normally too low to force switching in a neighbour cell; second, circuits composed by too many cascaded cells are subjected to error propagation due to electromagnetic and thermal noises. To solve these problems an external control flow, the so-called clock (12), is introduced. A modified cell with six dots (shown in figure 1.B) is needed in this case. When an external electric field is applied, the cell is forced to an unstable state called NULL, lowering the potential barrier between the two stable states. When the field is removed the cell switches to 0 or 1, depending on the neighbour cells. Since only circuits composed by a limited number of cells can work without error propagation, a spatial flow control system is introduced. The circuit is divided in small areas, composed by a limited number of cells, called clock zones. Every zone is separately controlled using a time varying clock signal as shown in figure 4. In the classical definition circuits are divided in four clock zones, the circuits partition and the clock signal waveforms are in figure 4.

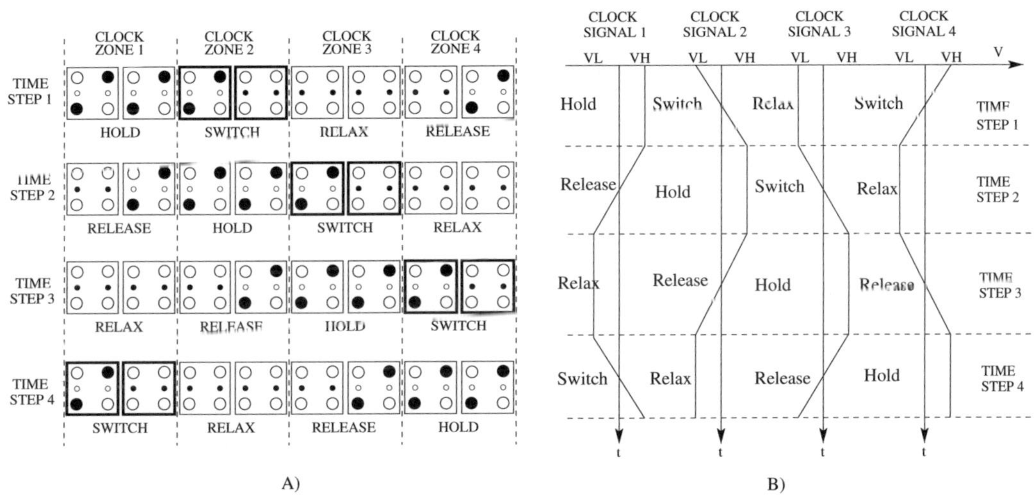

Fig. 4. Clock mechanism. A) Clock zones. B) Clock signals.

When the clock signal is high (V = VH) the potential barrier between the two logic states is risen and therefore the cell switch is impossible. In this case the cells are in HOLD state. When the clock signal decreases from VH to VL the potential barrier decreases its value slowly, cells start to switch from a stable state to an unstable one. Cells are in the RELEASE phase. When the clock signal is low (V = VL) the potential barrier is zero, the two logic states are not separated. Cells are in the RELAX state. Finally when the clock signal rises from -1 to +1 the potential barrier increases its value slowly forcing cells in a stable state: cells therefore are in the SWITCH state. As clear from figure 4.B, the clock signal is always identical, but applied with a different phase to other clock zones. This allows the spatial propagation of the signal through the circuit as shown in figure 4.A. During the first time step the clock zone number 2 is in the switch phase, they are in an unstable state and are read to switch to one of the stable states. Cells at its left are in the hold state and act like an input, while cells on its right are in an unstable state so they have no influence, allowing the correct switching of the cells in clock zone 2. During the second time step the situation is the same, but in this case the clock zone number 3 is in the switch phase.

Signals in this way propagate correctly through the circuit, however the signal flow is monodirectional. In order to propagate signals in every directions a complex clock zone layout is required (13), for example the one shown in figure 5 which assures signal propagation in every direction. Such layouts require that the clock signal must be confined perfectly to the clock zone, and do not interfere with the neighbour zones.

Fig. 5. Complex QCA clock zones layout.

The theoretical principle of the QCA can be implemented in different ways. Four are the proposals in literature for a real QCA implementation; they are briefly mentioned in the following.

Metal QCA (10)(12). The base cell is constituted by six metal lines, that act like quantum dots, on a substrate of silicon oxide. Metal lines are separated by tunnel-junction, which allow the electrons to exchange between neighbour dots. The charge configuration of the cell is read using a single electron transistor (SET). The cell works properly, unfortunately only at temperatures near the absolute zero.

Semiconductor QCA (14)(15). Complex eterostructures of Si-Ge or GaAs are used to create quantum dots that are able to trap electrons. The operation temperature is higher than the metal QCA but is always too low for practical uses. In order to increase the operation temperature cell dimensions must be reduced at some nanometers, but this is impossible with current technology. Moreover, one condition necessary for proper operations of QCA circuits is that every cell must be identical, but, if a so complex structure is realized with the desired resolution, the impact of defect rate caused by the fabrication process will make QCA inoperable, limiting every practical possibility of this implementation.

Molecular QCA (16)(17)(18)(19). In this case, complex molecules with many oxide-reduction centres, which act like quantum dots, are used as base cell. Electrons can react with every centre inside the molecule, changing the spatial distribution of the electric charge, and the logic value associated to it. The use of molecules bring many advantages, like that every QCA cell is identical to each others and the fact that molecules circuits can work at room temperature. However the most interesting aspect of the use of molecules is that the switching speed expected, from one charge configuration to another: it grants the possibility to obtain operating frequency of some THz; moreover the dimensions of such molecules are very small (a few nanometers), allowing the generation of circuits with a very high device densities. Molecular QCA are very attracting but their realization requires the ability of manipulating single molecules, which is not possible with up-to-date technology.

Magnetic QCA (20). The base cell is a single domain nanomagnet, with only two possible magnetizations which represent the two logic value 0 and 1. This is the second promising implementation of the QCA principle, because also in this case circuits can work at room temperature. Unfortunately the expected speed is lower not only than the molecular case, but also than CMOS circuits. However magnetic QCA have some specific advantages which make them attractive, in particular the low power consumption and the possibility to realize them with current technology: this allows to experiment and study the QCA principle so that most of the achievements can be adapted in a near future to molecular QCA, as soon as this solution becomes feasible.

3. Magnetic QCA

The idea of building a logic completely based on magnetic elements is not new, as it dates back to sixty years ago. However at that time it was not possible to realize such circuits, due to technology limitations; on the contrary today QCA principle seems the perfect way to implement a fully magnetic logic. In the Magnetic Quantum dot Cellular Automata (MQCA) implementation the basic cell is a nanoscale nanomagnets, with sizes between 50nm and 100nm. Magnetic materials are composed by magnetic domains, small areas with a uniform magnetization, and the behaviour is governed by the hysteresis cycle, which represents how material magnetization (M) changes if an external magnetic field (H) is applied, see figure 6.A. If the dimensions of the magnetic materials are less then approximately 100nm, there is only one magnetic domain and the hysteresis cycle change as shown in figure 6.B. In this case at the equilibrium only two magnetizations are possible, and they represent the two logic values 0 and 1. At the same time dimensions must be bigger than approximately 50nm, to avoid the superparamagnetic effect, which makes the magnetization varying with thermal fluctuations. Another important aspect is that nanomagnets must have one side bigger than the others, with an aspect ratio of almost 2, so that the magnetization is forced along the long side, the so-called easy axis. This is due to the shape anisotropy: when a magnetic material is magnetized a demagnetization field is generated, this field reaches its minimum along the longer axis of the materials, therefore the magnetization, at the equilibrium, tend to stay parallel to the easy axis.

Magnetic QCA can reach a speed of about 1GHz; however they have some significant advantages:

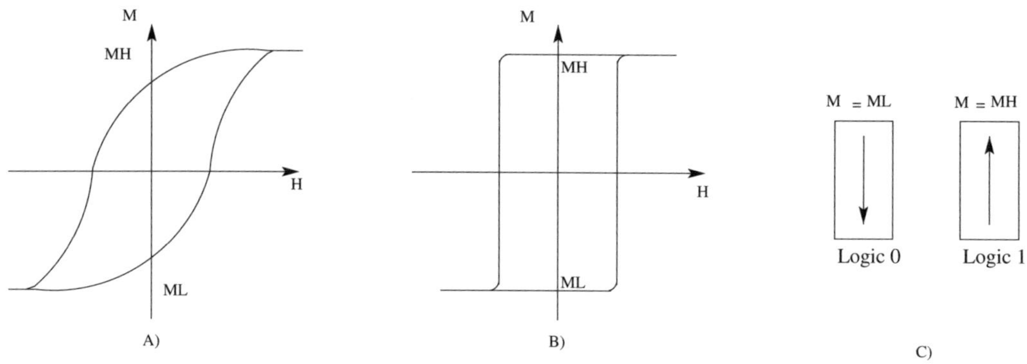

Fig. 6. A) Multidomain magnetic material hysteresis cycle. B) Singledomain magnetic material hysteresis cycle. C) Magnetic Quantum dot Cellular Automata (MQCA) cells.

- they are one of the only two implementations of the QCA principle that works at room temperature;
- they can be realized with current technology, with high end electron beam lithography;
- they have a very low power absorption, requiring an energy of 15-30$K_b T$ for every nanomagnets to switch, granting the possibility to obtain very low power electronic devices;
- they have an intrinsic memory ability, as, due to their magnetic nature they maintain the information stored also without power supply, enabling thus to define circuits with mixed computational-storage abilities;
- most of the high level research related to MQCA can be transposed to the molecular QCA, once technology will be ready.

4. A feasible three phases clock

It has been demonstrated (see (21)) that for MQCA, as well as for molecular QCA, an adiabatic switching is preferred to assure a correct information propagation. This means that switching of a nanomagnet from state "up" to state "down" is favoured if an intermediate state is reached first. That is, similarly to what mentioned in section 2, an external field is applied so that the pill "memory" (previous magnetization state to "up" or "down") is erased (magnetization become a perpendicular to "up" or "down" direction), and, at this point, as soon the external field is released, an input can more easily and with lower power loss force the new "up" or "down" magnetization to the pill. This is particularly important when the input of nanomagnet-B is another nanomagnet-A, which can force on the coupled nanomagnet-B only a limited magnetic field due to its intrinsic characteristics (shape and material).
Such external field is meant as a clock, as it is iteratively switched on and off and allows the evaluation phase, even though it has not the "traditional" function of a clock signal. One of the related aspects is the clock organization in complex computational structures. In this chapter, thus, we propose, starting from (22), a solution to clock distribution, "snake-clock", initially presented in our works in (23),(24) which we judge more feasible for the multiple-phases clock distribution, necessary to allow the information propagation without losses in complex nanomagnets arrays previously described. First, phases are three, differently from the four ones introduced for the molecular case: in figure 7.a the RESET, SWITCH and HOLD sequence

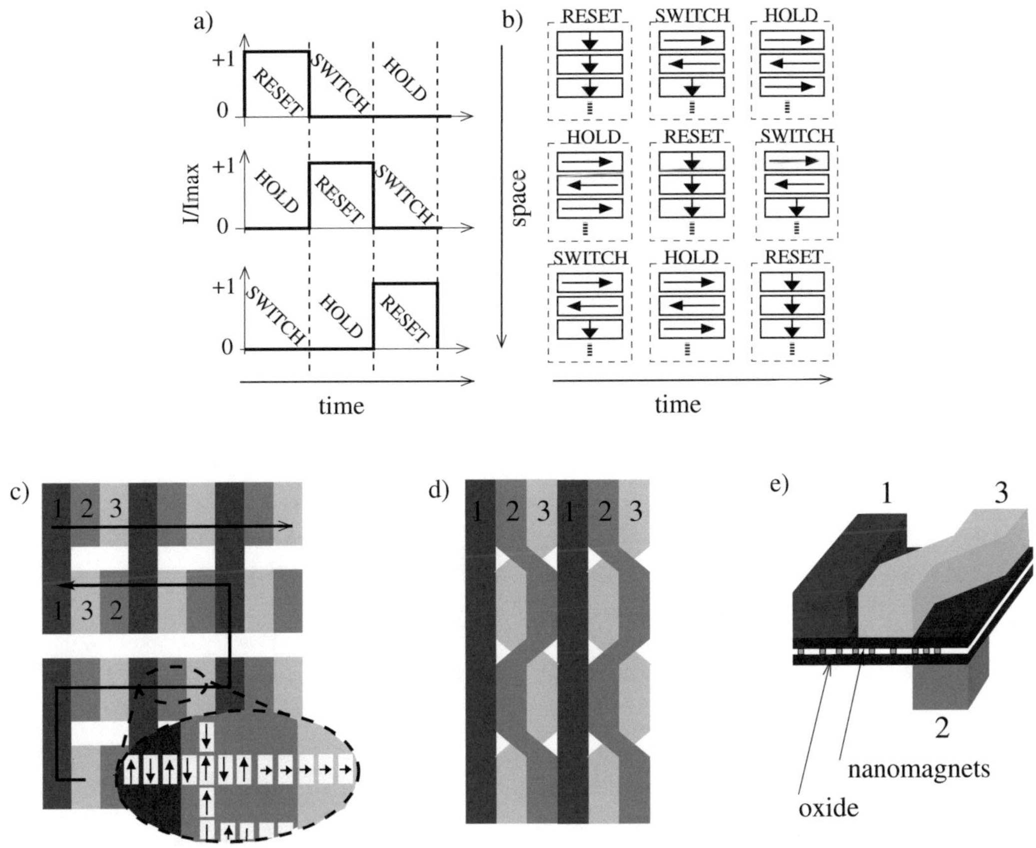

Fig. 7. Proposed clock organisation: a) Threes phases sequence, b) MQCA behaviour in three zones, c) Snake clock logic zones view, d) Snake clock layout top view e) Snake clock physical distribution.

is shown both in time and space. In figure 7.b the behaviour of nanomagnets grouped (each clock phase should serve a group of pills for the unavoidable size difference between the pills and the metal line generating such a phase) in the correspondent clock zones is depicted: when a cell group is in the HOLD phase the stable "up" and "down" states own the digital information; thus they can force it toward the near group which is in the SWITCH state, that is, its previous state has been previously "erased" thanks to a reset, and now these pills are ready to be influenced. The group in the following region is itself in the RESET state. In figure 7.c the top view of the clock zones is sketched together with the information flow: this style still allows the information flow in both the horizontal and vertical directions, but, as the correct phase sequence (1,2,3 in figure) must be assured, only a "snake" like propagation is possible. Even if this seems a limitation, it is feasible with current technology, differently from previously proposed solutions. This is also evident in the layout and physical views 7.d and 7.e respectively. The nanomagnets arrays can be sandwiched between two thin oxide layers, and on the top and bottom of this structure metal wires carrying the clock signal can be routed. One stripe (phase 1) can be straight, while the others (phases 2 and 3) should be routed in a zig-zig style, interlaced as they were twisted but belonging to two different metal layers. Active nanomagnet pills cannot be present in zones where metal wires are oblique. As proposed in (22), clock lines could be based on copper wires of an height to be accurately tailored, as demonstrated in (25), in order to trade off between the correct magnetic field generated to assure reset and the power consumption due to current flowing.

5. Snake-clock NCL-HDL MQCA model description

The proposed structure influences the circuit model we describe. We use VHDL, as proposed in (2) and (26) for general QCA, to model the circuit behaviour, but we also renew the description specifically to the magnetic implementation and to the "snake-clock" related information propagation. An example of a logic gate described in the following is in figure 8, where registers are associated to phase transitions (each register is indeed placed on a different phase zone), and combinational gates (in this case a Majority Voter, that is the basic QCA component) to the "computational" part of a clock zone (in this example, due to problems with available space, phase three only has one computational block). Wires and blocks are composed of arrays and structures of nanomagnets as in the "arrow" example in figure 7.c detail.

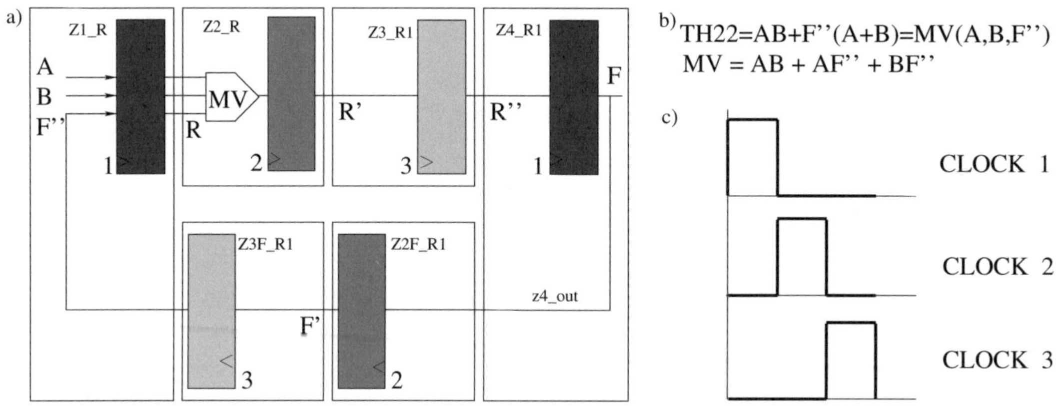

Fig. 8. Th22 behavioural model: a) Schematic, b) Th22 and majority voter logic equations, c) Registers clock signals.

One of the most critical problem in QCA is the "layout=timing" one, that is the overall timing and correct behaviour of QCA depends on the circuit layout. As an example, inputs to a generic Majority Voter (MV) should change synchronously to assure a correct computation. This can be easily assured in simple circuits by equalizing the number of magnets carrying the three signals to the MV so that no skew is sensed. But in complex circuits it could be impossible to assure such requirement.

In (27)(28)(29),(30) NCL is proposed as a possible solution. Null Convention Logic^{TM} (NCL, (31)), is an asynchronous logic where the delay insensitivity is reached through the encoding of every signal with two bits. In this way a signal can assume two different states, a DATA state, where DATA can be either '01' (which stands for '0' logic value), or '10' (which stands for '1' logic value), and a NULL state, characterized with '00'. The '11' state is forbidden. The delay insensitivity is assured by the fact that the gate changes its status from NULL to DATA only when all the input signals switch from NULL to DATA. In this way a circuit works properly even if there is a large difference in the propagation delay of signals.

Here we adapt NCL logic to the magnetic and snake-clock case with our HDL representation (24) starting from the proposal in (32). Therefore we have implemented all the NCL logic gates.

Figure 8 shows the simplest NCL gate, the Th22. The pipelined behaviour of QCA circuits is modeled using one register for each clock phase with the signal shown in figure 8.c, while the majority voter is an ideal combinational gate with no delay. The logic function of both the Th22 and the majority voter (MV) are detailed in figure 8.b.
The VHDL code for the MV modeling is straightforward and is reported in the following: a simple boolean function and an implicit process as signal assignment is used.

```
entity mv is
port (
      a, b, c: in std_logic;
      y: out std_logic
     );
end mv;


architecture behavioural of mv is
begin
  y <= (a and b) or (a and c) or (b and c);
end behavioural;
```

Registers are implemented in a generic way (entity *reg*), so it is possible to use the same entity in every clock zone.

```
entity reg is
generic (n_bit_reg : integer := 32);
port (d_in: in std_logic_vector (n_bit_reg - 1 downto 0);
      d_out: out std_logic_vector (n_bit_reg - 1 downto 0);
      reset, clock: in std_logic);
end reg;

architecture behavioural of reg is
begin
  p: process (clock, reset)
  begin
    if reset='1' then
       d_out <= (others => '0');
    elsif (clock'event and clock='1') then
          d_out <= d_in;
    end if;
  end process;
end behavioural;
```

These components are then used for modeling the TH22 (entity *th*22) in the following code: each register belongs to a specific clock zone, thus its clock input pin is connected to the proper external clock phase. Port maps are labelled according to the registers name in figure, while signals are not detailed in figure for sake of clarity.

```
entity th22 is
port (a, b: in std_logic;
      y: out std_logic;
      clk1, clk2, clk3: in std_logic);
end th22;

architecture behavioural of th22 is

  component mv
```

```
      port (a, b, c: in std_logic;
            y: out std_logic);
   end component;

   component reg
      generic (n_bit_reg : integer := 32);
      port (d_in: in std_logic_vector (n_bit_reg - 1 downto 0);
            d_out: out std_logic_vector (n_bit_reg - 1 downto 0);
            reset, clk: in std_logic);
   end component;

signal z2_m_out, z2_out, z3_out, z4_out: std_logic;
signal z2f_out, z3f_out: std_logic;
signal z1_out: std_logic_vector (2 downto 0);

begin

Z1_R: reg
     generic map (n_bit_reg => 3)
     port map (d_in(0) => a,    d_in(1) => b, d_in(2) => z2f_out,
               d_out => z1_out, reset => '0', clk => clk1);

Z2_M: mv
     port map (a => z1_out(0), b => z1_out(1), c => z1_out(2), y => z2_m_out);

Z2_R: reg
     generic map (n_bit_reg => 1)
     port map (d_in => z2_m_out, d_out => z2_out, reset => '0', clk => clk2);

Z3_R1: reg
     generic map (n_bit_reg => 1)
     port map (d_in => z2_out, d_out => z3_out, reset => '0', clk => clk3);
Z4_R1: reg
     generic map (n_bit_reg => 1)
     port map (d_in => z3_out, d_out => z4_out, reset => '0', clk => clk1);
Z2F_R1: reg
     generic map (n_bit_reg => 1)
     port map (d_in => z4_out, d_out => z3f_out, reset => '0', clk => clk2);
Z3F_R1: reg
     generic map (n_bit_reg => 1)
     port map (d_in => z3f_out, d_out => z2f_out, reset => '0', clk => clk3);

y <= z4_out;

end behavioural;
```

Simulation results, obtained using Modelsim (33), are shown in figure 9. The output of a MV is '1' when at least two inputs are '1', and similarly the output is '0' when at least two inputs are '0'. The input of the MV is signal R (3 bit), which represents signals A, B and F'' delayed of one clock phase. When two of them (signals R(0) and R(1) corresponding to inputs A and B) switch from '0' to '1' the output of the majority voter switches to '1'. Signals R', R'' and also the output F corresponds to the MV output delayed by one, two and three phases, respectively. So from this, it is possible to see that output F changes to '1' only when all inputs A and B go to '1', with a delay of one three-phase clock period which correspond to the time necessary to pass through three clock phases. When the output F is '1' this signal propagates back to the MV input (signals F', F'' and R(2)), so also when one of the inputs A and B change from '1' to

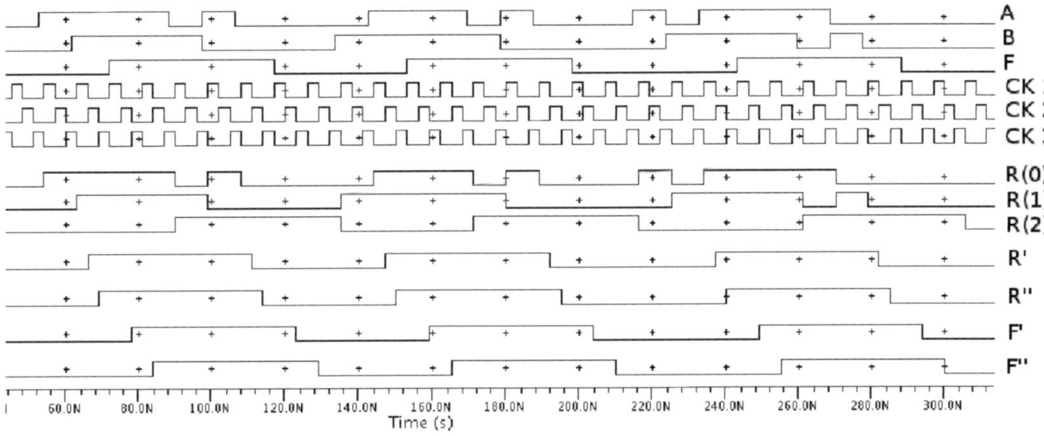

Fig. 9. TH22 simulation.

'0', the output F still remains '1'. Only when A and B switch to '0' the output F changes to '0', again with a delay of one clock period. Therefore this simulation confirms the logical equation of the TH22 shown in figure 8.

6. NCL-HDL magnetic QCA circuit example

To demonstrate the use of this modeling, and this logic, we implemented a more complex fully magnetic QCA circuit. One of the most simple and meaningful circuit is the full adder, which is the base computational block of every digital machine. Figure 10 shows the NCL full adder circuit. The circuit is splitted in two parts which calculates the two coded bits of the output. The behaviour of NCL gates can be understood looking at its symbols: a gate changes

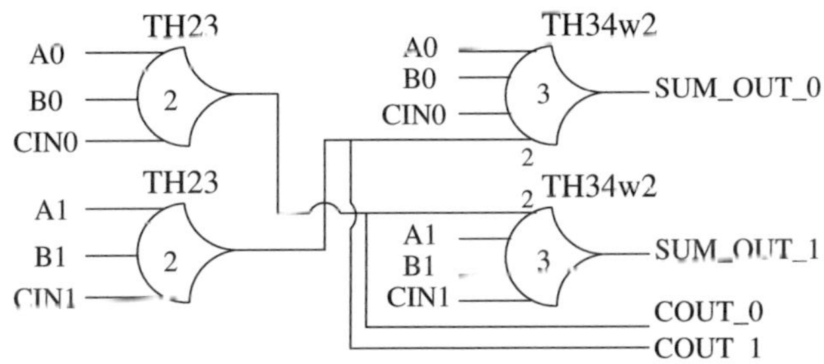

Fig. 10. Full adder NCL implementation. The circuit is splitted in two parts following the two bit coding of the NCL logic.

from 0 to 1 only when a number of inputs equal to the number written inside the gate symbol switches from 0 to 1. The small number written before some of the inputs means that this very input has a weight double than others inputs.

The VHDL code of the full adder, reported below, allows to understand the globally asynchronous locally synchronous (GALS) behaviour of the circuit. The NCL gates are ruled by a three phases synchronous clock, while the connections among the gates are asynchronous.

```
entity FA is
  port (
    A0, A1, B0, B1            : in  std_logic;
    cin0, cin1                : in  std_logic;
    sum0, sum1                : out std_logic;
    cout0, cout1              : out std_logic;
    clk1, clk2, clk3 : in  std_logic);
end FA;

architecture structural of FA is

  component th23
    port (a, b, c                  : in  std_logic;
          y                        : out std_logic;
          clk1, clk2, clk3            : in  std_logic);
  end component;

  component th34w2
    port (a, b, c, d               : in  std_logic;
          y                        : out std_logic;
          clk1, clk2, clk3         : in  std_logic);
  end component;

  signal th1_out, th2_out    : std_logic;

begin

  Th23_1 : th23  port map (
      a => A0,     b => B0,     c => cin0,    y => th1_out,
      clk1 => clk1,   clk2 => clk2,   clk3 => clk3);

  Th23_2 : th23 port map (
      a => A1,     b => B1,     c => cin1,    y => th2_out,
      clk1 => clk1,   clk2 => clk2,   clk3 => clk3);

  Th34w2_1 : th34w2 port map (
      a => th2_out,    b => A0,     c => B0,     d => cin0,     y => sum0,
      clk1 => clk1,   clk2 => clk2,   clk3 => clk3);

  Th34w2_2 : th34w2 port map (
      a => th1_out,    b => A1,     c => B1,     d => cin1,     y => sum1,
      clk1 => clk1,   clk2 => clk2,   clk3 => clk3);

cout0 <= th1_out;
cout1 <= th2_out;

end structural;
```

We employed the full adder to implement a 4 bit ALU, which is the fundamental block of every digital circuit. The circuit architecture is composed of two main parts (figure 11), a logic block which performs the logic OR and the logic AND, and an arithmetical unit which is able to add and subtract fixed point numbers, connected using two multiplexers for the operation selection. The logic block internal structure is shown in figure 11 upper detail, where two NCL gates for every bit implement the desired function (symbol X indicates the bit number, from 0 to 3). The arithmetic block is a ripple carry adder, where 4 full adders are connected serially. The upper-right detail of figure 11 shows the internal structure of the multiplexers, the same structure is repeated for each bit. The subtraction is performed with an addition between input A and the inverse of the input B, while the selection bit is sent to the first multiplexer and to the carry in input of the ripple carry adder. The inversion in NCL logic does not require any gate, because the two bits which represent the encoded signal can be simply switched (in NCL the inverse of 01 is 10). The two logic gates Th12 and Th22 assure that the overflow signal is always zero when the logic block is selected.

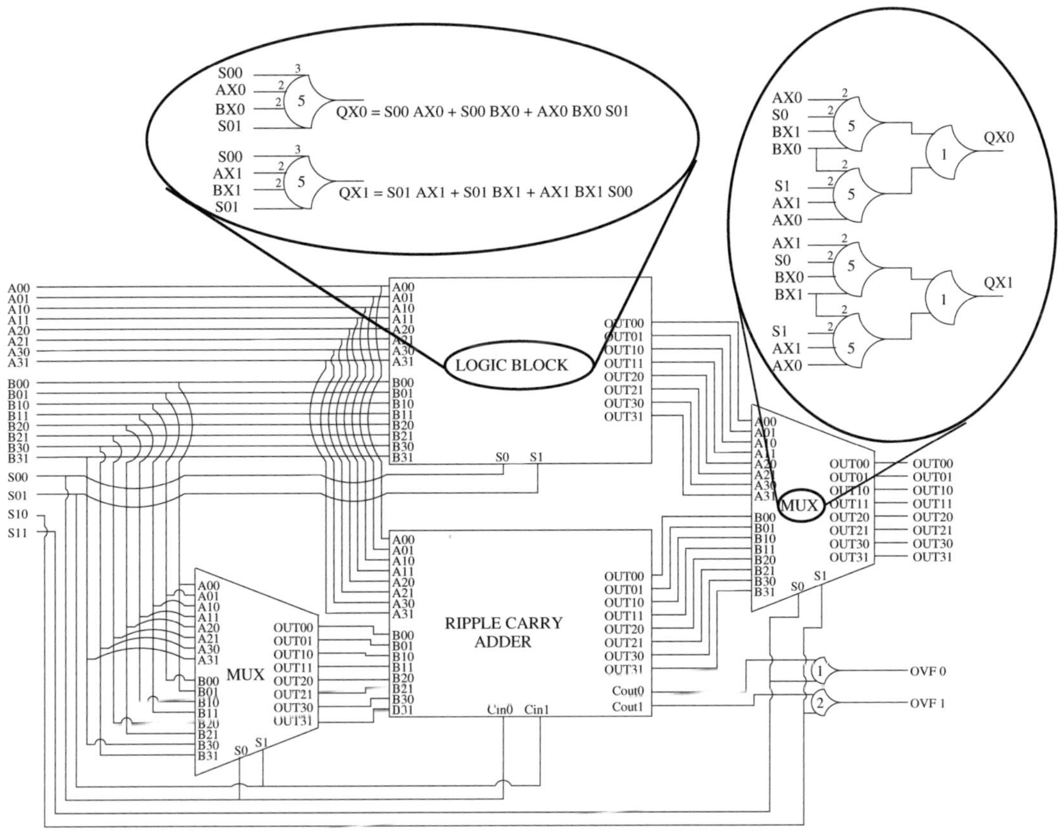

Fig. 11. Alu complete schematic. In the two details are shown respectively the schematic of the logic block and the multiplexer. The structure is repeated identically for every bit, the X indicates the bit number.

The simulation waveforms in figure 12 show all the possible ALU operations: note that the entire structure is organized in phases correspondent to the the snake clock and the basic cells are reorganized and based on the MV block. More in detail, the information is not a sequence of data, but, as visible in the simulation bottom line, is an alternative sequence of data (D) and null state (N). The N-D-N sequence assures that before a new data is evaluated, both inputs must go to 0, independently on their delay. The NULL state works as a timing reference for the circuit. This solves the layout–timing problem. It is worth noticing that the detailed signal propagation is assured by the sequence of the three clock phases mentioned in figure 8 and 7. For this reason our architecture is locally synchronous and globally asynchronous.
From figure 12 the correctness of the circuit behaviour can be established. The timing performance are not representative because our aim was only to demonstrate the feasibility

of the MQCA structure and not to evaluate their maximum speed. Thus a full magnetic and snake-clock NCL structure has been demonstrated here and assures promising potentialities for further architectures developments, as it solves a critical limitation of MQCA and is also based on a practicable clock structure.

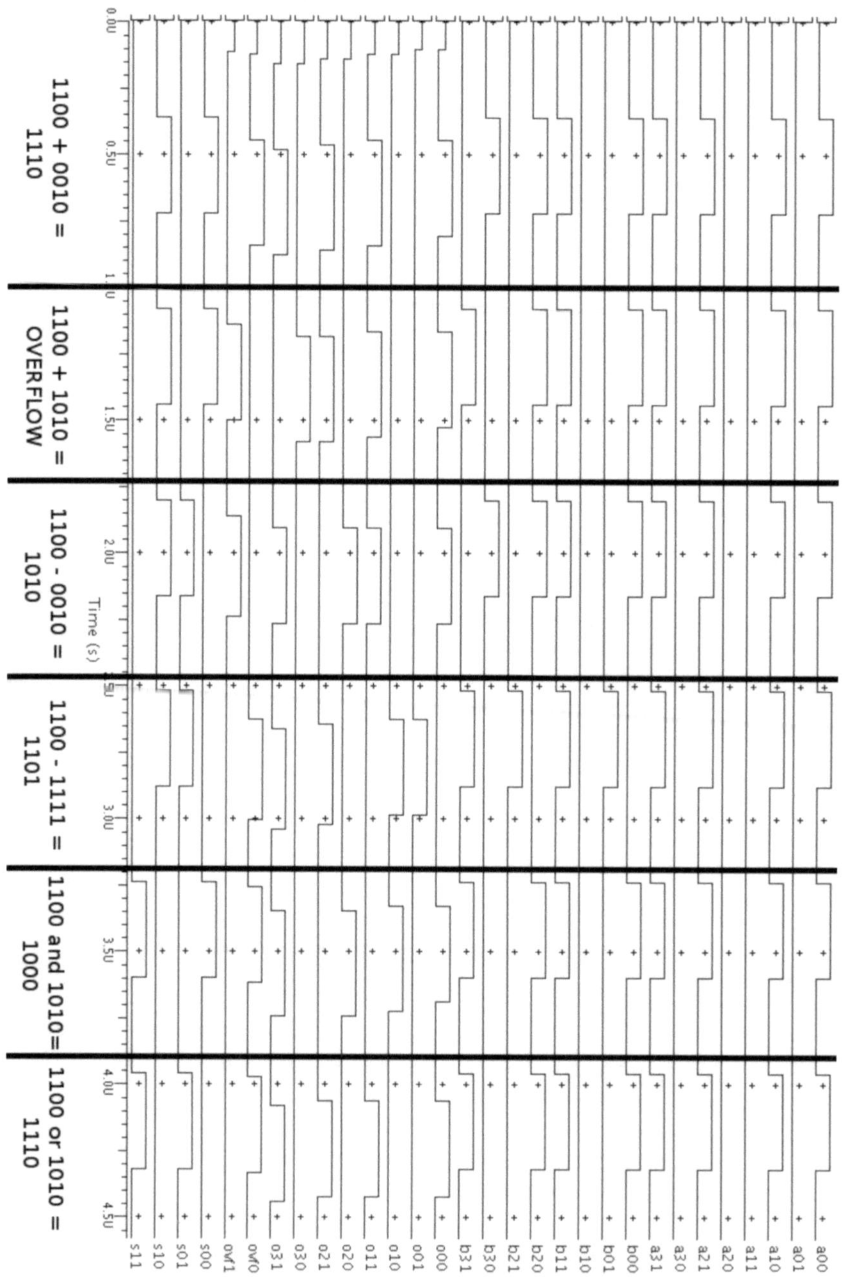

Fig. 12. Alu simulation results. Numbers indicate the operation performed and the NULL cycle (all waves at zero) represents the time reference of the circuit.

The description has been also enriched with other physical related information as *power* dissipation, based on values in (34),(35), (36) and using a VHDL-AMS description, and *layout*, as a dependency on the number of magnets necessary to carry a signal from a gate to the other is inserted in the model (detail in figure 13). Figure 13 shows the estimation of how the power dissipation changes increasing the complexity of the circuit: the obtained value are very promising for low power architectures.

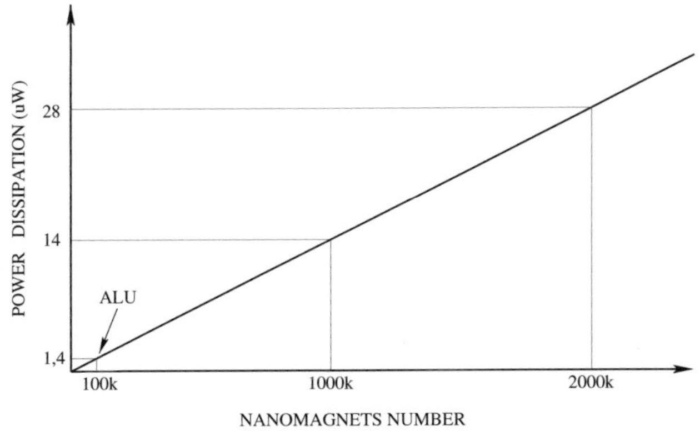

Fig. 13. Power dissipation estimation. The energy dissipated by each nanomagnet during the switching is supposed $30K_BT$ while the clock frequency used is 110 MHz.

We plan to further improve these descriptions related to the physical implementation as we believe that not only the architecture is more physically meaningful and variations to it can be decided on a technology basis, but also feedbacks to technology solutions can be generated, so that they can evolve towards usable actions.
This is the reason why we are setting up our own experiments, still at the preliminary phase at present time and driven by results partially presented in literature (e.g. (4)), but with the aim of jointly proof the feasibility of architectures and specifying meaningful objectives to physical experiments.

7. Preliminary experiments

Investigating a so advanced nanotechnology require a strong link between the high level design phase and the low level technological realization. Results in this direction have been obtained by previous works and reported in (4), (37), (38) and (39). We believe this to be a very important step, and thus we are setting up our own experiments, which preliminary results are in (24) and based on (40), to verify our proposed clock solution and to deeply investigate nanomagnetic circuits. The process for the creation of the nanomagnet structure is represented in figure 14. First a copper wire is created with sputtering, and an insulating layer of SiO_2 is deposed. Then, after the deposition of a PMMA (polymethylmethacrylate) trenches are opened using electron beam lithography (EBL), figure 14.a. At this point the ferromagnetic material, mainly cobalt, is deposed using RF magnetron sputtering, figure 14.b. Finally with a lift-off process the PMMA is removed with the excess of ferromagnetic material, figure 14.c, leaving only the desired nanomagnets. The magnetic state of nanomagnets is read using a magnetic force microscope (MFM).

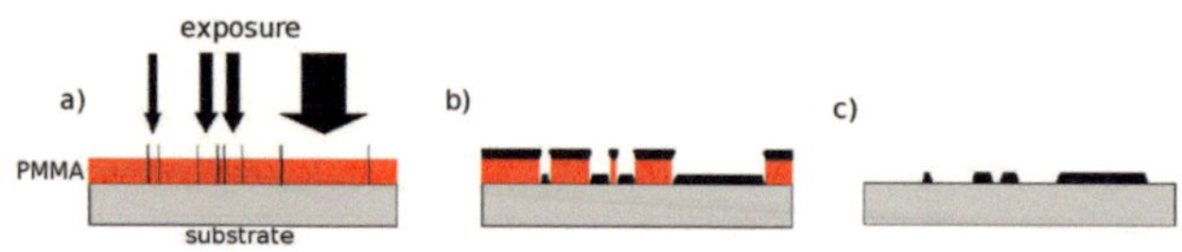

Fig. 14. Magnetic QCA realization process. a) PMMA deposition and EBL trench creation. b) Deposition of magnetic material. c) Lift-off.

8. Conclusions and future work

The work described in this chapter represents the first attempt to integrate high level description and technological level information, in order to obtain a practically feasible solution for Quantum dot Cellular Automata circuits. However a lot of work is still required. In particular, our research will focus on three different levels: a logic/synthesis level, a simulation level and a technological level, to be carried on simultaneously and taking into account feedbacks from others levels. We believe this is a mandatory step because, as we have seen from the work presented in this chapter, separately considering one single aspect of the design in this technology can lead to wrong or physically infeasible results.

From the logical point of view a first problem that must be addressed is the development of a synthesis methodology. The problem is twofold: first the basic gate is the majority voter, therefore logic circuits should be optimized upon this gate (41); second the layout=timing problem requires a dedicated approach: synthesizers must assure that the length of the input wires of each majority voter (the number of clock zones crossed by the wires) must be identical. A proposed synthesizer structure is shown in figure 15. Starting from a VHDL description, which can be either structural or behavioural, circuits are synthesized on a universal two-level logic, in this way the tool can be adapted also to different nanotechnologies. From this point the logic net is mapped on an optimized logic set, which in the case of QCA circuits is composed by the majority voter and the inverter. An intermediate step is possible at this point, because if a delay insensitive logic, like the NCL, or others types of logic, like a mixed boolean-NCL logic, are selected, the circuit net can be previously mapped on these logics, and then the logic gates must be implemented using majority voters. When the majority voter netlist is obtained, the circuit layout can be generated. If the two-level logic was mapped directly on majority voters, without the use of a delay insensitive logic, when the layout is generated the propagation delay of the inputs, expressed in terms of clock cycles, of every majority voter must be equalized, to avoid the layout=timing problem. A few works on these points have been proposed (42), (43),(44) but none of them undertakes at the same time layout=timing, NCL/boolean cohesistance, high and low level synthesis on majority voters. Thus the need of a comprehensive synthesis and layout methodology still arises from literature.

Another problem that must be addressed at logic level is the clock zone layout, which should be designed in order to guarantee the feasibility of the clock generation structure, as we have shown in this chapter. However other problems must be considered during the clock zone layout generation, like the clock zones sizes, the maximum number of nanomagnets for each zone, the crosstalk among neighbour clock zones and the reduction of the wasted area.

From the simulation point of view a lot of work is necessary; in particular there is the need of better understanding, using classical micromagnetic simulation tools, the basic interactions among nanomagnets. For example the interaction between nanomagnets coupled with the long side could be different from the interaction between nanomagnets coupled with the short side. Also the basic logic gates require more investigation, as for example the crosswire,

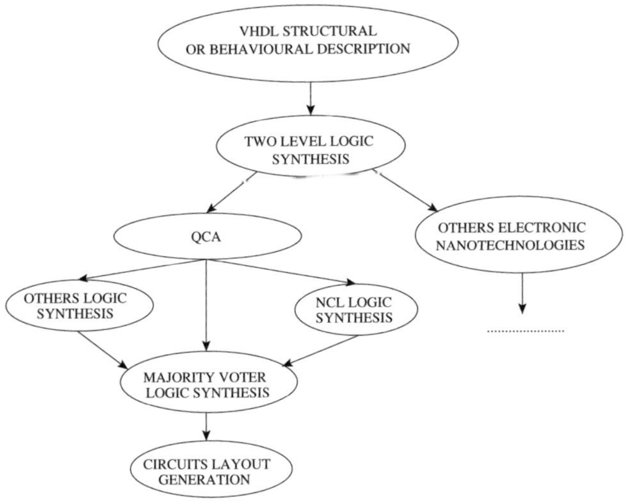

Fig. 15. Nanotechnologies circuit synthesizer.

the block which allows that two different wires cross without interferences on the same plane, is critical for the development of this technology (45). However classical micromagnetic tools are not well suited for simulations on nanomagnets. Micromagnetic tools, solve the micromagnetism dynamic equation, the so-called LLG (Landau-Lifschitz-Gilbert), applying the finite element method. The magnetic material is divided in small areas, the finite elements, and on every elements a system of equation is solved. This is a good approximation of a multidomain material, because each finite element represents a magnetic domain. However when a nanomagnet is analyzed, it is divided into finite elements, but in this case it is a bad approximation, because nanomagnets are single domain magnets. This leads to results that are physically not feasible. To solve this problem it is necessary to modify micromagnetic simulation tools or to develop a simulator dedicated to magnetic QCA. Even in this case many works focused on micromagnetic simulations contributing to understand a few of the abovementioned problems (37). Anyway still many aspects remain unclear and have not been tackled with a real implementation point of view. Our research plan, started with Comsol (46) and Magsimus (47) simulations includes this step too (25).
Finally, for what concerns technology, the work should follow the guide lines obtained from the low level simulations. The interaction between nanomagnets coupled with the long side or the short side must be deeply analyzed, the time performance must be evaluated and also the crosstalk between adjacent nanomagnets must be carefully inspected. Another point of analysis are the basic logic gates, in particular the crosswire which is critical to asses the further development of this technology. The clock system is another part which requires deep investigations: its feasibility and its effective behaviour must be verified on the field (48). However, since magnetic QCA circuits are indicated for low power circuits design, other clock solutions, for example to drive nanomagnets using electric field, must be studied, because the power consumption of the magnetic field generation system can erase the advantages of the low power dissipation of nanomagnets.

9. References

[1] H. Cho and E.E. Swartzlander, "Adder Designs and Analyses for Quantum-Dot Cellular Automata", IEEE Transactions on Nanotechnology, vol. 6, no. 3, May 2007.

[2] J. Huang and F. Lombardi, "Design and Test of Digital Circuits by Quantum-Dot Cellular Automata", Artech House Publishers, 2007.

[3] M. Xiaojun, J. Huang and F. Lombardi, "A model for computing and energy dissipation of molecular QCA devices and circuits", J. Emerg. Technol. Comput. Syst., Vol. 3, N. 4, pp. 1–30, 2008

[4] A. Imre, G. Csabaa, G.H. Bernstein, W. Porod and V. Metlushkob, "Investigation of shape-dependent switching of coupled nanomagnets", Superlattices and Microstructures, 34, 513-518, 2003.

[5] C. S. Lent, P. D. Tougaw, W. Porod and G. H. Bernstein "Quantum cellular automata", Nanotechnology, Vol. 4, 49, 1993

[6] P. Tougaw, C.S. Lent, W. Porod, "Bistable Saturation In Coupled Quantum-Dot Cells". Journal Of Applied Physics 1993, 74, (5), 3558-3566.

[7] P. Tougaw, C.S. Lent, "Dynamic behavior of quantum cellular automata", Journal Of Applied Physics 1996, 80, (8), 4722-4736.

[8] G. Toth, C.S. Lent, "Role of correlation in the operation of quantum-dot cellular automata". Journal Of Applied Physics 2001, 89, (12), 7943-7953.

[9] Joel L. Schiff, "Cellular Automata: A Discrete View of the World", Wiley & Sons, Inc.

[10] R. K. Kummamuru, A. O. Orlov, R. Ramasubramaniam, C. S. Lent, G. H. Bernstein, and G. L. Snider "Operation of a Quantum-dot Cellular Automata (QCA) shift register and analysis of errors", IEEE Trans. On Electron Devices, Vol. 50, 1906, 2003

[11] A. I. Csurgay, W. Porod, and C. S. Lent "Signal processing with near-neighborcoupled time-varying quantum-dot arrays", IEEE Trans. On Circuits and Systems, Vol. I47, 1212, 2000

[12] A.O. Orlov, R. Kummamuru, R. Ramasubramaniam, C.S. Lent, G.H. Bern- stein, G.L. Snider Clocked Quantum-dot Cellular Automata Devices: Experi- mental Study Dept. of Electrical Engineering, University of Notre Dame, Notre Dame, Indiana, USA.

[13] M.T. Niemier, M.J. Kontz, P.M. Kogge "A Design of and Design Tools for a Novel Quantum Dot Based Microprocessor" Presentation, University of Notre Dame, Notre Dame, Indiana, USA, 2006.

[14] A. Khitun., K.L. Wang Multi-functional edge driven nano-scale cellular au- tomata based on semiconductor tunneling nano-structure with a self-assembled quantum dot layer Superlattices and Microstructures, 37, 55-76, 2005.

[15] C.G. Smitha, S. Gardelisa, A.W. Rushfortha, R. Crooka, J. Coopera, D.A. Rit- chiea, E.H. Linfielda, Y. Jinb, M. Peppera Realization of quantum-dot cellular automata using semiconductor quantum dots Superlattices and Microstructures, 34, 195-203, 2003.

[16] C.S. Lent, B. Isaksen Clocked Molecular Quantum-Dot Cellular Automata IEEE Transactions on Electron Device, vol. 50, no. 9, september 2003.

[17] U. Lu and C. S. Lent, "Theoretical Study of Molecular Quantum-Dot Cellular Automata", J. of Computational Electronics, 4: 115118, 2005

[18] H. Qi, S. Sharma, Z.H. Li, G.L. Snider, A.O. Orlov, C.S. Lent, T.P. Fehlner, "Molecular quantum cellular automata cells. Electric field driven switching of a silicon surface bound array of vertically oriented two-dot molecular quantum cellular automata". Journal Of The American Chemical Society 2003, 125, (49), 15250-15259.

[19] J.Y. Jiao, G.J. Long, F. Grandjean, A.M. Beatty, T.P. Fehlner, "Building blocks for the molecular expression of quantum cellular automata. Isolation and characterization of a covalently bonded square array of two ferrocenium and two ferrocene complexes". Journal Of The American Chemical Society 2003, 125, (25), 7522-7523.

[20] W. Porod, "Magnetic Logic Devices Based on Field-Coupled Nanomagnets", Nano & Giga 07, Tempe, AZ, 12-16 March 2007.

[21] G. Csaba and W. Porod, "Simulation of Coupled Computing Architectures based on Magnetic Dot Arrays", Journal of Computational Electronics, Kluwer, 1:87-91, 2002

[22] M.T. Alam, J.DeAngelis, M. Putney, X.S. Hu, W. Porod, M. Niemier and G.H. Bernstein, "Clock Scheme for Nanomagnet QCA", *Proc.* of IEEE Int. Conf on Nanotechnology, 2007.

[23] M. Vacca "Magnetic QCA Nanoarchictures", *M*aster Thesis, Politecnico di Torino, November 2008.

[24] M. Graziano, A. Chiolerio and M. Zamboni "A Technology Aware Magnetic QCA NCL-HDL Architecture", Proc. IEEE Conf. on Nanotechnology, Genova, July 2009.

[25] M. Mascarino "Analysis and simulation of Circuits Based Magentic QCA", *M*aster Thesis, Politecnico di Torino, November 2009.

[26] M. Ottavi, L. Schiano abd F. Lombardi, *H*DLQ: A HDL Environment for QCA Design, ACM Journal on Emerging Technologies in Computing Systems, Vol.2, No.4, 2006

[27] M. Choi, M. Choi, Z. Patiz and N. Park, "Efficient and Robust Delay-Insensitive QCA (Quantum-Dot-Cellular-Automata) Design", *Proc. IEEE Int. Symp. on Defect and Foult-Tolerance in VLSI Systems*, 2006

[28] M. Choi, Z. Patitz, B. Jin, F. Tao, N. Park and M. Choi, "Designing layout-timing independent quantum-dot cellular automata (QCA) circuits by global asynchrony", Journal of System Architecture, Elsevier, 53, 2007, pp. 551-567.

[29] E. Tabrizizadeh, H.R. Mohaqeq and A. Vafaei, "Designing QCA Delay-Insensitive Serial Adder", Proc. IEEE International COnference on emerging trends in Engineering and Technology, 2008.

[30] S.C. Smith "Gate And Throughput Optimizations For Null Convention Self-timed Digital Circuits " *Doctor of Philosophy, Dissertation*, University of missouri, Columbia, USA, spring term 2001.

[31] K.M. Fant and S.A. Brandt., NULL Convention Logic^{TM}: "A Complete and Consistent Logic for Asynchronous Digital Circuit Synthesis", Proc. Int. Conf. on Application Specific Systems, Architectures, and Processors, 1996.

[32] S. Henderson, E.W.Johnson, J.R.Janulis and P.D. Tourgaw, "Incorporating Standard CMOS Design Process Methodologies into the QCA Logic Design Process", *I*EEE Trans. on Nanotechnology, Vol. 3, No.1, 2004.

[33] http://www.model.com/

[34] G. Csaba, P. Lugli, A. Csurgay and W. Porod, "Simulation of Power Gain and Dissipation in Field-Coupled Nanomagnets", *J*ournal of Computational Electronics, Springer, Vol. 4, 2005.

[35] G. Csaba, P. Lugli and W. Porod, "Power Dissipation in Nanomagnetic Logic Devices", proc. IEEE Conference on Nanotechnology, July 2004

[36] G. Csaba, P. Lugli, A. Csurgay and W. Porod, "Simulation of Power Gain and Dissipation in Field-Coupled Nanomagnets", *Journal of Computational Electronics*, Springer, Vol. 4, 2005.

[37] G.H. Bernstein, A. Imre, V. Metlushko, A. Orlov, L. Zhou, L. Ji, G. Csaba, W. Porod, "Magnetic QCA systems", *Microelectronics Journal*, Elsevier, vol. 36, 2005.

[38] A. Orlov, A. Imre, G. Csaba, L. Ji, W. Porod and G.H. Bernstein, "Magnetic Quantum-Dot Cellular Automata: Recent Developments and Prospects", *ASP J. of Nanoelectronics and Optoel.*, Vol3, N. 1, 2008.

[39] J.F. Pulecio and S. Bhanja, "Reliability of Bi-stable Single Domain Nano Magnets for Cellular Automata", Proc. IEEE Conference on Nanotechnology, August 2007.

[40] A. Chiolerio, E. Celasco, F. Celegato, S. Guastella, P. Martino, P. Allia, P. Tiberto and F. Pirri, "Enhanced imaging of magnetic structures in micropatterned arrays of Co dots and antidots", *J. of Magnetism and Magnetic Materials*, Vol. 320, e669-e673, 2008.

[41] R. Zhang, P. Gupta, N.K. Jha "Majority and Minority Network Synthesis With Application on Nanotechnologies" in IEEE Transactions on Computer-Aided Design of Integrated Circutis and Systems, vol. 26, no. 7, july 2007.

[42] T. Teod and L. Sousa QCA-LG: A tool for the automatic layout generation of QCA combinational circuits INESC-ID/IST, TU Lisbon, Portugal, IEEE, 2007.

[43] M.R.Azghadi, O. Kavehei and Keivan Navi, "A Novel Design for Quantum-dot Cellular Automata Cells and Full Adders". Journal of Applied Sciences 7(22) 3460-3468 , 2007

[44] R. Zhang, K. Walus, W.Wang and G.A. Jullien, "A Method of Majority Logic Reduction for Quantum Cellular Automata." IEEE Transactions on Nanotechnology Vol.3 No.4 December 2004.

[45] A. Chaudhary, D.Z. Chen, X.S. Hu, K. Whitton, M. Niemier, R. Ravichan- dran Eliminating Wire Crossings for Molecular Quantum-dot Cellular Automata Implementation University of Notre Dame, Notre Dame, USA, College of Computing Georgia Institute of Technology, Atlanta, USA, 2005.

[46] http://www.comsol.com/

[47] http://www.magoasis.com/magsimus.htm

[48] M.T. Alam, M.J. Siddiq, G.H. Bernstein, M. Niemier, W. Porod, X.S. Hu "On-Chip Clocking for Nanomagnet Logic Devices" University of Notre Dame, Notre Dame, Indiana, USA, IEEE, 2010.

4

Conservative Reversible Elementary Cellular Automata and their Quantum Computations

Anas N. Al-Rabadi
Computer Engineering Department, The University of Jordan
The Office of Graduate Studies and Research (OGSR), Portland State University

1. Introduction

Cellular automata (CA) are discrete spatially extended dynamical systems that are used as models of physical processes and as computational devices. An Elementary Cellular Automaton (ECA) is a collection of "colored" cells on a grid of specified shape that evolves through a number of discrete time steps according to a set of rules which are based on the states of neighboring cells and the previous state of the evolved cell. The next state of any cell in ECA depends only upon its present "neighborhood," which includes the state of the cell itself and those of its immediate neighbors to the left and right. The rules are then applied iteratively for as many time steps as desired. ECA model has been used as a "universal constructor" and were studied as one possible model for natural and engineered systems where comprehensive studies of CA have been performed in which a gigantic collection of results and discoveries concerning automata are presented [4,5,11,21,22,25,26,28,30,37,38,41,45,49,50,51,53,60,62,71,74,78,79,80,81,83,86,87,92,93,94,97,99, 100,106,107,108,109,110,111,112,113,114,115]. Several types of CA have been used extensively in several science and engineering applications such as: Image Processing [69,72], Finite State Machine (FSM) and VLSI circuit testing [2,13,17,19,20,29,30,32,46,48,56,75, 88,89,90,91,96,103], Encryption [39,59,61,85], Pattern Classification and Recognition [15,26,51,52,57,73, 77,95,104], Error Correcting Codes [16,68], Neural Networks [7,18,105], Fault Diagnosis [70,91], Fault Tolerance [65], Data Compression [39,69], Game Theory [37], Random Number Generator (RNG) [102], Number Sorting [64], and set-theoretic Reconstructability Analysis (RA) [117].

Motivations for pursuing the possibility of implementing ECA using Reversible Logic (RL) would include items such as [1,3,4,9,23,31,40,47,54,55,63,76,81,101]: (1) power: the fact that, theoretically, the internal computations in hardware RL-based systems consume no power. It was proven in [40], it is a necessary (but not sufficient) condition for not dissipating power in any physical circuit that all system circuits must be built using fully reversible logical components. For this reason, different technologies have been studied to implement reversible logic in hardware such as adiabatic CMOS and quantum [3,63,76]. Fully reversible discrete systems will greatly reduce the power consumption (theoretically eliminate) through three conditions: (a) logical reversibility: the vector of input states can always be uniquely reconstructed from the vector of output states, (b) physical reversibility: the physical switch operates backwards as well as forwards, and (c) the use of "ideal-like" switches that have no parasitic resistances; (2) size: since the newly emerging quantum computing technology must be reversible [3,40,63], the current trends related to more dense hardware implementations are heading towards 1 Angstrom, at which quantum mechanical effects have to be accounted for; (3) speed: if the properties of superposition and entanglement of quantum mechanics can be usefully employed in the reversible ECA (RECA) context, significant computational speed enhancements can be expected; and (4) mapping: since RECA produces new constraint types of maps, it is interesting to explore the new dynamics and advantages of modeling discrete systems using such RL maps in contrast to the classical irreversible maps.

This research extends and implements several of the reversible and quantum computing concepts that were developed earlier [3] to the context of ECA and this includes a new method for modeling and processing via the reversibility property in the existence of noise. The main contribution of this research is the creation of a new algorithm that can be used in noisy discrete systems modeling using conservative reversible elementary cellular automata (CRECA) and the corresponding quantum modeling of such discrete systems. One of the advantages of the use of new families of CRECA is their potential utilization in reconfigurable low-power (adiabatic) VLSI circuit designs [76] in contrast to the role of classical ECA circuits in classical (non-adiabatic) VLSI systems. M-ary quantum representations in ECA of: (1) *m*-ary orthonormal computational basis states quantum decision trees (QDTs) and (2) *m*-ary orthonormal composite basis states QDTs are also introduced as possible quantum representations for the modeling and manipulation of the quantum ECA (QECA) dynamics.

Although several approaches were introduced previously in dealing with reversible ECA [23,31,33,34,35, 36,47,54,55], none of these approaches considered the important modeling and processing case which uses Swap-based operations (primitives) to represent reversible ECA even in the presence of noise. Modeling using Swap-based circuits is important since many of the two-valued (binary) and many-valued (*m*-ary) quantum circuit implementations use two-valued and many-valued quantum *Swap*-based and *Not*-based gates. This can be important, since the Swap and Not gates are basic primitives in quantum computing, from which many other *m*-valued fundamental gates are built such as [3,63]: (1) *m*-valued Not gate, (2) *m*-valued Controlled-Not gate (C-Not gate or Feynman gate), (3) *m*-valued Controlled-Controlled-Not gate (C^2-Not gate or Toffoli gate), (4) *m*-valued Swap gate, and (5) *m*-valued Controlled-Swap gate (C-Swap gate or Fredkin gate).

The remainder of this research is organized as follows: basic backgrounds on RL and ECA are given in Sections 2 and 3. An algorithm for the synthesis of Swap-based CRECA is presented in Section 4. Quantum computation (QC) of CRECA is presented in Section 5. The extension to the *m*-ary (*m*-valued) case is introduced in Section 6. Conclusions and future work are presented in Section 7.

2. Fundamentals of reversible logic

A (*k*, *k*) reversible circuit is a circuit that has the same number of inputs (*k*) and outputs (*k*) and is a one-to-one mapping between the vectors of inputs and the vectors of outputs, thus the vector of input states can be always uniquely reconstructed from the vector of output states [3,9,40,63,101]. Thus, a (*k*, *k*) *reversible* map is a *bijective* function which is both injective ("one-to-one") and surjective ("onto"). The *auxiliary* outputs and inputs that are needed *only* for the purpose of reversibility are called "garbage" outputs and "garbage" inputs respectively. These are auxiliary outputs and inputs from which a reversible map is

constructed (cf. Table 1 in Example 1). If a circuit is composed of interconnecting reversible elements (primitives or gates) then the overall circuit is also reversible [3].
A (*k*, *k*) conservative circuit has the same number of inputs (*k*) and outputs (*k*) and has the same number of values in inputs and outputs (e.g., the same number of ones in inputs and outputs for binary, the same number of ones and twos in inputs and outputs for ternary, etc).
An algorithm called conservative reversible Boolean function (CRBF) that produces a conservative reversible Boolean map from its irreversible counterpart is as follows:

Algorithm CRBF

1. Augment the number of outputs to become equal the number of inputs: add a sufficient number of auxiliary output variables such that the number of outputs equals the number of inputs. Allocate a new column in the mapping table for each auxiliary variable.
2. For the construction of the first auxiliary output, assign a constant C_1 to half of the cells in the corresponding table column (e.g., zeros), and the second half as another constant C_2 (e.g., ones). For convenience, one may assign C_1 to the first half of the column, and C_2 to the second half of the column (cf. Table 1, column Y_1).
3. For the next auxiliary output, **If** non-reversibility still exists, **Then** assign for *identical* output tuples (irreversible map entries) values which are half zeros and half ones (cf. Table 1, bottom two entries of column Y_2), and then assign a constant for the remainder that are already reversible (cf. first two entries of Y_2).
4. **If** number of inputs *i* is now less than number of outputs *j*, **Then** add new auxiliary inputs ($j - i$) with constant column entries that will retain conservativeness (cf. Table 1, constant "0" as first two entries of column c and constant "1" as bottom two entries of column c).
5. **Goto** steps 3 and 4 until the total map entries are reversible and conservative.

Example 1. The standard two-variable Boolean OR: $Y = a + b$ is irreversible as in the following map:

a	b	Y
0	0	0
0	1	1
1	0	1
1	1	1

Following the above CRBF algorithm, the following is one possible reversible two-variable Boolean OR:

c	a	b	Y	Y_1	Y_2
0	0	0	0	**0**	**0**
0	0	1	1	**0**	**0**
1	1	0	1	**1**	**0**
1	1	1	1	**1**	**1**

Table 1. A (3, 3) conservative reversible map for the Boolean inclusive OR.

Using CRBF algorithm, the construction of the conservative reversible map in Table 1 is obtained as follows: Since Y is irreversible, assign garbage output Y_1 and assign the first half of its values as constant "0" and the second half as another constant "1". Since the new map is still irreversible, assign garbage output Y_2 and assign the 3rd cell value to constant "0" and the 4th cell value to constant "1". Since by now the new map is a reversible 2-input 3-output non-conservative map (i.e., Boolean (2, 3) non-conservative OR), add a new garbage input c that converts the map to be a Boolean (3, 3) conservative OR. One notes that the solution in Example 1 is not unique, i.e., several other conservative reversible maps can be obtained as well.

As data in real life situations can be exposed to noise sources: (1) environmental (external) noise, (2) structural (internal) noise, (3) interfacing (measurement; data acquisition) noise, (4) a system output state that will never occur (i.e., don't care state), or (5) unknown data (undecided), it is important to produce a conservative reversible mapping method that could incorporate noise in input or/and output data. This problem can be stated as: *given that certain cells in a map are acceptable to be noisy (i.e., can take values "0" or "1"), generate a conservative reversible map from the corresponding irreversible counterpart.*

An observation that can be noted is that if noise occurs, value "0" can turn to value "1" or value "1" can turn to value "0", and thus the reversible map obtained can become irreversible. One method to solve this problem is by adding *redundant* input/output variables that will maintain (1) reversibility and (2) conservativeness even with the existence of noise.

Example 2. Let us assume in a simplified noise situation that input data in Table 1 has been corrupted with noise as follows: $\{Y=1, Y_1=0, Y_2=0\} \rightarrow \{Y=1, Y_1=1, Y_2=0\}$. One can note that the map in Table 1 becomes irreversible since two input sets {c=0,a=0,b=1} and {c=1,a=1,b=0} has the same output $\{Y=1, Y_1=1, Y_2=0\}$. To obtain a reversible and conservative map while incorporating noise, one may add another *redundant* output Y_3 and input *k* (cf. CRBF):

k	c	a	b	Y	Y_1	Y_2	Y_3
1	0	0	0	0	0	0	1
1	0	0	1	1	$0 \rightarrow 1$	0	0
1	1	1	0	1	1	0	1
1	1	1	1	1	1	1	1

The previously illustrated procedure can handle as many cell changes that have altered values due to noise. In the most straightforward case a redundant variable is added for each noisy cell as an upper extreme. Yet, if the number of noisy cells is *N* and the number of needed added cells (to maintain reversibility) is *A*, then in general one may need $A \leq N$ iff the bijective mapping is still maintained. To achieve this, a simple exhaustive search algorithm using the CRBF algorithm over groups of cells may be utilized to obtain the constraint {*min* (*A*) *for max* (*N*)}, and this depends on the *distribution (i.e., type) of noise* that affects the map.

Example 3. The following map demonstrates an example for the use of the CRBF algorithm for achieving reversibility in the simultaneous presence of three erroneous cells.

k	c	a	b	Y	Y_1	Y_2	Y_3
1	0	0	0	0	0	0	**1**
1	0	0	1	1	**0→1**	0	**0**
1	1	1	0	1	**1→0**	0	**1**
1	1	1	1	1	1	**1→0**	**1**

As mentioned previously, in general, the errors (i.e., changes) in the cells may follow a pattern of certain noise distribution or may not. The important issue of noise distribution, and its direct effect on the method of selecting the needed added auxiliary variables, is to be addressed in a future publication.

3. Basics of elementary cellular automata

A cellular automaton is a decentralized computing model that provides an excellent platform for performing complex computations with the help of only local information [14,20,44,48,59,62,93,99,111,112,113,115]. A CA consists of a spatial *lattice* of cells, each of which, at time t, can be in one m states.

The lattice starts out with some initial configuration of local states (where configuration means the pattern of states over the entire lattice) and at each time step, the states of all cells in the lattice are synchronously updated [84]. We denote the lattice size (or number of cells) as d. For a 2-valued (binary) finite lattices, there is only a finite number of 2^d of possible configurations. In one-dimensional CA, the neighborhood of a cell includes the cell itself and some number of neighbors on either side of the cell. The number of neighbors on either side of the center cell is referred to as the CA's radius r. For example, an elementary one-dimensional CA is of radius $r = 1$. The motion equations for a CA are often expressed in the form of a *rule table*, which is a look-up table listing each of the neighborhood patterns and the state to which the central cell in that neighborhood is mapped [113].

The communication in CA between constituent cells is limited to local interaction, and the overall structure can be viewed as a parallel processing device. CA exhibits the same dynamics behaviors (including fractals and chaos) which is seen in systems of continuous differential equations [25,42,49,66,98,106]. Elementary Cellular Automata (ECA) as a special type of CA has been proven to be a powerful computing paradigm for the following properties [62,113,115]: (1) universality: an ECA can model any discrete system, and thus it is a powerful logically *complete* system from which all functions can be obtained and can be used to model complex systems; (2) simplicity: an elementary cellular automaton is the building block of the elementary cellular automata, which is a simple structure that evolves over time using specific evolution rules, that leads to modeling complex discrete systems using such simple structures; and (3) regularity: the evolution of ECA to generate discrete time systems consists of geometrically evolving cellular grids. Set-theoretically, a regular ECA rule is a mapping of $(s_t(i-1)\otimes s_t(i)\otimes s_t(i+1))$ onto $s_{t+1}(i)$, where $\otimes$ is the Cartesian product.

An ECA consists of an array of cells in one dimension (1-D). In a Boolean ECA, each cell can take on one of two state {0, 1} where the binary string representing the array changes at discrete time steps (intervals). The Boolean ECA dynamics is commonly represented: (1) *spatially*: by a horizontal sequence of 0's and 1's or of white and black cells, and (2) *temporally*: time, in successive rows, is the vertical axis. The next state of any cell in ECA depends only upon its present "neighborhood," which includes (a) the state of the cell itself and (b) those of its immediate neighbors to the left and right. That is, if $s_t(i)$ is the state of cell i at time t, the dynamic law governing the Boolean ECA is described by the Boolean mapping (function):

$$s_{t+1}(i) = f(s_t(i-1),\ s_t(i),\ s_t(i+1)) \tag{1}$$

Since there are $2^3 = 8$ possible neighborhoods and since each neighborhood can map into either of the two states of $s_t(i+1)$, then there are $2^8 = 256$ mappings (or ECA rules).
Example 4. Table 2 shows the binary string representation of ECA Rule #30.

$s_t(i-1)$	$s_t(i)$	$s_t(i+1)$	$s_{t+1}(i)$
0	0	0	0→Automaton1
0	0	1	1→Automaton2
0	1	0	1→Automaton3
0	1	1	1→Automaton4
1	0	0	1→Automaton5
1	0	1	0→Automaton6
1	1	0	0→Automaton7
1	1	1	0→Automaton8

Rule

Table 2. An illustrative example of ECA rule (Rule #30).

Figure 1 shows the dark and white cells as a second representation of ECA Rule #30.

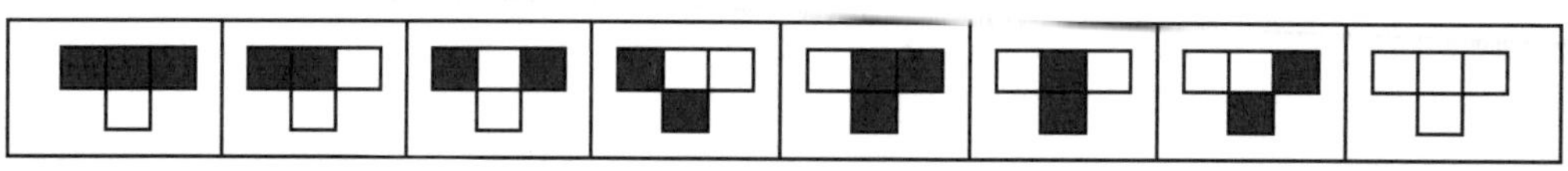

0 0 0 1 1 1 1 0

Fig. 1. A second ECA representation of Rule #30.

The 256 possible mappings are indexed by the binary number defined by $s_{t+1}(i)$ for the set of all neighborhoods, where the lowest order bit of this index is $f\,(0,0,0)$ and the highest order bit is $f\,(1,1,1)$. For example, by using binary number expansion over base 2, the mapping of Table 2 is indexed by the number $(00011110)_2$ and is Rule #30.
A discrete dynamics using Rule #30 can be shown by evolving specific length grid l for n steps starting from an initial condition. An example can be shown from [113] as in Figure 2a where the total evolution occurs after 15 steps starting from a centered single black cell. The temporal behavior in a classical ECA, as shown in Figure 2a, is generally performed using *overlapping* neighborhoods for obtaining the automata evolution, and (as stated previously) from the algebraic mathematical modeling perspective, an overlapping-based ECA evolution using Equation (1) is a lattice.
As shown in [111,112,113], the 256 mappings are divided into 88 equivalence classes, given that one considers maps to be equivalent if they are related: (1) by *reflection* , i.e., by left-right inversion of their arguments (which, if the dynamics were shown on transparency, would

merely involve turning the transparency over), (2) by *complementing*, i.e., negating the arguments and the function (which merely produces a photographic negative reversal), or (3) by *both reflection and complementing*. In general, an equivalence class will have 4 members, but *f* may generate itself under reflection and/or complementing, so that an equivalence class may have 1, 2, or 4 members. A representative rule that is chosen consistently is used to label the CA classes.

Other ECA *complexities* of discrete dynamics also have been reported, and efforts have been undertaken to characterize the CA rule space, which is trying to understand and characterize the global dynamics from the local CA rules. CA evolution can lead to various dynamics that exhibits emergent behaviors such as fractals (Sierpinski triangle or Sierpinski gasket in Figure 2c), chaos (Figure 2a), randomness, complexity, and particles [113]. Additive CA (Figures 2b, 2c, 2d, 2f, and 2g) and linear CA gained popularity in the VLSI field [6,12,14,20,48,58,59] due to local interaction of simple cells, each having two states "0" or "1" which are the elements of the second radix Galois field GF(2) [3,67]. Also, it has been shown that Rule #110 (as shown in Figure 2e), like the game of life, which is an extremely simple one-dimensional system and one which is difficult to engineer to perform specific behavior, is universal [113]. From applications point of view, for instance, Rule #30 which generates randomness has been proposed to be used for pseudo-random number generator (PRNG) and as a possible stream cipher for the use in cryptography [39,59,61,85].

One can note that the characteristic features of an ECA are: (1) size: (1a) spatial size l and (1b) temporal size n, (2) initial condition, (3) evolution rule, (4) number of cell's states (colors), (5) number of neighbors, and (6) evolution strategy (i.e., the way one conducts evolution such as top-to-down and left-to-right, top-to-down and center-to-sides, etc). For the ECA evolution using overlapping neighbors, the same evolution result is obtained when one uses the same rule and the same initial condition, regardless of the evolution strategy used. Thus, one can note that for example for the same evolution rule and different initial conditions one would obtain distinct automata evolutions, and equivalently for different evolution rules and same initial conditions one would obtain distinct automata evolutions.

The CA local rules applied to each cell can be either identical or different. These two different possibilities are termed as uniform and hybrid CA, respectively [12,32,58,92]. While the next state function (rule) in general is deterministic, there are variations in which the rule sets are probabilistic [8,10,27] or fuzzy [24]. CA rules can be time-independent rules or time-dependent rules in which alternate rules at different time steps are used.

As mentioned previously, the ECA is divided into 88 classes where the dynamics of these classes are governed by different attractors [113]. Several approaches have been investigated for the automatic classification of CA [116]. In [113], four attractor types are identified: (1) homogeneous (where the dynamics settles (relaxes) to a fixed configuration which is uniform that consists of all 1's or 0's), (2) Fixed point or periodic (but not uniform), (3) chaotic, or (4) complex. An alternate classification has been also provided [43]: (a) null, (b) fixed point, (c) periodic, (d) locally chaotic (chaotic in some parts of the cell array but regular in other parts), and (e) chaotic. Several approaches were proposed to characterize the average behavior of rules passing from one CA regime (class) to another (e.g., fixed point $\rightarrow$ periodic $\rightarrow$ complex $\rightarrow$ chaotic) [42].

CA are also studied as computational devices, both as theoretical tools and as practical highly efficient parallel machines. Computing in the CA context may mean: (a) CA does a useful computational task where the rule is interpreted as a "program", the initial configuration is the "input", and the CA runs for specific number of time steps or until it

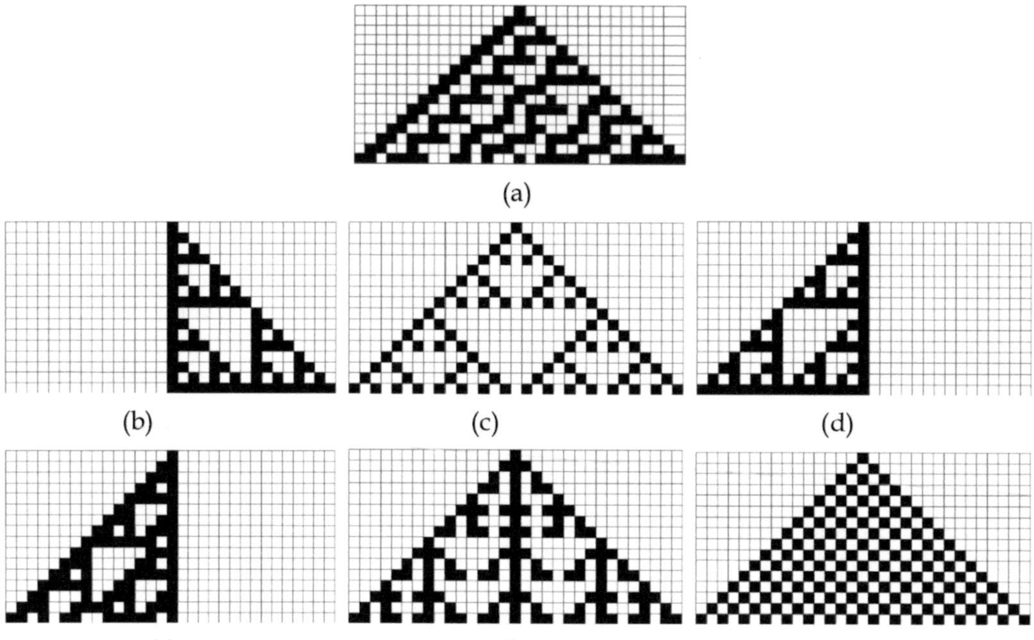

Fig. 2. Space-time diagram of the dynamical ECA which is temporally discrete and spatially discrete that can possess the following evolution dynamics where each row is an evolved Automata: (a) Rule #30, (b) Rule #60, (c) Rule #90, (d) Rule #102, (e) Rule #110, (f) Rule #150, and (g) Rule #250. All of the shown evolutions have started from an initial condition of a single black cell.

reaches a final goal "output" pattern (e.g., CA that performs image processing tasks [69,72]), or (b) a CA is capable of universal computing given specific initial configuration, which means (given the correct initial configuration) a CA can simulate a programmable computer, complete with logic gates, timing devices, etc (e.g., Conway's Game of Life, and the speculation that all Class 4 rules have the capacity for universal computing [113]).

Since real-life data is in general many-valued, the general case of many-valued ECA is used to model natural systems and their dynamics [113]. The following example shows an example of a ternary ECA.

Example 5. Discrete dynamics using ternary (i.e., 3-valued) Rule #322 in Figure 3a can be shown by the overlapping-neighborhood evolution of the grid of length 9 for 5 steps starting from an initial condition as shown in Figure 3b, where color-based values are as follows: "white" represents value (state) "0", "grey" represents value (state) "1", and "black" represents value (state) "2".

Note that the number of colors (values) allowed for the input cells defines the input radix (m_i) and the number of colors (values) allowed in the output cell defines the output radix (m_o). For the previous cases in Examples 4 and 5, the input radix equals the output radix since they use the same number of colors (i.e., values), and for this case the number represented by the ECA rule can be expressed by the radix m number expansion $N = \sum_{n=0}^{k-1} c_n m^n$, where c_n is the expansion coefficient which takes the value (color) of the

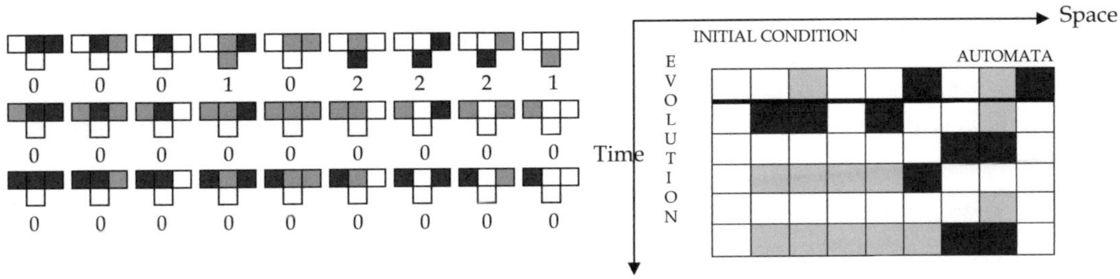

(a) (b)

Fig. 3. Three-valued ECA evolution: (a) Rule #322 which is obtained as: $1 \cdot 3^0 + 2 \cdot 3^1 + 2 \cdot 3^2 + 2 \cdot 3^3 + 1 \cdot 3^5 = 322$, and (b) ECA evolution using Rule #322 for the given initial condition.

output of the automaton at index n for number of automata $k = m^3$, and the index n is computed using the number expansion over the input colors (values or states).

Other important types of CA rules were proposed such as the Gacs-Kurdyumov-Levin (GKL) CA in which the evolution rule is the "majority vote" rule with $m = 2$, $r = 3$ as follows:

$$\begin{cases} If \;\; s_i(t) = 0, then \;\; s_i(t+1) = majority[s_i(t), s_{i-1}(t), s_{i-3}(t)] \\ If \;\; s_i(t) = 1, then \;\; s_i(t+1) = majority[s_i(t), s_{i+1}(t), s_{i+3}(t)] \end{cases}$$

where $s_i(t)$ is the state of site i at time t. The GKL rule states that for each neighbor for seven adjacent cells (that is $r = 3$), if the state of the central cell is "0", then its new state is decided by a majority vote among itself, its left neighbor, and the cell two cells to the left away, else if the state of the central cell is "1", then its new state is decided by a majority vote among itself, its right neighbor, and the cell two cells to the right away.

4. The synthesis of conservative reversible ECA

The evolution that results from Equation (1) is an irreversible evolution; the evolution of ECA according to Equation (1) in general leads to *irreversible dynamics*, i.e., result is not a one-to-one mappings between vectors of inputs and outputs, and thus the vector of input states cannot be always uniquely reconstructed from the vector of output states. To achieve reversible discrete dynamics, one may use the following alternative definition of ECA evolution [4]:

$$s_{cr,t+1}(i-1) = f_1(s_t(i-1),\, s_t(i),\, s_t(i+1)) \tag{2}$$

$$s_{cr,t+1}(i) = f_2(s_t(i-1),\, s_t(i),\, s_t(i+1)) \tag{3}$$

$$s_{cr,t+1}(i+1) = f_3(s_t(i-1),\, s_t(i),\, s_t(i+1)) \tag{4}$$

where subscript c means conservative and subscript r means reversible, such that the (3, 3) mappings from one step to the next are conservative and reversible and thus producing a CRECA.

One of the advantages of the use of new families of CRECA is their potential direct utilization in reconfigurable adiabatic (i.e., low-power) VLSI circuit designs [76] in contrast to the role of classical ECA circuits in classical (non-adiabatic) VLSI systems. This can be an important application goal, especially that classical (irreversible) ECA have already proven their use in the irreversible VLSI applications such as in the testing of VLSI circuits and Finite State Machines (FSM) [2,13,17,19,20,29,30,32,46,48,56,75,88,89,90,91,96,103].

Example 6. Using the algorithm CRBF, Table 3 shows a (3, 3) conservative reversible map for Rule #170.

$s_t(i\text{-}1)$	$s_t(i)$	$s_t(i+1)$	$s_{t+1}(i\text{-}1)$	$s_{t+1}(i)$	$s_{t+1}(i+1)$
0	0	0	0	0	0
0	0	1	1	0	0
0	1	0	0	0	1
0	1	1	1	0	1
1	0	0	0	1	0
1	0	1	1	1	0
1	1	0	0	1	1
1	1	1	1	1	1

Table 3. An example of CRECA for s_{t+1}(i-1) Rule #170.

The (3, 3) conservative reversible mapping in Table 3 for Rule #170 can be represented by the set of three binary strings as follows $\{10101010,11110000,11001100\}_2$, which produces the set of Rule #{170, 240, 204}.

Figure 4 shows an example of ECA discrete system dynamics for irreversible Rule #240 (Figure 4a) versus reversible Rule #{170, 240, 204} (cf. Table 3) using the same initial condition {110010101} (Figure 4b). While the evolution in Figure 4a is a non-overlapping neighbor evolution, the evolution in Figure 4c is an overlapping neighbor evolution. One notes that the irreversible overlapping-based neighbor ECA evolution for Rule #240 in Figure 4c leads to a more complex evolution than the irreversible non-overlapping-based neighbor ECA evolution for Rule #240 in Figure 4a. One can also observe that if one conducts a 3-block reversible evolution with overlapping neighbor (Figure 4d) then several cell(s) will result with conflict values inside it, and this case will be forbidden (avoided) since the value and its "opposite" cannot possess the same spatial location (address) at the same time. Therefore, 3-block reversible non-overlapping neighbor ECA evolutions (such as in Figure 4b) will be only used.

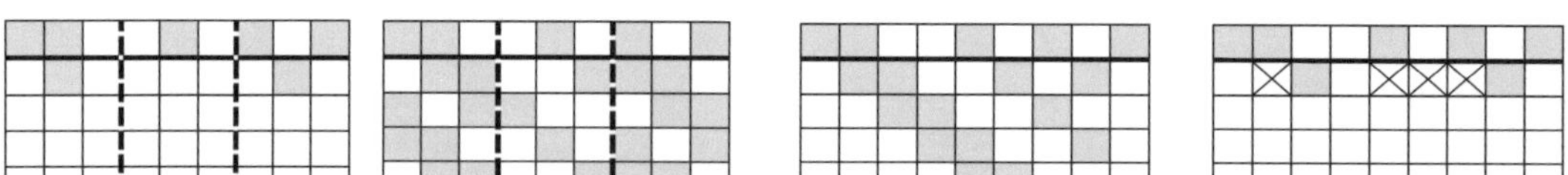

(a) (b) (c) (d)

Fig. 4. Discrete system dynamics for: (a) *irreversible* non-overlapping neighbor ECA evolution for Rule #240, (b) *reversible* non-overlapping neighbor ECA evolution for Rule #{170,240,204}, (c) *irreversible* overlapping neighbor ECA evolution for Rule #240, and (d) *reversible* overlapping neighbor ECA evolution for Rule #{170,240,204} where x means a cell with contradictory values, i.e., a cell with more than one value at the same spatial location.

Utilizing Figure 4b as an example, one can note that by incorporating the property of reversibility in the ECA, one obtains after a single forward pass, using reversible maps, a new relatively complex discrete dynamics that can be obtained with *irreversible* ECA, for the same initial conditions, only with much higher complexity in terms of the need to perform many forward iterations (i.e., several forward passes). For example, this can be seen in Figure 4, in order to achieve the evolved ECA in Figure 4b from Figure 4a, that one needs to evolve the ECA in Figure 4a using the individual evolution Rules {#170, #240, #204} at a time in each level and thus one needs a total of $3\frac{iterations}{level}\cdot 4levels = 12$ forward passes. This fact can reflect itself in the circuit design as an optimization tradeoff between spatial complexity (memory used) and time (i.e., temporal) complexity of number of iterations, and thus depending on the cost one could select the type of optimization, i.e., *spatial optimization in irreversible maps versus temporal optimization in reversible maps.*

Given: (1a) 1-D array length l, (1b) time steps n, (2) initial condition (distribution), and (3) reversible maps $\{f_1, f_2, f_3\}$, the *analysis* of CRECA refers to the finding of the CRECA evolution at step $(t+1)$ from step t. While analysis is useful to explore the whole space of all potential reversible system dynamics, the opposite problem of *synthesis* is the more interesting problem. The synthesis problem can be stated as follows: Given (1a) 1-D array length l, (1b) discrete time steps n, (2) a priori *known* or *assigned* initial condition, and (3) the result of a *total* spatial evolution over time, produce the reversible maps $\{f_1, f_2, f_3\}$. It turns out that, while CRECA analysis is relatively an easy problem, CRECA synthesis is a more difficult one.

Different types of reversible ECA have been studied [23,31,33,34,35, 36,47,54,55]. Yet, none of these approaches considered the important modeling and processing case which uses Swap-based operations (primitives) to represent reversible ECA even in the presence of noise. As mentioned previously, modeling and processing using Swap-based circuits is important since many of the two-valued and many-valued quantum circuit implementations use two-valued and multiple-valued quantum *Swap*-based and *Not*-based gates. This can be important, since the Swap and Not gates are basic primitives in quantum computing, from which many other m-valued fundamental gates are built, such as [3,63]: (1) m-valued Not gate, (2) m valued Controlled-Not gate (m-valued C-Not gate or m-valued Feynman gate), (3) m-valued Controlled-Controlled-Not gate (m-valued C^2-Not gate or m-valued Toffoli gate), (4) m-valued Swap gate, and (5) m-valued Controlled-Swap gate (m-valued C-Swap gate or m-valued Fredkin gate). The following is an algorithm to generate one possible Swap-based CRECA (SCRECA).

The SCRECA Algorithm can be used for the representation (i.e., modeling) and the operation (i.e., processing) reversibly on the final resulting lattice of the ECA evolution, whether that evolution was conducted using a non-overlapping neighbor ECA evolution or an overlapping neighbor ECA evolution.

Since the elementary cellular automaton in its fundamental form is a 3-cell block, then the SCRECA algorithm is based on mapping a partition of the spatial state of the automata in blocks of three cells and then finding a suitable permutation matrix reflecting the behavior of the conservative reversible system. This simplicity of the Swap-based SCRECA algorithm is also the reason for its ability to model complex evolutions.

As SCRECA is (1) reversible and (2) conservative, the output of each automaton $\vec{a}_{k,t+q}^{T}$ can be always obtained as a *permutation* of input $\vec{a}_{k,t+p}^{T}$. Therefore, the matrix $\left[\left[M_{(q-1)q}\right]\cdots\left[M_{(p+1)(p+2)}\right]\left[M_{p(p+1)}\right]\right]^{T}$ (i.e., the total matrix that results from multiplying the

Algorithm SCRECA

1. For a BECA (Boolean ECA or binary-input binary-output ECA) map specified as follows: (1) spatial length (i.e., array length) is l, and (2) temporal length (i.e., number of steps) is n.
2. **If** the length l is not a multiplication of 3, **Then** add minimum number of columns with zero values to make the length ($l/3$) is an integer, **Else** goto 3.
3. For temporal (row) index $K = 1,2,3,\ldots,n$, spatial automaton a_k with index $k = 0,1,2,\ldots,(l/3)-1$, and evolution matrix from an arbitrary time (z-1) to time z: $[M_{(z-1)z}]$, find transformation matrix from time (row) p (i.e., $t + p$) to time (row) q (i.e., $t + q$) as follows:

$$\vec{a}_{k,t+q}^{T} = \vec{a}_{k,t+p}^{T}\left[\left[M_{(q-1)q}\right]\ldots\left[M_{(p+1)(p+2)}\right]\left[M_{p(p+1)}\right]\right]^{T} \quad \text{or}$$

$$\vec{a}_{k,t+q} = \left[\left[M_{(q-1)q}\right]\ldots\left[M_{(p+1)(p+2)}\right]\left[M_{p(p+1)}\right]\right]\vec{a}_{k,t+p}$$

   where t, p, and q are positive integers.
4. For top-to-down and left-to-right evolution, **Goto** 5.
5. Since the CRECA is *conservative*, then by using the Swap-based reversible primitives, synthesize a reversible circuit for the CRECA map as follows:

5a. **For** ($m = 0;\ m < n;\ m$++)

   For ($k = 0;\ k \le \frac{l}{3}-1$; k++)

5b. Perform one-to-one spatial mapping of permuted automaton cell a_k between levels m and (m+1) into (3, 3) Swap-based reversible primitive (cf. Figure 5) between stages m and (m+1) in the corresponding reversible circuit.

6. **End**

matrices $\left\{\left[M_{(q-1)q}\right],\ldots,\left[M_{(p+1)(p+2)}\right],\left[M_{p(p+1)}\right]\right\}$) is always a *permutation matrix*. For example, for a 3-input 3-output permutation, Figure 5 shows all possible reversible (3, 3) Swap-based permutations using the Wire (Buffer) and Swap reversible logic primitives. The matrix representation in Figure 5 is obtained by solving for the output spatial state (vector) permutation from the input state (vector). This is shown for Figure 5d as an example as follows: $\begin{pmatrix}1&0&0\\0&0&1\\0&1&0\end{pmatrix}\begin{pmatrix}u\\v\\w\end{pmatrix}=\begin{pmatrix}u\\w\\v\end{pmatrix}$, where $\begin{pmatrix}u\\v\\w\end{pmatrix}$ is the input vector and $\begin{pmatrix}u\\w\\v\end{pmatrix}$ is the output vector in Figure 5d, respectively.

One notes that the above algorithm SCRECA can be used *spatially* for any of the following three cases: (a1) evolving a single automaton, (b1) evolving any set of automata at the same time, and (c1) evolving all of automata at the same time. Also, one notes that the above algorithm SCRECA can be used *temporally* for any of the following three cases: (a2) step-by-step automata evolution between two consecutive times (i.e., steps) (k-1) and k, (b2) automata evolution between any two times (steps) p and q, and (c2) total automata evolution for all of steps n. While temporal complexity in methods (a2) through (c2) result in step-by-step evolution matrix transformations (i.e., matrix multiplications), methods (a1) through (c1) result in spatial complexity that determines the number of input-output permutation primitive, e.g., (3, 3), (6, 6), (9, 9), etc. The determining factor for using methods (a1) - (c2) can be, for example, the complexity of possible circuit implementation of the resulting reversible circuit models.

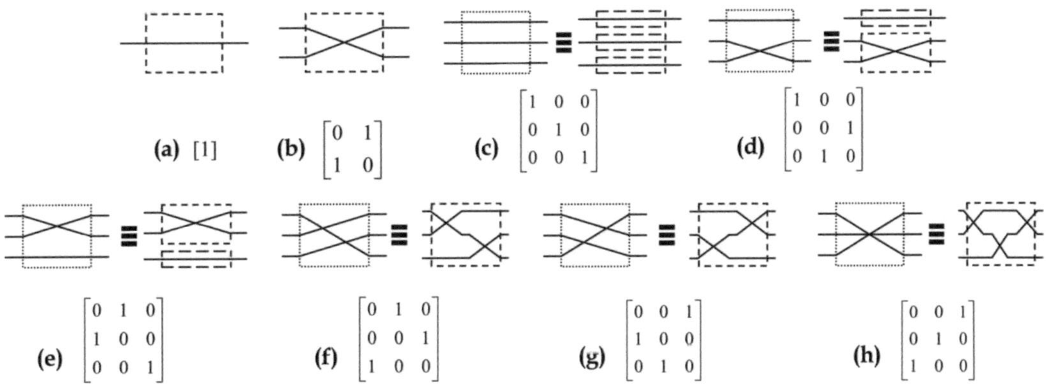

Fig. 5. Two-valued (binary) reversible and conservative permutation-based circuits: (a) (1, 1) Wire (i.e., Buffer), (b) (2, 2) Swap, and (c) - (h) all possible reversible (3, 3) Swap-based primitives.

Example 7. For a discrete system defined as follows: (1) Object: set of two objects $\{I_1, I_2\} \rightarrow$ automata; (2) Characteristic Features: location $\rightarrow$ automaton; (3) Data: spatial grid locations $\rightarrow$ cells, given an initial condition as {01010}, Figure 6a shows a possible top-to-down and left-to-right discrete dynamics of the two objects over 3-step period of time, where the tuple (t, s) indicate the cell indices in ECA. A possible conservative reversible discrete dynamics for Figure 6a can be obtained using Table 3 as shown in Figure 6b by adding an auxiliary cell C.

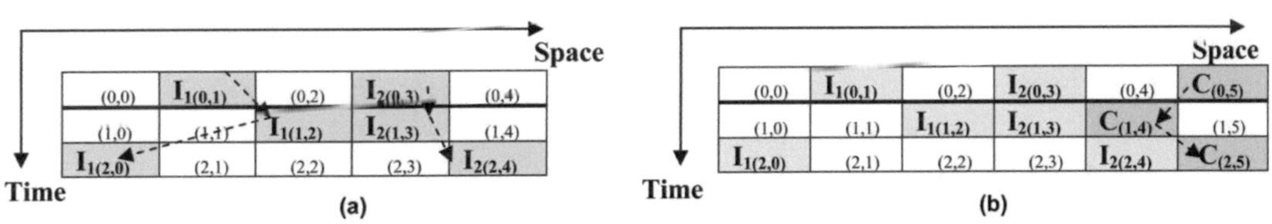

Fig. 6. An example of an evolution dynamics: (a) evolution of two objects, and (b) *reversible* discrete dynamics for Figure 6a that is obtained using Table 3.

The reversible circuit model for the evolution in Figure 6b can be obtained by interconnecting reversible *Swap*-based primitives from the permutation circuits that are shown in Figure 5. The two-stage *step-by-step* evolution of the conservative reversible discrete dynamics in Figure 6b can be modeled using the *Swap*-based reversible circuit in Figure 7a, and the two-stage *total* conservative reversible evolution can be modeled using the *Swap*-based reversible circuit in Figure 7b.

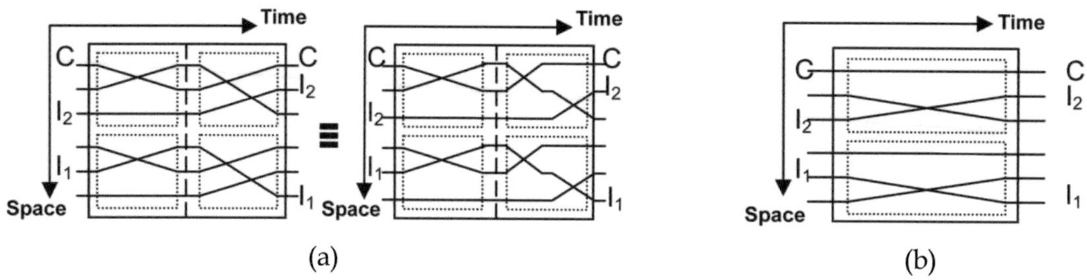

Fig. 7. Conservative and reversible Swap-based circuit model for the reversible dynamics in Figure 6b: (a) (6,6) conservative reversible circuit for the two-stage *step-by-step* evolution of the discrete dynamics in Figure 6b, and (b) (6,6) circuit for the two-stage *total* evolution in Figure 6b.

One notes that the two objects I_1 and I_2 and the additional object C are of the same type, i.e., logically can be represented as value "1". The two-stage *step-by-step* evolution of the conservative reversible discrete dynamics in Figure 7a is mathematically represented by the following transformation matrices (cf. Figures 5d and 5e), where 0_{3x3} is a zero-value matrix of dimension 3x3:

$$\text{Stage 1: } \begin{bmatrix} \begin{bmatrix} 0 & 1 & 0 \\ 1 & 0 & 0 \\ 0 & 0 & 1 \end{bmatrix} & 0_{3x3} \\ 0_{3x3} & \begin{bmatrix} 0 & 1 & 0 \\ 1 & 0 & 0 \\ 0 & 0 & 1 \end{bmatrix} \end{bmatrix}, \text{ Stage 2: } \begin{bmatrix} \begin{bmatrix} 0 & 1 & 0 \\ 0 & 0 & 1 \\ 1 & 0 & 0 \end{bmatrix} & 0_{3x3} \\ 0_{3x3} & \begin{bmatrix} 0 & 1 & 0 \\ 0 & 0 & 1 \\ 1 & 0 & 0 \end{bmatrix} \end{bmatrix}$$

and the two-stage *total* evolution of the reversible discrete dynamics in Figure 7b is represented by the following transformation:

$$\begin{bmatrix} \begin{bmatrix} 1 & 0 & 0 \\ 0 & 0 & 1 \\ 0 & 1 & 0 \end{bmatrix} & 0_{3x3} \\ 0_{3x3} & \begin{bmatrix} 1 & 0 & 0 \\ 0 & 0 & 1 \\ 0 & 1 & 0 \end{bmatrix} \end{bmatrix} = \begin{bmatrix} \begin{bmatrix} 0 & 1 & 0 \\ 0 & 0 & 1 \\ 1 & 0 & 0 \end{bmatrix} & 0_{3x3} \\ 0_{3x3} & \begin{bmatrix} 0 & 1 & 0 \\ 0 & 0 & 1 \\ 1 & 0 & 0 \end{bmatrix} \end{bmatrix} \begin{bmatrix} \begin{bmatrix} 0 & 1 & 0 \\ 1 & 0 & 0 \\ 0 & 0 & 1 \end{bmatrix} & 0_{3x3} \\ 0_{3x3} & \begin{bmatrix} 0 & 1 & 0 \\ 1 & 0 & 0 \\ 0 & 0 & 1 \end{bmatrix} \end{bmatrix}$$

Suppose now, due to an external unknown stimulus in Figure 6b (which is modeled using Table 3) that it is acceptable for the output vector $\{s_{t+1}(i-1)=0, s_{t+1}(i)=0, s_{t+1}(i+1)=1\}$ in the conservative reversible map in Table 3 to be $\{s_{t+1}(i-1)=0, s_{t+1}(i)=1, s_{t+1}(i+1)=1\}$, i.e., one does not care if $s_{t+1}(i)$ has value "0" or value "1", (which happens a lot in circuit design [82] for instance), and thus one would like to re-use the same map in Table 3. A sub-map of such (1) reversible and (2) conservative map would be as shown in Table 4a. One way to make Table 4a conservative and reversible is by using the method suggested in Section 2, i.e., by incorporating redundancy in inputs (K_t) and outputs (K_{t+1}).

Each row in the new map is a (4, 4) automaton and thus the new map would have 16 possible automata (i.e., each Rule is made of 16 "0/1" entries).

K_t	$s_t(i-1)$	$s_t(i)$	$s_t(i+1)$	$s_{t+1}(i-1)$	$s_{t+1}(i)$	$s_{t+1}(i+1)$	K_{t+1}
0	0	0	0	0	0	0	0
0	0	0	1	1	0	0	0
0	0	1	0	**0**	**0→1**	**1**	**0**
0	0	1	1	1	0	1	0
0	1	0	0	0	1	0	0
0	1	0	1	1	1	0	0
0	1	1	0	**0**	**1**	**1**	**1**
0	1	1	1	1	1	1	0

(a)

K_t	$s_t(i-1)$	$s_t(i)$	$s_t(i+1)$	$s_{t+1}(i-1)$	$s_{t+1}(i)$	$s_{t+1}(i+1)$	K_{t+1}
0	0	0	0	0	0	0	0
0	0	0	1	1	0	0	0
0	0	1	0	0	**0→1**	1	0
0	0	1	1	1	0	**1→0**	1
0	1	0	0	0	1	0	0
0	1	0	1	1	1	0	0
0	1	1	0	0	1	1	1
0	1	1	1	1	1	**1→0**	1

(b)

Table 4. Reversible and conservative maps in the existence of noise: (a) reversible conservative noisy map model for Table 3 with single erroneous cell, and (b) reversible conservative noisy map model for Table 3 with multiple-errors.

Note that Table 4a will be reversible for both cases if the value of the output noisy cell $s_{t+1}(i)$ is "0" or "1". The CRECA and its conservative reversible circuit model can be obtained for Table 4 by using the SCRECA algorithm utilizing (4, 4) Swap-based reversible primitives that can be obtained using all possible input-output permutations similar to the (3, 3) Swap-based primitives in Figure 5. *Table 4 shows that one way to incorporate noise while maintaining reversibility is to add more spatial complexity in terms of adding extra hardware (sub-circuits) that correspond to the redundant input/output variables.* The problem of obtaining a reversible map from an irreversible map is important because, as will be seen in the next section, quantum circuits are inherently reversible and thus does not consume power, while irreversible circuits and systems, due to an irreversible mapping, do consume power [9,40,63].

5. Quantum computing for the conservative reversible ECA

Quantum computing (QC) is a method of computation that uses a dynamic process governed by the Schrödinger Equation (SE) [3,63]. The one-dimensional time-dependent SE (TDSE) takes the following general form:

$$-\frac{(h/2\pi)^2}{2m}\frac{\partial^2|\psi\rangle}{\partial x^2}+V|\psi\rangle=i(h/2\pi)\frac{\partial|\psi\rangle}{\partial t} \tag{5}$$

$$or \quad H|\psi\rangle=i(h/2\pi)\frac{\partial|\psi\rangle}{\partial t} \tag{6}$$

where h is Planck constant ($6.626{\cdot}10^{-34}$ J·s), $V(x, t)$ is the potential, m is particle mass, $i=\sqrt{-1}$, $|\psi(x, t)>$ is the quantum state, H is the Hamiltonian operator ($H = -[(h/2\pi)^2/2m]\nabla^2 + V$), and ∇^2 is the Laplacian operator.

Although more complex forms of the Schrödinger Equation were proposed such as (1) the *relativistic* TDSE, and (2) the *master* TDSE, Equation (5) is still a good and acceptable useful form to model systems' dynamics utilizing quantum mechanical principles.

While the above holds for all physical systems, in the quantum computing (QC) context, the time-independent SE (TISE) is normally used [3,63]:

$$\nabla^2 \psi = \frac{2m}{(h/2\pi)^2}(V - E)\psi \tag{7}$$

where the solution $|\psi>$ is an expansion over orthogonal basis states $|\phi_i>$ defined in a complex linear vector space called Hilbert space **H** as follows:

$$|\psi\rangle = \sum_i c_i |\phi_i\rangle \tag{8}$$

where the coefficients c_i are called *probability amplitudes*, and $|c_i|^2$ is the *probability* that the quantum state $|\psi>$ will collapse into the (eigen) state $|\phi_i>$. The probability is equal to the inner product $|<\phi_i|\psi>|^2$, with the unitary condition $\sum|c_i|^2 = 1$. In QC, a linear and unitary operator $\Im$ is used to transform an input vector of quantum binary digits (qubits) into an output vector of qubits [3,63]. In two-valued QC, a qubit is a vector of bits defined as follows:

$$\text{qubit}_0 \equiv |0\rangle = \begin{bmatrix} 1 \\ 0 \end{bmatrix}, \text{qubit}_1 \equiv |1\rangle = \begin{bmatrix} 0 \\ 1 \end{bmatrix} \tag{9}$$

A two-valued quantum state $|\psi>$ is a superposition of quantum basis states $|\phi_i>$, such as those defined in Equation (9). Thus, for the orthonormal computational basis states $\{|0>,|1>\}$, one has the following quantum state:

$$|\psi\rangle = \alpha|0\rangle + \beta|1\rangle \tag{10}$$

where $\alpha\alpha^* = |\alpha|^2 = p_0 \equiv$ the probability of having state $|\psi>$ in state $|0>$, $\beta\beta^* = |\beta|^2 = p_1 \equiv$ the probability of having state $|\psi>$ in state $|1>$, and $|\alpha|^2 + |\beta|^2 = 1$. The calculation in QC for multiple systems (e.g., the equivalent of a register) follows the tensor (Kronecker) product ($\otimes$) [3]. For example, given two states $|\psi_1>$ and $|\psi_2>$ one has the following QC:

$$\begin{aligned} |\psi_1\psi_2\rangle &= |\psi_1\rangle \otimes |\psi_2\rangle \\ &= (\alpha_1|0\rangle + \beta_1|1\rangle) \otimes (\alpha_2|0\rangle + \beta_2|1\rangle) \\ &= \alpha_1\alpha_2|00\rangle + \alpha_1\beta_2|01\rangle + \beta_1\alpha_2|10\rangle + \beta_1\beta_2|11\rangle \end{aligned} \tag{11}$$

A physical system, describable as follows:

$$|\psi\rangle = c_1|\text{Spinup}\rangle + c_2|\text{Spindown}\rangle \tag{12}$$

(such as the Hydrogen atom), can be used to physically implement a two-valued QC. Another common alternative form of Equation (12) is:

$$|\psi\rangle = c_1\left|+\frac{1}{2}\right\rangle + c_2\left|-\frac{1}{2}\right\rangle = c_1|0\rangle + c_2|1\rangle \tag{13}$$

A Quantum circuit, that implements specific mapping, can be modeled as interconnects of certain quantum primitives [3]. As quantum circuits must be reversible, the conservative reversible primitives in Figures 5a and 5b are used for quantum circuit synthesis [3,63], and therefore the reversible circuits in Figure 5 can be used for QC. Yet, since inputs in the quantum domain are vectors of bits rather than scalar bits as in the classical domain, the quantum evolution of inputs to outputs in Figure 7 (as an example) is modeled in QC differently. In QC, a (1, 1) Wire and a (2, 2) Swap quantum primitives are modeled as in Figure 8.

$$\text{(1, 1) Wire: } \begin{bmatrix} 1 & 0 \\ 0 & 1 \end{bmatrix} \qquad \text{(2, 2) Swap: } \begin{bmatrix} 1 & 0 & 0 & 0 \\ 0 & 0 & 1 & 0 \\ 0 & 1 & 0 & 0 \\ 0 & 0 & 0 & 1 \end{bmatrix}$$

(a) (b)

Fig. 8. Quantum modeling of: (a) Wire (Buffer) gate and (b) Swap gate.

In Figure 8, the matrix representation is equivalent to the input-output (I/O) mapping representation of quantum gates, and we consider the example of the Swap gate to illustrate this point as follows. The Swap gate performs the following I/O mapping:

00	00
01	10
10	01
11	11

If one considers each *row* in the input side of the I/O map as an input vector represented by the natural binary code of 2^{index} with row index starting from "0", and similarly for the output row of the I/O map, then the matrix transforms the input vector to the corresponding output vector by transforming the code for the input to the code for the output. For example, the following matrix equation is the I/O mapping that uses the Swap matrix from Figure 8b:

$$[\text{Swap matrix}] \cdot [\text{input code}] = [\text{output code}]$$

$$\begin{bmatrix} 1 & 0 & 0 & 0 \\ 0 & 0 & 1 & 0 \\ 0 & 1 & 0 & 0 \\ 0 & 0 & 0 & 1 \end{bmatrix} \cdot \begin{bmatrix} 1 & 0 & 0 & 0 \\ 0 & 1 & 0 & 0 \\ 0 & 0 & 1 & 0 \\ 0 & 0 & 0 & 1 \end{bmatrix} = \begin{bmatrix} 1 & 0 & 0 & 0 \\ 0 & 0 & 1 & 0 \\ 0 & 1 & 0 & 0 \\ 0 & 0 & 0 & 1 \end{bmatrix}$$

One notes from this example, that the Swap gate, and similarly the Buffer (Wire) quantum gate in Figure 8a, is merely a permuter, i.e., it produces output vectors which are permutations of the input vectors. Another method for obtaining the matrix representations in Figure 8 is as follows [3]: Utilizing the algebraic addition and multiplication operations over the 2nd-radix (two-valued) Galois field [3,67], one obtains the following quantum transformations of the binary input qubits into the output qubits using the two-valued Swap quantum gate:

$$|00\rangle \rightarrow |00\rangle, |01\rangle \rightarrow |10\rangle, |10\rangle \rightarrow |01\rangle, |11\rangle \rightarrow |11\rangle$$

and by solving for the set of linearly independent equations over the two-valued Galois field, one obtains the Swap evolution matrix in Figure 8b. Therefore, the evolution of input to output for QC in Figure 7a is performed as follows, where ⊗ is the tensor (i.e., Kronecker) product, | is the quantum parallel interconnection, and — is the quantum serial interconnection [3]:

$$\text{Input}_1 = |C0I_2\rangle = |101\rangle = |1\rangle \otimes |0\rangle \otimes |1\rangle = \begin{bmatrix} 0 \\ 1 \end{bmatrix} \otimes \begin{bmatrix} 1 \\ 0 \end{bmatrix} \otimes \begin{bmatrix} 0 \\ 1 \end{bmatrix} = |0 \ \ 0 \ \ 0 \ \ 0 \ \ 0 \ \ 1 \ \ 0 \ \ 0\rangle^T$$

$$\text{Input}_2 = |0I_1 0\rangle = |010\rangle = |0\rangle \otimes |1\rangle \otimes |0\rangle = \begin{bmatrix} 1 \\ 0 \end{bmatrix} \otimes \begin{bmatrix} 0 \\ 1 \end{bmatrix} \otimes \begin{bmatrix} 1 \\ 0 \end{bmatrix} = |0 \ \ 0 \ \ 1 \ \ 0 \ \ 0 \ \ 0 \ \ 0 \ \ 0\rangle^T$$

Sub-System$_1$ = Sub-System$_2$ = [(Swap | Wire) — ((Swap | Wire) — (Wire | Swap))]

$$\rightarrow (\text{Swap} \,|\, \text{Wire}) = \begin{bmatrix} 1 & 0 & 0 & 0 \\ 0 & 0 & 1 & 0 \\ 0 & 1 & 0 & 0 \\ 0 & 0 & 0 & 1 \end{bmatrix} \otimes \begin{bmatrix} 1 & 0 \\ 0 & 1 \end{bmatrix} = \begin{bmatrix} \begin{bmatrix} 1 & 0 \\ 0 & 1 \end{bmatrix} & \begin{bmatrix} 0 & 0 \\ 0 & 0 \end{bmatrix} & \begin{bmatrix} 0 & 0 \\ 0 & 0 \end{bmatrix} & \begin{bmatrix} 0 & 0 \\ 0 & 0 \end{bmatrix} \\ \begin{bmatrix} 0 & 0 \\ 0 & 0 \end{bmatrix} & \begin{bmatrix} 0 & 0 \\ 0 & 0 \end{bmatrix} & \begin{bmatrix} 1 & 0 \\ 0 & 1 \end{bmatrix} & \begin{bmatrix} 0 & 0 \\ 0 & 0 \end{bmatrix} \\ \begin{bmatrix} 0 & 0 \\ 0 & 0 \end{bmatrix} & \begin{bmatrix} 1 & 0 \\ 0 & 1 \end{bmatrix} & \begin{bmatrix} 0 & 0 \\ 0 & 0 \end{bmatrix} & \begin{bmatrix} 0 & 0 \\ 0 & 0 \end{bmatrix} \\ \begin{bmatrix} 0 & 0 \\ 0 & 0 \end{bmatrix} & \begin{bmatrix} 0 & 0 \\ 0 & 0 \end{bmatrix} & \begin{bmatrix} 0 & 0 \\ 0 & 0 \end{bmatrix} & \begin{bmatrix} 1 & 0 \\ 0 & 1 \end{bmatrix} \end{bmatrix}.$$

$$\rightarrow (\text{Wire} \,|\, \text{Swap}) = \begin{bmatrix} 1 & 0 \\ 0 & 1 \end{bmatrix} \otimes \begin{bmatrix} 1 & 0 & 0 & 0 \\ 0 & 0 & 1 & 0 \\ 0 & 1 & 0 & 0 \\ 0 & 0 & 0 & 1 \end{bmatrix} = \begin{bmatrix} \begin{bmatrix} 1 & 0 & 0 & 0 \\ 0 & 0 & 1 & 0 \\ 0 & 1 & 0 & 0 \\ 0 & 0 & 0 & 1 \end{bmatrix} & \begin{bmatrix} 0 & 0 & 0 & 0 \\ 0 & 0 & 0 & 0 \\ 0 & 0 & 0 & 0 \\ 0 & 0 & 0 & 0 \end{bmatrix} \\ \begin{bmatrix} 0 & 0 & 0 & 0 \\ 0 & 0 & 0 & 0 \\ 0 & 0 & 0 & 0 \\ 0 & 0 & 0 & 0 \end{bmatrix} & \begin{bmatrix} 1 & 0 & 0 & 0 \\ 0 & 0 & 1 & 0 \\ 0 & 1 & 0 & 0 \\ 0 & 0 & 0 & 1 \end{bmatrix} \end{bmatrix}.$$

$$\Rightarrow [(\text{Swap} \,|\, \text{Wire}) — ((\text{Swap} \,|\, \text{Wire}) — (\text{Wire} \,|\, \text{Swap}))] =$$

$$\begin{bmatrix} \begin{bmatrix} 1 & 0 \\ 0 & 1 \end{bmatrix} & \begin{bmatrix} 0 & 0 \\ 0 & 0 \end{bmatrix} & \begin{bmatrix} 0 & 0 \\ 0 & 0 \end{bmatrix} & \begin{bmatrix} 0 & 0 \\ 0 & 0 \end{bmatrix} \\ \begin{bmatrix} 0 & 0 \\ 0 & 0 \end{bmatrix} & \begin{bmatrix} 0 & 0 \\ 0 & 0 \end{bmatrix} & \begin{bmatrix} 1 & 0 \\ 0 & 1 \end{bmatrix} & \begin{bmatrix} 0 & 0 \\ 0 & 0 \end{bmatrix} \\ \begin{bmatrix} 0 & 0 \\ 0 & 0 \end{bmatrix} & \begin{bmatrix} 1 & 0 \\ 0 & 1 \end{bmatrix} & \begin{bmatrix} 0 & 0 \\ 0 & 0 \end{bmatrix} & \begin{bmatrix} 0 & 0 \\ 0 & 0 \end{bmatrix} \\ \begin{bmatrix} 0 & 0 \\ 0 & 0 \end{bmatrix} & \begin{bmatrix} 0 & 0 \\ 0 & 0 \end{bmatrix} & \begin{bmatrix} 0 & 0 \\ 0 & 0 \end{bmatrix} & \begin{bmatrix} 1 & 0 \\ 0 & 1 \end{bmatrix} \end{bmatrix} \cdot \left[\begin{bmatrix} \begin{bmatrix} 1 & 0 \\ 0 & 1 \end{bmatrix} & \begin{bmatrix} 0 & 0 \\ 0 & 0 \end{bmatrix} & \begin{bmatrix} 0 & 0 \\ 0 & 0 \end{bmatrix} & \begin{bmatrix} 0 & 0 \\ 0 & 0 \end{bmatrix} \\ \begin{bmatrix} 0 & 0 \\ 0 & 0 \end{bmatrix} & \begin{bmatrix} 0 & 0 \\ 0 & 0 \end{bmatrix} & \begin{bmatrix} 1 & 0 \\ 0 & 1 \end{bmatrix} & \begin{bmatrix} 0 & 0 \\ 0 & 0 \end{bmatrix} \\ \begin{bmatrix} 0 & 0 \\ 0 & 0 \end{bmatrix} & \begin{bmatrix} 1 & 0 \\ 0 & 1 \end{bmatrix} & \begin{bmatrix} 0 & 0 \\ 0 & 0 \end{bmatrix} & \begin{bmatrix} 0 & 0 \\ 0 & 0 \end{bmatrix} \\ \begin{bmatrix} 0 & 0 \\ 0 & 0 \end{bmatrix} & \begin{bmatrix} 0 & 0 \\ 0 & 0 \end{bmatrix} & \begin{bmatrix} 0 & 0 \\ 0 & 0 \end{bmatrix} & \begin{bmatrix} 1 & 0 \\ 0 & 1 \end{bmatrix} \end{bmatrix} \cdot \begin{bmatrix} \begin{bmatrix} 1 & 0 & 0 & 0 \\ 0 & 0 & 1 & 0 \\ 0 & 1 & 0 & 0 \\ 0 & 0 & 0 & 1 \end{bmatrix} & \begin{bmatrix} 0 & 0 & 0 & 0 \\ 0 & 0 & 0 & 0 \\ 0 & 0 & 0 & 0 \\ 0 & 0 & 0 & 0 \end{bmatrix} \\ \begin{bmatrix} 0 & 0 & 0 & 0 \\ 0 & 0 & 0 & 0 \\ 0 & 0 & 0 & 0 \\ 0 & 0 & 0 & 0 \end{bmatrix} & \begin{bmatrix} 1 & 0 & 0 & 0 \\ 0 & 0 & 1 & 0 \\ 0 & 1 & 0 & 0 \\ 0 & 0 & 0 & 1 \end{bmatrix} \end{bmatrix} \right] = \begin{bmatrix} 1 & 0 & 0 & 0 & 0 & 0 & 0 & 0 \\ 0 & 0 & 1 & 0 & 0 & 0 & 0 & 0 \\ 0 & 1 & 0 & 0 & 0 & 0 & 0 & 0 \\ 0 & 0 & 0 & 1 & 0 & 0 & 0 & 0 \\ 0 & 0 & 0 & 0 & 1 & 0 & 0 & 0 \\ 0 & 0 & 0 & 0 & 0 & 0 & 1 & 0 \\ 0 & 0 & 0 & 0 & 0 & 1 & 0 & 0 \\ 0 & 0 & 0 & 0 & 0 & 0 & 0 & 1 \end{bmatrix}.$$

$$\Rightarrow \text{Output}_1: \begin{bmatrix} 1&0&0&0&0&0&0&0\\ 0&0&1&0&0&0&0&0\\ 0&1&0&0&0&0&0&0\\ 0&0&0&1&0&0&0&0\\ 0&0&0&0&1&0&0&0\\ 0&0&0&0&0&0&1&0\\ 0&0&0&0&0&1&0&0\\ 0&0&0&0&0&0&0&1 \end{bmatrix}\begin{bmatrix}0\\0\\0\\0\\0\\1\\0\\0\end{bmatrix} = \begin{bmatrix}0\\0\\0\\0\\0\\0\\1\\0\end{bmatrix} = |1\rangle\otimes|1\rangle\otimes|0\rangle = |110\rangle = |CI_2 0\rangle,$$

$$\text{Output}_2: \begin{bmatrix} 1&0&0&0&0&0&0&0\\ 0&0&1&0&0&0&0&0\\ 0&1&0&0&0&0&0&0\\ 0&0&0&1&0&0&0&0\\ 0&0&0&0&1&0&0&0\\ 0&0&0&0&0&0&1&0\\ 0&0&0&0&0&1&0&0\\ 0&0&0&0&0&0&0&1 \end{bmatrix}\begin{bmatrix}0\\0\\1\\0\\0\\0\\0\\0\end{bmatrix} = \begin{bmatrix}0\\1\\0\\0\\0\\0\\0\\0\end{bmatrix} = |0\rangle\otimes|0\rangle\otimes|1\rangle = |001\rangle = |00I_1\rangle.$$

One can note that the classical method using Figure 5 and the quantum method using Figure 8 produce formally the same output in two distinct ways: *the first uses linear transformation upon classical bits while the second uses (equivalently) distinct linear transformation upon qubits.* While the previous example considered that the probability of the quantum system is 100% in one state and 0% in the rest (i.e., $|\psi_i\rangle = 1.0|0\rangle + 0.0|1\rangle$ or $|\psi_i\rangle = 0.0|0\rangle + 1.0|1\rangle$), the following example illustrates the evolution of a general superimposed quantum state.

Example 8. Feynman gate is the quantum XOR and plays a fundamental role in quantum computing [63]. The fundamental Swap gate (cf. Figure 8b) can be decomposed into serially-interconnected Feynman-based primitives. This example illustrates the evolution of the input superimposed quantum states into output quantum states using the quantum circuit in Figure 9d which is related to the fundamental Swap gate via using the quantum circuit in Figure 9c. The quantum matrix representations for the basic gates in Figures 9a and 9b is shown within the two Figures respectively, and is obtained using any of the two methods that were shown previously for obtaining the quantum matrix representation for the Swap gate. The quantum matrix representation for the circuit in Figure 9d is obtained using the regular matrix multiplication of the matrix representations of the serially interconnected C-Not and flipped C-Not gates.

For the two quantum input states: $|\psi_1\rangle = \frac{1}{\sqrt{2}}(|0\rangle + |1\rangle)$, $|\psi_2\rangle = a|0\rangle + b|1\rangle$, the evolution of the superimposed input quantum state:

$$|\psi\rangle = |\psi_1\psi_2\rangle = |\psi_1\rangle\otimes|\psi_2\rangle = \frac{1}{\sqrt{2}}(|0\rangle+|1\rangle)\otimes(a|0\rangle+b|1\rangle) = \frac{1}{\sqrt{2}}(a|00\rangle+b|01\rangle+a|10\rangle+b|11\rangle)$$

using the circuit in Figure 9d is obtained as follows:

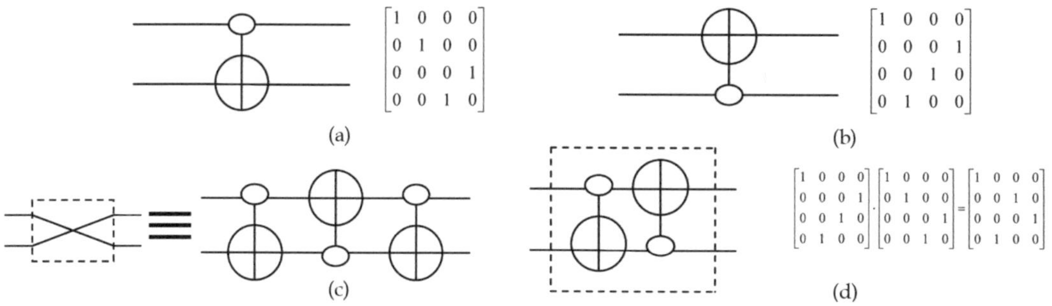

Fig. 9. Quantum gates and circuits and their quantum matrix representations: (a) 2-valued Controlled-Not gate (2-valued C-Not gate or 2-valued Feynman gate), (b) flipped 2-valued Controlled-Not gate (flipped 2-valued C-Not gate or flipped 2-valued Feynman gate), (c) Swap gate as an equivalent to a serial cascading of CNot-FlippedCNot-CNot gates, and (d) a sub-circuit of the quantum circuit in Figure 9c which is composed of a serial interconnection between a C-Not gate and a flipped C-Not gate.

$$\begin{bmatrix}1&0&0&0\\0&0&1&0\\0&0&0&1\\0&1&0&0\end{bmatrix}\begin{bmatrix}a/\sqrt{2}\\b/\sqrt{2}\\a/\sqrt{2}\\b/\sqrt{2}\end{bmatrix}=\begin{bmatrix}a/\sqrt{2}\\a/\sqrt{2}\\b/\sqrt{2}\\b/\sqrt{2}\end{bmatrix}$$

Thus, the superimposed output quantum state is:

$$|\psi'\rangle=\frac{a}{\sqrt{2}}|00\rangle+\frac{a}{\sqrt{2}}|01\rangle+\frac{b}{\sqrt{2}}|10\rangle+\frac{b}{\sqrt{2}}|11\rangle=\left(a|0\rangle+b|1\rangle\right)\frac{1}{\sqrt{2}}\left(|0\rangle+|1\rangle\right)=|\psi_2\rangle\otimes|\psi_1\rangle=|\psi_2\psi_1\rangle$$

One can note from Example 8 that the quantum matrix holds the orthonormal axes in the corresponding quantum space that define that particular quantum space, the quantum state is a vector of probabilities in that quantum space, and the quantum evolution is a transformation of the vector of probabilities in the corresponding quantum space. Equivalently, one may interpret the quantum evolution as the application of the transformed quantum space (that is the transformed orthonormal axes) upon the input vector of probabilities. This can be directly observed from the following Equation:

$$|\psi'\rangle=\left[|00\rangle\ |01\rangle\ |10\rangle\ |11\rangle\right]\left[\begin{bmatrix}1&0&0&0\\0&0&0&1\\0&0&1&0\\0&1&0&0\end{bmatrix}\cdot\begin{bmatrix}1&0&0&0\\0&1&0&0\\0&0&0&1\\0&0&1&0\end{bmatrix}\right]\begin{bmatrix}a/\sqrt{2}\\b/\sqrt{2}\\a/\sqrt{2}\\b/\sqrt{2}\end{bmatrix}=\left[|00\rangle\ |01\rangle\ |10\rangle\ |11\rangle\right]\begin{bmatrix}1&0&0&0\\0&0&1&0\\0&0&0&1\\0&1&0&0\end{bmatrix}\begin{bmatrix}a/\sqrt{2}\\b/\sqrt{2}\\a/\sqrt{2}\\b/\sqrt{2}\end{bmatrix}$$

$$=\left[|00\rangle\ |01\rangle\ |10\rangle\ |11\rangle\right]\begin{bmatrix}a/\sqrt{2}\\a/\sqrt{2}\\b/\sqrt{2}\\b/\sqrt{2}\end{bmatrix}=\left[|00\rangle\ |11\rangle\ |01\rangle\ |10\rangle\right]\begin{bmatrix}a/\sqrt{2}\\b/\sqrt{2}\\a/\sqrt{2}\\b/\sqrt{2}\end{bmatrix}=\frac{1}{\sqrt{2}}\left(a|00\rangle+b|11\rangle+a|01\rangle+b|10\rangle\right)$$

Although Example 8 demonstrates the method for evolving the input superimposed quantum states into output quantum states for two-valued quantum circuit, the same method is straightforward extended to the many-valued case that will be introduced in the following section.

For the superposition of quantum states in the corresponding quantum ECA (QECA), one can spatially obtain the total superimposed quantum state from the individual quantum cells (quantum states), by superimposing *recursively* two quantum cells (states) at a time, due to the fact that the tensor (Kronecker) product possesses the associative property, as follows:

$$|\psi\rangle = |\psi_1\psi_2...\psi_n\rangle = |\psi_1\rangle \otimes |\psi_2\rangle \otimes ... \otimes |\psi_n\rangle = (...(((|\psi_1\rangle \otimes |\psi_2\rangle) \otimes |\psi_3\rangle) \otimes |\psi_4\rangle) \otimes ... \otimes |\psi_n\rangle) \quad (14)$$

The decomposition in Equation (14) can be directly utilized in using a binary tree for the representation of each pair of the quantum states' tensor product, and the resulting quantum decision tree (QDT) [3] can be used as a data structure for simulating the evolution dynamics in the corresponding QECA. This is shown in Figure 10 for the two quantum states of the Wire (Buffer) in Equations (15) and (16), respectively.

$$|\psi_A\rangle = [|0\rangle \quad |1\rangle]\begin{bmatrix}1 & 0\\0 & 1\end{bmatrix}\begin{bmatrix}\alpha_1\\\beta_1\end{bmatrix} \quad (15)$$

$$|\psi_B\rangle = [|0\rangle \quad |1\rangle]\begin{bmatrix}1 & 0\\0 & 1\end{bmatrix}\begin{bmatrix}\alpha_2\\\beta_2\end{bmatrix} \quad (16)$$

Where $\begin{bmatrix}1 & 0\\0 & 1\end{bmatrix}$ is the Buffer quantum operator [3].

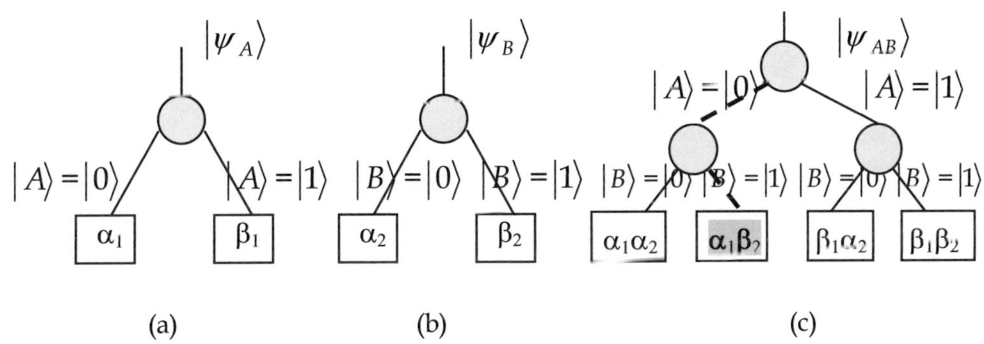

Fig. 10. Two-valued computational basis states QDT representations for: (a) Equation (15), (b) Equation (16), and (c) Equation (11).

As an example, Figure 10c shows the quantum decision path $|AB\rangle = |01\rangle$ in a dashed dark line that leads to the *highest* probability $\alpha_1\beta_2$ into which the QECA spatially superimposed state will collapse.

The QDTs in Figure 10 use the quantum computational basis states to model the ECA dynamics. Other quantum basis states such as the 1-qubit quantum systems' orthonormal composite basis states $\left\{\frac{|0\rangle+|1\rangle}{\sqrt{2}}, \frac{|0\rangle-|1\rangle}{\sqrt{2}}\right\}$ and the 2-qubit quantum systems' Einstein-

Podolsky-Rosen (EPR) basis states $\left\{\frac{|00\rangle+|11\rangle}{\sqrt{2}},\frac{|00\rangle-|11\rangle}{\sqrt{2}},\frac{|01\rangle+|10\rangle}{\sqrt{2}},\frac{|01\rangle-|10\rangle}{\sqrt{2}}\right\}$ can be used [3,63] for the quantum representation of ECA, where various tree representations will lead to different computational optimizations in terms of (1) number of internal nodes used (i.e., memory used or spatial complexity) and (2) the speed of implementation operations using such representation (i.e., temporal complexity). For instance, by using the quantum Walsh-Hadamard operator $\frac{1}{\sqrt{2}}\begin{bmatrix}1 & 1\\ 1 & -1\end{bmatrix}$ [3,63], Equations (17) and (18) represent the equivalence of Equations (15) and (16) in terms of the orthonormal composite basis states $\left\{\frac{|0\rangle+|1\rangle}{\sqrt{2}},\frac{|0\rangle-|1\rangle}{\sqrt{2}}\right\}$ as follows [3]:

$$\begin{aligned}|\Psi_A\rangle &= \alpha_1|0\rangle+\beta_1|1\rangle=\alpha_1\frac{|+\rangle+|-\rangle}{\sqrt{2}}+\beta_1\frac{|+\rangle-|-\rangle}{\sqrt{2}},\\ &=\frac{\alpha_1+\beta_1}{\sqrt{2}}|+\rangle+\frac{\alpha_1-\beta_1}{\sqrt{2}}|-\rangle=\lambda_1|+\rangle+\mu_1|-\rangle.\end{aligned} \tag{17}$$

$$\begin{aligned}|\Psi_B\rangle &= \alpha_2|0\rangle+\beta_2|1\rangle=\alpha_2\frac{|+\rangle+|-\rangle}{\sqrt{2}}+\beta_2\frac{|+\rangle-|-\rangle}{\sqrt{2}},\\ &=\frac{\alpha_2+\beta_2}{\sqrt{2}}|+\rangle+\frac{\alpha_2-\beta_2}{\sqrt{2}}|-\rangle=\lambda_2|+\rangle+\mu_2|-\rangle.\end{aligned} \tag{18}$$

where $\left\{|+\rangle=\frac{|0\rangle+|1\rangle}{\sqrt{2}},|-\rangle=\frac{|0\rangle-|1\rangle}{\sqrt{2}}\right\}$ and $\left\{|0\rangle=\frac{|+\rangle+|-\rangle}{\sqrt{2}},|1\rangle=\frac{|+\rangle-|-\rangle}{\sqrt{2}}\right\}$.

Consequently, measuring $|\Psi_A\rangle$ with respect to the new basis $\{|+\rangle,|-\rangle\}$ will result in the state (basis) $|+\rangle$ with probability $\frac{|\alpha_1+\beta_1|^2}{2}$ and the state (basis) $|-\rangle$ with probability $\frac{|\alpha_1-\beta_1|^2}{2}$. Similarly, measuring $|\Psi_B\rangle$ with respect to the new basis $\{|+\rangle,|-\rangle\}$ will result in the state (basis) $|+\rangle$ with probability $\frac{|\alpha_2+\beta_2|^2}{2}$ and the state (basis) $|-\rangle$ with a probability of $\frac{|\alpha_2-\beta_2|^2}{2}$. Figure 11 shows the corresponding QDTs using Equations (17) and (18), respectively [3].

As an example, Figure 11c shows the quantum decision path $|AB\rangle=|+-\rangle$ in a dashed dark line that leads to the *highest* probability $\lambda_1\mu_2$ into which the QECA spatially superimposed state will collapse.

The representation in Equation (14) is the quantum superposition over the spatial axis of QECA and leads to the tensor (Kronecker) matrix multiplication for all of the 3-block cells, and the quantum evolution (dynamics) is performed over the time (temporal) axis of QECA that transforms the input qubits into the corresponding output qubits using the spatially-obtained evolution matrix.

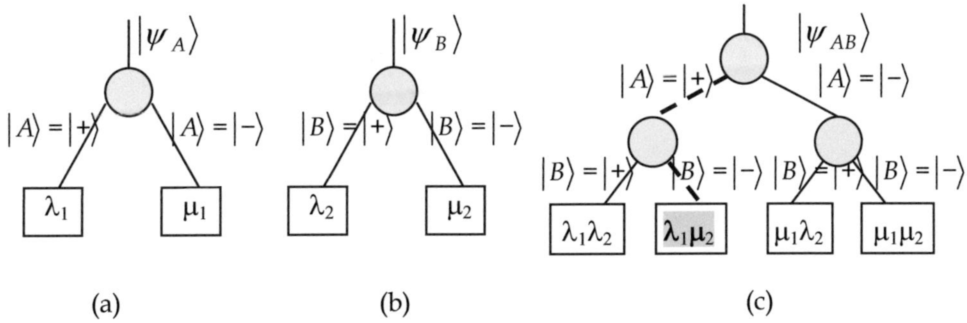

Fig. 11. Two-valued orthonormal composite basis states QDT representation for:
(a) Equation (17), (b) Equation (18), and (c) Equation (11).

6. Extensions to the many-valued conservative reversible ECA

Binary ECA that was introduced previously (cf. Figures 1 and 2) can be extended to the general case of many-valued ECA [113], where each ECA cell can take any value of "many" different values (cf. Figure 3). The next state of any cell in the many-valued ECA depends upon its present "neighborhood," which includes (a) the state of the cell itself and (b) those of its immediate neighbors to the left and right which also can take one of "many" values.
Many-valued QC can also be accomplished for the case of many-valued ECA. For the three-valued QC, the qubit becomes a 3-dimensional vector, called quantum discrete digit (qudit), and in general, for many-valued QC (MVQC) the qudit is of dimension "many". For example, one has for 3-state QC (in Hilbert space H) the following qudits:

$$\text{qudit}_0 \equiv |0\rangle = \begin{bmatrix}1\\0\\0\end{bmatrix}, \text{qudit}_1 \equiv |1\rangle = \begin{bmatrix}0\\1\\0\end{bmatrix}, \text{qudit}_2 \equiv |2\rangle = \begin{bmatrix}0\\0\\1\end{bmatrix} \tag{19}$$

A three-valued quantum state is a superposition of three quantum orthonormal basis states (vectors). Thus, for the orthonormal computational basis states $\{|0\rangle,|1\rangle,|2\rangle\}$, one has the following quantum state $|\psi\rangle = \alpha|0\rangle + \beta|1\rangle + \gamma|2\rangle$, where $\alpha\alpha^* = |\alpha|^2 = p_0 \equiv$ probability of having state $|\psi\rangle$ in state $|0\rangle$, $\beta\beta^* = |\beta|^2 = p_1 \equiv$ the probability of having state $|\psi\rangle$ in state $|1\rangle$, $\gamma\gamma^* = |\gamma|^2 = p_2 \equiv$ the probability of having state $|\psi\rangle$ in state $|2\rangle$, and $|\alpha|^2 + |\beta|^2 + |\gamma|^2 = 1$.
The calculation in QC for many-valued multiple systems follow the tensor product in a manner similar to the one demonstrated for the higher-dimensional qubit in two-valued QC [3]. It has been shown that a physical system comprising trapped ions under multiple-laser excitations can be used to reliably implement MVQC [3]. A physical system in which an atom (particle) is exposed to a specific potential field (function) can also be used to implement MVQC (two-valued being a special case). In such an implementation, the resulting distinct energy states are used as the orthonormal basis states.

In ternary QC, as a special case of the general many-valued (m-valued or m-ary) QC, a (1, 1) Wire and a (2, 2) Swap quantum primitives are modeled as in Figure 12 [3] (as compared to the binary case in Figure 8).

$$W = \begin{bmatrix} 1 & 0 & 0 \\ 0 & 1 & 0 \\ 0 & 0 & 1 \end{bmatrix} \qquad S = \begin{bmatrix} 1 & 0 & 0 & 0 & 0 & 0 & 0 & 0 & 0 \\ 0 & 0 & 0 & 1 & 0 & 0 & 0 & 0 & 0 \\ 0 & 0 & 0 & 0 & 0 & 0 & 1 & 0 & 0 \\ 0 & 1 & 0 & 0 & 0 & 0 & 0 & 0 & 0 \\ 0 & 0 & 0 & 0 & 1 & 0 & 0 & 0 & 0 \\ 0 & 0 & 0 & 0 & 0 & 0 & 0 & 1 & 0 \\ 0 & 0 & 1 & 0 & 0 & 0 & 0 & 0 & 0 \\ 0 & 0 & 0 & 0 & 0 & 1 & 0 & 0 & 0 \\ 0 & 0 & 0 & 0 & 0 & 0 & 0 & 0 & 1 \end{bmatrix}$$

(a) (b)

Fig. 12. The ternary unitary matrices as mathematical representations of: (a) Wire (i.e., Buffer) (**W**) quantum gate and (b) Swap (**S**) quantum gate.

In the many-valued ECA context, the general m-valued QC will be performed as one-to-one mapping permutation-based automaton cell between levels m and (m+1) into (3, 3) Swap-based reversible primitive (cf. Figure 13) between stages m and (m+1) in the corresponding reversible circuit. The idea of the previously introduced Algorithms CRBF and SCRECA (in Sections 2 and 4, respectively) can be generalized in a straightforward manner from the case of binary to the case of many-valued. The only difference would be that all Swap-based gates must be of "many" valued in their (a) representations and (b) operations.

The many-valued quantum circuits obtained through the implementation of the new quantum logic synthesis method in this Section *evolve* (i.e., *transform*) the input qudits into output qudits using the underlying mathematical transformation that is demonstrated in the following example.

Example 9. The following circuit in Figure 14 represents a parallel quantum interconnect between ternary Wire (**W**) (i.e., Buffer) and ternary Swap (**S**) quantum primitives from Figures 12 and 13.

Let us evolve the ternary input qubit $|120\rangle = |1\rangle \otimes |2\rangle \otimes |0\rangle$ using the ternary quantum circuit in Figure 14 (which is also the special permutation circuit in Figure 13d). This is done using the following general two quantum synthesis rules [3]: (1) the total multiple-valued quantum evolution transformation $[M]$ of the total serially-interconnected quantum circuit is equal to the matrix multiplication of the individual evolution matrices $[N_q]$ that correspond to the individual quantum primitives, i.e., $[M]_{serial} = \prod_q [N_q]$, and (2) the total evolution transformation $[M]$ of the total parallel-interconnected quantum circuit is equal to the tensor (i.e., Kronecker) product of the individual evolution matrices $[N_q]$ that correspond to the individual quantum primitives, i.e., $[M]_{parallel} = \otimes [N]_q$.

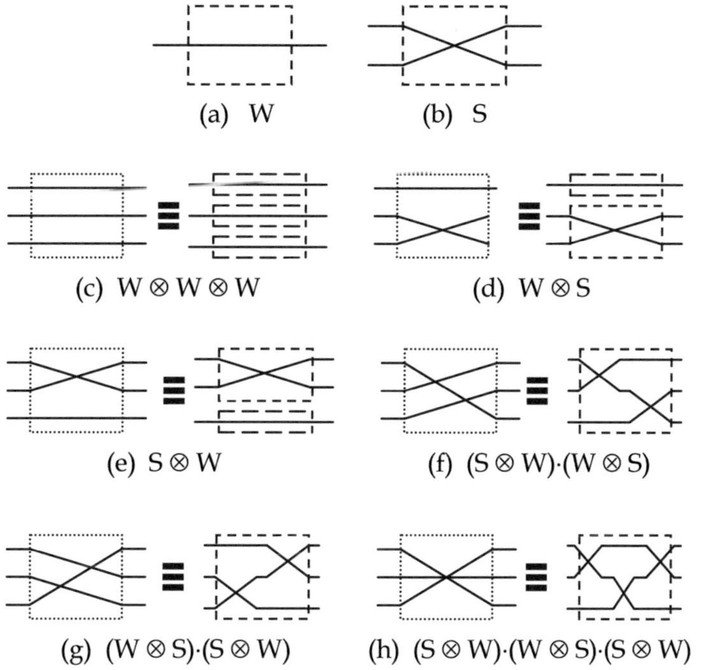

Fig. 13. Many-valued (m-ary) reversible and conservative permutation-based circuits: (a) m-ary (1, 1) Wire (W), (b) m-ary (2, 2) Swap (S), and (c) - (h) all possible m-ary reversible and quantum (3, 3) Swap-based primitives. The symbol ⊗ is the Kronecker (i.e., tensor) product.

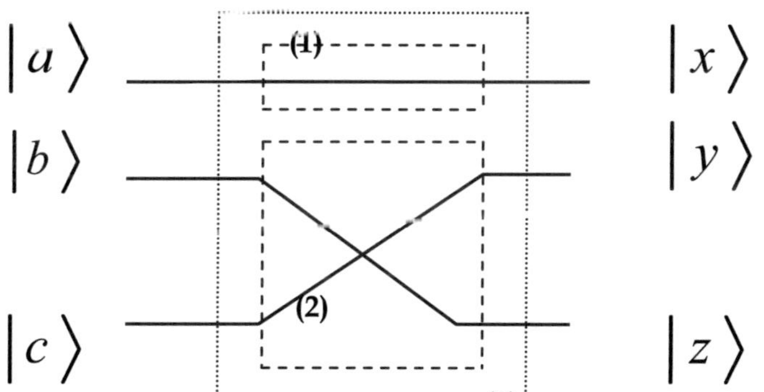

Fig. 14. A ternary quantum circuit composed of a parallel interconnect of a ternary Wire (**W**) and a ternary Swap (**S**) quantum gates.

The evolution matrices (transformations) of the parallel-interconnected dashed boxes in (1) and (2) in Figure 14 are as follows, where the symbol | means a parallel interconnection, and the utilized *unitary* matrices are the mathematical representations of the quantum gates in Figures 12 and 13 in the quantum domain [3,63].

$$\Rightarrow (3) = (1) \mid (2) = \text{Wire} \otimes \text{Swap} \Rightarrow \mathbf{M} = \mathbf{W} \otimes \mathbf{S} =$$

$$\begin{bmatrix} 1 & 0 & 0 \\ 0 & 1 & 0 \\ 0 & 0 & 1 \end{bmatrix} \otimes \begin{bmatrix} 1&0&0&0&0&0&0&0&0 \\ 0&0&0&1&0&0&0&0&0 \\ 0&0&0&0&0&0&1&0&0 \\ 0&1&0&0&0&0&0&0&0 \\ 0&0&0&0&1&0&0&0&0 \\ 0&0&0&0&0&0&0&1&0 \\ 0&0&1&0&0&0&0&0&0 \\ 0&0&0&0&0&1&0&0&0 \\ 0&0&0&0&0&0&0&0&1 \end{bmatrix}.$$

$$\therefore \mathbf{M} = \begin{bmatrix} \begin{bmatrix} 1&0&0&0&0&0&0&0&0 \\ 0&0&0&1&0&0&0&0&0 \\ 0&0&0&0&0&0&1&0&0 \\ 0&1&0&0&0&0&0&0&0 \\ 0&0&0&0&1&0&0&0&0 \\ 0&0&0&0&0&0&0&1&0 \\ 0&0&1&0&0&0&0&0&0 \\ 0&0&0&0&0&1&0&0&0 \\ 0&0&0&0&0&0&0&0&1 \end{bmatrix} & & \\ & \begin{bmatrix} 1&0&0&0&0&0&0&0&0 \\ 0&0&0&1&0&0&0&0&0 \\ 0&0&0&0&0&0&1&0&0 \\ 0&1&0&0&0&0&0&0&0 \\ 0&0&0&0&1&0&0&0&0 \\ 0&0&0&0&0&0&0&1&0 \\ 0&0&1&0&0&0&0&0&0 \\ 0&0&0&0&0&1&0&0&0 \\ 0&0&0&0&0&0&0&0&1 \end{bmatrix} & \\ & & \begin{bmatrix} 1&0&0&0&0&0&0&0&0 \\ 0&0&0&1&0&0&0&0&0 \\ 0&0&0&0&0&0&1&0&0 \\ 0&1&0&0&0&0&0&0&0 \\ 0&0&0&0&1&0&0&0&0 \\ 0&0&0&0&0&0&0&1&0 \\ 0&0&1&0&0&0&0&0&0 \\ 0&0&0&0&0&1&0&0&0 \\ 0&0&0&0&0&0&0&0&1 \end{bmatrix} \end{bmatrix}.$$

For the input qudit

$$\vec{I} = |120\rangle = |1\rangle \otimes |2\rangle \otimes |0\rangle = \begin{pmatrix} 0_{3x1} & 0_{3x1} & 0_{3x1} & 0_{3x1} & 0_{3x1} & 1 & 0 & 0 & 0_{3x1} & 0_{3x1} & 0_{3x1} \end{pmatrix}^T$$

∴ The output qudit

$$\vec{O} = [M]\vec{I} = \begin{pmatrix} 0_{3x1} & 0_{3x1} & 0_{3x1} & 0 & 0 & 1 & 0_{3x1} & 0_{3x1} & 0_{3x1} & 0_{3x1} & 0_{3x1} \end{pmatrix}^T$$

$$= |1\rangle \otimes |0\rangle \otimes |2\rangle = |102\rangle .$$

By observing the transformed output qudit from Example 9, one can note that the output qudit is a Swap-based transformation of the input qudit, i.e., the element values of the input qudit has been permuted within the output qudit. Similarly, all the fundamental m-valued (m-ary) Swap-based circuits in Figure 13 do this basic quantum operation of permutations. If a circuit is composed of interconnecting m-valued reversible elements (primitives or gates) then the overall m-valued circuit is also reversible. Thus, analogously to the binary case, and due to the permutation operations, the many-valued ECA circuits that are constructed from such basic elements as in Figure 13 are both conservative and reversible.

For the superposition of quantum states in the corresponding many-valued quantum ECA (m-valued QECA), then one can obtain the total superimposed quantum state from the individual quantum cells (quantum states), by superimposing *recursively* two quantum cells (states) at a time according to Equation (14). The decomposition in Equation (14) can be directly utilized in using an m-ary tree for the representation of each pair of the quantum states' tensor product, and the resulting many-valued quantum decision tree (MVQDT) [3] can be used as a data structure for simulating the evolution dynamics in the corresponding QECA. As an example, for the ternary case, the ternary Wire (Buffer) QDT is shown in Figure 15 for the two quantum states in Equations (20) and (21), respectively.

$$|\psi_A\rangle = \begin{bmatrix} |0\rangle & |1\rangle & |2\rangle \end{bmatrix} \begin{bmatrix} 1 & 0 & 0 \\ 0 & 1 & 0 \\ 0 & 0 & 1 \end{bmatrix} \begin{bmatrix} \alpha_1 \\ \beta_1 \\ \gamma_1 \end{bmatrix} \tag{20}$$

$$|\psi_B\rangle = \begin{bmatrix} |0\rangle & |1\rangle & |2\rangle \end{bmatrix} \begin{bmatrix} 1 & 0 & 0 \\ 0 & 1 & 0 \\ 0 & 0 & 1 \end{bmatrix} \begin{bmatrix} \alpha_2 \\ \beta_2 \\ \gamma_2 \end{bmatrix} \tag{21}$$

Analogously to the two-valued case, the QECA superimposed state $|\psi_{AB}\rangle$ in Figure 15 will collapse into the quantum state with the highest probability.

The ternary QDTs in Figure 15 use the quantum computational basis states to model QECA dynamics. For instance, by using the quantum Chrestenson gate $C^{(3)}_{(1)normalized} = \frac{1}{\sqrt{3}} \begin{bmatrix} 1 & 1 & 1 \\ 1 & d_1 & d_2 \\ 1 & d_2 & d_1 \end{bmatrix}$ [3], Equation (24) presents the equivalence of Equations (20) and (21) in terms of the ternary orthonormal composite basis states as follows [3]: by using the ternary quantum signal $|\Psi\rangle = \alpha|0\rangle + \beta|1\rangle + \gamma|2\rangle$ as an input to the ternary normalized quantum Chrestenson gate, one obtains the following quantum signal at the output of the gate [3]:

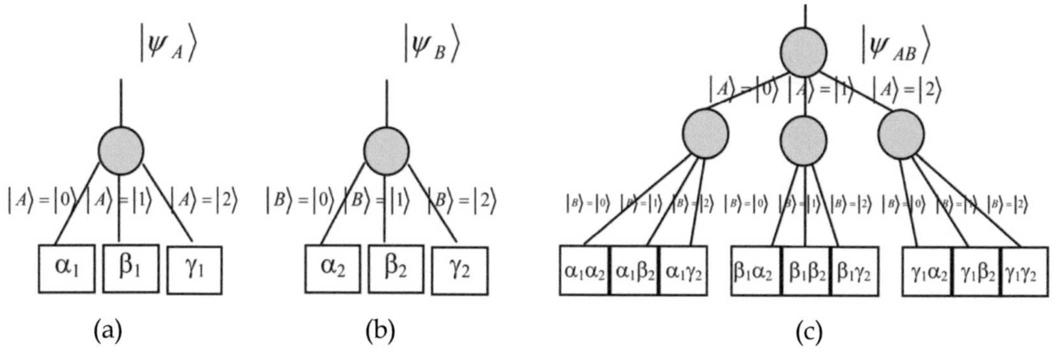

Fig. 15. Ternary computational basis states QDT representations for: (a) Equation (20), (b) Equation (21), and (c) the superposition of Equations (20) and (21): $|\psi_{AB}\rangle = |\psi_A\rangle \otimes |\psi_B\rangle$.

$$|\Psi\rangle' = \begin{bmatrix}|0\rangle & |1\rangle & |2\rangle\end{bmatrix} \frac{1}{\sqrt{3}} \begin{bmatrix} 1 & 1 & 1 \\ 1 & d_1 & d_2 \\ 1 & d_2 & d_1 \end{bmatrix} \begin{bmatrix} \alpha \\ \beta \\ \gamma \end{bmatrix} = \begin{bmatrix}|0\rangle & |1\rangle & |2\rangle\end{bmatrix} \begin{bmatrix} \frac{\alpha+\beta+\gamma}{\sqrt{3}} \\ \frac{\alpha+d_1\beta+d_2\gamma}{\sqrt{3}} \\ \frac{\alpha+d_2\beta+d_1\gamma}{\sqrt{3}} \end{bmatrix},$$

$$= \frac{\alpha+\beta+\gamma}{\sqrt{3}}|0\rangle + \frac{\alpha+d_1\beta+d_2\gamma}{\sqrt{3}}|1\rangle + \frac{\alpha+d_2\beta+d_1\gamma}{\sqrt{3}}|2\rangle. \tag{22}$$

$$|\Psi\rangle' = \begin{bmatrix}|0\rangle & |1\rangle & |2\rangle\end{bmatrix} \frac{1}{\sqrt{3}} \begin{bmatrix} 1 & 1 & 1 \\ 1 & d_1 & d_2 \\ 1 & d_2 & d_1 \end{bmatrix} \begin{bmatrix} \alpha \\ \beta \\ \gamma \end{bmatrix},$$

$$= \begin{bmatrix} \frac{|0\rangle+|1\rangle+|2\rangle}{\sqrt{3}} & \frac{|0\rangle+d_1|1\rangle+d_2|2\rangle}{\sqrt{3}} & \frac{|0\rangle+d_2|1\rangle+d_1|2\rangle}{\sqrt{3}} \end{bmatrix} \begin{bmatrix} \alpha \\ \beta \\ \gamma \end{bmatrix}, \tag{23}$$

$$= \begin{bmatrix}|\|\rangle & |+\rangle & |-\rangle\end{bmatrix} \begin{bmatrix} \alpha \\ \beta \\ \gamma \end{bmatrix} = \alpha|\|\rangle + \beta|+\rangle + \gamma|-\rangle.$$

Where:

$$\{\ |+\rangle = \frac{|0\rangle+d_1|1\rangle+d_2|2\rangle}{\sqrt{3}}, |\|\rangle = \frac{|0\rangle+|1\rangle+|2\rangle}{\sqrt{3}}, |-\rangle = \frac{|0\rangle+d_2|1\rangle+d_1|2\rangle}{\sqrt{3}}\ \}$$ and

$$\{|0\rangle = \frac{|+\rangle+|\|\rangle+|-\rangle}{\sqrt{3}}, |1\rangle = \frac{d_2|+\rangle+|\|\rangle+d_1|-\rangle}{\sqrt{3}}, |2\rangle = \frac{d_1|+\rangle+|\|\rangle+d_2|-\rangle}{\sqrt{3}}\}.$$

Thus, one obtains at the input of the quantum Chrestenson gate the following quantum state:

$$\begin{aligned}\therefore |\Psi\rangle &= \alpha|0\rangle + \beta|1\rangle + \gamma|2\rangle, \\ &= \alpha\frac{|+\rangle + ||\rangle + |-\rangle}{\sqrt{3}} + \beta\frac{d_2|+\rangle + ||\rangle + d_1|-\rangle}{\sqrt{3}} + \gamma\frac{d_1|+\rangle + ||\rangle + d_2|-\rangle}{\sqrt{3}}, \\ &= \frac{\alpha + d_2\beta + d_1\gamma}{\sqrt{3}}|+\rangle + \frac{\alpha + \beta + \gamma}{\sqrt{3}}||\rangle + \frac{\alpha + d_1\beta + d_2\gamma}{\sqrt{3}}|-\rangle = \lambda|+\rangle + \mu||\rangle + \eta|-\rangle\end{aligned} \tag{24}$$

$$\therefore \{ \sqrt{p_{||\rangle}} = \frac{\alpha+\beta+\gamma}{\sqrt{3}}, \sqrt{p_{|-\rangle}} = \frac{\alpha + d_1\beta + d_2\gamma}{\sqrt{3}}, \sqrt{p_{|+\rangle}} = \frac{\alpha + d_2\beta + d_1\gamma}{\sqrt{3}} \}.$$

Consequently, measuring $|\Psi\rangle$ with respect to the new basis $\{| \,|>, |+>, |->\}$ will result in the state (basis) $\{||\rangle\}$ with probability equals to $\frac{|\alpha+\beta+\gamma|^2}{3}$, will result in the state (basis) $\{|-\rangle\}$ with probability equals to $\frac{|\alpha + d_1\beta + d_2\gamma|^2}{3}$, and will result in the state (basis) $\{|+\rangle\}$ with probability equals to $\frac{|\alpha + d_2\beta + d_1\gamma|^2}{3}$, where:

$$d_2 = -(1+d_1) = -\frac{1}{2}(1+\sqrt{3}i) = e^{\frac{4\pi i}{3}}, \quad d_1 = -(1+d_2) = -\frac{1}{2}(1-\sqrt{3}i) = e^{\frac{2\pi i}{3}}.$$

Similar to the composite-based QDT in Figure 11, one can use the ternary composite basis states {| | >, | + >, | - >} to construct the ternary orthonormal composite basis states QDT as shown in Figure 16. Analogously to the two-valued case, the QECA superimposed state $|\psi_{AB}\rangle$ in Figure 16 will collapse into the quantum state with the highest probability.

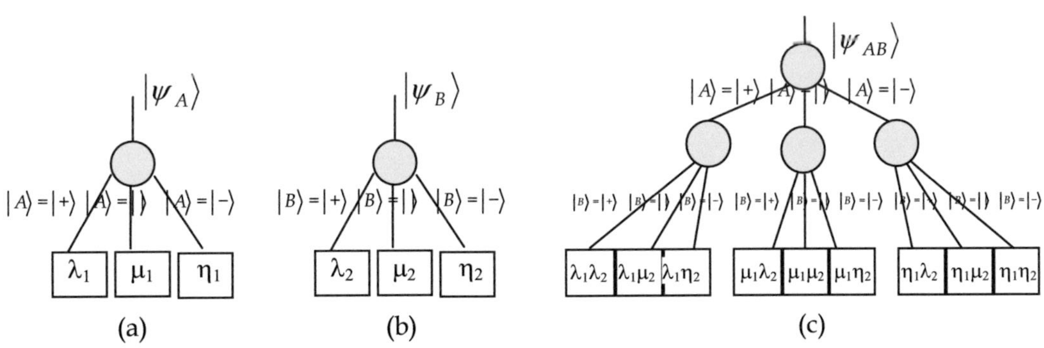

Fig. 16. Ternary computational basis states QDT representations for: (a) Equation (24) for $|\psi_A\rangle$, (b) Equation (24) for $|\psi_B\rangle$, and (c) the superposition of: $|\psi_{AB}\rangle = |\psi_A\rangle \otimes |\psi_B\rangle$.

In general, a data structure called multiple-valued quantum decision diagrams (MvQDDs) can be constructed for the corresponding multiple-valued quantum decision trees [3]. The rules for such quantum decision diagrams are the same as in classical decision diagrams [3]: (1) *join* isomorphic nodes, and (2) *remove* redundant nodes. MvQDDs can result in a more efficient representation than the corresponding MvQDTs in terms of memory space (more compact) and faster processing speed [3].

For any quantum evolution matrix (i.e., the quantum superposition over the spatial axis of QECA that leads to the tensor (Kronecker) matrix multiplication for all of the 3-block cells) the evolution (as was shown in Example 8) leads to: (a1) the permutation of the probability amplitudes or (b1) the permutation of the orthonormal bases. Consequently, in terms of the QDT representation, either: (a2) the evolution matrix leads to the permutation of the QDT leaves (probability amplitudes) while retaining the order of the QDT paths or (b2) the paths in the corresponding QDT will be permuted while retaining the order of the QDT leaves.

The state in the general case of m-valued (m-ary) QECA (which is the spatial superposition of the individual states) can be either: (1) *decomposable* as shown in Equation (25), or (2) *non-decomposable* (i.e., *entangled*) as shown in Equation (26).

$$|\psi_{12\ldots n}\rangle = \prod_{p=1}^{n}\left(\sum_{k=1}^{d}\alpha_k|D_k\rangle\right)_p \tag{25}$$

$$|\psi_{12\ldots n}\rangle \neq \prod_{p=1}^{n}\left(\sum_{k=1}^{d}\alpha_k|D_k\rangle\right)_p \tag{26}$$

where α_k is the probability amplitudes and $|D_k\rangle$ is the elementary (fundamental) basis states.

As an example of the entanglement in the QECA context, for the two-valued case, if the state vectors of quantum systems A and B were entangled with each other, then if one changes the state vector of one system A, then the corresponding state vector of the other system B is also changed, instantaneously, and independently of the medium through which some communicating signal must travel. By measuring one of the state vectors of a quantum system A, the state vector collapses into a knowable state. Instantaneously and automatically, the state vector of the other quantum system B will collapse into the other knowable state.

7. Conclusions and future work

In this research, an algorithm to model noisy discrete systems utilizing conservative reversible elementary cellular automata (CRECA) is introduced and the corresponding m-ary quantum computing is presented. The ECA representations in the quantum domain of (a) m-ary orthonormal computational basis states quantum decision trees (QDTs) and (b) m-ary orthonormal composite basis states QDTs are also introduced as quantum representations for the modeling and manipulation of the quantum ECA (QECA) dynamics. The new CRECA circuits and systems can play an important role in the synthesis of future reversible circuits and systems that consume minimal power such as in the quantum technology.

As was introduced in this research, the new method of adding auxiliary variables, to incorporate the effect of noise while retaining conservativeness and reversibility, is costly in terms of the resulting structural complexity. Therefore, future work will include the creation of other less complex and more efficient CRECA algorithms to incorporate the effect of noise.

Future work will also include items such as: (1) The investigation of implementing the proposed new synthesis algorithms using Quantum Dot Cellular Automata; (2) The investigation of using the new reversible and quantum ECA algorithms that were introduced in this research for testing logical reversible and quantum circuits to (a) test, (b) localize and (c) correct circuit errors; (3) The investigation of chaos in reversible ECA and quantum ECA; (4) The investigation of the previously introduced methods for the case of rule-varying ECA; (5) The incorporation of the reversibility property in error correcting codes to correct for noisy cells within the context of ECA; (6) Some CAs are considered to conserve a kind of energy measure, a Hmiltonian, and these are reversible, thus the investigation of defining a Hamiltonian that is conserved within the context of reversible and quantum ECA that has been presented in this research will be conducted; (7) The generalization of the results introduced in this research to the general case of reversible *m*-valued *k*-dimensional CA; (8) Exploration of using genetic algorithm (GA) and genetic programming (GP) to evolve reversible CA rules to perform particular computational tasks; (9) The investigation of configuring the local settings (rules and initial conditions) of a CRECA from a given prescribed global situation (behavior) which is generally called the *inverse problem* will also be performed; (10) The development of a 3-block reversible overlapping-based neighborhood ECA evolution algorithm that doesn't result in conflict values inside map cells (which is naturally forbidden since the value and its "opposite" cannot possess the same spatial location (address) at the same time); (11) Since CA are increasingly being studied as a class of efficient parallel computers, and as the main bottleneck in applying CA more widely to parallel computing is programming, future work will involve the investigation of the automatic programming of reversible CA using GA and GP; and (12) The implementation of Soft Computing (i.e., Computational Intelligence) techniques for the newly introduced types of Reversible Cellular Automata (RCA) such as: (a) Fuzzy Reversible Cellular Automata (FRCA), (b) Fuzzy Evolutionary Reversible Cellular Automata (FERCA), and (c) Neuro-Fuzzy Reversible Cellular Automata (NFRCA).

8. References

[1] A. Adamatzky (Ed.), *Collision-Based Computing*, Springer-Verlag, 2002.

[2] A. Albicki and M.Khare, "Cellular Automata used for Test Pattern Generation," *Proc. ICCD*, pp. 56-59, 1987.

[3] A. N. Al-Rabadi, *Reversible Logic Synthesis: From Fundamentals to Quantum Computing*, Springer-Verlag, N.Y., 2004.

[4] A. N. Al-Rabadi and W. Feyerherm, "Reversible Conservative Noisy Elementary Cellular Automata (ECA) Circuits and their Quantum Computation", *Proc. of the IEEE/ACM*

International Workshop on Logic and Synthesis (IWLS), pp. 273-279, Temecula, California, June 2-4, 2004.

[5] M. Arabib, "Simple Self-Reproducing Universal Automata," *Information and Control*, 9:177-189, 1966.

[6] H. Aso and N. Honda, "Dynamical Characteristics of Linear Cellular Automata," *J. Comput. Syst. Science*, 30:291-317, 1958.

[7] J. Austin, "The Cellular Neural Network Associative Processor, C-NNAP," *Proc. 5th Intl. Conf. on Image Processing and its Application*, pp. 622-626, July 1995.

[8] F. Bagnoli, F. Franci, and R. Rechtman, "Opinion Formation and Phase Transitions in a Probabilistic Cellular Automaton with Two Absorbing States," *Proc. of the 5th International Conference on Cellular Automata for Research and Industry (ACRI)*, Switzerland, pp. 249-258, October 2002.

[9] C. Bennett, "Logical Reversibility of Computation," *IBM J. of Research and Development*, 17, pp. 525-532, 1973.

[10] S. A. Billings and Y. Yang, "Identification of Probabilistic Cellular Automata," *IEEE Trans. on System, Man, and Cybernetics*, Part B, 33(2):1-12, 2002.

[11] C. Burks and D. Farmer, "Towards Modeling DNA Sequences as Automata," *Physica D*, 10:157-167, 1984.

[12] K. Cattel and J.C. Muzio, "Synthesis of One-dimensional Linear Hybrid Cellular Automata," *IEEE Trans. on CAD*, 15:325-335, 1996.

[13] S. Chakraborty, D. Roy Chowdhury, and P. Pal Chaudhuri, "Theory and Application of Non-Group Cellular Automata for Synthesis of Easily Testable Finite State Machines," *IEEE Trans. on Computers*, 45(7): 769-781, July 1996.

[14] S. Chakraborty, *Some Studies on Theory and Applications of Additive Cellular Automata*, Ph.D. Thesis, I.I.T., Kharagpur, India, 1996.

[15] S. Chattopadhyay, S. Adhikari, S. Sengupta, and M. Pal, "Highly Regular, Modular, and Cascadable Design of Cellular Automata-based Pattern Classifier," *IEEE Trans. on VLSI Systems*, 8(6):724-735, 2000.

[16] D. R. Chowdhury, S. Basu, I. S. Gupta, and P. Pal Chaudhuri, "Design of CAECC-Cellular Automata based Error Correcting Code," *IEEE Trans. on Computers*, 43(6):759-764, June 1994.

[17] D. R. Chowdhury, S. Chakraborty, B. Vamsi, and Pal Chaudhuri, "Cellular Automata based Synthesis of Easily and Fully Testable FSMs," *Proc. ICCAD*, pp. 650-653, Nov. 1993.

[18] L. O. Chua and L. Yang, "Cellular Nellular Networks: Application," *IEEE Trans. on Circuits and Systems*, 35(10):1273-1290, 1988.

[19] F. Corno, M. S. Reorda, and G. Squillero, "Evolving Effective CA/CSTP: BIST Architectures for Sequential Circuits," *Proc. ACM Symposium on Applied Computing*, pp. 345-350, ACM Press, 2001.

[20] A. K. Das, *Additive Cellular Automata: Theory and Application as Built-in Self-test Structure*, Ph.D. Thesis, I.I.T., Kharagpur, India, 1990.

[21] A. K. Das, A. Sanyal, and P. Pal Chaudhuri, "On Characterization of Cellular Automata with Matrix Algebra," *Information Sciences*, 61(3): 251-277, 1992.

[22] S. Dormann, A. Deutsch, and A. T. Lawniczak, "Fourier Analysis of Turing-like Pattern Formation in Cellular Automaton Models," *Future Generation Computer Science*, 17:901-909, 2001.

[23] J. Durand-Lose, "Representing Reversible Cellular Automata with Reversible Block Cellular Automata," *Discrete Mathematics and Theoretical Computer Science Proceedings*, AA (DM-CCG), pp. 145-154, 2001.

[24] P. Flocchini, F. Geurts, A. Mingarelli, and N. Santoro, "Convergence and Aperiodicity in Fuzzy Cellular Automata: Revisiting Rule 90," *Physica D: Nonlinear Phenomena*, 142(1-2):20-28, August 2000.

[25] U. Frisch, B. Hasslacher, and Y. Pomeau, "Lattice Gas Automata for the Navier-Stokes Equation," *Phys. Rev. Lett.*, 56(14): 1505-1508, 1986.

[26] N. Ganguly, P. Maji, S. Dhar, B. K. Sikdar, and P. Pal Chaudhuri, "Evolving Cellular Automata as Pattern Classifier," *Proc. 5th International Conference on Cellular Automata for Research and Industry (ACRI)*, Switzerland, pp. 56-68, October 2002.

[27] G. Grinstein, C. Jayaprakash, and Y. He, "Statistical Mechanics of Probabilistic Cellular Automata," *Phys. Rev. Lett.*, 55: 2527-2530, 1985.

[28] H. Gutowitz, "A Hierarchical Classification of CA," *Physica D*, 45:136-156, 1990.

[29] P. D. Hortensius, R. D. McLeod, W. Pries, D. M. Miller, and H. C. Card, "Cellular Automata based Pseudo-Random Number Generators for Built-in Self-Test," *IEEE Tans. on CAD*, 8(8): 842-859, August 1989.

[30] P. D. Hortensius, R. D. McLeod, and H. C. Card, "Cellular Automata Based Signature Analysis for Built-in Self-Test," *IEEE Trans. on Computers*, C-39(10): 1273-1283, October 1990.

[31] K. Imai, "Reversible Cellular Automata," *Information Epistemology and Computation (IEC) Laboratory*, Graduate School of Engineering, Hiroshima University, Japan.

[32] D. Kagaris and S. Tragoudas, "Von Neumann Hybrid Cellular Automata for Generating Deterministic Test Sequences," *ACM Trans. on Design Automation of Electronic Systems (TODAES)*, 6(3): 308-321, 2001.

[33] J. Kari, "Reversibility of 2D Cellular Automata is Undecidable," *Physica D*, 45:379-385, 1990.

[34] J. Kari, "Reversibility and Surjectivity Problems of Cellular Automata," *J. of Comp. and Sys. Science*, 48(1): 149-182, 1994.

[35] J. Kari, "Representation of Reversible Cellular Automata with Block Permutations," *Math. Sys. Theory*, 29: 47-61, 1996.

[36] J. Kari, "On the Structural Depth of Reversible Cellular Automata," *Fundamenta Informaticae*, 38(1-2): 93-107, 1999.

[37] O. Kirchkamp, *Spatial Evolution of Automata in the Prisoners' Dilemma*, Manuscript, Bonn University, 1994.

[38] P. Kurka, "Languages, Equicontinuity and Attractors in Cellular Automata," *Ergodic Theor., Dynamic System*, 17: 229-254,1997.

[39] O. Lafe, "Data Compression and Encryption using Cellular Automata Transforms," *IEEE International Joint Symposia on Intelligence and Systems (IJSIS)*, pp. 234-241, 1996.

[40] R. Landauer, "Irreversibility and Heat Generation in the Computational Process," *IBM J. of Research and Development,* 5, pp. 183-191, 1961.

[41] C. Langton, "Self-Reproduction in Cellular Automata," *Physica D,* 10:134-144, 1984.

[42] C. Langton, "Computation at the Edge of Chaos," *Physica D,* 42:12-37, 1990.

[43] W. Li, N. H. Packard, and C. G. Langton, "Transition Phenomena in Cellular Automata Rule Space," *Physica D,* 45: 77-94, 1990.

[44] M. Mahajan, *Studies in Language Classes Defined by Different Time-Varying Cellular Automata,* Ph.D. Thesis, I.I.T., Madras, 1992.

[45] O. Martin, A. M. Odlyzko, and S. Wolfram, "Algebraic Properties of Cellular Automata," *Comm. Math. Phys.,* 93: 219-258, 1984.

[46] M. Matsumoto, "Simple Cellular Automata as Pseudorandom *m*-Sequence Generators for Built-in Self-Test," *ACM Trans. on Modeling and Computer Simulation (TOMACS),* 8(1): 31-42, 1998.

[47] H. V. McIntosh, "Reversible Cellular Automata," *Departamento de Aplicación de Microcomputadoras, Instituto de Ciencias,* Universidad Autónoma de Puebla, México, 1991.

[48] S. Misra, *Theory and Application of Additive Cellular Automata for Easily Testable VLSI Circuit Design,*Ph.D. Thesis, I.I.T., Kharagpur, India, 1992.

[49] M. Mitchell, P. T. Hraber, and J. P. Crutchfield, "Revisiting the Edge of Chaos: Evolving Cellular Automata to Perform Computations," *Complex Systems,* 7: 89-130, 1993.

[50] E. Moore (editor), *Sequential Machine: Selected Papers,* Addison-Wesley Publishing Company Inc.,Redwood City, CA, 1964.

[51] J. H. Moore and L. W. Hahn, "A Cellular Automata-based Pattern Recognition Approach for Identifying Gene-Gene and Gene-Environment Interactions," *American Journal of Human Genetics,* 67(52), 2000.

[52] F. J. Morales, J.P. Crutchfield, and M. Mitchell, "Evolving Two-dimensional Cellular Automata to Perform Density Classification: A Report on Work in Progress," *Parallel Computing,* 27:571-585, 2001.

[53] J. Moreira and A. Deutsch, "Cellular Automaton Models of Tumor Development: A Critical Review," *Advances in Complex Systems,* 5(2&3): 247-269, 2002.

[54] K. Morita and S. Ueno, "Parallel Generation and Parsing of Array Languages using Reversible Cellular Automata," *International Journal of Pattern Recognition and Artificial Intelligence,* 8: 543-561, 1994.

[55] K. Morita, "Reversible Simulation of One-Dimensional Irreversible Cellular Automata," *Theoretical Computer Science,* 148: 157-163, 1995.

[56] G. Mrugalski, J. Rajski, and J. Tyszer, "Cellular Automata-based Test Pattern Generators with Phase Shifter," *IEEE Trans. on CAD,* 19(8): 878-893, August 2000.

[57] M. Mukherjee, N. Ganguly, and P. Pal Chaukhuri, "Cellular Automata Based Authentication," *Proc. 5th International Conference on Cellular Automata for Research and Industry (ACRI),* Switzerland, pp. 259-269, October 2002.

[58] J. C. Muzio *et. al.,* "Analysis of One-dimensional Linear Hybrid Cellular Automata over GF(q)," *IEEE Trans. on Computers,* 45(7): 782-792, July 1996.

[59] S. Nandi, *Additive Cellular Automata: Theory and Application for Testable Circuit Design and Data Encryption,* Ph.D. Thesis, I.I.T., Kharagpur, India, 1994.

[60] S. Nandi *et. al.*, "Analysis of Periodic and Intermediate Boundary 90/150 Cellular Automata," *IEEE Trans. on Computers*, 45(1): 1-12, January 1996.

[61] S. Nandi, B. K. Kar, and P. Pal Chaudhuri, "Theory and Application of Cellular Automata in Cryptography," *IEEE Trans. on Computers*, 43(12): 1346-1357, December 1994.

[62] J. V. Neumann, *The Theory of Self-Reproducing Automata*, A. W. Burks (ed.), Univ. of Illinois Press, Urbana and London, 1966.

[63] M. Nielsen and I. L. Chuang, *Quantum Computation and Quantum Information*, Cambridge University Press, 2000.

[64] H. Nishio, "Real Time Sorting of Binary Numbers by One-Dimensional Cellular Automata," *Technical Report*, Kyoto University, 1981.

[65] H. Nishio and Y. Kobuchi, "Fault Tolerant Cellular Space," *J. Comp. Sys. Science*, 11:150-170, 1975.

[66] S. Omohundro, "Modeling Cellular Automata with Partial Differential Equations," *Physica D*, 10: 128-134, 1984.

[67] C. Paar, P. Fleischmann, and P. Roelse, "Efficient Multiplier Architectures for Galois Fields GF(2^{4n})," *IEEE Trans. on Computers*, 47(2): 162-170, 1998.

[68] K. Paul and D. R. Chowdhury, "Application of GF(2^P) CA in Burst Error Correcting Codes," *Proc. VLSI*, INDIA, pp. 562-567, January 2000.

[69] K. Paul, D. R. Chowdhury, and P. Pal Chaudhuri, "Cellular Automata Based Transform Coding for Image Compression," *Proc. HiPC*, INDIA, pp. 269-273, December 1999.

[70] K. Paul, A. Roy, P. K. Nandi, B. N. Roy, M. D. Purkhayastha, S. Chattopadhyay, and P. Pal Chaudhuri, "Theory and Application of Multiple Attractor Cellular Automata for Fault Diagnosis," *Proc. Asian Test Symposium*, pp. 388-392, December 1998.

[71] Y. Pomeau, "Invariants in Cellular Automata," *J. Phys. A*, 17, 1986.

[72] K. Preston, M. J. Duff, S. Levialdi, Ph. E. Norgren, and J. I. Toriwaki, "Basics of Cellular Logic with Some Applications in Medical Image Processing," *Proc. IEEE*, 67: 826-856, 1979.

[73] R. Raghavan, "Cellular Automata in Pattern Recognition," *Information Science*, 70: 145-177, 1993.

[74] F. C. Richards, T. P. Meyer, and N. H. Packard, "Extracting Cellular Automata Rules directly from Experimental Data," *Physica D*, 45: 189-202, 1990.

[75] M. Roncken, K. Stevens, and P. Pal Chaudhuri, "CA-BIST for Asynchronous Circuits: A Case Study on RAPPID Asynchronous Instruction Length Decoder," *Proc. 6th International Symposium on Advanced Research in Asynchronous Circuits and Systems*, Eilat, Israel, pp. 62-72, 2000.

[76] K. Roy and S. Prasad, *Low-Power CMOS VLSI Circuit Design*, John Wiley & Sons Inc., 2000.

[77] S. Saha, P. Maji, N. Ganguly, B. K. Sikdar, and P. Pal Chaudhuri, "Evolution of Cellular Automata Based Pattern Classifier and Recognizer," *IEEE Conference on System, Man & Cybernetics*, pp. 114-119, 2002.

[78] R. M. Z. D. Santos and S. Coutinho, "Dynamics of HIV Infection: A Cellular Automata Approach," *Phys.Rev. Lett.*, 87(16), 168102, 2001.

[79] P. Sarkar, "A Brief History of Cellular Automata," *ACM Computing Systems*, 32(1):80-107, March 2000.

[80] P. Sarkar. and R. Barua, "Multi-dimensional σ- Automata, π- Polynomial and Generalized s-Matrices," *Theoretical Computer Science*, 197(1-2): 111-138, 1998.

[81] P. Sarkar. and R. Barua, "The Set of Reversible 90/150 Cellular Automata is Regular," *Discrete Applied Math.*, 84(1-3): 199-213,1998.

[82] T. Sasao, *Logic Synthesis and Optimization*, Kluwer Academic Publishers, 1993.

[83] B. Schonfisch and M. Kinder, "A Fish Migration Model," *Proc. 5th International Conference on Cellular Automata for Research and Industry (ACRI)*, Switzerland, pages 210-219, October 2002.

[84] B. Schonfisch and A. D. Ross, "Synchronous and Asynchronous Updating in Cellular Automata," *Biosystems*, 51: 123-143, 1999.

[85] S. Sen, C. Shaw, D. R. Chowdhuri, N. Ganguly, and P. Pal Chaudhuri, "Cellular Automata Based Cryptosystem," *Proc. ICICS*, Singapore, pp. 303-314, December 2002.

[86] M. Serra, T. Slater, J. C. Muzio, and D. M. Miller, "Analysis of One Dimensional Cellular Automata and their Aliasing Probabilities," *IEEE Trans. on CAD*, 9(7): 767-778, July 1990.

[87] M. Shereshevsky, "Lyapunov Exponent for One-dimensional Cellular Automata," *J. Nonlinear Science*, 2: 1-8, 1992.

[88] B. K. Sikdar, D. K. Das, V. Boppana, C. Yang, S. Mukherjee, and P. Pal Chaudhuri, "GF(2^p) Cellular Automata as a Built-In Self-Test Structure," *Proc. ASP-DAC*, Japan, pp. 319-324, 2001.

[89] B. K. Sikdar, N. Ganguly, and P. Pal Chudhuri, "Design of Hierarchical Cellular Automata for On-Chip Test Pattern Generator," *IEEE Trans. on CAD*, 21(12): 1530-1539, Dec. 2002.

[90] B. K. Sikdar, N. Ganguly, A. Karmakar, S. Chowdhury, and P. Pal Chaudhuri, "Multiple Attractor Cellular Automata for Hierarchical DIAGNOSIS of VLSI Circuits," *Proc. Asian Test Symposium*, pp. 385-390, November 2001.

[91] B. K. Sikdar, N. Ganguly, P. Majumder, and P. P. Chaudhuri, "Design of Multiple Attractor GF(2^p) Cellular Automata for Diagnosis of VLSI Circuits," *Proc. Int. Conf. on VLSI Design*, India, pp. 454-459, January 2001.

[92] M. Sipper, "Co-evolving Non-Uniform Cellular Automata to Perform Computations," *Physica D*, 92: 193- 208, 1996.

[93] A. Smith, *Introduction to and Survey of Polyautomata Theory. Automata, Languages, Development*, North Holland Publishing Co., 1976.

[94] S. Smith, R. Watt, and R. Hameroff, "Cellular Automata in Cytoskeletal Lattices," *Physica D*, 10: 168-174, 1984.

[95] A. R. Smith(III), "Real-time Language Recognition by One-Dimensional Cellular Automata," *J. Computer Sys. Science*, 6: 233-253, 1972.

[96] S. Tezuka, "A Method of Designing Cellular Automata as Pseudorandom Number Generators for Built-In Self-Test for VLSI," *Finite Fields: Theory, Applications and Algorithms*, pp. 363-367, 1994.

[97] T. Toffoli, "CAM: A High-Performance Cellular Automata Machine," *Physica D*, 10: 195-204, 1984.

[98] T. Toffoli, "Cellular Automata as an Alternative to (rather than an approximation of) Differential Equations in Modeling Physics," *Physica D*, 10: 117-127, 1984.

[99] T. Toffoli and N. Margolus, *Cellular Automata Macjomes: A New Environment for Modeling*, MIT Press, Cambridge, Mass, 1987.

[100] T. Toffoli and N. Margolus, *Invertible Cellular Automata: A New Environment for Modeling*, MIT Press, Cambridge, Mass., 1987.

[101] T. Toffoli and N. Margolus, "Irreversible Cellular Automata: A Review", *Physica D*, 45: 229-253, 1993.

[102] M. Tomassini, M. Sipper, and M. Perrenoud, "On the Generation of High-Quality Random Numbers by Two-dimensional Cellular Automata," *IEEE Trans. on Computers*, 49(10):1146-1151, 2000.

[103] Ph. Tsalides, T. A. York, and A. Thanailakis, "Pseudo-Random Number Generators for VLSI Systems Based on Linear Cellular Automata," *IEE Proc. E. Comp. Digit. Tech.*, 138(4): 241-249, 1991.

[104] P. Tzionas, P. Tsalides, and A. Thanailakis, "A New Cellular Automaton-Based Nearest Neighbor Pattern Classifier and its VLSI Implementation," *IEEE Trans. on VLSI Implementation*, 2(3): 343-353, 1994.

[105] P. Tzionas, Ph. Tsalides, and A. Thanailakis, "A Cellular Neural Network Predicting the Behavior of a Complex System Modeled as a Cellular Automaton," *Proc. 15th Annual International Symposium on Forecasting (ISF)*, Toronto, Canada, June 4-7 1995.

[106] G. Vchniac, "Simulating Physics with Cellular Automata," *Physica D*, 10: 96-115, 1984.

[107] A. Winfree, E. Winfree, and H. Seifert, "Organizing Centers in Cellular Excitable Meduim," *Physica D*, 17: 109-115, 1985.

[108] S. Wolfram, "Statistical Mechanics of Cellular Automata," *Rev. Mod. Phys.*, 55(3): 601-644, July 1983.

[109] S. Wolfram, "Universality and Complexity in Cellular Automata," *Physica D*, 10: 1-35, 1984.

[110] S. Wolfram, "Undecidability and Intractability in Theoretical Physics," *Phys. Rev. Lett.*, 54: 735-738, 1985.

[111] S. Wolfram, *Theory and Applications of Cellular Automata*, World Scientific, Singapore, 1986.

[112] S. Wolfram, *Cellular Automata and Complexity*, 2002.

[113] S. Wolfram, *A New Kind of Science*, Wolfram Media, 2002.

[114] F. Wu, "A Linguistic Cellular Automata Simulation Approach for Sustainable Land Development in a Fast Growing Region," *Computers, Environment and Urban Systems*, 20(6): 367-387, Nov. 1996.

[115] A. Wuensche and M. Lesser, *The Global Dynamics of Cellular Automata*, Volume 1, Addison-Wesley, 1992.

[116] A. Wuensche, "Classifying Cellular Automata Automatically," *Complexity*, 4(3): 47-66, 1999.

[117] M. Zwick and H. Shu, "Set-Theoretic Reconstructability of Elementary Cellular Automata," *Advances in Systems Science and Applications*, 1, pp. 31-36, 1995

5

Quadra-Quantum Dots and Related Patterns of Quantum Dot Molecules: Basic Nanostructures for Quantum Dot Cellular Automata Application

Somsak Panyakeow
Semiconductor Device Research Laboratory (SDRL),
CoE Nanotechnology Center of Thailand,
Department of Electrical Engineering, Faculty of Engineering
Chulalongkorn University, Bangkok 10330,
Thailand

1. Introduction

The concept of quantum dot cellular automata (QCA) was proposed by C. S. Lent et al., in 1993 based on current switch with a cell having a bi-stable charge configuration representing either "1" or "0" in a binary system. This function is operated without current flow into or out of the cell. The basic mechanism is "Coulomb repulsion force" among

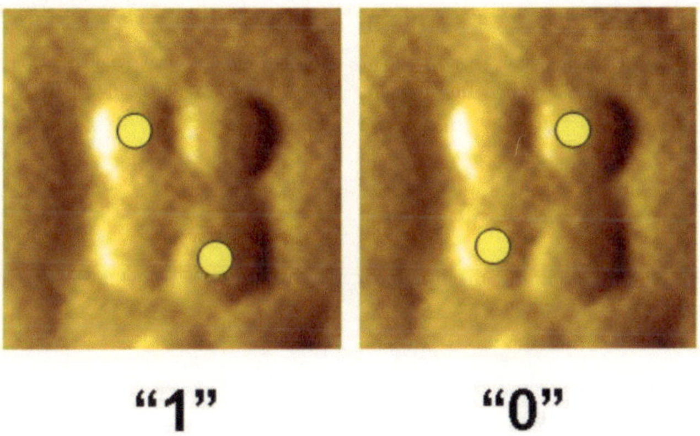

Fig. 1. Basic QAC cells represent digital data "1" and "0"

distributed charges in the individual QCA cells. Each charge configuration provides the field from one QCA cell to adjacent cells. The transfer of charge configuration, therefore, consumes very small power and occurs at a very high speed. QCA approach would break the limitation in shrinking of CMOS technology, which is normally based on "top-down technology". Quantum dots (QDs) in QCA cells are created by self assembly approach, which is "bottom-up technology". Each quantum dot in a QCA cell localizes charge because of its zero dimensional nanostructure. However, the barrier between dots has to be narrow enough so that a charge can quantum mechanically tunnels from one dot to another.

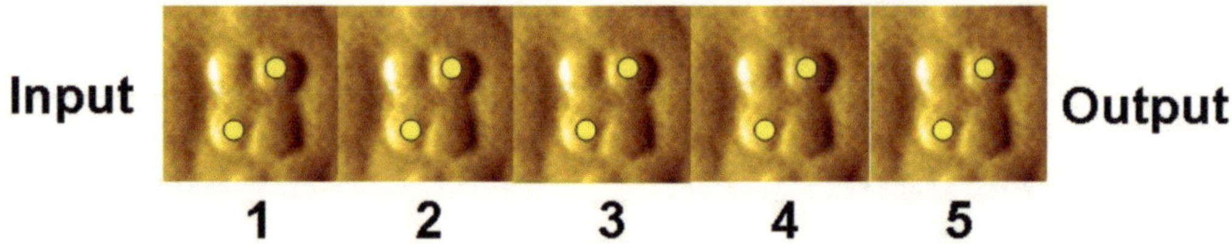

Fig. 2. Schematic display of QCA wire transferring data at high speed and low power consumption

Quantum dots are technically created from several semiconductor materials having lattice mismatch like InAs/GaAs (7% lattice mismatching). When InAs is grown on GaAs at monolayer (ML) scale by molecular beam epitaxy (MBE), strain is created at the interface. At a critical thickness of InAs called wetting layer, strain relaxation occurs and leads to quantum dot formation (J. Timler et al., 2003). The semiconductor quantum dots grown by self-assembly are defect free and provide good electrical and optical properties. They are potential nanostructures for several electronic and photonic device applications. Self-assembly of QDs is natural process. Therefore, the QD creation sites are random. QD size is not uniform. However, when the MBE growth parameters are precisely controlled, QD uniformity is improved and is applicable for many devices. The dot sizes and dot separations are normally in the order of tens of nanometers.

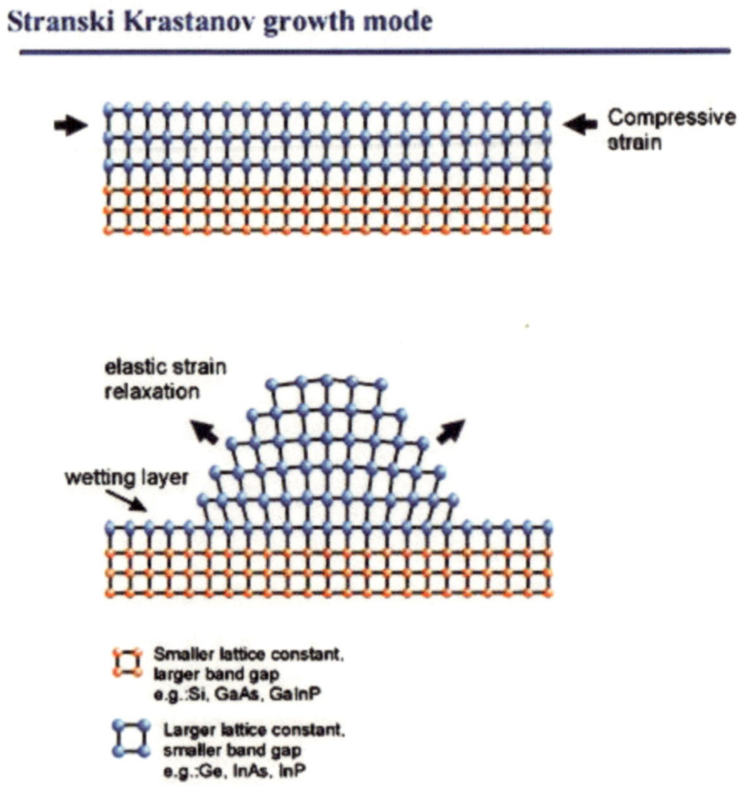

Fig. 3. Quantum dots grown by strained semiconductors

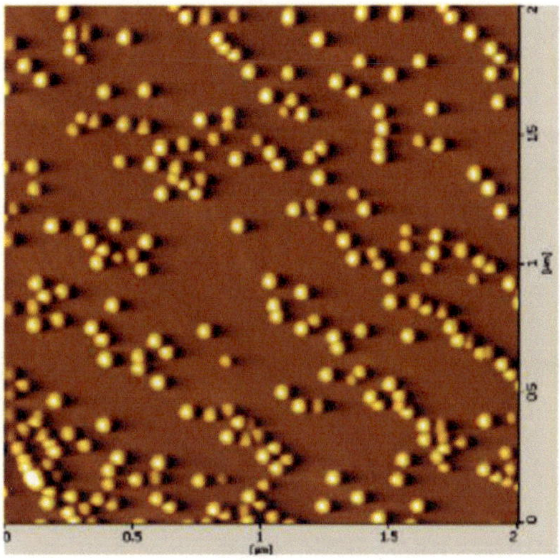

Fig. 4. Self-assembled quantum dots are naturally random.

The design feature of QCA cell is quadra-quantum dots (QQDs), which are composed of two stable orientations. Electrons in these two orientations are used to represent the two binary digits "1" and "0". The four dots in a QCA cell are at the corners of a square having two mobile charges. These two mobile charges or electrons can quantum mechanically tunnel between dots but not between cells.

QCA concept is performed on different patterns of QCA cells. Linear array of QCA cells works as binary wire where Coulomb interaction induces all QCA cells in the wire into the same polarization. Therefore, QCA data can be transferred from one end of the wire to the other. Corner interaction of QCA cells having anti-voting can perform as an inverter, where polarization changes from one diagonal direction to another or alters QCA data from "1" to "0" or from "0" to "1". Logic gates having three inputs and one output are realized by using a cross-over of QCA cells. They can work like a majority gate. Combinations of different QCA patterns are used in the design of QCA memory bits (Y. Lu et al., 2007). QCA is a promising tool for future computation using semiconductor quantum nanostructures.

Fig. 5. Schematic display of QCA inverter changing data from "1" to "0" or from "0" to "1"

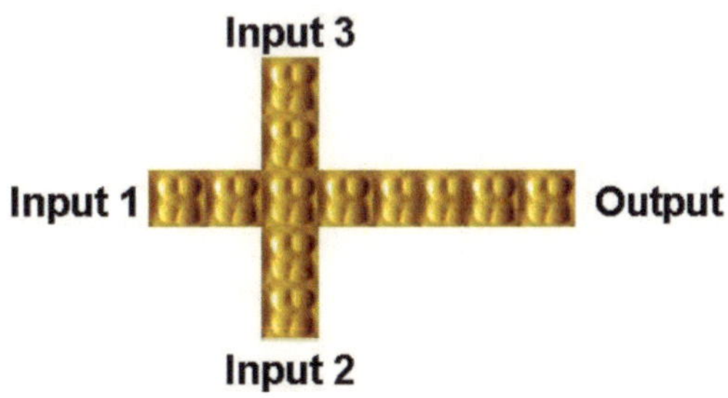

Fig. 6. Schematic display of a QCA logic working as a majority gate

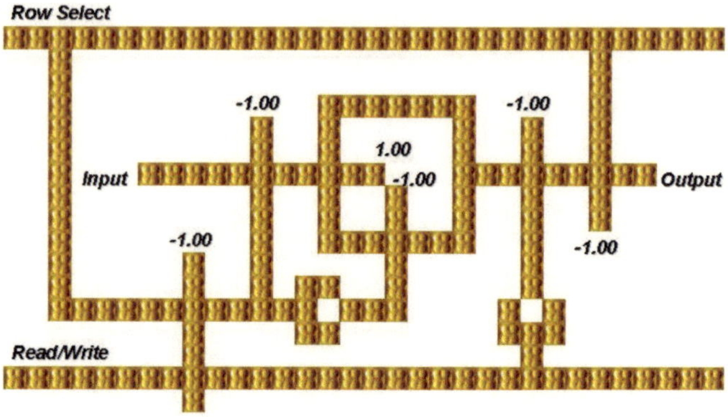

Fig. 7. Schematic design of a QCA circuit having one bit memory

2. Semiconductor quantum nanostructures

2.1 Quantum dot molecules

Self-assembled quantum dots are widely studied due to their unique properties such as zero dimensionality and the resultant delta-function energy states (O. Suekano et al., 2002, L.G. Wang et al., 2000, K. Jacobi et al., 2003). These properties lead to an improved device performance, such as quantum dot lasers with an ultra-low threshold current density (M. Asada et al., 1986, Y. Arakawa et al., 1982) and single electron devices with a high speed response and a low power consumption (Y. Ono et al., 2005). Self-assembly of quantum dots using various semiconductor systems including strained InAs/GaAs, always results in random dot formation with a variation of dot size (D. Leonard et al., 1993, T. v. Lippen et al., 2005). In many applications, it is desirable to have uniform quantum dots, and, thus, there is a need to develop some growth techniques which can provide some degree of dot alignment and uniformity. In order to obtain aligned dots, many approaches have been proposed and demonstrated (Z. M. Wang et al., 2004, T. Mano et al., 2004, Z. M. Wang et al., 2004), but those based on self-assembly are preferred over other techniques due mainly to the simplicity of the processes involved.

It has been demonstrated that thin capping of quantum dots provides anisotropic strain fields which lead to the elongation of capped nanostructures after annealing (S. Suraprapapich et al., 2005). The regrowth of quantum dots on elongated nanostructures results in aligned quantum dots and aligned quantum dot molecules (QDMs).

Lateral quantum dot molecules are closely packed quantum dots in the growth plane. Quantum dot molecules have several unique features, i.e., uniform dot sets with specific patterns, high dot density, and anisotropic nanostructure (T. v. Lippen et al., 2004, T. v. Lippen et al., 2005, W. Sheng et al., 2002). Therefore, they are potential candidates for nanoelectronic applications, such as that in quantum dot cellular automata because of their potential in obtaining four quantum dots arranged in a rectangular pattern (C. S. Lent et al., 1993). Lateral quantum dot molecules can be realized by several growth techniques (R. Songmuang et al., 2003, T. Mano et al., 2004). The thin-capping-and-regrowth molecular beam epitaxial process, which can be used to obtain quantum dot molecules in one continuous growth, has been demonstrated (S. Suraprapapich et al., 2005). Multiple cycles of the thin-capping-and-regrowth process of the quantum dots give improved dot alignment

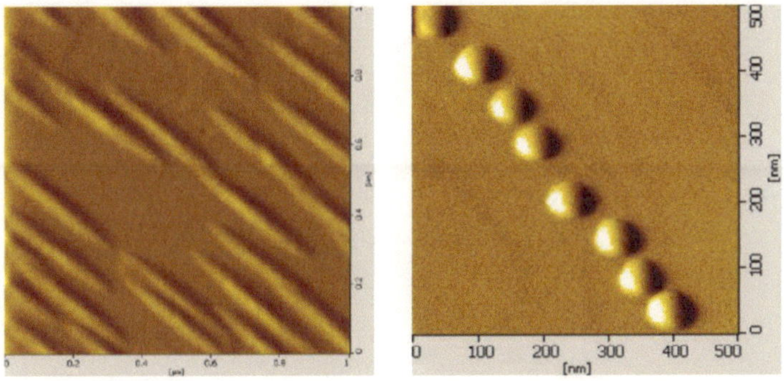

Fig. 8. Aligned quantum dots grown on elongated nanostructures after thin capping of as-grown quantum dots

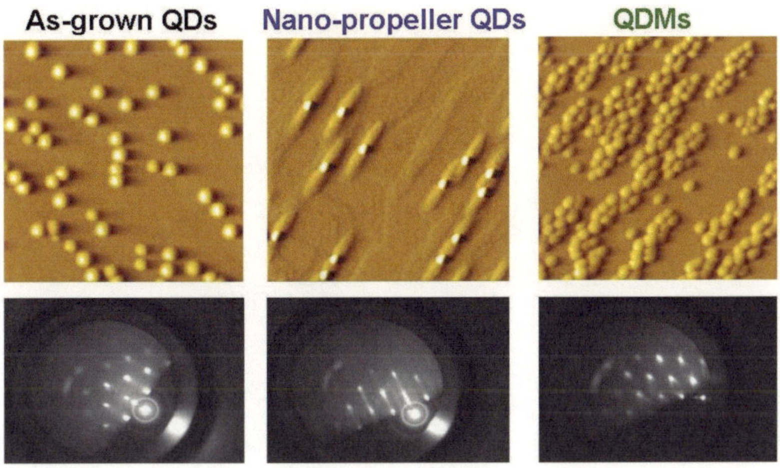

Fig. 9. As-grown QDs are transformed to nano-propellers and QDMs respectively after thin-capping-and-regrowth process as confirmed by RHEED patterns

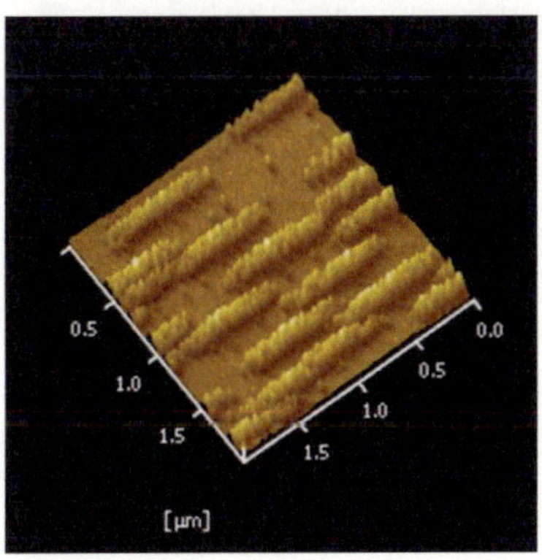

Fig. 10. Laterally close packed quantum dot molecules grown by thin-capping-and-regrowth MBE process

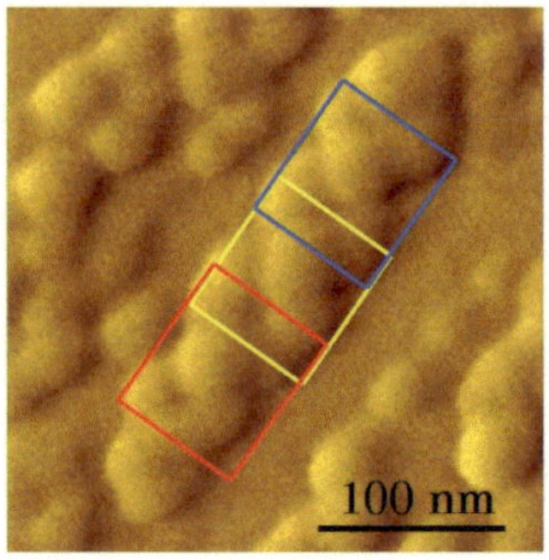

Fig. 11. Chain of overlapping quantum dot molecules grown by multiple thin-capping-and regrowth process

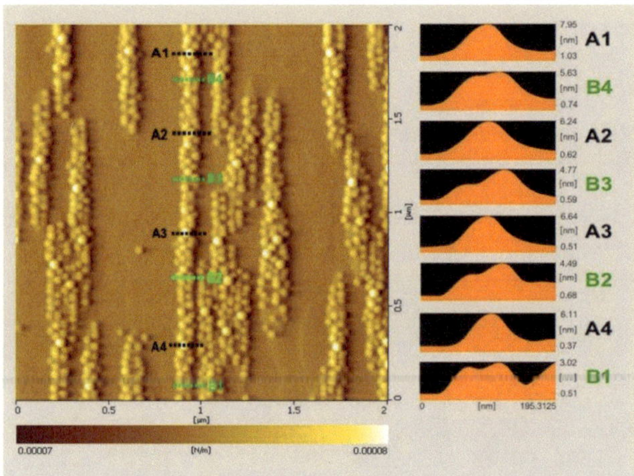

Fig. 12. Long chain of QDMs

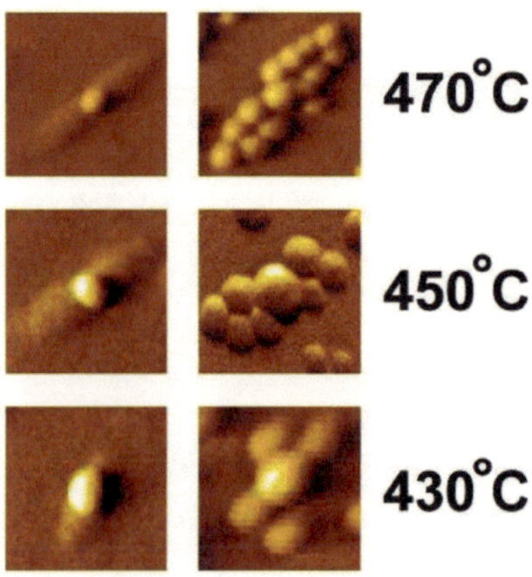

Fig. 13. Dot number per quantum dot molecule is controlled by different capping temperatures of as-grown quantum dots

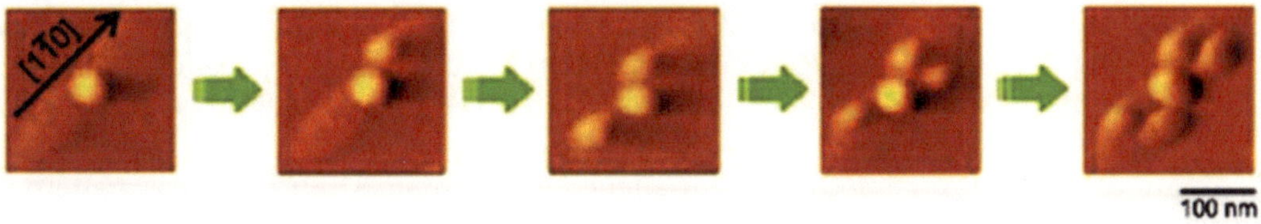

Fig. 14. Formation of 4 satellite dots on nano-propeller template along $[1\bar{1}0]$ crystallographic direction

up to a certain number of growth cycles. In addition, with aligned quantum dots as templates, aligned quantum dot molecules can be obtained by this growth technique.
The dot number in quantum dot molecules grown by thin-capping-and-regrowth MBE process can be controlled by varying the capping temperature and the capping thickness (N. Siripitakchai et al., 2007). Quantum dot molecules with a small number of quantum dots per quantum dot molecule ensemble can be grown and used as a basic building block for quantum computation in accordance with the quantum dot cellular automata principle (M. Macucci et al., 2006). A quantum dot molecule with four to five dots per molecule can be grown with GaAs capping thickness and InAs regrowth thickness of 25 ML and 1.5 ML respectively (N. Siripitakchai et al., 2008). However, nonlinear strain distribution originated from underlying templates results in the center dot and satellite dots of each molecule having different dot size. By increasing the regrowth temperature, an optimized condition is found to reduce the size difference between the satellite dots and the center dot. By repeating the quantum dot molecule growth cycles several times, certain degree of dot alignment is obtained. An alignment of quantum dots is used as a template in creating aligned quantum dot molecules at the topmost surface albeit with increased size difference between the center dot and the satellite dots.

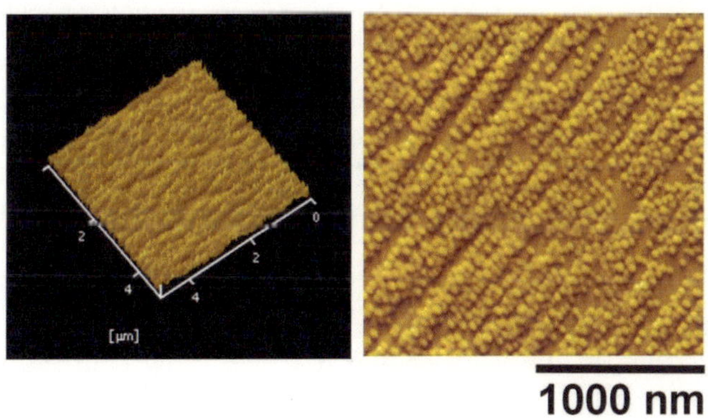

Fig. 15. High density quantum dot molecules is preferable for quantum dot solar cell application

2.2 Quantum dot alignment and cross-hatch

The statistical nature of quantum dot formation by conventional Stranski-Krastranow mode results in random dot position. In some applications, such as in quantum dot solar cells, the random dot positions and uniformity are not of major concerns, as long as dot density is high (S. Suraprapapich et al., 2006). Yet in certain applications, such as super luminescent light emitting diodes, quantum dots are preferred to be large and non-uniform for efficient light emission (C. Y. Ngo et al., 2007). But in quantum dot based quantum cellular automata (C. S. Lent et al., 1997) and bit-patterned media (B. D. Terris et al., 2005), the positions of active elements or quantum dots must be deterministic.

In order to develop a growth technique for aligned quantum dots and cross-over pattern of aligned quantum dots, which are useful in the design of various functions of quantum dot cellular automata, self-assembled InAs quantum dots are grown on cross-hatch GaAs/InGaAs templates via molecular beam epitaxy with controlled parameters such as degree of excess growth, growth rate and capping of the quantum dot layer (S. Kanjanachuchai et al., 2009). The InAs quantum dots are grown on an InGaAs cross-hatch layer without any excess growth, the dot alignments are formed both along the [110] and $[1\bar{1}0]$ directions as a result of chemical potential gradient and anisotropic strain fields. When the underlying InGaAs cross-hatch layer is covered by a thick GaAs spacer layer, subsequent growth of InAs quantum dots results in preferential alignment of quantum dots along either the [110] or $[1\bar{1}0]$ direction, respectively.

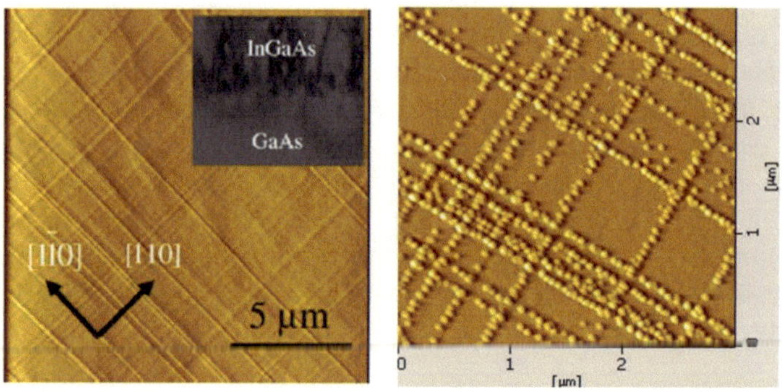

Fig. 16. Cross hatched substrate leads to quantum dot alignment and cross hatch

The MBE growth technique using cross-hatch substrates is a method for the self-assembly of dot alignment either in [110] or $[1\bar{1}0]$ direction and the cross-over of quantum dot lines in perpendicular configuration, i.e., in the [110] and $[1\bar{1}0]$ directions. This bottom-up approach is useful for the design of different QCA building blocks for various QCA applications.

2.3 Quantum Rings and Bi-Quantum dot molecules

Quantum dot molecules, in the form of a pair of vertically coupled quantum dots, are proposed and demonstrated to be a quantum gate controlling qubits in quantum computation (M. Bayer et al., 2001). In vertically coupled quantum dots, the upper self-assembled quantum dots are formed on top of the lower self-assembled quantum dots due to the strain field around the lower quantum dots. The vertical separation between the upper and the lower quantum dots controls the degree of coupling. In principle, however, laterally coupled quantum dots are preferred because they allow a large number of quantum gates in a two dimensional array on the surface (G. J. Beirne et al., 2006). Such lateral quantum dot molecules are more applicable-wise. Lateral quantum dot molecules have been achieved by several growth techniques, such as a combination of in situ etching and self-assembly (S. Kiravittaya et al., 2003), self-assembly by anisotropic strain engineering on an InGaAs/GaAs (311 B) super-lattice templates and droplet epitaxy (J. H. Lee et al., 2006).

An uninterrupted molecular beam epitaxy process comprising partial capping and regrowth to obtain lateral quantum dot molecules within a single growth run has been developed. The key processing step is the partial capping of InAs quantum dots by thin GaAs layer. The surface morphology after the capping process is affected by several parameters such as as-grown quantum dot size and capping temperature. The same growth process is used in both solid source and gas source molecular beam epitaxies. Dramatically different lateral quantum dot molecules are obtained. As-grown quantum dots are transformed to camel-like nanostructures when As4 overpressure from a conventional Arsenic solid source is used in the molecular beam epitaxy machine. But when As2 overpressure from a gas source is used, quantum rings (QRs) are formed. The Arsenic species is a crucial parameter to in forming different shapes of nanostructures (S. Suraprapapich et al., 2007).

Under As2 overpressure, the migration length of Indium adatoms is shorter than under As4. Therefore, the shape of transformed nanostructures is less anisotropic, resulting in InGaAs quantum ring formation after the partial capping of as-grown InAs quantum dots. The surface migration of Indium adatoms, however, is still anisotropic, leading to higher Indium concentrations on the two regions of the InGaAs quantum ring in the $[1\bar{1}0]$ direction. At these particular parts of InGaAs quantum ring, strain becomes higher. When the amount of deposited InAs is increased during the regrowth process over InGaAs quantum ring template, the strain at these two regions relaxes, leading to the formation of InAs quantum dots which become a bi-quantum dot molecule (Bi-QDM). Bi-quantum dot molecules are formed on strained InGaAs quantum ring nanostructures; therefore, the amount of InAs required in bi-quantum dot molecules is less than that required on the flat GaAs surface. The formation of bi-quantum dot molecules starts at an InAs thickness of 0.6 ML compared to 1.8 ML InAs quantum dots conventionally grown on flat GaAs buffer layer. Hence, the individual dots making up the bi-quantum dot molecule are smaller than those of as-grown quantum dots.

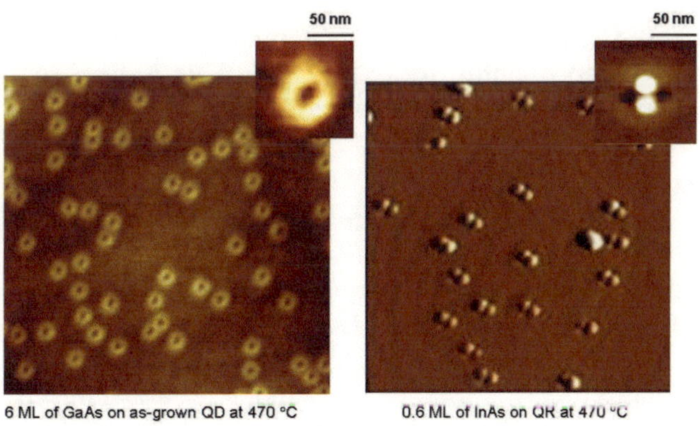

Fig. 17. Quantum rings and bi-quantum dot molecules grown by As_2 gas source MBE

Bi-quantum dot molecules are useful basic nanostructures for spintronic applications. The electron spins in coupled quantum dots of a bi-quantum dot molecule can work as a spin qubit, spin-up and spin-down. The semiconductor material of bi-quantum dot molecules needs to be magnetic semiconductor like GaMnAs (K. S. Ryu et al., 2008, U. Wurstbauer et al., 2008, M. Bozkurt et al., 2010) for practical use in spintronics.

Fig 18. Bi-quantum dot molecule grown on quantum ring

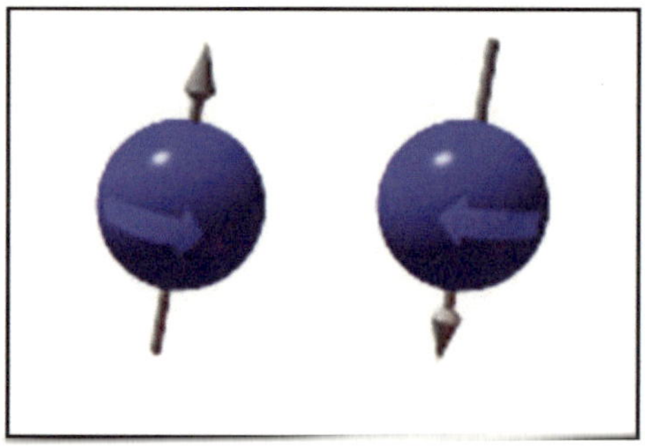

Fig. 19. Electron spins in bi-quantum dots work as a qubit

When InGaAs quantum rings are created after the partial capping of as-grown InAs quantum dots by As2 overpressure in gas source MBE, InAs bi-quantum dot molecules are achieved by the regrowth process at a low temperature of 470°C. But when the substrate temperature is increased to as high as 520°C, the number of quantum dots on a quantum ring becomes five to seven quantum dots per ring. This is how to form another InAs quantum nanostructure called quantum dot rings (QDRs).

Quantum dot rings

Quantum dot rings are created on the quantum ring templates with less anisotropy. InAs quantum rings always have unsymmetrical shapes due to high migration of Indium adatoms in Arsenic environment. When the quantum dot material is changed from Indium Arsenide (InAs) to Indium Phosphide (InP), Indium adatoms in Phosphorous environment change and become less migrating. This leads to InP ring shaped quantum dot molecules.

Instead of using Stranski-Krastranow growth mode, self-assembled InP ring shaped quantum dot molecules can be fabricated by solid source molecular beam epitaxy using the droplet epitaxy technique. This droplet epitaxy involves two processes, i.e., the deposition process of group III elemental droplets without the presence of group V element and the crystallization or incorporation process of group V element into droplets to form the III-V nanostructures (T. Mano et al., 2005, T. Mano et al., 2005). InP is chosen as a material for

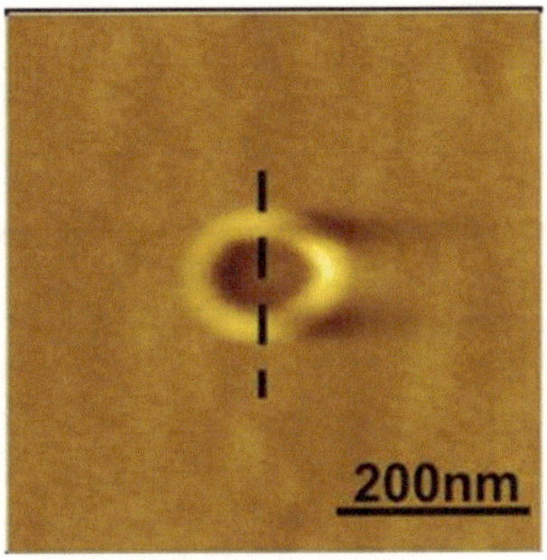

Fig. 20. InGaAs quantum ring grown by droplet epitaxy

quantum dot structure because of its lattice mismatch with In0.49Ga0.51P layer. In addition, droplet epitaxy technique can provide the circular ring shaped structure due to isotropic migration property of Indium adatoms under P2 pressure on the In0.49Ga0.51P layer during crystallization process (W. Jevasuwan et al., 2007). Therefore, the droplet epitaxy technique is favorable for the growth of ring shaped quantum dot molecule structure. In droplet epitaxy growth, the initial dimension of the Indium droplets, the Phosphorous atom migration and diffusion process determine the size and shape of the Indium Phosphide nanostructure. It is found that the crystallization temperature can affect the quantum dot size and density on the ring as well as the ring size and density (W. Jevasuwan et al., 2010). At a high crystallization temperature, the quantum dots on the ring and the ring itself become bigger; meanwhile the dot density as well as ring density is decreased. The explanation for this is that, with high crystallization temperature, initial Indium droplets can efficiently incorporate with each other and Indium adatoms can migrate farther from the center of droplets to minimize the energy of the system; thus, bigger InP quantum dots and bigger InP ring shaped quantum dots molecules are obtained.

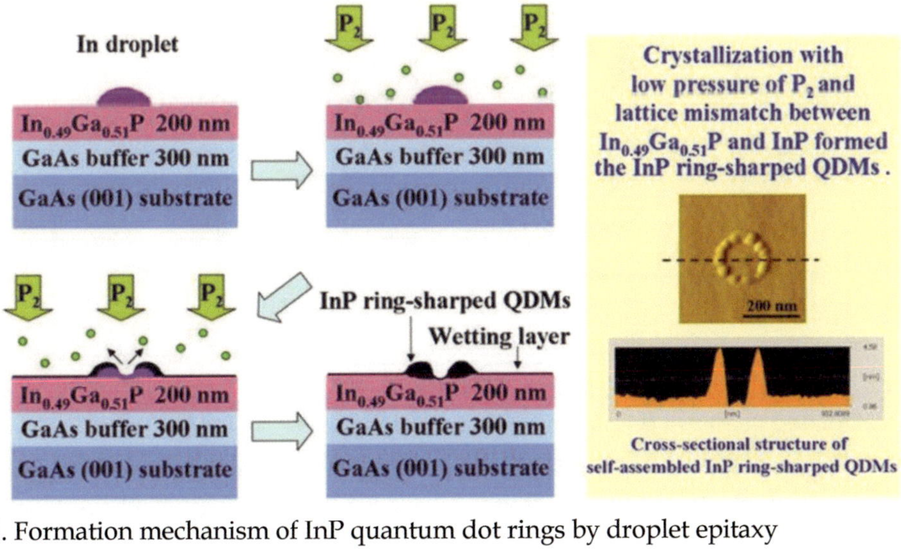

Fig. 21. Formation mechanism of InP quantum dot rings by droplet epitaxy

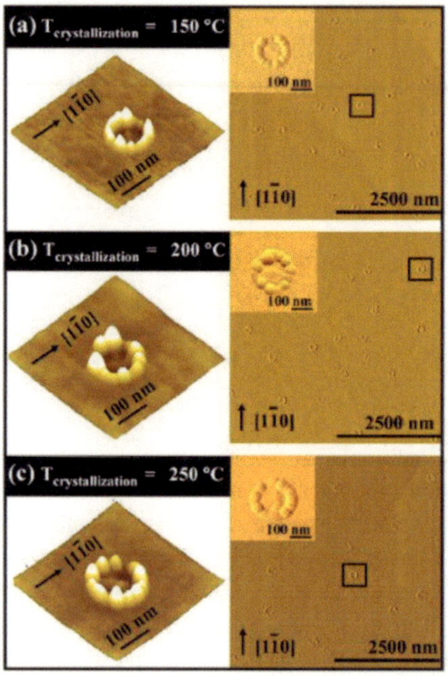

Fig. 22. InP quantum dot rings grown at different crystallization temperatures

This ring shaped quantum dot molecules called quantum dot rings (QDRs) have an interesting feature when the number of quantum dots on each ring is controlled. Quantum dot rings with eight dots are useful in extended quantum dot cellular automata (I. L. Bajec et al., 2006) where three encode values of "1", "0" and "1/2" are possible. By adding

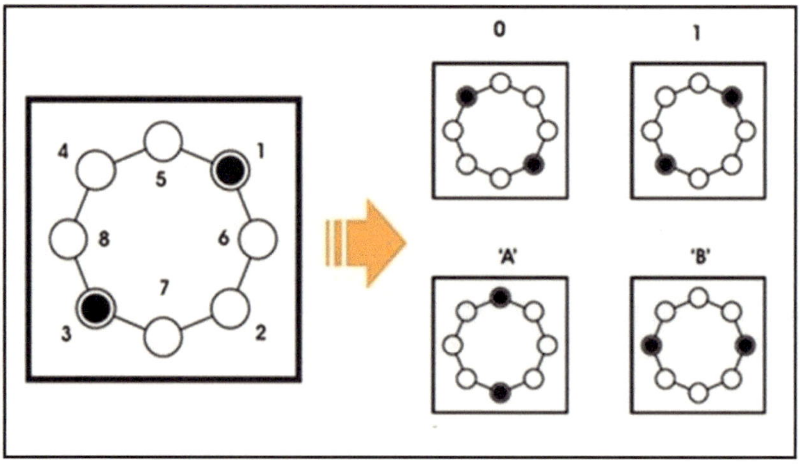

Fig. 23. Octa quantum dot molecule with ring-shape gives 3 logic values of "1", "0" and "1/2" in extended quantum cellular automata

four more quantum dots to classical four quantum dot sets, quantum dot cellular automata can be extended to enlarged range of states. This leads to wider aspects of future quantum computation based on quantum dot nanostructures.

3. Quadra quantum dots

Quantum rings can be created by droplet epitaxy both in InAs and InP material systems. Nanoholes at the center of the quantum rings are used as templates for several patterns of quantum dot molecules. Several approaches using artificial substrate process methods, such as atomic force microscope (AFM) tip and scanning tunneling probe-assisted nanolithography have been developed to obtain nanohole templates for growing quantum dot molecules (J. S. Kim et al., 2006, S. Kohmoto et al., 1999, E. S. Moskalenko et al., 2005). These methods, however, require complicated and expensive substrate processing equipment and are also prone to defects and contamination. A combination of two different techniques is developed to create quantum dot molecules from quantum ring templates. The first technique is droplet epitaxy, which is used to grow InGaAs quantum ring structures having non-uniform ring stripes and deep square shaped nanoholes. The second is conventional Stranski-Krastanow growth mode, which creates four InAs quantum dots on the InGaAs nanoholes. Combining these two techniques has helped overcoming a few of limitations of individual technique, thus leading to a novel fabrication of four quantum dots in one quantum dot molecule.

When Indium-Gallium (In-Ga) droplets are used in the droplet epitaxy and become crystallized by arsenic pressure, quantum rings with square shaped nanoholes can be achieved at a specific growth condition (P. Boonpeng et al., 2010). The square shape of nanoholes is oriented along both the $[110]$ and $[1\bar{1}0]$ crystallographic directions. Most of the square-like nanoholes exhibit a V-shape profile along $[110]$ and a U-shape profile along $[1\bar{1}0]$. The difference in shape profiles is due to anisotropic behavior of the atomic diffusion from the center of the In-Ga droplet under As_4 flux during crystallization of the ring structure. The substrate temperature (330-390°C) during droplet deposition process is a key parameter for controlling the size of nanoholes. At a high substrate temperature of 390°C, larger In-Ga droplets are deposited and transformed to bigger quantum rings with larger nanoholes. Consequently, anisotropic behavior is pronounced leading to a difference in the height of ring lobes between those along $[110]$ and $[1\bar{1}0]$. The bigger nanoholes at 390°C give higher ring lobes along $[1\bar{1}0]$, nearly double compared with the shorter ring lobes along $[110]$. It is also clear that nanohole density is reduced at a higher temperature during droplet deposition in which small droplets are merged into large droplets having a small number of transformed nanostructures per unit area. Despite the larger nanoholes at high substrate temperature, the hole-depth is slightly shallower at 4nm. It is found that nanoholes prepared at 360°C are the most uniform with smallest deviation in their dimension. The formation mechanism of square-like nanoholes is based on the As4 diffusion in InGa droplets during the supply of As4 flux (P. Boonpeng et al., 2009).

Square-like nanoholes have a high strain at each corner of the nanostructure. Therefore, when quantum dots are grown on this square-like nanohole template, four quantum dots called quadra quantum dots (QQDs) are created. In the fabrication process of quadra quantum dots, the substrate temperature is increased to 450°C. InGaAs square-like nanoholes are transformed to the InGaAs nano-mounds. Then, InAs quadra quantum dots are grown on InGaAs nano-mound at the substrate temperature of 450°C. It is noticeable that quadra quantum dots in each group are not uniform in dot size depending on crystallographic directions in which respective lobes around nanohole templates prior to quantum dot growth are not the same in volume and shape.

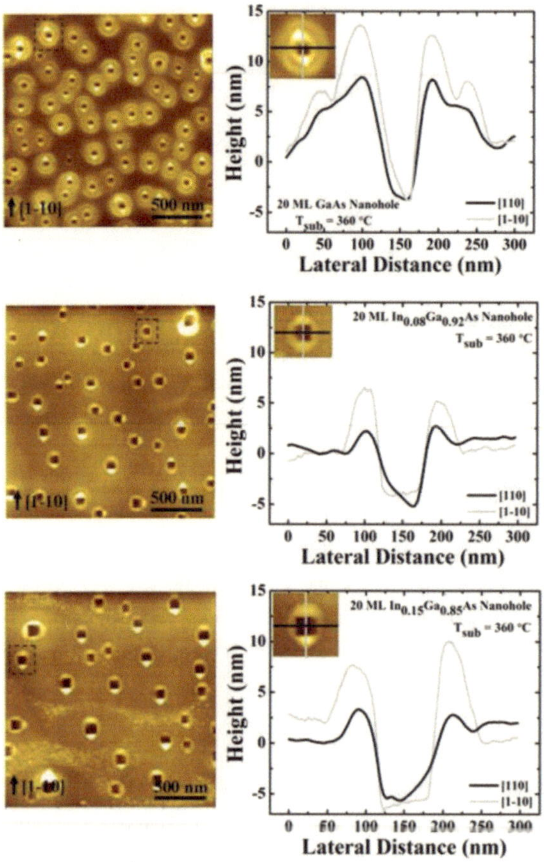

(a) Double quantum rings grown by using GaAs droplet epitaxy

(b) In0.08 Ga0.92As quantum rings with square-shaped nanoholes

(c) In$_{0.15}$Ga$_{0.85}$As quantum rings with deep square-shaped nanoholes

Fig. 24.

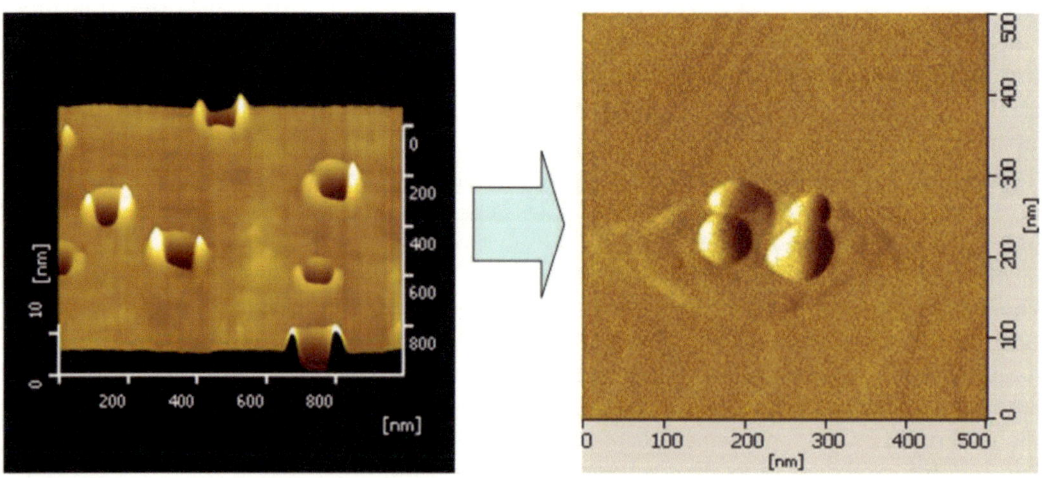

Fig. 25. Square-shaped nanoholes are used as templates for the formation of quadra quantum dots

These square shape quadra quantum dots can be used as a basic cell of quantum dot cellular automata in which two electrons are localized at two quantum dots along either diagonal direction representing either "1" or "0" in a qubit system. However, application-wise, uniform quadra quantum dots are required. Therefore, the square-like nanohole templates of which the holes exhibit the U-shape profile along both directions will be key nanostructures providing uniform quantum dot molecules. In addition, uniform square-like nanoholes with good alignment and cross-hatched are also required for practical design of QCA cells. Overlapping of nano-mounds along the [1$\bar{1}$0] crystallographic direction is a demonstration of aligned quadra quantum dots by self-assembly approach. In engineering point of view, though, the self-assembly of nanostructures is a simple approach and needs few sophisticated fabrication instruments. The precise control of quantum dot molecules at designated sites is very important and makes quantum computation workable. Therefore, the final approach would be the combination of "bottom-up" and "top-down" at optimal requirement.

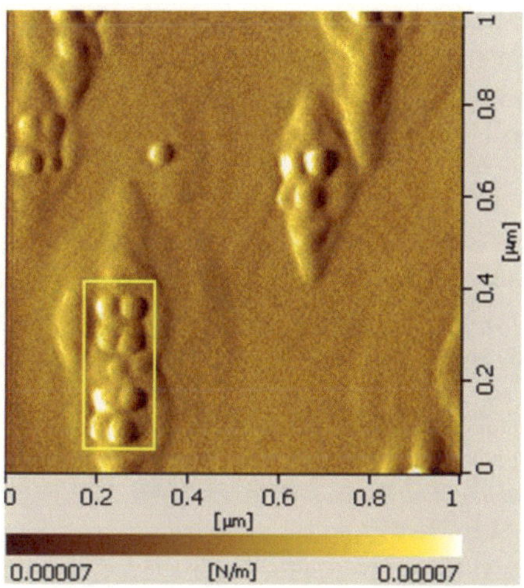

Fig. 26. Two sets of quadra quantum dots are aligned along [1$\bar{1}$0] by oriented templates

4. Summary

Self-assembly of InAs quantum dot molecules with different features fabricated by the combination of conventional Stranski-Krastanow growth mode and modified MBE technique using thin or partial capping as well as droplet epitaxy has been reviewed. Quantum dot alignment and cross-hatch are demonstrated by using modified InGaAs/GaAs substrates. Partial capping of as-grown quantum dots leads to an elongation of the nanostructure having nanoholes at the original sites of the dots. Under some specific conditions, i.e. dot materials, growth parameters, these techniques can provide quantum ring nano-templates for InAs bi-quantum dot molecules and InP quantum dot rings. InGaAs quantum rings with square shaped nanoholes are realized by droplet epitaxy. They are utilized as nano-templates for quadra quantum dot molecules where four InAs quantum dots are situated at the four corners of a square. This quadra quantum dot set is a basic QCA cell for future quantum computation. For practical use, precise control of quantum dot molecules both in their dot uniformity and dot sites needs further research and development.

5. Acknowledgement

This review article was prepared for a chapter of the book "Cellular Automata" to be published. The article was kindly proved by Prof. Dr. Mongkol Dejnakarin at the stage of manuscript preparation.

This review article is a result of my continuous research activity at Chulalongkorn University. I am indebted to many of my colleagues at the Semiconductor Device Research Laboratory (SDRL): Dr. Montri Sawadsaringkarn, Dr. Banyong Toprasertpong, Dr. Choompol Antarasen, Dr. Somchai Rattanathammaphan, Dr. Songphol Kanjanachuchai, Dr. Chanin Wissawinthanon; my technical research assistants: Mr. Supachok Thainoi, Mr. Pornchai Changmoang; and all my graduate students as well as my supporting staffs: Mrs. Kwanruan Thainoi, Mr. Pattana Phuntuwong, Mr. Preecha Bunamphai.

This research project on quantum nanostructures is financially supported by the Thailand Research Fund (TRF), Office of High Education Commission (OHEC) of Thailand, Asian Office of Aerospace Research and Development (AOARD), Nanotechnology Center of Thailand and Chulalongkorn University.

6. References

C. S. Lent, P.D. Tougaw, and W. Porod, (1993). Appl. Phys. Lett. 62, 741.

J. Timler and C. S. Lent, (2003). J. Appl. Phys. Vol. 94, No. 2, 1050.

Y. Lu, M. Lui and C. S. Lent, (2007). J. Appl. Phys. 102, 034311.

O.Suekano, S. Hasekawa, I. Okui, M. Takata, and H. Nakashima, (2002). Jpn. J. Appl. Phys., Part 1 41, 1022.

L. G. Wang, P. Kratzer, N. Moll, and M. Scheffler, (2000). Phys. Rev. B 62, 1897.

K. Jacobi, (2003). Prog. Surf. Sci. 71, 185.

M. Asada, Y. Miyamoto, and Y. Suematsu, (1986). IEEE J. Quantum Electron. QE-22, 1915.

Y. Arakawa and M. Sakaki, (1982). Appl. Phys. Lett. 40, 39.

Y. Ono, A. Fujiwara, K. Nishiguchi, H. Inokawa, and Y. Takahashi, (2005). J. Appl. Phys. 97, 031101.

D. Leonard, M. Krishnamurthy, C. M. Reaves, S. P. Denbaars, and P. M. Petroff, (1993). Appl. Phys. Lett. 63, 3203.

T. v. Lippen, R. Notzel, G. J. Hamhuis, and J. H. Wolter, (2005). J. Appl. Phys. 97, 044301.

Z. M. Wang, H. Churchill, C. E. George, and G. J. Salamo, (2004). J. Appl. Phys. 96, 6908.

T. Mano, R. Notzel, G. J. Hamhuis, T. J. Bijkemans, and J. H. Wolter, (2004). J. Appl. Phys. 95, 109.

Z. M. Wang, K. Holmes, Y. I. Mazur, and G. J. Salamo, (2004). Appl. Phys. Lett. 84, 1931.

S. Suraprapapich, S. Thainoi, C. Laliew, S. Kanjanachuchai, and S. Panyakeow, (2005). Int. J. Nanosci. 4, 1.

T. v. Lippen, R. Notzel, G. J. Hamhuis, and J. H. Wolter, (2004). Appl. Phys. Lett. 85, 118.

T. v. Lippen, [, R. Notzel, G. J. Hamhuis, and J. H. Wolter, (2005). J. Appl. Phys. 97, 044301.

W. Sheng and J. P. Leburton, (2002). Appl. Phys. Lett. 81, 4449.

C. S. Lent and P. D. Tougaw, (1993). J. Appl. Phys. 74, 6227.

R. Songmuang, S. Kiravittaya, and O. G. Schmidt, (2003). Appl. Phys. Lett. 82, 2892.

T. Mano, R. Notzel, G. J. Hamhuis, T. J. Bijkemans, and J. H. Wolter, (2004). J. Appl. Phys. 95, 109.

S. Suraprapapich, S. Thainoi, S. Kanjanachuchai, and S. Panyakeow, (2005). J. Vac. Sci. Technol. B 23, 1217.

N. Siripitakchai, S. Suraprapapich, S. Thainoi, S. Kanjanachuchai, and S. Panyakeow, (2007). J. Cryst. Growth, 301-302, 812.

M. Macucci (Ed.), (2006). Quantum Cellular Automata: Theory, Experimentation and Prospects, Imperial College Press, London.

N. Siripitakchai, C. C. Thet, S. Panyakeow, and S. Kanjanachuchai, (2008). Microelectronic Engineering 85, 1218-1221.

S. Suraprapapich, S. Thainoi, S. Kanjanachuchai, and S. Panyakeow, (2006). Sol. Energy Mater. Sol. Cells 90, 2968-2974.

C. Y. Ngo, S. F. Yoon, W. J. Fan, and S. J. Chua, (2007). Appl. Phys Lett. 90, 113103.

C. S. Lent and P. D. Tougaw, (1997). Proc. IEEE 85, 541-557.

B. D. Terris and T. Thomson, (2005). J. Phys. D: Appl. Phys. 38, R199-R222.

S. Kanjanachuchai, M. Maitreeboriraks, C. C. Thet, T. Limwongse, and S. Panyakeow, (2009). Microelectronic Engineering 86, 844-848.

M. Bayer, P. Hawrylak, K. Hinzer, S. Fafard, M. Korkusinski, Z. R. Wasilewski, O. Stern, and A. Forchel, (2001). Science 291, 451.

G. J. Beirne, C. Hermannstadter, L. Wang, A. Rastelli, O. G. Schmidt, and P. Michler, (2006). Phys. Rev. Lett. 96, 137401.

S. Kiravittaya, R. Songmuang, N. Y. Jin-Phillipp, S. Panyakeow, and O.G. Schmidt, (2003). J. Cryst. Growth 251, 258.

J. H. Lee, Z. M. Wang, N. W. Strom, Y. I. Mazur, and G. J. Salamo, (2006). Appl. Phys. Lett. 89, 202101.

S. Suraprapapich, S. Panyakeow, and C. W. Tu, (2007). Appl. Phy. Lett. 90, 183112.

K. S. Ryu, J. B. Kim, Y. P. Lee, H. Akinaga, T. Managa, R. Viswan, and S. C. Shin, (2008). Appl. Phys. Lett. 92, 082503.

U. Wurstbauer, M. Sperl, M. Soda, D. Neumaier, D. Schuh, G. Bayreuther, J. Zweck, and W. Wegscheider, (2008). Appl. Phys. Lett. 92, 102506.

M. Bozkurt, V. A. Grant, J. M. Ulloa, R. P. Campion, C. T. Foxon, E. Marega, Jr., G. J. Salamo, and P. M. Koenraad, (2010). Appl. Phys. Lett. 96, 042108.

T. Mano and N. Koguchi, (2005). J. Cryst. Growth 278, 108-112.

T. Mano, T. Noda, M. Yamagiwa, and N. Koguchi, (2005). Thin Solid Films 515, 531-534.

W. Jevasuwan, S. Panyakeow, and S. Rattanathammaphan, (2007). Microelectronic Engineering 84, 1548-1551.

W. Jevasuwan, P. Boonpeng, S. Panyakeow, and S. Rattanathammaphan, (2010). Microelectronic Engineering 87, 1416-1419.

I. L. Bajec, N. Zimic, and M. Mraz, (2006). Microelectronic Engineering 83, 1826-1829.

J. S. Kim, M. Kawabe, and N. Noguchi, (2006). Appl. Phys. Lett. 88, 072107.

S. Kohmoto, H. Nakamura, T. Ishikawa, and K. Asakawa, (1999). Appl. Phys. Lett. 75, 3488.

E. S. Moskalenko, F. K. Karlsson, V. T. Donchev, P. O. Holtz, B. Monemar, W. V. Schoenfield, and P. M. Petroff, (2005). Nano Lett. 5, 2117.

P. Boonpeng, W. Jevasuwan, S. Panyakeow, and S. Rattanathammaphan, (2010). Jpn. J. Appl. Phys. 49, 04DH09.

P. Boonpeng, W. Jevasuwan, S. Suraprapapich, S. Rattanathammaphan, and S. Panyakeow, (2009). Microelectronic Engineering 86, 853-856.

6

Quantum Cellular Automata Controlled Self-Organizing Networks

Laszlo Gyongyosi and Sandor Imre
Department of Telecommunications, Budapest University of Technology
Hungary

1. Introduction

Every process of our universe is based on the fundamental elements of nature: information and computation. The basic motivation behind the study of quantum cellular automata (QCA) is the wish to analyze the processes of nature. QCA provide a natural framework within which to describe many classically undescribable and uncomputable physical phenomena, such as the properties of quantum physical systems and the complex background of quantum dynamics. Quantum cellular automata models are based on the working mechanism of classical cellular automata models and use the power of reversible quantum computation. Cellular automata can be used in many fields of science, such as parallel computation, artificial intelligence, image processing, biological systems, simulation of physics systems, hardware design, algorithm theory, and many more.

In the first part of this chapter, we give a brief overview of the basic properties of quantum information processing and analyze the quantum versions of classical cellular automata models. We present all materials in a clear, perspicuous, and comprehensible manner, without using a complex mathematical background. After reviewing physical QCA implementations, we sketch future directions, and then conclude the first part.

In the second part of the chapter, we examine one possible application of QCA, which uses quantum computing to realize real-life based, truly random network organization. This abstract machine is called a Quantum Cellular Machine (QCM), and we design it for controlling a truly random biologically-inspired network, and to integrate quantum learning algorithms and quantum searching into a controlled, self-organizing system. The self-organizing processes in classical systems cannot be truly random. Using our quantum probabilistic QCM unit, we can add truly random behavior to the self-organizing processes of biological networks. A quantum mechanical-based quantum cellular machine (QCM) controls the self-organizing processes of the network and uses a closed, non-classical quantum mechanical-based language inside the QCM. The proposed QCM solution has deep relevance in the evolution of truly random quantum probabilistic self-organizing network structures. The QCM controls the evolution of the system, changes its environment and creates plans without any human interaction, using truly random quantum probabilistic decisions. In a classical system, the classical circuits can only exhibit deterministic behavior. In a quantum probabilistic control system, the quantum circuits can follow both deterministic and quantum probabilistic quantum cellular machine control behaviors. The QCM has classical and quantum communication layers, it uses the classical layer to detect the network environment. The lower layer of the quantum cellular machine contains the non-deterministic quantum probabilistic decisions and interacts with the classical level. The quantum cellular machine model with the power of quantum computing can be used for the development of a real-life based network organism. We show, that a real, biologically inspired, non-deterministic, truly random network model can be achieved by the discussed QCM model.

In the third part of this chapter, we show that a very efficient quantum searching algorithm can be integrated into the QCM, to find the best solution to a given network input command. We present a quantum searching based method specially designed for quantum probabilistic self-organizing networks, to reduce the complexity of the classical traditional search in the network. The proposed QCM can process both quantum and classical information, and accomplish both deterministic and quantum probabilistic tasks. The information unit is a quantum bit, which can lie in a coherent superposition state of logical states zero and one, and can thus simultaneously store zero and one. Using quantum bits, we can speed up the solutions of classical problems, and even solve some hard problems that classical computers can't solve. The key aspect behind the optimal decisions of a QCM is to design a high-efficiency searching algorithm. A QCM updates the probability amplitudes of its quantum register, according to a given reward value, derived from the network environment. The QCM repeatedly applies a unitary transformation to the quantum states, thus it can enhance, for example, the probability amplitude of the optimal path in the self-organizing network environment, while suppressing the amplitude of all other solutions. The QCM's quantum searching algorithm can help resolve many hard tasks, for example it could be applied to find an optimal logical path, using the effects of quantum mechanics. In the numerical analysis we will show that the quantum communication layer could improve the performance of classical systems.

2. Quantum Cellular Automata

The field of quantum information processing is growing dynamically, and the revolutionary properties of quantum dynamics can be exploited in many fields of science. The classical cellular automata (CA) model uses a discrete and infinite network, equipped with cells. The working mechanism of a CA can be described through the change of states of these discrete cells. The classical automata is deterministic and the state of the cells depends on the states of the neighbouring cells. The state of the automata is determined by the state of all its cells. The quantum version of the classical cellular automata has many advantages over the classical model. The quantum cellular automata (QCA) uses quantum parallelism, which makes it possible to address the cells simultaneously, in parallel, hence the behaviour of a QCA can be controlled globally. The global updating mechanism of the QCA model makes its physical implementation easy in practice, hence the individual manipulation of the quantum bits of the quantum register is not required (Watrous, 1995).

2.1 Related work

In classical computation, the automata—which in general describes parallel processes — could easily become very complex. Using the power of quantum computation and quantum parallelism, the complexity of these structures can be decreased dramatically (Perez-Delgado and Cheung, 2005). As we will see, the phenomena of quantum mechanics can be exploited and can be integrated into the quantum cellular machine. According to the physical attributes of the quantum cellular machine, the evolution of quantum systems can be analysed and discussed by the framework of the QCA, which is a hard task in many physical quantum systems (Dam, 1996).

In a quantum cellular machine, the information processing is realized by quantum operations and transformations. These quantum transformations are called unitary transformations, and these processes are applied on quantum bits, instead of classical bits. Quantum bits represent the fundamental basic unit of quantum information. In practice, quantum states can be realized by photons, electrons, atoms or half-spin particles (Grössing and Zeilinger, 1988). One of the most important properties of quantum states is that these qubits can be in a superposition state, which cannot be imagined for classical bits. This property means that a quantum state can be simultaneously in the logical state of 0 and 1. However, to convert the superponated information into 'useful' information, we have to apply a measurement to the qubit, which converts the quantum information encoded in the position of the state into classical information (Benioff, 1980), (Gyongyosi et al., 2009), (Imre and Balazs, 2005), (Nielsen and Chuang, 2000). The output of the measurement is not completely determined by the position of the qubit, hence its result is not deterministic, but probabilistic (Curtis and Meyer, 2004), (Miller et al., 2006). We will call this property, quantum probabilistic output or behaviour. The measurement destroys the state of the qubit, and changes its state to a "classical" or orthogonal state—according to the basis of the measurement, and the logical value of the classical output. Quantum algorithms, which exploit quantum parallelism, use quantum registers—the collection of superponated quantum states. Using a quantum register, tasks can be computed with an exponential speed up as the number of quantum states in the quantum register increases linearly (Margolus, 1991).

The idea of a cellular automata, or machine, was formulated by von Neumann, a Hungarian mathematician, who showed that a cellular automata based system was capable of self-reproduction (Neumann, 1966). Later, a two-dimensional cellular automata model became extremely popular—later known as the 'Game of Life' (Gardner, 1970). The model uses 'alive' and 'dead' cells, and there are many rules for the state 'dead' and for the state 'alive'. The cells can change between these two states, according to the properties of their neighbours. After the Game of Life had become so popular, new ideas have been presented. As has been shown, the physical properties of the processes of the classical world can be traced back to the fundamental properties of cellular automata behaviour. Later, the one dimensional cellular automata also was introduced (Watrous, 1995). The cellular automata models the world through parallel processes—hence, it is natural to apply the results of quantum information processing to cellular automata models. The idea of a Quantum Cellular Automata (QCA) was first mentioned by Toffoli and Margolus (Toffoli et al., 1990), (Margolus, 1991). Later, Feynman (Feynman, 1982), Grössing and Zeilinger (Grössing and Zeilinger, 1988), and Watrous (Watrous, 1995) have published some formalized results on the subject. The term QCA was first used by Grössing and Zeilinger, and the model of Watrous is based on Feynman's ideas. Based on these works, Richter and Werner (Richter and Werner, 1996) showed some new results in the field.

Parallelism of processes can be exploited dramatically with the help of quantum parallelism, since the transformations of the QCA's are applied in parallel on all the qubits of the quantum register. It also means that the quantum states of the QCA do not have to be addressed separately, since all the quantum states can be used simultaneously in the processes (Vollbrecht and Cirac, 2008). From an engineering viewpoint, the QCA machine can be regarded as a natural extension of the original classical CA model, since the working mechanism of the CA is defined as the combination of parallel processes (Benioff, 1980), (Neumann, 1966), (Miller et al., 2006). Since all the unitary transformations can be realized simultaneously in the model, the quantum states of the quantum register can be handled as an indistinguishable quantum register, where it is not required to control all the qubits in a separate manner, individually (Arrighi et al., 2007), (Toth and Lent, 2001).

2.2 Quantum computing

In this section, we give a brief overview of quantum mechanics, and we introduce the basic definitions of quantum information processing which will be used in the text.

2.2.1 Brief overview of quantum information processing

In quantum information processing, the logical values of classical bits are replaced by state vectors $|0\rangle$ and $|1\rangle$, - called the Dirac notation. Contrary to classical bits, a qubit $|\psi\rangle$ can also be in a linear combination of basis vectors $|0\rangle$ and $|1\rangle$.
The state of a qubit can be expressed as

$$|\psi\rangle = \alpha|0\rangle + \beta|1\rangle, \tag{1}$$

where α and β are complex numbers, which is also called the superposition of the basis vectors, with probability amplitudes α and β. A qubit $|\psi\rangle$ is a vector in a two-dimensional complex space, where the basis vectors $|0\rangle$ and $|1\rangle$ form an orthonormal basis. The orthonormal basis $\{|0\rangle, |1\rangle\}$ forms the computational basis, in Fig. 1 we illustrate the computational basis for the case where the probability amplitudes are real (Imre and Balazs, 2005).

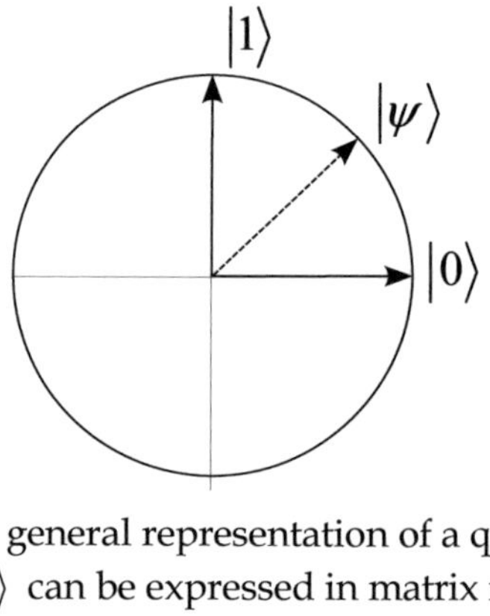

Fig. 1. Computational basis and general representation of a qubit in superposition state.
The vectors or states $|0\rangle$ and $|1\rangle$ can be expressed in matrix representation by

$$|0\rangle = \begin{bmatrix} 1 \\ 0 \end{bmatrix} \text{ and } |1\rangle = \begin{bmatrix} 0 \\ 1 \end{bmatrix}. \tag{2}$$

If $|\alpha|^2$ and $|\beta|^2$ are the probabilities, and the number of possible outputs is only two, then for $|\psi\rangle = \alpha|0\rangle + \beta|1\rangle$ we have $|\alpha|^2 + |\beta|^2 = 1$, and the norm of $|\psi\rangle$ is $\||\psi\rangle\| = \sqrt{|\alpha|^2 + |\beta|^2} = 1$.

The most general transformation of $\| |\psi\rangle \|$ that respects this constraint is a linear transformation U that takes unit vectors to unit vectors.
A *unitary* transformation can be defined as

$$U^\dagger U = UU^\dagger = I, \tag{3}$$

where $U^\dagger = \left(U^*\right)^T$, hence the adjoint is equal to the transpose of complex conjugate, and I is the identity matrix.
The tensor product has an important role in quantum computation, here we quickly introduce the concept of tensor product. If we have complex vector spaces V and W of dimensions m and n, then the tensor product of $V \otimes W$ is an mn dimensional vector space. The tensor product is non-commutative, thus the notation preserves the ordering. The concept of a linear operator also can be defined over the vector spaces. If we have two linear operators A and B, defined on the vector spaces V and W, then the linear operator $A \otimes B$ on $V \otimes W$ can be defined as $(A \otimes B)(|v\rangle \otimes |w\rangle) = A|v\rangle \otimes B|w\rangle$, where $|v\rangle \in V$ and $|w\rangle \in W$. In matrix representation, $A \otimes B$ can be expressed as

$$A \otimes B = \begin{bmatrix} A_{11}B & \dots & A_{1m}B \\ \vdots & \ddots & \vdots \\ A_{m1}B & \dots & A_{mm}B \end{bmatrix}, \tag{4}$$

where A is an $m \times m$ matrix, and B is an $n \times n$ matrix, hence $A \otimes B$ has dimension $mn \times mn$.
The state $|\psi\rangle$ of an n-qubit quantum register is a superposition of the 2^n states $|0\rangle, |1\rangle, \ldots, |2^n - 1\rangle$, thus

$$|\psi\rangle = \sum_{i=0}^{2^n-1} \alpha_i |i\rangle, \tag{5}$$

with amplitudes α_i constrained by

$$\sum_{i=0}^{2^n-1} |\alpha_i|^2 = 1. \tag{6}$$

The state of an n-qubit length quantum register is a vector in a 2^n-dimensional complex vector space, hence if the number of the qubits in the quantum register increases linearly, the dimension of the vector space increases exponentially.
A complex vector space V is a Hilbert space $\mathcal{H}$ if there is an *inner product*

$$\langle \psi | \varphi \rangle \tag{7}$$

with $x, y \in \mathbb{C}$ and $|\varphi\rangle, |\psi\rangle, |u\rangle, |v\rangle \in V$ satisfying the rules $\langle \psi | \varphi \rangle = \langle \varphi | \psi \rangle^*$, $\langle \varphi | (a|v\rangle + b|v\rangle)\rangle = a\langle \varphi | u\rangle + b\langle \varphi | v\rangle$, and $\langle \varphi | \varphi \rangle > 0$ if $|\varphi\rangle \neq 0$. If we have vectors

$|\varphi\rangle = a|0\rangle + b|1\rangle$ and $|\psi\rangle = c|0\rangle + d|1\rangle$, then the inner product in matrix representation can be expressed as

$$\langle\varphi|\psi\rangle = \begin{bmatrix} a^* & b^* \end{bmatrix}\begin{bmatrix} c \\ d \end{bmatrix} = a^*c + b^*d. \tag{8}$$

The norm of the vector $|\varphi\rangle$ can be expressed as $\||\varphi\rangle\| = \sqrt{\langle\varphi|\varphi\rangle}$, and the dual of the vector $|\varphi\rangle$ is denoted by $\langle\varphi|$. The *dual* is a linear operator from the vector space to the complex numbers, defined as $\langle\varphi|(|v\rangle) = \langle\varphi|v\rangle$. The outer product between two vectors $|\varphi\rangle$ and $|\psi\rangle$ can be defined as

$$|\psi\rangle\langle\varphi|, \tag{9}$$

satisfying $(|\psi\rangle\langle\varphi|)|v\rangle = |\psi\rangle\langle\varphi|v\rangle$. The matrix of the outer product $|\psi\rangle\langle\varphi|$ is obtained by usual matrix multiplication of a column matrix by a row matrix, however the matrix multiplication can be replaced by tensor product, since:

$$|\varphi\rangle\langle\psi| = |\varphi\rangle \otimes \langle\psi|. \tag{10}$$

If we have vectors $|\varphi\rangle = a|0\rangle + b|1\rangle$ and $|\psi\rangle = c|0\rangle + d|1\rangle$, the outer product in matrix representation can be expressed as

$$|\varphi\rangle\langle\psi| = \begin{bmatrix} a \\ b \end{bmatrix}\begin{bmatrix} c^* & d^* \end{bmatrix} = \begin{bmatrix} ac^* & ad^* \\ bc^* & bd^* \end{bmatrix}. \tag{11}$$

In Fig 2. we illustrate the general description of a unitary transformation on an n-length quantum state, where the input state $|\psi_i\rangle$ is either $|0\rangle$ or $|1\rangle$, generally. After the application of a unitary transformation U on the input states, the state of the quantum register can be given by a state vector $|\psi\rangle$.

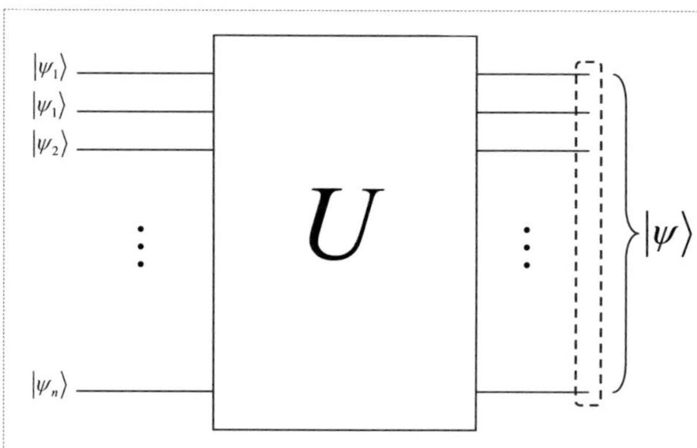

Fig. 2. General sketch of a unitary transformation on an n-length quantum register.

The unitary operator U is a $2^n \times 2^n$ matrix, with, in principle, an infinite number of possible operators. The result of the measurement of the state $|\psi\rangle$ results in zeros and ones that form the final result of the quantum computation, based on the n-length qubit string stores in the quantum register.

The quantum circuit of a QCM realizes a reversible operation, and any reversible quantum operation can be expressed as a unitary matrix. For a unitary transformation U, the following property holds:

$$(U^T)^* = U^{-1}, \tag{12}$$

where T denotes transposition and * denotes complex conjugation. The inverse transformation of U also can be expressed by the adjugate $U^\dagger$, which is equal to U^{-1}. One of the most standard quantum gates is the Controlled-NOT (CNOT) gate (Nielsen and Chuang, 2000), (Toffoli et al., 1990).

The CNOT gate is a very important gate in quantum computation, since from the one qubit quantum gates and the CNOT gates every unitary transformation can be expressed, hence these gates are universal. This gate is a two-qubit gate and it contains two qubits, called the control and the target qubit. If the control qubit is $|1\rangle$, then the gate negates the second qubit—called the target qubit. The general CNOT gate is illustrated in Fig. 3.

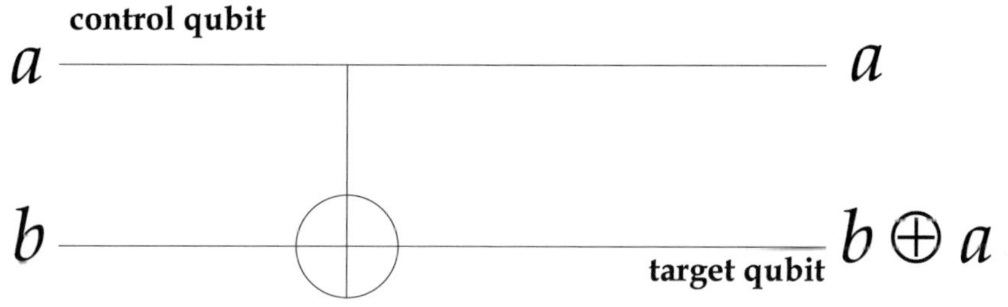

Fig. 3. The Controlled-NOT (CNOT) gate.

As can be verified, the quantum CNOT gate can be regarded as the generalization of the classical XOR transformation, hence $\mathbf{CNOT}|a, b\rangle = |a, b \oplus a\rangle$, which unitary transformation can be expressed in matrix form as follows:

$$\mathbf{CNOT} = \begin{bmatrix} 1 & 0 & 0 & 0 \\ 0 & 1 & 0 & 0 \\ 0 & 0 & 0 & 1 \\ 0 & 0 & 1 & 0 \end{bmatrix}. \tag{13}$$

The controlled behaviour of the CNOT gate can be extended to every unitary transformation, and the generalized control quantum gate can be defined. In Fig. 4, we show a controlled U transformation, the U transformation is applied to the target qubit b only if the control qubit a is in high logical state. We note that the CNOT gate cannot be used to copy a quantum state, while the classical XOR gate can be applied to copy a classical bit.

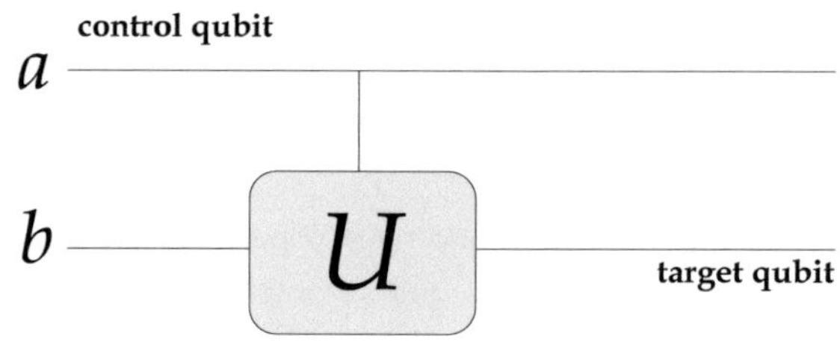

Fig. 4. A controlled-*U* gate.

As can be seen easily, for the CNOT gate, this unitary transformation U is equal to the NOT-transformation, hence the CNOT gate is a controlled-X gate, actually. We can also define the inverse of this transformation as the controlled-$U^{\dagger}$ transformation, as follows:

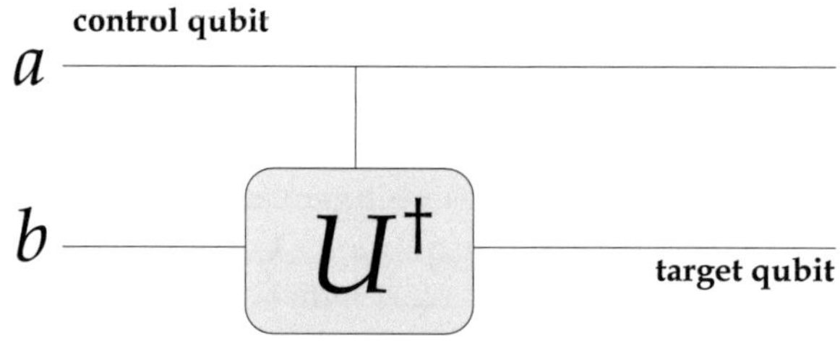

Fig. 5. A controlled inverse *U* gate.

Another important issue in the QCMs quantum circuit is the measurement operator M. The measurement operator converts the quantum information to classical, since after the measurement of a quantum state, the quantum information which is encoded in the quantum state becomes classical, and can be expressed as a logical 0 or 1. The general measurement circuit is illustrated in Fig. 6.

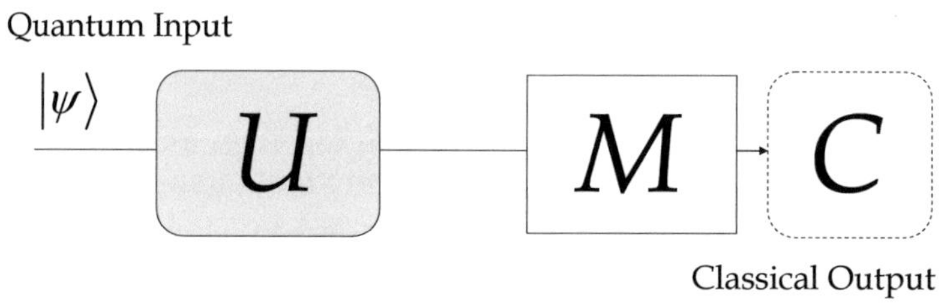

Fig. 6. The measurement of quantum information. The *M* measurement converts the quantum information to classical.

If we measure the quantum state $|\psi\rangle = \alpha|0\rangle + \beta|1\rangle$, then the output will be $M = 0$ with probability $|\alpha|^2$ or $M = 1$ with probability $|\beta|^2$.

For the general case, if we measure the n-length quantum register $|\psi\rangle = \sum_{i=0}^{2^n-1} \alpha_i |i\rangle$, with possible states $|0\rangle, |1\rangle, \ldots, |2^n - 1\rangle$, then the quantum measurement can be described as a set of $\{M_m\}$ of linear operators. The number of the possible outcomes is n, hence the number m of possible measurement operators is between $1 \le m \le n$.

If we measure the quantum register in state $|\psi\rangle = \sum_{i=0}^{2^n-1} \alpha_i |i\rangle$, then the outcome i has a probability of

$$\Pr(i) = \langle \psi | M_i^\dagger M_i | \psi \rangle . \tag{14}$$

The sum of the probabilities of all possible outcomes is $\sum_{i=1}^{m} \Pr(i) = \sum_{i=1}^{m} \langle \psi | M_i^\dagger M_i | \psi \rangle = 1$, according to the completeness of the measurement operators, since $\sum_{i=1}^{m} M_i^\dagger M_i = I$.

After the measurement of outcome *i*, the state of the quantum register collapses to

$$|\psi'\rangle = \frac{M_i |\psi\rangle}{\sqrt{\langle \psi | M_i^\dagger M_i | \psi \rangle}} = \frac{M_i |\psi\rangle}{\sqrt{\Pr(i)}} . \tag{15}$$

Using the previous example, if we have single quantum state $|\psi\rangle = \alpha|0\rangle + \beta|1\rangle$, then the measurement operators can be defined as

$$M_0 = |0\rangle\langle 0| \text{ and } M_0 = |1\rangle\langle 1| , \tag{16}$$

since the unknown qubit is defined in the orthonormal basis of $|0\rangle$ and $|1\rangle$.

2.3 Properties of Quantum Cellular Automata

The main idea behind QCA models can be stated as follows: exploit maximally the phenomena of quantum mechanics to outperform the classical model. It seems to be a natural extension to use the properties of quantum information processing, since all the operations of the classical version are parallelized. The QCA models have the advantage, that its can be used to simulate any quantum circuit, or the quantum Turing machine, or can be used to simulate the properties of entanglement transmission. This property is called the *universality* of the quantum cellular automata models, (Curtis and Meyer, 2004), (Grössing and Zeilinger, 1988).

The definition of the QCA model was formalized by Watrous (Watrous, 1995). The QCA can be described as a four-tuple, which consists of a *d*-dimensional construction of cells, a finite set of states, a finite set of neighbours, and a local transaction function. The quantum version of the classical CA uses discrete time and discrete space, however in the quantum case, the transitions are realized by unitary transformations. Moreover, according to quantum parallelism, each of the transformations of the QCA are realized simultaneously on all cells of the QCA. On the other hand, the transformations can be applied only for a small set of local neighbourhoods, in this case, the updating is achieved locally. The updating transformations operate probabilistically on the cells, and for a *well-formed* QCA, all the probabilities of the unitary transformations have to preserve the squared sum of these properties, which is equal to one. As has also been shown, this 'well-formed' property can be verified algorithmically (Dam, 1996), (Perez-Delgado and Cheung, 2005).

In the classical CA model, the processes and the cell updating mechanisms are achieved on classical bits, and the transformations are classical transformation. In a quantum system, the processes are realized by unitary transformations, and the transition functions of these unitary transformations are slightly different from the classical approach. Moreover, according to the no-cloning theorem (Wootters and Zurek, 1982), an unknown quantum state cannot be cloned perfectly, hence the quantum states cannot be split into two quantum registers, and then spliced into one quantum register again. In classical CA, this synchronization method can be applied easily, since the classical bits can be copied freely, an unlimited number of times. The quantum states of the QCA are updated without the possibility of register duplication, using different approaches, such as the partitioning of the quantum register. The partitioning scheme is used to construct a reversible version of the classical cellular automata model. A cellular automata is called *reversible* if there exists only one possible configuration for every actual configuration. The QCA is a reversible automata, however to define the QCA we have to extend the reversibility property and we have to add other properties.

2.3.1 The formal model of the QCA

The transition function of the QCA realizes the map instantaneously and for all the qubits of the quantum register simultaneously (Watrous, 1995). Watrous's one-dimensional QCA consists of the finite set of all possible states, the finite set of the automata's neighborhoods, and a local transition function. The cells of the quantum automata are described in a Hilbert space, and the cells are in superposition states, hence all the possible classical CA states can be handled simultaneously in the QCA model. The results of the transition functions are described as complex numbers in the Hilbert space (Arrighi et al., 2007), (Meyer, 1996).

In a QCA, the transformations are generally achieved by physical processes, hence they can be naturally described as unitary transformations. The unitarity of the one-dimensional QCA can be verified by algorithmic tools, checking whether the sum-squared probabilities of the transformations is equal to 1, or not.

2.3.2 Partitioned and Block-partitioned QCA

The main purpose of the quantum cellular automata model is the realization of the computation of all computable functions in a parallel way, using the fundamental properties of quantum mechanics. After Watrous published the one-dimensional QCA model, the *partitioned* version of this automata was also introduced (Dam, 1996), (Meyer, 1996), (Toffoli et al., 1990).

The partitioned QCA model uses cells, which can be divided into *sub-cells*: these cells are the left, right and centre cells. In a partitioned QCA model, the next state of a cell is determined by the right sub-cell of the left neighbour of the cell, and by the middle sub-cell of itself and by the left sub-cell of the right cell. The cell structure of the partitioned QCA is illustrated in Fig. 7. The local transition function is denoted by μ.

In the partitioned one-dimensional QCA model, the transition function μ can be divided into many permutations of the sub-cells in the neighbourhood of a given cell. The decomposition of μ is based on the fact that transition function can be expressed as unitary transformations, which transformations act on the given cell.

The decomposed transformation function μ can be described as these unitary transformations and by swap transformations between the sub-cells of different cells. A swap transformation between the sub-cells of the neighbouring cells is illustrated in Fig. 8.

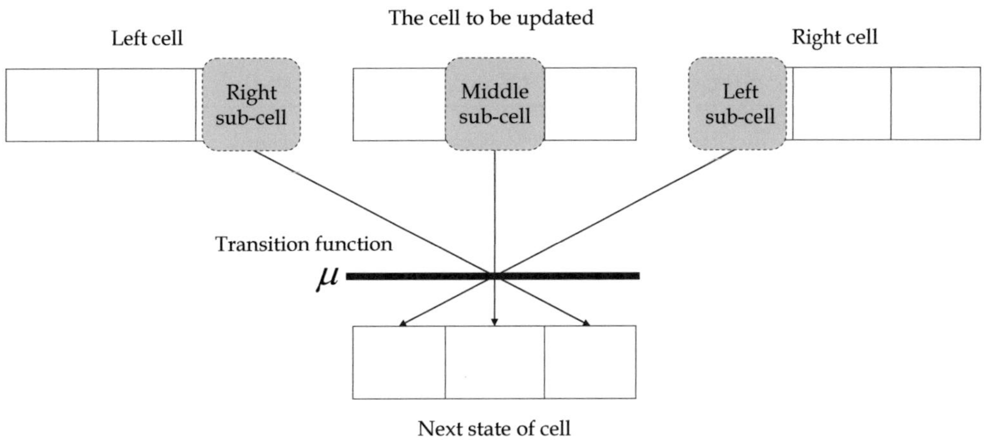

Fig. 7. The one-dimensional QCA. Each cell can be decomposed into three sub-cells.

The cells are divided into three sub-cells. In the updating process, the quantum automata swaps the left and right sub-cells of the neighbouring cells. Next, it updates each cell internally, with the help of a unitary operation, which acts on the three sub-cells of every cell. The partitioned QCAs form a subclass of QCA. There exist several other important subclasses, such as the Block-partitioned QCA (Dam, 1996).

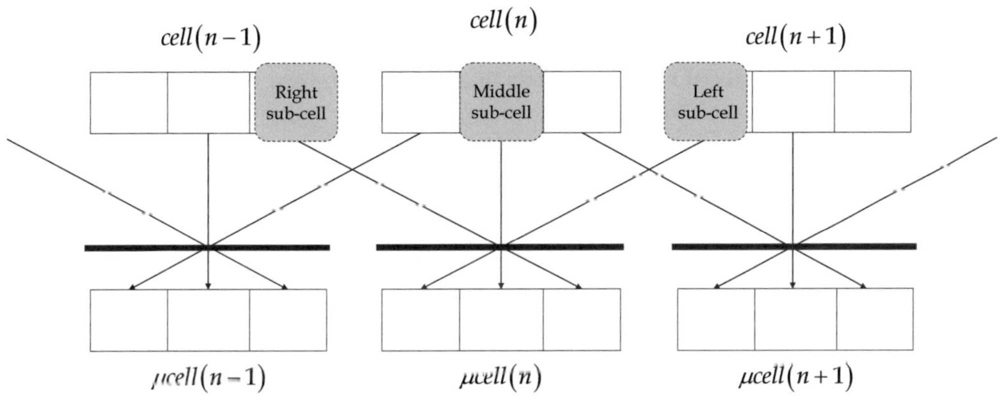

Fig. 8. The updating rule of the QCA. The position of the left and right sub-cells of the neighbouring cells are changed in the next state of the given cell. The updating process is realized by unitary operations applied to each sub-cell of the cells.

The block-partitioned model was introduced by Margolus and Toffoli (Margolus, 1991), (Toffoli et al., 1990) and in this type of model, the cells are divided into blocks, where each block contains two cells. This subclass has deep relevance in practice, since it can be applied to model the properties of physical systems, and other properties also can be explored with this model. The transition function is achieved on *block-level*, hence the maps are realized between the blocks, or the states of the blocks (Dam, 1996), (Meyer, 1996). In the communication process, the blocks can be shifted, and the unitary transformations are applied to the blocks. The rules can be realized by quantum gates as we will see in the second part of this chapter, in which we will define the most important quantum gates.

As a natural generalization of the block-partitioned QCA model, every one-dimensional QCA can be expressed as a set of local unitary operations. According to the Margolus partitioning scheme, a one-dimensional QCA can be expressed by unitary operations (Nielsen and Chuang, 2000), (Watrous, 1995).
In Fig. 9, we show a one-dimensional QCA, partitioned into unitary transformations. The unitary transformations belong to the blocks of the QCA.

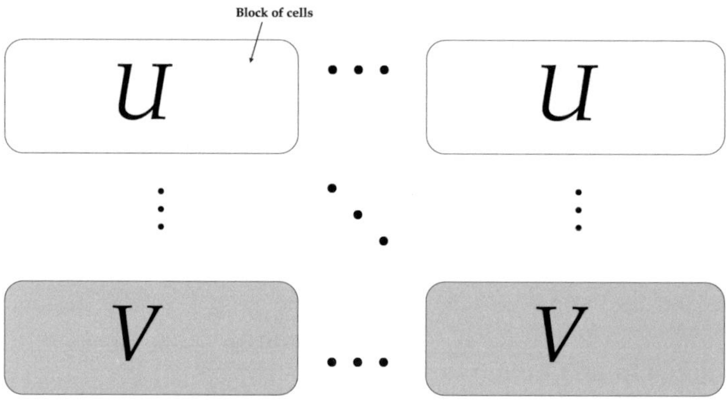

Fig. 9. Block-partitioned QCA. The blocks can be used to realize unitary transformations.

As a result of the decomposition of quantum transformations into elementary quantum gates, every quantum transformation and behaviour can be expressed using one-qubit and two-qubit quantum gates. In the second part of this chapter, we show a *reduction method*, which is able to find the most simple version of a given quantum transformation. It makes the circuits of the quantum cellular automata very easy to implement in practice, using basic quantum devices and tools. The rules of the quantum cellular automata can be viewed as elementary quantum gates applied to the cells, hence the quantum circuit of a QCM can be expressed as the concatenation of different rules, which rules are applied to the cells of the automata model.
Using Margolus's result (Margolus, 1991), in the second part of this chapter we will show, that any quantum probabilistic controller logic can be constructed from elementary unitary quantum transformations. Moreover, an intelligent self-organizing structure can be constructed from these results, as we will see in the second and the third parts of this chapter.
In the next part of this chapter, we show a quantum cellular automata based approach, called the *Quantum Cellular Machine* (QCM), which uses reversible quantum probabilistic quantum circuits to vest quantum probabilistic, truly random behaviour in a self-organized network structure. The QCM combines the basic properties of the block partitioned QCA model and adds many extended functions, according to its quantum circuit realization. The QCM's quantum circuit can realize any unitary transformation, using one- and two-qubit elementary quantum gates, and combines classical and quantum information processing.

2.3.3 Physical QCA Implementations

In this section, we have reviewed the basic properties of Quantum Cellular Automata (QCA). The QCA model refers to the quantum computational analogy with conventional classical models of cellular automata. The physical implementation of a 'classical' cellular automata—called the quantum dot cellular automata—can be exploited by the fundamental properties of the phenomena of quantum mechanics. The quantum dots are nano-structures, which can be constructed from standard semi conductive materials. In these structures, the electrons are trapped inside the dot, however the smaller physical quantum dot requires a higher potential energy for an electron to escape. In a quantum dot QCA, the quantum dots respond to the charge state of their neighbours.

In the quantum dot implementation, the working processes of the logic are based on neighbour interactions, or the movement of charge. The main advantage of these implementations is their very low power, however in these implementations the input and the output is not isolated well.

As in Fig. 10, there are two energetically equivalent ground state polarizations, which can be labelled as logical '0' and logical '1' (Arrighi et al., 2007), (Meyer, 1996), (Toth and Lent, 2001).

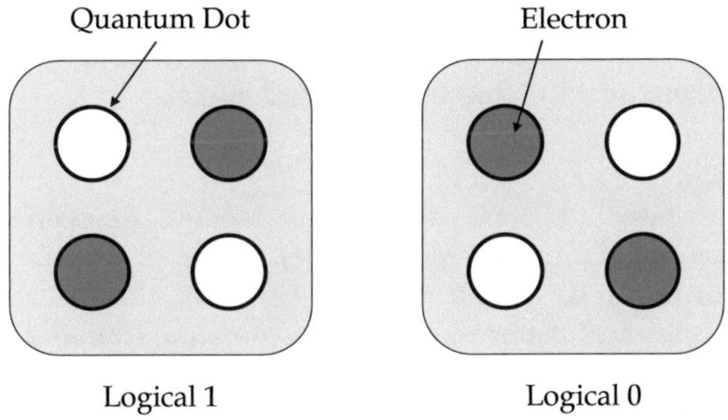

Fig. 10. The basic logic unit of the QCA is the cell. The QCA cell contains four quantum dots.

In experimental realizations, the quantum dot can be described as a nanometre sized structure. The quantum dot has the capability of trapping electrons. To represent the logical zero and one states, the quantum dot confines these electrons, which can escape only if a high potential is available.

The first implementation of physical quantum dot QCA machine was introduced by Toth and Lent (Toth and Lent, 2001). In their method, the state of the system converges to the lowest energy state, which state can be regarded as a uniquely defined state in the system. Later, the construction of a physical QCA model was extended to tunnel junctions and other phase changer nano-technological devices, using correlated magnetic and electrical states, or other magnetic and non-magnetic particles such as the metal tunnel junction QCA or the molecular and magnetic QCA (Arrighi et al., 2007), (Richter and Werner, 1996).

3. Quantum probabilistic control of self-organizing networks

A novel approach to future network communication is the quantum probabilistic self-organizing network structure. The main component of this kind of network structure is the QCM (*Quantum Cellular Machine*). The QCM uses a classical language to communicate with the components of the quantum probabilistic self-organizing networks, and uses a closed, non-classical quantum mechanical based language inside the component model. The proposed QCM model uses quantum computing for the development and the control of a truly random network organism.

In this part, we propose the QCM model to use quantum computing for the development of a real-life based network organism. The QCM model applies quantum mechanics and quantum computing to act on the QCM's internal self model and on its lower quantum layer. The particular quantum effects such as superposition or entanglement can be used to represent a real-life based self-organism and to demonstrate the quantum mechanically based unpredictable logical behaviour. The non-deterministic effects of quantum mechanics can be implemented well in the QCM model by the probabilistic outputs and quantum measurements. The QCM's internal self quantum state cannot be formalized classically; however its internal state machine can be implemented as a cellular automaton. The cells communicate directly by the real inputs and outputs and general transformations are performed on a global level by quantum circuits and quantum algorithms. The proposed quantum model's goal is to demonstrate the quantum mechanical based model's superiority to classical cellular automata based self-organizing networks.
In this part of this chapter, we define the theoretical basis of the QCM's quantum logic; then we give an example of implementation of the QCM module. Finally we conclude with the results and benefits of our quantum mechanical based model.

3.1 Properties of QCM

In the biologically inspired network organization models, the non-repeating output is desired for the same input (Curtis and Meyer, 2004), (Miller et al., 2006) and thus the QCM component behaviour has to be *non-deterministic*. However, the classical cellular automata model has no more dynamical patterns, only the information from the environment and its local state. Thus, if we want to construct a real biologically inspired non-deterministic model, we have to use quantum mechanics and a mapping that allows the QCM to use quantum level communication on a higher, logical level (Gyongyosi et al., 2009). The QCM can redefine the classical-level actions by this lower quantum control level, by applying the rules of the quantum level.
The two layers use two different communication methods. The classical level describes the QCM and network interacting using the classical communication layer. The QCM uses the classical layer to perceive the network environment through the data and information sent by other network components and to execute the given instructions. The lower layer of the QCM represents the non-deterministic quantum probabilistic decisions. The quantum level evolves dynamically, and it represents the properties of the biological organizations and interacts with the classical level.
Our purpose is to implement quantum mechanics based probabilistic decisions in biologically inspired network organizations and network adaptation, and to use them in problems where real non-deterministic behaviour is needed.
The logical output function remaps the network's actual logical state and the internal self model according to either the self model or the logical output function. The logical output function is used by the QCM's self model to modify both the network's state and the internal self model state. The logical output function affects the execution of the network commands, and hence the results of the quantum learning algorithm are converted back to classical ones.
In Fig. 11 we illustrated the hierarchical structure of the QCM. The decisions are based on the internal state and network model, and the output of the QCM is propagated back to the classical layer. The output of the QCM is determined by quantum learning and quantum

searching algorithms. The network model and the self model variables are stored as qubits in the quantum layer of the QCM. The other network variables are stored and handled on the classical layer.

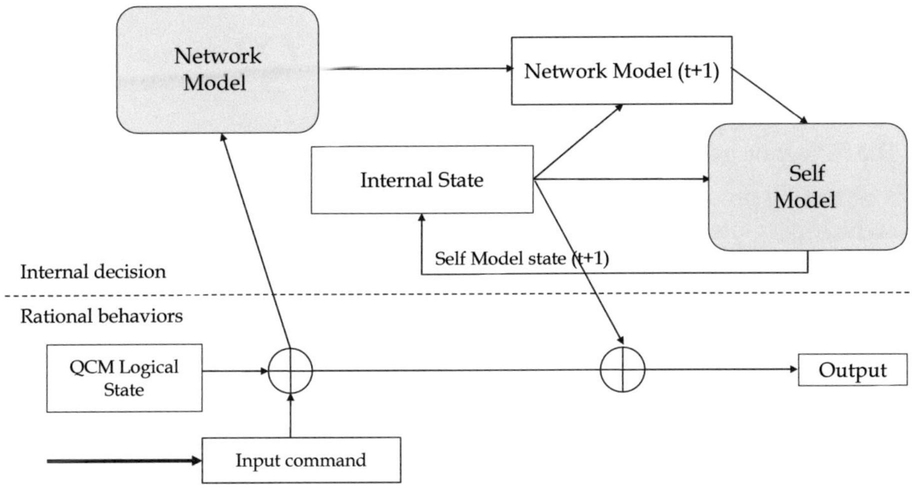

Fig. 11. The hierarchical structure of the QCM model.

In classical systems, the classical network elements can realize only deterministic behaviour. In our quantum probabilistic control system, the quantum circuits can realize both deterministic and quantum probabilistic behaviours. The quantum control based QCM forms a quantum system exploiting the superposition of the state of the QCM with the state of the network environment.

The quantum probabilistic controlled QCM uses automated methods to synthesize quantum behaviours from the examples, the *cares* of the quantum controlled QCM's quantum control table. The minterms not given as examples are the *don't knows*. The minterms not given as examples are converted to output values with various probabilities (Miller et al., 2006). We use the *simplicity principle* by seeking circuits of *reduced complexity*. We extend the QCM's logic synthesis approach to a *learning method* using quantum circuits (Nielsen and Chuang, 2000), (Curtis and Meyer, 2004).

3.1.1 Learning quantum behaviours from network examples

Logic synthesis methods applied to binary functions with many *don't cares* are used as the basis of various learning approaches. The *learning process* creates a circuit description and converts *don't cares* to *cares* trying to satisfy the simplicity. The method of logic synthesis based learning has already been applied to binary and multiple-valued circuits; however it has not been applied to quantum circuits.

In our learning method we use the EPR circuit to realize entanglement. The EPR-generator circuit is illustrated in Fig. 12. The circuit contains a Hadamard gate and a Controlled-NOT (CNOT) gate.

Our QCM *controller's unitary matrix* is the mapping between QCMs inputs and outputs. The unitary mapping is closely related to the behaviour observed on the QCM. The behaviours of the QCM combine quantum probabilistic and deterministic behaviours given by the unitary controller matrix.

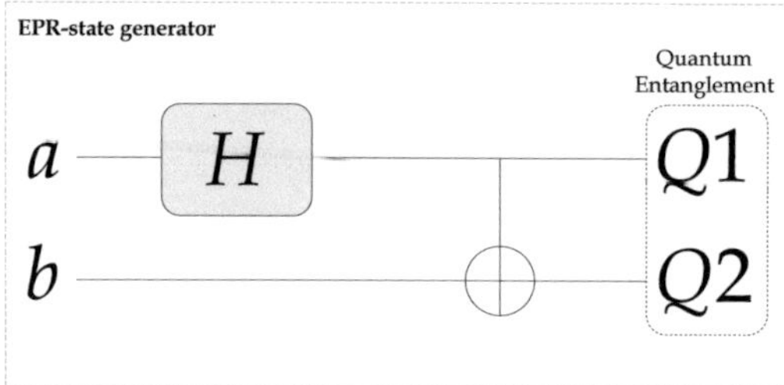

Fig. 12. The EPR-state generator quantum circuit.

The self-organizing processes of the network can be modelled as many cellular automata in parallel, which permute the cells and apply the rules in parallel for many cells. From this viewpoint, the constructed QCM model can be described as a cellular automata model, which uses permutation and parallel quantum transformations on the quantum register. The permutations and unitary transformations are realized in two individual steps, sequentially. The automata repeats the sequences, until the evolution of the quantum system reaches its desired output (Dam, 1996).
The abstract cellular automata-based model of the QCM is illustrated in Fig. 13.

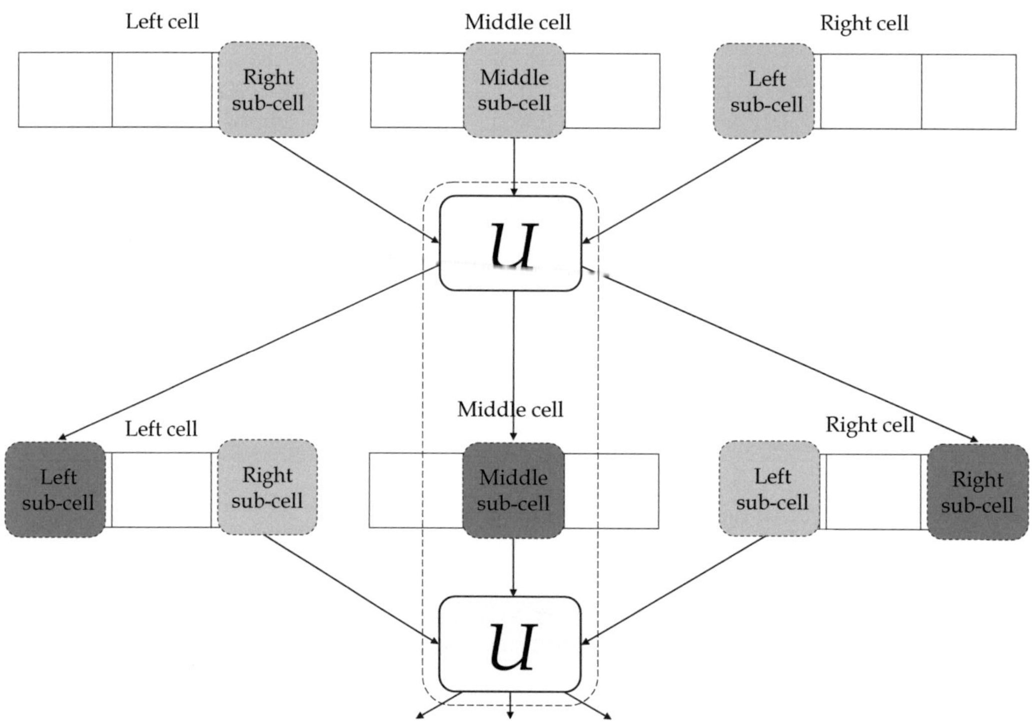

Fig. 13. Extended parallel gate construction. The unitary transformations of the QCA are realized by the quantum gates in parallel.

In this abstract cellular automata representation, the quantum transformations can be changed in every step, and the sequence of the gates can be different in every transformations.

3.1.2 Learning incompletely specified quantum functions

In the quantum probabilistic controlled system, any quantum control function is constructed in the complex Hilbert space $H^{\otimes N}$ from a set of a single-quantum bit and two-quantum bit operators

$$G = \{[I],[controlled - U],[controlled - U^{\dagger}],[CNOT]\}. \tag{17}$$

In general the synthesis problem is to find the simplest circuit for a *Unitary Control Map* (UCM) table with *few given examples* and *many don't cares*. The given examples are mean *cares* in the *UCM* table. Let G be a set of *single-qubit* and *two-qubit* unitary operators on complex H^N ; then the process of synthesis can be expressed as a minimization of the given function with respect to the width of the QCM's circuit and the amount of elementary operators used inside the QCM's unitary control mechanism. Thus, this synthesis S_{H^N} can be written as follows (Miller et al., 2006):

$$S_{H^N}(n,G) \xrightarrow{\min} V(n,G), \tag{18}$$

where $V(n,G)$ is the cost of the QCM's circuit constructed of gates from set G. We use only single-qubit and two-qubit gates, and thus the QCMs learned by this method are directly implementable in quantum hardware, have low hardware costs, and satisfy the simplicity criteria (Curtis and Meyer, 2004).

3.2 Quantum probabilistic controlling system

We define the quantum probabilistic QCM controlling system. Let I be a set of vectors such that

$$I_k^p = \{i_0, i_1, \dots, i_n\}, \; n = 2^N \tag{19}$$

is the *k*-th input vector of an *N* quantum bit length state of pattern P or function specification, and

$$f : I \to O \tag{20}$$

is a *reversible* function. The output vector

$$O_k^p = \{o_0, o_1, \dots, o_n\} \tag{21}$$

is the expected *result vector* for the *input pattern* I_k^p and O is the set of all output vectors. Let $i_k \in \{0,1\}$ and $o_k \in \{0,1\}$ be the elements of the input and output vectors respectively. Let $|\psi\rangle$ be a *three-qubit* quantum state and G be the set of possible operators, and thus *quantum gates* (Curtis and Meyer, 2004). Then, there exists a quantum logic circuit U_f such that for any pair of input patterns I_i^p and output patterns

$$(I_i^p, O_i^p) \; : \; I_i^p \in I^p, \; O_i^p \in O^p, \tag{22}$$

where $\forall O_i^p \in O \exists I_i^p \in I$ such that $f\left(I_i^p\right) = O_i^p$ is a *one-to-one* mapping. This means that there is a *unitary transform* on a quantum system $U_f|\psi\rangle \to |\psi'\rangle$ for $|\psi\rangle \in I^p$, $|\psi'\rangle \in O^p$. The learning of such a function implies finding the *minimal set* of quantum gates implementing function f and realizing unitary control matrix U_f. The *unspecified* outputs are denoted by *X*; these values represent a *don't care* logic value and correspond to an unknown output. The set of examples is given as a set of pairs

$$P = \{i_k, o_k\}, k = 1, \ldots, n \le 2^N. \tag{23}$$

For the *incompletely* specified functions, the QCM uses a process to *explicitly find* a mapping or function satisfying each pair $\left(I_k^p, O_k^p\right)$ from the given set P such that

$$f\left(I_k^p\right) = O_k^p. \tag{24}$$

The goal of the QCM's learning process is to find a circuit that realizes a *complete* mapping with *incomplete* specifications and that agrees with the set of input-output pairs from the specification examples. The result of the QCM's learning process is thus a circuit that describes a *complete mapping* that agrees with the set of input-output pairs from the specification examples (Miller et al., 2006).
Thus, let f be a three-qubit *incompletely specified* reversible function defined in Table 1.

Target	0	1
Control: ab		
00	000	001
01	X	X
11	100	101
10	X	X

Table 1. An incompletely specified UCM table of the QCM.

The function can be completed as a *reversible* map since all output *care* values $\{000, 001, 100, 101\}$ are different. The table thus represents the set of learning examples, also called the *problem specification*. Then an *arbitrary* unitary transformation U satisfies all the *specified* transitions $U|000\rangle \to |000\rangle$, $U|001\rangle \to |001\rangle$, $U|110\rangle \to |100\rangle$ and $U|111\rangle \to |101\rangle$. Together, these transformations are a *valid solution* to the *learning problem* specified in Table 1. Using simplicity criteria, the circuit is reduced and its *UCM* unitary matrix is simplified as well (Miller et al., 2006).

3.2.1 The difference between classical and quantum learning

In the classical learning method the QCMs learn a deterministic function. In our probabilistic quantum learning, the QCM learns a unitary mapping to a quantum state that is quantum-deterministic only before the measurement. However the observer never knows to which classical state this deterministic state will collapse as the result of the measurement. Thus, when we design the network, we set certain constraints for the QCM's behaviour but we can only probabilistically predict how the QCM will behave within the constraints (Curtis and Meyer, 2004).

The QCM's UCM unitary control map represents the learned function using the quantum probabilistic learning. The *don't cares* are denoted by U_0 and U_1, where the subindex denotes the desired output value. The quantum probabilistic learning has similar results to standard probabilistic learning with the difference that the probabilities are calculated from quantum states, which are complex vectors.

Assume a single output function defined by the QCM's UCM table specifying the *desired* outputs as would result by observing values *0* and *1* on the QCM's quantum output in some special cases of the state of the environment. The UCM table contains *don't cares* and *cares*, and assuming there is a method to synthesize the cares, the problem that remains to be solved is the manner in which it is possible to specify the values of *don't cares*. The unitary operators used in the quantum probabilistic control based QCM network model are:

$$\left\{[NOT],[U],\left[U^{\dagger}\right],[CNOT],[controlled-U],\left[controlled-U^{\dagger}\right]\right\}. \tag{25}$$

How the *don't cares* are filled with respect to the QCM's learning method should be specified. For this, let $S_{out}=\{0,1,U_0,U_1\}$ be the set of all possible symbolic outputs of the given single output function. The $U_0=U|0\rangle$ and $U_1=U|1\rangle$ symbols represent quantum states, vectors, or complex numbers that correspond to measuring or observing the QCM's system in state $M(U_0)$ and $M(U_1)$, where M is the quantum measurement operator (Curtis and Meyer, 2004).

The QCM's expected input-output mapping can be changed by replacing the *controlled-U* operators by controlled-Hadamard gates. The well defined input values *0* and *1* remain the same; however the *don't care input* specifications can be mapped to four different symbols: $0,1,U_0,U_1$. The *X don't cares* will be replaced with $0,1,U_0$ or U_1. The well defined inputs remain the same, while the *don't cares* are mapped to one of the four possible values $X\rightarrow 0,1,U_0,U_1$. The probabilities of the output states depend directly on the *logic of the QCM* and thus on the quantum gates selected by the learning algorithm (Miller et al., 2006). We use the reversible quantum gates, CNOT, Controlled-U, and Controlled-$U^{\dagger}$ gates. In our quantum probabilistic based control system, if the controlled quantum bit is an eigenvalue of the unitary transformation, the behaviour is deterministic. Otherwise the behaviour is probabilistic, according to the rules of quantum measurement (Curtis and Meyer, 2004).

3.2.2 Deterministic solution to the QCM's learning

In that case, if the QCM has a global three-qubit state in superposition, for example for state $|110\rangle$, the transition can be expressed as follows:

$$|110\rangle\xrightarrow{U}\frac{1-i}{2}|101\rangle+\frac{1+i}{2}|111\rangle. \tag{26}$$

At the end of the transition, the first and last qubits are unaffected by the measurement process, but if we assume deterministic learning, the required quantum circuit also satisfies the incomplete function for a single qubit (Miller et al., 2006). The more detailed view of the implementation allows us to make the next analysis based on symbols $U, U^{\dagger}$, and their algebra

$$UU = NOT,\ U^{\dagger}U^{\dagger} = NOT,\ UU^{\dagger} = U^{\dagger}U = I. \tag{27}$$

The *deterministic* quantum circuit is shown in Fig. 14.

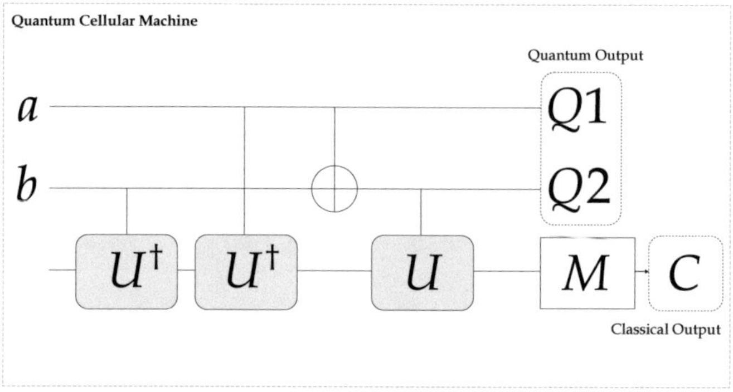

Fig. 14. A deterministic circuit to realize the learning of the QCM with incomplete function specification. The *don't cares* will be selected deterministically.

In Table 2, the example of analysis of the QCM's target signal C in the circuit from Fig. 14 is shown.

Target	0	1
Control: ab		
00	I	I
01	$UU^{\dagger}$	$UU^{\dagger}$
11	$U^{\dagger}U^{\dagger}$	$U^{\dagger}U^{\dagger}$
10	$U^{\dagger}U$	$U^{\dagger}U$

Table 2. Analysis of the QCM's target qubit in the circuit. The mapping of the UCM table for the incompletely defined specifications is deterministic.

Let us assume that the QCM gets an $|110\rangle$ input from the environment. The output of its quantum circuit can be derived as follows:

1. Since the second qubit is the control of the first $U^{\dagger}$ transformation, the QCM applies the *controlled-*$U^{\dagger}$ transformation on the third qubit.

$$\xrightarrow{controlled-U^{\dagger}} |11\rangle \frac{1-i}{\sqrt{2}}(|0\rangle + |1\rangle). \tag{28}$$

2. Since the first qubit is the control of the second $U^{\dagger}$ transformation, the QCM applies the *controlled-*$U^{\dagger}$ transformation on the third qubit.

$$\xrightarrow{controlled-U^{\dagger}} |110\rangle. \tag{29}$$

3. The QCM applies the *controlled-NOT* transformation:

$$\xrightarrow{CNOT} |101\rangle . \tag{30}$$

On the other hand, if the input is $|111\rangle$, then the output of the circuit is $|100\rangle$. As can be concluded from the results, the QCM generates the inverse of the target as the output only if $ab = 11$; otherwise it makes an identity transformation.

As we have seen, the QCM's quantum circuit realizes a deterministic output for input $|110\rangle$; on the other hand – as we will see here – it becomes quantum probabilistic for input $|100\rangle$. However, to achieve the quantum probabilistic behaviour of the QCM, we have to make a small modification on the circuit, as follows (Curtis and Meyer, 2004):

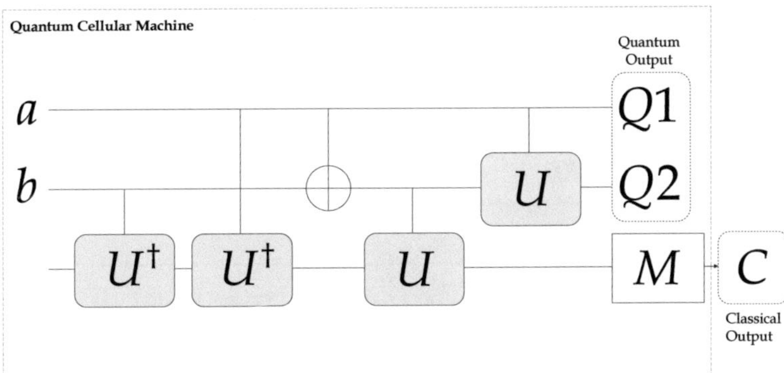

Fig. 15. The quantum probabilistic circuit.

Compared to the previous quantum circuit, we have added the *controlled-*U transformation to the circuit. As a result, after a measurement on the third qubit, the state of the second qubit becomes quantum probabilistic (Miller et al., 2006).

The new quantum circuit can generate *deterministic* output; however it also has quantum *probabilistic behaviour*. To see it, we analyze the QCM's transition for the input state $|100\rangle$ as follows.

1. Since the first qubit is the control of the $U^{\dagger}$ transformation, the QCM applies the *controlled-*$U^{\dagger}$ transformation on the third qubit.

$$\xrightarrow{controlled-U^{\dagger}} |10\rangle \frac{1-i}{\sqrt{2}}\left(|0\rangle + |1\rangle\right). \tag{31}$$

2. The QCM applies the *controlled-NOT* transformation:

$$\xrightarrow{CNOT} |11\rangle \frac{1-i}{\sqrt{2}}\left(|0\rangle + |1\rangle\right). \tag{32}$$

3. Then, the QCM applies the *controlled-*U transformation on the third qubit, since the CNOT gate has changed the value of its control qubit b:

$$\xrightarrow{controlled-U} |110\rangle . \tag{33}$$

Finally, the QCM applies the gate's *controlled-U* on the second qubit:

$$\begin{aligned}&\xrightarrow{controlled-U}|1\rangle\frac{1+i}{\sqrt{2}}(|0\rangle+|1\rangle)|0\rangle\\&\rightarrow\frac{1+i}{\sqrt{2}}(|100\rangle+|110\rangle).\end{aligned} \tag{34}$$

The original *three-to-one incompletely specified function* is mapped to a *reversible* quantum *three-by-three* circuit. The map of the deterministic circuit with incomplete function specification will have *probabilistic behaviour* from the multiple qubit measurement. The output value of the second qubit is not determined after the measurement made on the third qubit. This output can be used to control other parts of the network or to realize truly random behaviour in the network.

Target	0	1
Control: ab		
00	$\|000\rangle$	$\|001\rangle$
01	$\|010\rangle$	$\|011\rangle$
11	$\|1\rangle\left[\frac{1+i}{\sqrt{2}}(\|0\rangle+\|1\rangle)\right]\|1\rangle$	$\|1\rangle\left[\frac{1+i}{\sqrt{2}}(\|0\rangle+\|1\rangle)\right]\|0\rangle$
10	$\|1\rangle\left[\frac{1+i}{\sqrt{2}}(\|0\rangle+\|1\rangle)\right]\|0\rangle$	$\|1\rangle\left[\frac{1+i}{\sqrt{2}}(\|0\rangle+\|1\rangle)\right]\|1\rangle$

Table 3. The map of the deterministic circuit with incomplete function specification and quantum probabilistic behaviour.

The quantum control based QCM forms a quantum system exploiting the *superposition* of the state of the QCM with the state of the network environment. In the presented quantum probabilistic QCM network the focus is not on how the QCM is implemented with respect to its environment, but rather on the *strategies* for learning the QCM network behaviours based on quantum circuit structures (Miller et al., 2006).

3.3 Conclusion and future work

The QCM's internal self model modifies the classical commands and the logical behaviour of the QCM on different levels. The QCM's internal self model is generated on the lowest level; the expressed logical behaviour is based on quantum measurements. The proposed quantum model demonstrates the quantum mechanical based model's superiority to classical cellular automata based self-organizing networks. We constructed a real biologically inspired non-deterministic network model, based on quantum mechanics, allowing the QCM to use quantum level communication on a higher logical level.

As future work we would like to extend our novel quantum mechanical based control mechanism to other biologically inspired self-organizing structures and to publish simulation results on the convergence rate of our quantum probabilistic learning method.

4. Quantum learning algorithm based controller QCM

In this part we define the extended version of the QCM - called the *controller QCM* - and show that it can be used for solving hard problems, such as network controlling, routing, and network organizing, using very efficient quantum searching and quantum learning algorithms. We define quantum algorithms for controlling the truly quantum probabilistic network structure, and we demonstrate the performance of the quantum-learning based QCM over the classical network controlling solutions.

4.1 Introduction

In this part, we define the extended version of QCM as the main controller element. This QCM is able to interact with the other network components - using both quantum and classical information - and can dynamically reorganize the activities to serve the dynamic needs in an adaptive and goal-oriented way. Moreover, the QCM has a deep impact on the self-organizing capability of the network.

The main component of the quantum probabilistic self-organizing network structure is the *controller QCM*, which offers and uses services that adapt without any human interaction to the changes of environment of the network, and creates plans and a knowledge map. The knowledge map represents a snapshot of the current network state. The primary task of the controller QCM is to use and provide services. It monitors the internal and external environment of the self-organizing network's structure, adapts itself to the changing conditions, and knows its capabilities and how to adapt. The model consists of two parts. The common part contains the same functionalities as a common QCM. The specific part contains advanced functions, such as the implementation of the quantum-learning algorithm. The controller QCM uses quantum computing for the development of network controlling, routing, path finding, and other problems relating to the effectiveness of self-organizing. The elements of the quantum probabilistic self-organizing networks are other, simpler QCMs, without integrated advanced quantum searching and learning methods. In the QCM model, quantum mechanics and quantum computing act on the QCM's quantum registers and it modifies its output. The quantum based communication appears in two major forms in our quantum network model, since both the self-organizing processes in the network are truly random and the controlling and routing tasks are also solved quantum mechanically. We present the quantum mechanical based learning and controlling algorithm of the QCM component model, which is the core of the quantum probabilistic self-organizing framework.

The actual *part* of this chapter is organized as follows. First, we introduce the basic properties of the controller QCM. In the section, we describe the properties of the extended version of the QCM module. At the end of this part, we conclude with the results and benefits of our quantum mechanical based model.

4.2 Related work

The quantum searching algorithm was presented by Grover et al. for quantum database searching (Imre and Balazs, 2005), (Nielsen and Chuang, 2000). The effectiveness of quantum searching is based on a fundamental property of quantum information processing, the quantum parallelism. The problem of quantum searching was developed to solve the problem of identification of an item in an unsorted database with N elements. This kind of sorting problem generally requires $N/2$ steps in classical systems, and hence the complexity of the problem is $\mathcal{O}(N)$ classically. With the help of quantum information processing the searching can be solved with complexity $\mathcal{O}(\sqrt{N})$; hence, with the quantum based approach a quadratic increase can be achieved in the speed of the searching process (Imre and Balazs, 2005).

In this section we present an extended version of the QCM shown in the previous part of this chapter, using quantum searching and quantum learning algorithms to speed up the steps of self-organizing and other hard problems such as routing in self-organizing systems or path selection, and so on. One of the most important properties of quantum searching methods is that it can be implemented by elementary quantum circuit elements, and hence the implementation of the algorithm can be realized easily in practice. We implement a more advanced version of the quantum algorithm, compared to the original searching algorithm. We call it the quantum learning algorithm, and it is able to use the fundamental properties of quantum searching and can combine it with service and environment demands. The extended version of the QCM has the capability to control and sense the network and can find solutions for network-related problems using the quantum-searching based quantum learning method.

4.3 Problem discussion and motivation

The controller QCM reads the classical command from the self-organizing network, builds a map from the current network structure, and applies a unitary transform to modify the current state of the network. After the transformation the QCM measures the state of its final quantum register that affects the output. The actual state of the network model is stored in the QCM's initial quantum register. The result of the advanced quantum learning algorithm and the results of the quantum iteration processes are stored in the QCM's final quantum register, which then realizes a direct contact with the network. The structure of the network controller QCM has a different structure from the one presented in Section 2, since it is *equipped with advanced quantum-learning algorithms*. From an engineering point of view, the controller QCM is an extended version of the traditional QCM, equipped with advanced quantum learning methods. The traditional QCM is not implemented with the quantum-searching algorithm, hence its complexity is much higher than the controller QCMs.

In Fig. 16 we illustrated the decision mechanism of the controller QCM module. The input command is modified by the state of the internal quantum state, and the decisions are based on the result of the quantum learning algorithm. As can be concluded, the controller QCM can be viewed as an extended QCM with extended functions – such as quantum learning and quantum probabilistic decisions. The other parts of the self-organizing network structure can be realized by simpler QCMs, which are responsible only for simpler tasks such as self-organizing and so on.

The QCM uses the logical function to determine its output. The logical output is processed from the value of the QCM's final quantum register, which stores the result of the quantum learning algorithm. The result of the QCM's quantum probabilistic decision acts mainly on he network command language by rewriting the network structure.

In Fig. 17 we illustrate the connection between controller-QCMs and ordinary QCMs. The controller-QCMs have extended capabilities such as advanced quantum searching and learning methods. The ordinary QCMs communicate with each other and the controller-QCMs to realize the self-organizing network structure.

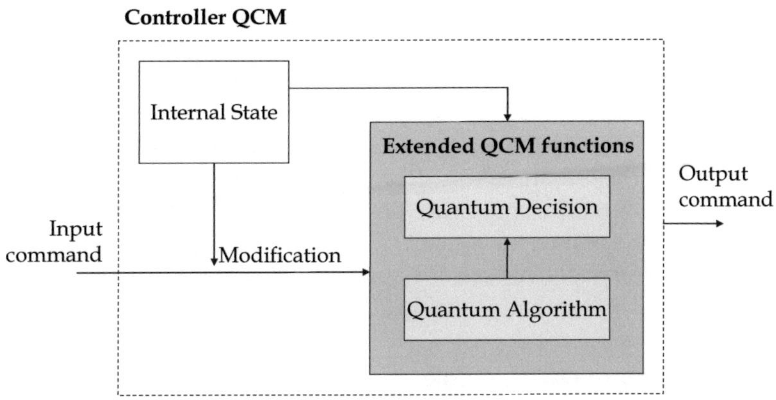

Fig. 16. The decision and output determination of the extended QCM.

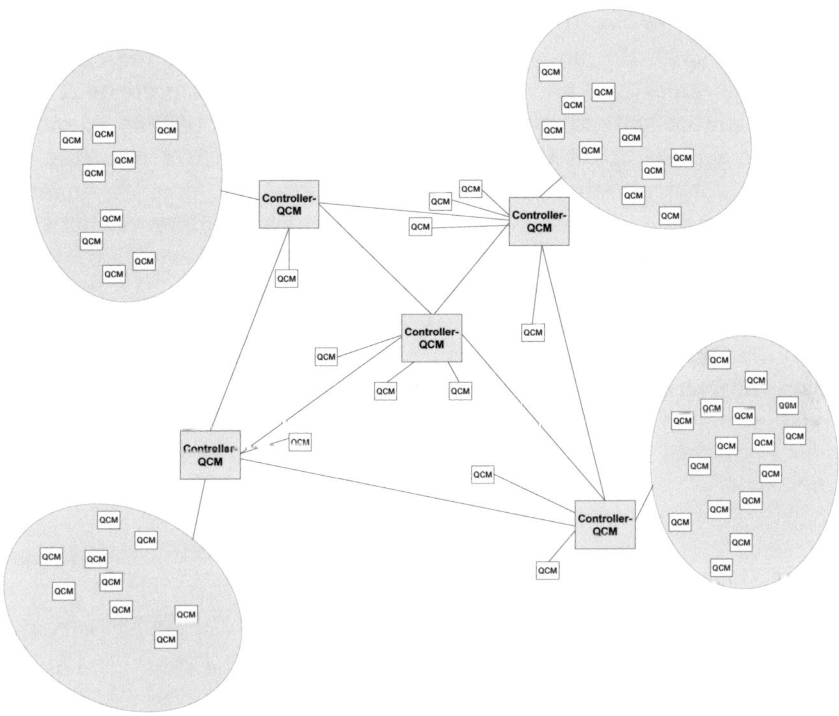

Fig. 17. The controlled self-organizing quantum probabilistic network structure.

To realize the controlling of the network, we implement a very efficient $\mathcal{O}\left(\sqrt{N}\right)$ quantum searching algorithm to control the self-organizing processes of the network and to find the best solution to the input command (Arrighi et al., 2007).

4.3.1 Extended QCM functions

The controller QCM senses and processes information from its external network environment. In this model, the external network is a quantum probabilistic self-organizing system. The QCM can also process quantum and classical information and accomplish deterministic and quantum probabilistic tasks. The information unit is a quantum bit, which can lie in the coherent superposition state of logical states zero and one, and thus it can simultaneously store zero and one. Using quantum bits, we can effectively speed up the solutions of the classical problems and even solve some hard problems that a classical computer cannot solve (Feynman, 1982). The key aspect behind the optimal decisions of QCM is the design of a high-efficiency searching algorithm. In our model, we use the ability of quantum parallel processing to design a corresponding quantum learning control algorithm, which can effectively reduce the complexity of solving problems and speed up information processing (Nielsen and Chuang, 2000).

4.3.2 Parallel processing of QCM module

As we mentioned before, our QCM is basically a complex quantum system, its state is also represented by the quantum state, and thus we encode all information according to quantum bits. The state of the QCM's internal $|\psi\rangle$ quantum state can be written into a superposition state as $|\psi\rangle = \alpha|0\rangle + \beta|1\rangle$, where α and β are complex coefficients and $|\alpha|^2 + |\beta|^2 = 1$. The states $|0\rangle$ and $|1\rangle$ are two orthogonal states; the eigenstates of $|\psi\rangle$ correspond to logic states zero and one. The $|\alpha|^2$ represents the occurrence probability of $|0\rangle$ when the quantum state is measured, and $|\beta|^2$ is the probability of obtaining result $|1\rangle$. The value of a classical bit is either zero or one; however a quantum state can be prepared in the coherent superposition state of zero and one. A quantum bit can simultaneously store zero and one, which is one of the main differences between quantum and classical information processing. If the QCM applies a unitary transformation U to a superposition state, the transformation will act on all eigenstates of the superposition state $|\psi\rangle$, and the output will be a new superposition state obtained by superposing the results of eigenstates. If the QCM processes function $f(x)$, the transformation U can simultaneously work out many different results for a certain input x.

The ability of strong parallel processing is a very important advantage of our QCM's module over traditional QCM. Let us consider an n-qubit quantum state which lies in a superposition state:

$$|\psi\rangle = \sum_{x=00\ldots0}^{11\ldots1} c_x |x\rangle, \tag{35}$$

where $\sum_{x=00\ldots0}^{11\ldots1} |c_x|^2 = 1$, and c_x are the complex coefficients. The state $|x\rangle$ has 2^n values; it contains all integers from 1 to 2^n. Since U is linear, processing function $f(x)$ can be expressed as follows:

$$U \sum_{x=00\ldots0}^{11\ldots1} c_x |x,0\rangle = \sum_{x=00\ldots0}^{11\ldots1} c_x U |x,0\rangle = \sum_{x=00\ldots0}^{11\ldots1} c_x U |x, f(x)\rangle, \tag{36}$$

where $|x,0\rangle$ represents the input joint state and $|x, f(x)\rangle$ is the output joint state. The controller QCM uses the superposition principle of quantum states, and hence with an n-qubit quantum register it can simultaneously process 2^n states.

4.4 Quantum circuits of quantum searching

In our quantum searching algorithm, the controller QCM updates the probability amplitudes of the quantum register according to a given reward value derived from the network environment. The quantum searching process can be implemented using the Hadamard-transformations and conditional phase shift operations. Through the Hadamard-gate, a quantum bit in the state $|0\rangle$ or $|1\rangle$ is transformed into a superposition state of two states as

$$H|0\rangle = \frac{1}{\sqrt{2}}(|0\rangle + |1\rangle) \text{ or } H|1\rangle = \frac{1}{\sqrt{2}}(|0\rangle - |1\rangle), \tag{37}$$

that is, the magnitude of the amplitude in each state is $\frac{1}{\sqrt{2}}$, but the phase of the amplitude in the state $|1\rangle$ is inverted. Let us consider a quantum system described by n quantum bits which has 2^n possible states. To prepare an equally weighted superposition state, the controller QCM performs the transformation H on each qubit independently. The state transition matrix representing this operation will be of the dimensions $2^n \times 2^n$ and can be implemented by n Hadamard-gates. The process can be represented as:

$$H^{\otimes n}\left|\overbrace{00\ldots0}^{n}\right\rangle = \frac{1}{\sqrt{2^n}} \sum_{a=00\ldots0}^{\overbrace{11\ldots1}^{n}} |x\rangle. \tag{38}$$

According to the above method, we can accomplish the initialization of state and action. To realize quantum searching, the controller QCM has to make a Hadamard-transformation on the initial quantum register. In the searching process, it selects the solutions from the quantum register using probability amplitude amplification, and finally applies a Hadamard-transformation to obtain the answer sought for the input problem.

In Fig. 18 we illustrated the general scheme of the controller QCM's searching process. The classical network input is stored in its internal quantum register, and the Hadamard-transformations and the searching process are defined only in quantum space.

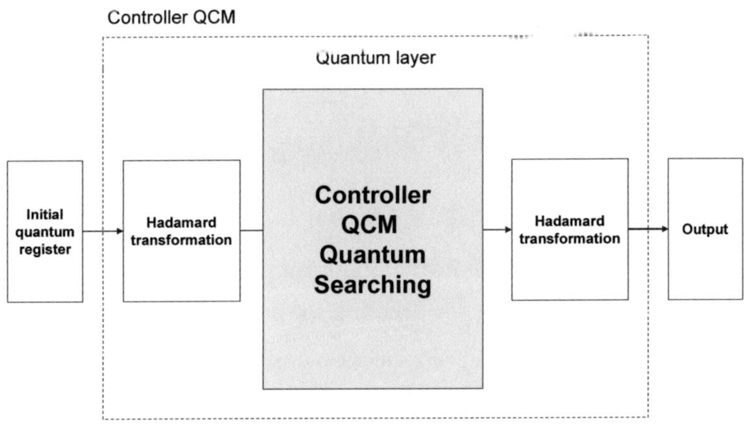

Fig. 18. The general model of the controller QCM's quantum searching module

The conditional phase-shift operation is an important element to carry out the quantum searching iteration. The phase-shift transformation ϕ for a two-state system can be expressed as

$$\phi = \begin{pmatrix} e^{i\phi_1} & 0 \\ 0 & e^{i\phi_2} \end{pmatrix}, \tag{39}$$

where $i = \sqrt{-1}$ and ϕ_1, ϕ_2 are arbitrary real numbers. The conditional phase-shift operation does not change the probability of each state, since the square of the absolute value of the amplitude in each state is the same. To update probability amplitudes we reinforce the selected decision corresponding to a larger reward value through repeating the quantum searching process T times. We initialize the action

$$f(s) = \left|x_s^{(n)}\right\rangle = \frac{1}{\sqrt{2^n}} \sum_{a=00\ldots0}^{\overbrace{11\ldots1}^{n}} |x\rangle. \tag{40}$$

Then we construct a reflection transform

$$U_x = 2\left|x_s^{(n)}\right\rangle\left\langle x_s^{(n)}\right| - I, \tag{41}$$

which preserves $\left|x_s^{(n)}\right\rangle$, but flips the sign of any vector orthogonal to $\left|x_s^{(n)}\right\rangle$.

Geometrically, if U_a acts on an arbitrary vector, it preserves the component along $\left|x_s^{(n)}\right\rangle$ and flips the component in the hyperplane orthogonal to $\left|x_s^{(n)}\right\rangle$, and thus it can be viewed as an operation of inversion about the mean value of the amplitude (Nielsen and Chuang, 2000). The controller QCM exchanges $\left|x_s^{(n)}\right\rangle$ with the k-th computational basis state $\left|x_k\right\rangle$, and constructs another reflection transformation $U_{x_k} = I - 2\left|x_k\right\rangle\left\langle x_k\right|$. Thus we can form a unitary transformation

$$U_I = U_s U_k = U_x U_{x_k}. \tag{42}$$

It repeatedly applies the transformation U_I on $\left|x_s^{(n)}\right\rangle$, and thus it can enhance the probability amplitude of the k-th path in the quantum probabilistic self-organizing network environment, denoted by $\left|x_k\right\rangle$, while suppressing the amplitude of all other actions.

In Fig. 19 we illustrated the realization of reflection and rotation transformations. The initial state is denoted by $|\psi\rangle$, and the reflected state along the L-axis is denoted by $|\psi'\rangle$. The angle of the rotation process is denoted by θ.

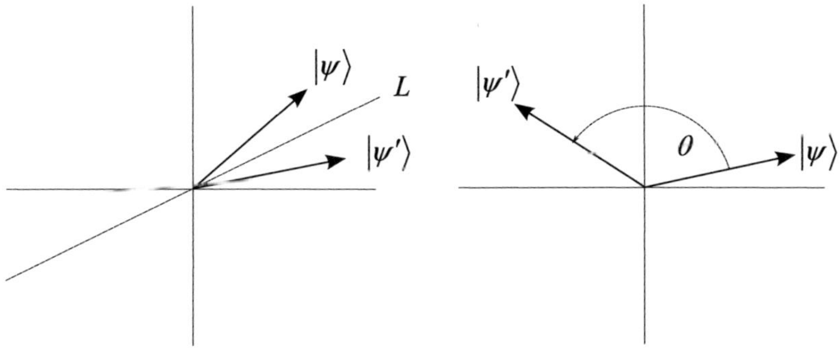

Fig. 19. The geometrical representation of reflection and rotation.

This process can be viewed as a rotation in a two-dimensional space, and the initial decision $f(s)$ can be expressed as (Nielsen and Chuang, 2000):

$$f(s)=\left|x_s^{(n)}\right\rangle=\frac{1}{\sqrt{2}}\left|x_k\right\rangle+\sqrt{\frac{2^n-1}{2^n}}|\varphi\rangle, \tag{43}$$

where $|\varphi\rangle=\sqrt{\frac{1}{2^n-1}}\sum_{a\neq a_k}|x\rangle$. We define the rotation angle θ satisfying $\sin\theta=\frac{1}{\sqrt{2^n}}$, and thus

$$f(s)=\left|x_s^{(n)}\right\rangle=\sin\theta\left|x_k\right\rangle+\cos\theta|\varphi\rangle. \tag{44}$$

The controller QCM applies the quantum searching iteration U_I T times on $\left|x_s^{(n)}\right\rangle$, and thus

$$U_I^T\left|x_s^{(n)}\right\rangle=\sin((2T+1)\theta)\left|x_k\right\rangle+\cos((2T+1)\theta)|\varphi\rangle. \tag{45}$$

By repeating the quantum iteration operator, the controller QCM can reinforce the probability amplitude of the corresponding decision according to the feedback value (Gyongyosi et al., 2009). The QCM's searching algorithm only applies the quantum iteration operator to reinforce the possible paths in the network environment.

4.4.1 General description of searching problem

In classical computation, an unstructured searching problem of *searching space N*, the classical algorithm complexity is $\mathcal{O}(N)$. In our network it is an important task to search for a suitable decision from quantum probabilistic self-organizing network space, based on the current state of the QCM.

If the complexity of the state or *decision space* is $\mathcal{O}(N)$, the problem complexity in a traditional QCM is $\mathcal{O}(N^2)$; since it is not equipped with the quantum searching algorithm. The extended QCM can reduce the complexity to $\mathcal{O}(N\sqrt{N})$ by using a quantum searching algorithm. It means, that for the *searching space N*, the QCM has to apply only $\sqrt{N}$ steps to find the solution, instead of the classical N steps. Thus, if the QCM has N possible actions, where $2^n \geq N \geq 2^{n-1}$, we can prepare an equally weighted superposition quantum state

$$|s\rangle = \frac{1}{\sqrt{2^n}} \sum_{i=1}^{2^n} |i\rangle. \tag{46}$$

This quantum state can be accomplished by applying the Hadamard-transformation to each quantum bit of the n-qubit state $|00\ldots00\rangle$. Then, we construct a reflection transform

$$U_s = 2|s\rangle\langle s| - I. \tag{47}$$

If the QCM applies U_s on an arbitrary vector, it preserves the component along $|s\rangle$ and flips the component orthogonal to $|s\rangle$, and thus if we apply U_s to $|\psi_0\rangle$ we get

$$\begin{aligned} U_s|\psi_0\rangle = 2|s\rangle\langle s|\psi_0\rangle - |\psi_0\rangle = 2|s\rangle\sqrt{2^n}\frac{1}{2^n}\sum_{i=1}^{2^n} x_i - |\psi_0\rangle = \\ 2\frac{1}{\sqrt{2^n}}\sum_{i=1}^{2^n}|i\rangle\sqrt{2^n}\frac{1}{2^n}\sum_{i=1}^{2^n} x_i - \sum_{i=1}^{2^n} x_i|i\rangle = \sum_{i=1}^{2^n}\left(2\frac{1}{2^n}\sum_{i=1}^{2^n} x_i - x_i\right)|i\rangle. \end{aligned} \tag{48}$$

Then, we use another reflection transform

$$U_k = -2|k\rangle\langle k| + I, \tag{49}$$

where $|k\rangle$ is the k-th eigenstate, and by applying U_k to state $|\psi_0\rangle$, we obtain

$$U_k|\psi_0\rangle = -2|k\rangle\langle k|\psi_0\rangle + |\psi_0\rangle = -2|k\rangle x_k + |\psi_0\rangle = \sum_{i=1, i\neq k}^{2^n} x_i|i\rangle - x_k|k\rangle. \tag{50}$$

The transformation U_k only changes the amplitude's sign of $|k\rangle$ in the superposition quantum state, and thus we can form a U_I unitary quantum iteration transformation:

$$U_I = U_s U_k. \tag{51}$$

If the QCM repeatedly applies the iteration transformation U_I on $|\psi_0\rangle$, it enhances the probability amplitude of $|k\rangle$, while suppressing the amplitude of all other states $|i \neq k\rangle$. By applying the iteration transformation enough times, the QCM can make state $|\psi_0\rangle$ collapse into state $|k\rangle$ with a probability of almost 1. In the description of the iteration process, we define an angle θ, which satisfies the equation $\sin^2\theta = \frac{1}{2^n}$. After applying the iteration U_I to $|\psi_0\rangle$ j times, the probability amplitude of state $|k\rangle$ becomes

$$x_k^j = \sin\left((2j+1)\theta\right). \tag{52}$$

The QCM's rotation process is illustrated in Fig. 20. In every iteration step, the QCM rotates state $|\psi\rangle$ into $G|\psi\rangle$.

4.4.2 Changing the probability amplitude through the Iterations

The "good" and "bad" answers to the input problem are denoted by basis states $|A\rangle$ and $|B\rangle$, respectively. In every iteration step, the QCM tries to get closer to the good answer, denoted by state $|A\rangle$.

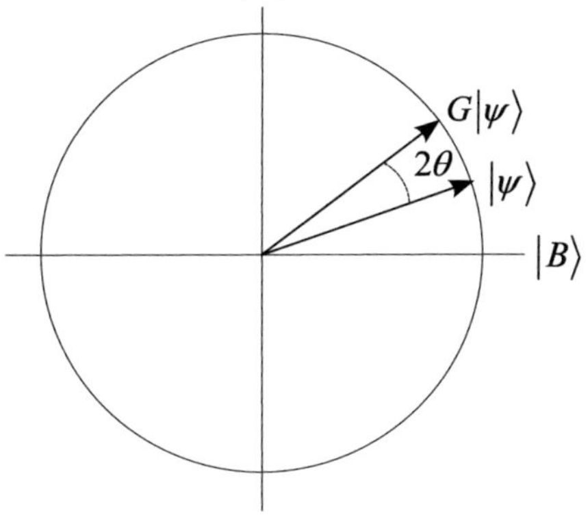

Fig. 20. In every iteration step, the QCM rotates the initial state by a given phase.

If the QCM applies the iteration U_I to $|\psi_0\rangle$ $j=\frac{\pi-2\theta}{4\theta}$ times, then $(2j+1)\theta\approx\frac{\pi}{2}$, and thus

$$x_k^j=\sin\left(\frac{\pi}{2}\right)=1, \tag{53}$$

However, the QCM must perform an integer number of iterations (Nielsen and Chuang, 2000), and thus we have to calculate with some probability of failure, which is no more than $1/2^N$, if the QCM performs the iteration U_I $\operatorname{int}\left[\frac{\pi}{4\theta}\right]$ times.

In Fig. 21 we illustrated the searching process as a series of different rotations. The angle between two lines L_1 and L_2 is θ. Rotation of state $|\psi\rangle$ by angle 2θ can be realized by two reflections. We reflect $|\psi\rangle$ first about L_1 and then about L_2, and we can conclude that state $|\psi\rangle$ is rotated by angle 2θ.

The QCM uses quantum searching to make the optimal decision, and the theoretical results show that QCM can reduce the complexity of $\mathcal{O}(N^2)$ in traditional QCM to

$$\mathcal{O}(N\sqrt{N}) \tag{54}$$

using the quantum searching algorithm. If N is large the QCM can find the optimal decision with a high probability of $1-\mathcal{O}\left(\frac{1}{N}\right)$.

Using the quantum iteration, the QCM can find the needed result with a probability of almost 1 in $\sqrt{N}$ steps. As we can conclude, the QCM dramatically reduces the complexity of the searching process, and it can make a suitable decision based on the current state of the QCM.

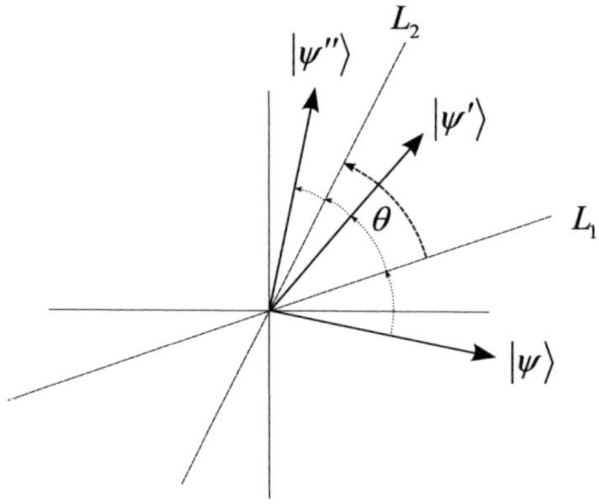

Fig. 21. At the end of the iteration process, the QCM rotates the initial state close to the right basis state.

4.5 Optimal QCM decisions

In the searching problem, the QCM wants to find a logical path from a given network node A to network node B in the network environment, while no available data source tells it how to achieve the goal. The QCM must accumulate experience by itself and become more intelligent through learning from its self-organizing network environment. At a certain iteration step, the QCM observes the state of the environment S_t, inside and outside the QCM.

The QCM makes a decision d_t in which the QCM chooses a path in the network environment, and afterwards the QCM receives feedback g_{t+1} which reflects how good that selected path is. The goal of the QCM decision is to realize a mapping from states to decisions, and to make a connection from logical state A to logical state B in the quantum probabilistic self-organizing network environment, with a minimum cost. The QCM makes the decisions based on the policy

$$\pi : S \times \cup_{i \in S} D_{(i)} \to [0,1], \tag{55}$$

so that the expected (E) sum of the discounted feedback of each state will be maximized (Nielsen and Chuang, 2000):

$$\begin{aligned} V_{(s)}^{\pi} &= E\left\{ g_{t+1} + \gamma g_{t+2} + \gamma^2 g_{t+3} + \ldots \middle| s_t = s, \pi \right\} = E\left[g_{t+1} + \gamma V_{(s_{t+1})}^{\pi} \middle| s_t = s, \pi \right] \\ &= \sum_{d \in D_s} \pi(s,d) \left[g_s^d + \gamma \sum_{s'} p_{ss'}^d V_{(s')}^{\pi} \right], \end{aligned} \tag{56}$$

where $\gamma \in [0,1]$ is the discount factor and $\pi(s,d)$ is the probability of selecting a given path in the self-organizing structure. The output of the path selection is based on decision d

according to state s. Under policy π, the probability of state transition is $p_{ss'}^{d} = \Pr\{s_{t+1} = s' | s_t = s, d_t = d\}$ and the expected one-step feedback is $g_s^d = E\{g_{t+1} | s_t = s, d_t = d\}$. The QCM's quantum searching algorithm could help to find an optimal logical path from network node A to node B using the effects of quantum mechanics. The output of the controller QCM is propagated back to the classical network layer as we have illustrated in Fig. 22.

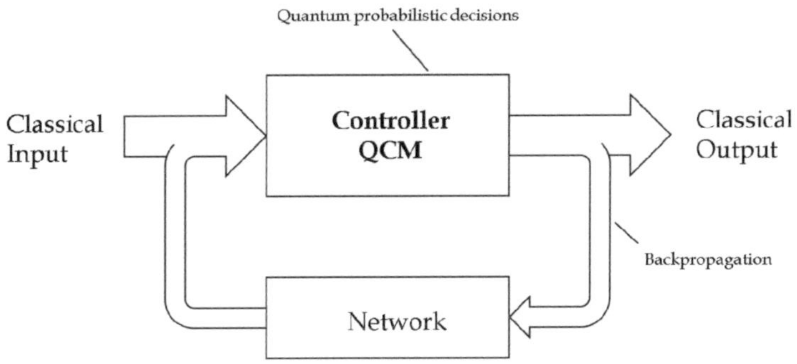

Fig. 22. The QCM communicates with the classical network layer.

The QCM can be represented as a dynamical quantum system which is controlled by the classical network layer (Gyongyosi et al., 2009).

4.5.1 Finding the optimal solution

The output of the QCM is based on a state-decision pair $\{State(t), Decision(t)\}$. The QCM's quantum decision process uses a scalar value, named feedback, to reflect how good that selected path is.

We propose a novel quantum learning method inspired by quantum superposition and quantum parallelism. Let N_S and N_d be the number of states and decisions of the QCM, and let m,n be numbers which are characterized by the following equations:

$$N_S \leq 2^m \leq 2N_S,\ N_d \leq 2^n \leq 2N_d. \tag{57}$$

The QCM uses m and n quantum bits to represent state set $S = \{s\}$ and decision set $D = \{d\}$. The learning procedure was inspired by the superposition principle of quantum states and quantum parallel computation. The occurrence probability of the eigenvalue is denoted by the probability amplitude of the quantum state, which is updated according to feedback. To realize the searching process, the QCM first initializes state $\left|s^{(m)}\right\rangle = \sum_{s=00\ldots0}^{\overbrace{11\ldots1}^{m}} c_S |s\rangle$, thus mapping from states to decisions as $f(s) = \pi : S \rightarrow D$, where $f(s) = \left|d_s^{(n)}\right\rangle = \sum_{a=00\ldots0}^{\overbrace{11\ldots1}^{n}} c_d |d\rangle$, and c_s, c_d are the probability amplitudes of state $|s\rangle$ and decision $|d\rangle$.

In the learning process, the QCM initializes the state and decision to the equal superposition state $\left|s^{(m)}\right\rangle$ as follows:

$$\left|s^{(m)}\right\rangle = \frac{1}{\sqrt{2^m}} \sum_{s=00\ldots0}^{\overbrace{11\ldots1}^{m}} |s\rangle, \tag{58}$$

with map function

$$f(s) = \left|d_s^{(n)}\right\rangle = \frac{1}{\sqrt{2^n}} \sum_{s=00\ldots0}^{\overbrace{11\ldots1}^{n}} |d\rangle. \tag{59}$$

After the initialization phase, the QCM repeats for all states

$$\left|s^{(m)}\right\rangle = \sum_{s=00\ldots0}^{11\ldots1} c_S |s\rangle = \frac{1}{\sqrt{2^m}} \sum_{s=00\ldots0}^{\overbrace{11\ldots1}^{m}} |s\rangle \tag{60}$$

the following algorithm:

Algorithm

1. Observe $f(s) = \left|d_s^{(n)}\right\rangle$ and get decision $|d\rangle$;
2. Take decision $|d\rangle$ and observe next state $\left|s'^{(m)}\right\rangle$ and reward g from the network
   2.1. The QCM updates state value $V(s)$:
   $V(s) \leftarrow V(s) + \alpha\left(g + \gamma V(s') - V(s)\right).$
3. Update probability amplitudes by repeating the quantum searching iteration U_I T times:
   $U_I^T \left|d_s^{(n)}\right\rangle = \left[U_x U_{x_k}\right]^T \left|d_s^{(n)}\right\rangle$, and $c_x \leftarrow e^{\lambda(r+V(s'))} c_x$.

The initial register of the QCM is illustrated in Fig. 23. In the initial phase, the QCM's quantum register contains

$$|\psi\rangle = H|0\rangle = \frac{1}{\sqrt{N}} \sum_{x=0}^{N-1} |x\rangle, \tag{61}$$

where every state has the same probability amplitude $\frac{1}{\sqrt{N}}$.

In Fig. 24 we illustrate the QCM's quantum register after the iteration steps of the searching process. The state which represents the answer to the question of the QCM has higher

probability while the "bad" states have lower probability amplitudes than the average probability amplitude in the initial quantum register.
The QCM's quantum searching algorithm is inspired by the superposition principle of quantum states and the power of parallel quantum computations.

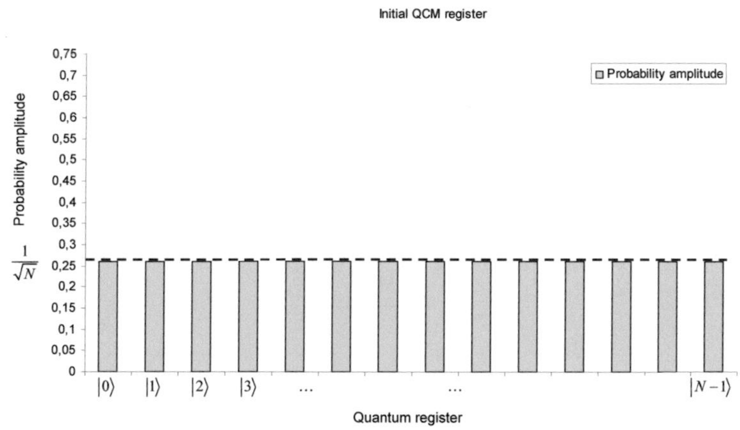

Fig. 23. The probability amplitudes of the QCM's initial quantum register.

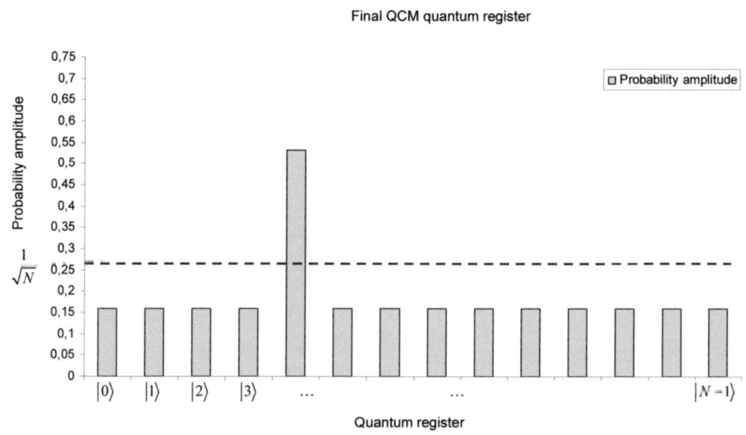

Fig. 24. The probability amplitudes of the QCM's states after the quantum searching process.

4.6 Numerical analysis

Our numerical analysis is based on the shortest path problem, in which the QCM has to find the shortest path in the network environment from communication element A to network element B. The problem can be stated as a searching problem in an unsorted database.
In the numerical analysis we compare the performance of traditional QCM and QCM. The QCM has to find the shortest path in the network from a given network element to a given network component, determined by the classical network command. The QCM puts the initial input network command into a quantum register, and it applies the quantum searching. The searching process is based on the classical input command and the QCM's internal state. The internal state describes the actual network state, and the quantum

searching algorithm seeks the best solution which describes the shortest path between the network elements.
In Fig. 25 we illustrate the inputs of the QCM's searching module.

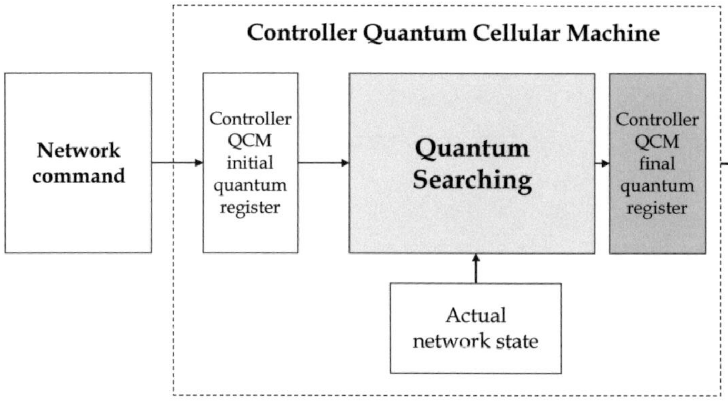

Fig. 25. The realization of the QCM's quantum searching process.

In the numerical analysis, we have assumed that the *shortest path* between nodes *A* and *B* defined in the input command contains *20 network nodes*.
In Fig. 26 we illustrate the number of required steps as function iterations. As we can conclude, the traditional QCM converges after 2500 steps, while the QCM finds the optimal path after 20 steps.

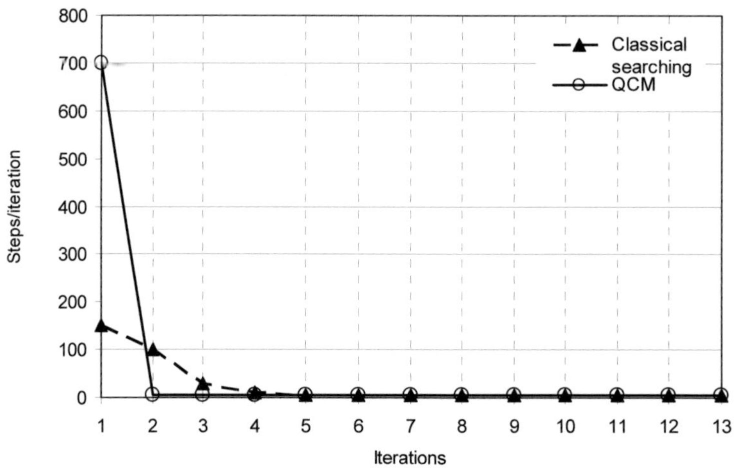

Fig. 26. The number of iterations required to find the optimal solution with traditional and extended QCM.

The QCM converges very fast to the optimal solution; however in the initial phase of the searching process, the number of steps per iteration is significantly higher. We can conclude that in the initial phase the QCM has higher uncertainty than the traditional QCM. The QCM finds the solution exponentially faster, and can find the solution much faster than the classical implementation. From the simulation results, we can conclude that the QCM's

quantum searching method needs only a few iteration steps to find the optimal way in the network environment.
The numerical results for the number of steps per iteration with traditional QCM are illustrated in Fig. 27.

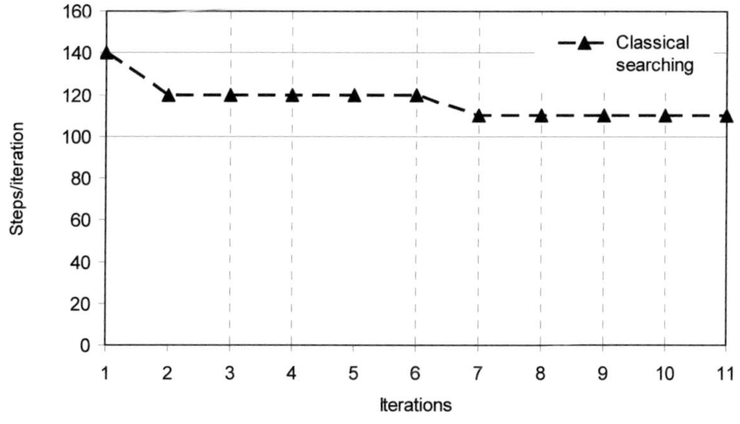

Fig. 27. The required number of classical searches after 50 iterations is still much higher than the optimal one.

We conclude that the quantum searching based QCM converges much faster than the classical one and the speed of the iteration process increments dramatically.

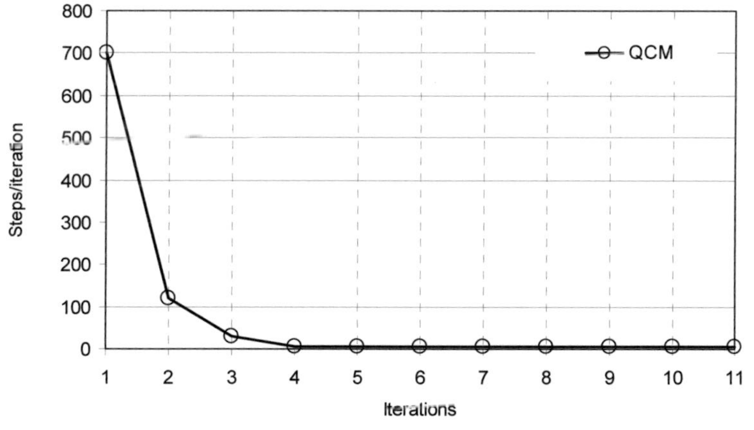

Fig. 28. The QCM finds the solution after 20 iterations, while the classical solution converges only after 2500 iterations.

From our numerical results we can conclude that the QCM module can help to improve he performance of truly random networks such as the described quantum probabilistic self-organizing networks and the overall performance of quantum probabilistic self-organizing communication systems and future Internet services.

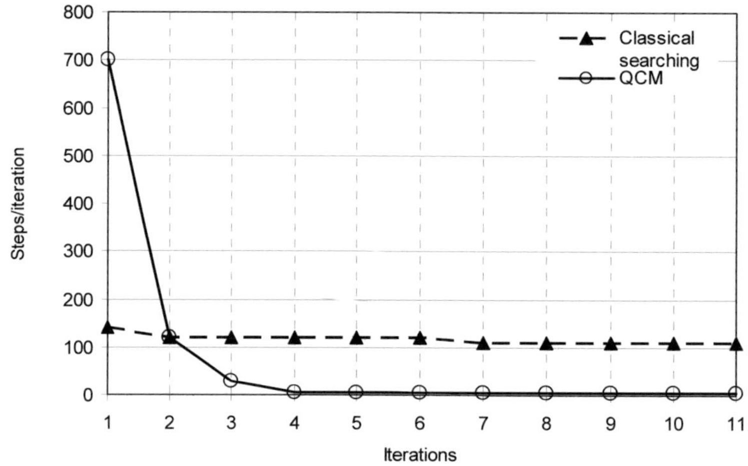

Fig. 29. Comparison of the performance of classical searching and QCM.

The QCM module can be used to dramatically speed up network controlling and it can be integrated efficiently into classical architectures.

4.7 Conclusion and future work

The QCM's internal self model modifies the classical commands and the logical behaviour of the QCM on different levels. The QCM's internal self model is generated on the lowest level, and the expressed logical behaviour is based on quantum measurements.
In this part we constructed a truly random non-deterministic network model based on quantum mechanics, allowing the QCM to use quantum level communication and quantum searching. The speed of QCM decision mechanisms can be increased using powerful parallel computing and fast searching ability. In our model, we integrate quantum searching to find the best solution to the given problem, encoded in the input network command of the QCM. In the numerical analysis we showed that the quantum communication layer could improve the performance of classical systems. The performance of the communication elements of quantum probabilistic self-organizing networks could be increased dramatically by quantum searching. The QCM's searching algorithm is based on the superposition principle of quantum states, whose behaviour cannot be described classically.

5. Conclusions

Quantum computing offers fundamentally new solutions in the field of computer science. The classical biologically inspired self-organizing systems have increasing complexity and these constructions do not seem to be suitable for handling the service demands of the near future. The cell-organized, quantum mechanics based cellular automata models have many advantages over classical models and circuits. As we have seen, for a quantum cellular machine, every cell is a finite-dimensional quantum system with unitary transformations, and there is a difference between the axiomatic structure of classical and quantum versions of cellular automata. To see clearly the advantages of quantum information processing based solutions, we have discussed the parallel address mechanisms of quantum cellular machines.

In Section 2, we have given a brief overview of quantum mechanics, such as the definition of a quantum bit, the postulates of quantum mechanics, and the basics of quantum algorithms. In Sections 3 and 4, we have exhibited an application of a quantum cellular automata model to a quantum probabilistically controlled, self-organizing biological network structure. The network control mechanisms of this self-organizing structure are performed by an extended version of a quantum cellular machine, with integrated quantum searching processes and built-in quantum learning algorithms. In the proposed searching process, a QCM selects the solutions from the quantum register, using probability amplitude amplification, and finally applies a Hadamard-transformation, to get the searched-for answer to the input problem. As we have presented, the performance of the communication of self-organizing biological networks could be increased dramatically by quantum searching. The QCM's searching algorithm is based on the superposition principle of quantum states, which behavior cannot be described classically.

As future work we would like to extend our quantum learning algorithm to other network elements, and we would like to integrate our method into truly random self-organizing networks.

6. References

Arrighi, P.; Nesme, V. & Werner, R. (2007). N-dimensional quantum cellular automata. 0711.3975.

Benioff, P. (1980). The computer as a physical system: A microscopic quantum mechanical hamiltonian model of computers as represented by Turing machines. *Journal of Statistical Physics*, 22:563–591.

Curtis, D. & Meyer, D. (2004). Towards quantum template matching, pp. 134–141.

Dam, W. (1996). Quantum cellular automata. Master's thesis, University of Nijmegen.

Feynman, R. (1982). Simulating physics with computers. *International Journal of Theoretical Physics*, 21:467–488.

Gardner, M. (1970). "Mathematical Games: The fantastic combinations of John Conway's new solitaire game "Life"". *Scientific American* 223: 120–123

Grössing, G. & Zeilinger, A. (1988). Quantum cellular automata. *Complex Syst.*, 2:197–208.

Gyongyosi, L.; Bacsardi, L. & Imre, S. (2009). Novel Approach for Quantum Mechanical Based Autonomic Communication, In *FUTURE COMPUTING 2009 Proceedings*, The First International Conference on Future Computational Technologies and Applications, pp. 586-590., Athen, Greece.

Imre, S. & Balazs, F. (2005). *Quantum Computing and Communications – An Engineering Approach*, Published by John Wiley and Sons Ltd.

Margolus, N. (1991). Parallel quantum computation. In: W. H. Zurek, editor, *Complexity, Entropy, and the Physics of Information, Santa Fe Institute Series*, pages 273–288. Addison Wesley, Redwood City, CA.

Meyer, D. A. (1996). From quantum cellular automata to quantum lattice gases. *Journal of Statistical Physics*, 85:551–574.

Miller, D. M.; Maslov, D. & Dueck, G. W. (2006). Synthesis of quantum multiple-valued circuits, *Journal of Multiple-Valued Logic and Soft Computing*, vol. 12, no. 5-6, pp. 431–450.

Neumann, J. (1966). *Theory of Self-Reproducing Automata*. University of Illinois Press, Champaign, IL, USA.

Nielsen, M. A. & Chuang, I. L. (2000). *Quantum Computation and Quantum Information*, (Cambridge University Press.

Perez-Delgado, C. A. & Cheung, D. (2005). Models of quantum cellular automata.

Richter & Werner. (1996). Ergodicity of quantum cellular automata. *Journal of Statistical Physics*, 82:963–998.

Toffoli, T. & Margolus, N. H. (1990). Invertible cellular automata: A review. *Physica D: Nonlinear Phenomena*, 45:229–253.

Toth, G. & Lent, C. S. (2001). Quantum computing with quantum-dot cellular automata. *Physical Review A*, 63:052315.

Vollbrecht, K. G. H. & Cirac (2008), J. I. Quantum simulators, continuous-time automata, and translationally invariant systems. *Phys. Rev. Lett.*, 100:010501, 2008.

Watrous, J. (1995). On one-dimensional quantum cellular automata. In: *Proceedings of the 36th Annual Symposium on Foundations of Computer Science*, pages 528–537.

Wootters, W. K. & Zurek, W. H. (1982). A single quantum cannot be cloned. *Nature*, 299:802–803.

7

Quantum-Chemical Design of Molecular Quantum-Dot Cellular Automata (QCA): A New Approach from Frontier Molecular Orbitals

Ken Tokunaga
General Education Department, Faculty of Engineering, Kogakuin University
Japan

1. Introduction

Recently, research and development of next-generation devices have been very active (1). Quantum-dot cellular automata (QCA) (2) which is constructed from many quantum dot cells (QDC, Fig. 1) is one of such new-generation devices. The QCA devices such as a majority logic gate and a signal transmission wire (Fig. 2) are expected to achieve a dramatic saving of energy and an increase in processing speed of computing since these devices are free from a current flow. Successful operations of several QCA devices have been already demonstrated (3; 4). However, for improvement in operation temperature and size of the QCA devices, the idea of molecular quantum-dot cellular automata (molecular QCA) devices (5), in which a QDC constructed from small metallic dots is replaced by a single molecule, was proposed. Toward the experimental operation of molecular QCA devices, syntheses of tetranuclear complexes (6–10) and simplified dinuclear complexes (11; 12), and single-molecule observation of the dinuclear complexes (13–16) have been paid attention. However, the capacity of molecular QCA devices for molecular computing is still not clear.

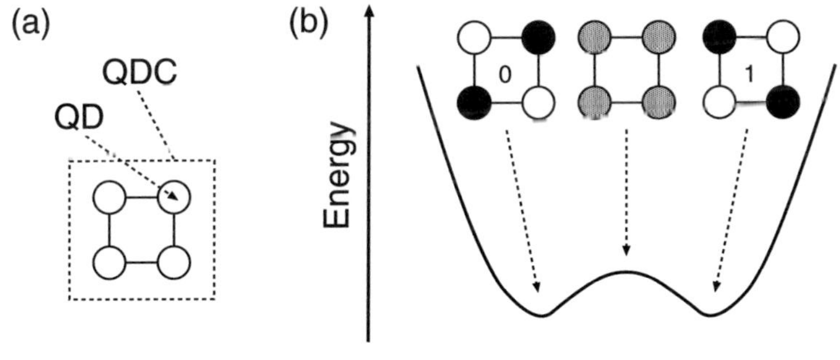

Fig. 1. (a) Quantum dot (QD) and quantum-dot cell (QDC) constructed from four QDs. (b) Schematic energy curve of two localized degenerate states, "0" and "1", and one delocalized transition state of QDC after injection of two electrons into QDC. Charge of open circles is positive relative to that of filled circles. In the transition state, charges of four dots are all equivalent.

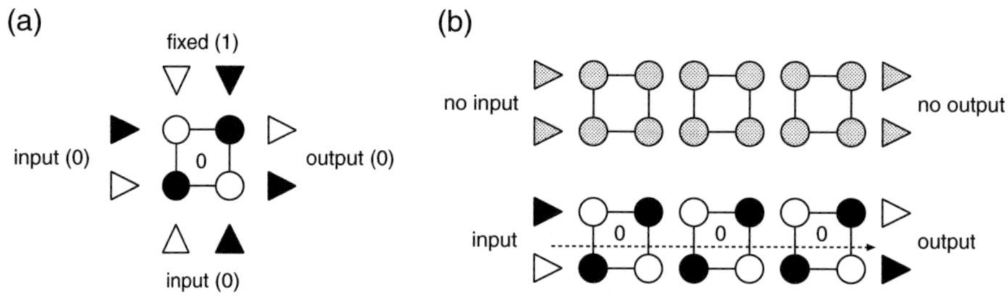

Fig. 2. Examples of QCA devices constructed from many QDCs: (a) QCA logic gate (OR gate) and (b) QCA signal transmission wire.

Braun-Sand and Wiest (17; 18) have reported theoretical studies on the electronic response of Ru dinuclear complexes to Li^+ in order to propose molecular QCA candidates. Lent *et al.* took up hydrocarbons with allyl end-groups (19; 20) and tetranuclear complex (21). In these studies, however, only the static response of molecular QCA to the switch of input was focused, and dynamic properties such as signal transmission time after the switch had not been discussed. About this point, Timler and Lent (22), and Lu and Lent (23) have reported the dynamic behavior of multi-cellular systems using model Hamiltonian. However, the detailed discussion about a relation between the electronic structure and dynamic properties had not been made in their studies. For understanding the behavior and performance of molecular QCA devices and development of high-efficient devices, it is necessary to clear the relation.

Very recently, I have proposed the simple method for an analysis of dynamic behavior of QCA devices, taking Creutz-Taube complexes $[L_5M\text{-}BL\text{-}ML_5]^{n+}$ (M=Ru, BL=pyrazine(**py**) and 4,4′-bipyridine(**bpy**), L=NH_3, n=5) as examples (24), based on the methods proposed by Remacle and Levine (25; 26). These analyses are all based on the simple one electron theories, density functional theory (DFT) and Hartree-Fock theory (HF). Time evolution of the wave function is expressed by the *initial* and *final* stationary states. *Initial* wave function is expanded by *final* wave function. Using this method, main properties concerning the signal transmission such as the signal period T, the signal amplitude A, and the signal transmission time t_{st} (see Fig. 3) can be interpreted as follows (24):

- Signal period (T) is inverse proportional to an orbital energy gap, $\Delta\varepsilon_{HL}$, between HOMO (the highest occupied molecular orbital, H) and LUMO (the lowest unoccupied molecular orbital, L) of the *final* stationary state.
- Signal amplitude (A) is proportional to an overlap integral, $d_{LH'}$, between HOMO of the *initial* stationary state (H') and LUMO of the *final* stationary state (L).
- Signal transmission time (t_{st}) is determined depending on the balance of A and T.

This method has advantage that signal transmission behavior can be analyzed from the viewpoint of one electron properties, which are shapes of molecular orbitals (MOs) and MO energies. Thus, the proposed method is suitable for simple design of high-performance molecular QCA. Additionally, in my next paper (27), metal-dependence of dynamic behavior of signal transmission through metal complexes $[L_5M\text{-}BL\text{-}ML_5]^{n+}$ (M=Fe, Ru, and Os, BL=**py** and **bpy**, L=NH_3, n=5), was discussed.
In this Chapter, I review my approaches (24; 27) for the theoretical study on the two-site molecular QCA (Fig. 3) . Additionally, I discuss the influence of complex charge n on the signal transmission through molecular QCA. The reason why mixed-valence complexes are

suitable for molecular QCA is shown from the calculation of complexes with charge n=4, 5, and 6. Summarizing these results, I propose a new and simple approach for designing high-performance molecular QCA.

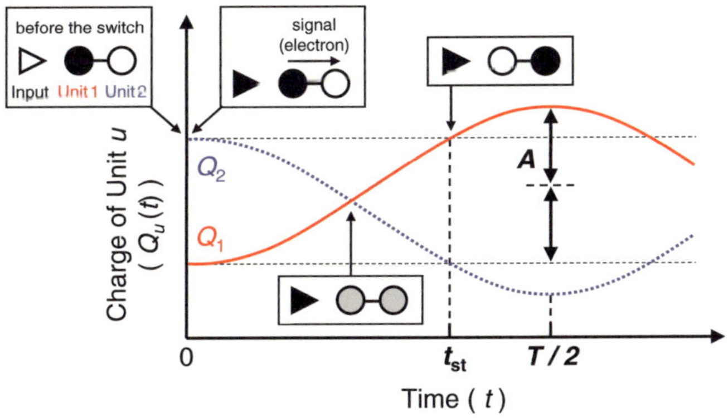

Fig. 3. Simplified two-site QCA and schematic picture of signal transmission between two units after the switch of input. A, T, and t_{st} are the signal amplitude, the signal period, and the signal transmission time, respectively.

This Chapter is organized as follows. In section 2, model, theory, and computational method of dynamic simulations are presented. A detailed explanation about the time evolution of the Mulliken charge (28) is also given. Calculated results of geometric parameters and molecular orbitals of selected complexes are shown in section 3. In section 4, the dynamic responses of molecular QCA cell upon the switch are calculated by the DFT and HF methods. In subsection 4.1, the relation between "input position" and signal transmission behavior is discussed. Detailed procedure of analysis from MOs are explained in this subsection. Relation between "switch power" and signal transmission behavior is shown in subsection 4.2. "Complex charge" also have great influence on the signal transmission (subsection 4.3). Lastly in subsection 4.4, the influence of "metal kind" on the signal transmission is discussed. In all subsections of section 4, factors which determine the dynamic properties of molecular QCA cell are discussed from the viewpoint of MOs and orbital energies. Finally, this Chapter is summarized in section 5.

2. Model, theory, and computation

2.1 Model

Schematic picture of signal transmission behavior is shown in Fig. 3. Before the switch (input charge is positive), unit 1 (U1) and unit 2 (U2) have negative and positive charges, respectively. U1 is constructed from one M atom near to the input plus five NH_3 ligands, and U2 is constructed from one M atom far from the input plus five NH_3 ligands (see Fig. (4). The moment of the switch of input corresponds to t=0. After the switch of the input charge from q^i to q^f, as time flows after the switch, $Q_2(t)$ decreases and $Q_1(t)$ increases, namely, signal (electron) is transmitted from U1 to U2 by the Coulombic repulsion. Via transition state, signal transmission is completed when Q_1 becomes almost same to $Q_2(t$=0), and Q_2 becomes almost same to $Q_1(t$=0). This time is called the signal transmission time (t_{st}). After the signal transmission, periodic behavior is repeated with a period of T and an amplitude of A.

Like the previous work by Braun-Sand and Wiest (18), dinuclear metal complexes shown in Fig. 4 are used to understand the essence of signal transmission through the molecular QCA cell. Bridging ligand (BL) of the complexes is pyrazine (**py**) or 4,4′-bipyridine (**bpy**), and ligand is NH_3. Total charge of the whole molecule is $n+$, excluding the input charge. Metal atoms (M) are selected as Fe, Ru, and Os and charges ($n+$) of the complexes are 4+, 5+, and 6+. These complexes are well-known to have mixed-valence electronic state when $n = 5$, and such complexes are called Creutz-Taube complexes (29; 30). Point charge q placed parallel to M-N_{BL} axis at a distance of r_{q-M} = 5, 10, and 15 Å from the M atom is used as an input to the complexes. For the discussion of switch power, three kinds of switch patterns, (q^i, q^f) = (+0.1, -0.1), (+0.3, -0.3), (+0.5, -0.5) (in e unit), are selected.

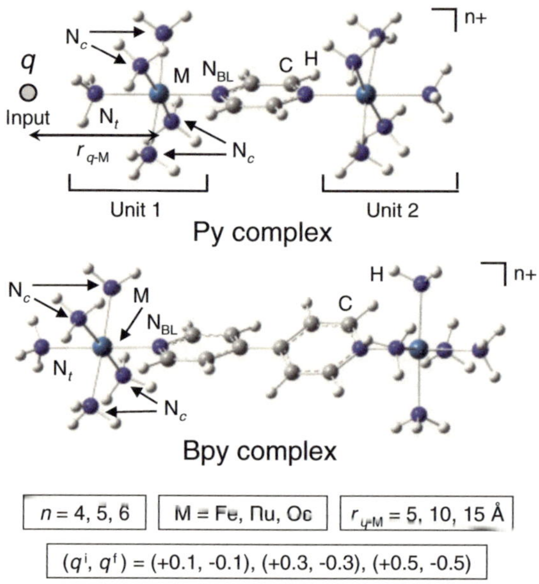

Fig. 4. Input and structures of **py** and **bpy** complexes.

2.2 Theory

Dynamic calculation for the simulation of signal transmission is all based on one-electron theories. A method of time evolution is similar to that of Remacle and Levine (24–27). All procedures shown below are repeated for both α and β MOs.

In *initial* stationary state before the switch, the following one-electron equation

$$h^{\mathrm{i}}|\psi_n^{\mathrm{i}}\rangle = \varepsilon_n^{\mathrm{i}}|\psi_n^{\mathrm{i}}\rangle \tag{1}$$

is satisfied, where h^{i}, $|\psi_n^{\mathrm{i}}\rangle$, and $\varepsilon_n^{\mathrm{i}}$ denote one-electron Hamiltonian, nth MO, and nth orbital energy when q=q^{i}, respectively. Similarly, in *final* stationary state after the switch, the following equation

$$h^{\mathrm{f}}|\psi_n^{\mathrm{f}}\rangle = \varepsilon_n^{\mathrm{f}}|\psi_n^{\mathrm{f}}\rangle \tag{2}$$

is satisfied, where h^{f}, $|\psi_n^{\mathrm{f}}\rangle$, and $\varepsilon_n^{\mathrm{f}}$ denote one-electron Hamiltonian, nth MO, and nth orbital energy when q=q^{f}, respectively. At the moment ($t = 0$) of switch of input (q=$q^{\mathrm{i}} \rightarrow q$=$q^{\mathrm{f}}$), one-electron Hamiltonian h suddenly changes from h^{i} to $h^{\mathrm{f}}(0)$ (31) but MOs are remaining $|\psi_n^{\mathrm{i}}\rangle$, so that time evolution of nth MO $|\psi_n(t)\rangle$ is represented by the following time-dependent Schrödinger equation (in atomic unit)

$$i\frac{\partial|\psi_n(t)\rangle}{\partial t} = h^{\mathrm{f}}(t)|\psi_n(t)\rangle, \tag{3}$$

where $|\psi_n(0)\rangle$ corresponds to $|\psi_n^{\mathrm{i}}\rangle$. Neglecting the time dependence of $h^{\mathrm{f}}(t)$ (assumed to be equal to h^{f} of Equation 2) and expanding $|\psi_n(t)\rangle$ in a complete set of the *final* stationary states $|\psi_j^{\mathrm{f}}\rangle$ of Equation 2, $|\psi_n(t)\rangle$ is written as

$$|\psi_n(t)\rangle = e^{-ih^{\mathrm{f}}t}|\psi_n(0)\rangle = \sum_j^{\mathrm{all}} e^{-ih^{\mathrm{f}}t}|\psi_j^{\mathrm{f}}\rangle\langle\psi_j^{\mathrm{f}}|\psi_n(0)\rangle = \sum_j^{\mathrm{all}} |\psi_j^{\mathrm{f}}\rangle e^{-i\varepsilon_j^{\mathrm{f}}t} d_{jn}, \tag{4}$$

where $d_{jn} = \langle\psi_j^{\mathrm{f}}|\psi_n(0)\rangle = \langle\psi_j^{\mathrm{f}}|\psi_n^{\mathrm{i}}\rangle$ is the overlap integral between MOs and j runs over all MOs when $q = q^{\mathrm{f}}$. This approximation gives not only a drastic reduction of computational time but also a simple picture of signal transmission based on MOs. Then, an inner product of $|\psi_n(t)\rangle$ is

$$\langle\psi_n(t)|\psi_n(t)\rangle = \sum_{j,j'}^{\mathrm{all}} d_{jn} d_{j'n} e^{i\Delta\varepsilon_{jj'}t}\langle\psi_j^{\mathrm{f}}|\psi_{j'}^{\mathrm{f}}\rangle = 1, \tag{5}$$

where $\Delta\varepsilon_{jj'} = \varepsilon_j^{\mathrm{f}} - \varepsilon_{j'}^{\mathrm{f}}$. In actual calculation, $|\psi_j\rangle$ and $|\psi_{j'}\rangle$ are expressed by localized gaussian functions $|\phi\rangle$ and molecular coefficients c as

$$|\psi_j\rangle = \sum_\mu^{\mathrm{all}} c_{j\mu}|\phi_\mu\rangle, \tag{6}$$

$$|\psi_{j'}\rangle = \sum_\nu^{\mathrm{all}} c_{j'\nu}|\phi_\nu\rangle, \tag{7}$$

where μ and ν run over all basis functions. Total number of electrons N is defined as

$$N = \sum_n^{\mathrm{occ.}} \langle\psi_n(t)|\psi_n(t)\rangle. \tag{8}$$

Substituting Equations 5 and 7 into Equation 8, N can be explicitly rewritten like the form of Mulliken population as (32; 33)

$$\begin{aligned} N &= \sum_{\mu,\nu}^{\mathrm{all}} \left[\sum_n^{\mathrm{occ.}} \sum_{j,j'}^{\mathrm{all}} d_{jn} d_{j'n} \cdot c_{j\mu} c_{j'\nu} \cdot \cos(\Delta\varepsilon_{jj'}t) \right] \langle\phi_\mu|\phi_\nu\rangle \\ &= \sum_{\mu,\nu}^{\mathrm{all}} P_{\nu\mu} S_{\mu\nu} = \sum_\nu^{\mathrm{all}} (\mathbf{PS})_{\nu\nu}, \end{aligned} \tag{9}$$

where $\mathbf{S}$ is an overlap matrix of $S_{\mu\nu} (= \langle\phi_\mu|\phi_\nu\rangle)$, and $\mathbf{P}$ is a population matrix of $P_{\nu\mu}$:

$$P_{\nu\mu} = \sum_n^{\mathrm{occ.}} \sum_{j,j'}^{\mathrm{all}} d_{jn} d_{j'n} \cdot c_{j\mu} c_{j'\nu} \cdot \cos(\Delta\varepsilon_{jj'}t). \tag{10}$$

Then, the time-dependent Mulliken charge of unit u is defined as

$$Q_u(t) = \sum_{a \in u}^{\text{Atom}} \left\{ Z_a - \sum_{\nu \in a}^{\text{Basis}} (\mathbf{PS})_{\nu\nu} \right\}, \tag{11}$$

where Z_a is a nuclear charge of an atom a. The value in the braces of Equation 11 corresponds to the Mulliken charge of a.

2.3 Computation

All dynamic calculations were performed by the restricted DFT method for 4+ and 6+ complexes, and unrestricted DFT method for 5+ complexes, using B3LYP functional. It is well-known that DFT method generally over-estimate the electron delocalization (35), so that the HF method which generally under-estimate the electron delocalization was also checked. However, detailed results of HF method are not shown in this chapter (see my previous paper, ref. 24). Conventional basis set was used for H, C, and N atoms (6-31G(d) for C and N atoms, and 6-31G for H atoms). All-electron 3-21G basis set was used for Fe and Ru atoms, and LANL2DZ basis set and LANL2 pseudo potential were used for Ru and Os atoms. It was confirmed about Ru complexes that there is only a small difference between the results obtained by 3-21G and LANL2DZ basis sets. Therefore, the comparison between Fe (3-21G), Ru (3-21G), and Os (LANL2DZ) complexes will be valid. All results of Ru complexes shown in this chapter are those obtained by 3-21 basis set for Ru atom.

Gaussian 03 program package (34) was used for geometrical optimizations and self-consistent field electronic calculations. Fortran 77 program for the time evolution of the Mulliken charge and its analysis was coded by myself.

3. Structures

3.1 Geometries

Geometrical optimizations were performed for only 5+ complexes. The schematic structures of **py** and **bpy** complexes with are shown in Fig. 4. N_{BL}, N_c, and N_t represent N atoms of M-BL, *cis*-M-NH_3, and *trans*-M-NH_3 bonds, respectively. Geometrical optimizations of **py** and **bpy** complexes have already been studied by other research groups, imposing or without imposing symmetry (35–39). In this chapter, all possible symmetries (including C_1 point group) were checked in the search of the stable structures, and it was confirmed that the most stable structures have no vibrational modes with imaginary frequencies.

Table 1 shows a summary of the computed geometries of this work. For **py** complex, imposing C_{2h}, C_{2v}, C_2, C_s, and C_i symmetries, the most stable symmetries were obtained as C_{2h} symmetry (^2B_g state) for Ru complex and C_2 symmetry (^2B state) for Fe and Os complexes. Some calculations starting from C_1 symmetry also converged into these symmetries, so that stable structures of **py** complex were concluded to be symmetric. Energy differences between the most stable structures in each symmetry are very small that the symmetry of the stable structure will strongly depend on a selection of calculation method and basis set. Two M atoms of the complex are equivalent so that **py** complexes are regarded as Class III of Robin-Day's classification (40). The results of this work about Ru complexes are very similar to the results obtained by Braun-Sand and Wiest (17), but Ru-N_{BL} bond lengths are estimated a little longer due to the polarization basis function of N atoms. Compared with X-ray crystal structure (42; 43), computed bond lengths, especially Ru-N_{BL} bond length, are over-estimated by about 0.2 Å. This is because that inter-molecular interactions are neglected in calculations of this article.

	py			bpy		
Metal	Fe	Ru	Os	Fe	Ru	Os
Symmetry	C_2	C_{2h}	C_2	C_2	C_2	C_2
Electronic State	^2B	^2B_g	^2B	^2B	^2B	^2B
M-N_{BL}	1.939	2.206	2.099	1.927	2.169	2.115
M-N_c	2.028	2.210	2.197	2.026	2.205	2.192
M-N_t	2.075	2.191	2.211	2.071	2.208	2.214
dihedral angle	-	-	-	15.1	28.3	23.0

Table 1. Summary of symmetries, irreducible representations of electronic state, and computed M-N bond lengths (Å) of **py** and **bpy** complexes with charge $n = 5$. M-N_c bond length is averaged over all M-N_c bonds.

For **bpy** complex, the most stable symmetries finally converged to C_2 symmetry (^2B state). Another structure starting from C_1 symmetry also converged into this structure, so that C_2 symmetry was concluded to be the most stable structure. Computed bond lengths of Ru complexes in Table 1 is similar to the results obtained by Braun-Sand and Wiest (17). The dihedral angles between two C_5N rings are 15.1°, 28.3°, and 23.0° for Fe, Ru, and Os complexes, respectively. These calculation predicts **bpy** complex to be classified into Class III. Contrast to above results by DFT method, HF method gives C_1 symmetry as stable structure of **bpy** complexes (not shown in the text)(24). HF calculation predicts large difference between two M-N_{BL} bond lengths. This result is consistent with the fact that Ru-**bpy** complex is thought to belong to Class II due to the experimental result of near-IR spectrum (41). These calculated results are not surprising because HF method tends to give more localized electronic structures than DFT method.
In my previous paper (24), **bpy** complexes were classified into Class III and Class II by DFT and HF methods, respectively. And it was found that signal transmission does not take place in Class II complex by HF method. Therefore, I focused only on the Class III result by DFT method in order to analysis signal transmission behavior and expand knowledge about molecular design of QCA even though the classification of **bpy** complex into Class III is contradict to the experimental observation.

3.2 Frontier molecular orbitals

Frontier molecular orbitals of Ru complexes (BL = **py** and **bpy**, $n = 5$) are shown in Fig. 5. Be careful that no input charge is put at the side of complex in this figure. Other orbitals do not contribute to the signal transmission so that are not shown here. For **py** complexes, 112α and 113α orbitals are linear combinations of $4d_{x^2-y^2}$ orbitals of Ru atoms. 112β and 113β orbitals are constructed from $4d_{yz}$ orbitals of Ru atoms and π^* orbital of BL. In 112β orbitals, $4d_{yz}$ and π^* forms bonding orbital so that it has lower energy than 113β orbital. Both 114α and 114β orbitals are almost same to the π^* orbitals of BL and have anti-bonding character between metals and BL. Similar to the frontier orbitals of **py** complex, those of **bpy** complexes are also constructed from $4d_{yz}$ and $4d_{x^2-y^2}$ orbitals of Ru atoms and π^* orbital of BL. However, contribution of BL $\pi*$ orbital to 132β orbital in **bpy** complex is smaller than that of BL $\pi*$ orbital to 112β orbital in **py** complex. Orbitals of Fe and Os complexes are not shown here but are qualitatively same to those of Ru complexes. 3*d* and 5*d* orbitals contribute to frontier MOs of Fe and Os complexes, respectively.

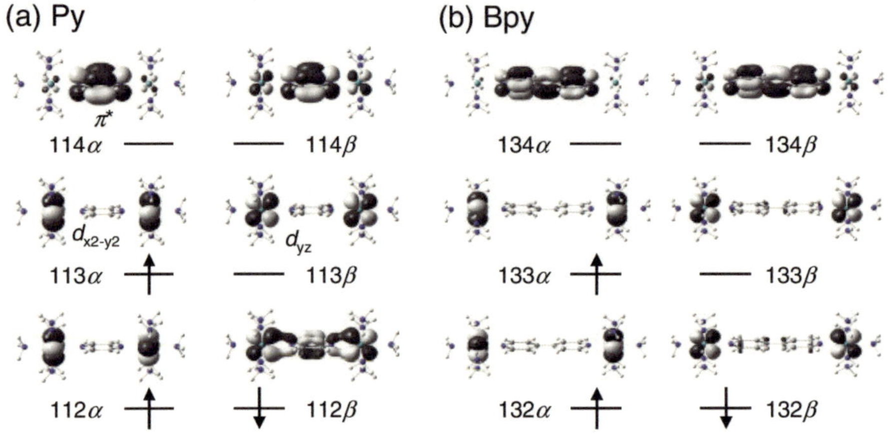

Fig. 5. Frontier molecular orbitals of (a) **py** and (b) **bpy** complexes without input charge.

4. Signal transmission

4.1 Input position

The relation between input position and signal transmission behavior is discussed. About Ru complexes with 5+ charge, switch position $r_{q-\mathrm{Ru}}$ is changed from 5 Å to 15 Å. Input charge is switched from q^{i}=+0.5 to q^{f}=-0.5.

4.1.1 Ru-py complexes

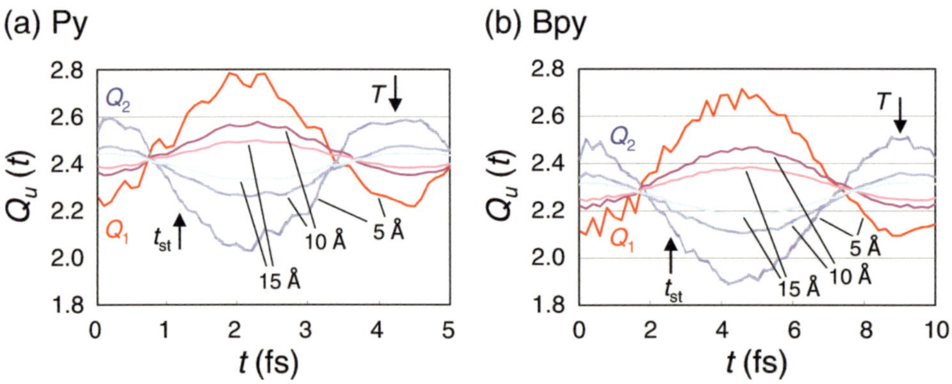

Fig. 6. Dependence of dynamic behavior on input position. Results of (a) **py** and (b) **bpy** complexes.

Figure 6 shows time-evolution of $Q_1(t)$ and $Q_2(t)$ after the switch of the input. The moment of the switch of input corresponds to t=0. Summation of Q_1, Q_2, and charge of LB is always exactly +5. Time evolution of the charge of BL is very small so that is not shown here. As time

flows after the switch, Q_2 decreases and Q_1 increases, namely, signal (electron) is transmitted from U1 to U2 by the Coulombic repulsion.
In **py** results shown in Fig. 6(a), Q_1 becomes almost same to Q_2 at $t \approx 0.8$ fs. At $t \approx 1.2$ fs, Q_1 becomes almost same to $Q_2(0)$, and Q_2 becomes almost same to $Q_1(0)$. Signal transmission is completed at this time, so that the signal transmission time (t_{st}) is estimated as $t_{st} \approx 1.2$ fs. After the signal transmission, periodic behavior is repeated with a period of $T \approx 4.3$ fs.
As a whole, the amplitude of the time evolution (signal amplitude: A) is strongly dependent on r_{q-Ru}, on the other hand, signal transmission time (t_{st}) and period of the evolution (signal period: T) are almost independent of r_{q-Ru}. Charge of BL remains almost constant throughout the time evolution, so that signal transmission is said to occur via a hopping mechanism (26). When r_{q-Ru}=5 Å, dynamic behavior is a little complicated because that electric field originated from q is so strong that electronic structure is strongly perturbed.

4.1.2 Ru-bpy complexes

Fig. 6(b) shows time-evolution of $Q_1(t)$ and $Q_2(t)$ after the switch of the input. Charge of BL (not shown) remains almost constant throughout the time evolution, so that signal transmission is said to occur via a hopping mechanism as **py** complex. At $t \approx 1.8$ fs, Q_1 and Q_2 become almost the same. At $t \approx 2.6$ fs, Q_1 becomes almost same to $Q_2(0)$, and Q_2 becomes almost same to $Q_1(0)$, so that the signal transmission time is estimated as $t_{st} \approx 2.6$ fs. Periodic behavior is repeated with $T \approx 9.1$ fs. A is strongly dependent on r_{q-Ru}, but t_{st} and T are almost independent of r_{q-Ru}. It should be noted that A of **bpy** complex is a little larger than that of **py** complex, and t_{st} and T of **bpy** complex are about twice as large as those of **py** complex. Thus, signal transmission through **bpy** complex with long BL is slower than that through **py** complex with short BL. From the viewpoint of signal amplitude, **bpy** complex is better suited for molecular QCA, but from the viewpoint of signal transmission time, dynamic calculation gives the opposite result. This means that for the simulation and design of molecular QCA, dynamic consideration is indispensable.
Signal transmission time t_{st} is 1-2 fs at the maximum. On the other hand, the period T of nuclear motion is usually several tens - several hundreds fs. Therefore, nuclear vibration will have only a small influence on the signal transmission and can be neglected.

4.1.3 Analysis from molecular orbitals (MOs)

It was found that signal amplitude (A) is strongly dependent on r_{q-Ru}, on the other hand, signal transmission time (t_{st}) and signal period (T) are almost independent of r_{q-Ru}. Here, these points are discussed from the viewpoint of MOs and orbitals energies.

4.1.3.1 Molecular orbitals

Figures 7 and 8 show frontier MOs and orbital energies of stationary states of **py** and **bpy** complexes before (q=q^{i}) and after (q=q^{f}) the switch of the input when $n = 5$.
For **py** complex (Fig. 7), 112α and 113α orbitals dramatically change before and after the switch. Two d_{zx} orbitals, 112α of (a) and 112α of (b), are originally degenerated when q=0.0. This is also applied to a set of 113α of Fig. 7 (a) and 113α of Fig. 7 (b). When q=+0.5, one of two orbitals in which U1 has large distribution is stable due to the Coulombic attraction to the positive q. Inversely, when q=−0.5, the other orbital in which U2 has larger distribution is stable due to the Coulombic repulsion to the negative q. 112β and 113β are almost same to the 112β and 113β orbitals without input charge shown in Fig.5 and are constructed mainly from a linear combination of two $4d_{yz}$ orbitals of two Ru atoms, one bonding and the other anti-bonding. 112β has larger distribution on U1 when q=+0.5 and on U2 when q=−0.5 due

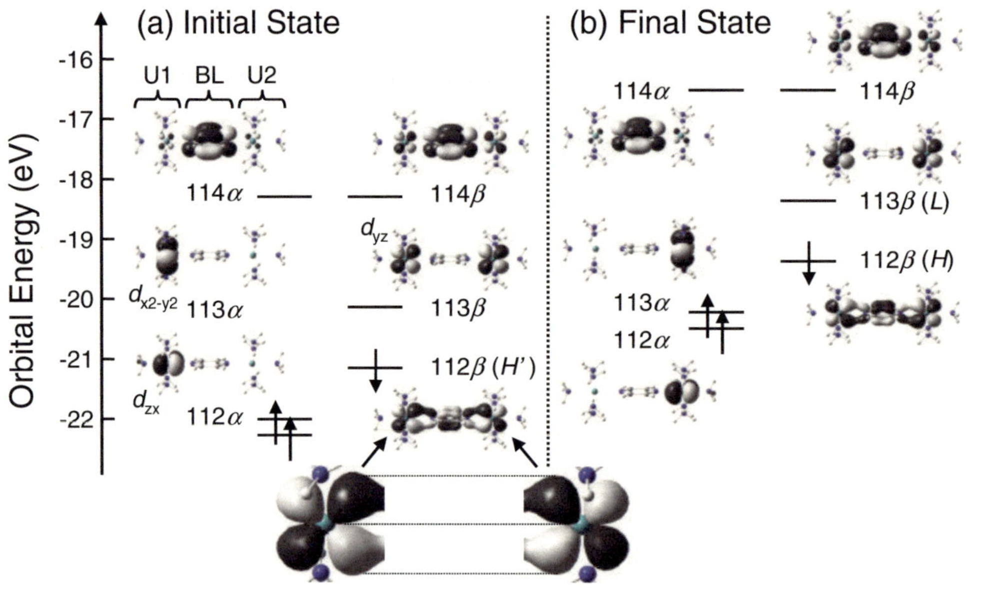

Fig. 7. Frontier molecular orbitals and orbital energies of **py** complex when $n = 5$. (a) *Initial* stationary state ($|\psi^i\rangle$) with q=q^i=+0.5 and (b) *final* stationary state ($|\psi^f\rangle$) with q=q^f=−0.5. In this figure, input q is placed at a distance of $r_{q-\mathrm{Ru}}$=10Å on the left of the complexes (also see Fig. 4).

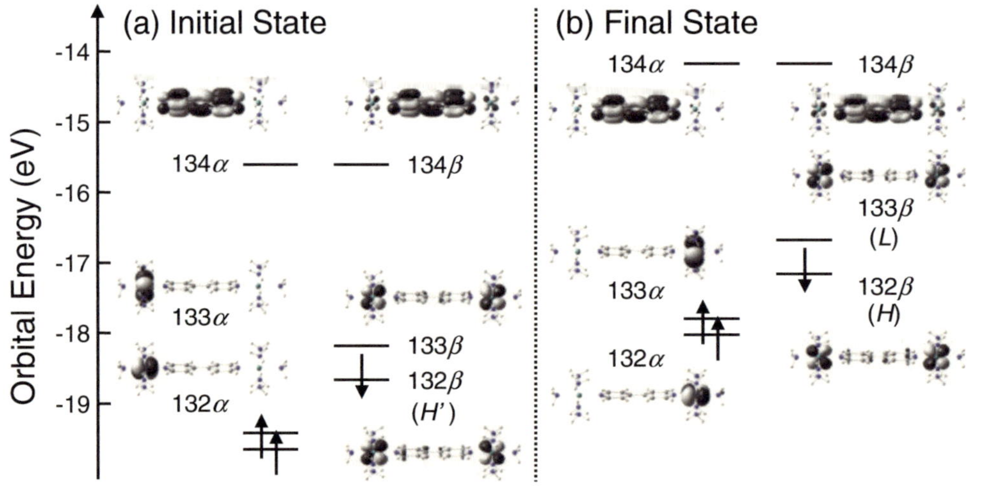

Fig. 8. Frontier molecular orbitals and orbital energies of **bpy** complex when $n = 5$. (a) *Initial* stationary state ($|\psi^i\rangle$) with q=q^i=+0.5 and (b) *final* stationary state ($|\psi^f\rangle$) with q=q^f=−0.5.

to the Coulombic interaction to the input (see enlarged figures in Fig. 7). However, 113β has opposite character, that is larger distribution on U2 when q=+0.5 and on U1 when q=−0.5, because 112β and 113β are a pair of bonding and anti-bonding orbitals. Larger distribution on one unit of 112β naturally results in smaller distribution on the same unit of 113β.

The same interpretation can be applied to results of **bpy** complex in Fig. 8. 132α and 133α are localized on U1 when q=+0.5 and are localized on U2 when q=−0.5 due to Coulombic interaction. 132β and 133β have bonding and anti-bonding character, respectively, and are mainly constructed from two $4d_{yz}$ orbitals.

4.1.3.2 Signal period (T)

Time-dependent part of Equation 11 is extracted as

$$\sum_{j,j'\neq j}^{\text{all}} -A_{ujj'} \cos(2\pi t/T_{jj'}), \tag{12}$$

where

$$T_{jj'} = 2\pi/\Delta\varepsilon_{jj'}, \tag{13}$$

$$A_{ujj'} = \sum_{a\in u}^{\text{Atom}} \sum_{\nu\in a}^{\text{Basis}} \sum_{\mu}^{\text{all}} \sum_{n}^{\text{occ.}} d_{jn}d_{j'n} \cdot c_{j\mu}c_{j'\nu} \cdot s_{\mu\nu}. \tag{14}$$

$T_{jj'}$ and $A_{ujj'}$ are the signal period and signal amplitude of unit u of the time evolution, respectively. The term $-A_{ujj'}\cos(2\pi t/T_{jj'})$ represents the contribution of the interaction between $|\psi_j^{\mathrm{f}}\rangle$ and $|\psi_{j'}^{\mathrm{f}}\rangle$ to the time evolution of $Q_u(t)$. All terms with $j = j'$ are excluded because they are time-independent ($\Delta\varepsilon_{jj'} = 0$). In Table 2, two values of $T_{jj'}$ are tabulated in order of $|A_{ujj'}|$. For both **py** and **bpy** complexes, (j, j')=(H, L) term is dominant in U1 and U2 so that the transmission character is almost determined by H and L, where H and L denote HOMO(β) and LUMO(β) of the *final* stationary state (q=q^{f}=−0.5). The values of the second largest $A_{ujj'}$ are negligibly small. Thus, consideration of only (H, L) term is enough to reproduce Fig. 6.
The $T_{jj'}$ (or $\Delta\varepsilon_{jj'}$) with the largest $A_{ujj'}$ mainly determines the period (T) of the time evolution. $T_{jj'}$ is almost independent of $r_{q-\mathrm{Ru}}$ because orbital energies $\varepsilon_j^{\mathrm{f}}$ are influenced by the strength of electric field originated from the input but energy gaps $\Delta\varepsilon_{jj'}$ between frontier MOs are almost determined by the interaction between Ru atoms, bridging ligand, and ligands, and are little influenced by the strength of electric field originated from the input (see orbitals energies of Figs. 7 and 8).

4.1.3.3 Signal amplitude (A)

In dynamic behavior, signal amplitude (A) is almost determined by the value of A_{uHL}. A_{uHL} is divided into two terms as

$$A_{uHL} = C_{uHL}D_{HL}, \tag{15}$$

where

$$C_{uHL} = \sum_{a\in u}\sum_{\nu\in a}\sum_{\mu} c_{H\mu}c_{L\nu}s_{\mu\nu}, \tag{16}$$

$$D_{HL} = \sum_{n} d_{Hn}d_{Ln}. \tag{17}$$

Absolute values of A_{uHL}, C_{uHL}, and D_{HL} are tabulated in Table 3. As seen from the time evolution in Fig. 6, A_{uHL} sharply decreases as $r_{q-\mathrm{Ru}}$ increases. C_{uHL} changes only a little as

		Unit 1			Unit 2		
	$r_{q-\text{Ru}}$	j, j'	$A_{1jj'}$	$T_{jj'}$	j, j'	$A_{2jj'}$	$T_{jj'}$
py	5Å	$112\beta, 113\beta$	0.128	4.26	$112\beta, 113\beta$	-0.140	4.26
		$106\alpha, 115\alpha$	0.006	0.57	$111\alpha, 114\alpha$	0.008	1.03
	10Å	$112\beta, 113\beta$	0.052	4.47	$112\beta, 113\beta$	-0.053	4.47
		$112\beta, 114\beta$	0.001	1.47	$109\alpha, 114\alpha$	0.002	0.94
	15Å	$112\beta, 113\beta$	0.027	4.47	$112\beta, 113\beta$	-0.028	4.49
		$109\alpha, 114\alpha$	-0.001	0.92	$109\alpha, 114\alpha$	0.001	0.92
bpy	5Å	$132\beta, 133\beta$	0.143	9.06	$132\beta, 133\beta$	-0.145	9.06
		$123\beta, 135\beta$	0.006	0.53	$131\alpha, 134\alpha$	0.004	1.04
	10Å	$132\beta, 133\beta$	0.061	9.34	$132\beta, 133\beta$	-0.061	9.34
		$114\alpha, 135\alpha$	-0.001	0.44	$131\alpha, 134\alpha$	0.001	0.93
	15Å	$132\beta, 133\beta$	0.033	9.36	$132\beta, 133\beta$	-0.033	9.36
		$114\beta, 135\beta$	0.000	0.43	$130\alpha, 134\alpha$	0.001	0.91

Table 2. Contribution of a set of (j, j') orbitals to the time-evolution of Mulliken charge. Two values of $T_{jj'}$ (fs) are shown in order of $|A_{ujj'}|$ (e). For all complexes, the set of (HOMO(β), LUMO(β)) gives the largest $A_{ujj'}$.

$r_{q-\text{Ru}}$ increases, but D_{HL} sharply decreases as $r_{q-\text{Ru}}$ increases. Thus, the decrease in A_{uHL} attendant on the increase of $r_{q-\text{Ru}}$ is mainly due to the decrease in D_{HL}. Although D_{HL} is defined as a summation over all MOs n as seen in Equation 17, $d_{HH'}d_{LH'}$ among all $d_{Hn}d_{Ln}$ has the dominant contribution to D_{HL}, where H' is HOMO(β) of the *initial* stationary state (q=q^{i}=+0.5), because d_{Hn} is almost zero except for $n = H'$. Additionally, although the values of $d_{HH'}$ are almost constant ($0.926 < d_{HH'} < 0.998$) for all BL and $r_{q-\text{Ru}}$, $d_{LH'}$ is strongly dependent on $r_{q-\text{Ru}}$ as shown in Table 3. As $r_{q-\text{Ru}}$ becomes smaller, the values of $d_{HH'}$ deviate from 1. The values of $d_{LH'}/A_{uHL}$ are almost constant for all $r_{q-\text{Ru}}$. Consequently, we can approximate Equation 15 as

$$|A_{uHL}| \propto |d_{LH'}|. \qquad (18)$$

H' and L have been already shown in Figs. 7 and 8. In both complexes, larger distribution of H' is located on U1. Similarly, larger distribution of L is on U1. For both complexes, the function $\psi^{\text{f}}_{L}\psi^{\text{i}}_{H'}$ has positive value around U1 and negative value around U2. $\psi^{\text{f}}_{L}\psi^{\text{i}}_{H'}$ has larger distribution on U1 than on U2, so that the overlap integral $d_{LH'} = \langle\psi^{\text{f}}_{L}|\psi^{\text{i}}_{H'}\rangle$ has non-zero value in total. If the input is positioned considerably far from the complex (this situation is equivalent to $q^{\text{i}} \approx q^{\text{f}} \approx 0$), the value of $d_{LH'}$ is almost zero because L and H' are almost orthogonal. Namely, the input placed nearer to the molecule leads to more asymmetric H' and L, so that $d_{LH'}$, in other words, A_{uHL} tends to be large. All complexes with **bpy** BL have small coefficients on BL and MOs distribute mainly on the metal atoms. Thus, the distribution of frontier orbitals of **bpy** complexes is strongly influenced by the switch of the input and signal amplitude A of **bpy** complexes is larger than that of py complexes.

4.2 Switch power

The relation between switch power and signal transmission behavior is discussed. Switch power corresponds to the difference between q^{i} and q^{f}. About Ru complexes with $n = 5$ and $r_{q-\text{Ru}} = 10$ Å, three kinds of switch, (q^{i}, q^{f}) = (+0.1, -0.1), (+0.3, -0.3), and (+0.5, -0.5), are simulated.

	py			bpy		
$r_{q-\mathrm{Ru}}$	5Å	10Å	15Å	5Å	10Å	15Å
A_{uHL}	0.128	0.052	0.027	0.143	0.061	0.033
C_{uHL}	0.378	0.418	0.424	0.412	0.444	0.448
D_{HL}	0.338	0.125	0.065	0.348	0.137	0.075
$d_{HH'}d_{LH'}$	0.338	0.125	0.065	0.348	0.137	0.075
$d_{HH'}$	0.931	0.992	0.998	0.926	0.990	0.997
$d_{LH'}$	0.364	0.126	0.065	0.376	0.139	0.075
$d_{LH'}/A_{uHL}$	2.84	2.42	2.41	2.63	2.28	2.27

Table 3. Absolute values of A_{uHL}, C_{uHL}, D_{HL}, $d_{HH'}d_{LH'}$, $d_{HH'}$, $d_{LH'}$, and $d_{LH'}/A_{uHL}$ of unit 2.

4.2.1 Ru-py and Ru-bpy complexes

Figure 9(a) shows the results of **py** complex. Signal period (T) is 4.3 fs and signal transmission time (t_{st}) is 1.2 fs, and both are independent of (q^i, q^f). On the other hand, signal amplitude (A) decreases as (q^i, q^f) becomes small. This is because that MOs become more symmetric as (q^i, q^f) becomes small so that values of $d_{LH'}$ becomes small. Figure 9(b) shows the results of **bpy** complex. Signal period (T) is 9.1 fs and signal transmission time (t_{st}) is 2.6 fs. Dependence of A and T on the switch power is same to the result of **py** complex.

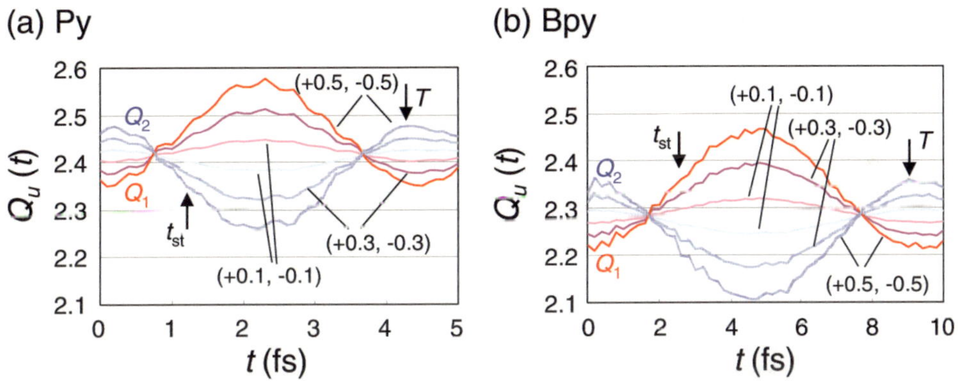

Fig. 9. Dependence of dynamic behavior on switch power. Results of (a) **py** and (b) **bpy** complexes

4.2.2 Analysis from MOs

In Table 4, the largest $|A_{ujj'}|$ and corresponding $T_{jj'}$ are tabulated. Similar to the discussion about the input position, $(j, j') = (H, L)$ term is dominant so that the transmission behavior is almost determined by H and L. The $T_{jj'}$ (or $\Delta\varepsilon_{jj'}$) with the largest $A_{ujj'}$ mainly determines the period (T) of the time evolution of Figure 9.

Absolute values of A_{uHL}, C_{uHL}, and D_{HL} are tabulated in Table 5. We can see that the order of D_{HL} qualitatively correspond to that of A_{uHL}. Therefore, the analysis of D_{HL} is necessary for understanding the values of A_{uHL}. $d_{HH'}d_{LH'}$ term among all $d_{Hn}d_{Ln}$ terms has the dominant contribution to D_{HL}. Although the values of $d_{HH'}$ are almost an unit ($0.990 < d_{HH'} < 1.000$) for all complexes, $d_{LH'}$ is strongly dependent on the switch power.

		Unit 1			Unit 2		
	(q^{i}, q^{f})	j, j'	$A_{1jj'}$	$T_{jj'}$	j, j'	$A_{2jj'}$	$T_{jj'}$
py	(+0.1,-0.1)	$112\beta, 113\beta$	0.011	4.50	$112\beta, 113\beta$	-0.011	4.50
	(+0.3,-0.3)	$112\beta, 113\beta$	0.032	4.49	$112\beta, 113\beta$	-0.032	4.49
	(+0.5,-0.5)	$112\beta, 113\beta$	0.052	4.47	$112\beta, 113\beta$	-0.053	4.47
bpy	(+0.1,-0.1)	$132\beta, 133\beta$	0.012	9.37	$132\beta, 133\beta$	-0.012	9.37
	(+0.3,-0.3)	$132\beta, 133\beta$	0.037	9.36	$132\beta, 133\beta$	-0.037	9.36
	(+0.5,-0.5)	$132\beta, 133\beta$	0.061	9.34	$132\beta, 133\beta$	-0.061	9.34

Table 4. Dependence of dynamic parameters, $|A_{ujj'}|$ and $T_{jj'}$, on switch power.

Consequently, we can qualitatively discuss the values of $|A_{uHL}|$ from those of $|d_{LH'}|$. As the switch power increases, asymmetry of H' and L increases. Therefore, signal amplitude A also increase. These discussions about switch power are qualitatively same to those of input position in the subsection 4.1. Thus, a decrease in (q^{i}, q^{f}) is equivalent to an increase in $r_{q-\mathrm{Ru}}$.

	py			**bpy**		
(q^{i}, q^{f})	(+0.1,-0.1)	(+0.3,-0.3)	(+0.5,-0.5)	(+0.1,-0.1)	(+0.3,-0.3)	(+0.5,-0.5)
A_{uHL}	0.011	0.032	0.053	0.012	0.037	0.061
C_{uHL}	0.429	0.429	0.429	0.449	0.448	0.445
D_{HL}	0.025	0.075	0.125	0.028	0.083	0.137
$d_{HH'}d_{LH'}$	0.025	0.075	0.125	0.028	0.083	0.137
$d_{HH'}$	1.000	0.997	0.995	1.000	0.997	0.990
$d_{LH'}$	0.025	0.075	0.126	0.028	0.083	0.139
$d_{LH'}/A_{uHL}$	2.27	2.34	2.38	2.33	2.24	2.28

Table 5. Absolute values of A_{uHL}, C_{uHL}, D_{HL}, $d_{HH'}d_{LH'}$, $d_{HH'}$, $d_{LH'}$, and $d_{LH'}/A_{uHL}$ of U2.

4.3 Complex charge

The relation between complex charge and signal transmission behavior is discussed about Ru complexes. Complex charge $n+$ is set at 4+, 5+, and 6+. Electronic structures of complexes with $n+ = 4+, 6+$ charges were obtained by the single point calculations of the complex with the optimized geometry in $n+ = 5+$ charged state. Complex with 5+ charge is open-shell systems, and those with 4+ and 6+ are closed-shell system. In the calculation, other parameters are fixed at $r_{q-\mathrm{Ru}} = 10$Å and (q^{i}, q^{f})=(+0.5, -0.5).

4.3.1 Ru-py and Ru-bpy complexes

Figure 10(a) shows time evolution of $Q_1(t)$ and $Q_2(t)$ of **py** complexes with 4+, 5+, and 6+ charges. Signal transmission time t_{st} is estimated as 0.3 fs (4+) $<$ 1.2 fs (5+) $<$ 1.5 fs (6+) and values of signal amplitude A are estimated as 0.01 e (6+) $<$ 0.02 e (4+) $<$ 0.05 e (5+). After the signal transmission, periodic behavior is repeated with a period (T) of 1.5 fs (4+) $<$ 4.5 fs (5+) $<$ 5.7 fs (6+). From the viewpoint of operation speed of QCA device, 4+ complex is most useful. On the other hand, from the viewpoint of signal amplitude of QCA device, 5+ complex is most useful.

Figure 10(b) shows time evolution of $Q_1(t)$ and $Q_2(t)$ of **bpy** complexes. Signal transmission time t_{st}, signal amplitude A, and signal period T are estimated as 0.2 fs (4+) $<$ 2.2 fs (5+) $\approx$

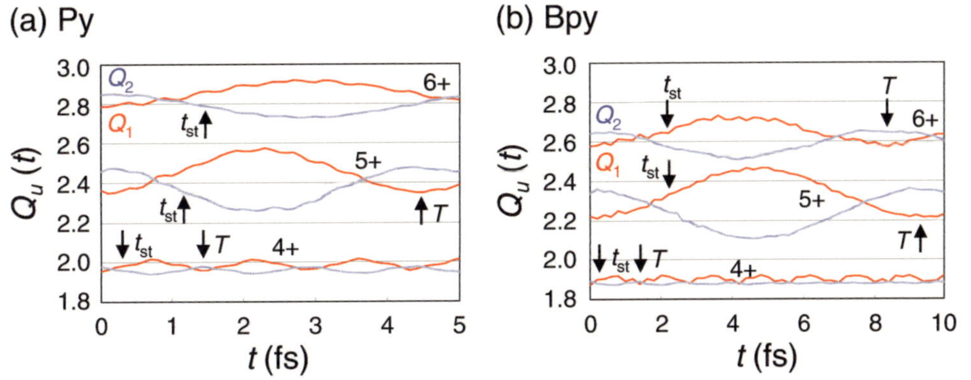

Fig. 10. Dependence of dynamic behavior on complex charge. Results of (a) **py** and (b) **bpy** complexes

2.2 fs (6+), 0.01 e (4+) $<$ 0.02 e (6+) $<$ 0.06 e (5+), and 1.4 fs (4+) $<$ 8.3 fs (6+) $<$ 9.3 fs (5+), respectively. From the viewpoint of operation speed of QCA device, 4+ complex is most useful. On the other hand, from the viewpoint of signal power of QCA device, 5+ complex is most useful. This result is qualitatively same to the results of **py** complex.

4.3.2 Analysis from MOs

Figures 11 and 12 show frontier MOs and orbital energies of stationary states of **py** and **bpy** complexes before and after the switch of the input. Only HOMO and LUMO are shown here since other orbitals play almost no role in signal transmission (24). These MOs are almost same to the orbitals shown in Fig. 5. However, LUMO of 6+ complexes are different between *initial* and *final* stationary states for **py** and **bpy** complex.

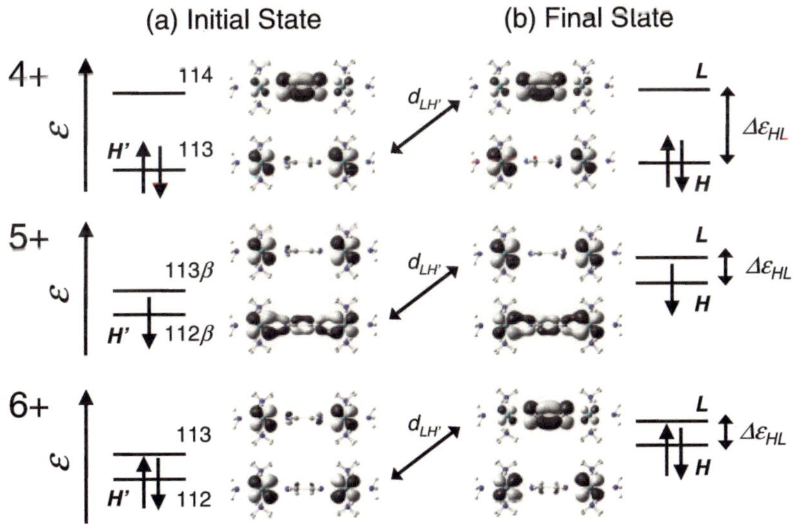

Fig. 11. Frontier molecular orbitals and orbital energies of **py** complex. (a) *Initial* stationary state ($|\psi^{i}\rangle$) with q=q^{i}=+0.5 and (b) *final* stationary state ($|\psi^{f}\rangle$) with q=q^{f}=−0.5.

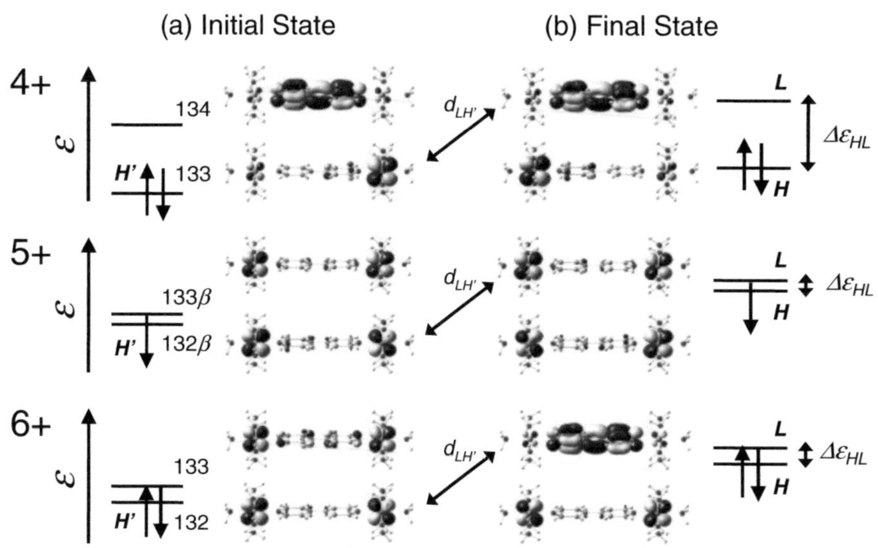

Fig. 12. Frontier molecular orbitals and orbital energies of **bpy** complex. (a) *Initial* stationary state ($|\psi^{\mathrm{i}}\rangle$) with q=q^{i}=+0.5 and (b) *final* stationary state ($|\psi^{\mathrm{f}}\rangle$) with q=q^{f}=−0.5.

In Table 6, two values of $T_{jj'}$ are tabulated in order of $|A_{ujj'}|$. Except for **bpy** complex with 4+ charge, $(j, j') = (H, L)$ term is dominant so that the transmission behavior is almost determined by H and L except for **bpy** complex with 4+ charge. The $T_{jj'}$ (or $\Delta\varepsilon_{jj'}$) with the largest $A_{ujj'}$ mainly determines the period (T) of the time evolution of Figure 10. H-L energy gap (ε_{HL}) of 4+ complexes is very large so that signal period T is very short.

		Unit 1			Unit 2		
	n+	j, j'	$A_{1jj'}$	$T_{jj'}$	j, j'	$A_{2jj'}$	$T_{jj'}$
py	4+	113, 114	0.005	1.45	113, 114	-0.004	1.35
		106, 119	0.001	0.48	101, 117	0.000	0.45
	5+	112β, 113β	0.052	4.47	112β, 113β	-0.053	4.47
		112β, 114β	0.001	1.47	109α, 114α	0.002	0.94
	6+	112, 113	0.015	5.74	112, 113	-0.015	5.74
		102, 115	0.001	0.58	101, 116	-0.001	0.53
bpy	4+	133, 134	0.003	1.36	130, 134	-0.001	1.24
		124, 143	0.002	0.47	133, 134	-0.001	1.36
	5+	132β, 133β	0.061	9.34	132β, 133β	-0.061	9.34
		114α, 135α	-0.001	0.44	131α, 134α	0.001	0.93
	6+	132, 133	0.017	8.29	132, 133	-0.017	8.29
		125, 133	0.002	2.11	125, 133	0.002	2.11

Table 6. Dependence of dynamics parameters, $|A_{ujj'}|$ and $T_{jj'}$, on complex charge.

Absolute values of A_{uHL}, C_{uHL}, and D_{HL} are tabulated in Table 7. In previous sections, the values of $|A_{uHL}|$ were proportional to those of $|d_{LH'}|$ since the values of C_{uHL} were almost constant for all cases (24). In this section, however, the values of $|A_{uHL}|$ are not exactly proportional to those of $|d_{LH'}|$ since the values of C_{uHL} also depend on the number of occupied orbitals. We can see that the order of D_{HL} qualitatively corresponds to that of $d_{LH'}$. 4+ and 6+ complexes have much smaller $d_{LH'}$ than 5+ complexes. This is because that 4+ and 6+ complexes have closed-shell electronic structures, therefore, input switch has little influence on the shapes of H' and L. On the other hand, 5+ complexes have open-shell electronic structures, so that the molecular orbital is sensitive to the input charge. These results mean that mixed-valence complexes are suitable for QCA application.

	py			**bpy**		
$n+$	4+	5+	6+	4+	5+	6+
A_{uHL}	0.004	0.053	0.015	0.001	0.061	0.017
C_{uHL}	0.122	0.429	0.461	0.037	0.445	0.428
D_{HL}	0.029	0.125	0.033	0.023	0.137	0.039
$d_{HH'}d_{LH'}$	0.025	0.088	0.033	0.009	0.137	0.039
$d_{HH'}$	0.926	0.996	0.999	0.497	0.990	0.999
$d_{LH'}$	0.027	0.088	0.033	0.018	0.139	0.039

Table 7. Absolute values of A_{uHL}, C_{uHL}, D_{HL}, $d_{HH'}d_{LH'}$, $d_{HH'}$, and $d_{LH'}$ of U2

4.4 Kind of metals

The relation between metal atoms and signal transmission behavior is discussed. Metal is changed Fe, Ru, and Os. Complex charge and switch power are selected as 5+ and (+0.5, -0.5), respectively.

4.4.1 M-py and M-bpy complexes

Figure 13(a) shows time evolution of $Q_1(t)$ and $Q_2(t)$ of **py** complexes after the switch of the input from $q = +0.5$ to $q = -0.5$. Signal transmission time t_{st} is estimated as 0.6 fs (Fe) < 0.7 fs (Os) < 1.1 fs (Ru). After the signal transmission, periodic behavior is repeated with a period (T) of 2.0 fs (Fe) < 2.5 fs (Os) < 4.5 fs (Ru). From the Figures, values of signal amplitude A are estimated as 0.05 e (Fe) < 0.06 e (Os) < 0.10 e (Ru). All t_{st}, T, and A are dependent on the kind of metal. From the viewpoint of operation speed of QCA device, Fe complex is most useful. On the other hand, from the viewpoint of signal power of QCA device, Ru complex is most useful.

Figure 13(b) shows time-evolution of $Q_1(t)$ and $Q_2(t)$ of **bpy** complexes. Signal transmission time t_{st} is estimated as 1.4 fs (Fe) < 1.7 fs (Os) < 2.5 fs (Ru). After the signal transmission, periodic behavior is repeated with a period (T) of 5.2 fs (Fe) < 6.3 fs (Os) < 9.3 fs (Ru). These values of T are almost twice as large as those of **py** complexes, and are valid considering the difference in molecular size between **py** and **bpy** bridging ligands. The values of A are estimated as 0.11 e (Os) < 0.12 e (Ru) < 0.13 e (Fe). From the viewpoints of both operation speed and signal power of QCA device, Fe complex shows good result.

4.4.2 Analysis from MO

Figures 14 and 15 show frontier MOs and orbital energies of stationary states of **py** and **bpy** complexes before (a) and after (b) the switch of the input. Only HOMO and LUMO with β spin are shown here since other orbitals play almost no role in signal transmission (24). These MOs are mainly constructed from π^* orbital of BL and d_{yz} orbital of M atom. HOMOs have larger distribution on U1 when $q = +0.5$ e due to the Coulombic attraction. On the other hand, when $q = -0.5$ e, HOMOs have smaller distribution on U1 due to the Coulombic repulsion.

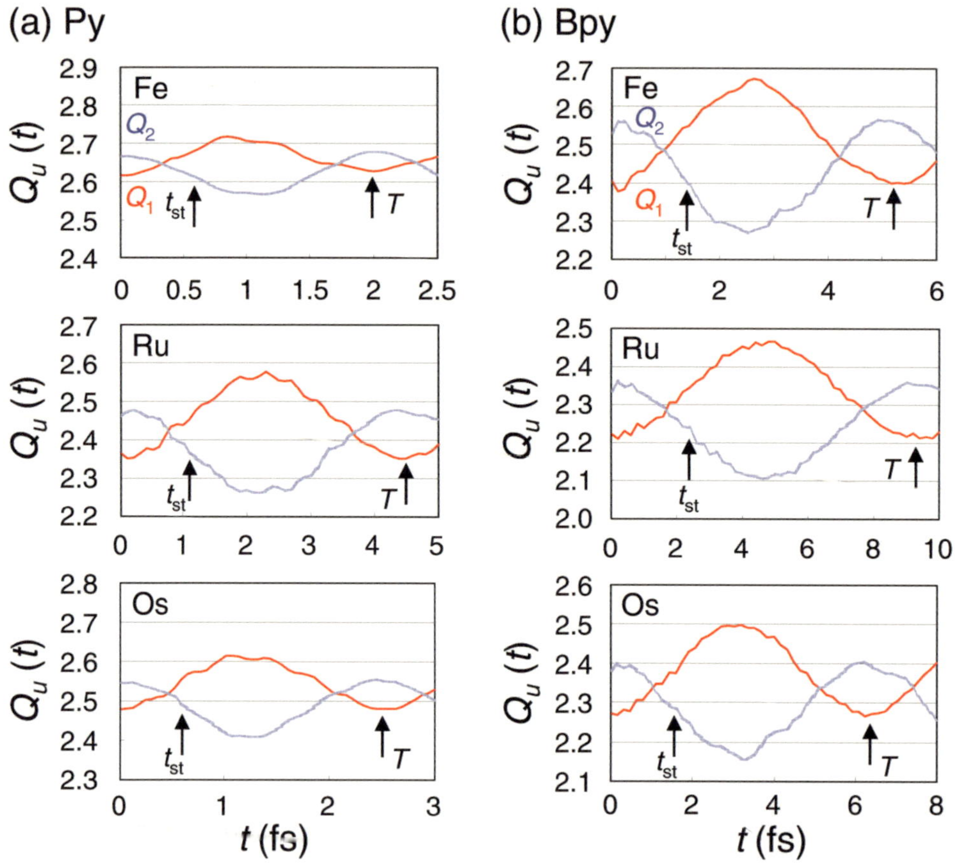

Fig. 13. Dependence of dynamic behavior on metal atoms. Results of (a) **py** and (b) **bpy** complexes.

In Table 8, the largest $|A_{ujj'}|$ and corresponding value of $T_{jj'}$ are tabulated. For all complexes, $(j, j') = (H, L)$ term is dominant so that the transmission behavior is almost determined by H and L. The $T_{jj'}$ (or $\Delta\varepsilon_{jj'}$) with the largest $A_{ujj'}$ mainly determine the period (T) of the time evolution of Figure 13. Orbital energies $\varepsilon_j^{\mathrm{f}}$ are influenced by the strength of electric field originated from the input, but energy gaps $\Delta\varepsilon_{jj'}$ between frontier MOs are almost determined by the interaction between metal atoms, bridging ligand, and ligands. Difference in the kind of metal atoms results in the difference in this interaction ($\Delta\varepsilon_{jj'}$ and $T_{jj'}$).
Absolute values of A_{uHL}, C_{uHL}, and D_{HL} are tabulated in Table 9. We can see that the order of D_{HL} qualitatively correspond to that of A_{uHL}. Therefore, the analysis of D_{HL} is necessary for understanding the values of A_{uHL}. $d_{HH'}d_{LH'}$ term among all $d_{Hn}d_{Ln}$ terms has the dominant contribution to D_{HL}. Additionally, although the values of $d_{HH'}$ are almost an unit ($0.980 < d_{HH'} < 0.996$) for all complexes, $d_{LH'}$ is strongly dependent on the kind of metal. Consequently, we can qualitatively discuss the values of $|A_{uHL}|$ from that of $|d_{LH'}|$. H' and L have been already shown in Figures 14 and 15. The values of $|A_{uHL}|$ are not exactly proportional to those of $|d_{LH'}|$ since the values of C_{uHL} also depend on the kind of metal atoms. In all complexes, larger distribution of H' is located on U1 (left-hand side). Similarly,

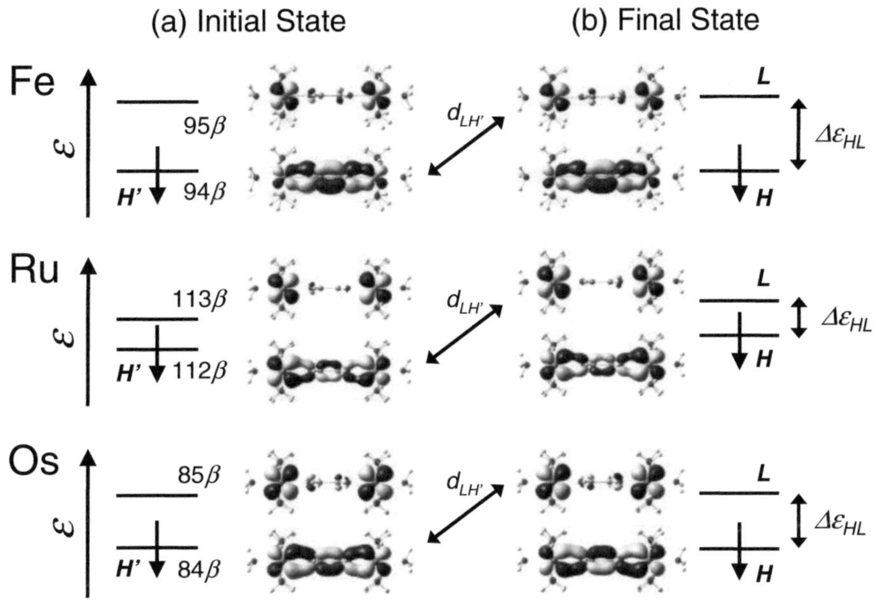

Fig. 14. Frontier molecular orbitals and orbital energies of **py** complex. (a) *Initial* stationary state ($|\psi^{\mathrm{i}}\rangle$) with q=q^{i}=+0.5 and (b) *final* stationary state ($|\psi^{\mathrm{f}}\rangle$) with q=q^{f}=−0.5.

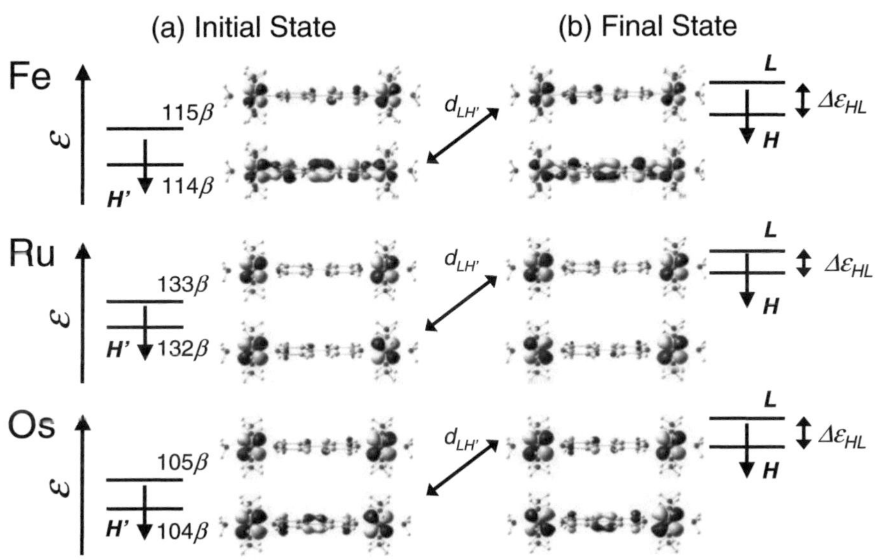

Fig. 15. Frontier molecular orbitals and orbital energies of **bpy** complex. (a) *Initial* stationary state ($|\psi^{\mathrm{i}}\rangle$) with q=q^{i}=+0.5 and (b) *final* stationary state ($|\psi^{\mathrm{f}}\rangle$) with q=q^{f}=−0.5.

larger distribution of L is on U1. For all complexes, $\psi_L^{\mathrm{f}}\,\psi_{H'}^{\mathrm{i}}$ has larger distribution on U1 than on U2, so that the overlap integral $d_{LH'} = \langle\psi_L^{\mathrm{f}}|\psi_{H'}^{\mathrm{i}}\rangle$ has non-zero value in total.
About **py** complexes, H' and L of Ru complex have large distribution on the Ru metal but those of Fe complex have small distribution on the Fe metal from Figure 7. Therefore,

		Unit 1			Unit 2		
	M	j, j'	$A_{1jj'}$	$T_{jj'}$	j, j'	$A_{2jj'}$	$T_{jj'}$
py	Fe	$94\beta, 95\beta$	0.021	2.00	$94\beta, 95\beta$	-0.026	2.00
	Ru	$112\beta, 113\beta$	0.052	4.47	$112\beta, 113\beta$	-0.053	4.47
	Os	$84\beta, 85\beta$	0.031	2.48	$84\beta, 85\beta$	-0.033	2.48
bpy	Fe	$114\beta, 115\beta$	0.065	5.15	$114\beta, 115\beta$	-0.071	5.15
	Ru	$132\beta, 133\beta$	0.061	9.34	$132\beta, 133\beta$	-0.061	9.34
	Os	$104\beta, 105\beta$	0.056	6.26	$104\beta, 105\beta$	-0.057	6.26

Table 8. Dependence of dynamics parameters, $|A_{ujj'}|$ and $T_{jj'}$, on kind of metals.

	py			**bpy**		
M	Fe	Ru	Os	Fe	Ru	Os
A_{uHL}	0.026	0.053	0.033	0.071	0.061	0.057
C_{uHL}	0.295	0.429	0.352	0.372	0.445	0.401
D_{HL}	0.088	0.125	0.093	0.192	0.137	0.141
$d_{HH'}d_{LH'}$	0.088	0.125	0.093	0.192	0.137	0.141
$d_{HH'}$	0.996	0.992	0.996	0.980	0.990	0.990
$d_{LH'}$	0.088	0.126	0.094	0.195	0.139	0.143

Table 9. Absolute values of $A_{uHL}, C_{uHL}, D_{HL}, d_{HH'}d_{LH'}, d_{HH'}$, and $d_{LH'}$ of U2.

the distribution of frontier orbitals of Ru complexes is strongly influenced by the switch of the input. Consequently, strongly deformed H' and L give large $d_{LH'}$ and A. About **bpy** complexes, simple interpretation like **py** complexes are a little difficult because the difference in MO coefficients between metals of **bpy** complexes is smaller than that of **py** complexes. All complexes with **bpy** BL have small coefficients on BL and MOs distribute mainly on the metal atoms. Thus, signal amplitude A of **bpy** complexes is larger than that of **py** complexes and the difference in A between **bpy** complexes is small.

5. Summary

With a view to analysing the dynamic behavior of molecular QCA device and designing molecular QCA candidate, a new theoretical approach from frontier molecular orbitals are discussed. From the detailed analysis of the dynamic behavior based on MOs and orbital energies, the following three general points were found:

- Signal amplitude (A) through the complexes strongly depends on (q^{i}, q^{f}) and $r_{q-\mathrm{M}}$, and its magnitude is explained from the asymmetry of MOs due to the input charge and the overlap between MOs.
- Signal period (T) is independent of (q^{i}, q^{f}) and $r_{q-\mathrm{M}}$ because T is determined from energy gaps between MOs ($\Delta\varepsilon$) which is independent of (q^{i}, q^{f}) and $r_{q-\mathrm{M}}$.
- Signal transmission time (t_{st}) is determined depending on the balance of A and T.

For dinuclear complexes discussed in this Chapter, discussions mainly about $d_{LH'}$ and $\Delta\varepsilon_{HL}$ are valid except for only one system, **bpy** complex with 4+ charge. These results could be useful guidelines for molecular design of molecular QCA candidates. Generally, Class III

complexes with large A (large overlap) and small T (large $\Delta\varepsilon$) tend to give small t_{st}, and could be good molecular QCA candidates.
This analysis method was applied to many varieties of QCA pattern, input position, switch power, complex charge, and kind of metals, and we found that

- **bpy** complexes generally have stronger signal amplitude (A), but waste longer time (t_{st}) for signal transmission than **py** complexes
- Strong switch power (q^{i}, q^{f}) results in the large signal amplitude (A). Change in switch power corresponds to the change in input position (r_{q-M}).
- MOs of mixed-valence complexes ($n = 5$) are sensitive to the change in input charge q. Thus, these complexes are suitable for molecular QCA from the viewpoint of signal amplitude (A).
- Large MO coefficient on metal atoms leads to the large A since shapes of such MOs are greatly influenced by the switch.

Lastly, it should be noted that these method can be easily applied to the reverse switch (24). Results by HF method can be discussed similarly, but signal transmission is difficult to occur since HF method tends to overestimate the electron localization.

6. Acknowledgements

Theoretical research shown in this Chapter was supported by the Joint Studies Program (2010) of the Institute for Molecular Science (IMS). The author would like to thank Dr. Hiroshi Kawabata of Hiroshima University for helpful comments to this chapter. Theoretical calculations were mainly carried out using the computer facilities at Research Center for Computational Science (Okazaki, Japan) and Research Institute for Information Technology, Kyushu University (Fukuoka, Japan).

7. References

[1] Zhirnov, V.V.; Hutchby, J.A.; Bourianoff, G.I.; Brewer, J.E. Emerging research logic devices. An assessment of new field-effect transistor, resonant tunnel device, single-electron transistor, and quantum cellular automata technologies. *IEEE Circ. Dev. Mag.* 2005, *21*, 37–46.

[2] Lent, C.S.; Tougaw, P.D.; Porod, W.; Bernstein, G.H. Quantum cellular automata. *Nanotechnology* 1993, *4*, 49–57.

[3] Orlov, A.O.; Amlani, I.; Berstein, G.H.; Lent, C.S.; Snider, G.L. Realization of a functional cell for quantum-dot cellular automata. *Science* 1997, *277*, 928–930.

[4] Amlani, I.; Orlov, A.O.; Toth, G.; Berstein, G.H.; Lent, C.S.; Snider, G.L. Digital logic gate using quantum-dot cellular automata. *Science* 1999, *284*, 289–291.

[5] Lent, C.S. Molecular electronics: Bypassing the transistor paradigm. *Science* 2000, *288*, 1597–1599.

[6] Lau, V.C.; Berben, L.A.; Long, J.R. $[(Cyclen)_4Ru_4(pz)_4]^{9+}$: A Creutz-Taube square. *J. Am. Chem. Soc.* 2002, *124*, 9042–9043.

[7] Yao, H.; Sabat, M.; Grimes, R.N.; de Biani, F.F.; Zanello, P. Metallacarborane-based nanostructures: A carbon-wired planar cctagon. *Angew. Chem. Int. Ed.* 2003, *42*, 1002–1005.

[8] Jiao, J.; Long, G.J.; Grandjean, F.; Beatty, A.M.; Fehlner, T.P. Building blocks for the molecular expression of quantum cellular automata. Isolation and characterization of a covalently bonded square array of two ferrocenium and two ferrocene complexes. *J. Am. Chem. Soc.* 2003, *125*, 7522–7523.

[9] Jiao, J.; Long, G.J.; Rebbouh, L.; Grandjean, F.; Beatty, A.M.; Fehlner, T.P. Properties of a mixed-valence $(Fe(II))_2(Fe(III))_2$ square cell for utilization in the quantum cellular automata paradigm for molecular electronics. *J. Am. Chem. Soc.* 2005, *127*, 17819–17831.

[10] Berben, L.A.; Faia, M.C.; Crawford, N.R.M.; Long, J.R. Angle dependent electronic effects in 4,4-bipyridine-bridged Ru_3 triangle and Ru_4 square complexes. *Inorg. Chem.* 2006, *45*, 6378–6386.

[11] Qi, H.; Sharma, S.; Li, Z.; Snider, G.L.; Orlov, A.O.; Lent, C.; Fehlner, T.P. Molecular quantum cellular automata cells. Electric field driven switching of a silicon surface bound array of vertically oriented two-dot molecular quantum cellular automata. *J. Am. Chem. Soc.* 2003, *125*, 15250–15259.

[12] Qi, H.; Gupta, A.; Noll, B.C.; Snider, G.L.; Lu, Y.; Lent, C.; Fehlner, T.P. Dependence of field switched ordered arrays of dinuclear mixed-valence complexes on the distance between the redox centers and the size of the counterions. *J. Am. Chem. Soc.* 2005, *127*, 15218–15227.

[13] Wei, Z.; Guo, S.; Kandel, S.A. Observation of single dinuclear metal-complex molecules using scanning tunneling microscopy. *J. Phys. Chem. B* 2006, *110*, 21846–21849.

[14] Manimaran, M.; Snider, G.L.; Lent, C.S.; Sarveswaran, V.; Lieberman, M.; Li, Z.; Fehlner, T.P. Scanning tunneling microscopy and spectroscopy investigations of QCA molecules. *Ultramicroscopy* 2003, *97*, 55–63.

[15] Lu, Y.; Quardokus, R.; Lent, C.S.; Justaud, F.; Lapinte, C.; Kandel, S.A. Charge Localization in Isolated Mixed-Valence Complexes: An STM and Theoretical Study. *J. Am. Chem. Soc. 2010, 132*, 13519-13524

[16] Guo, S.; Kandel, S.A. Scanning Tunneling Microscopy of Mixed Valence Dinuclear Organometallic Cations and Counterions on Au(111). *J. Chem. Phys. Lett. 2010, 1*, 420-424.

[17] Braun-Sand, S.B.; Wiest, O. Theoretical studies of mixed-valence transition metal complexes for molecular computing. *J. Phys. Chem. A* 2003, *107*, 285–291.

[18] Braun-Sand, S.B.; Wiest, O. Biasing mixed-valence transition metal complexes in search of bistable complexes for molecular computing. *J. Phys. Chem. B* 2003, *107*, 9624–9628.

[19] Lent, C.S.; Isaksen, B.; Lieberman, M. Molecular quantum-dot cellular automata. *J. Am. Chem. Soc.* 2003, *125*, 1056–1063.

[20] Lent, C.S.; Isaksen, B. Clocked molecular quantum-dot cellular automata. *IEEE Trans. Electron Devices* 2003, *50*, 1890–1896.

[21] Lu, Y.; Lent, C.S. Theoretical study of molecular quantum-dot cellular automata. *J. Comput. Electron.* 2005, *4*, 115–118.

[22] Timler, J.; Lent, C.S. Maxwell's demon and quantum-dot cellular automata. *J. Appl. Phys.* 2003, *94*, 1050–1060.

[23] Lu, Y.; Liu, M.; Lent, C. Molecular quantum-dot cellular automata: From molecular structure to circuit dynamics. *J. Appl. Phys.* 2007, *102*, 034311–1–6.

[24] Tokunaga, K. Signal transmission through molecular quantum-dot cellular automata: A theoretical study on Creutz-Taube complexes for molecular computing. *Phys. Chem. Chem. Phys.* 2009, *11*, 1474–1483.

[25] Remacle, F.; Levine, R.D. The time scale for electronic reorganization upon sudden ionization of the water and water-methanol hydrogen bonded dimers and of the weakly bound NO dimer. *J. Chem. Phys.* 2006, *125*, 133321–1–7.

[26] Remacle, F.; Levine, R.D. Time-resolved electrochemical spectroscopy of charge migration in molecular wires: computational evidence for rich electron dynamics. *J. Phys. Chem. C* 2007, *111*, 2301–2309.

[27] Tokunaga, K. Metal dependence of signal transmission through molecular quantum-dot cellular automata (QCA): A theoretical study on Fe, Ru, and Os mixed-valence complexes. *Materials* 2010, *3*, 4277–4290.

[28] Mulliken, R.S. Electronic population analysis on LCAO-MO molecular wave function, I. *J. Chem. Phys.* 1955, *23*, 1833–1840.

[29] Creutz, C.; Taube, H. Binuclear complexes of ruthenium ammines. *J. Am. Chem. Soc.* 1973, *95*, 1086–1094.

[30] Tom, G.M.; Creutz, C.; Taube, H. Mixed valence complexes of ruthenium ammines with 4,4′-bipyridine as bridging ligand. *J. Am. Chem. Soc.* 1974, *96*, 7827–7829.

[31] At the moment of the switch, $h^{\mathrm{f}}(0)$ is not exactly equal to h^{f} of Equation 2 because one-electron Hamiltonian itself depends on $|\psi_n\rangle$. After the switch, $h^{\mathrm{f}}(t)$ gradually approaches h^{f}.

[32] Szabo, A.; Ostlund, N.S. (1982) Modern Quantum Chemistry: Introduction to Advanced Electronic Structure Theory, Macmillan (New York).

[33] The $e^{i\Delta\varepsilon_{jj'}t}$ term gives not only cosine term but also sine term. The sine term is neglected in this work because imaginary charge represented by the term has no physical meaning.

[34] Frisch, M.J.; Trucks, G.W.; Schlegel, H.B.; Scuseria, G.E.; Robb, M.A.; Cheeseman, J.R.; Montgomery, Jr., J.A.; Vreven, T.; Kudin, K.N.; Burant, J.C.; Millam, J.M.; Iyengar, S.S.; Tomasi, J.; Barone, V.; Mennucci, B.; Cossi, M.; Scalmani, G.; Rega, N.; Petersson, G.A.; Nakatsuji, H.; Hada, M.; Ehara, M.; Toyota, K.; Fukuda, R.; Hasegawa, J.; Ishida, M.; Nakajima, T.; Honda, Y.; Kitao, O.; Nakai, H.; Klene, M.; Li, X.; Knox, J.E.; Hratchian, H.P.; Cross, J.B.; Adamo, C.; Jaramillo, J.; Gomperts, R.; Stratmann, R.E.; Yazyev, O.; Austin, A.J.; Cammi, R.; Pomelli, C.; Ochterski, J.W.; Ayala, P.Y.; Morokuma, K.; Voth, G.A.; Salvador, P.; Dannenberg, J.J.; Zakrzewski, V.G.; Dapprich, S.; Daniels, A.D.; Strain, M.C.; Farkas, O.; Malick, D.K.; Rabuck, A.D.; Raghavachari, K.; Foresman, J.B.; Ortiz, J.V.; Cui, Q.; Baboul, A.G.; Clifford, S.; Cioslowski, J.; Stefanov, B.B.; Liu, G.; Liashenko, A.; Piskorz, P.; Komaromi, I.; Martin, R.L.; Fox, D.J.; Keith, T.; Al-Laham, M.A.; Peng, C.Y.; Nanayakkara, A.; Challacombe, M.; Gill, P.M.W.; Johnson, B.; Chen, W.; Wong, M.W.; Gonzalez, C.; Pople, J.A. *Gaussian 03, Revision C.02*. Wallingford CT, 2004.

[35] Hardesty, J.; Goh, S.K.; Marynick, D.S. A comparative DFT-MP2 study of the Creutz-Taube ion and related systems. *J. Mol. Struct. (Theochem)* 2002, *588*, 223–226.

[36] Zhange, L.-T.; Ko, J.; Ondrechen, M.J. Electronic structure of the Creutz-Taube ion. *J. Am. Chem. Soc.* 1987, *109*, 1666–1671.

[37] Sizova, O.V.; Panin, A.I.; Ivanova, N.V.; Baranovskii, V.I. Electronic structure, spectrum, and intramolecular electron transfer model of $[(NH_3)_5Ru\text{-}(4,4'\text{-bipy})\text{-}Ru(NH_3)_5]^{5+}$. *J. Struct. Chem.* 1997, *38*, 366–374.

[38] Bencini, A.; Ciofini, I.; Daul, C.A.; Ferretti, A. Ground and excited state properties and vibronic coupling analysis of the Creutz-Taube ion, $[(NH_3)_5Ru\text{-pyrazine-}Ru(NH_{3)})_5]^{5+}$, using DFT. *J. Am. Chem. Soc.* 1999, *121*, 11418–11424.

[39] Broo, A; Larsson, S. Ab initio and semi-empirical studies of electron transfer and spectra of binuclear complexes with organic bridges. *Chem. Phys.* 1992, *161*, 363–378.
[40] Robin, M.B.; Day, P. Mixed valence chemistry - A survey and classification. *Adv. Inorg. Chem. Radiochem.* 1967, *10*, 247–422.
[41] Creutz, C. Mixed valence complexes of d5-d6 metal centers. *Prog. Inorg. Chem.* 1983, *30*, 1–73.
[42] Beattie, J.K.; Hush, N.S.; Taylor, P.R.; Raston, C.L.; White, A.H. Crystal structure of μ-pyrazine-bis(penta-ammineruthenium) penta-(bromide chloride)-water (1/4). *J. Chem. Soc., Dalton Trans.* 1977, 1121–1124.
[43] Fürholz, U.; Fürgi, H-.B.; Wagner, F.E.; Stebler, A.; Ammeter, J.H.; Krausz, E.; Clark, R.J.H.; Stead, M.J.; Ludi, A. The Creutz-Taube complex revisited. *J. Am. Chem. Soc.* 1984, *106*, 121–123.

Part 2

Materials Science

8

Modeling of Macrostructure Formation during the Solidification by using Frontal Cellular Automata

Dmytro S. Svyetlichnyy
AGH University of Science and Technology
Poland

1. Introduction

Prediction of the microstructure and properties is one of the most important problems in materials science. There are different methods that are used for modeling of the microstructure evolution, among them are the front tracking method (Thompson et al., 1987; Frost et al., 1988), the phase-field models (Fan & Chen, 1997), the cellular automata (CA) models (Davies, 1997), vertex models (Weygand at al., 2001), Monte Carlo Potts models (Holm at al., 2001) and the finite element method (FEM) based models (Bernacki at al. 2007). Application of CA models, for simulation of the different phenomena in materials, has increased significantly in the resent years. CA approach is used for modeling of solidification (Rappaz & Gandin, 1993; Raabe, 2004), dynamic and static recrystallization (Kumar et al., 1998; Hurley & Humphreys, 2003; Qian & Guo, 2004), phase transformation (Das et al., 2002), grain refinement (Svyetlichnyy et al., 2008), micro-shear band and shear band propagation. The main asset of CA based methods is their ability for a close correlation between the microstructure and the mechanical properties during both micro- and meso-scale simulation. The joint methods based on CA and FEM improve accuracy of the coupled phenomena simulation during the forming processes. CA based models have been developed and are being used mostly as two-dimensional (2D) versions. However, three-dimensional (3D) models have been published as well.

The 2D CA models are simpler and faster. They also include less elements and connections. They are based on less complicated algorithms. They are also simpler for design, implementation and more useful for visualization. However, there are some problems which have been solved in the 2D CA, but are still unsolved in 3D CA. Microstructure evolution is in general the three-dimensional problem and the results obtained by 2D CA cannot always be directly transferred to a real 3D process. However, the 3D models require significantly more memory and time for the calculation. This is because they have more cells and each cell has more neighbors. The memory and also the processing time problems can be potentially solved by parallelization using several processors or computers working in the network. Another approach that has been applied recently, along with the parallelization, is based on development of different algorithms capable of using appropriate properties of the special CA types. One of these algorithms, known as the frontal CA (FCA) and developed for simulation of the microstructure evolution, is described by Svyetlichnyy (2010).

The objective of the paper is development of a model and tools for modeling the macroscopic structure formation during the solidification in continuous casting line, based on technique of cellular automata, which can cooperate with finite element model.
The model is described in the paper, as well as some examples of simulation of the macrostructure formation during the continuous casting simulation using the developed model are presented.

2. Frontal cellular automata

The first CA model was developed as the 2D version. The simulation using this model can be carried out with good resolution on the relatively big space, for example 1000x1000 cells. However, the real microstructure evolution is mainly the 3D process. Hence, appropriate CA should be applied for the modeling. At this point, "the curse of dimensionality" is reached also known as the Hughes effect, when both the number of the cells and the calculation time arise enormously (Svyetlichnyy, 2010). The more cells are used, the shorter is the step of calculation. Thus, the calculation time for the 3D space can be evaluated as the fourth power of the number of cells on a side. As a result, the first trial of the classical CA application in 3D space could be the last one because of its impracticality. The 2D calculation lasts for several minutes, while the same calculation in 3D space lasts for several days.
Let's consider a process of the grain growth. There are three areas that can be picked out in each process variant. In the first area, there are no changes of the initial state. The changes are completed in the second one. In the third area, the cells change their state. These areas are unlabeled and can be used in the calculations. The first and also the second area have to be excluded from the calculation in the current step because no change is expected. The main idea of the FCA is that the only thin cell layer located near the front of the changes, i.e. near the moving boundary, can be utilized in the calculations.
The use of frontal cellular automata instead of conventional ones makes possible to reduce the computation time significantly, especially for three-dimensional models, because considerable regions are excluded from the calculations in current time step and the front of the changes is studied only. The principles of FCA, has been presented in detail by Svyetlichnyy (2010).
Accurate modeling of macrostructure formation during the solidification processes is complex task that relies on proper choice of the appropriate method. The choice is depended on intended effect, accuracy, computation costs and so on. Use of the CA joining with other methods make possible to obtain more accurate, more reliable results. Often the CA are jointed with finite differences or finite element method (FEM). Schemes of mutual use of the CA and FEM, according to their role in the model, can be divided between two groups. The first one contains solution, in which simulations are carried out independently, without feedback. Systems with co-operation of both components can be included to the second group. The one component is primary; another is secondary, served to deliver parameters and variables for proper calculations by primary method. CA can be secondary one only provided it is of simple structure and does not require much calculation costs, i.e. memory and calculation time. CA used for microstructure evolution simulation, especially tree-dimensional, in view of computational requirements cannot be applied as the secondary method. Thus, the CA play primary role in theoretical research, uneven deformation on the level of crystals or properties of polycrystalline structures.
Many efforts have so far been devoted to modeling of dendrite growth behaviors (Zhu & Hong, 2001; Beltran-Sanchez & Stefanescu, 2003; Burbelko at al, 2010; Yuan & Lee,

2010). Two main types of CA models for dendrite growth are used. The first ones are based on numerical solution of dendrite growth and the second ones are based on numerical solution of the transport equations. However, consideration of the dendrite growth is limited to small domain or for few dendrites. Another approach, which provided for hypothetical grain shape, is used in the paper. Here is considered anisotropic growth and reduction of anisotropy of the cellular space, as well. To assume that internal structure of each dendrite can be obtained by other method, efforts on the paper has focused on the macrostructure formation, which can be created for relatively large domain.
Then the variant of independent simulations by FEM and CA, without feedback, is chosen. Post-processing based on information about macrostructure formation is developed. Process is modeled by FEM in the macro-scale; the results of FEM simulation are used by CA. An arbitrary FEM code can be used in such a scheme. It is enough to meet the requirements for data needed for post-processing calculations.
General model of microstructure evolution during the solidification processes is based on universal FCA and covers such aspects of microstructure evolution or macrostructure formation. The universal cell automaton M is presented schematically in figure 1 (Svyetlichnyy, 2010). The set of the states $Q = \{q_0, q_1, q_2, q_3, q_b, q_t\}$ comprises the initial matrix state q_0, the "frontal cell" q_1, the "boundary cell" q_2, the "cell inside the grain" q_3, the buffer q_b and the transient states q_t.

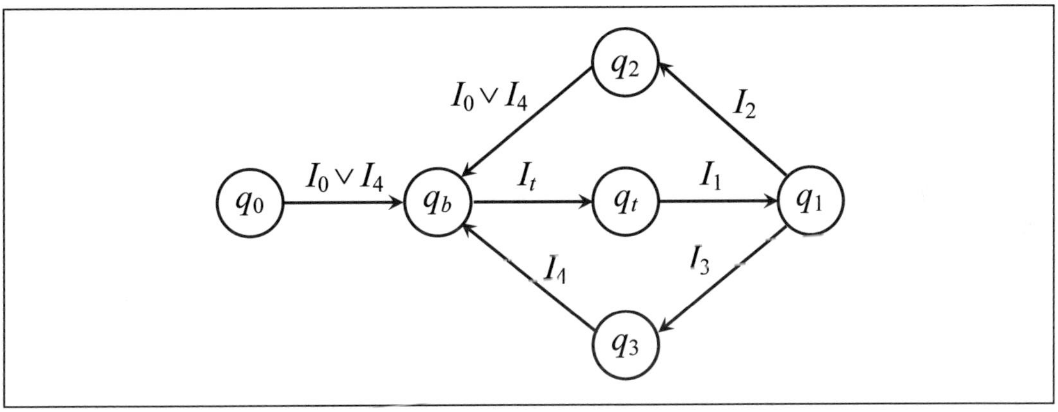

Fig. 1. Universal frontal cellular automaton M (q – states, I – transition conditions)

Initial state can be either $Q_{in} = \{q_0\}$ for creation of initial microstructure, or $Q_{in} = \{q_2, q_3\}$ for other algorithms. Final state always is $Q_f = \{q_2, q_3\}$. Alphabet contains "letters" $\Sigma = \{I_0, I_1, I_2, I_3, I_4, I_t\}$, which are treated as conditions for transition. Then, transition rules define the current q_i, and the next q_{i+1} states and letter I_k (transition condition). Such rules are commonly presented either in a table or by description. Actually conditions have following meanings. I_0 is defined by nucleation conditions and depends on process that is modeled, I_t serves for synchronization, it is vestige of previous versions of CA, in the FCA is not necessary and will be excluded further, I_1 introduces time delay and allows for control of boundary motion, I_2 and I_3 determines either cell will be inside (I_2) grain or on its boundary (I_3), I_4 is a function of I_1 or the state q_1 in the cell neighboring to considered cell and transfers it in the state q_b. Namely, the dependence of I_4 on I_1 or the state q_1 makes the CA as frontal ones. Instead of testing every neighboring cells for every cells in every time step (in classic

CA) only cells in state q_1 forms condition I_4 for their neighbors (in FCA). "Language" of CA consists of some "words", which contain several letter and mean cell transition from initial to final state. For example, four words $(I_0 \vee I_4)I_tI_1(I_2 \vee I_3)$ define creation or formation micro- or macrostructure.

The universal automaton is characterized by the closed circuit of the states. The states q_2 and q_3 can be not only the final states, but also the initial states for the next cycle of the modeling and the states of every cell can be repeated for several times. This property is useful for the modeling of some processes, but in modeling of macrostructure formation is not used.

In order to modeling solidification in continuous casting line with the mold of arbitrary shape, some changes are fulfilled in the automaton (figure 2).

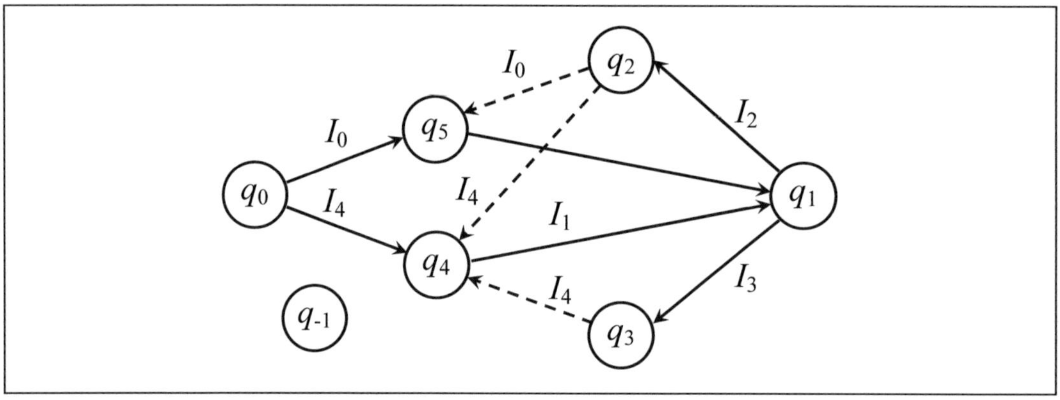

Fig. 2. New frontal cellular automaton

Firstly, states q_b and q_t were united into the state q_4, as well as conditions I_t and I_1. Condition I_t is excluded because of sequential type of calculations in FCA, which are different from calculations in classic CA. In the classic CA, a sequence of study of the cell state is defined spatially and it threatens to expand influence of the current cell beyond its neighborhood. In the FCA, sequence is set according to the cells state and any loop cannot be closed in one time step and influence of the cell cannot be extended beyond the neighborhood.

Then, connections from q_2 and q_3 to $q_{4(b)}$ are hold on, but remain deactivated.

And finally, new two states q_5 and q_{-1} are added. State of "nucleon" q_5 is added for more clear presentation and disjunction of the transition conditions I_0 (nucleation) and I_4 (boundary motion). Transition from the "nucleon" state q_5 into the state of "frontal cell" q_1 fulfills without any conditions. The other new state q_{-1} determines the cells, which do not participate in calculations, can be named "empty" and serve for consideration of real shape of the modeled space that must not be always parallelepiped. The cells in the state q_{-1} never change state and only mark boundary of the space. Due to this state round corner can be easily introduced for the modeled slab.

3. Isotropy of the cellular space and anisotropy of grain growing

Because of cubical shape of cell, cellular space demonstrates some anisotropy; some algorithms were used to reduce effect of the cell shape on the properties whole space (Svyetlichnyy, 2010).

According to the scheme in figure 2, words $(I_0 \vee I_4I_1)(I_2 \vee I_3)$ with initial state q_0 and final states q_2 and q_3 are responsible for formation of macrostructure. Letter I_0 describes nucleation; I_4 is appeared, when moving boundary of the growing grain has passed the neighboring cell. Letters I_0 and I_4 set cell into the "nucleon" state q_5 or "transient" state q_4 respectively. The transient state q_4 introduces delay, which is the time needed for the motion of a grain boundary through the cell with reckoning of cell shape and sizes. It defines grain growth rate, which can be arbitrary function of direction of growing, normal to boundary, disorientation angle or other parameters. Another effect of introduction of transient state is reduction of anisotropy of the cellular space. After passing the front thru whole cell (delay in several steps), the letter I_1 appears, and the cell is transferred into the state q_1. Cells pass from the "nucleon" state q_5 into the "frontal" state q_1 at the end of the step without any delay. The letters I_2 and I_3 emerge when all cells in its von Neumann neighborhood are in the state of q_1, q_2 or q_3. If all neighboring cells belongs to the same grain, a new state of cell is the "inside grain" q_3 otherwise "on the boundary" q_2. States q_3 and q_2 are the final states of the algorithm.

The more cells are used and the finer resolution is obtained, the more isotropic space could be received. As a test mainly growing of spherical grain is studied. Isotropic space allows for easy control of the grain or crystal shape. Several examples of free crystal growth are presented in figure 3. Shapes of the crystal shown in the picture are spheres, ellipsoids, cylinders, octahedrons, cubes and parallelepipeds respectively. At the beginning of the project, the same shapes of the crystals have been tried in the modeling of the solidification process. Some examples of the final structure are presented in figure 4.

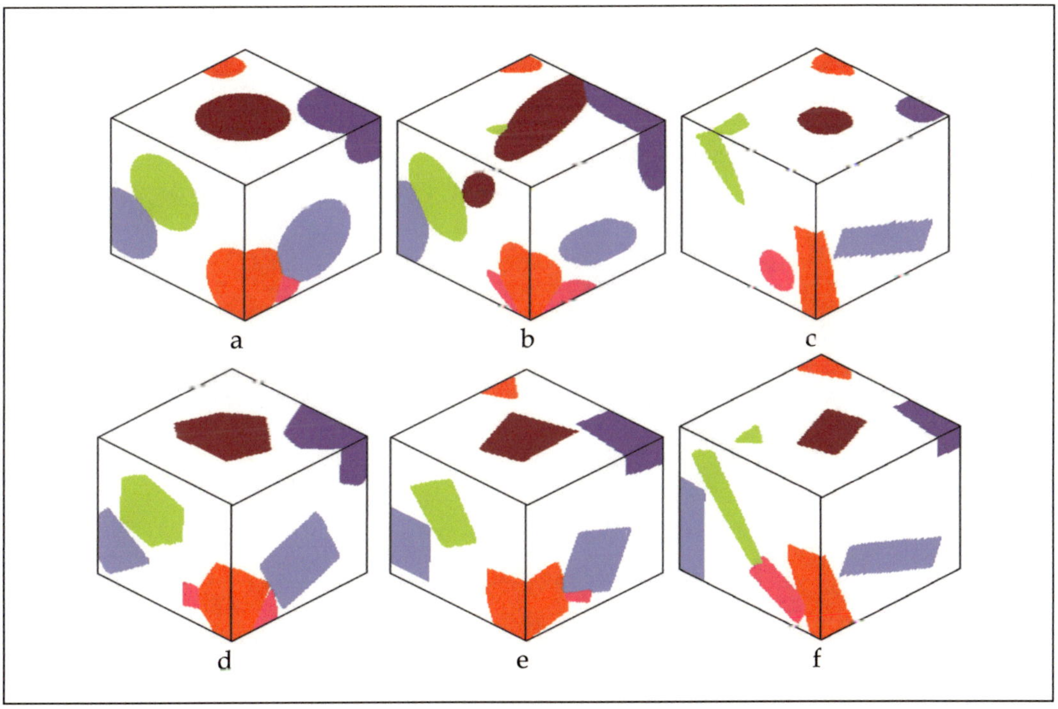

Fig. 3. Examples of free growing crystal of different shapes: a – spheres, b – ellipsoids, c - cylinders, d – octahedrons, e - cubes, f - parallelepipeds

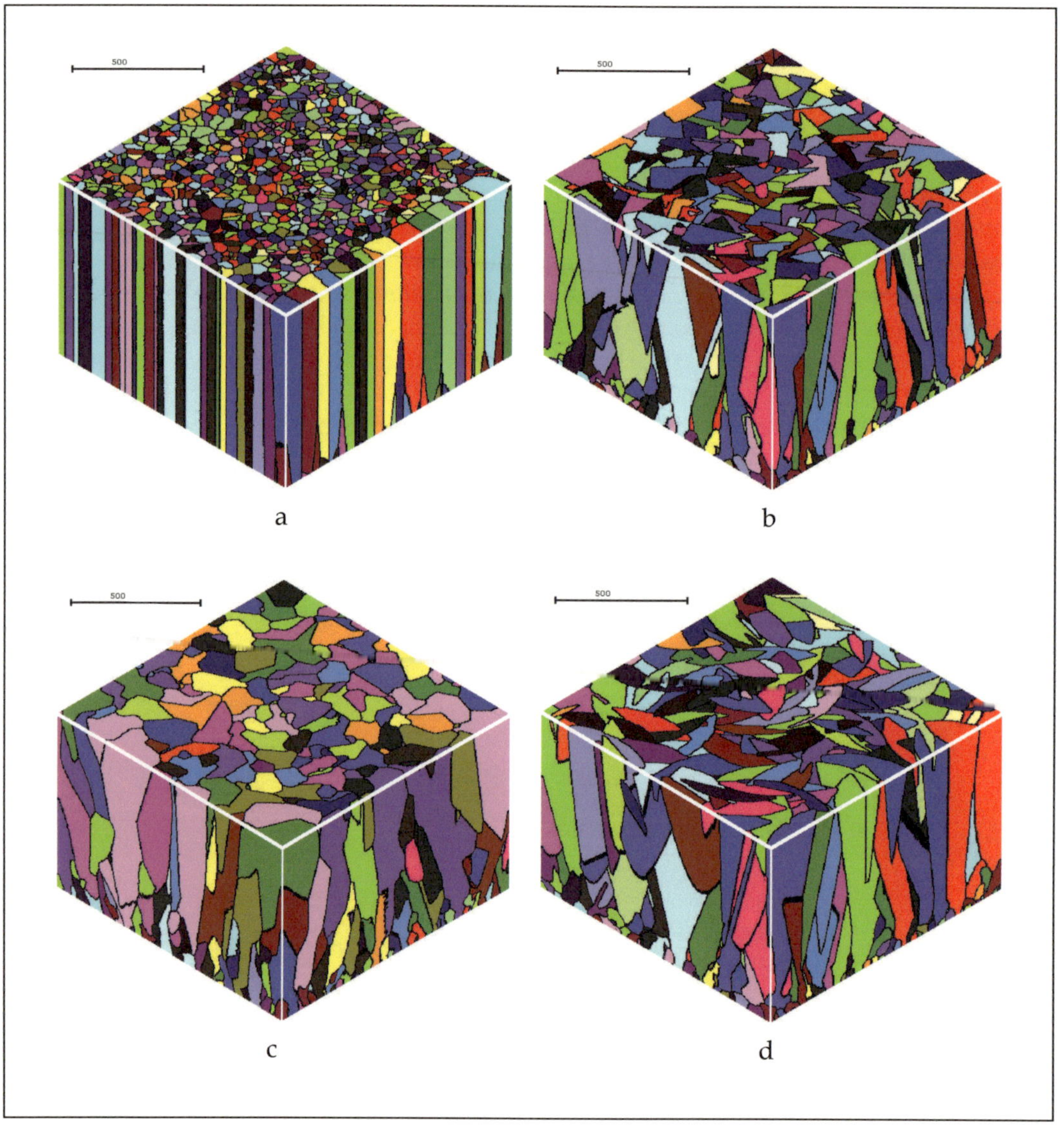

Fig. 4. Final structure for different shapes of growing crystals: a - sphere, b - parallelepiped, c - cube, d - cylinder

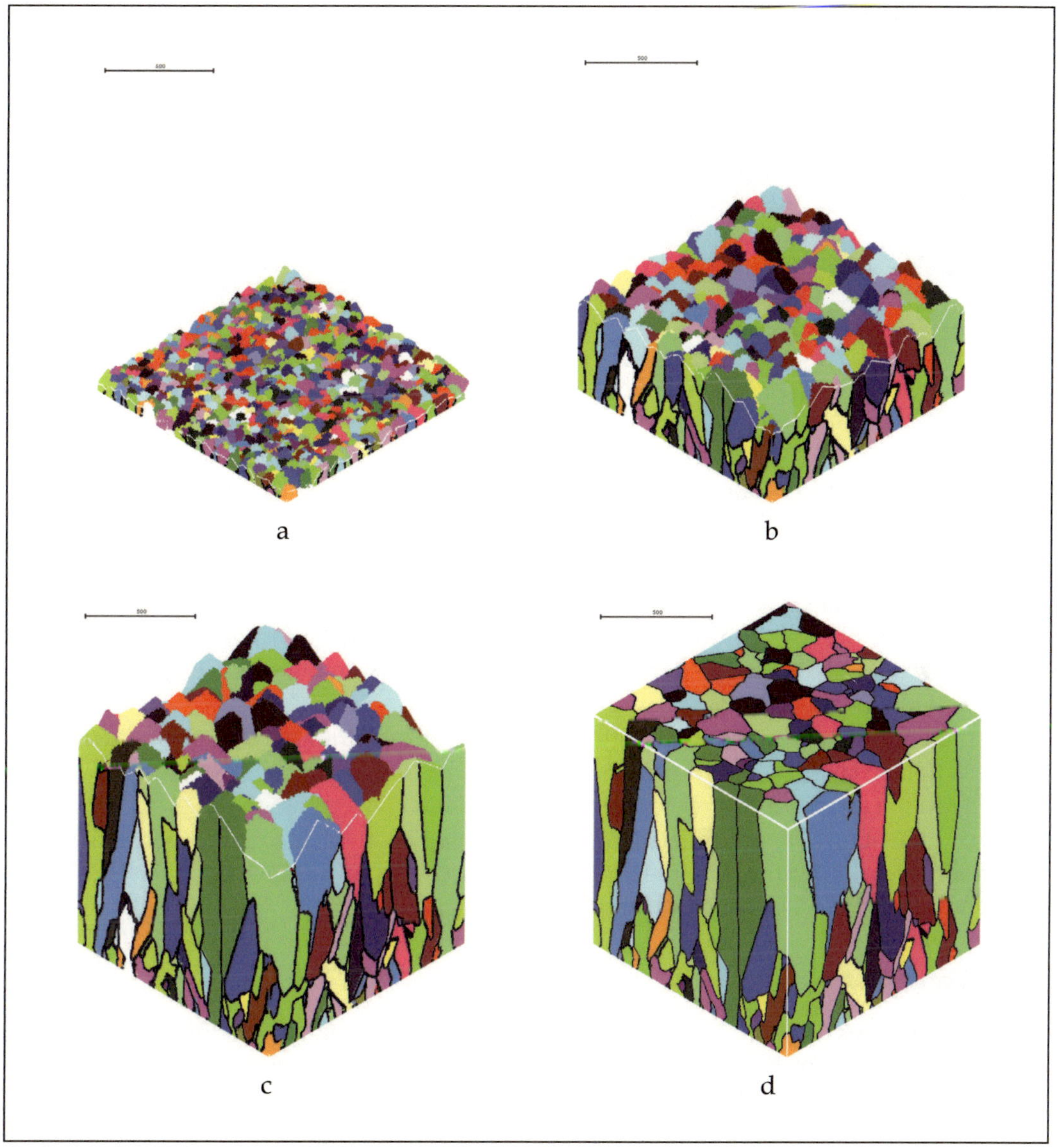

Fig. 5. Growing of the octahedral crystals

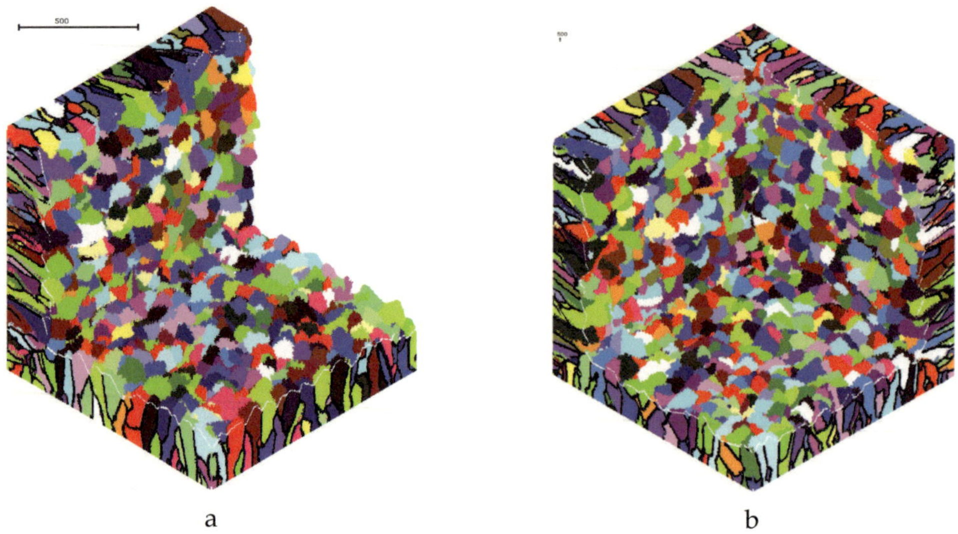

Fig. 6. Growing of the crystals from two (a) and three (b) surfaces

For spherical shape of growing crystals, symmetry does not prefer any direction for any crystals, and every grain grows in the same way. As result number of active growing crystal remains constant along whole process and structure with boundaries parallel to growing direction can be observed. Introduction of whichever asymmetry causes that some crystals grow faster then other, and it depends on their initial crystallographic orientation. Final structure depends on shape of growing crystal as well.

Then simulations were carried out with the shape of octahedron only, as more suitable for the steel. Some stages of growing of the octahedral crystal are shown in figure 5. Variants with nucleation on two and three surfaces were modeled as well (figure 6).

The first simulations were fulfilled without accounting of the real solidification conditions. Surface or the solidification tip was assumed to be parallel to the surface, where nuclei are appeared i.e. with the constant solidification speed in any point.

4. FEM and FCA

In the real processes, crystallization tip is determined by the temperature distribution in the metal. Then results of FEM calculations were used for simulation of the macrostructure formation during the solidification.

Possibilities of that calculation are limited mainly by the computer RAM. Bigger sizes require more space and more memory, because resolution cannot be changed. Maximal size, which can be modeled now, is about 15x15x1.8 mm. That's why only part of the slab is modeled. A rounded slab corner is also taken into account in design of cellular space.

As mentioned above, the variant of independent simulations by FEM and CA, without feedback, is chosen. Process is modeled by FEM code developed by Malinowski (Hadała & Malinowski, 2009) in the macro-scale. FEM solution is three-dimensional

stationary temperature distribution in the slab that moves with constant speed in consideration of all constructive and technological conditions.
Two external files are used for communication between FEM and FCA. The first one carries information about main parameters of modeled process, such as slab shape and sizes, number of FEM elements, coordinates of the FEM mesh nodes, temperature of solidus and liquidus, casting speed and so on. The second one contains temperature distribution. The distribution has to be suited to the cellular space. Though FEM solution is stationary temperature field, FCA considers the solution as hundreds locations of cross-section of the slab along casting line. Instead of spatial coordinate along the slab, FCA uses time, taking into account casting speed.
Every location of cross-section is studied before FCA calculations. Simulation of macrostructure formation begins when temperature at least in the one FEM node, which belongs to the point inside cellular space, decreases below the temperature of solidus. When temperature drops below the temperature of solidus in whole cellular space, the simulation is stopped. The simulation is carried out from one cross-section location to other. It makes timing easy, because internal time step is not of absolute value, but relative only in that case.
Before FCA calculations for current location, discrete temperature distribution must be transferred into two continuous lines, which present isotherms of liquids and solidus. A cross-section, FEM nodes, FCA space and isotherm are shown on the left part of figure 7. After lines are obtained for cross-section, they are carried to the cellular space. The right part of figure 7 demonstrates further calculations for one line. Hachure lines present new isotherm transferred from FEM and solidification tip obtained in previous step. New isotherm is replaced by several (up to eight) legs marked as "front lines". Then cellular space is divided on segments contiguous to the appropriate front line. "Segment line" is a border that separates one segment from another.

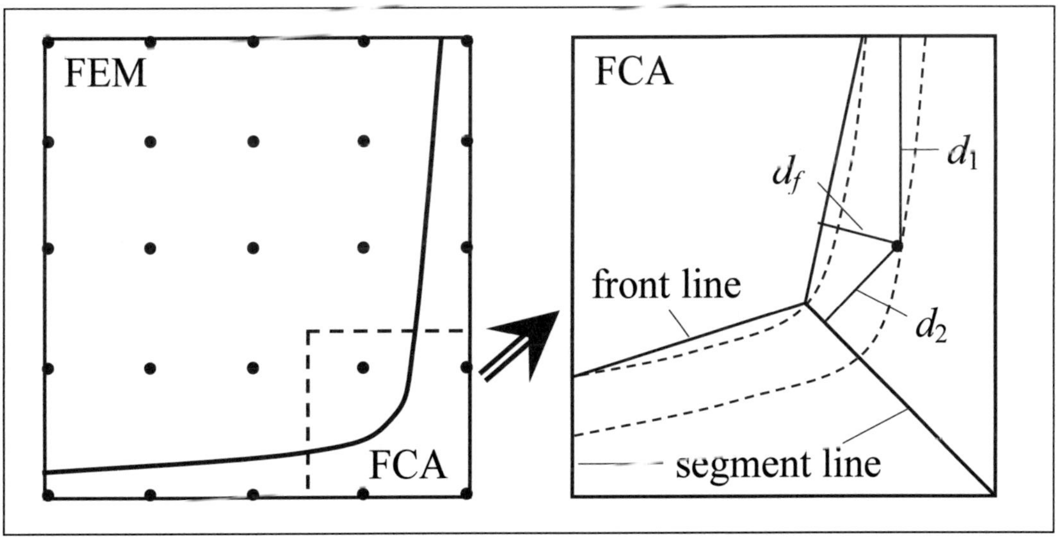

Fig. 7. Scheme for calculations of the grain growth rate factor

Segmentation of the cellular space is used to differentiate growing rate in different part of the space. Growing rate is additionally controlled by introduction of factor, which depends on location of a point in appropriate segment. The factor is not constant inside the segment, but linear function of local relative coordinate x. Coordinate x is defined from the equation: $x = d_1 / (d_1 + d_2)$ and can changes in diapason 0 to 1, where d_1 and d_2 - distance from the point to segment lines. Because solidification tip must reach the next location determined by front line simultaneously on all line length, growing rate must be depended on initial distance of solidification tip from the front line. Thus, for every cells on the front of solidification (in state q_4) three distances d_f (from front line), d_1 and d_2 (from segment lines) are calculated. It allows to obtain dependence of distance d_f on local coordinate x for every segment. Generally obtained dependence for whole cellular space has discontinuities on the border of segments; and the discontinuities must be eliminated. Then dependence is normalized by division on maximal value (distance) and constrains on minimal value are introduced. Such a transformation as a result gives a growing rate factor. New cells involved in solidification process inherit from the neighboring cells number of segment, its local coordinate is calculated, and time delay for the state q_4 is computed in view of growing rate factor correspondent to its location.

Calculations are finished for current location of cross-section when solidification tip reaches the front line. Then new location is chosen and calculations are repeated.

5. FCA code

Code for FCA modeling has been designed in Department of Heat Engineering and Environment Protection, Faculty of Metal Engineering and Industrial Computer Science, AGH University of Science and Technology (Poland). It is still developing now. Several processes with microstructure evolution can be chosen for modeling (figure 8), they are: creation new initial structure with arbitrary grain shapes, flat rolling in several passes, continuous forming processes with varied deformation conditions (shape rolling, forging an so on), cold deformation with grain refined, phase transformation (austenite-ferrite), solidification and modeling of macrostructure formation in continuous casting.

A module of modeling of macrostructure formation in continuous casting has been designed in the frame of the program for modeling whole process of continuous casting which consist of several modules. The main module based on FEM code serves for calculations of the

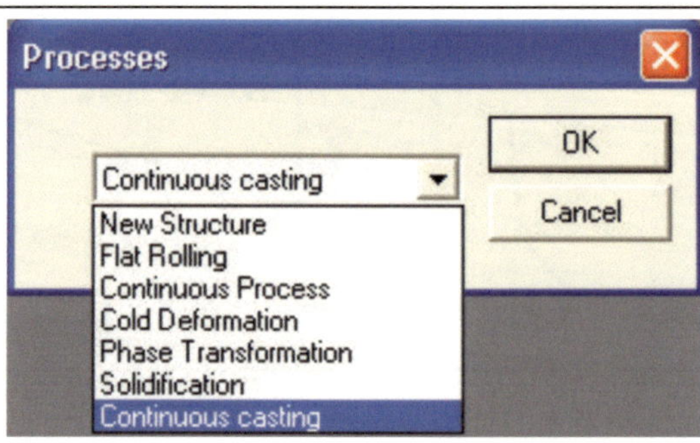

Fig. 8. Processes menu of FCA code

temperature distribution of the whole slab in consideration with all process conditions. FEM solution is saved in the external file, and the file is used as interface between FEM and FCA codes without feedback.

After the choice of the modeled process, user has two options for further work (figure 9). They are modeling the process or review results. When modeling is being carried out, information about the process is being saved in several files. The first one stores basic information, such as type of modeled process, sizes of cellular space (both in cells and in micrometers), initial number of grains, modeled point number and so on. The second file contains initial information about grains: grain number, crystallographic orientation and location where the grain appears. The next file is a list of the cells that has passed from liquid state to solid one. It is the list of coordinates (in cells) and grain number, which it belongs to, being written in the sequence of their state changes. Such three files allow for presentation whole modeled process or for continuation a broken process (figure 10).

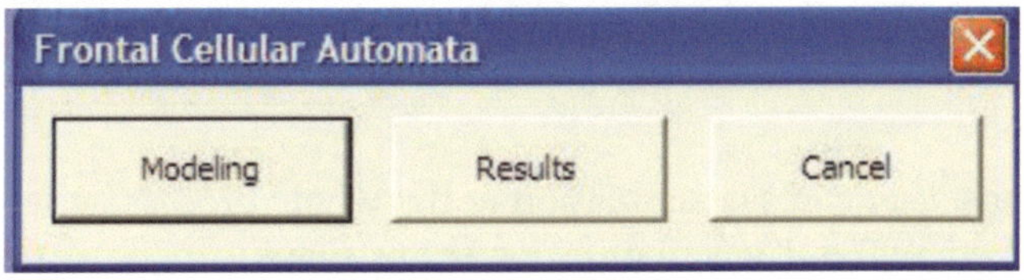

Fig. 9. Choice of modeling the process or review results

Fig. 10. Menu for choice of modeling the new process or continuation a broken process

Thus, choice of the option "modeling" gives two possibilities: new modeling or continuation of broken calculations (figure 10). New modeling can be fulfilled at any time. Continuation of the broken calculations could be realized as soon as at least one process had been started; independently the calculations have been finished or not. In fact information stored in the files is a snapshot of the last state of calculations, then their interruption is not critical and they can be renewed from the last saved point. Simultaneously with the saving information to the files, it can be outputted on display, fully visualizing calculations. This option can be selected by marking appropriate box. But full visualization elongates calculations essentially and is not recommended. If such option is not selected, visualization during modeling is limited to a few snaps, which is saved as well. After modeling is completed, structure obtained in the process is written in the file and can be used in the other models for further modeling.

User has some choice for control of modeling in dependence of computer power, mainly RAM memory. Because of limits on sizes of the cells, which connected with resolution, accessible memory determines sizes of modeled space. Usually, whole cross-section of the slab cannot be modeled, thus only some part can be chosen for calculations. Now program allows for calculation macrostructure formation in parallelepiped specimen from the sizes

3.5x3.5x0.875 mm (1GB RAM) to 15.0x15.0x.1.8 mm (16 GB RAM) (figure 11). It uses from 3.5 millions to 115 millions cells. Accordingly, time of calculation is varied in wide range from two minutes to 1-2 hours.

Because of sizes of the slab, only part of cross-section can be modeled by FCA. There are four options for choice: right or bottom side, right bottom edge or center of the slab (figure 12).

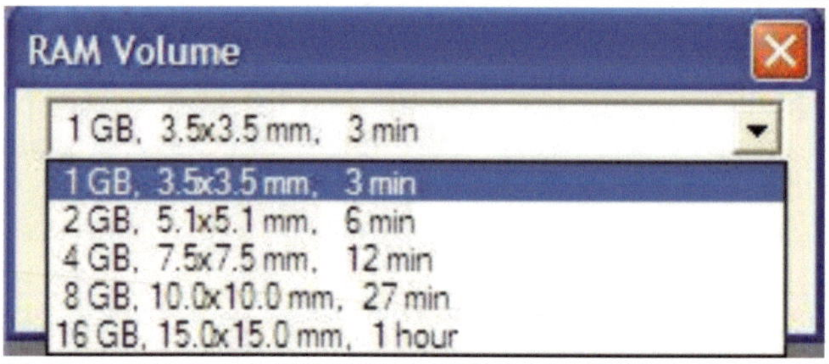

Fig. 11. Memory choice menu

After the calculations, user can see simulation of the whole process, when information from the files is visualized without calculation, or some snaps can be seen (figure 13). Final macrostructure can be presented as well. All structures are shown in isometric view. Final macrostructure is pointed on the faces of the rectangular cellular space or on few parallel cross-sections. Picture of partially solidified macrostructure is filled up by solidification tip. Appropriate macrostructure is inputted from the files, saved during the modeling.

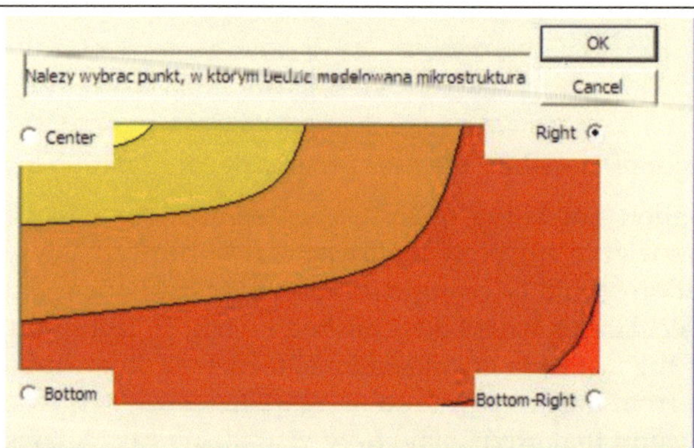

Fig. 12. Point choice menu

Fig. 13. Menu for results demonstration

6. Results

Modeling of the casting process has been carried out. Sizes of cross-section are 100x100 mm. Radius of round corner is 5 mm. FEM solution has received for quarter of cross-section on whole length of casting line. Full solution has 313 locations of cross-section along the slab with 17x17 nodes in each. Not every cross-sections has been used by FCA, several the first ones have temperature over the temperature of solidus, while the last ones have its below temperature of solidus in whole cellular space. Because of sizes of the slab, only part of cross-section can be modeled by FCA. There are four options for choice: right or bottom side, right bottom edge or center of the bloom.

There are three snapshots of the process of macrostructure formation, when nucleation is on the right side of the slab, in figure 14.

Firstly, intensive heterogeneous nucleation in the mold gives many new grains with random crystallographic orientation. A solidification tip is parallel to surface of the slab. Further, some grains with orientation close to growing direction receive advantage over others, and number of growing grains decreases. The front of solidification becomes gradually non-parallel. The same pictures, one can see, when modeled the bottom side of the slab (figure 15).

Other three snapshots of the process are presented in figure 16. Here is shown right bottom corner of the slab. Grains grow preferentially perpendicular to the surface of mold. Then, area near the corner closes up, and two main direction of growing remain.

Formation of macrostructure at the center of the slab is sown in figure 17. When the process of solidification draws to a close, a zone of equi-axis grains is formed. Basis of such grains is homogeneous nucleation during the process. The grains on the early stages of solidification either contact with the dendrites or not. When they touch formed structure, they joint to dendrite structure and receive preferential direction of growing; they become

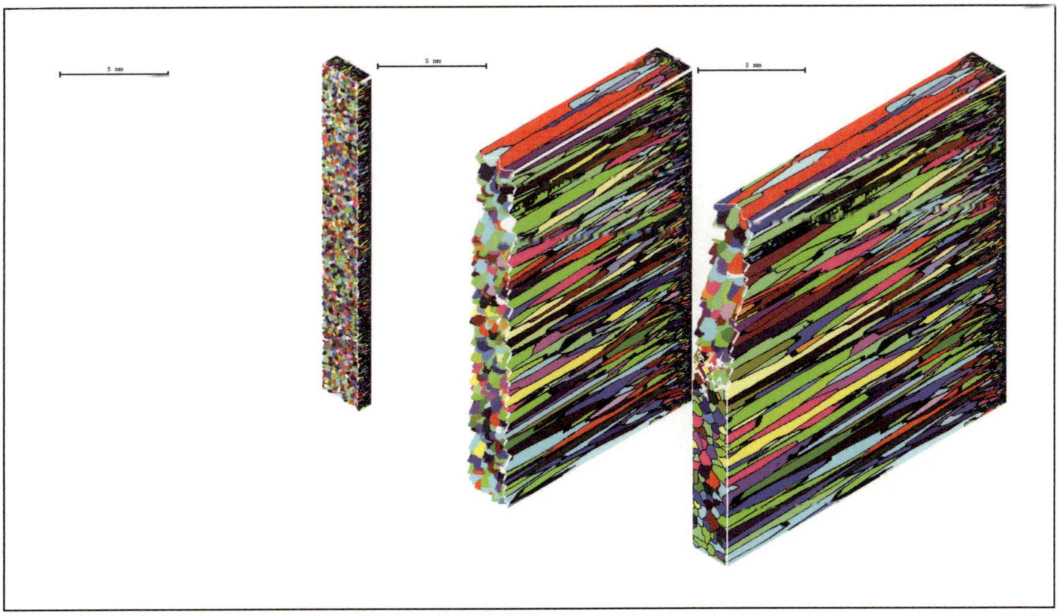

Fig. 14. Growing of the crystals from the right side

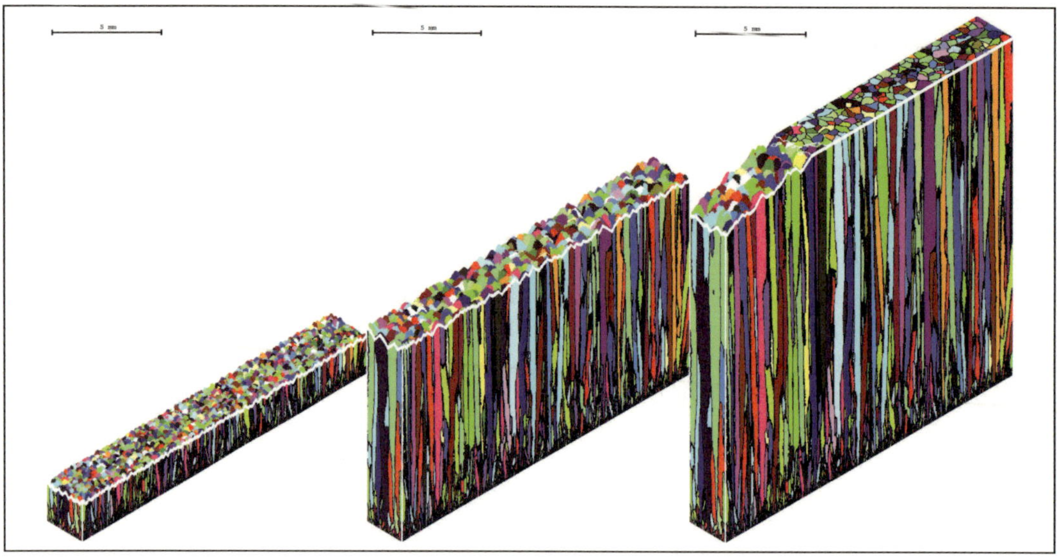

Fig. 15. Growing of the crystals from the bottom side

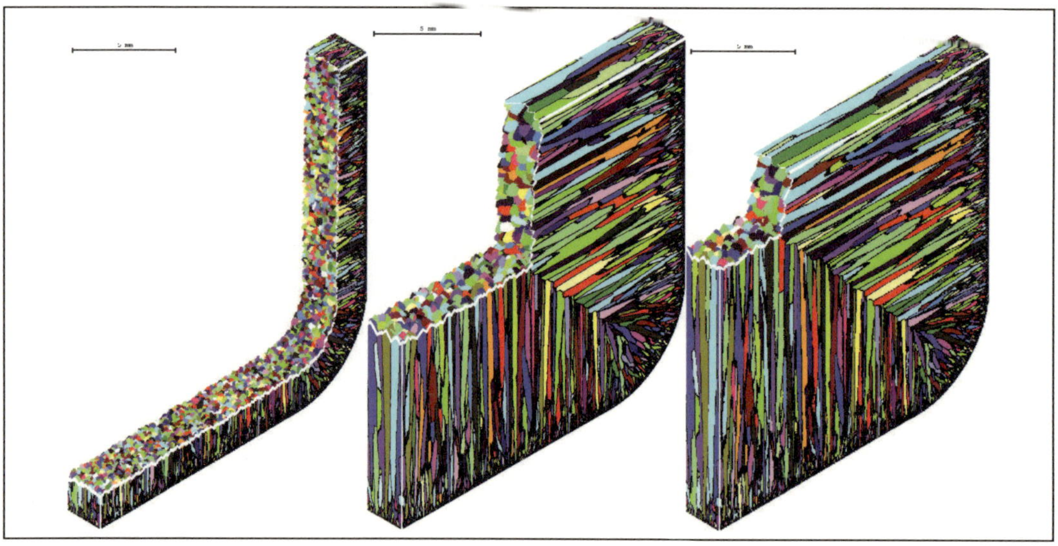

Fig. 16. Formation of macrostructure at the corner

Fig. 17. Formation of macrostructure at the center

undistinguishable from the other grains. Growing of free grains is braked till the end of solidification process. Then fast growing of the equi-axis grains begins. Three stages of the process can be seen in figure 17.

6. Future research

There are two directions of the development present project planed. The first one is connected with researches of effect processes parameters on formation macrostructure. Mainly attention will be paid on nucleation, crystal growth rate, chemical composition, melt convection and mixing.

The second direction is extension of modeled space. New principles of cellular space is developed, but not implemented into the code. Results presented in the chapter have been obtained in the stationary cellular space, when every cell has invariable spatial coordinates.

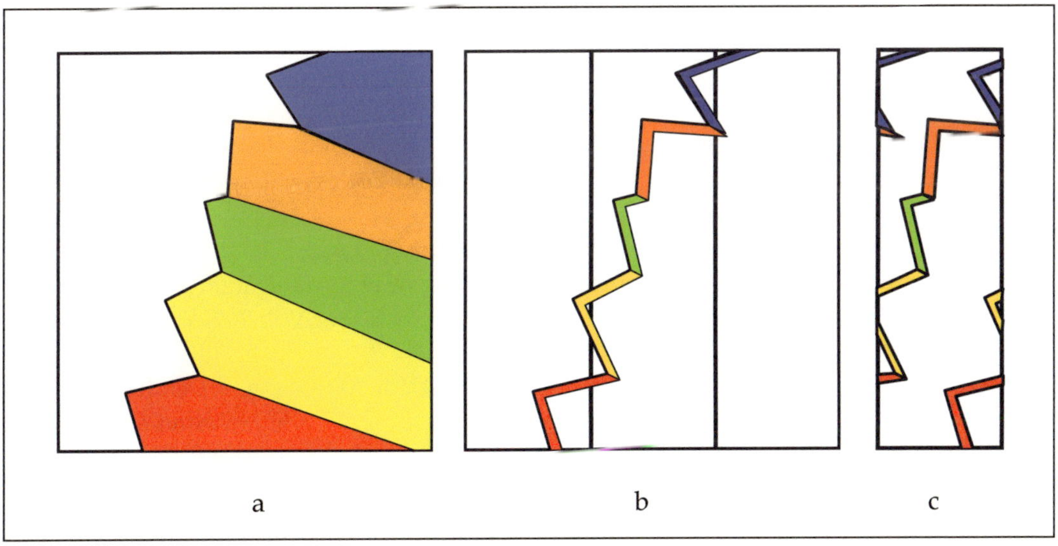

Fig. 18. Space in the new frontal cellular automaton

Every cell exists during the whole modeling and therefore it requires memory. In the proposed variant, cellular space can remains stationary, but cell will be consequently assigned to different point of the modeled space during the modeling. The cell will have the same coordinates (in cells) in the cellular space, but different spatial coordinates in modeled space. A transition can be explained with aid of figure 18.

In figure 18a a fragment of modeled and cellular space is shown. Two regions not only can be excluded from calculations, but also their points can be non-existent. Actually only thin layer shown in figure 18b is important for calculations. Behind the solidification front cells are need not further. Information has already been saved in the files, and cells can be cleaned, prepared and assigned for the next point of modeled space. Thus, instead large cellular space can be used only thin layer of several cells in thickness. An example of the layer is presented in figure 18c.

7. Conclusions

The developed three-dimensional FCA model for modeling of macrostructure formation during the continuous casting is discussed in the paper. Reduction of the effect of anisotropy on the grain growth allows for better control of the shape of dendrites. In the model, the CA space, the shape and the sizes of the cells remain constant and can be of arbitrary shape. The joint FCA with FEM has allowed to improve accuracy of modeling. Calculated distribution of the temperature gives a basis for simulation of macrostructure formation close to the real one because FEM modeling has carried out with consideration all technological and process conditions. The presented results favored the conclusion that the FCA model can be applied for such a simulation of the macrostructure formation.

8. Acknowledgement

Support of the Polish Ministry of Education and Science is greatly appreciated (Grant no. N R07 0018 04).

9. References

Beltran-Sanchez L., Stefanescu D. (2003). Growth of Solutal Dendrites: A Cellular Automaton Model and Its Quantitative Capabilities, *Metall. Mater. Trans. A*, Vol. 34A, No. 2, pp.367-382, ISSN 1073-5615

Bernacki, M., Chastel, Y., Digonnet, H., Resk, H., Coupez, T., Loge, R.E. (2007). Development of numerical tools for the multiscale modeling of recrystallization in metals, based on a digital material framework, *Comp. Meth. Mat. Sci.*, Vol. 7, No. 1, pp. 142-149, ISSN 1641-8581.

Burbelko A.A., Fraś E., Kapturkiewicz W., Gurgul D. (2010). Modelling of Dendritic Growth During Unidirectional Solidification by the Method of Cellular Automata, *Mat. Sci. Forum*, Vol. 649, pp. 217-222, ISSN 0255-5476.

Das, S., Palmiere, E.J., Howard, I.C. (2002). CAFE: a Tool for Modeling Thermomechanical Processes, *Proc. of Thermomech. Processing: Mechanics, Microstructure & Control,* pp. 296-301, ISBN 0-9522507, The University of Sheffield, June 2002, The University of Sheffield, Sheffield.

Davies, C. H. J. (1997). Growth of Nuclei in a Cellular Automaton Simulation of Recrystallization, *Scr. Mater.*, Vol. 36, No.1, pp. 35-40, ISSN 1359-6462.

Fan, D., Chen, L.Q. (1997). Computer simulation of grain growth using a continuum field model. *Acta Mat.* Vol.45, No.2, pp. 611–622, ISSN 1359-6454.

Frost, H.J., Thompson, C.V., Howe, C.L., Whang, J. (1988). A Two-Dimensional Computer Simulation of Capillary-Driven Grain Growth: Preliminary Results, *Scripta Metall.* Vol. 22, No.1, pp. 65-70, ISSN 1359-6454.

Holm, E.A., Hassold, G.N., Miodownik, M.A. (2001). On misorientation distribution evolution during anisotropic grain growth, *Acta Mater.* Vol.49, No.15, pp. 2981-2991, ISSN 1359-6454.

Hurley, P.J., Humphreys, F.J. (2003). Modelling the Recrystallization of Single-Phase Aluminium, *Acta mater.*, Vol.51, No.13, pp. 3779-3793, ISSN 1359-6454.

Kumar, M., Sasikumar, R., Kesavan Nair, P. (1998). Competition between nucleation and early growth of ferrite from austenite – studies using cellular automation simulations, *Acta Mater.*, Vol.46, No.17, pp. 6291-6303, ISSN 1359-6454.

Hadała B., Malinowski Z. (2009). Accuracy of the finite element solution to steady convection-diffusion heat transport equation in continuous casting problem, *Comp. Meth. Mat. Sci.*, Vol. 9, No. 2, pp. 302-308, ISSN 1641-8581.

Qian, M., Guo, Z.X. (2004). Cellular Automata Simulation of Microstructural Evolution during Dynamic Recrystallization of an HY-100 Steel, *Mater. Sci. Eng. A*, Vol.A365, No.1-2, pp. 180-185, ISSN 0921-5093.

Raabe, D. (2004). Mesoscale simulation of spherulite growth during polymer crystallization by use of a cellular automaton, *Acta Mater.*, Vol. 52, No.9, pp. 2653-2664, ISSN 1359-6454.

Rappaz, M., Gandin, C.-A. (1993). Probabilistic Modelling of Microstructure Formation in Solidification Processes, *Acta Metal. Mater.*, Vol. 41, No.2, pp. 345-360, ISSN 1359-6454.

Svyetlichnyy, D.S., Majta, J., Muszka, K. (2008). Modeling of microstructure evolution of BCC metals subjected to severe plastic deformation, *Steel Res. Int.*, Vol.79, pp. 452–458, ISSN 1611-3683.

Svyetlichnyy D.S. (2010). Modeling of the Microstructure: From Classical Cellular Automata Approach to the Frontal One, *Comp. Mater. Sci.*, doi:10.1016/j.commatsci.2010.07.011, ISSN 0927-0256.

Thompson, C.V., Frost, H.J, Spaepen, F., 1987, *The Relative Rates of Secondary and Normal Grain Growth, Acta Metall.*, Vol.35, No.4, pp. 887-890, ISSN 1359-6454.

Weygand, D., Brechet,Y., Lepinoux, J. (2001). A Vertex Simulation of Grain Growth in 2D and 3D, *Adv. Eng. Mater.*, Vol. 3, No.1-2, pp. 67-71, ISSN 1527-2648.

Yuan L., Lee P.D. (2010). Dendritic solidification under natural and forced convection in binary alloys: 2D versus 3D simulation, *Modelling Simul. Mater. Sci. Eng.*, Vol. 18, No.5, 055008, ISSN 0965-0393.

Zhu M.F., Hong C.P. (2001). A Modified Cellular Automaton Model for the Simulation of Dendritic Growth in Solidification of Alloys, ISIJ Int., Vol. 41, No. 5, pp 436-445, ISSN 0915-1559.

9

Point Automata Method for Dendritic Growth

Agnieszka Zuzanna Lorbiecka and Božidar Šarler
University of Nova Gorica
Slovenia

1. Introduction

Solidification microstructure is very important since it influences the properties of the final casting. Because of that has understanding and modelling of microstructures large industrial relevance. However, the understanding of solidification processes and related microstructures involves very complicated relationships. This is because it is affected by many interacting phenomena on different scales, such as heat and solute transfer, fluid flow, thermodynamics of interfaces and so on (Rettenmayr & Buchmann, 2006). Experiments that allow direct visualization of microstructure formation are difficult to perform. In the last decade, several numerical models, which can solve complicated transport phenomena and phase transformation under different boundary and initial conditions, were developed to calculate various microstructure features of solidifying materials such as grain growth with details of solidification interface morphology. Among of all numerical approaches Cellular Automata (CA) modeling (Wolfram, 2002) and phase field modeling (Qin & Wallach, 2003) are the most popular and widely used. We focus on the CA based approach in this chapter. A considerable progress on solidification microstructure simulation (Boettinger et al., 2000; Miodownik, 2002) has been made by the CA approach.

Rappaz and Gandin (Rappaz & Gandin, 1993) were the pioneering researchers who developed the CA model for modelling microstructure where the nucleation and the growth kinetics could be considered and grain structure with certain shapes and size were predicted. Gandin and Rappaz (Gandin & Rappaz, 1994; Gandin & Rappaz, 1997) simulated the grain structure by coupling the CA technique for the grain growth with the finite element method (FEM) solver for the heat flow (CA-FEM). Later Spittle and Brown (Spittle & Brown, 1995) coupled the CA with a finite difference solver (CA-FDM) for solute diffusion during the solidification of casting to predict the microstructure.

Unfortunately, the simple CA models for dendritic growth suffer from the strong impact of the anisotropy of the numerical grid. Consequences are that they tend to grow only in the grid direction (Zhan et al., 2008). It does not matter which crystallographic orientation will be chosen the CA method will always shift the dendrite with respect to the grid axis. During growth have the crystallographic orientation axes of different grains different divergence angles with respect to the coordinate system. In these cases is the growth stage difficult to simulate by the CA method. It is because the configuration of the CA mesh has a direct influence on simulated structure and shape. Anderson (Anderson et al., 1984) and later Spittle and Brown (Spittle & Brown, 1989) used a hexagonal, rather than the standard square 2-D lattice in order to better represent the grain anisotropy. But in general even now it is still difficult to properly model the preferred crystallographic orientation. Rappaz and Gandin developed a decentered square method (Rappaz & Gandin, 1993) to try to solve this problem, which turns out to be very complicated.

We elaborate a novel Point Automata (PA) method in this chapter which follows the CA concept and is able to solve the mentioned crystallographic orientation problem. A basic feature of this method is to distribute nodes randomly in the domain instead of using regular cells, which leads to different distances between the nodes and different neighborhood configurations for each of them. This new approach was first proposed by Janssens for modelling the re-crystallisation (Janssens, 2000, 2003, 2010; Raabe et al., 2007). (Lorbiecka et al., 2009) were the first to couple the classical CA method with a meshless method instead of the FEM or FDM. They successfully predicted the grain structure in continuously cast steel billets. Subsequently, they replaced the CA method by the PA method in the same physical system (Lorbiecka & Šarler, 2009) and demonstrated the suitability of the PA method for cellular to equiaxed and equiaxed to cellular transition simulation in steel strands. The preliminary results of the dendritic growth based on the PA approach have been presented in (Lorbiecka & Šarler, 2009). This approach is explained and evaluated in details in the present chapter where we cope with a simple physical model which can simulate the dendritic forms during the solidification of pure metals from the undercooled melt. The developed algorithm is able to obtain the dendritic morphology by solving the heat transfer equation coupled with the solid fraction field evolution through the calculations of crystal growth velocity, interface curvature, thermodynamic and kinetic anisotropy, respectively.

The present chapter is structured in the following way: the CA and the PA methods are defined first, followed by the description of the governing equations of the heat transfer model and the stochastic model. The solution of temperature field and solid fraction is explained afterwards. The differences in numerical implementation of the classical CA and the new PA solution procedure are compared and discussed. The dendritic growth is simulated for two different orientations with the same random node arrangement with the PA method. Afterwards, the influence of two different random node arrangements as well as different node randomness was tested on two different crystallographic orientations. Finally, the numerical results are shown for seven dendrites growing simultaneously with the orientations 0° or 45° by the classical CA method and with different, more realistic orientations for the PA method. This demonstrates the flexibility of the new method for simulation of realistic dendritic structures. Conclusions with systematically listed characteristics of the PA method and future developments of the PA method complete the present chapter.

2. CA and PA definitions

Numerical models for solving the microstructure equations can briefly be divided into two categories: deterministic and stochastic (Stefanescu, 2009). Stochastic modelling represents a system where the physical phenomena are described by the random numbers. As a consequence the output data can vary from one simulation to another. The most popular stochastic methods used to simulate the microstructure formations are: Monte Carlo methods, Random Walker and CA approach. CA stochastic method (Wolfram, 2002) represents one of the numerical techniques, widely applied in modelling solidification and re-crystallization processes. This algorithm was first established by Neumann (Neumann, 1987) and is nowadays commonly used in materials science. What follows are the basic elements of the CA method

- n-D (n=1, 2, 3) space is divided into a discrete number of n-dimensional elements which are named cells (polygons and polyhedrons).
- a state is assigned to each CA cell,
- the neighbourhood configuration is defined deterministic or stochastic for each CA cell,
- transition rules are defined which create a new state of the cell as a function of the states(s) of the cell(s) consisting of the previously defined local neighbourhood of the cell.

The above presented basic features of the CA system are commonly implemented in the literature. In the present work an alternative formulation to a common CA method is introduced. What follows are the basic elements of this novel PA method

- the starting point is to distribute PA nodes (not cells) randomly on the n-D computational domain,
- a state is assigned to each PA node,
- the neighbourhood configuration is defined for each node separately with respect to the chosen neighbourhood configuration,
- the neighbourhood of the node includes all random nodes whose positions are located in the domain of a circle in 2D or sphere in 3D. The number of the neighbours can vary locally. The transition rules are defined and they create a new state of the point as a function of the states(s) of the points(s) consisting the local neighbourhood configuration.

The irregular (also named random) PA cellular transitions rules can be used in exactly the same way as for the regular approach. In this sense the PA approach is not much different from the conventional one, despite bringing many advantages listed in the conclusions.

3. Governing equations

Thermally induced dendritic growth is considered in this example. It is physically described by the heat conduction and phase change kinetics. The temperature field is solved by the classical deterministic method and the phase change kinetics by the stochastic method.

3.1 Temperature field

Consider a two dimensional domain Ω with boundary Γ filled with a phase change material which consists of at least two phases, solid and liquid, separated by an interfacial region, which is usually very thin in pure substances. The thermal field in such a system is governed by the following equation (Xu et al., 2008)

$$\frac{\partial}{\partial t}(\rho h) = \nabla \cdot (\lambda \nabla T) \tag{1}$$

where ρ, h, λ, T represent material density, specific enthalpy, thermal conductivity and temperature, respectively. The specific enthalpy is constituted as

$$h = c_p T + f_l L \tag{2}$$

where c_p , L , f_l represent the specific heat, the latent heat and liquid fraction, respectively. All material properties are assumed constant for simulation simplicity. The solid and liquid fractions follow the rules

$$f_s + f_l = 1;\; f_s(T) = \begin{cases} 1 & for\ T \le T_s \\ \dfrac{T_l - T}{T_l - T_s} & for\ T_s < T < T_l \\ 0 & for\ T \ge T_l \end{cases} \tag{3}$$

where T_s , T_l , f_s represent the solidus temperature, liquidus temperature and the solid fraction, respectively. In case of a pure substance are the solidus and the liquidus temperature equal to the melting temperature T_m . However, for the computational purposes a narrow melting interval $T_l > T_m > T_s$ is always involved. The melting temperature T_m is defined as $T_m = \frac{1}{2}(T_s + T_l)$. We search for the temperature at time $t_0 + \Delta t$ by assuming the initial conditions

$$T(\mathbf{p},t_0) = T_0(\mathbf{p});\ \mathbf{p} \in \Omega;\ f_s(\mathbf{p},t_0) = f_{s0}(\mathbf{p});\ \mathbf{p} \in \Omega \tag{4}$$

(where $\mathbf{p}$ represents the position vector) and Neumann boundary conditions

$$\frac{\partial T}{\partial n}(\mathbf{p},t) = F(\mathbf{p},t);\ \mathbf{p} \in \Gamma,\ t_0 < t \le t_0 + \Delta t \tag{5}$$

where $\mathbf{n}$ represents the normal on Γ and T_0 , f_{s0} , F represent known functions.

3.2 Phase change kinetics

3.2.1 Interface undercooling

The phase change situation can be achieved by undercooling a liquid below its melting temperature. When a solid seed is placed in such an undercooled melt, solidification will be initiated. Due to crystal anisotropy and perturbations in the system, the growth of the solid from the seed will not be uniform and an equiaxed dendritic crystal will form. Solid liquid interface is undercooled to the temperature T_f defined as (Saito et al., 1988; Nakagawa, et al., 2006)

$$T_f = T_m - \Gamma K \tag{6}$$

where Γ and K are the Gibbs-Thomson coefficient and the interface curvature, respectively.

3.2.2 Dendrite growth kinetics

The growth process is driven by the local undercooling. The interface growth velocity is given by the classical sharp model (Shin & Hong, 2002)

$$V_g^*(\mathbf{p},t) = \mu_K\left(T_f - T(\mathbf{p},t)\right);\ \mathbf{p} \in \Gamma_{s,l} \tag{7}$$

where V_g^* , μ_K , $\Gamma_{s,l}$ are the growth velocity, interface kinetics coefficient and the solid liquid interface, respectively.

Dendrites always grow in the specific crystallographic orientations. Therefore, it is necessary to consider anisotropy in either the interfacial kinetics or surface energy (or both). The present model accounts for the anisotropy in the both kinetics.

3.2.3 Thermodynamic anisotropy

The Gibbs-Thomson coefficient can be evaluated (Krane et al., 2009) by taking into account the thermodynamic anisotropy related to the crystal orientation and type as follows

$$\Gamma = \overline{\Gamma}\left[1 - \delta_t \cos\left[S\left(\theta - \theta_{def}\right)\right]\right] \tag{8}$$

where S, θ, θ_{def}, δ_t, $\overline{\Gamma}$ represent factors which control the number of preferential directions of the material's anisotropy ($S = 0$ for the isotropic case, $S = 4$ for four fold anisotropy and so on), growth angle (angle between the y coordinate and the line that connects the centre of the mass of the dendrite and point at $\Gamma_{s,l}$, see Fig. 1), the preferential crystallographic orientation, thermodynamic anisotropy coefficient and the average Gibbs-Thomson coefficient, respectively.

3.2.4 Kinetic anisotropy

The crystal growth velocity is calculated according to the crystal orientation by taking into the consideration the crystal growth direction θ and the preferred orientation θ_{def}. The crystal growth velocity follows the equation (Shin & Hong, 2002)

$$V = V_g^*(\mathbf{p},t)\left[1 + \delta_k \cos\left(S\left(\theta - \theta_{def}\right)\right)\right] \tag{9}$$

where δ_k represents the degree of the kinetic anisotropy.

3.3 Coupling

The movement of the solid-liquid interface is governed by the evolution of the temperature field in the computational domain (Fig. 1).

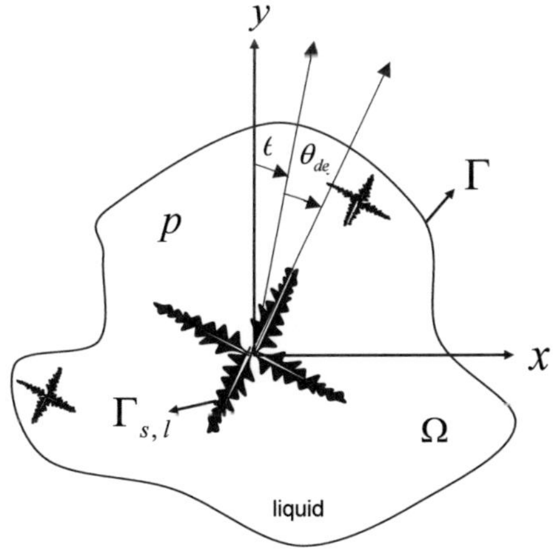

Fig. 1. Scheme of the dendritic growth

The dendritic structures are modelled by the stochastic method to track the interface motion coupled to the determinate heat transfer calculations. We first describe the solution of the temperature field based on the FDM method and subsequently the transition rules for the CA (PA) methods for calculation of solid fraction field. The flowchart of the calculations is given in Fig. 12.

4. Solution of the temperature field

A square domain is considered with length l. The number of points in FDM mesh in x and y directions is N. The total number of FDM grid points is N^2 - 4, since the four corner nodes are not considered.
A uniform FDM discretization is made with mesh distance $\Delta x = \Delta y = a = l/(N-1)$ as seen in Fig. 5 (left). The solution for the temperature field is performed by the simple explicit FDM. Solution of the temperature field in the domain nodes is thus

$$T_{i,j} = T_{0\,i,j} + \frac{\Delta t \lambda}{\rho c_p}\left(\left[\left(T_{0\,i-1,j} - 2T_{0\,i,j} + T_{0\,i+1,j}\right)/\left(\Delta x^2\right)\right] + \left[\left(T_{0\,i,j-1} - 2T_{0\,i,j} + T_{0\,i,j+1}\right)/\left(\Delta y^2\right)\right]\right) + \\ + \frac{L}{c_p}\left(f_{s\,i,j} - f_{0s\,i,j}\right) \tag{10}$$

for $i = 2,3,...,N-1$ and $j = 2,3,...,N-1$
The boundary nodes are calculated (the Neumann boundary conditions are set to $F = 0$ W/m²) as: west $T_{1,j} = T_{2,j}$ for $j = 2,...,N-1$, east $T_{N,j} = T_{N-1,j}$ for $j = 2,...,N-1$, north $T_{i,N} = T_{i,N-1}$ for $i = 2,...,N-1$ and south $T_{i,1} = T_{i,2}$ for $i = 2,...,N-1$, where Δt, $f_{0s\,i,j}$, $T_{0\,i,j}$, $T_{0\,i+1,j}$, $T_{0\,i-1,j}$, $T_{0\,i,j+1}$, $T_{0\,i,j\,1}$ are the time step, initial solid fraction, initial temperature in the FDM central, east, west, north and south nodes, respectively.

5. Solution of the solid fraction field

We now define and discuss the elements of the classical CA and the novel PA methods in details.

5.1 Definition of mesh and neighbourhood configuration

Square cells with length $\Delta x = \Delta y = a = l/n$ where $n = N-1$ represents the number of cells in x and y directions are considering in the CA approach. In the PA approach the square is divided in uniform or nonuniformy distributed nodes. Cells are not defined.

5.1.1 Mesh and neighbourhood in the CA method

A basic definition of neighborhood originates from the classical CA approach which operates on the grid divided into the square cells (Neumann, 1987; Nastac, 2004). The cell structure is depicted in Fig. 2. In our calculations the Neumann configuration which takes into account only the closest neighbor's cells during the computation is applied.
The conventional square mesh structure is commonly applied in the CA calculations. It represents a square domain covered by the CA cells $x_{CA\,i,j}$, $y_{CA\,i,j}$ located exactly in the middle of four FDM nodes, as it is depicted in Fig. 5 (left).

$$x_{CA\,i,j} = \frac{1}{2}\left[x_{FDM\,i,j} + x_{FDM\,i+1,j}\right]; \quad y_{CA\,i,j} = \frac{1}{2}\left[y_{FDM\,i,j} + y_{FDM\,i,j+1}\right] \tag{11}$$

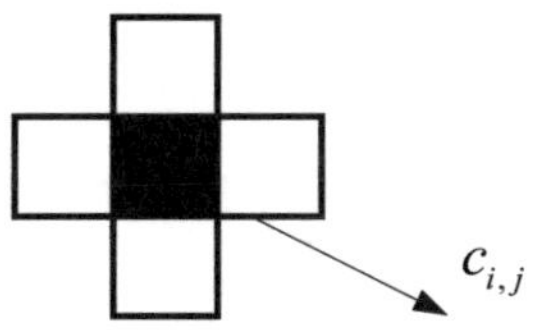

$$c_{i,j} = \left\{c_{i+1,j}, c_{i,j+1}, c_{i-1,j}, c_{i,j-1}\right\}$$

Fig. 2. Graphical representation of the Neumann neighbourhood configuration for the conventional CA method

5.1.2 Mesh and neighborhood in the PA method

The PA node grows with respect to the heat flow and with respect to the 'neighbourhood' configuration which is now associated with the position of the neighbouring PA nodes which fall into a circle (Janssens, 2000, 2003) with radius R_H in 2-D or a sphere in 3-D. It means that each PA node can in case of the random mesh contain different number and position of the neighbours, which give various possibilities of neighbourhood configurations for each node. For the novel PA method the random node arrangement is in the present chapter generated from the regular CA mesh.

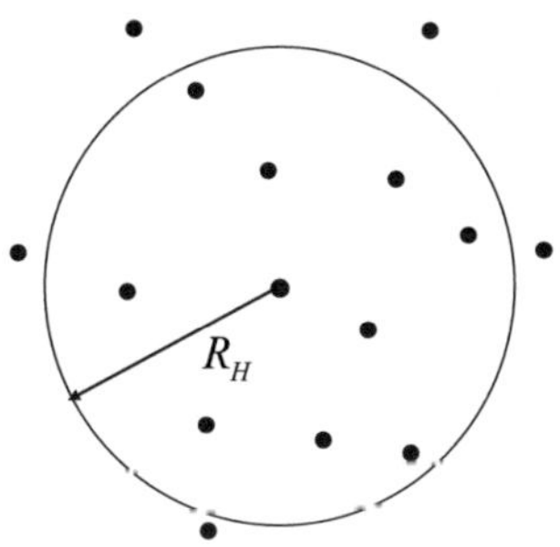

$$c_{i,j} = \left\{c_{i,j}; \left|r_i - r_j\right|_{i \neq j} < R_H\right\}$$

Fig. 3. Graphical representation of the neighbourhood configuration proposed for the new PA method

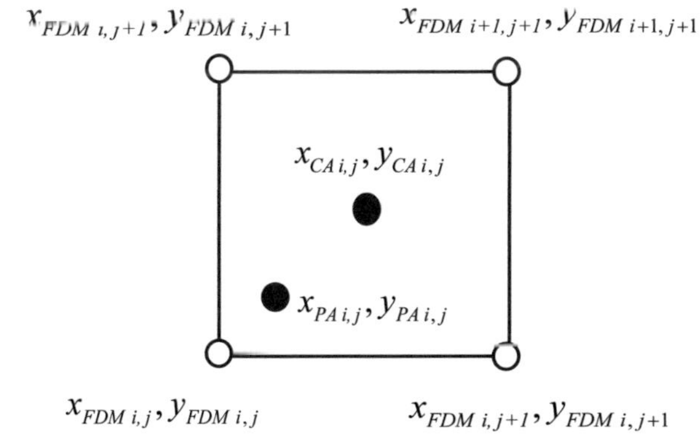

Fig. 4. Schematic representation of the relationship between FDM nodes (4 corners), CA cell (center) and the random PA node

To construct the random node arrangements, the CA cell centres are displaced to the randomly chosen positions and become random PA nodes $x_{PA\,i,j}, y_{PA\,i,j}$ on the computational domain (see Fig. 5 bottom).
The displacement of each CA centre is assumed only in the square area limited by the four FDM nodes. The following procedure is applied

$$x_{PA\,i,j} = x_{CA\,i,j} + \varepsilon[2rand - 1]; \quad y_{PA\,i,j} = y_{PA\,i,j} + \varepsilon[2rand - 1] \tag{12}$$

where $x_{PA_{i,j}}$, $y_{PA_{i,j}}$, ε represent coordinates of PA nodes and the scaling value $0 \le \varepsilon \le 0.49$, respectively. It must be emphasized that the PA procedure is established on the random nodes in general. The heat transfer calculations are performed on the regular FDM nodes, which is explained in Section 6.

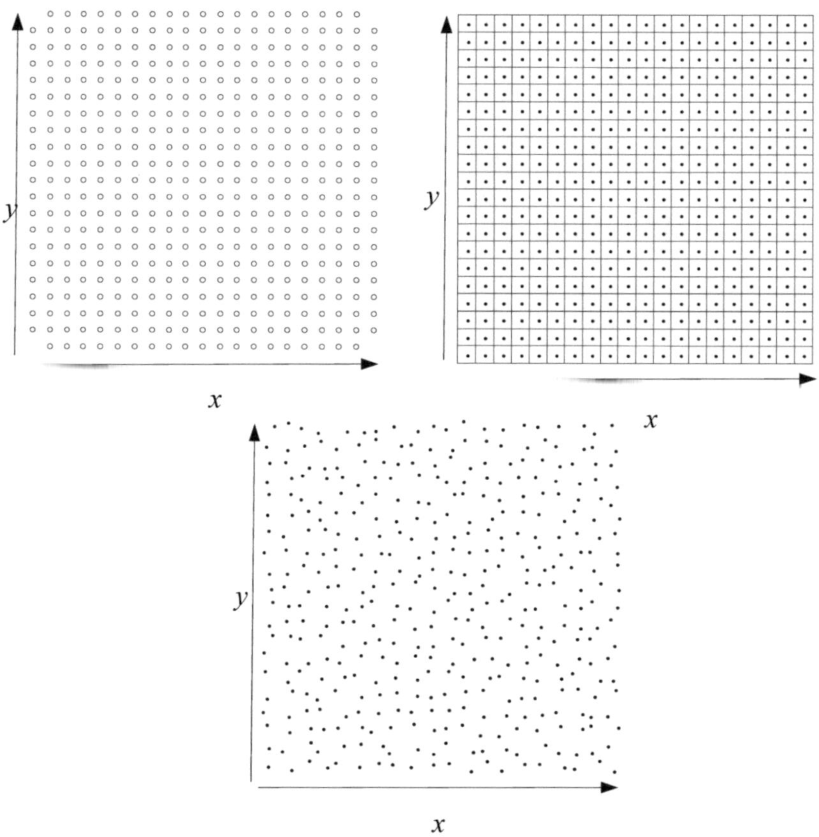

Fig. 5. Scheme of the space discretization: (top left) FDM nodes with $N = 21$, (top-right), CA cells with $n = 20$, (bottom) PA nodes with $n = 20$

5.2 Curvature calculations

The interface curvature is approximated by the counting cell procedure developed by Sasikumar and Sreenivasan (Sasikumar & Sreenivasan, 1994).

5.2.1 Calculation of curvature in the CA method

The expression for curvature K is given by the formula (Krane et al., 2009)

$$K = \frac{1}{a}\left(1 - \frac{2N_{s\,CA}}{N_{t\,CA}}\right) \tag{13}$$

where $N_{s\,CA}$ and $N_{t\,CA}$ are the number of solid CA cells whose centres fall inside the circle of assumed radius R_c and the total number of CA cells whose centres fall inside the circle, respectively (see Fig. 6 (top)).

5.2.2 Calculation of curvature in the PA method

The expression for PA is derived from the expression for the CA method (equation 13) by assuming the average node distance $\bar{a}$ instead of a (see Fig. 6 (bottom)).

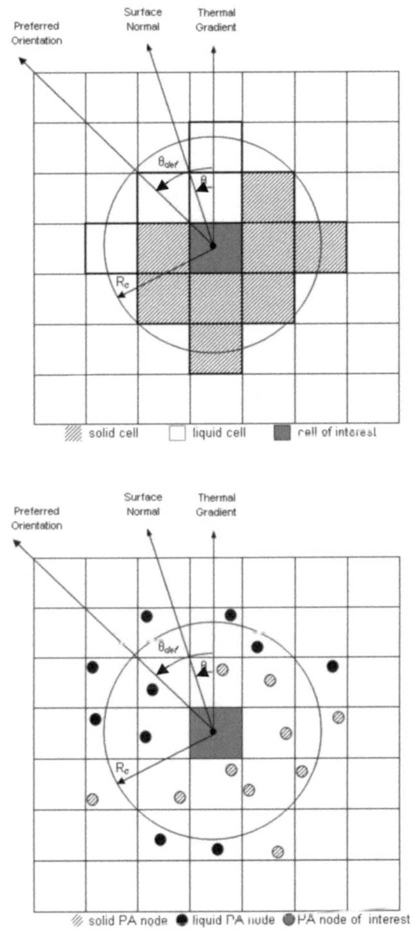

Fig. 6. Top: scheme showing a circle sample with $R_c = 2a$ for calculating the curvature in the conventional CA method (example: $N_{s\,CA} = 8$ and $N_{t\,CA} = 12$); bottom: in the PA method (example: $N_{s\,PA} = 7$ and $N_{t\,PA} = 11$)

5.3 Phase change

The crystal growth velocity is calculated according to the crystal orientation. The envelope of the grain can be expressed by the equation 9 which is depicted in Fig. 7.
Once a CA cell (or PA node) becomes solid it starts to grow with respect to the 'neighbourhood' configuration (see Fig. 2 and Fig. 3). Each of the CA cells (or the random nodes) can have two possible states: liquid or solid. The CA cell (or PA node) becomes solid through the growth process. The change of the solid fraction of the CA cell or PA node is calculated from the crystal growth velocity.

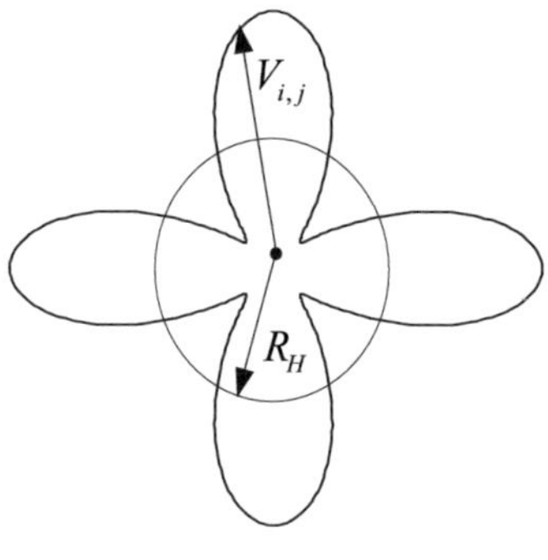

Fig. 7. Schematic representation of the shape function (for parameters see Table 1)

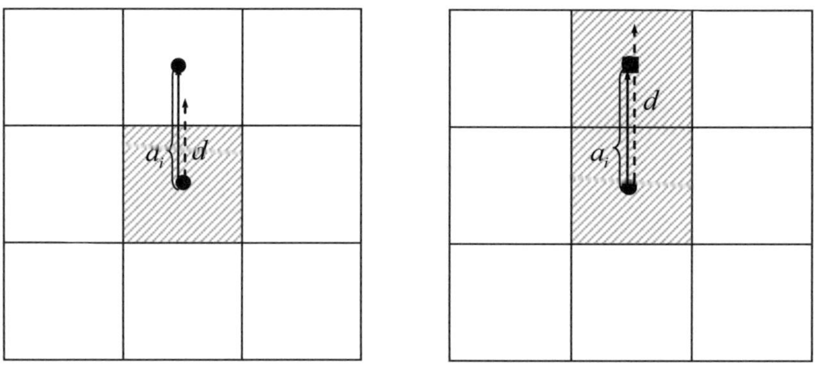

Fig. 8. Left: growth front will not reach the closest neighbour $d < a_i$. The CA cell will not be converted to solid (example for the Neumann neighbourhood configuration); left: growth front will reach the closest neighbour $d \geq a_i$. The CA cell will be converted to solid (example for the Neumann neighbourhood configuration)

For all neighbours of the treated solid CA cell (or solid PA node), general criterion d is checked which is represented by the following formula

$$d = \frac{l(t)}{a_i} \tag{14}$$

$$l = \int_{t_0}^{t} V_{i,j}\, dt \tag{15}$$

where a_i represent lengths from the analyzed CA cell or PA node to the nearest one.
If neighbour is one of the four nearest east, north, west, south neighbours then in the CA method this distance becomes $a_i = a$. In the PA method a_i $(a_i < R_H)$ represents the different distances to the neighbouring PA nodes which fall into the circle with radius R_H (see Fig. 9).
When $d \geq a$ or $d \geq a_i$ (Fig. 8 (right) and Fig. 9 (right)) the growing solid touches the centre of the neighbouring CA cell or PA node and this cell/node transforms its state from liquid to solid $f_{sPA} = 1$.

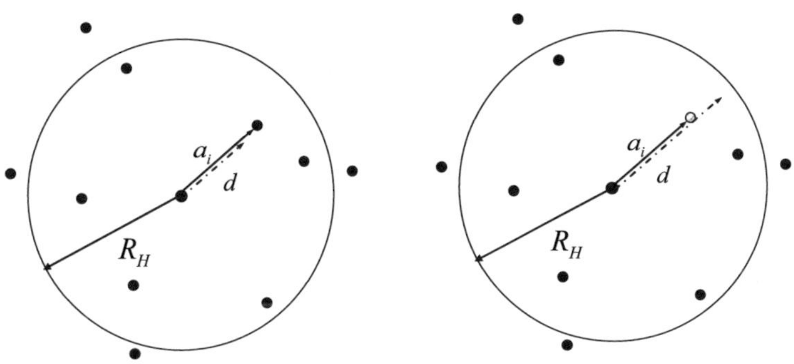

Fig. 9. Left: growth front will not reach the closest neighbour $d < a_i$. The PA node will not be converted to solid; right: growth front will reach the closest neighbour $d \geq a_i$. The PA node will be converted to solid

6. FDM-PA-FDM transfer of temperature and solid fraction

6.1 FDM-PA transfer of temperature

The obtained values of temperature on regular FDM grid (see Section 4) are in each time step transferred to random PA grid according to the described scheme (Fig. 12). The following simple interpolation formula (Xu & Liu, 2001) is used in the present chapter

$$T_{PA\,i,j} = \left(T_{i,j+1}l_1 + T_{i+1,j+1}l_2 + T_{i+1,j}l_3 + T_{i,j}l_4\right) / \sum_{i=1}^{4} l_i \tag{16}$$

In case of FDM-CA the equation 16 reduces to

$$T_{CA\,i,j} = \left(T_{i,j+1} + T_{i+1,j+1} + T_{i+1,j} + T_{i,j}\right) / 4 \tag{17}$$

where $T_{PA\,i,j}$, $T_{i,j}$, $T_{CA\,i,j}$ and l_i represent the temperature of the PA node, the temperatures of the four closest FDM nodes, the temperature for the centre CA cell and the distances to the nearest four FDM nodes, respectively. The calculation is repeated in each time step (see Fig. 10).

6.2 PA-FDM transfer of solid fraction

The temperature field at time $t_0 + \Delta t$ can be calculated from the equation 10 for all FDM nodes. Then these values are recalculated to all PA nodes according to the equation 16. Afterwards the PA procedure takes place (see Section 3). The output information from this

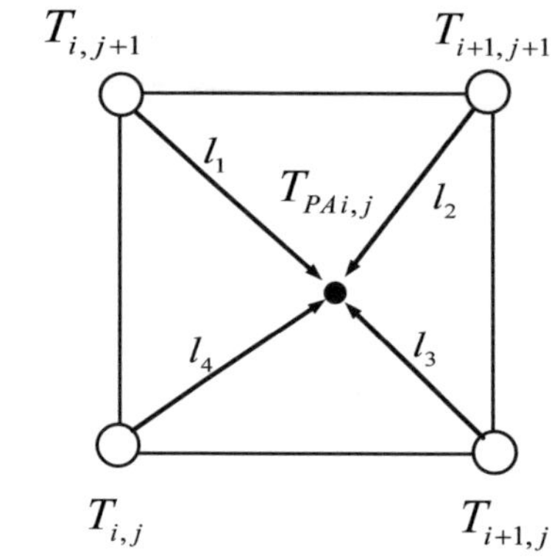

Fig. 10. Relationship between four FDM nodes and PA node for the calculation of the temperature values

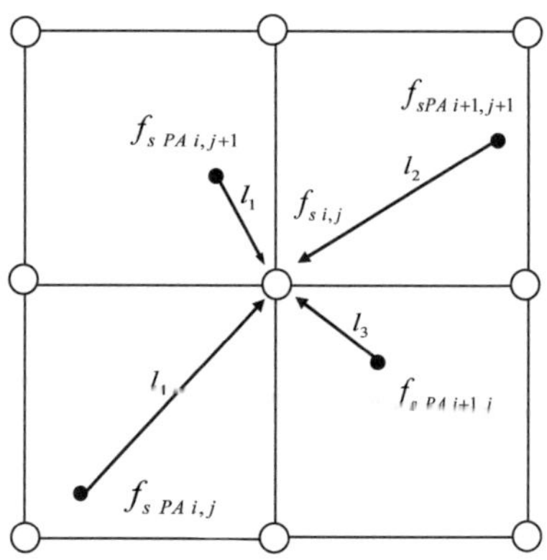

Fig. 11. Relationship between the FDM node and four neighbouring PA nodes for the transfer of solid fraction

level of calculation is the value of solid fraction for all random PA nodes $f_{s\,PA\,i,j}$ which have to be transferred to the FDM nodes to be able to calculate the new values of temperature (Fig. 11). The following equation is applied

$$f_{s\,i,j} = (f_{s\,PA\,i,j+1} l_1 + f_{s\,PA\,i+1,j+1} l_2 + f_{s\,PA\,i+1,j} l_3 + f_{s\,PA\,i,j} l_4) / \sum_{i=1}^{4} l_i \tag{18}$$

In case of FDM-CA the equation 18 reduces to

$$T_{CA\,i,j} = \left(T_{i,j+1} + T_{i+1,j+1} + T_{i+1,j} + T_{i,j}\right) / 4 \tag{19}$$

where $f_{s\,i,j}$ and $f_{s\,PA}$ represent the solid fraction for the FDM nodes and for the PA nodes, respectively.

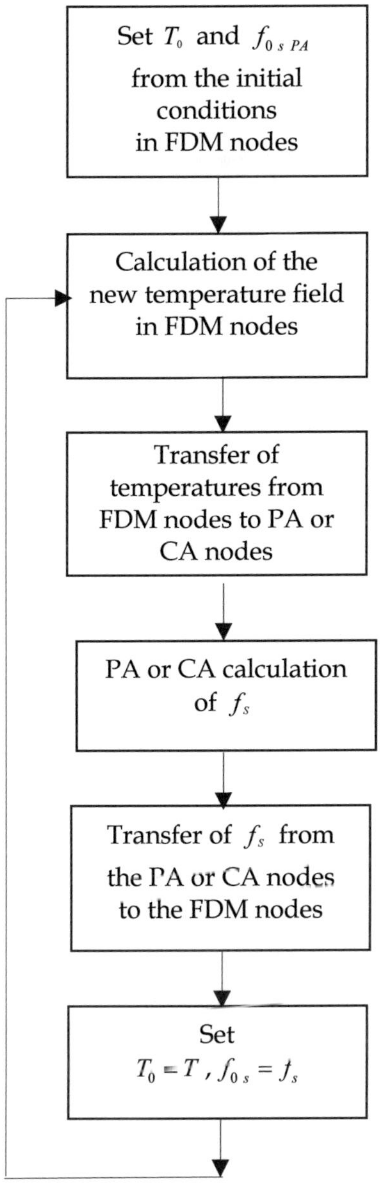

Fig. 12. Flowchart of the thermal field and solid fraction calculations

7. Numerical example

7.1 Numerical implementation

The model was coded in Fortran. For the dendritic growth in Figs. 13-17, the CPU time varies from 10 to 15 minutes depending on the input data. The solid PA nodes or CA cells are depicted by a colour pixel which can be observed on the screen during the simulation.

7.2 Problem definition and distretization

Initial conditions. Simplified material properties presented in Table 1 for pure aluminium (Kammer, 1999) are used in all prepared numerical examples. The process starts from the predetermined solid seed position in one single PA or CA node in the middle of the computational domain with the following initial conditions of temperature $933.45\,\mathrm{K} - 1.5\,\mathrm{K}$ and solid fraction $f_s = 1$. All other PA nodes are assumed to be liquid $f_s = 0$ and FDM nodes with the temperature $770.23\,\mathrm{K}$. This data is constant with the problem defined in the article. The numerical examples in the present chapter are solved by the FDM based temperature calculations and CA or PA based solid fraction calculations. The computational domain is the square with length $l = 350\ \mu\mathrm{m}$ and uniform discretization $N = 701$.

Mesh generation. FDM and CA methods are always constructed on a regular node arrangement in the present chapter. In the PA approach the random node arrangement needs to be constructed. The PA approach was tested first with the predetermined node arrangement PA-(A), see Fig. 14 and then with different types of random node arrangements: PA-(B), PA-(C), see Fig. 15, respectively (Table 2).

Time step. The time step used in FDM calculation of the temperature field is limited by the formula (Zhu & Hong, 2001)

$$\Delta t_{FDM} = \frac{a^2}{4.5D};\ D = \frac{\lambda}{\rho c_p} \tag{20}$$

where D represents the thermal diffusivity. For the calculations of the solid fraction field by the CA and PA method the following relation is used (Daming et al., 2004) for assuming stability

$$\Delta t_{CA} = \eta \min\left(\frac{a}{V^*_{\max}}, \frac{a^2}{D}\right) \tag{21}$$

where η and $V^*_{\max}$ represent the positive constant less then 1 and the maximum growth velocity of all interface cells, respectively.

For the stability of the coupled FDM-CA-PA procedure a minimum of Δt_{CA} and Δt_{FDM} should be used. All depicted results of simulations are shown for the different crystallographic angles after 1500 time steps of the length $\Delta t_{FDM} = 6.82x10^{-10}$ s.

Thermal fluctuations. In order to avoid the symmetric shape of the dendrite (in the conventional CA approach) some fluctuations need to be introduced into the calculations. The following equation is commonly applied $P = 1 + \lambda^* rand$. Thermal noises are usually present by putting the random fluctuations F into the calculations of the latent heat, undercooling temperature or velocity (Voller, 2008). It this chapter we use them in the velocity calculations $V = V \times P$.

Neighbourhood configuration. In the CA approach only the closest neighbourhood configuration has been analyzed. Larger the value of R_H is chosen in the PA method more dendritic and irregular structures can be observed. A more extended area of neighbours needs to be taken into the consideration in the PA method. The radius of neighbourhood should be kept at a minimum of 1.5 μm in case of $a = 0.5\,\mu\mathrm{m}$. For smaller values the dendritic shapes become distorted and the preferred orientations lost as well.

Symbol	Value	Unit
ρ	2700	kg/m^3
T_m	933.45	K
T_s	933.45-1.5	K
T_l	933.45+1.5	K
λ	210	W/mK
c_p	955.56	J/kgK
L	259259.26	J/kg
η	0.222	1
$\overline{\Gamma}$	1.6 x 10^{-7}	Km
δ_t	0.3	1
δ_k	0.75	1
S	4	1
R_c	1.5	μm
R_H	2	μm
μ_K	2	m/sK
l	350	μm
n	700	PA nodes/ CA cells
N	701	FDM nodes

Table 2. Nominal parameters used in the calculations

7.3 Simulated results

The dendritic morphologies were calculated by the classical FDM-CA and the novel FDM-PA approaches. The following numerical examples were prepared

- From CASE 1 to CASE 2 the dendritic growth process is simulated by the PA method with the same random node arrangement denoted (PA-(A)) for the following two orientations $\theta_{def} = 22^\circ$ and $\theta_{def} = 37^\circ$.
- From CASE 3 to CASE 4 the dendritic growth process is simulated by the PA method with different random node arrangements (PA-(B), PA-(C)) for the orientation $\theta_{def} = 10^\circ$.
- From CASE 5 to CASE 6 the dendritic growth process is simulated by the PA method with different randomness of the node arrangement $\varepsilon = 0.10$ and $\varepsilon = 0.49$, for the orientation $\theta_{def} = 8^\circ$.
- From CASE 7 to CASE 8 the dendritic growth process is simulated by the PA method including the factor responsible for the correction in the lengths of the x and y branches for different random node arrangements (PA-(F)-F, PA-(G)-F).

The results have been arranged and represented in the following way. Fig. 13 represents seven dendrites growing simultaneously at orientations 0° and 45° as the grid is constructed by the classical FDM-CA method. The FDM-PA calculations with different orientations of the crystallographic axis are depicted in Fig. 14 based on the same node arrangement. Then Fig. 15 shows the FDM-PA results with the varied random mesh structure for a single dendrite with orientation $\theta_{def} = 10°$. Fig. 16 represents dendritic growth for a single dendrite with $\theta_{def} = 8°$ for a different node arrangement randomness. In Fig. 17 the results for the PA method, where the randomness correction factor is applied, are represented (see discussion in the next paragraph). Finally, Fig. 18 represents seven dendrites growing simultaneously at different orientations by the FDM-PA method.

CASE	θ_{def}	λ^*	ε	node arrangement
1	22°	0	0.49	PA-(A)
2	37°	0	0.49	PA-(A)
3	10°	0	0.49	PA-(B)
4	10°	0	0.49	PA-(C)
5	8°	0	0.49	PA-(D)
6	8°	0	0.10	PA-(E)
7	0°	0	0.49	PA-(F)-F
8	0°	0	0.49	PA-(G)-F

Table 1. Parameters used in the calculations

7.4 Discussion of the results

The orientations of crystallographic axes of different dendrites have different orientations in general. It is commonly recognized that this process is difficult to simulate by the classical CA method since the dendrite will always switch to 0° or 45° direction during the growth. Our testing is thus primarily focused on the growth of the dendrite at different orientations by the novel PA method. Simulated examples are for the random node arrangements PA-(A),..., PA-(F) presented in Figs. 14-17, respectively. They show that when employing the PA method any of the crystallographic orientation can easily be achieved. Results show that the proper growth direction is always observed with increasingly random ($\varepsilon \rightarrow 0.49$) node arrangement.

For the same input parameters the dendritic growth process simulated by the CA and PA method for the $\theta_{def} = 0^\circ$ preferential crystallographic orientation gives the different lengths of x and y branches. This is due to the influence of the random node arrangement and subsequent variable distances between the nodes. In the CA method the same value of a is taken while for the PA method this distances are different and might vary between maximum $\Delta x = \Delta y = 2\varepsilon a$ and minimum $\Delta x = \Delta y = 2(1-\varepsilon)a$.

It can be concluded that the differences in the length between x and y directions with respect to the random node arrangement are almost constant and kept below $\approx 5\%$.

The average length of the dendrite at ten different orientations and some random node arrangement with $\varepsilon = 0.49$ is 152.8 ± 5.18 μm. The average length of the dendrite calculated with four different random node arrangement for the fixed angles 5°, 15° and 30° is 153.37 $\pm$ 5.39 μm, 156.12 $\pm$ 6.44 μm and 151.75 $\pm$ 5.36 μm, respectively (Lorbiecka & Šarler, 2010). From this one can conclude that the errors caused by the rotation of the dendrite are at the same order as the errors cussed by different random node arrangements. Fig. 16 demonstrates that when reducing ε from 0.49 to 0.1 the PA starts to behave like the CA and the proper simulation of the dendrite is not possible. We are too close to the classical node structure in such case and CA limitations appear.

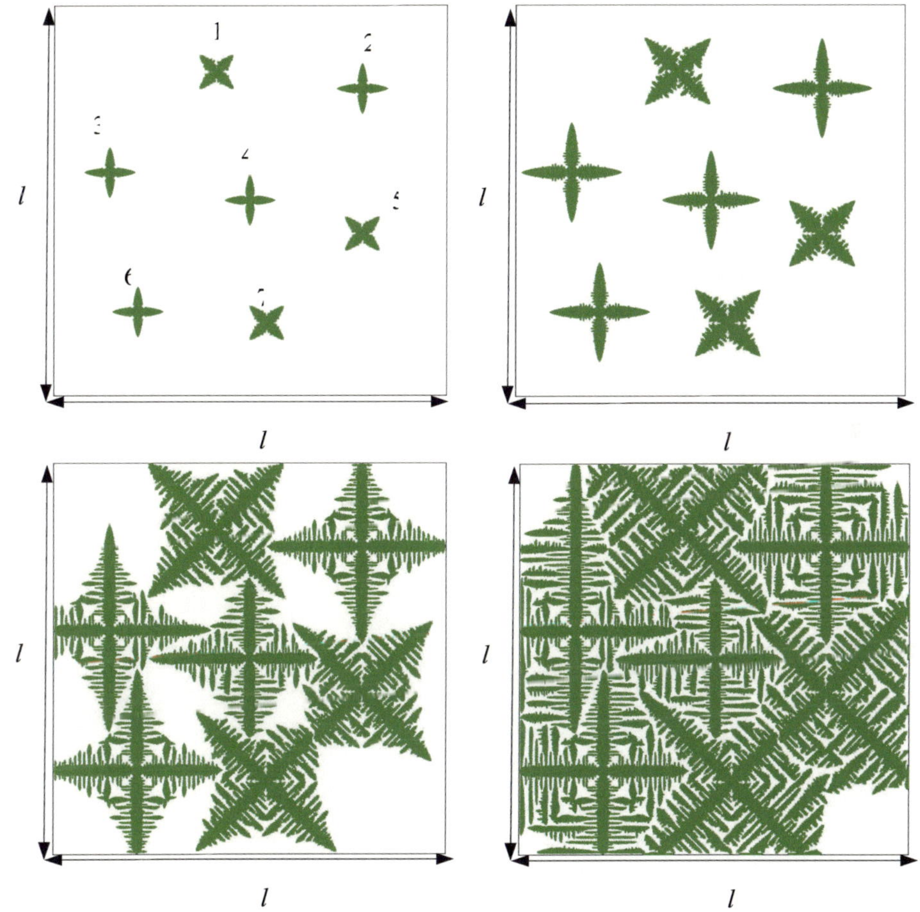

Fig. 13. Seven dendrites growing simultaneously at orientations 0° and 45° after 350, 700, 1500 and 2500 time steps of the length $6.82\text{x}10^{-10}$ s. FDM-CA solution procedure

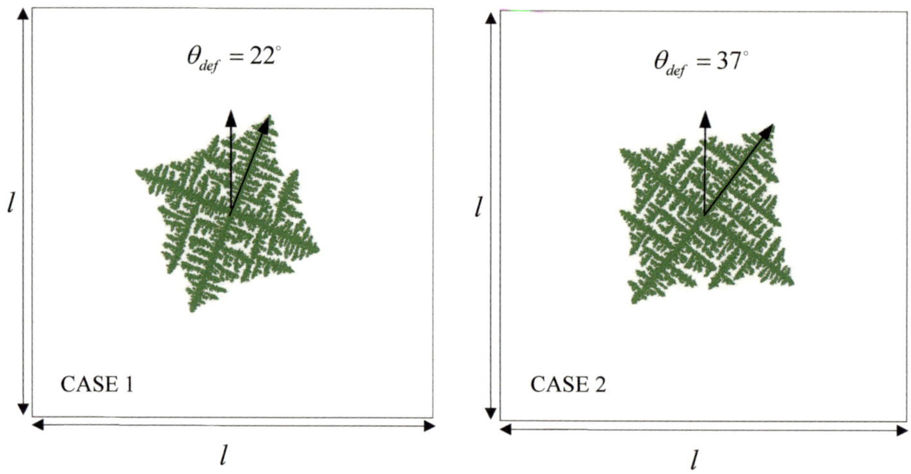

Fig. 14. Simulated dendritic growth for a single dendrite for two orientations by the PA method for the same PA-(A) random node arrangement $\theta_{def} = 22°$ and $\theta_{def} = 37°$

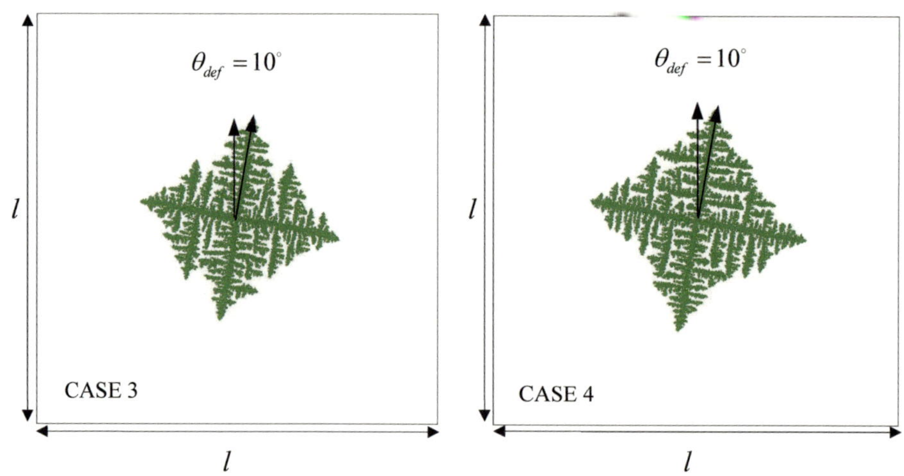

Fig. 15. Simulated dendritic growth for a single dendrite with $\theta_{def} = 10°$ for different random node arrangement structures: PA-(B), PA-(C), respectively

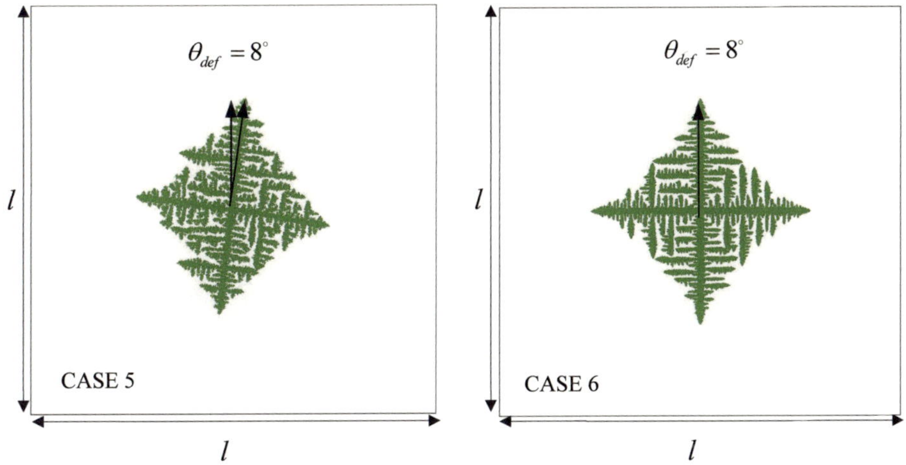

Fig. 16. Simulated dendritic growth for a single dendrite with $\theta_{def} = 8^\circ$ for different node arrangement randomness $\varepsilon = 0.49$ PA-(D) and $\varepsilon = 0.1$ PA-(E).

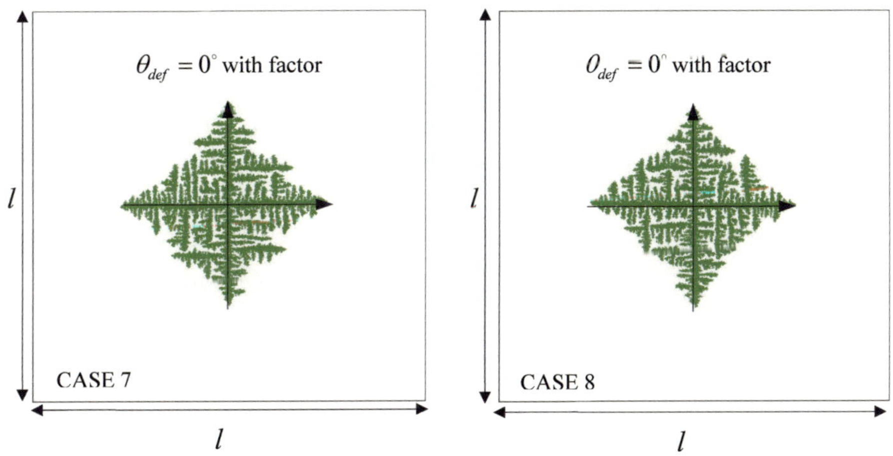

Fig. 17. Simulated dendritic growth for a single dendrite by the PA method with factor 1.25

To achieve the same dendrite length in PA method as in the CA method, an empirical factor, which multiplies the calculated velocity in the PA method, was added in the code. It can be shown that putting factor 1.25, (for the random node arrangement ε = 0.49) in the PA calculations, the branches will have the same length in both methods (see Fig. 17).

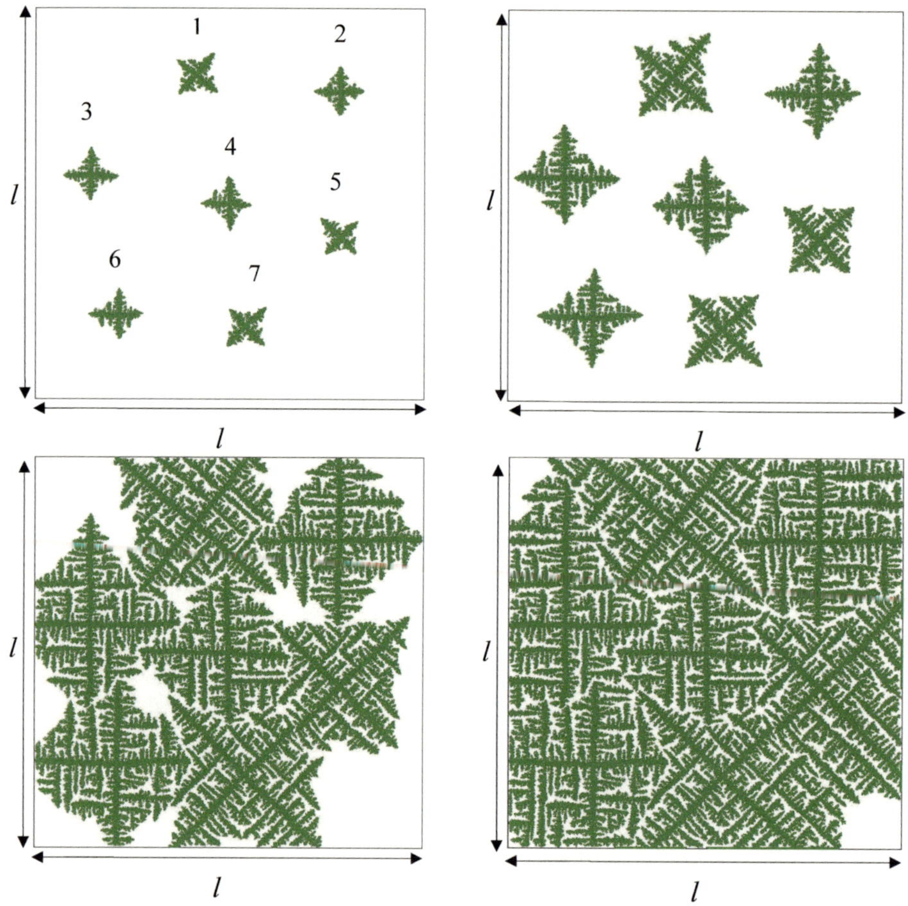

Fig. 18. Seven dendrites growing simultaneously at different orientations after 350, 700, 1500 and 2500 time steps of the length $6.82x10^{-10}$ s. FDM-PA solution procedure

In the present study it is not necessary to put any thermal fluctuations in the PA method. The random node arrangements in the PA method replace the thermal fluctuations of the CA method.

8. Conclusions

In this chapter a novel PA method is developed and applied to model the dendritic growth process. The principal characteristics and advantages of the developed PA method are

- No need for mesh generation or polygonisation. Only the node arrangement has to be generated, but without any geometrical connection between nodes.
- In the new PA method the governing equations are solved with respect to the location of points (not polygons) on the computational domain.
- The random grid PA method allows to rotate dendrites in any direction since it has a limited anisotropy of the node arrangements.
- PA method offers a simple and powerful approach of CA type simulations. It was shown that both methods are able to qualitatively and quantitatively model a diverse range of solidification phenomena in almost the same calculation time.
- The dimension of the neighborhood radius and generation of the random node arrangement has to be chosen carefully in order to be able to rotate the dendrite.
- Straightforward node refinement possibility.
- Straightforward extension to 3-D.

The use of FDM-PA method instead of FDM-CA method implies transfer of the results from the regular FDM mesh to the irregular PA node arrangements and vice versa. This is not the case in the classical FDM-CA method. A replacement of the FDM method with a meshless (Atluri, 2004; Liu & Gu, 2005; Šarler et al., 2005; Šarler & Vertnik, 2006) method that is able to directly cope with irregular node arrangement is underway.

9. Acknowledgment

The first author would like to thank the EU Marie Curie Research Training Network INSPIRE for position to study and research at the University of Nova Gorica, Slovenia. The second author would like to thank the Slovenian Research Agency for funding in the framework of the project J2-0099 Multiscale modelling of liquid-solid systems.

10. Reference

Atluri, S.N. (2004). The Meshless Method (MLPG) for Domain and BIE Discretization, Tech Science Press, Forsyth

Anderson, M.P.; Srolovitz, D.J. & Grest, S.G. (1984). Computer simulation of grain growth. I. Kinetics. *Acta Metall*, Vol.32, pp. 783-791

Boettinger, W.J.; Coriell, S.R.; Greer, A.L.; Karma, A.; Kurz, A.; Rappaz, M. & Trivedi, R. (2000). Solidification microstructure recent developments, future directions. *Acta Metall.*, Vol.48, pp. 43-70

Daming, L.; Ruo, L. & Zhang, P. (2004). A new coupled model for alloy solidification. *Science in China Ser. A. Mathematics.*, Vol. 47, pp. 41-52

Gandin, Ch.A. & Rappaz, M. (1994). A coupled finite element-cellular automaton model for the prediction of dendritic grain structures in solidification processes. *Acta Metall.*, Vol.42, No.7, pp. 2133-2246

Gandin, Ch.A. & Rappaz, M. (1997). A 3D cellular automaton algorithm for the prediction of dendritic grain growth. *Acta Metall.*, Vol. 45, pp. 2187-2195.

Janssens, K.G.F. (2000). *Irregular cellular automata modeling of grain growth.* Continuum Scale Simulation of Engineering Materials, Germany

Janssens, K.G.F. (2003). Random Grid, Three Dimensional, Space-Time Coupled Cellular Automata for the Simulation of Recrystallization and Grain Growth. *Modelling Simul. Mater. Sci. Eng,* Vol.11, No.2, pp.157-171

Janssens, K.G.F.; Raabe, D.; Kozeschnik, E.; Miodownik, M.A. & Nestler, B. (2007). *Computational Materials Engineering*, Elsevier Academic Press, Great Britain

Janssens, K.G.F. (2010). An introductory review of cellular automata modeling of moving grain boundaries in polycrystalline materials. *Mathematics and Computers in Simulations,* Vol.80, No.7, pp. 1361-1381

Krane, M.J.M.; Johnson, D.R. & Raghavan, S. (2009). The development of a cellular automaton - finite volume model for dendritic growth. *Applied Mathematical Modelling,* Vol.33, No.5, pp. 2234-2247

Kammer, K. (1999). *Aluminium Handbook1.* Aluminium-Verlag Marketing & Kommunikation GmbH

Liu, G.R. & Gu, Y.T. (2005). *An Introduction to Meshfree Methods and Their Programming,* Springer, Dordrecht

Lorbiecka, A.Z.; Vertnik, R., Gjerkeš, H.; Manojlović, G.; Senčič, B.; Cesar, J. & Šarler, B. (2009): Numerical modelling of Grain Structure in Continuous Casting of Steel. *Computers, Materials & Continua,* Vol. 8, No. 3, pp. 195-208

Lorbiecka, A.Z.& Šarler, B. (2009). Modelling grain growth processes by the conventional Cellular Automata and New Point Automata method. In: G. Tsatsaronis and A. Boyano (ed) *International conference of Optimization Using Exergy- based Methods and Computational Fluid Dynamics*, Berlin, Germany, pp.243-252

Lorbiecka, A.Z.& Šarler, B. (2009). Point automata method for prediction of grain structure in the continuous casting of steel. In: L. Andreas (ed) *3nd International Conference of Simulation and Modelling of Metallurgical Processes in Steelmaking, Steelsim 2009,* ASMET, Leoben, Austria, pp. 192-197

Lorbiecka, A.Z. & Šarler, B. (2010). Simulation of dendritic growth with different orientation by using the point automata method. *CMC: Computers, Materials & Continua,* Vol. 18, No.1, pp. 69-104.

Midownik, M.A. (2002). A review of microstructural computer models used to simulate grain growth and recrystallisation in aluminium alloys. *J.Light. Met,* Vol.2, No.3, pp. 125-135

Nastac, L. (2004). *Modeling and Simulation of Microstructure Evolution in Solidifying Alloys.* Kluwer Academic Publishers

Nakagawa, M.; Narsume, Y.; Ohsasa, K. (2006): Dendrite Growth Model Rusing Front Tracking Technique with New Growth Algorithm. *ISIJ International,* Vol.46, No.6, pp. 909-913

Neumann, J.V. (1987). The general and logical theory of automata, 1963. In: W. Aspray and A. Burks, Editors, *Chapters of John von Neumann on Computing and Computer Theory. The Charles Babbage Institute Reprint Series for the History of Computing,* Vol.12, pp. 477-490

Rappaz, M. & Gandin, Ch.A. (1993). Probabilistic modeling of microstructure formation in solidification processes. *Acta Metall.*, Vol.41, pp. 345-360

Rettenmayr, M.; Buchmann, M. (2006): Solidification and Melting - Asymmetries and Consequences. *Materials Science Forum.*, Vol.508, pp. 205-210

Saito, Y. Goldbeck-Wood, G. & Muller-Krumbhaar, H. (1988). Numerical simulation of dendritic growth. *Physical Review*, Vol. 33, pp. 2148-2157.

Sasikumar, R. & Sreenivasan, R. (1994). Two-dimensional simulation of dendrite morphology. *Acta metall. mater*, Vol.42, No.7, pp. 2381-2386.

Shin, Y.H. & Hong, C.P. (2002). Modeling of Dendritic Growth with Convection Using a Modified Cellular Automata Model with a Diffuse Interface. *ISIJ International*, Vol. 42, No.4, pp. 359-367

Spittle, J.A. & Brown, S.G.R. (1989). Computer simulation of the effect of alloy variable on the grain structures of castings. *Acta. Metall.*, Vol.37, pp. 1803-1810

Spittle, J.A. & Brown, S.G.R. (1995). A cellular automaton model of steady state columnar dendritic growth in binary alloys. *J.Mater. Sci*, vol. 30, pp. 3989-3994

Stefanescu, D. M. (2009). *Science and Engineering of Casting Solidification.* Springer Science

Šarler, B.; Vertnik, R. & Perko, J. (2005). Application of diffuse approximate method in convective diffusive solidification problems, *Computers, Materials & Continua,* Vol. 2, pp. 77-83

Šarler, B. & Vertnik, R. (2006). Meshfree local radial basis function collocation method for diffusion problems. *Computers and Mathematics with Application*, Vol.51, pp. 1269-1282

Qin, R.S. & Wallach, E.R. (2003). A phase-field model coupled with a thermodynamic database. *Acta Materialia*, Vol.51, pp. 6199-6210

Wolfram, S. (2002). *A New Kind of Science.* Wolfram Media, Inc

Voller, V.R. (2008). An enthalpy method for modeling dendritic growth in a binary alloy. *Science Direct, International Journal of Heat and Mass Transfer*, Vol.52, pp. 823-834

Xu, Q.; Li, B.; Liu, Y. & Liu, B. (2008). Numerical modelling of microstructure evolution and dendrite growth in alloy solidification process. *International Journal of Materials and Product Technology*, Vol.33, pp. 37-49

Xu, Q.Y. & Liu, B.C. (2001). Modeling of As-Cast Microstructure of Al Alloy with a Modified Cellular Automaton Method. *Materials Transactions*, Vol.42, No.11, pp. 2316-2321

Zhan, Z.; Wei, Y. & Dong, D. (2008). Cellular automaton simulation of grain growth with different orientation angles during solidification process. *Journal of Materials Processing Technology*, Vol.208, No.1, pp. 1-8

Zhu, M.F. & Hong, C.P. (2001). A modified cellular automaton model for the simulation of dendritic growth in solidification of alloys. *ISIJ International*, Vol.41, No.5, pp. 436-445

10

Simulation of Dendritic Growth in Solidification of Al-Cu alloy by Applying the Modified Cellular Automaton Model with the Growth Calculation of Nucleus within a Cell

Hsiun-Chang Peng and Long-Sun Chao
National Defense University, National Cheng Kung University
Taiwan

1. Introduction

Solidification microstructure is an important index to evaluate the mechanical properties and qualities of the casting. The modeling of microstructure is one of the important aspects of solidification simulation. With the rapid development of computational technique and solidification theory, there is a continuously increasing interest in simulating the microstructure evolution during a solidification process in recent years.

Dendritic microstructure is a common solidification structure whose morphology features affect the properties of product. Dendrite evolution involves the heat, solute transfer and phase transition etc., and these processes always interact with each other, so it is difficult to exactly predict the microstructure evolution. In the past, there are several methods used to simulate the dendrite morphology, including the phase field method, front-tracking method, and the classical and modified cellular automaton methods. The phase field method (Boettinger et al., 2001) has an advantage of dealing with complex topology variation. On the other hand, a phase function has to be introduced into the model that has no much physical meaning. In addition, the mesh size must be smaller than the thickness of interface layer, which limits the computational scale. Furthermore, the thickness of interface layer is a variable that has different values at different positions, which is not consistent with the experiments. The front-tracking method (Juric & Tryggvason, 1996) needs to know the precise position of solid-liquid interface and the velocity of the interface to predict the position of the interface in the next step, so that too much calculation time is consumed on the iteration of the precise interface position.

The classical cellular automaton method (Rappaz & Gandin, 1993; Gandin et al., 1999) has the advantages of simple rules and clear physical backgrounds. Moreover, the mesh size can be much coarser than that of the phase field method. However, the dendrite growth velocity in the method is referenced only to the local temperature in the solidifying region for a fixed alloy composition. Therefore, the individual grains do not interact directly until they touch each other and it is unable to describe the more detail features such as the side branches and the formation of second phases (eutectic). Being different from the classical one, several modified cellular automaton methods (Nastac, 1999; Zhu & Hong, 2001; Beltran-Sanchez &

Stefanescu, 2003) were developed to simulate dendrite morphology with more detailed local conditions, which includes the thermal diffusion and solute redistribution, curvature effect, latent heat release, and the change of solid fraction according to the minute calculation of the growth velocity.

In the presented work, the modified cellular automaton method (Zhu & Hong, 2001) with KGT model is used to simulate the crystal growth of Al-Cu alloy. The mesh size used here is larger than the critical radius of a nucleus. If a mesh (or cell) is chosen as a nucleation site, the growth mechanism is then applied to the mesh instead of regarding it as completely solidified. The directional solidification processes for different solutal concentrations are simulated and compared with the experimental results.

2. Mathematical models

Nucleation. The continuous nucleation condition is considered in the present work where different Gaussian distributions account for the nucleation both on the mold wall and in the bulk liquid. The increase of grain density d_n is induced by an increase in the undercooling $d(\Delta T)$ according to the following Gaussian distribution (Rappaz & Gandin, 1993):

$$\frac{d_n}{d(\Delta T)} = \frac{n_{\max}}{\sqrt{2\pi}\Delta T_\sigma} \exp\left[-\frac{1}{2}\left(\frac{\Delta T - \Delta T_{mn}}{\Delta T_\sigma}\right)^2\right] \tag{1}$$

where ΔT_{mn} is the mean nucleation undercooling, ΔT_σ is the standard deviation, and n_{max} is the maximum density of nuclei given by the integral of this distribution from 0 to ∞. Thus, the density of grains $n(\Delta T)$ formed at any undercooling ΔT is given by

$$n(\Delta T) = \int_0^{\Delta T} \frac{d_n}{d(\Delta T')} d(\Delta T') \tag{2}$$

Growth kinetics and orientation. The growth velocity of a dendrite tip under a certain undercooling ΔT is calculated according to the KGT model (Kurz et al., 1986), which is $v(\Delta T) = k_1\Delta T^2 + k_2\Delta T^3$. k_1 and k_2 are the functions of the initial concentration. The total undercooling at the dendrite tip is given by the sum of the various contributions to undercooling (Rappaz & Gandin, 1993):

$$\Delta T = \Delta T_c + \Delta T_t + \Delta T_r + \Delta T_k \tag{3}$$

where ΔT_c, ΔT_t, ΔT_r, ΔT_k are the solutal, thermal, curvature, and kinetic undercooling, respectively. The kinetic undercooling is small for the metallic alloy under normal solidification, so that the effect is neglected. Nuclei formed on the mold wall or in the bulk liquid grow along the preferential growth direction, which corresponds to $\langle 10 \rangle$ for cubic metals in the present two-dimensional model.

Solute Transport. The local equilibrium at the solid-liquid interface is assumed to balance the interfacial concentrations that are described as follow.

$$C_s^* = kC_l^* \tag{4}$$

where k is the partition coefficient, C_s^* and C_l^* are the interface equilibrium concentrations in the solid and liquid phases, respectively.

As the solidification proceeds, the solidified region rejects solute to the neighboring liquid according to Eq. (4). Diffusion within the entire liquid domain is redistributed by the following equation.

$$\frac{\partial C_l}{\partial t} = \frac{\partial}{\partial x}\left(D_l \frac{\partial C_l}{\partial x}\right) + \frac{\partial}{\partial y}\left(D_l \frac{\partial C_l}{\partial y}\right) + C_l(1-k)\frac{\partial f_s}{\partial t} \tag{5}$$

where D_l is the solute diffusion coefficient in the liquid phase, f_s is the solid fraction, and k is the partition coefficient. The last term of the right hand side of the equation indicates the amount of solute rejected at the solid-liquid interface.
The governing equation for diffusion in the solid phase is given by

$$\frac{\partial C_s}{\partial t} = \frac{\partial}{\partial x}\left(D_s \frac{\partial C_s}{\partial x}\right) + \frac{\partial}{\partial y}\left(D_s \frac{\partial C_s}{\partial y}\right) \tag{6}$$

where D_s is the solute diffusion coefficient in the liquid phase.
Thermal transport. The governing equation for two-dimensional transient heat conduction is

$$\rho C_p \frac{\partial T}{\partial t} = \frac{\partial}{\partial x}\left(\lambda \frac{\partial T}{\partial x}\right) + \frac{\partial}{\partial y}\left(\lambda \frac{\partial T}{\partial y}\right) + \rho \Delta H \frac{\partial f_s}{\partial t} \tag{7}$$

where ρ is the density, C_p is the specific heat, λ is the thermal conductivity, and ΔH is the latent heat.

3. Numerical method

The modified cellular automaton model used to predict the evolution of dendritic structures is based on the coupling of the macroscopic heat and microscopic mass transport. The designation of a nucleus site in a mesh (cell) is followed by applying the growth mechanism to the mesh instead of regarding it as completely solidified.
Nucleation and growth algorithm. The cellular automaton model for the nucleation and growth simulation consists of (1) the geometry of a cell, (2) the state of a cell, (3) the neighborhood configuration, and (4) the transition rule that determines the state of a given cell during any time step. The calculation domain is divided into uniform square arrangement of micromeshes, called cells. Each cell is characterized by different variables such as temperature, concentration, crystallographic orientation, solid fraction and state (i.e. solid or liquid). Two kinds of cells are necessary according to Eq. (5) and (6). One is the liquid cell including the solid-liquid interface and the other is the solid cell. If a cell is a predetermined nucleation cite according to Eq. (1) by the local undercooling, the nucleus in the cell will grow along the preferential direction until the growth touches the boundaries of the cell. Then the state of the cell changes from liquid to solid with a reference index. The cell will grow continuously along the preferential direction corresponding to its crystallographic orientation if the undercooling of any adjacent liquid cell is sufficient to initiate the growth. The growth length L at a given time t_n from the nucleus to the boundaries of nucleation cell or the solid cell to its liquid neighbors can be calculated by

$$L(t_n) = \frac{\{v_1[\Delta T(t_1)] \times \Delta t_1\} - r^0 + \sum_{i=2}^{n}\{v_i[\Delta T(t_i)] \times \Delta t_i\}}{(\cos\theta + |\sin\theta|)} \tag{8}$$

where Δt_i is the time step size, θ is the angle of the cell's preferential growth direction $\langle 10 \rangle$ with respect to the line between the solid cell to its liquid neighbors or the nucleus to each boundary of the nucleation cell, and n indicates the time step number. r^0 is the critical radius forming a nucleus only effective in the nucleation cell and is zero elsewhere. $v_1\left[\Delta T(t_1)\right]$ and $v_i\left[\Delta T(t_i)\right]$ are the growth rates at time t_1 and t_i. The growth rate in any liquid or nucleation cell can be calculated by using the KGT model depending upon the local undercooling $\Delta T(t_i)$. The neighborhood of 8 cells around a liquid cell is considered to estimate the liquid-to-solid state transition of the liquid cell. The local undercooling $\Delta T(t_i)$ is given by

$$\Delta T(t_i) = T_l - T_{s/l}(t_i) + \left(C_{s/l}(t_i) - C_0\right) - \Gamma \overline{K}_{s/l}(t_i) \tag{9}$$

where T_l is the equilibrium liquidus temperature, m is the liquidus slope, C_0 is the initial concentration, and Γ is the Gibbs-Thomson coefficient. $\overline{K}_{s/l}$, $C_{s/l}(t_i)$ and $T_{s/l}(t_i)$ are the mean curvature, the concentration and the temperature of the solid-liquid interface in the liquid cell at time t_i. Then, the solid fraction $f_s(t_n)$ contributed from a solid cell to the liquid cell at a given time can be expressed as

$$f_s(t_n) = L(t_n) / \ell \tag{10}$$

where ℓ is the length between the solid cell and the liquid cell or half the size (dx/2) of the nucleation cell. Since the neighborhood of 8 cells around a liquid cell is considered, for example, $\ell = dx$ if the solid cell is located at one of the four nearest east, west, south and north neighbors, and $\ell = \sqrt{2}dx$ if the solid cell is located at one of the corner neighbors. When $f_s(t_n) \geqq 1$, which means that the growth front of the solid cell touches the center of the liquid cell.

The transformation of state from liquid to solid depends on the total solid fraction $f_s^t(t_n)$, which can be written as

$$f_s^t(t_n) = \frac{1}{M} \sum_{i=1}^{M} f_s^i(t_n) \tag{11}$$

where M is the total number of the contributed solid neighbors to the liquid cell or total number of the growth components in a nucleation cell. When $f_s^t(t_n) \geq 1$ means that the state of the liquid or nucleation cell changes from liquid to solid and the newly solidified cell gets the same orientation index as the group of the solid cells.

The primary dendrite will grow and coarsen along the preferential $\langle 10 \rangle$ direction by the means of the algorithm described above. As the growing and the coarsening processes of the primary trunk proceed, the solute will be enriched in the liquid near the solid-liquid interface due to the solute redistribution, which will destroy the interface stability and therefore form the side branching or the secondary arms along the primary trunk.

Calculation of the interface curvature. The interface curvature in a cell with the solid fraction f_s is calculated by the counting cell method (Sasikumar & Sreenivasan, 1994), which is expressed as

$$\overline{K}_i = \frac{1}{dx}\left\{1 - \frac{2}{n+1}\left[f_s^t(i) + \sum_{j=1}^{n} f_s^t(j)\right]\right\} \tag{12}$$

where dx is the cell size and n is the number of the neighboring cells. The values of the curvature vary from 1/dx to 0 for convex surfaces and from 0 to -1/dx for concave surfaces.

Calculation of the solute transport. An explicit finite difference scheme is applied for calculating the solute diffusion in both the solid and liquid phases, and the zero-flux boundary conditions are used for the cells located at the surface of the calculation domain. The mesh arrangement is the same as the growth algorithm described above. When a cell transforms its state from liquid to solid by nucleation or growth, its concentration is changed according to Eq. (4). The rejected amount of solute $(C_l^* - kC_s^*)$ will accumulate in the neighboring liquid cell(s).

Solution scheme for macroscopic thermal transport. As the thermal diffusivity of metallic alloys is 3-4 orders of magnitudes greater than the solute diffusivity, the kinetics for microstructure evolution can be assumed to be solute transport-controlled, and therefore the thermal diffusion can be considered to be complete in the microscopic scale. Thus the thermal transport is calculated through the arrangement of macroscopic meshes. The governing equation (Eq. (7)) and related boundary conditions are solved by the explicit finite difference algorithm. The value of temperature simulated is located in the center of the square mesh. The latent heat effect in the last term of Eq. (7) is dealt with by using the temperature recovery method depending on the total variation of the solid fraction in the macroscopic mesh, which is contributed from the change of the liquid-to-solid state in the microscopic cells included. Therefore, the equivalent temperature ΔT_L recovered from a liquid cell due to the latent heat release during nucleation or growth is evaluated by

$$\Delta T_L = \left(\Delta H_V \times dx^2\right) / \left(\rho C_P \times \Delta X^2\right) \tag{13}$$

where ΔH_V is volumetric latent heat release, ρC_P is the volumetric specific heat, and ΔX and dx are the mesh sizes for the macroscopic and microscopic schemes, respectively. Temperature of the macroscopic mesh is then recovered based on Eq. (13) by the newly solidified macroscopic cells. Using these updated temperatures, macroscopic heat transfer calculation can be continued.

Integration of the macroscopic and microscopic schemes. The present model consists of two schemes: the combination of solute transport in FDM and modified cellular automaton model for simulating the evolution of dendritic structures and the macroscopic heat transport in FDM. Based on the calculated temperature profile in the cells, the calculation of nucleation and growth as well as the solute redistribution are carried out by the modified cellular automaton model as described above.

For two different schemes, two kinds of time step are used; one for the macroscopic heat transfer calculation based on the macroscopic mesh, and the other for the modified cellular automaton model, based on microscopic cells, as follows:

Macroscopic time step:

$$\Delta t_{macro} = \left(\Delta X^2 \times \rho C_p\right) / \left(4.5 \times \lambda\right) \tag{14}$$

where λ is the thermal conductivity.
Microscopic time step:

$$\Delta t_{micro} = (1/4.5)\min\left[\left(dx/V_{\max}\right),\left(dx^2/D_l\right)\right] \tag{15}$$

where V_{max} is the maximum growth velocity within all liquid cells during each time step and D_l is the solute diffusion coefficient in the liquid phase. Within a Δt_{macro}, the relationship between both time steps is $\Delta t_{micro} \leqq \Delta t_{macro}$.

4. Results and discussion

The Al-Cu alloy is chosen to simulate the several microstructures of dendritic growth in the present work with the material properties listed in table 1.

Free dendritic growth in an undercooled melt. In order to simulate free dendritic growth in an undercooled melt, the calculating domain is divided into 320×320 cells with a cell size of 0.2 μm, which is fine enough to resolve a dendrite tip radius (Zhu & Hong, 2001). The size is larger than the critical radius r^0 of a crystal, which is approximated by the following equation (Kurz & Fisher, 1998)

$$r^0 = (2\Gamma)/\left(\Delta T_{r^0}\right) \tag{16}$$

where Γ is the Gibbs-Thomson coefficient and ΔT_{r^0} is the undercooling for the occurrence of nucleation. Based on the calculation of the Gaussian distribution in the bulk liquid, the nucleation will appear if the simulated temperature is lowered by the amount of ΔT_{mn}. Thus, for simplicity, the mean nucleation undrecooling ΔT_{mn} in the bulk is used for ΔT_{r^0}. In the beginning of simulation, one nucleus with the preferential growth direction of 0° or 45° with respect to the horizontal direction is assigned in the center of the area. The initial concentration of the calculation domain is assumed to be C_0.

The simulated dendrite morphology of an Al-2.0mass%Cu alloy solidified into an undercooled melt is shown in Fig. 1 for three stages: (a) the initial growth stage before emitting the side branch, (b) the initial of the secondary arms emitting from the primary trunk, and (c) the dendrite morphology with well-developed secondary and even tertiary arms. The different levels of darkness in the figure indicate the concentration profiles in both the solid and liquid phases. Within the solid region, along the centerline of primary trunks or side arms, there exists a spine with lower concentration, which is considered as the result of the combined effect of curvature and interface kinetics (Warren & Boettinger, 1995). The concentration in solid near the solid-liquid interface shows the higher concentration where the final solidification occurs. It could be seen from Fig. 1 (c) that the tertiary arm branching occurs only at one side of the secondary arms. These phenomena have been consistent with the observation of experiments and also simulated by the modified cellular automaton (Fig. (d)-(f)) (Zhu & Hong, 2001) and phase field models (Warren & Boettinger, 1995). The results of Fig. 1 illustrates the similar capability of the model with the present modification to depict the dendrite evolution features, including the growing and coarsening of the primary trunk, the branching of the secondary and tertiary dendrite arms, as well as the solute segregation patterns.

T_l	Liquidus temperature [K]	928.0 (2mass%Cu) 922.0 (4.5mass%Cu)
T_m	Melting temperature [K]	933.0
k	Partition coefficient	0.17
m	Slope of the liquidus line [K/mass%]	-3.36
C_p	Specific heat [J/kg·K]	1086
ρ	Density [kg/m^3]	2780
λ	Thermal conductivity [W/m·K]	192.5
ΔH_v	Volumertic latent heat [J/m^3]	1.107×10^9
D_l	Solute diffusion coefficient in liquid [m^2/sec]	10^{-9}
D_s	Solute diffusion coefficient in solid [m^2/sec]	10^{-12}
Γ	Gibbs-Thomson coefficient [mK]	2.4×10^{-7}

Table 1. Thermal and physical properties of Al-Cu alloy (Zhu & Hong, 2001; Kurz & Fisher, 1998) used in the present calculation.

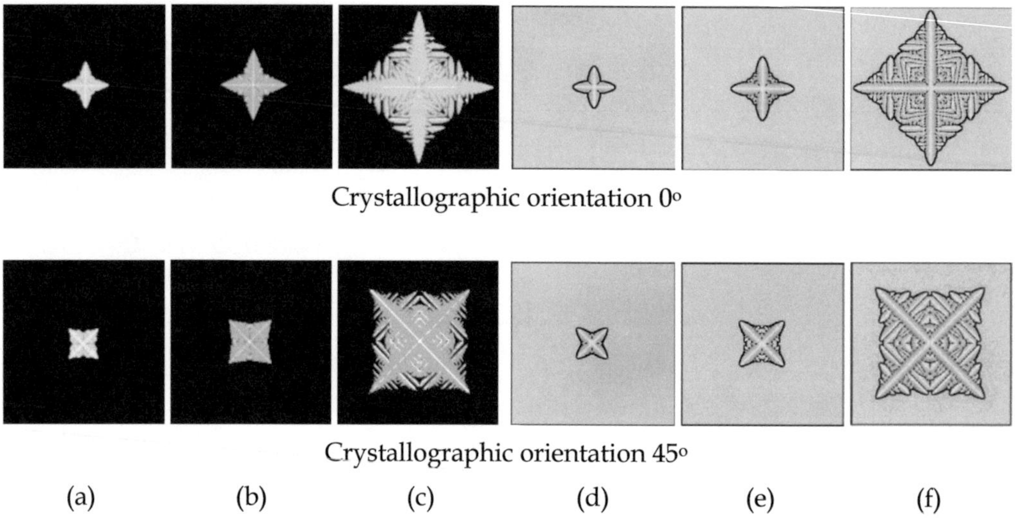

Fig. 1. The simulated dendritic shapes during the isothermal growth of an Al-2.0mass%Cu alloy

Prediction of the Structures formed in the directional solidification. The present model is applied to predict the evolution of dendritic grain structures of Al-2.5mass%Cu and Al-4.5mass%Cu alloys unidirectionally solidified over a copper chill plate with a constant temperature of 298 K. the nucleation parameters are listed in table 2. The symbols indexed "s" and "b" correspond to nucleation parameters on the mold surface and in the bulk liquid, respectively. Fig. 2 indicates the simulated and experimental macro- and micro- structures of Al-Cu alloys unidirectionally solidified with a pouring temperature of 1013 K. Fig. 2(c) and 2(f) indicate the simulated structures by the proposed method and Fig. 2(a), 2(b), 2(d) and 2(e) the experimental ones (Zhu & Hong, 2001). The left three figures indicate the case of the Al-2.5mass%Cu and the others for the case of the Al-4.5mass%Cu. Fig. 2(c) and 2(f), indicating the dendritic structures simulated by the proposed method, are also in good agreement with 2(c) and 2(f). The case of Al-4.5mass%Cu has smaller undercooling in the

	$n_{max,s}$ [m^{-2}]	$\Delta T_{mn,s}$ [K]	$\Delta T_{\sigma,s}$ [K]	$n_{max,b}$ [m^{-3}]	$\Delta T_{mn,b}$ [K]	$\Delta T_{\sigma,b}$ [K]
Al-2.5mass%Cu	1.8×10^{8}	0.5	0.1	8×10^{9}	5.0	0.1
Al-4.5mass%Cu	1.8×10^{8}	0.5	0.1	1.6×10^{10}	2.0	0.1

Table 2. The nucleation parameters of Al -Cu alloy (Zhu & Hong, 2001) used in the present calculation.

(a) (b) (c)

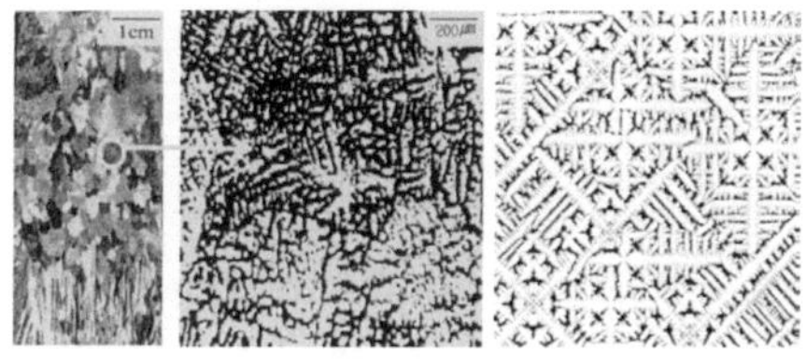

(d) (e) (f)

Fig. 2. Simulated and experimental results in directional casting of Al-Cu alloys.

bulk liquid, resulting in the nucleaction of equiaxed structures. For this simulation, a calculation domain is divided into 400×400 cells with a cell size of 3 μm, which is larger than the critical radius calculated by Eq. (16). It is seen that the proposed method can be applied to predict both the columnar and equiaxed dendritic morphology in a casting process of a binary alloy.

5. Conclusions

The proposed model, which is based upon the coupling of a modified cellular automaton model with the growth calculation of a nucleus in a given nucleation cell, has been developed to simulate the evolution of the dendritic structure in solidification of alloys. For a free dentritic growth in the undercooled melt, it is found that the proposed model can quantitatively describe the evolution of dendritic growth features, including the growing and coarsening of the primary trunks, the branching of the secondary and tertiary dendrite arms, as well as the solute segregation patterns. Moreover the directional solidification with the columnar and equiaxed grains is simulated by the proposed method and the evolution from nucleation to impingement between grains is observed.

6. References

Beltran-Sanchez, L. & Stefanescu, D. M. (2003). Growth of solutal dendrites: A cellular automaton model and its quantitative capabilities. *Metall. Mater. Trans. A*, Vol. 34A, p367-382.

Boettinger, W. J.; Warren, C.; Beckermann, C. & Karma, A. (2001). Phase-field simulation of solidification. *Annu. Rev. Mater. Res.*, Vol. 132, p163-194.

Gandin, Ch.-A.; Desbiolles, J.-L.; Rappaz, M. & Thevoz, Ph. (1999). A three-dimensional cellular automaton-finite element model for the prediction of solidification grain structures. *Metall. Mater. Trans. A*, Vol. 30A, No. 12, p3153-3165.

Juric, D. & Tryggvason, G. (1996). A front-tracking method for dendritic solidification. *J. Comput. Phys.*, Vol. 123, p127-148.

Kurz, W. & Fisher, D. J. (1998). *Fundamentals of Solidification*, Trans Tech Publication, Switzerland.

Kurz, W.; Giovanola, B. & Trivedi, R. (1986). Theory of Microstructural Development during Rapid Solidification. *Acta Metall.*, Vol. 34, p823-830.

Nastac, L. (1999). Numerical modeling of solidification morphologies and segregation patterns in cast dendritic alloys. *Acta Mater.*, Vol. 47, p4253-4262.

Rappaz, M. & Gandin, Ch.-A. (1993). Probabilstic modeling of microstructure formation in solidification processes. *Acta Metall. Mater.*, Vol. 41, No. 2, p345-360.

Sasikumar, R. & Sreenivasan, R. (1994). 2-dimensional simulation of dendrite morphology. *Acta Metall. Mater.*, Vol. 42, No. 7, p2381-2386.

Warren, J. A. & Boettinger, W. J. (1995). Prediction of dendritic growth and microsegregation patterns in a binary alloy using the phase-field method. *Acta Metall. Mater.*, Vol. 43, p689-703.

Zhu, M. F. & Hong, C. P. (2001). A modified cellular automaton model for the simulation of dendritic growth in solidification of alloys. *ISIJ Int.*, Vol. 41, No. 5, p436-445.

11

Mesoscopic Modelling of Metallic Interface Evolution Using Cellular Automata Model

Abdelhafed. Taleb and Jean Pierre Badiali
UPMC, Laboratoire d'Electrochimie,
Chimie des Interfaces et Modélisation pour l'Energie
ENSCP, Chimie ParisTech, CNRS/UMR 7575.11 rue P. et M. Curie,
75231 Paris cedex 05
France

1. Introduction

The evolution of metallic surfaces in contact with aggressive environment results from a large number of coupled phenomena operating over wide ranges of time and length scales. Indeed we deal with a large number of chemical species, a combination of many processes (chemical, electrochemical, mechanical ...) and we have to perform a multi-scale analysis both in space and time. To understand and reproduce the rich phenomenology of such systems various approaches are developed from microscopic to mesoscopic and macroscopic levels.

At the atomic scale the main task consists to describe elementary processes involved in a specific metal interface (Arrouvel et al., 1996); (Balazs, 1996); (Balazs, 1995), in this case all the chemical specificities are considered. However the elementary processes are not directly observable but they underlie other phenomena for instance transport phenomena that depend on boundary conditions. This introduces a coupling between microscopic and macroscopic levels of description.

Therefore leaving the microscopic scale some scientists - mainly physicists - have developed an approach in which the main goal (Balazs, 1996); (Balazs & Gouyet, 1995); (Vazquez et al., 1995) is to focus on the general aspects of the processes involved in metal surface evolution. Many processes developed at the level of the interface are considered as irrelevant. This leads to analyse the results in terms of universality classes and scaling laws. These models allow for investigating the morphology of the surface (roughness, dendrites formation, etc …).

Besides these rather recent approaches a huge literature that we call electrochemical to be short, has been developed. It is based on models combining a set of electrochemical and chemical reactions coupled with transport phenomena and an electric potential distribution. These models lead to solve a set of partial differential equations that are purely deterministic.

Hereafter we want to develop an approach that is intermediate between the one developed by physicists and that corresponding to the traditional electrochemical literature. Thus, our main goal is to investigate the evolution of metal surface related to stochastic processes but including realistic electrochemical point of view. However, we do not want to describe a specific system but rather to analyse how the combination of a small number of basic processes very well accepted by electrochemists might determine general features. Since we do not consider all the processes that may have an important role for a specific system we work at a mesoscopic scale i.e. we assume that a coarse graining is performed on processes at a microscopic scale. Hereafter mesoscopic approaches are considered as a way to combine the macroscopic phenomenology with the stochastic character of the processes originating from the microscopic scale phenomena. The cellular automata (CA) models are particularly suited for describing the physics at a mesoscopic scale. There is also another reason justifying the use of CA models. A large literature concerning the corrosion experiments reveals the stochastic character of some quantities like the incubation time, the corrosion rate, the pit morphology, etc .... Thus using a cellular automata model we have a theoretical tool from which we may expect to reproduce a stochastic behavior.

In parallel, Monte Carlo (MC) simulations (Malki & Baroux, 2005); (Reigada et al., 1994) have been performed, they exhibit some strong similarities with a CA description. An important advantage of CA is that it saves computing time when compared with the MC lattice dynamics where sites are updated randomly in a sequential manner (Kortlük, 1998). CA and MC have found to be in good quantitative agreement for several surface catalytic reactions models once the initial inherent difficulties to an implementation of a parallel procedure has been overcome (Cordoba et al., 2001). However, CA does not seem to have been used extensively in modeling metal electrolyte interface, although this approach has been recognized more efficiency than their MC counterparts (Nishidate et al., 1996), and of course, more suitable for high speed parallel computers.

In recent works we have shown that a cellular automata model is a simple and convenient way to describe interface evolution in contact with aggressive environment taking into account the diffusion (Taleb et al., 2001); (Taleb et al., 2006); (Taleb et al., 2007); (Stafiej et al., 2006); (Vautrin et al., 2007), (Vautrin et al., 2008). A combination of simple processes involving diffusion and chemical reactions represents a typical example of what we want to investigate; this is justified because such phenomena are present in the formation of any oxide layer. The richness of behaviours we observe does not result from the existence of a huge number of processes but from an apparent very simple algorithm. Our main goal is to describe the gross features, which appear in the formation of oxide layers on a metallic surface in the presence of corrosion, precipitation of some reaction products and pH distribution. In particular we will focus on the evolution of the corrosion front and a description of its morphology via its roughness.

The mesoscopic approach is efficient to discover some general tendencies or the coupling between several phenomena. However the weak points of this approach concern the coarse graining procedure that it supposes and the connection with the microscopic scale. In general we are not able to perform this coarse graining explicitly. In some cases it is possible to have a mapping between simulation and experimental results then we may estimate the size of the lattice spacing and to check the consistency of the approach. This has been done in one of our paper (Taleb et al., 2001); (Taleb et al., 2006) in which we have predicted the law of oxide layer growth on a metal surface. This is much more difficult in other cases.

In Section 2 we will develop the main ingredients that are necessary to develop a cellular automata model in general. This implies to define what we mean by the mesoscopic scale, and to give the general conditions needed to realize a CA approach. In Section 3 we describe some simulation results in the case of a planar interface. We will start from the simplest model in which there is no diffusion, this model is equivalent to a double Eden model. Then we introduce the diffusion of corrosion product and also the Pilling Bedworth coefficient, the feedback effect of the layer in formation on the corrosion rate will be analyzed via several quantities like the evolution of the front, the distribution of walkers and the surface roughness. In Section 4 we improve the previous models by introducing more explicitly some basic chemical and electrochemical processes. This will be illustrated by considering a heterogeneous process in which a metal recovered by an insulating film is put in contact with an aggressive medium due to a local rupture in the film. In Section 5 we present the conclusions and give some perspectives.

2. The main ingredients in a cellular automata description

In this Section we develop the main ingredients that are involved in the cellular automata model.

2.1 The mesoscopic scale

Today the mesoscopic scale is largely developed in the domain of chemical physics associated with the so-called the soft matter physics (De Gennes, 1991). Mesoscopic scale results from a coarse graining procedure which is rarely performed explicitly.

To elaborate a mesoscopic description we are inspired by two archetypal examples in which the coarse graining is performed more or less explicitly. The first one is the Brownian motion (Le Bellac, 1988). To investigate the motion of an ion in a solution we may forget the detailed dynamics associated with the solvent molecules provided the ion mass is much larger than the one of a solvent molecule. Then focusing on the ionic dynamics the solvent gives rise to the sum of a frictional and a random force. In this case the coarse graining (Le Bellac, 1988) can be performed analytically because it is assumed that the ion mass is infinitely large compare to the solvent mass. In our approach, we retain only a given number of processes that are treated explicitly; others generate the stochastic evolution. As in the case of Brownian motion we assume that the neglected processes have a characteristic time much smaller than the ones on which we focus. The second example that we have in mind is the ferromagnetism (Kortlüt, 1988). The spins responsible of the magnetism are localized on the sites of a lattice for which the order of magnitude of the lattice spacing is few angstroms. However if we focus on the long range structure near a critical point for instance we forget the microscopic structure, we replace the spins by larger entities the so called spin block that are localized on a supper lattice for which the lattice spacing is few nanometers. The same idea is used here; instead of all the chemical or electrochemical reactions that take place on the metal sites when we are at a microscopic level we consider that an effective process reminiscent of what happens at a microscopic scale but localized on the sites of a lattice for which the lattice spacing is at a mesoscopic scale. The metal atoms, for instance, are replaced by a given number of metal atoms that behaves as a quasi -particle and the information corresponding to a scale smaller than the lattice spacing are considered as irrelevant.

2.2 Realization of a cellular automata model

In a CA model we represent the system by a discrete lattice and then define its dynamic by rules of transformation of the lattices sites during discrete time steps named simulation time step δt. Our CA model is a combination of several stochastic processes characterized by their

probabilities representing electrochemical and chemical reactions. Depending on the considered corrosion system, the number of species and the local chemistry, the stochastic processes involved will be different.
To perform the simulation we used a two dimensional (2D) lattice. This reduced dimensionality is chosen mostly to save computational time. Certainly, the simulation of a three dimensional system would produce a richer class of behaviors but as we shall see a two dimensional approach is sufficient to describe a lot of processes that are expected to take place in real systems. There is no doubt that a 3D calculation will change the order of magnitude of some quantities but we expect that some phenomena may remain qualitatively the same. On the same footing we may expect that the results quantitatively depend on the geometry of the lattice but that any lattice is sufficient for describing the main features in which we are interested. Here we use a squared lattice (connectivity 4).

2.3 Definition of the lattices sites

For a given interface we define a certain number of species. As mentioned above in the case of metal, we do not consider particles but quasi-particles. The species are quasi-particles that move or are transformed as well defined entities. The state of each lattice site is determined by the dominating species at this point. Some of them are common to all corrosion systems. Usually the lattice sites representing the bulk material are denoted M and we call them metal sites or shortly M sites. Such sites are never in contact with the external aggressive environment by definition. We define two other types of metallic sites, R and P located on the surface of the corroded material and exposed to the aggressive environment. R represents a reactive site, which can be transformed in a passive site P. A P site mimics the presence of a solid entity on the metal surface, which can be dissolved. Other sites may exist but they are related to a specific model as we shall see below.
Each site is referred by two indexes one noted "i" is associated with the column and the other "j" is associated with the position of the row. We assume that the lattice is a cell having N_x columns while the number of rows is not limited; outside this cell we assume periodic boundary conditions.

2.4 Transformation rules of the lattices sites

During one simulation time step, δt, different processes take place. Among the processes associated with different electrochemical or chemical reactions considered some of them correspond to a change in the solid, others take place on the corrosion front but on the liquid side and the last ones appear in the bulk solution. To these different phenomena are associated different time scales. The estimation of these different characteristic times ratio leads to a given ordering in the algorithm associated with the processes. This represents an important part of the model but it is also a quite general problem unavoidable in any theoretical description. For instance, in standard deterministic approaches we have to deal with a series of differential equations each one being characterized by a given time. Then from physical arguments we may compare the characteristic time and select the processes that are relevant for a given time scale. In what follows we assume that the long time is related to the transformation of fresh metal sites M into reactive metal R, δt is the time needed to produce this transformation of the solid. The characteristic time associated with chemical or electrochemical reactions is assumed to be vanishingly small in comparison with δt. On the same way we assume that the interfacial processes producing H^+ or OH^- are very short.

The interfacial properties will be investigated as a function of time $t = N_t\ \delta t$, where N_t is the number of simulation time step. Hereafter δt will be considered as our unit of time and the time will be simply measured by N_t.

2.5 Diffusion process

As mentioned in the introduction the diffusion is a basic process in the formation of oxide layers. Hereafter the diffusion will be described by a random walk process. Since the concentration of the diffusion species may be very high in the neighbourhood of the metal surface we will introduce a steric interaction assuming that at most one diffusing species can occupy a given site. This kind of modeling of the steric interaction is commonly used in the literature (Nicolis et al., 2001) and is referred to as the simple exclusion rule. In order to characterize the diffusion we have to decide how many diffusion steps can be performed during δt. We assume that an elementary diffusion step takes a time $\delta t/N_{diff}$ or that N_{diff} diffusion can be performed during δt. During each time interval $\delta t/N_{diff}$ all walkers noted D attempt to execute one step. Among the four nearest neighbors of a given walker, one is selected at random. If this nearest neighbor is a metal site (M, R), no move is made. If the selected nearest neighbor is a P site free of D species, then the walker is moved to it. The walker stays at its initial position when the selected nearest neighbor is already occupied by a D species. In the simulations the list of walkers (D) is permuted randomly at each time step to avoid spurious correlations with the initial setting of the list.

3. Results on planar interfaces.

To mimic the formation of a layer on a metal surface we consider three main processes: corrosion, diffusion and precipitation. Since these phenomena take place in two different regions of the interface we have to deal with a film which is developing with two fronts: one for the growth and the other one for the corrosion. This leads to investigate the coupling between the two fronts; of course the diffusion will play an important role in this coupling.
In this section we first consider a basic model in which there is no diffusion and then we introduce the diffusion and the Pilling Bedworth coefficient which combines with steric hindrance may produce a layer feedback effect on the corrosion rate.

3.1 A basic model

In Section 2.3 we have defined two kinds of metal sites; those in contact with the aggressive medium noted R and the others corresponding to the bulk metal and noted M. We assume that in contact with the aggressive medium the reactive site R can be transformed into a species P. Thus all the chemical transformations that appears at a microscopic scale are replaced by the transformation that is noted

$$E + R \rightarrow P \qquad (1)$$

In which E represents a solution site located in the neighbourhood of the reactive site R that is replaced by the reaction product P. This P is put at random on a growth site that is a E site in contact with a P site. By this process we generate at random a compact layer of connected P sites.
Formally such a description of corrosion can be considered as the reverse of a growth process described via the Eden model (Eden, 1961). The basic model is in fact similar to a double Eden model. An example of layer resulting from this process is shown in Figure 1a-

b. The black part represents the bulk metal, the grey part the layer already formed and the white part is occupied only by E species. The conditions of the simulation are given in the figure captions. In order to give a quantitative information on the growth and the corrosion front we define their mean position. After N_t simulation steps the mean position of the growth and the corrosion front are given according to

$$\langle h_{growth}(N_t)\rangle = \frac{1}{N_x}\sum_{i=1,N_x} h_{growth}(i) \tag{2}$$

$$\langle h_{corr}(N_t)\rangle = \frac{1}{N_x}\sum_{i=1,N_x} h_{corr}(i) \tag{3}$$

In which $h_{growth}(i)$ and $h_{corr}(i)$ are, respectively, for the column i the highest value of j for which there is an P site and a corrosion site. As expected from a simple mean field approach the profiles are linear function of N_t. This also shows that the size of the cell $N_x = 2000$ is large enough to produce very well defined average; in other words although we have a random process the average appears as deterministic quantities. In the model considered there is no natural time step. For instance if we decide that during δt we proceed to N_{corr} time we we may predict that

$$\langle h_{corr}(N_t)\rangle = h(0) - \frac{N_t N_{corr}}{N_x} \tag{4}$$

which is in total agreement with the simulation results. From (4) we may define a corrosion rate $k(N_t)$ as

$$k(N_t) = \frac{d}{dN_t}\left[h(0) - \langle h_{corr}(N_t)\rangle\right] = \frac{d}{dN_t}\Delta h_{corr}(N_t) \tag{5}$$

Here, the corrosion rate is constant and we have $k(N_t)=N_{corr}/N_x$. This represents the number of corroded sites counted per unit of the initial area, N_x, and per unit of time. Although the random choice of the reactive sites does not affect the evolution of $<h_{gowth}(N_t)>$ and $<h_{corr}(N_t)>$, it determines the geometrical roughness of the fronts defined according to

$$\sigma_{growth}(N_t) = \left[\frac{1}{N_x}\sum_{i=1,N_x}(h_{growth}(i) - \langle h_{growth}(N_t)\rangle)^2\right]^{1/2} \tag{6}$$

and

$$\sigma_{corr}(N_t) = \left[\frac{1}{N_x}\sum_{i=1,N_x}(h_{corr}(i) - \langle h_{corr}(N_t)\rangle)^2\right]^{1/2} \tag{7}$$

for which we observe the scaling law of the Eden model $\sigma_{growth}(N_t) \sim N_t^{1/3}$ and the same for the corrosion front. In parallel it is well known that the front exhibits a fractal dimension d_f=1.5 (Barabasi & Stanley, 1995).

3.2 Introducing diffusion and feedback effect

In the previous model the diffusion plays no role this is equivalent to say that the diffusion is infinitely rapid, the P entity just formed may reach any growth site into the layer in formation. Now we may improve the previous model by assuming that the P site performs a random walk before to reach a growth site. In addition we will take into account that the species P has a volume larger than the R one. We take this into account by assuming that a site occupied by the metal contains a number (Φ +1) of M species. Instead of Eq. scheme (1) the corrosion reaction is now formally represented by the following reaction scheme.

$$E + (\Phi + 1)\, M \rightarrow P + (\Phi)\, D \quad (8)$$

where D denoted the diffusing species, it arises as an intermediate in the conversion of the M species into the corrosion product. Its role is then to redistribute the excess volume arising from (Φ) M via a diffusion process that we mimic as a random walk with steric interaction between the D species as explained in subsection 2.5. In Eq. (8), Φ is the traditional Pilling-Bedworth coefficient. The Eq. scheme (8) is basically different from Eq. Scheme (1). In Eq. scheme (1) the corrosion process is certain when a R site has been chosen, when we use Eq scheme (8) we decide that the corrosion is possible provided we can introduce Φ sites in the neighbourhood of M taking into account that R and D cannot occupied the same site. This steric hindrance produces a feedback effect of the layer on the corrosion rate; this is equivalent to say that the layer induces a overpotential in the corrosion rate.

For a given time step, δt, we select at random a given number, $N_{corr,}$ of reactive sites that we attempt to transform. If Φ=1, for each selected reactive site, now represented by (Φ +1) M, two D species have to be inserted in the oxide layer. Then we adopt the following rule. The selected reactive site R is transformed to a layer site (P) that takes the place of the R initial site. At the same time step one D species starts executing its random walk in the following way. From among the four nearest neighbors of the transformed site, the D species is moved till it reaches a E site connected with a P site i.e. a growth site then it replaces E and it is transformed in a P site integrated in the layer in formation. Each attempt to corrode is successful because we can always place the D species at the newly created layer site without breaking the simple exclusion rule. Thus, N_{corr} reactive sites are transformed at a time step.

If Φ=2, we have to attempt insertion of two new D species. One of the nearest neighbors of the site to be corroded is selected at random. If it is a free layer site both sites are converted to D sites. In the other case we attempt the random selection for the remaining three and then two nearest neighbor sites. If it turns out with the last one that none of the nearest neighbors is a free layer site, we have decided to adopt the rule that the corrosion is impossible. This seems to us the simplest and most physical of a handful of the possibilities one can consider here to remain consistent with the exclusion rule. Thus, in the case of Φ=2, the outcome of an attempt to perform scheme reaction is not a priori certain and depend on the situation in the immediate vicinity of the site selected for corrosion. We have created a feedback effect of the oxide layer in formation on the reaction rate. In this simple case we mimic a limitation of the corrosion rate by a concentration overpotential well known in electrochemistry (Bard & Faulkner, 1980).

The snapshots corresponding to Φ=1 are given in Figure 2a. In the layer the white point correspond to the D species. We can see immediately that the diffusion reduces the roughness of the growth front as already reported in ref (Taleb et al., 2004). A similar result is obtained experimentally with the anodization of copper in thiourea containing acid

solution (Hasseb et al., 2001). The mean positions of the corrosion front are not modified by the diffusion, and in particular the corrosion rate defined in (5) is unchanged. In contrast the position of the growth front is no more a linear function of N_t as we can see on figure 3a. For largest values of N_t we observe $[<h_{growth}(N_t)>-h(0)] \sim (N_t)^{\alpha}$ where α is very close to 0.5 the usual signature for growth processes determined by diffusion (Cabrera & Mott, 1949). For Φ=2 the snapshot corresponds to the figure 2b. The growth front exhibits the same properties as in the case of Φ=1 (see figure 3a) while the evolution of the corrosion front is modified. The comparison of Figure 2a and 2b corresponding to the same value of $N_t = 9\ 10^4$ shows that the feedback effect has two main consequences: the thickness of the layer is reduced and a smoothing of the corrosion front is observed.
In the case of Φ=2 (Fig 3a), the value of $\Delta h_{corr}(N_t)$=125 is attained at the simulation time $N_t=10^5$, whereas in the case of Φ=1 when the feedback effect is absent the same value is already obtained at $N_t=2\ 10^4$. The corrosion rate is reduced by approximately 1 order of magnitude. For the case of Φ=2, we have continued the simulation up to $N_t=4.8\ 10^5$ time steps when $\Delta h_{corr}(N_t)$=310, and it is approximately 8 time smaller than the value extrapolated for the case of Φ=1. Thus, the doubling of the number of D species created by corrosion cannot compensate for the reduction rate, and the thickness of the layer is much larger in the case of Φ=1 than in the case of Φ=2.
For Φ=2 the corrosion front exhibit a parabolic evolution, except for times $N_t \rightarrow 0$, . As seen in Figure 3a, for the largest values of N_t we have $\Delta h_{corr}(N_t) \sim (N_t)^{\alpha}$ where α is 0.58, and longer simulation show a very slow evolution of α toward 0.5, which is the value obtained by the experiments in a similar situation (Hasseb et al., 2001). Figure 3a shows the crossover between two regimes. At short times, $N_t \rightarrow 0$, the corrosion front is not covered by D species and each attempt to corrode a site is successful as in the case of Φ=1. After a given number of corrosion steps the corrosion front is both covered by D species that block the corrosion and on average, $N_{corr}(N_t)$ becomes smaller than N_{corr}. However, the coverage of reactive sites by blocking D species may change because these D species may diffuse. This diffusion can be thought of as being due to other species moving more freely than the D species itself. We have in mind holes, which are free layer sites dispersed between the sites occupied primarily by D species when the concentration of D species is high. A hole can move as a result of swapping with the neighboring D species when they happen to step into it. At a distance away from the corrosion front the holes start penetrating the layer of D sites blocking the front. In this regime the corrosion rate or $N_{corr}(N_t)$ is determined partially by initial corrosion rate and by the motion of holes in the vicinity of the corrosion front. In the asymptotic regime in which almost all of the reactive sites are covered by D species, the corrosion rate is only determined by the diffusion of holes and square root dependence in time is expected. As we shall see in Figure 2, for $N_t=9.10^4$ we are not yet in the asymptotic regime, and therefore, the coefficient α=0.58 corresponding to that in Figure 2a describes a crossover situation.
The figure 3b shows how the front positions depend on the value of N_{corr} in the case Φ = 2. A linear behaviour should suggest that the value of $\Delta h_{corr}(N_t)$ obtained for N_{corr}=1 and $N_t = 10^5$ (curve a in Figure 3b) should be the same as the one obtained with N_{corr}=10 and $N_t=10^4$ (curve b in Figure 3b). This is clearly not the case; the value obtained for N_{corr}=10 is approximately one-half of the value resulting from a linear prediction. Because one-half of the prediction corrosion acts have been effectively performed but 10 walkers are injected into each effective corrosion, we might expect that the total thickness of the layer should be larger when N_{corr}=10 than in the case of N_{corr}=1. The simulations are not in agreement with

these predictions. Therefore, it seems difficult to predict in a quantitative way the effect of the initial corrosion rate on the behaviour of the system. The intricate coupling between the processes can be illustrated by investigating the distribution of walkers in the layer as a function of N_t.

The walker distribution $n_D(j)$ along the direction perpendicular to the initial layer plane is obtained by counting for each line j of the square lattice the total number of walkers on this line. In Figure 4, for N_{corr}=10, we compare $n_D(j)$, for Φ=1 and Φ=2, at two different times corresponding to $N_t=10^4$ (Figure 4a) and 9 10^4 (Figure 4b). The walker distributions given in Figure 4b correspond to the snapshots presented in parts a and b of figure 2. The two $n_D(j)$ have the same form; however for Φ=1 the faster advancement of the corrosion front compared to the case of Φ=2 and the slower advancement of the growth front are clearly visible. The part of the distribution located below the maximum corresponds to the corrosion front and we see that $n_D(j)$ tends to be larger when Φ is increased.

The area under the distribution $n_D(j)$ shows that the total number of walkers is strongly reduced by the feedback effect when we go from Φ=1 to Φ=2; however, the gradient of the walker concentration is higher in the later case. Accordingly, the diffusion process is more efficient in the case of Φ=2. Thus, we see that the structure of the diffusion efficiency. The stronger the blocking is, the smaller the number of diffusing species is and accordingly the larger the efficiency of the diffusion is that tends to move away the blocking D species. This illustrates how the simple algorithm that we use leads to a strong competition between processes and finally to results that are difficult to predict.

For Φ=1, and N_{corr}=3 several results concerning the walker distribution $n_D(j)$ are presented in Figure 5 (Saunier et al., 2005). Whatever the value of Φ, the occurrence of a point where the concentration remains constant during the corrosion process is observed. The results of simulation shown in Figures 5 suggest approximating the walker distribution in the region where $n_D(j)$ is decreasing by a linear dependence. For Φ=1, this is done in Figure 6 in which we have represented two walker distribution referred by 1 and 2. These distributions correspond to two different times $N_{(t1)}$ and $N_{(t2)}$. They intersect at a given position that we choose as the new origin x'=0 and where $n_D(j)=n_m$. For the distribution 1 and 2, the position of the growth fronts are noted X_1 and X_2 while Y1 and Y2 represents the positions for which the saturation appears. In the case Φ=2, the results given in Figure 5c show that the trapezoidal form of the walker distribution represented in Figure 6 should be transformed into a triangular one.

For each walker distribution from the geometrical consideration, we have:

$$\frac{n_m}{1} = \frac{X_i}{X_i + Y_i} \tag{9}$$

Where i=1 or 2. Since n_m is fixed from (9) we obtain

$$\frac{dY_i}{dX_i} = \frac{1 - n_m}{n_m} \tag{10}$$

Now, we consider the two distributions simultaneously. In the part of the layer corresponding to x'> 0, the net number of particles increases because X_2 is larger than X_1, i.e., the number of walkers also increasing the thickness of the layer by (X_2-X_1). Thus the number of particles injected in this part of the layer is given by.

$$(X_2 - X_1) + \frac{n_m}{2} X_2 - \frac{n_m}{2} X_1 \tag{11}$$

Because of mass conservation, this number must be equal to the number of particles that migrate from the part $x'<0$. This number depends on the value of Φ and can be readily estimated as follows. For Φ=1, we have

$$(Y_2 - Y_1)\frac{1-n_m}{2}, \tag{12}$$

While for Φ=2, we have

$$(Y_2 - Y_1)\frac{1-n_m}{2} + (Y_2 - Y_1)(\phi - 1), \tag{13}$$

Which reduces to Eq. (12) if Φ=1. Thus, we can write the conservation of particles as.

$$(Y_2 - Y_1)(1 + \frac{n_m}{2}) = (Y_2 - Y_1)[\frac{1-n_m}{2} + (\phi - 1)]. \tag{14}$$

If we take the derivative of this relation relative to X_2, for instance, and use the value of the derivative given in (10) we can get the value of n_m that only depends on Φ. We have immediately n_m =0.25 for Φ=1 and n_m=0.5 for Φ=2. The simulation results are very close to these theoretical predictions since we find n_m=0.28 for Φ=1 and n_m=0.51 for Φ=2. Thus, the previous analysis of the walker distribution predicts quite well the existence of a point where we have a fixed distribution. From simple arguments of symmetry we may expect that this point has to be located near the initial metal/solution plane. The simulations show that the deviations from the position of the initial plane separation are very small taking into account that the thickness of the layer in the saturation regime corresponds to several hundred units of length.

Another quantity characterizing this model is the surface roughness already defined from equations (6) and (7). The results obtained for N_{corr}=10 are given in Figure 7a. We can see that the influence of Φ is very important on σ_{corr}, for Φ = 1 there is no feedback effect and σ_{corr} increases with Δh_{corr} while for Φ = 2 we are in a regime of saturation in which the diffusion is determining and then the corrosion front is smooth and time independent for large values of Δh_{corr} . Now we may analyze σ_{growth} , this quantity is time independent and very small in comparison of what can be predicted with the Eden model, we conclude that the evolution is determined by a diffusion process. In Figure 7b we may see how the smoothing will results from a diffusion process From the left side of the Figure 7b we see that a rough front of Eden type is obtained after 430 simulation steps in the case Φ =1 while on the right side of the Figure 7b we can see the front in the case Φ = 2 and after 4000 simulation time steps. Points A mark the uppermost and points B the lowermost positions of the corrosion front they show that the roughness. In both cases for a hole the probability of arriving at the point A is larger than the probability of reaching point B. Therefore A is more readily corroded as the point B. As a consequence during the front evolution the front tends to move faster at the position of the site A than at the lower site B until the difference in the probability of corrosion between sites becomes insignificant.

The main results obtained in this Section can be summarized as follows. For a system in which the initial corrosion rate is high compared to the diffusion rate, the corrosion products can stay on the corrosion front and block the corrosion mechanism. The blocking of corrosion sites by the corrosion products can be associated with the concentration over-potential, and the feedback effect of the layer on the corrosion rate is similar to a passivation effect. However, the diffusion is not totally impeached because the holes may arrive in the vicinity of the corrosion front. Thus the long-time behaviour of corrosion rate is no longer determined by the initial corrosion rate but by the diffusion process. The simulation shows the transition between these two regimes. The diffusion of holes produces, as a consequence, a smoothing of the corrosion front.

4. Heterogeneous phenomena and localized corrosion

In order to improve the previous model we introduce explicitly some basic chemical and electrochemical processes and a more sophisticated description of the aggressive medium. This will be illustrated by considering a model of localized corrosion. In Subsection 4.1 the model will be presented and the results will be given in 4.2.

4.1 Model for the electrochemical and chemical.

We consider a piece of metal with a flat surface covered by an insulating layer. Due to a mechanical reason for instance we assume that a single punctual damage is performed in this layer putting in contact the metal with the aggressive environment. To be illustrative such environment is an ionic solution containing a given aggressive ion. Depending on the local acidity or basicity the reactions involved in the corrosion processes will be different. We list them below. There is metal anodic dissolution followed by metal cation hydrolysis in acidic or neutral medium.

$$M + H_2O \rightarrow MOH_{aq} + e + H^+ \tag{15}$$

with corrosion products detached from the surface. The reaction (15) exhibits the very well known autocaytalytic effect that is associated with pitting corrosion. Metal anodic oxidation in basic medium, can be written

$$M + OH^- \rightarrow MOH_{solid} + e \tag{16}$$

It leads to the formation of corrosion products MOH_{solid} on the metal surface. They are associated to cathodic reactions which correspond to reduction of the hydrogen ion or water

$$H^+ + e \rightarrow \tfrac{1}{2} H_2 \tag{17}$$

$$H_2O + e \rightarrow \tfrac{1}{2} H_2 + OH^- \tag{18}$$

depending on the acidity of the environment. When the oxidation and reduction are spatially separated, thereafter named SSE reactions, anodic reactions (cathodic reactions) increase the acidity (basicity) of the environment. This leads to the creation of a pH inhomogeneity in the solution. In contrast, when anodic and cathodic reactions occur simultaneously at the same place or at a distance below a certain length scale both electrochemical reactions compensate with no net acidity or basicity change.

$$M + H_2O \rightarrow MOH_{aq} + \tfrac{1}{2} H_2 \tag{19}$$

$$M + H_2O \rightarrow MOH_{solid} + \tfrac{1}{2} H_2 \tag{20}$$

The occurrence of reactions scheme of Eq. (19) and (20) depends also on acidity of the medium. We refer to the above reactions as localized electrochemical reactions (LE reactions). Note that considering the LE reactions or SSE reactions depends on the length scale selected for the modelling. In our previous work (Vautrin et al., 2007); (Vautrin et al., 2008) we have studied the influence of the LE reactions on the corrosion process. The present study is devoted to the effect of prevailing SSE reactions on the corrosion process.
We assume that the presence of aggressive anions that we do not take into account explicitly may induce additional chemical reactions of MOH_{solid} dissolution (Vautrin et al., 2007); (Vautrin et al., 2008)

$$MOH_{solid} \rightarrow MOH_{aq} \tag{21}$$

which occurs especially in acidic medium. In the following we consider MOH_{aq} as an implicit part of the environment solution; it does not appear explicitly in the model. The ions H^+ and OH^- generated in the solution by SSE reactions diffuse and when they encounter neutralisation occurs:

$$H^+ + OH^- \rightarrow H_2O \tag{22}$$

The previous processes are very well accepted in corrosion science; however we may point out some differences with traditional investigations. Hereafter we consider that the corrosion is initiated by an external factor and we do not investigate the processes producing a breakdown in the protective film. Second we assume that the concentration of the aggressive species is not a determining process. Here we analyse the role of diffusion processes on the local pH in solution. This kind of investigation is absent in many works in which it is assumed that the cathodic reaction does not take place inside the cavity but at the external surface of the material.
As it has been shown besides the direct dissolution of the material a detachment of islands occurs in the evolution of the corroding surface. To describe this phenomenon in the context of our lattice model we define the connectivity of the metallic pieces. The connectivity of two sites in our lattice model is defined such that there is a suite of nearest neighbour (nn) sites of the types M, P or R forming a path from one site to another (Chpard & Droz, 1998). Otherwise they are disconnected. The Von Neumann or 4 - connectivity is used except for the front. Two neighboring front sites are connected if they are both von Neumann nearest neighbors or they have an M site as a common von Neumann neighbour. This prevents the surface of a connected M piece from splitting into disconnected pieces. Thus an island in our model is a whole connected piece of metallic sites disconnected from the main corroding block.
In case of spatially separated electrochemical (SSE) reactions, we assume that anodic dissolution of a piece of metal is accompanied by a simultaneous cathodic reaction. The sites of the two reactions belong to the surface of a single connected piece of material.
The electrochemical and chemical reactions given in Eq. schemes (15) – (22) corresponds to description at a microscopic level, now we have to translate such reactions at the

mesoscopic level i.e. in terms of sites. In addition to the sites E we introduce extra solution sites denoted A and C. The site A (C) indicates that the environment at the position occupied by this site is more acidic (basic) than in the original solution E. To a given site we associate the difference in the numbers of acidic and basic sites, $N_{exc}=N_A-N_C$ located in the nearest neighbourhood of the site. Consequently we speak about acidic, neutral and basic environment for $N_{exc}>0$, $N_{exc}=0$ and $N_{exc}<0$, respectively. We mimic the anodic reactions by Eq. schemes (15) and (16) as

$$R \rightarrow A, \quad N_{exc} \geq 0 \tag{23}$$

$$R+C(nn) \rightarrow P+E(nn), \quad N_{exc} < 0 \tag{24}$$

The "(nn)" is put to indicate the nearest neighbor of the considered site. In Eq. scheme (24) the reactive site is changed into a passive site while C is consumed and a new E site appears. Here we adopt the rule that any surface site S, where S=R or S=P, mediates the cathodic processes with an *a priori* equal probability. We represent cathodic reactions by the Eq. schemes (17) and (18) by

$$S+A(nn) \rightarrow S+E(nn), \quad N_{exc} \geq 0 \tag{25}$$

$$S+E(nn) \rightarrow S+C(nn), \quad N_{exc} < 0 \tag{26}$$

We also adopt a simple exclusion rule. If the nearest neighbors of the surface site are neither E nor A it follows that the S site is blocked by nearest neighbors of C type and such an S site cannot mediate the cathodic process. Therefore the *a posteriori* probability of the SSE reaction depends on the blocking of its cathodic part by the presence of C sites. We repeat the selection from among the other S sites until a free site is found, whatever its position provided it is connected to the site on which the anodic reaction takes place, or until the list of connected surface sites is exhausted. If the cathodic reaction is impossible, the spatially separated anodic and cathodic reactions cannot be realized.
The reaction schemes of Eq. (23)-(26) corresponding to SSE reactions are assumed to be realized with a probability $p_{sse}=1$. It can be lower due the blocking of cathodic reaction discussed above. Finally we can mimic the dissolution of MOH_{solid} by Eq. scheme (21) as.

$$P \rightarrow E \tag{27}$$

The probability of this reaction is taken as $p_{PE}=0.25\ N_{exc}$ if $N_{exc} \geq 0$ and $p_{PE}=0$ otherwise. Similarly to Eq. scheme of (24) the Eq. scheme (28) implies that after the dissolution of a P sites some M sites which are in contact with the solution become fresh R site. To account for diffusion C and A sites created in the SSE reactions execute random walk. The target site is selected at random from the nearest neighbours of the walker. If the target site is E the walker is swapped to it. If the walker is C and the target site is occupied by the walker A or vice versa neutralization occurs that mimics the reaction scheme of Eq (22)

$$A + C \rightarrow E + E \tag{28}$$

In any other case the random walk remains in its initial position. We regulate the diffusion rate with respect to the corrosion rate with N_{diff} being an integer parameter indicating the number of steps random walk we perform for each time step of corrosion. We expect that N_{diff} plays an important role in the corrosion evolution as diffusion tends to smooth out the pH inhomogeneities created by SSE reactions.
The above schemes and the values that we use for the set of probabilities are only qualitative and conceived on what is generally known or accepted about corrosion processes in some class of materials. The number of species and the corrosion processes depend on the system considered. The generic features of the corrosion process should not depend, however, on the detailed form of our assumptions.
We may illustrate this procedure like this. Exploring at random the list of surface sites, we find that for the site i the reaction of anodic dissolution followed by metal cation hydrolysis in acidic or neutral medium can be realized. Then the reactive metal site is transformed in MOH_{aq} that disappears instantaneously in the solution and the i is replaced by H^+ that immediately changes the acidity in the interface i.e. the transformation of a site in the neighbourhood of i is now dependent of what happened in i. When all the possibilities of chemical or electrochemical reactions have been explored the diffusion of H^+ or OH^- and their eventual recombination takes place. Only when we restart a new time step we considered the fresh reactive site created during the previous step. The ordering of events considered in the algorithm describes a physical chemistry picture of a given number of metal corroded systems. However, other choice of ordering can be considered for other corroded system. For instance we may introduce a more sophisticated coupling between reactions and diffusion.

4.2 Results

In Figure 8 we present snapshots obtained at $N_{diff} = 6000$ as function of the time steps. The solution remains locally neutral and the corrosion front is characterized by a uniform roughness with hemispherical shape in the initial stage of the simulation (Fig 8a). We observe the separation of the solution into acidic and basic zones with an intermediate neutral zone after relatively few hundred simulations time steps (Fig 8b-c). The corrosion front is simultaneously separated into smooth and rough surface zone corresponding, respectively to acidic and basic zones in the solution side (Fig 8b-c). The smooth surface zone follows the lattice symmetry and the rough surface zone has an irregular form (Fig 8b-c). We observe the transition from a homogeneous state to an inhomogeneous one concerning the solution and the corrosion front for every N_{diff} is the earlier this transition appears. This suggests that for each N_{diff} value there exist a critical size of the corrosion cavity. Below this critical size the diffusion of A and C species is efficient enough to ensure the neutralization of all of them. Above this critical size the diffusion is too slow for A and C species to neutralize completely. We will discuss this in more detail later. The smooth and rough zones of the corrosion front can be justified as follows. The part of the corrosion front in contact with the basic solution contains P sites as predominant species. P sites cannot be dissolved in the basic medium and can only be used for cathodic reaction. However, for the P sites with totally basic environment the cathodic reactions cannot take place on it. Consequently the corrosion practically stops there. In contrast, the part of the corrosion front in contact with the acidic solution can undergo the anodic reaction. Because the probability of this reaction p_{sse}=1 is high the metal corrosion is rapidly developed there leading to a smooth front as already shown (Taleb et al., 2004). It is already interesting to notice that the coexistence of two or more regions that may qualify by smooth or rough has been observed in experiment with Al (Balazs, 1996); (Balazs, 1995).

The stochastic character of the phenomena occurring during the corrosion process can be observed in the Fig. 9a-d where we present the snapshots corresponding to a same choice of probabilities, N_{diff}=100 and approximately the same number of time steps. In Figure 9a we observe a deep cavity developing downwards in contrast to the cavities of Figure 9c-d and developing sideways. In figure 9c-d we can observe that the single anodic zone develops the corrosion either to right side or the left side, respectively depending on some initial asymmetry created by the fluctuation. We observe two anodic zones separated by one cathodic zone in Figure 9b. The evolution of this form leads practically to a double cavity and the two cavities develop sharing the same cathodic zone. The coalescence of theses cavities can be expected. Figure 8 and 9 show that a large class of morphology is already obtained and that it is difficult of characterizing the pits geometry in a simple way.

4.2.1 The critical radius

For a given number of corroded sites, $N_{corrded}$, we define an equivalent radius

$$R_{eq} = (\frac{2N_{corroded}}{\pi})^{1/2} \tag{29}$$

representing the radius of the semicircle that we would have if the $N_{corroded}$ sites were placed in it. This radius R_{eq} is just a quantitative quantity that allows a comparison of different results corresponding to very different underlying geometries. From our previous results it appears that R_{eq} is a simple quantity that depends linearly on time and can be interpreted in a simple way (Vautrin et al., 2007).

In Figure 10a we present R_{eq} as a function of simulation time steps, N_t, for several values of N_{diff}. In the initial stage of corrosion all the curves coincide and form a straight line characterized by a common universal slope whatever the N_{diff} value. After this initial stage the slope decreases: the smaller N_{diff} the earlier the decrease is obtained. This decrease occurs simultaneously to the appearance of zones in the solution and at the corrosion front. This can be seen by comparing the Figure 10a and 10b. In Figure 10b we present the relative concentration of A sites, n_A, with respect to all the solution sites as a function of the time steps. The A and C sites are created by an SSE reaction as a pair and disappear in pairs in the neutralization reaction. Consequently the number of A sites is equal to that of C sites. We observe that the fraction of A sites is practically negligible until a certain time step where it begins to grow. The time step for which the fraction of A sites grows corresponds to the time step on which the solution stops to be homogeneous and also to time where R_{eq} versus N_t changes its slope (Figure 10a). All these results illustrate the existence of a critical radius, Rc, separating two regimes in the pit growth.

At the beginning of the process we have a stationary regime for which at each time step we start with neutral solution. When R_{eq}>Rc we have a diffusion controlled regime, the diffusion cannot ensure the complete neutralization of A and C sites. As seen in Figure 8 the

A and C sites survive in the solution forming acidic and basic zones in the globally neutral solution. The fraction of A sites is smaller in the case of large N_{diff} because the diffusion and then the neutralization are very efficient.
There is not a unique definition of R_c, hereafter we decide to fit R_{eq} versus N_t according to two straight lines corresponding to the stationary regime or to the diffusion limited regime. We define the critical point by the coordinates (R_c, T_c) of the crossing point between these two straight lines. In figure 11 we show the behaviour of R_c as a function of N_{diff}. We may use a simple model to analyze these results. First, it seems obvious that larger is N_{diff} larger might be the value of R_c. Second, it is clear that R_c must depend on a characteristic length λthat we have to cover by diffusion in order to favour the occurrence of the neutralization via Eq. scheme (28), smaller is λ larger might be R_c. To estimate λ two limiting mechanisms can be considered in which the neutralization takes place near the surface or in the bulk of the cavity. For the first time (N_t) of the simulation, N_{create} represents the number of ions H^+ and OH^- created during this time step and, in the stationary regime, the only H^+ and OH^- ions present in the solution are those produced during the considered simulation time step. The number N_{create} is proportional to r time the value of the effective radius at time t. If the neutralization takes place on the surface, the distance λ is the mean distance between ions on the surface, we have $\lambda \sim R/\ N_{create}$ this is just a pure number depending on geometrical factor and we may expect $R_c \sim N_{diff}$. If the neutralization occurs in the bulk solution we may imagine a mechanism in one or two steps: the ions H^+ and OH^- diffuse into the bulk of the solution where they are neutralized or to reach by diffusion the solution bulk where they are uniformly distributed is not sufficient to the occurrence of the neutralization and additional time is needed to their collisions and neutralization. The first process leads to $\lambda \sim R_c$ leading to $R_c \sim N_{diff}{}^{1/2}$. If λ is determined by the mean distance between H^+ and OH^- when the homogenization is done we have $\lambda \sim (\pi R^2 / N_{create})^{1/2} \sim R^{1/2}$ leading to $R_c \sim (N_{diff} / R_c{}^{1/2})$ or $R_c \sim N_{diff}{}^{2/3}$. The simulation results show that a surface neutralization ($R_c \sim N_{diff}$) is excluded but we cannot decided between the two power laws $R_c \sim N_{diff}{}^{1/2}$ or $R_c \sim N_{diff}{}^{2/3}$, it is satisfactory to note that for each of these laws the order of magnitude of the prefactor is 1. The linear dependence between R_{eq} and N_t up to R_c suggests that the same power law must relate the critical time T_c and N_{diff}. Indeed we have verified that it is so. Thus the very crude description that we have proposed is certainly a part of simulation result.
At this level it is tempting to analyze the model by trying a mapping between our results and the real world. This task is not easy because our quantitative result is the couple (R_c, T_c) for which we have no experimental result. If our transition time T_c indicates the time after which we observe the growth of a stable regime we cannot associate T_c with the duration of a nucleation phenomena considered in (Ernst & Newman 2002) since the phenomena determining T_c are not taken into account explicitly in (Ernst & Newman 2002). Nevertheless it seems tempting to assume that the transition appears after T_c =1second and that the radius R_c is approximately 1μm. Let assume that the magnitude of the diffusion coefficient D of the species A and C is about 10^{-5} cm^2sec^{-1} as usually in liquid medium. In our simulation the expression of our diffusion coefficient is $D= 4a^2/\ \delta t$ in which a is the lattice spacing and δt the duration of an elementary diffusion step. In the approximation $\lambda \sim R_c \sim 1\mu m$ we have $R_c{}^2 \approx D\ N_{diff}\ \delta t$. From figure 10 we choose the case N_{diff} = 6000 for which we get $\delta t \approx (1/6)\ 10^{-6}$ second and a ≈ 10 nanometres. This approximate calculation gives just orders of magnitude

and shows the coherence of our approach provided the chemical and electrochemical reaction have a characteristic time much smaller than 1microsecond. In parallel we deduce that the time for metal restructuring is $6000\delta t \approx 10^{-3}$ second.

4.2.2 Auto catalytic reaction

One of the peculiar and interesting behaviour predicted by the present model is associated with the transition from what we call the stationary regime to diffusion limited regime described in the above section and characterized by the coexistence of rough and smooth zones. The peculiarity of the transition consists in the combination of two processes. First we have seen that the reaction scheme in the equation (15) or (24) is of autocatalytic type; it means that such reaction appears in acidic medium but the result of it is to increase the acidity. Finally it means that when such reaction appears in one place of the surface it favors the appearance of similar reaction in its neighborhood. These spatial correlations of chemical origin, initiate zones with homogeneous properties. Second, if the diffusion of H^+ and OH^- cannot perform a homogenization of the solution during one time step, i. e. after N_{diff} steps, these zones survive and may grow. Of course the distribution of these zones resulting from stochastic processes determines the pit geometry. Note that in the diffusion regime the size of the pit is three orders of magnitude larger than of the initial damage. Thus we can say that our simulations are able to describe the passage from a mesoscopic to a macroscopic scale.

Here we have an example illustrating the fact that the coupling of a surface autocatalytic reaction with a diffusion process may generate a symmetry breaking leading to spatial inhomogeneities at a macroscopic level. Similar phenomena have been extensively investigated by Prigogine and his coworkers (Glansdorff & Prigogine, 1971) and we are in qualitative agreement with their physical predictions. However we cannot describe quantitatively our results from equations used in (Glansdorff & Prigogine, 1971) based on traditional methods of chemical kinetics, so to say on a mean field approach. The stationary regime corresponds to the formation of a small system in which we have strong correlations between the events that take place on nearest neighbor sites. This is clearly outside the scope of a mean field approach. Undoubtedly our description of corrosion processes is realistic, even though only a part of the complicated phenomena is represented in the initiation of a pit and its evolution. But anyway to describe the beginning of a pit formation leads to consider a small volume where strong correlations exist between the reactants. It seems that this is very far from what is done with the theories developed today and accordingly only simulations can give an insight about the beginning of the pit formation.

5. Conclusions and perspectives

Modeling at a mesoscopic scale using cellular automata model appears as an interesting tool to understand general properties of corrosion processes. In this chapter there is two parts; in Section 3 we essentially focus on the diffusion and the feedback effect of the layer on the corrosion rate, in this part no explicit reactions are taking into account. An example of realistic electrochemical and chemical reactions have been introduced in Section 4, there are associated with a pitting corrosion.

The model developed in Section 3 gives a simple description of a phenomenon of passivation. The blocking of corrosion sites by diffusing species can be associated with the existence of concentration overpotential. For a system in which the initial corrosion rate is high compared to the diffusion rate, the corrosion products can stay on the corrosion front and slower the corrosion mechanism. In addition to an obvious decrease of the corrosion rate, we may also observe a flattening of the corrosion front. Moreover, if we measure the thickness of the layer relative to the initial position then it has been shown that we can find exactly the parabolic law predicted by Mott and Cabrera including the exact value of the prefactor. We show also that the distribution of diffusing species within the growing layer is characterized by two regimes for the growth. Initially the diffusing species are inserted in the layer at constant flux which increase their concentration and after a certain time it may reach a maximum value. The transition from a constant concentration regime results from the steric exclusion between the diffusing species.

Other aspect of corrosion described here is related to the processes that occur within the corroded cavities of pitting (Section 4). Our main difference with standard approaches is related to the fact that we use a stochastic approach in which the shape of the pit (hemisphere or cylinder) is not prescribed. We reproduce different morphologies of pitting corrosion and we observe the existence of a wall pit roughening transition. The simulations allow for a passage from a mesoscopic to a macroscopic scale. The different properties that we have investigated show a transition from a stationary regime to a diffusion limited regime. This transition is characterized by a morphology changing from a semicircular to an elongated shape. This change is accompanied by the appearance of a non uniform distribution in the wall roughness and by the coexistence of zones having different acidity in the solution. The pit surface is divided into two regions, in which anodic surface is smooth and cathodic one is rough, and these two regions are in contact respectively in the solution side with acidic and basic zones. Thus a global description of the surface neglecting these inhomogeneities will give a very poor description of the pitting corrosion.

The transition is characterized by a critical radius R_c depending on the number of diffusion steps N_{diff} during one simulation time step. By a simple analysis we have established several power laws which characterize quite well the critical behaviour observed in the simulation results. This shows that the correlations between different processes involved in our system are well understood. From our analysis, we can say that the neutralization of ions H^+ and OH^- does not take place on the surface of the pit. The pitting is associated with a autocatalytic reaction coupled with a diffusion process; however at the beginning of the pitting it exists strong correlations between the events and a mean field approximation is not able to reproduce the phenomena, probably only numerical simulations can be used to analyze the pit initiation.

In this chapter we focused on a few number of processes but a lot of other processes can be investigated by a cellular automata model. For instance we may investigate the deviations from the Faraday law, the corrosion of the grain boundaries. Another aspect concerns the surface roughness; the definition (7) is restricted to a mechanical description of the roughness but we may also introduce a chemical roughness showing how many reactive site exist on the surface. The relation between the two definitions of the roughness has not been investigated yet. Many other basic phenomena can be investigated as for instance the adsorption of a given inhibitor on the surface. Obviously some three dimensional approaches will be appreciated.

6. Figures

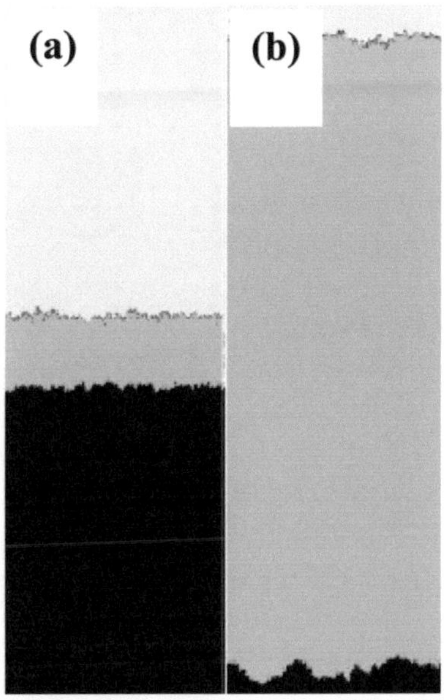

Fig. 1. Snapshots taken at different time step N_t for the double Eden model with N_{corr}=10, N_x = 2000 and (a)- N_t=10000, (b)- N_t=90000.

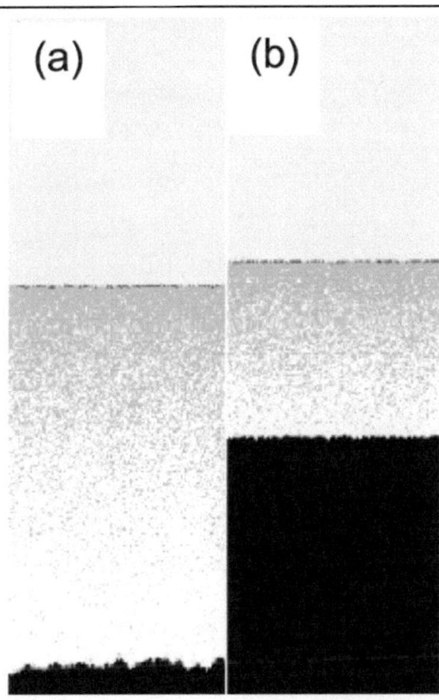

Fig. 2. Snapshots taken at time step N_t =90000, for a- the Eden model for corrosion front and diffusion model for growth with N_{corr}=10 and Φ =1, b- the diffusion model both for corrosion and diffusion front with N_{corr}=10 and Φ =2.

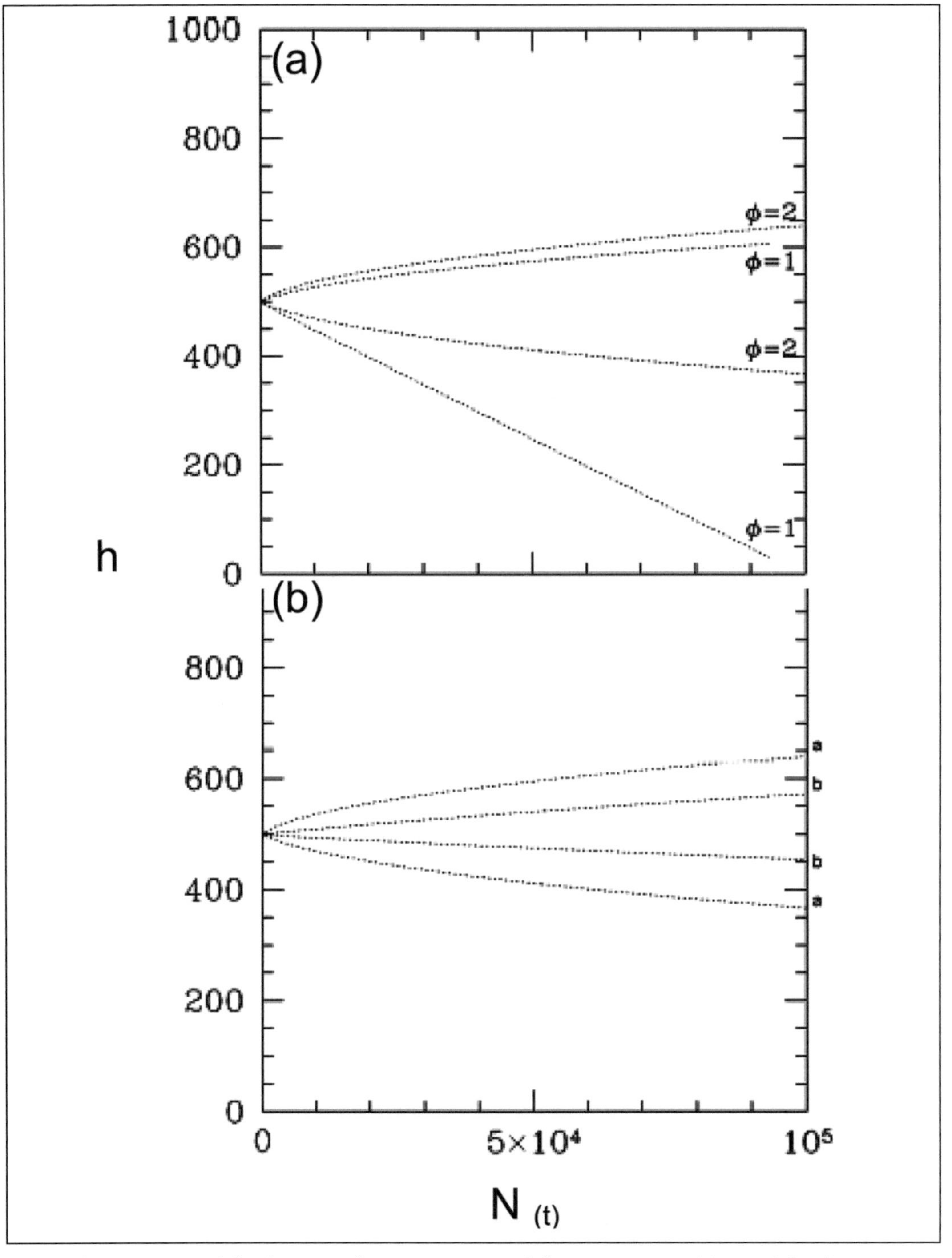

Fig. 3. Comparison of the front evolution in terms of the average positions of the fronts growth (the two upper curves) and corrosion (two lower curves) and for different conditions (a)- N_{corr}=10, Φ=2 and N_{corr}=10, Φ=1; (b)-Φ=2 and a-N_{corr}=10, b- N_{corr}=1.

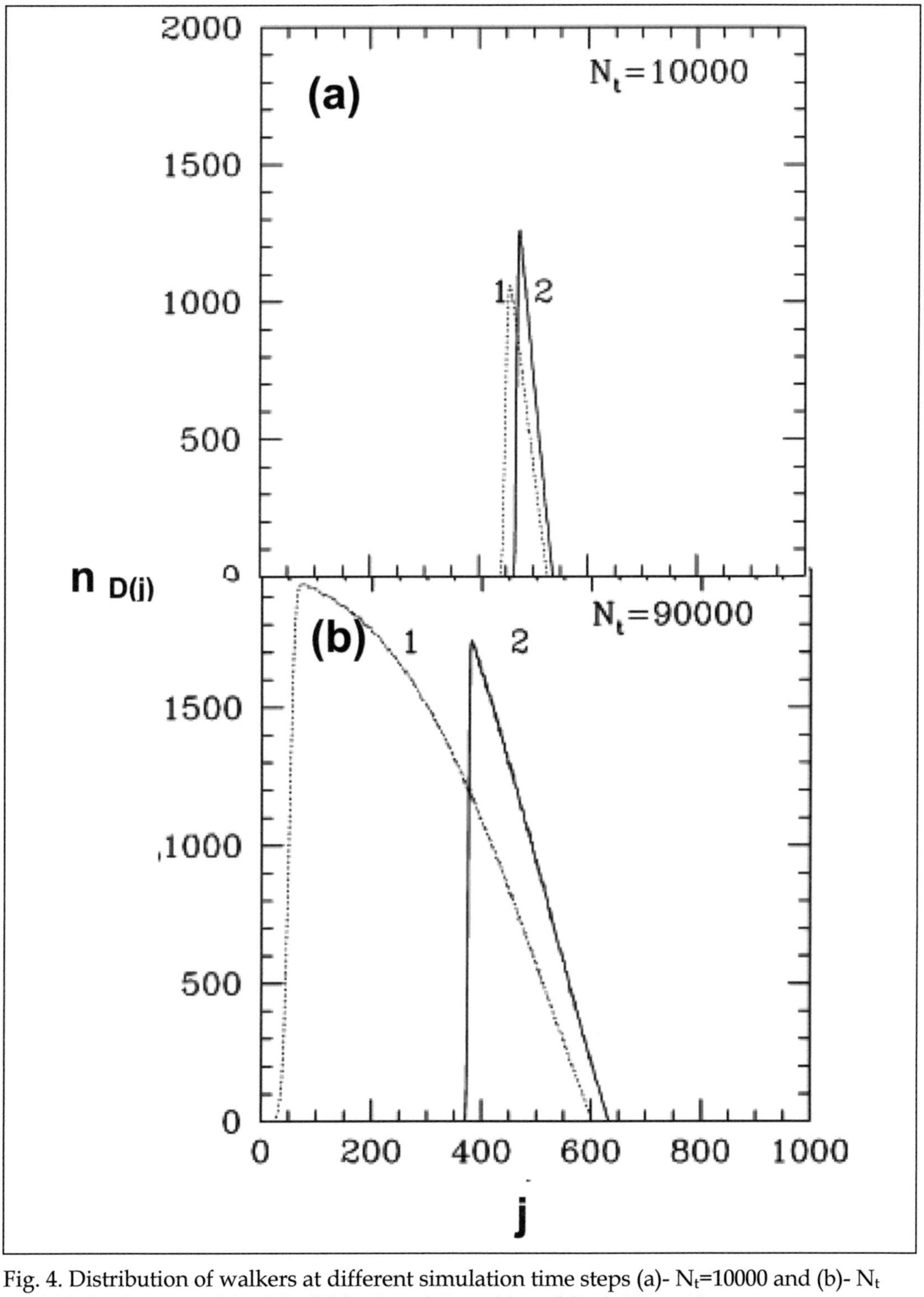

Fig. 4. Distribution of walkers at different simulation time steps (a)- N_t=10000 and (b)- N_t =90000 for the case of Φ =2 (solid line) and Φ =1 (dotted line), N_{corr}=10.

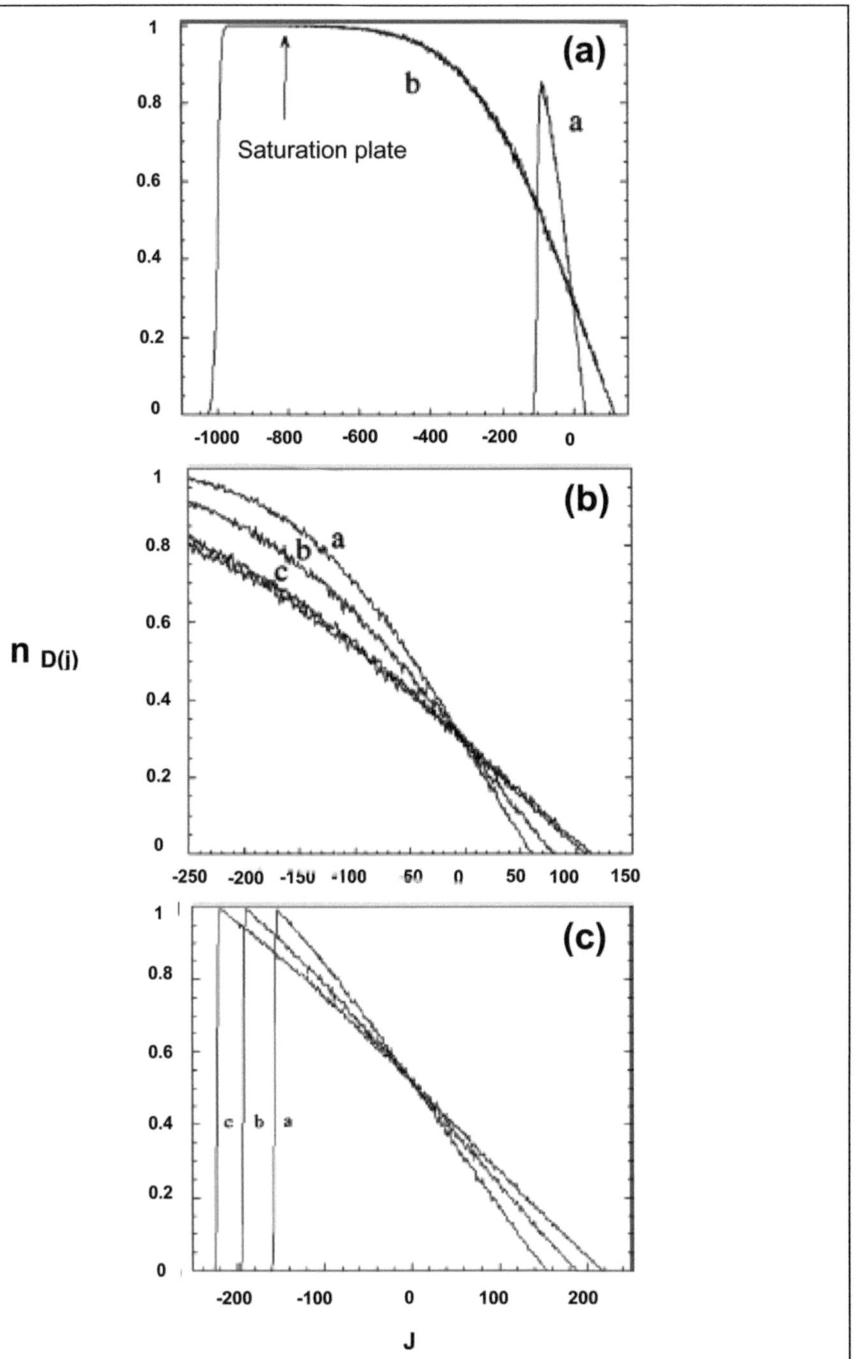

Fig. 5. Walker distribution in the layer obtained for different simulation conditions, (a) $N_{corr}=3$, $\Phi=1$, $N_x=600$ and for different times a- $N_t=10^4$ and b- $N_t=10^5$; (b) $N_{corr}=3$, $\Phi=1$, $N_x=600$ and for different times a- $N_t=5\ 10^4$, b- $N_t=9\ 10^4$, c- $N_t=10^5$; (c) $N_{corr}=150$, $\Phi=2$, $N_x=600$ and for different times a- $N_t=5\ 10^4$, b- $N_t=9\ 10^4$, c- $N_t=10^5$

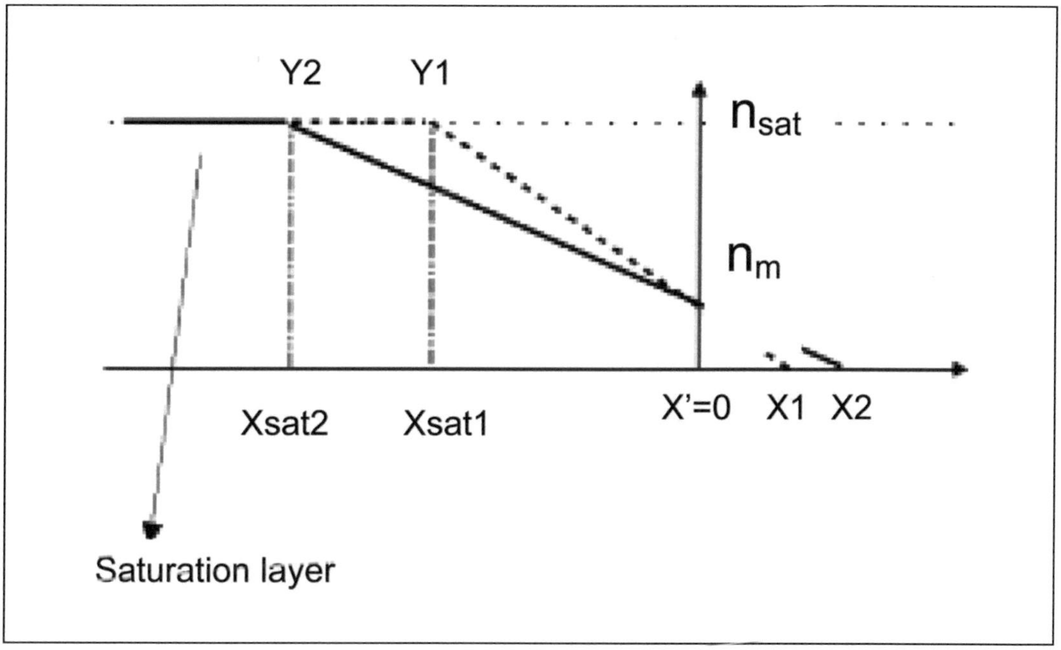

Fig. 6. Representation of the walkers distribution in the case Φ =1. Definition of the positions X_i and Y_i. $x'(0)$ refers to the position where the concentration C_m is constant.

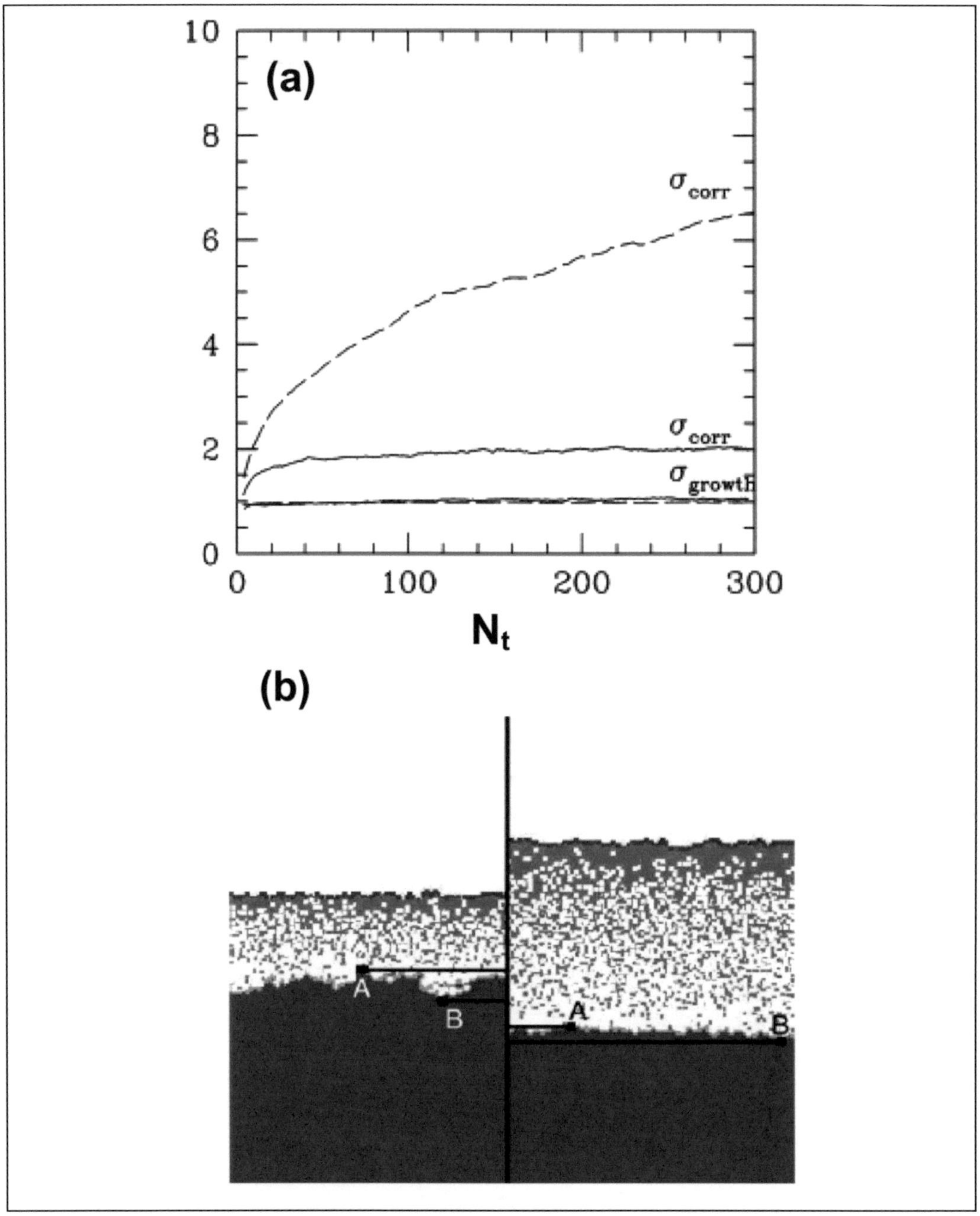

Fig. 7. Front roughness defined by (6) and (7). N_{corr}=10. (a) Φ =1 (dotted lines) and Φ =2 (solid lines) for the growth fronts (lower curves) and corrosion fronts (upper curves) as a function of the amount of material corroded Δh_{corr}. In figure 7(b) we can see the snapshot of the interface. Points A mark the uppermost and points B the lowermost positions of the corrosion front.

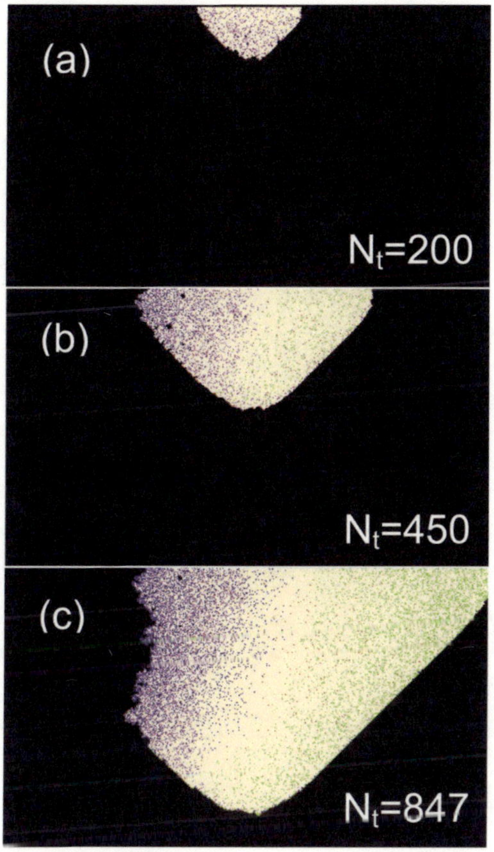

Fig. 8. Corresponding to the number of diffusion step N_{diff}=6000 and indicated simulation time steps (N_t). The green, blue and white colours correspond, respectively to acidic, basic and neutral zones.

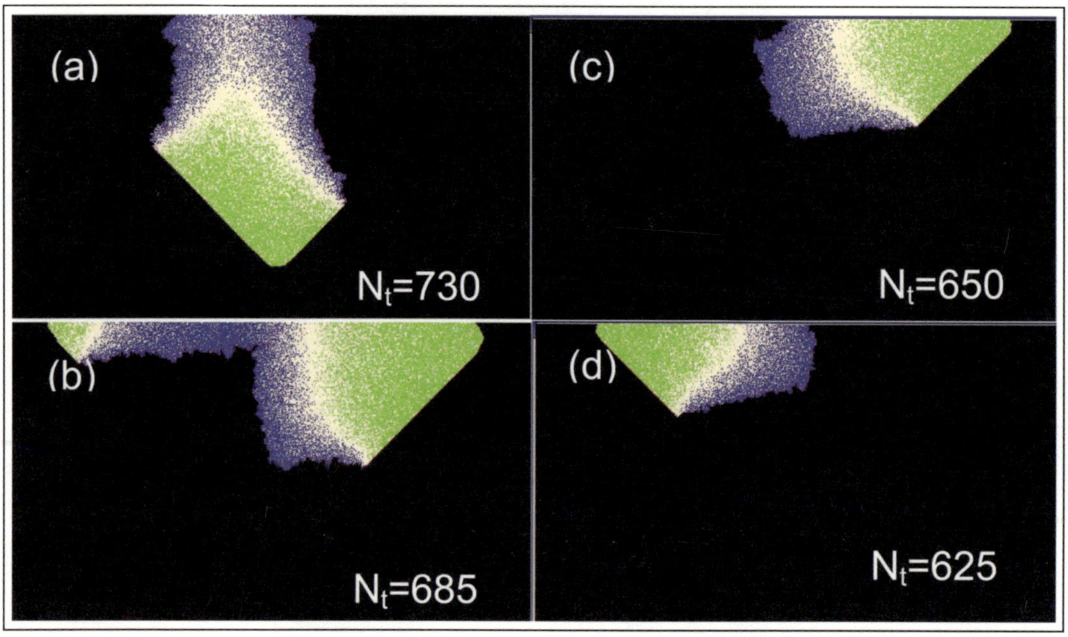

Fig. 9. Snapshots corresponding to the number of diffusion step N_{diff}=100 and indicated simulation time steps (N_t). The green, blue and white colours correspond respectively to acidic, basic and neutral zones.

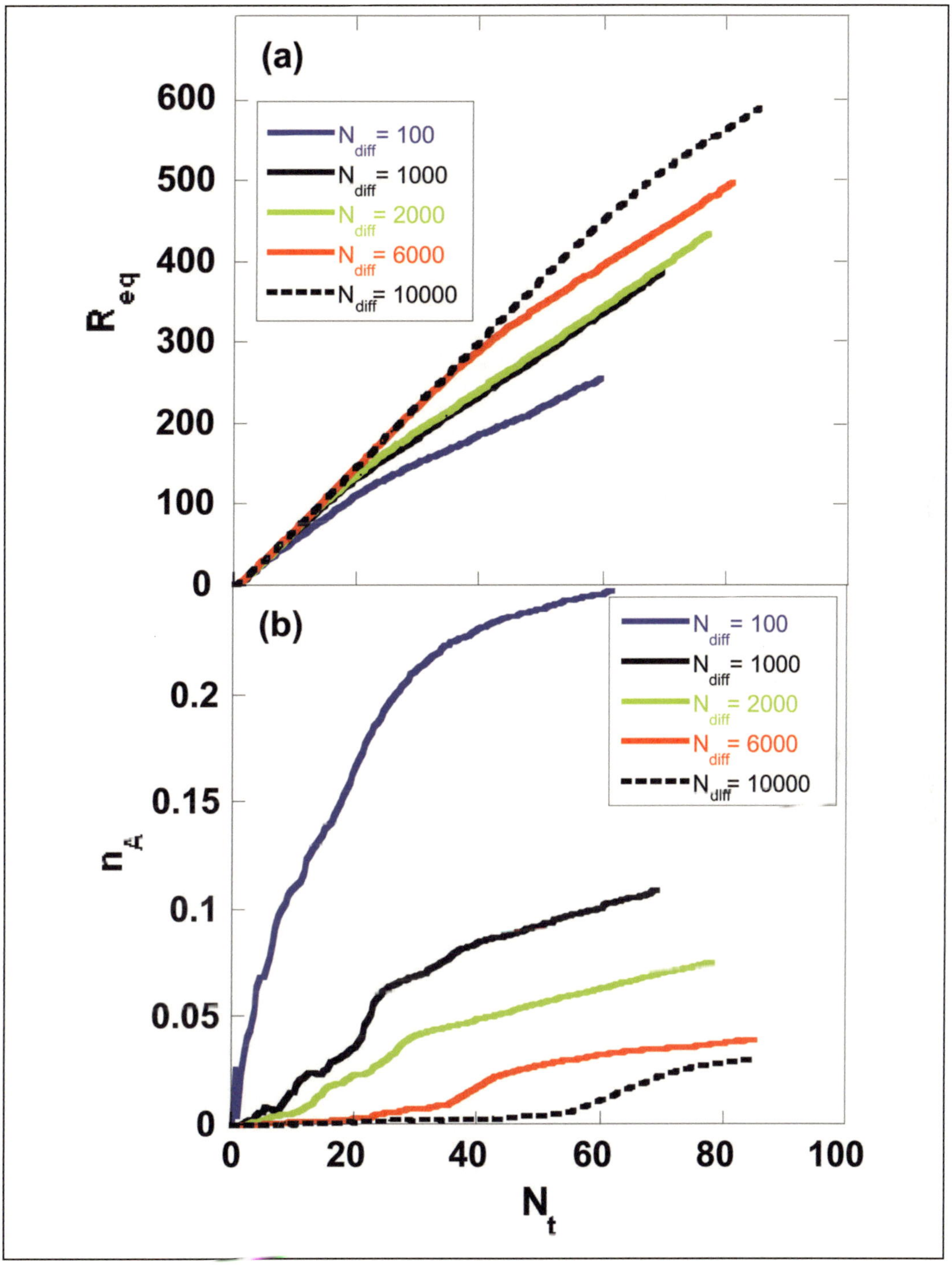

Fig. 10. (a)- Evolution of the equivalent radius (R_{eq}) versus the simulation time steps (N_t) for indicated number of diffusion step (N_{diff}). (b)- The evolution of the fraction of the acidic sites A (n_A) versus the simulation time steps, (N_t), for indicated number of diffusion step (N_{diff}).

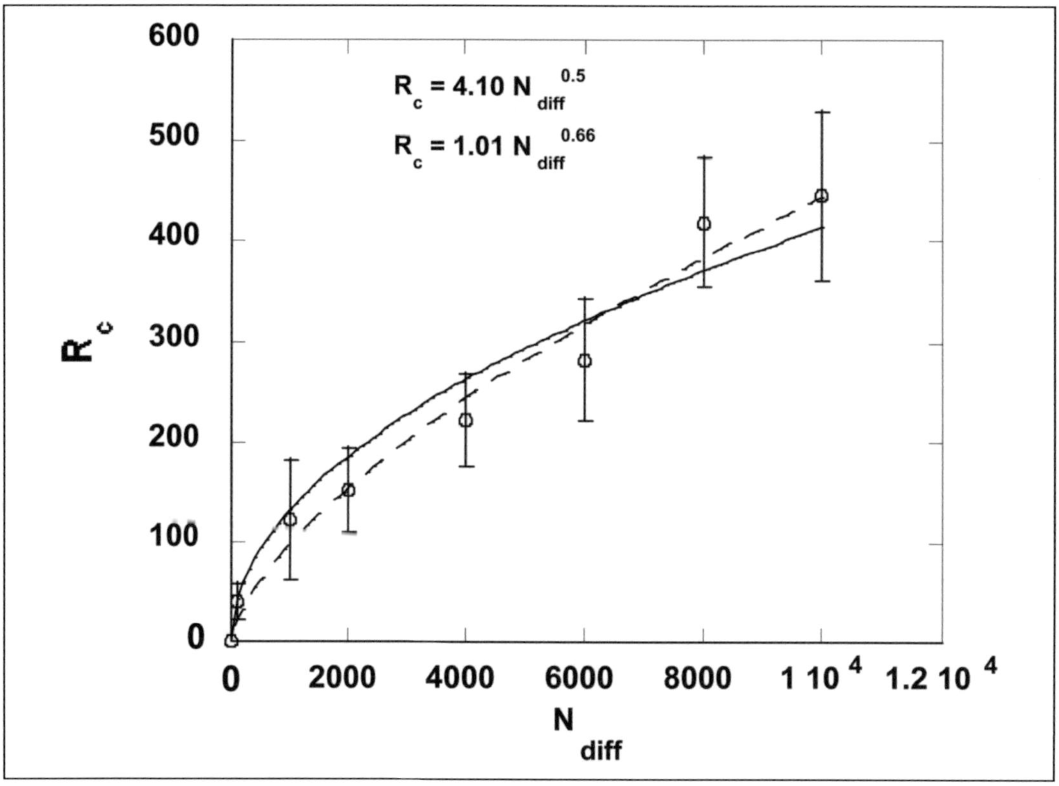

Fig. 11. Evolution of the critical radius (R_c), versus the diffusion step (N_{diff}). (_) the simulation data (o) the calculated result.

7. Equations

Equations are centred and numbered consecutively, from 1 upwards (Book Antiqua, 9pt).

$$E + R \rightarrow P \tag{1}$$

$$\langle h_{growth}(N_t)\rangle = \frac{1}{N_x}\sum_{i=1,N_x} h_{growth}(i) \tag{2}$$

$$\langle h_{corr}(N_t)\rangle = \frac{1}{N_x}\sum_{i=1,N_x} h_{corr}(i) \tag{3}$$

$$\langle h_{corr}(N_t)\rangle = h(0) - \frac{N_t N_{corr}}{N_x} \tag{4}$$

$$k(N_t) = \frac{d}{dN_t}\left[h(0) - \langle h_{corr}(N_t)\rangle\right] = \frac{d}{dN_t}\Delta h_{corr}(N_t) \tag{5}$$

$$\sigma_{growth}(N_t) = \left[\frac{1}{N_x}\sum_{i=1,N_x}(h_{growth}(i) - \langle h_{growth}(N_t)\rangle)^2\right]^{1/2} \tag{6}$$

$$\sigma_{corr}(N_t) = \left[\frac{1}{N_x}\sum_{i=1,N_x}(h_{corr}(i) - \langle h_{corr}(N_t)\rangle)^2\right]^{1/2} \tag{7}$$

$$E + (\Phi + 1)\, M \rightarrow P + (\Phi)\, D \tag{8}$$

$$\frac{n_m}{1} = \frac{X_i}{X_i + Y_i} \tag{9}$$

$$\frac{dY_i}{dX_i} = \frac{1 - n_m}{n_m} \tag{10}$$

$$(X_2 - X_1) + \frac{n_m}{2}X_2 - \frac{n_m}{2}X_1 \tag{11}$$

$$(Y_2 - Y_1)\frac{1 - n_m}{2}, \tag{12}$$

$$(Y_2 - Y_1)\frac{1 - n_m}{2} + (Y_2 - Y_1)(\phi - 1), \tag{13}$$

$$(Y_2 - Y_1)(1 + \frac{n_m}{2}) = (Y_2 - Y_1)[\frac{1 - n_m}{2} + (\phi - 1)] \tag{14}$$

$$M + H_2O \rightarrow MOH_{aq} + e + H^+ \tag{15}$$

$$M + OH- \rightarrow MOH_{solid} + e \tag{16}$$

$$H^+ + e \rightarrow \tfrac{1}{2} H_2 \tag{17}$$

$$H_2O + e \rightarrow \tfrac{1}{2} H_2 + OH^- \tag{18}$$

$$M + H_2O \rightarrow MOH_{aq} + \tfrac{1}{2} H_2 \tag{19}$$

$$M + H_2O \rightarrow MOH_{solid} + \tfrac{1}{2} H_2 \tag{20}$$

$$MOH_{solid} \rightarrow MOH_{aq} \tag{21}$$

$$H^+ + OH^- \rightarrow H_2O \tag{22}$$

$$R \rightarrow A, \quad N_{exc} \geq 0 \tag{23}$$

$$R + C(nn) \rightarrow P + E(nn), \quad N_{exc} < 0 \tag{24}$$

$$S + A(nn) \rightarrow S + E(nn), \quad N_{exc} \geq 0 \tag{25}$$

$$S + E(nn) \rightarrow S + C(nn), \quad N_{exc} < 0 \tag{26}$$

$$P \rightarrow E \tag{27}$$

$$A + C \rightarrow E + E \tag{28}$$

$$R_{eq} = \left(\frac{2N_{corroded}}{\pi}\right)^{1/2} \tag{29}$$

8. References

(Arrouvel et al., 2007) Arrouvel, C.; Diawara, B.; Costa, D. & Marcus, P. (2007). DFT periodic study of the adsorption of glycine on the anhydrous and hydroxylated (0001) surface of α Alumina J. Phys. Chem. C 111, 18164-1873.

(Balazs, 1996) Balazs, L. (1996). Corrosion front roughening in two dimensional pitting of aluminum thin layer. Phys Rev. E 54, 1183- 1189.

(Balazs & Gouyet, 1995) Balazs, L. & Gouyet, J. F. (1995). Two dimensional pitting corrosion of aluminium thin layer. Physica A 217, 319-338.

(Barabasi & Stanley, 1995) Barabasi, A. L. & Stanley, H. E. (1995). Fractal Concepts in Surface Growth, Cambridge University Press: Cambridge, NY.

(Bard & Foulkner, 1980) Bard, J. A. & Faulkner, L. B. (1980). Electrochemical Methods: Fundamentals and applications, John Wiley and Sons: NY.

(Cabrera & Mott, 1949) Cabrera, N & Mott, N. F. (1948). Theory of the oxidation of metals. Rep. Prog. Phys. 12, 163-184.

(Chopard & Droz, 1998) Chopard, B. & Droz, M. (1998). Cellular Automat Modelling of Physical Systems Cambridge University Press, NY.

(Cordoba-Torres et al 2001) Cordoba-Torres, P. ; Nogueira, R. P. ; De Miranda, L. ; Brenig, L. ; Wallenborn, J. & Fairen, V. (2001). Cellular automata simulation of asimple corrosion mechanism: mesoscopic heterogeneity versus macroscopic homogeneity. Electrochem. Acta 46, 2975-2989.

(De Gennes, 1991) De Gennes P. G. (1991). Scaling concepts in polymer physics Ed. Cornell University Press, NY.

(Eden, 1961) Eden, M. (1961). Proceeding of fourth Berkeley Symposium on Mathematical Stastics and Probability of California Press 1, Berkeley.

(Ernst & Newman, 2002) Ernst, P. & Newman, R. C. (2002). Pit growth studies instainless steel foils I. Introduction and pit growth kinetics. Corros. Sci. 44, 927-941.

(Glansdorff & Prigigine, 1971) Glansdorff, P. & Prigogine, I. (1971). (Eds), Structure Stabilité et Fluctuation Masson et Cie, Paris.

(Haseeb et al., 2001) Haseeb, A. S. M. A.; Schilardi, P. L.; Boltzan, A. E.; Piatti, R. C. V.; Salvarezza, R. R. & Arvia, A. J. (2001). Anodisation of copper in thiourea containing acid solution: part II in situ transversal imaging observations kinetics of anodic film growth. J. Electroanal. Chem. 500, 543-553.

(Kortlük, 1998) Kortlük, O. (1998). A general cellular automaton model for surface reactions. J. Phys. A: Math. Gren. 31, 9185-9189.

(Le Bellac, 1988) Le Bellac, M.; Barton, G. (1988) Quantum and Statistical Field Theory, Portland, OR: Booknew.

(Malki & Baroux, 2005) Malki, M. & Baroux, B. (2005). Computer simulation of corrosion pit growth. Corrs. Sci. 47, 171-182.

(Nicolis & Nicolis, 2001) Nicolis, C.; Kozak, J. J. & Nicolis, G. (2001). Encounter controlled reactions between intercating wlkers in finite lattices complex kinetics and many body effects. J. Chem. Phys. 115, 663-671.

(Nishida & Baba, 1996) Nishidate, K. & Baba, M. (1996). Cellular automaton model random walkers. Phys. Rev. Lett. 77, 1675-1678.

(Reigada et al., 1994) Reigada, R.; Sagués, F. & Costa, J. M. (1994). A Monte carlo simulation of localized corrosion. J. Chem. Phys. 101, 2329-2337.

(Saunier et al., 2005) Saunier, J. ; Dymitrowska, M. ; Chaussé, A. ; Stafiej, J. & Badiali, J. P. (2005). J. Electroanal. chem. 582, 267-273.

(Staficj et al., 2006) Stafiej, J.; Taleb, A.; Vautrin-Ul, C.; Chausse, A. & Badiali, J. P. (2006). Passivation of Metals and Semiconductors, and Properties of Thin Oxide Layers, P. Marcus, V. Maurice (Eds), Elsevier, paris, pp 667-673.

(Taleb et al., 2001) Taleb, A.; Stafiej, J.; Chausse, A.; Messina, R. & Badiali, J. P. (2001). Simulation of film growth and diffusion during the corrosion process. J. Electroanal. Chem. 500, 554-561.

(Taleb et al., 2004) Taleb, A.; Chausse, A.; Dymitrowska, M.; Stafiej, J. & Badiali, J. P. (2004). Simulation of corrosion and passivation phenomena: Diffusion feedback on the corrosion rate. J. Phys. Chem. B, 108, 952-958.

(Taleb et al., 2007) Taleb, A. Stafiej, & J. Badiali, J. P. (2007). Numerical simulation of crystallographic corrosion : Particle production and surface roughness. Phys Chem. C 11, 9086-9094.

(Vautrin et al., 2007) Vautrin-Ul, C.; Taleb, A.; Chaussé, A.; Stafiej, J. & Badiali, J. P. (2007). Mesoscopic modelling of corrosion phenomena : Coupling between electrochemical and mechanical processes, analysis of the deviation from the faraday law. Electriochemica Acta 52, 5368-5376.

(Vautrin et al., 2008) Vautrin-Ul, C. ; Mendy, H. ; Taleb, A. ; Chaussé, A. ; Stafiej, J. & Badiali, J. P. (2008). Numerical simulation of spatial heterogeneity formation in metal corrosion. Corros. Sci. 50, 2149-2158.

(Vazquez et al., 1995) Vazquez, L.; Vara, J. M.; Herrasti, P.; Ocon, P.; Savarezza, R. C. & Arvia, A. J. (1995). Methods of fractal analysis applied to STM imaging. Chaos, Solitons and Fractales 6, 569-573.

Part 3

Cryptography and Coding

12

Deeper Investigating Adequate Secret Key Specifications for a Variable Length Cryptographic Cellular Automata Based Model

Gina M. B. Oliveira, Luiz G. A. Martins and Leonardo S. Alt
Universidade Federal de Uberlândia
Brazil

1. Introduction

Cellular automata (CA) are particularly well suited for cryptographic application and there are several previous studies in this topic (Benkiniouar & Benmohamed, 2004; Gutowitz, 1995; Kari, 1992; Nandi et al., 1994; Oliveira et al., 2004; 2008; Seredynski et al., 2003; Tomassini & Perrenoud, 2000; Wuensche, 2008; Wolfram, 1986). Since CA rule is simple, local and discrete, it can be executed in easily-constructed massively-parallel hardware at fast speeds. Basically, the CA-based cryptographic models can be divided into three classes: (*i*) models that use CA to generate binary sequences with good pseudo-random properties, which are used as cryptographic keys, but the effective ciphering process is made by another function (Benkiniouar & Benmohamed, 2004; Seredynski et al., 2003; Tomassini & Perrenoud, 2000; Wolfram, 1986); (*ii*) models based on additive, non-homogeneous and reversible CA, that use algebraic properties of this kind of rules to generate automata of maximum and/or known cycle (Kari, 1992; Nandi et al., 1994); and (*iii*) models based on irreversible CA, which uses the backward interaction of cellular automata in the ciphering process and the forward interaction to decipher (Gutowitz, 1995; Oliveira et al., 2004; 2008; 2010a; Wuensche, 2008), as the cryptographic model discussed here.

Gutowitz has previously proposed a cryptographic model based on backward evolution of irreversible CA (Gutowitz, 1995). A toggle CA rule transition is used as the secret key in his model. A pre-image of an arbitrary lattice is calculated adding extra bits in each side of the lattice. This increment is pointed as the major flaw in the model. CA backward interaction is also known as pre-image computation and an efficient reverse algorithm was proposed by Wuensche and Lesser (Wuensche & Lesser, 1992) for a periodic boundary condition, keeping the pre-image with the same size of the image. Such algorithm was evaluated as encryption method in (Oliveira et al., 2008). However, its usage has the disadvantage that there is no guarantee of pre-image existence for any given lattice and any given rule. The only rules with assurance of pre-image existence are not appropriate for ciphering because they do not exhibit a chaotic dynamics.

Thus, a new approach was proposed, which alternates the original reverse algorithm and the variation that uses extra bits, using the second only when the pre-image computation fails. This variation is similar to pre-image computation adopted in Gutowitz model (Gutowitz, 1995). Although this approach needs to add bits to the ciphertext when a failure occurs, it is expected that in practice few failures happen and the ciphertext length will be equal or close to the plaintext. In the resultant method, encryption always succeeds and the final length of the ciphertext is not fixed. This method was named Variable-Length Encryption Method (VLE) (Oliveira et al., 2010a).

Initial experiments were performed using small sets of radius 2 and radius 3 toggle rules. Subsequent experiments were performed using a representative rule set formed by all radius 2 right-toggle rules, totalizing 65536 rules. These rules represent 50% of the possible secret keys in radius 2 space, being that the other 50% are the all radius 2 left-toggle rules, which are dynamically equivalent to the set analyzed. Based on an exhaustive analysis of this rule space we concluded that, considering a cryptographic purpose, there are a lot of undesirable behavior rules in the complete set that must be avoided as secret keys; they represent approximate 5% of the rule space investigated.

It was employed an analysis based on several CA static parameters, trying to capture a pattern associating such parameters to underperforming rules. Static parameters like Z, Sensitivity, Absolute Activity, Activity Propagation and Neighborhood Dominance (Oliveira et al., 2001) were investigated to capture the pattern associated to underperforming rules. A database was generated associating rules performance in VLE ciphering with their parameters. A genetic algorithm-based data mining was performed to discover adequate key specifications based on CA parameters. We deeper investigate these specifications using them as to filter the set of radius 2 rules as to elaborate new radius 3 rules. By applying such methodology it were able to discover good secret key specifications for VLE. Using such specifications, ciphertext length is short, encryption process returns high entropy and VLE has a good protection against differential cryptanalysis.

This chapter is organized as follows. Section 2 presents some concepts related to cellular automata with emphasis on forecast behaviour CA parameters. Section 3 reviews some previous CA models related to the cryptographyc model discussed here. Section 4 details the major steps of VLE cryptographic model. Section 5 presents results of experiments performed to evaluate VLE´s ciphering quality and to find a good specification of toggle rules to be used as secret keys. Section 6 presents the major conclusions.

2. Cellular automata definitions

Cellular automata (CA) are discrete complex systems that possess both a dynamic and a computational nature. A cellular automaton consists of two parts: the cellular space and the transition rule. Cellular space is a regular lattice of N cells subjected to boundary conditions. A state is associated to each cell at time t. The transition rule τ yields the next state for each cell as a function of its neighbourhood. At each time step, all cells synchronously update their states according to τ. For one-dimensional (1D) CA, the neighbourhood size m is usually written as $m = 2R + 1$, where R is CA radius. In binary-state CA, the transition rule τ is given by a state transition table which lists each possible neighbourhood together with its output bit, that is, the updated value for the state of the central cell.

A special kind of CA rule is used as the secret key in the cryptographic model discussed here: they are toggle transition rules. A CA transition table is said to be a toggle rule if it is sensible in respect to a specific neighborhood cell, that is, if any modification of the state on this cell necessarily provokes a modification on the new state of the central cell, considering all possible rule neighborhoods. Considering one-dimensional radius-1 CA, the neighborhood is formed by three cells and they can be sensible in respect to the left cell, to the right cell, and to

the central cell. For example, elementary rules 00101101, 10011010, 10010110 are left-toggle, right-toggle and left-and-right-toggle rules, respectively.
The dynamics of a cellular automaton is associated with its transition rule. In order to help forecast the dynamic behavior of CA, several parameters have been proposed in the literature, as the precursor lambda parameter (Langton, 1990). Some forecast parameters had shown to be important in the analysis of the key space related to the cryptographic model discussed here. They are briefly discussed following.

2.1 Z

The definition of Z parameter derived from the pre-image calculus algorithm and it is composed by Z_{left} and Z_{right}. Let us assume that a part of a pre-image of an arbitrary lattice configuration is known and that we want to infer the missing cell states, successively, from left to right. Z_{left} is defined as the probability that the next cell to the right in the partial pre-image has a unique value, and it is directly calculated from the transition table, by counting the deterministic neighborhoods. Z_{right} is the converse, from right to left. Z parameter is the greater of Z_{left} and Z_{right}. A detailed explanation about this parameter is given in (Wuensche, 1998). In (Oliveira et al., 2001) an analysis of Z parameter is presented and the main conclusions are: (i) it is good discriminators of the chaotic behavior (ii) rules with a Z value close to 1 have high probability to be chaotic. The components Z_{left} and Z_{right} have shown very important in the specification of the rule transitions used as secret keys in the method discussed in (Oliveira et al., 2008).

2.2 Symmetry

During the evaluation of reverse algorithm described in (Oliveira et al., 2008), a characteristic that have shown important to secret key specification was the symmetry of the output binary sequence representing a transition rule. Let m be the number of cells considered in the neighborhood of a binary cellular automaton and the rule transition defined by k output bits ($k = 2^m$): $b_0, b_1, ..., b_{k-1}$. The symmetry level (S) is the number of pair of bits b_i and b_{k-i-1} ($0 \leq i \leq k/2 - 1$) that have the same value. It can be normalized divided by the total number of pairs ($k/2$). For example, considering radius-1 CA rules, the symmetry level of rules 10111101, 10110010 and 10001111 is 1, 0 and 0.25, respectively. The importance of this parameter in the specification of CA rules suitable for encryption was first noted due to the low number of lattices with at least one pre-image when rules with S equal to 1 are used. That is, the secret key can not be a palindrome. This parameter has also demonstrated to be relevant in another classical problem in the context of cellular automata field: to find rules able to classify the density of 1s of a given lattice, the density classification task (DCT). Such kind of pattern was observed when analyzing good rules suitable to perform DCT (de Oliveira et al., 2006). Recently, when working with the equivalent dynamical transformations of a CA rule (reflection, complementary and complementary-plus-reflection) we perceived that this symmetry is directly related to the bits used to perform the complementary transformation. In this sense, a rule with $S = 0$ does not have a complementary equivalent rule, because when we apply the transformation it returns to the same rule. For example, rule 01101001 of elementary space. Conversely, rules with $S = 1$ has a complementary rule formed by the complement of the output bits. For example, equivalent elementary rules 01100110 and 10011001.

2.3 Absolute activity

This parameter came from the analysis of lambda parameter (or Activity) Langton (1990); it measures only the rule's activity level counting how many transitions lead to state 1, regardless of the states of the neighbors. The goal of Absolute Activity parameter was to improve the measure of activity verifying the transitions that lead to a different state of the central cell's state or it's neighbors (Oliveira et al., 2001). It quantifies how much change is entailed by the rule, in the state of the central cell, in relation to the current state of the central cell, and the states of the pair of cells which are equally apart from the centre (Oliveira et al., 2001).

2.4 Neighborhood dominance

It verifies whether the new value of the central cell "follows" the state that appears the most in the neighborhood (Oliveira et al., 2001). For example, in transition $100 \rightarrow 1$ there is no neighborhood dominance, although the central cell changes. Besides, a relative weight is associated to each neighborhood in such way that greater is the homogeneity, greater is the weight of dominance associated to this neigborhood. For example, in elementary space, the neighborhoods 000 and 111 have weigth 3, and the others, 1 (Oliveira et al., 2001).

2.5 Core entropy

Let τ be the CA transition rule, R the radius, $m = 2R + 1$ the neighborhood size and $n = 2^m$ the number of neighborhoods (size of the rule). In a toggle rule, we know that if the neighborhood T_i has output X, for $0 \leq i < n$:

- If it is right toggle:
  - If i is even, $T_{i+1} \rightarrow \overline{X}$;
  - If i is odd, $T_{i-1} \rightarrow \overline{X}$;
- If it is left toggle:
  - If i is $< n/2$, $T_{i+n/2} \rightarrow \overline{X}$;
  - If i is $\geq n/2$, $T_{i-n/2} \rightarrow \overline{X}$;

So, if we know half of the rule, we can generate the rule. A default rule generator is the sequence of the cells in even positions if the rule is right toggle, and the first half of the rule, if it is left toggle. This generator rule is called rule core. The Core Entropy is the spatial entropy associated to this core (Oliveira et al., 2010b).

3. Previous CA-based cryptographic models

A classification scheme of the previous approaches used in CA-based cryptographic models has been presented in the introductory section of this work. In the present section the methods which use irreversible CA are revised. In the first sub-section we revise the methods that use toggle rules, which return a strong and fixed increase in the ciphertext length in relation to the original plaintext. In the second sub-section we revise the methods that investigated the employment of the reverse algorithm proposed by (Wuensche & Lesser, 1992) as a ciphering process aiming to keep the ciphertext in the same length of the related plaintext. A comparative analysis of two similar proposes described in (Oliveira et al., 2008) and (Wuensche, 2008) are also presented.

3.1 Toggle rules-based methods

Gutowitz proposed and patented the first cryptographic model based on backward evolution of irreversible CA (Gutowitz, 1995). His model uses toggle transition rules (section 2) as secret keys. Gutowitz used irreversible CA with toggle rules - either to the right or to the left - for encrypting. Toggle rules turn possible to calculate a pre-image of any lattice starting from a random partial pre-image. Using this method, a pre-image of any lattice is calculated adding R extra bits in each side of the lattice, where R is the radius of the rule. Consider an initial lattice of N cells and a right-toggle transition rule with radius 1: the pre-image will have $N+2$ cells. Suppose that two initial bits X and Y are randomly chosen to start the pre-image calculation and they are positioned in the left border of the lattice. The state of the next right cell (the third one) is deterministically obtained because the only two possible transitions are $XY0 \rightarrow T$ and $XY1 \rightarrow \overline{T}$. One can check the value of first cell in the initial lattice to see if it is T or $\overline{T}$ and to determine if the third cell in the pre-image is 0 or 1. Once the state of the third cell is determined, the next step is to determine the state of the forth cell and the other cells successively up to completing the entire pre-image. The right-toggle property of the transition rule guarantees that the entire $N+2$ pre-image cells can be obtained, step-by-step, in a deterministic way. The same process can be done for left-toggle rules and in this case the initial cells must be positioned in the rightmost side. A fundamental characteristic in Gutowitz's model to guarantee pre-image for any lattice is the usage of a non periodic boundary condition. When the pre-image is obtained the extra bits are not discarded and they are incorporated to the lattice. Therefore, it is always possible to obtain a pre-image for any initial choice of bits. As the length of initial bits is $2R$, it is possible to obtain 2^{2R} different pre-images for each lattice. Therefore, the cellular automaton is irreversible. This pre-image calculus is specific to the ciphering method and it can be used only when applying toggle rules.

A toggle transition rule τ is used as the secret key in Gutowitz's cryptographic model. The plaintext is the initial lattice and P pre-images are successively calculated, starting with random initial bits ($2R$ cells) at each step. The ciphertext is given by the last pre-image obtained after P steps. The decryption process is based on the fact that the receptor agent knows both τ and P. By starting from the ciphertext the receptor just needs to apply the transition rule τ forward by P steps and the final lattice will be the plaintext. Let P be the number of pre-image steps, N the length of the original lattice and R the CA radius. The method adds $2R$ bits to each pre-image calculated and the size of the final lattice is given by $N+2RP$. For example, if 50 pre-images were calculated using a radius 2 rule starting from a plaintext of 128 bits, the size of the ciphertext would be 328. Clearly, it is not a negligible increment and it is pointed as the major flaw in Gutowitz's model.

A high degree of similarity between ciphertexts when the plaintext is submitted to a little perturbation was identified as another flaw in Gutowitz's model. The original model was altered by using bidirectional toggle CA rules (to the right and to the left simultaneously) in (Oliveira et al., 2004). The experiments with this model show that the similarity flaw was solved with such a modification and it is protected against differential cryptanalysis (Oliveira et al., 2004). However, the ciphertext increase in relation to the plaintext length remains in this model.

3.2 Reverse algorithm-based methods

An algorithm for a generic pre-image computation was proposed in (Wuensche & Lesser, 1992). This algorithm is known as reverse algorithm and it is based on the idea of partial neighborhoods. The complete description of this method can be found in (Wuensche & Lesser, 1992) and a summary in (Oliveira et al., 2008). Before starting the calculus, R cells are added to each side of the lattice corresponding to the pre-image, where R is the CA radius and the algorithm starts the calculus of the pre-image, randomly initializing the $2R$ leftmost cells. This procedure is similar to the start of the pre-image calculus used in Gutowitz's model. However, in a periodic CA boundary condition, the last cells need to be validated. The pre-image calculus is concluded verifying if the initial bits can be equal to the final $2R$ rightmost ones. If so, the extra bits added to each neighborhood side are discarded returning the pre-image to the same size of the original lattice. If no, the process returns again to use the last option stored in a stack, which contains the not evaluated possible values until this point of computation. The reverse algorithm finds all the possible pre-images for any arbitrary lattice and any arbitrary rule transition.

The reverse algorithm was evaluated as an encryption method in (Oliveira et al., 2008). An advantage of this method is that it can be applied to any kind of CA rule. So, it is not a specialized method as the one used in Gutowitz's model that works only with toggle rules. However, its application as a ciphering process has the disadvantage that there is no guarantee of pre-image existence for any given lattice and any given rule transition. On the other hand, it is well-known that for a fixed lattice the large majority of cellular automata rule space has a lot of lattice configurations with no pre-images; they are known as Garden-of-Eden states (Wuensche & Lesser, 1992). Therefore, the major challenge to apply the reverse algorithm as a viable cipher method is to find a manner to guarantee the existence of at least one pre-image for any possible initial lattice representing a possible plaintext to be encrypted.

The first attempt to solve this problem was to use Z parameter (Wuensche, 1998) in rule specification (Macêdo et al., 2008). It was already known that as higher is the Z value associated to a CA transition rule as higher is the probability of the cellular automation exhibits a chaotic behavior (Oliveira et al., 2001) and as higher is the probability of a pre-image existence for any lattice (Wuensche, 1998). Initially, the set of CA rules with Z equal to 1 was chosen as potential rules to use as secret keys in a cryptographic model based on the reverse algorithm. However, the first analysis of some simple $Z = 1$ rules (elementary rules and some other radius 2 binary rules manually constructed) have shown that this specification would not be enough to guarantee of pre-image existence. When this first $Z = 1$ set of rules was applied to encrypt random texts with usually cipher-block sizes (32, 64, 128 bits), it was not possible to cipher a lot of tested initial lattices. Aiming to discover the ideal specification for a 100% of pre-image existence rule, a simple genetic algorithm (GA) was implemented to find CA rules with a desirable characteristic (for example, as specific value of Z parameter). The implemented GA aids the process of generating rule sets to be evaluated as secret keys but it is not properly a part of the cipher method. Using GA it was possible to evaluate samples of rules with different specifications and several parameters related to the CA context have been evaluated as the dynamical forecast parameters Z (Wuensche, 1998), lambda (Langton, 1990), sensitivity (Binder, 1994), neighborhood dominance (Oliveira et al., 2001) and so on. The parameters that have presented more dependence to the 100% of pre-image existence problem was the components of Z known as Z_{right} and Z_{left} and the symmetry level parameter S explained in section 2. When a set of rules generated by GA with specification Z equal to 1 were applied to cipher some lattices samples with fixed length (32, 64 and 128 bits), a wide range of performance was obtained, from 0% to 100% of encrypted lattices. However, a clear characteristic have emerged from the analysis of these rules: the worst performance was obtained applying $Z_{left} = Z_{right} = 1$ rules and $S = 1$ rules.

Using this information, the set of $Z = 1$ rules could be improved, avoiding these characteristics. Due to Z definition (Wuensche, 1998), considering a rule with Z equal to 1, either Z_{right} or Z_{left} necessarily must be equal to 1. However, the other component is independent and can assume a value from 0 to 1. As we mentioned before, one component must be equal to 1 and the other must be different of 1 to avoid the worst performance. On the other hand, the symmetry level equal to 1 also has to be avoided. Following this observation, a set of rules was generated with the opposite characterization: rules with a low level of symmetry (< 0.25) and with one of the components of Z (Z_{left} or Z_{right}) equal to 1 and the other with a low value (< 0.25). Some initial experiments with this set have return in a first moment a mistaken conclusion that the "ideal rule specification" for a 100% of pre-image existence was found since they returned 100% of performance when tested in several samples of 32, 64 and 128 bits (Macêdo et al., 2008). However, an undesirable characteristic has been latter discovered when the dynamical behavior of some rules of this "ideal" set were analyzed: they are not chaotic rules as expected for $Z = 1$ rules; conversely, they are fixed-point behavior rules (with a spatial shift) (Oliveira et al., 2008) Some experiments using an entropy measure to characterize the difference between two ciphertexts obtained encrypting to very similar plaintexts have confirmed this observation for the majority of the rule set, because the associated entropy of this ciphering was very low. So, they cannot be used as secret keys since they are not able hide the original information, a primordial pre-requisite for any encryption process (Oliveira et al., 2008). Therefore, a trade-off was established when specifying a transition rule to be used with the reverse algorithm: if the rule is perfect in respect to the existence of pre-images, it does not have a chaotic behavior; if the rule is perfect in respect to the chaoticity, it can not be able to calculate the pre-image for a large range of possible plaintexts.

A new round of experiments were performed in (Oliveira et al., 2008) using $Z = 1$ rules with an intermediate level both for symmetry and Z_{left}/Z_{right} balance: $0.25 < S < 0.5$ and $0.25 < Z_{left} < 0.5$ and $Z_{right} = 1$. A sample of 100 radius-2 CA rules were evaluated calculating 128 consecutive pre-images starting from 1000 random lattices of 512 bits. All the rules were able to calculate the 128 consecutive pre-images for all 512-bits lattices. Besides, the average of the mean entropy obtained for all the rules was high (0.8857) indicating that they exhibit a chaotic behavior. An important final observation is that although it was possible to specify rules with a high probability to find at least one pre-image for any lattice and with a good perturbation spread, even the better rules evaluated can fail when the pre-image computation is applied to some lattice.

The major conclusion of the analysis in (Oliveira et al., 2008) is that the simple adoption of the reverse algorithm is not recommended because the possible rules with 100% guarantee of pre-image existence are not appropriate for ciphering. Two alternative approaches have been emerged. The first is the application of a variation of the reverse algorithm in which extra bits are added to the lattice in each cipher step, similar to the process adopted in Gutowitz's cryptographic model. Using this approach the 100% guarantee of pre-image existence was obtained with a good level of entropy. However, this approach is affected by the same disadvantage of Gutowitz's model: a considerable and fixed increase in the ciphertext in relation to the original one. The second propose in (Oliveira et al., 2008) is a method based on the original reverse algorithm adopting a contour procedure to apply when the pre-image calculus fail. As the secret key specification previous discussed gives a low probability to this failure occurrence, we expect to rarely use this contour procedure but it guarantees the possibility to cipher any plaintext. This method, which is the key point of the present work,

alternates the original reverse algorithm and the variation that uses extra bits in the ciphering process, using the second only when the pre-image calculus fails. Although this approach needs to add some bits to the ciphertext when a failure occurs, it is expected that in practice few failures happens and the ciphertext length will be equal or close to the plaintext. The general idea of this second approach was proposed in (Oliveira et al., 2008) but it has been redefined, implemented and tested first in (Oliveira et al., 2010a). Sections 4 and 5 details the method and presents experiments performed to evaluate and to improve its and the properly specification of the secret keys to have a reasonable final length.
In a certain sense, the method proposed in (Wuensche, 2008) is very similar to the initial method proposed in (Oliveira et al., 2008). It is also based on the employment of the reverse algorithm to encrypt a plaintext through successive pre-image computations, obtaining a lattice correspondent to the ciphertext. Deciphering method is performed by CA forward evolution. Therefore, in essence the idea is the same one applied in the original method described in (Oliveira et al., 2008), even so the methods have been proposed in an independent way. The problem of finding rules with 100% guarantee of pre-image existence was also addressed in (Wuensche, 2008). Aiming to guarantee a good performance of the algorithm in the ciphering process, the author indicates that keys must be chain-rules with $Z_{left} = 1$ and $0.5 < Z_{right} < 1$. The treatment given to failure occurrences when performing pre-image calculus is an important point to discern the two works in (Oliveira et al., 2008) and (Wuensche, 2008). The author in (Wuensche, 2008) said that: "*for big binary systems, like 1600, the state-space is so huge,* 2^{1600}, *that to stumble on an unencryptable state would be very unlikely, but if it were to happen, simply construct a different chain rule*". However, there is a practical viability of any cipher method only if this method assures the encryption of any plaintext and that the suggested secret key discarding in the case of failure cannot be adopted in a communication system. Moreover, even with the adoption of lattices with high length (as 1600 bits suggested in (Wuensche, 2008)) the use of rules with $Z_{right}/Z_{left} > 0.5$ do not avoid the occurrence of rules with a high number of Garden-of-Eden states. Systematic experiments were not presented in (Wuensche, 2008) to evaluate this possibility. We performed several experiments using different groups of rules with radius 3 and $Z_{left} = 1$. Approximate 200 rules have $0.75 < Z_{right} < 1$ and some of them do not return a good performance attempting to calculate 20 consecutive pre-images. Therefore, even using a large lattice and a rule within the specification suggested in (Wuensche, 2008), it is clear that a failure can happen during the ciphering process. As example of rule of such undesirable performance we can point rule 569A99965999596AA965666AA666A699. Thus, the alternative method discussed in (Oliveira et al., 2008) to deal with situations in which the reverse algorithm did not obtain the pre-image is a necessary approach. It is the key point of the method investigated in this work.

4. Variable length encryption method

Since the main conclusion of the analysis in (Oliveira et al., 2008) is that the simple adoption of the reverse algorithm is not possible, an alternative method was investigated in (Oliveira et al., 2010a). It is based on reverse algorithm adopting an alternative procedure to apply when the pre-image computation fails (Oliveira et al., 2008). It is expected that with an appropriate key specification there is a low probability to this failure occurrence. The alternative procedure adds extra bits only when the pre-image is not possible to calculate. Therefore, it is expected to rarely use this procedure but it guarantees the possibility to cipher any plaintext. For practical reasons related to encryption speed, it can be better to limit the method to operate with only toggle rules. The method works as it alternates rounds of pre-image computation performed by reverse algorithm (a variation of Gutowitz's model for periodic conditions) with few or none steps of pre-image computation performed by Gutowitz's model. Ciphering is made by computing P consecutive pre-images starting from a lattice of size N corresponding to the plaintext. The secret key is a radius-R CA rule τ generated with an appropriate specification based CA static parameters.

Suppose that it started to calculate pre-images using reverse algorithm and the secret key τ and it fails in the *K-th* pre-image such that $K \leq P$. In such situation the ciphering process uses the modified reverse algorithm with extra bits to calculate the *K-th* pre-image. Thus, the *K-th* pre-image will have $N + 2R$ cells. Ciphering returns again using the original reverse algorithm to calculate the remaining pre-images. If all the subsequent pre-images computation succeeds the final ciphertext will have a size of $N + 2R$. If the pre-image computation fails again, the ciphering process changes and adds $2R$ more bits to the lattice. If the process fails in F pre-images ($F \leq P$) the final lattice will have $N + 2FR$. Starting from a lattice of N cells, the size of the ciphertext after P pre-images computation is given by $N \leq$ *ciphertext size* $\leq N + 2PR$. Therefore, it is a variable-length encryption model, named *VLE*. However we expected that in practice the ciphertext size will be next to N due to the characteristics of the rule used as secrete key. It is important to note that the ciphertext obtained using Gutowitz's model will have exactly $N + 2PR$ bits – the worst and improbable situation in the proposed method. For example, if $N = 512$, $P = 64$ and $R = 5$ the size of the ciphertext using VLE will be situated between 512 and 1152 bits. However, we expected that in practice the ciphertext size will be next to 512 due to the characteristics of the rule used as secret key. On the other hand, the ciphertext obtained using Gutowitz model will be exactly 1152 bits.

Deciphering will be executed applying the forward interaction of cellular automata rules. By starting from the ciphertext the recipient needs to apply the transition rule τ forward by P steps and the final lattice will be the plaintext. He also needs to know in which pre-images failures happened to recover the original text. An improvement of the method in relation to the one proposed in (Oliveira et al., 2008) is the usage of a non-retroceding method in a case of failure. Tests performed in (Oliveira et al., 2008) have used the following retroceding strategy: when calculating a sequence of 10 consecutive pre-images to cipher a plaintext, suppose that a failure occurs in the 8th pre-image, for example. In this case, the algorithm returns to the last lattice in which there is a possibility to have another pre-image. So, when we try to calculate 10 consecutive pre-images starting from a given lattice and this process fail in the end we can affirm that all the possible backward trajectories were evaluated and it is really impossible to find 10 consecutive pre-images starting from the given lattice. Using this retroceding procedure the number of lattices possible to be ciphered by the original reverse algorithm is increased. However, during the experiments, we perceived that this procedure is high-time consuming as expected and with low actual return to the final performance of the rules. Besides, with the increase of the block size, this inefficient behavior is more probable. So for the simplicity and the speedy of the method, we decided to implement the variable-length ciphertext method using a non-retroceding method. When the pre-image computation fail, the method changes to the computation using extra bits without trying to backtrack to find another pre-image with lower order.

CA backward interaction-based ciphering method is more adjusted to encryption as a block-cipher method using a restricted lattice length instead of encryption as a stream cipher method with an arbitrarily large lattice. This argument is motivated by the fact that the pre-image computation is an algorithm of considerable computational cost. A major advantage of the pre-image calculus adopted is that the process never retrocedes when a pre-image is calculating and it always succeeds, although there is an increase of cells during the process. Using a parallel hardware in Gutowitz's model, it is possible to calculate simultaneously different pre-images to reduce significantly the final time of processing. Unfortunately, using the reverse algorithm with periodic boundary conditions this kind of parallelism is not possible. Using the simplification to apply only toggle rules (as in Gutowitz's model), it speeds up the pre-image computation, since that will be removed the ambiguities and there is no possibility of the algorithm to come back in the computation before arriving at the end of the lattice. However, various pre-image initializations are possible and typically only one will succeed. Using a stream cipher approach, since reverse calculus is essentially sequential, the idea to parallel the calculus of a unique pre-image starting from a specific initialization is probably unfeasible. On the other hand, if a block cipher approach is used, a parallel architecture can be used to perform the blocks ciphering in a distributed way increasing the throughput of the entire encryption method. Therefore, we claim that the employment of the reverse algorithm-based ciphering is more adequate as a block-cipher method and we suggested the following block sizes: 256 or 512 bits. Although the reverse algorithm-based block-cipher method can be applied using any operation mode already investigated in the literature for other block-cipher method (ECB, CBC, PCBC, OFB, CFB or CTR) (Stallings, 2003), we strongly suggest the use of counter operation mode (CTR) to increase the security and the throughput of the entire encryption process.

5. Experiments

Using VLE we have the guarantee that ciphering is possible even if an unexpected Garden-of-Eden state occurs. However a short length ciphertext depends on the secret key specification. Some initial experiments were performed to analyze method's performance and to evaluate rules specification proposed in (Oliveira et al., 2008) and (Wuensche, 2008). In these experiments small groups of radius 2 and radius 3 rules were used. Section 5.1 presents these experiments. Subsequently, a deeper investigation about an appropriate rule specification using a more representative key set was carried out. Aiming to perform a more exhaustive analysis, some experiments were conducted using the complete set of radius 2 right-toggle rules: it was used all possible radius 2 transition rules with $Z_{left} = 1$. Sections 5.2 and 5.3 report these experiments.

5.1 Small sets of radius 2 and 3 rules

A computational environment was implemented to analyze method's performance and to evaluate rules specification, starting from the information presented in (Oliveira et al., 2008) which uses Z_{left}, Z_{right} and S. The extreme parameters values ($Z_{right} \leq 0.05$, $Z_{right} \geq 0.95$, $S \leq 0.05$ and $S \geq 0.95$) were excluded due to rules in these ranges present low performance in relation to either pre-images existence or entropy. Two groups of rules with $Z_{left} = 1$ were established, each one containing 500 rules for each radius analyzed (2 and 3). The first group was formed by rules with Z_{right} specified in the range $0.25 < Z_{right} \leq 0.5$ as suggested in (Oliveira et al., 2008); it was named Group 0. The second group was formed by rules in the range $0.5 < Z_{right} < 0.95$ as suggested in (Wuensche, 2008); it was named Group 1. Each group was used in the ciphering process using samples of 256 bits plaintexts: 100 initial lattices randomly generated with a Gaussian distribution. The number of pre-images steps (P) was defined according to the rule radius (R) (considering the block size of 256 bits): it was used $P = 128$ for radius 2 rules and $P = 85$ for radius 3 ones. The results for each group of rules are presented in Table 1. The objectives of this investigation are: (i) to determine which is the average length of the final lattices (ciphertexts), related to the average number of failures occurred during the ciphering; and (*ii*) to determine which is the difference associated to two ciphertexts obtained starting from two very similar plaintexts, to evaluate the encryption quality and specially its protection against a differential cryptanalysis-like attack.

(i) Calculating ciphertexts final length: applying the method described in Section 4, any rule with $Z_{left} = 1$ is able to complete the ciphering process starting from any initial lattice, independently of the number of pre-image previously established. However, the final length of the ciphertext can be between N (best case) and $N + 2PR$ (worst case). We want to evaluate if the expected final length is in fact close to the best case and which is the behavior of each group in such evaluation. Table 1 presents group performances: the average length of the final lattice or ciphertext (L_{mean}) and the average number of failures occurred during ciphering process (F_{mean}). Table 1 shows L_{mean} and F_{mean} for each group of rules and for each radius size R. Each average was computed considering 50000 tests: 500 rules applied over 100 initial lattices.

(ii) Comparing ciphertexts generated by pairs of similar plaintexts: cryptanalysis methods try to find the plaintext after getting the ciphertext without knowing the secret key. The differential cryptanalysis is based on the analysis of some pairs of ciphertexts generated by similar plaintexts. Although the origins of differential cryptanalysis are related to studies in how to break ciphertexts encrypted by DES algorithm (Biham & Shamir, 1991), Sen et al. (2002) have used the same idea to analyze their CA cryptosystem named CAC and they compared their results with the results obtained with DES and AES cryptosystem (Sen et al., 2002). In this analysis, several pairs of plaintext (X, X') are used, which differ one of the other by a fixed and small difference D. Each pair (X, X') is used to generate a pair of ciphertexts (Y, Y') which differ one of the other by a difference D'. D and D' are obtained by applying the XOR operations between the pair members. For each pair (Y, Y'), the number of 1s in D' is counted, which corresponds to the number of different bits between Y and Y', and the standard deviation of this measure is calculated over all the analyzed pairs. As higher the deviation standard in D', as higher is the probability of the ciphertext be broken by differential cryptanalysis. An algorithm with standard deviation below 10% is said to be protected against differential cryptanalysis (Sen et al., 2002). Difference D between two plaintexts X and X' was fixed in only one bit in any arbitrary position over the lattice (single bit perturbation) and the value of D' was determined for each plaintext evaluated. D' was calculated to each pair (Y,Y') to obtain the standard deviation (σ) for each group set. The total number of tests is 200000: 50000 tests for each group and for each fixed radius. A standard deviation of 4.47% was obtained considering all the 200000 tests. Therefore, the proposed CA cryptographic model can be considered secure in relation to differential cryptanalysis. Considering groups 0 and 1, we obtained 4.81% and 4.13%, respectively. Table 1 shows the standard deviation (σ) for each group of rules (0 or 1) and for each radius size (2 or 3).

Additionally, to ensure that the final difference D' obtained between Y and Y' generated from two similar plaintexts X and X' does not keep any pattern which eventually could help a cryptanalyst using a differential cryptanalysis-like attack, a second measure was applied: we calculated the entropy associated to each D'. A measure of spatial entropy was applied on D' to evaluate the existence of some undesirable regularity on this difference. Entropy above 0.75 assures a random difference enough to affirm that ciphertexts Y and Y' do not maintain any similarity, even so they started from similar plaintexts. Entropy below 0.5 indicates a strong pattern in difference D'. Entropy values between 0.5 and 0.75 had been considered fuzzy, since it cannot guarantee the existence of an ordered or random pattern. Therefore, if any cryptography method is applied to similar texts returning an average of spatial entropy (E_{mean}) above 0.75 (with a low standard deviation), it indicates a good protection to differential cryptanalysis. Furthermore, it assures that the ciphering adds a high level of entropy during the process, a necessary characteristic in any encryption method.

R	N	P	Group	Z_{right}	L_{mean}	F_{mean}	E_{mean}	$\sigma_{mean}(\%)$
2	256	128	0	$0.25 < Z_{right} \leq 0.5$	256.19	0.047	0.89	5.29
			1	$0.5 < Z_{right} < 0.95$	269.80	3.449	0.87	4.32
3	256	85	0	$0.25 < Z_{right} \leq 0.5$	267.07	1.845	0.87	4.33
			1	$0.5 < Z_{right} < 0.95$	325.50	11.583	0.85	3.94

Table 1. Mean values obtained for all rules and for the 500 worst rules in each set in first experiment.

Looking over radius 2 rules in Table 1, rules of group 1 ($Z_{right} > 0.5$) have high entropy and a low standard deviation, confirming that these rules quickly spread any perturbation. However, they produce a significant increase in lattice size, confirming that these rules have high probability of failures during pre-image computation. The analysis of radius 2 rules indicated that group 0 presented the best results, i.e. the rules with Z_{right} between 0.25 and 0.5 also have high entropy and low standard deviation in the ciphertext pairs analysis and the number of expected failures in pre-images is very low (< 0.5), turning the texts ciphered starting from plaintexts with 256 bits very close to the original size. Analyzing the results using the radius 3 rules, one can observe that although the rules still presented good measures related to the pairs of ciphertexts analysis (high entropy and low standard deviation), the final size of the ciphertexts tend to increase when comparing with radius 2 rules, even that the number of pre-images used is smaller when using radius 3 rules. Rules with Z_{right} between 0.25 and 0.5 (Group 0) presented again the best performance in relation to the average number of failures. However, the number of expected failures is above 1 and the expected final length is almost 5% longer than the original lattice size: 267.07. Group 1 presented a high average number of failures (above 11 failures in 85 pre-image steps), returning ciphertexts 27% longer than the original size.

Therefore, Group 0 presented the best performance, despite having increased the average number of failures from radius 2 to 3; the number of failures is acceptable for both radius and the final lattices have an average size close the minimum. They represent the rules with $0.25 < Z_{right} \leq 0.5$ as suggested in (Oliveira et al., 2008). Group 1 is formed by the rules with $0.5 < Z_{right} \leq 0.95$; they represent the rules with $Z_{right} > 0.5$ as suggested in (Wuensche, 2008) and presented a non-satisfactory performance: although they returned good entropy values, they also returned the largest values of ciphertext length. Therefore, they were considered inappropriate to use in a block-ciphering system, at least in the block size investigated here: 256 bits. Similar experiments were performed in (Oliveira et al., 2010a) with other block sizes: as the block size increases, the adequacy of these rules also tends to increase in both groups. However, as a general conclusion, rules using Group 0 specification returns better performance than rules like Group 1. Despite of this comparative analysis between groups'specification, our expectative about the usage of the variable length method had been confirmed: it has a good quality of ciphering entropy and the ciphertext length is close to the original block size, specially using rules specified according to (Oliveira et al., 2008). However, a lot of open questions remained since the experiments were performed based on very limited samples of rules.

5.2 Investigating the complete radius 2 rule set with a variable number of pre-image steps

Subsequent experiments were conducted using the complete set of radius 2 right-toggle rules; all of them have $Z_{left} = 1$ and $0 \leq Z_{right} \leq 1$. Radius 2 toggle rules are defined by only 16 bits since the other 16 bits are deterministically defined. This set is composed by 65536 (2^{16}) rules, being that all of them have Z_{right} =1. These rules represent 50% of the possible keys in radius 2 space (restricted to use only toggle rules for faster encryption), being that the other 50% are the left-toggle rules ($Z_{left} = 1$), which are dynamically equivalent to the set analyzed. We employed the VLE environment to cipher one hundred 256-bits plaintexts using each right-toggle rule of the complete set. In previous experiments described in Section 5.1 the number of consecutive pre-images employed during ciphering was fixed: $P = 128$ for radius 2 rules and 256-bits plaintexts. Here, the number of consecutive pre-image steps was dynamically defined between 16 and 128, depending on the results obtained during ciphering. In that way, the ideal number of consecutive pre-images employed during ciphering was also experimentally investigated. Based on an exhaustive analysis of radius 2 right-toggle rule space we analyze the effects of using as secret keys the following sets of rules: *(i) Fullset* - the complete set of rules in which the unique restriction is the right-toggle property ($Z_{left} = 1$ is a consequence); *(ii)* $Subset_A$ - the restricted rule set defined by the specification $0.25 < Z_{right} \leq 0.5$ and $S = 1$ as proposed in (Oliveira et al., 2008). Fullset is formed by 65536 rules while $Subset_A$ is composed by only 21019 rules (32.1% of Fullset rules). Therefore, using $Subset_A$ specification, the reduction of possible keys is severe and the number of available secret keys is reduced to approximate $\frac{1}{3}$.

The objectives of this investigation are the same of those related on last subsection. The first objective is to calculate ciphertexts final length: Table 2 presents the performance of each set/subset: the average length of the final lattice or ciphertext (L_{mean}) and the average number of failures occurred during ciphering process (F_{mean}). Each average result was computed considering the application of each rule of the set to cipher 100 lattices of 256 bits. The second objective is to compare ciphertexts generated by pairs of similar plaintexts (X, X') aiming to verify if the method is secure against differential cryptanalysis-like attacks. D' was calculated to each pair of ciphertexts (Y,Y') to obtain the standard deviation (σ) for each rule set. Spatial entropy (E) (Oliveira et al., 2008) was calculated on D' to evaluate the existence of some undesirable regularity on this difference. E above 0.75 indicates a random difference enough to expect that ciphertexts Y and Y' do not maintain any similarity. Table 2 shows σ_{mean} and E_{mean} for each set of rules. We also used entropy E to determine when stop pre-image computation (P). D' entropy was calculated in some P steps to determine in which one the ciphering will be stopped. D' entropy (E) is first calculated in $P = 16$. If E is above 0.75 the pre-image computation stops and the 16th pre-image is the ciphertext. Otherwise, this process is repeated to $P = 32$, 64 and 128. If until $P = 128$ entropy E does not meet 0.75, the ciphertext is the 128th pre-image. A mean standard deviation (σ_{mean}) below 5% was obtained for all the sets of rules. Therefore, the proposed CA cryptographic model can be considered secure in relation to differential cryptanalysis. The mean number of faults (F_{mean}) during ciphering process is very low for all set - below 0.1 – which returns a mean ciphertext size very close to the original size 256 bits.

$Subset_A$ returned the smaller ciphertexts, indicating that this specification indeed reduce the final size as observed in last subsection. When considering the mean entropy of D' (E_{mean}), all sets returned high values, above 0.87, indicating that the rules are able to add a high entropy during ciphering. Therefore, considering only the mean values of each set analyzed, all of them returned good values on the measures analyzed and there was no need to reduce the set of keys. However, the worst performing rules in $Fullset$ indicate the existence of secret keys not appropriate for ciphering purpose. Such rules are highlighted in the right side of Table 2, in which only the 500 worst performing rules in each set are considered. The mean number of faults (F_{mean}) is above 5 in $Fullset$, indicating that these rules return ciphertexts with size superior to 276 bits in average. Moreover, F_{mean} represents the mean value size for each rule considering all the 100 lattices used to test it. However, if we consider the worst result in such lattices, we can find ciphertexts with a considerable size: column F_{max} shows the mean of the maximum ciphertext size obtained considering the 500 worst rules in each set. This metric highlights the existence of secret keys in $Fullset$ returning ciphertexts with size superior to 290 bits. It was possible to notice that there are more than 200 rules in $Fullset$ returning ciphertext lengths between 280 and 740 bits in the worst case and more than 270 bits in average. There are only 17 rules in $Subset_A$ that returns ciphertext length above 300 bits in the worst case and only 97 rules with mean value between 260 and 280 bits. Therefore, considering the final ciphertext length, rules of $Subset_A$ presented much better performance both in mean values considering the entire rule set and in mean and maximum values considering the worst rules (Table 2). Naturally, this better performance is a consequence of the low number of fails. No significant difference is clear in mean entropy considering all rules in Table 2. Only when observing 500 worst performing rules considering entropy values differences are highlighted. The mean entropy in D' (E_{mean}) is bellow 0.5 in $Fullset$ and $Subset_A$, indicating that they do not perform an actual encryption of the plaintexts in average. E_{min} represents the worst entropy found for each rule considering all the 100 lattices. E_{min} is below 0.1 for $Fullset$ and $Subset_A$. It indicates the existence of lattices that are not encrypted by some few rules. The most probable behavior of such CA rules is that they only shift the initial lattices, not performing an actual encryption of plaintexts. Although this behavior is a minor occurrence in the entire set of CA rules it cannot be allowed in a cryptosystem.

		All rules				500 worst rules			
Set	Number of rules	L_{mean}	F_{mean}	E_{mean}	$\sigma_{mean}(\%)$	F_{mean}	F_{max}	E_{mean}	E_{min}
$Fullset$	65536	256.38	0.095	0.879	3.66	5.851	13.448	0.170	0.036
$Subset_A$	21019	256.10	0.025	0.872	3.65	0.932	3.212	0.396	0.037

Table 2. Mean values obtained for all rules and for the 500 worst rules in each set.

Concluding our analysis: (*i*) There are a lot of undesirable behavior rules in $Fullset$ – considering a cryptographic purpose - that must be avoided as secret keys. Therefore the entire rule space formed by all radius 2 toggle rules (totalizing 130816 rules including left-toggle and right-toggle and the existence of 256 left-and-right-toggle) cannot be applied as secret keys in VLE method. Approximate 6000 rules must be avoided (3500 due to low entropy and 2500 due to long ciphertext length). (*ii*) The specification proposed in (Oliveira et al., 2008) and evaluated in last section try to filter such undesirable behavior keys. However, its application is not so effective. The specification in (Oliveira et al., 2008) was proposed with the major goal of reducing ciphertext lengths, what is really achieved. But, the reduction imposed in key space is high (approximate 66%) and it could not avoid a great number of low entropy rules.

In respect to the number of pre-images P used during ciphering, the average of the maximum number of P used for each radius 2 rule of the $Fullset$ was of 33.10 pre-images (considering the 100 plaintexts of 256-bits analyzed). Thus, we conclude that a fixed number of pre-images $P < 64$ could be enough to cipher 256-bits plaintexts although $P = 128$ was used in the first experiments using VLE (Oliveira et al., 2008; 2010a).

5.3 Investigating the complete radius 2 rules set with a fixed number of pre-image steps

A new experiment was performed using the complete radius 2 rules set to cipher samples of 256-bits plaintexts employing a fixed and predefined number of pre-image steps (P). Different values of P were considered in this analysis: 32, 40, 48, 56 and 64. Using $P = 64$, the best result related to perturbation spread was obtained as expected (that is, the highest entropy) but additionally the number of fails increased (when compared with $P = 32$). On the other hand, using $P = 32$, it was possible to observe that this number of steps was not enough to spread perturbations when using a considerable portion of rules of the entire set. Considering the trade-off between perturbation spread and number of fails we conclude that the best evaluated value of P was 48. VLE environment were used to cipher one hundred 256-bits plaintexts by calculating 48 consecutive pre-image steps. We obtained $L_{mean} = 257.90$ and $F_{mean} = 0.476$, which returns a mean ciphertext size very close to the original size (256 bits). We obtained $\sigma_{mean} = 3.83\%$ and $E_{mean} = 0.876$ for the complete set of right-toggle rules. Since σ_{mean} is below 10%, the proposed CA cryptographic model can be considered secure in relation to differential cryptanalysis. E_{mean} is above 0.85 indicating that rules were able to add a high entropy during ciphering, using $P = 48$. However, the analysis of the worst performing rules in the set indicates the existence of secret keys not adequate for ciphering purpose. The entire rule space formed by all radius 2 right-toggle rules is not appropriate to be applied as secret keys in VLE method. Approximate 4000 rules (6% of the key space) must be avoided: 3200 due to low entropy and 800 due to long ciphertext length.

Aiming to better understand the relation between CA static parameters and underperforming rules, several parameters was used trying to identify a pattern to filter such rules; they are: Z_{right}, Symmetry (S), Absolute Activity (AA), Neighborhood Dominance (ND), Core Entropy (CE), complementary-plus-reflection Symmetry ($BWLR$), reflection Symmetry (LR), Sensitivity and Activity Propagation (AP) (Oliveira et al., 2001; 2010b). These nine parameters were calculated for all the 65536 radius 2 rules. A database was elaborated in which each register corresponds to one right-toggle transition rule and the fields are composed by the values of the nine parameters calculated for the rule, and the values of the metrics calculated when the transition rule is applied to cipher 100 plaintexts: F_{mean} and E_{mean} (results obtained with 48 pre-image steps). We first analyze the fields F_{mean} and E_{mean} of each register of the database to characterize the underperformed rules in specific classes. Field Class was added to the database with the classification of each register in one of these classes: (1) 886 rules with low mean entropy (< 0.5); (2) 750 rules with large mean ciphertext length (> 300 bits); and (3) 63900 remaining rules. As a pattern associating parameters with the worst performing rules in ciphering was not possible to recognize by a simple visual inspection, it was applied a data mining process (Fidelis et al., 2000). A standard GA was elaborated to mining IF-THEN rules associating the parameters (antecedent) with the performance class (consequent) (Oliveira et al., 2010c). The antecedent part of such rules is composed by a conjunction of conditions of the type: IF <parameter> <operator> <value>, being that the operator can be $<$ (minor), $\geq$ (larger or equal) or $\neq$ (different). The consequent part is always in the format THEN <class> = C, being that C can be "(1) Low Entropy", "(2) Large Ciphertext" or "(3) Adequate". The classification rule that was indeed intended to be mined is Class 3, because it represents appropriate transition rules to be used in cryptography. However, the other two classification rules (classes 1 and 2) were also important to achieve our goal, because they better characterize low entropy transition rules and long ciphertext ones, given us some important information to prune the rules returned by GA for Class 3. After several executions and post-processing pruning procedures we have found the best rules following:

$Rule_{ND}$: IF $S \neq 1$ AND $ND < 0.54$ AND $CE > 0.645$ AND $Z_{right} \neq 1$ AND $Z_{right} > 0.35$ THEN $Class = Adequate$
$Rule_{AA}$: IF $S \neq 1$ AND $AA \geq 0.46$ AND $CE > 0.645$ AND $Z_{right} \neq 1$ AND $Z_{right} > 0.35$ THEN $Class = Adequate$
Both rules employ four of the nine CA parameters to characterize adequate secret keys, being that tree of them are Symmetry (S), Core Entropy (CE) and Z_{right} parameters. Additionally, the first uses Neighborhood Dominance (ND) parameter and the second one uses Absolute Activity (AA) parameter, then we named them as $Rule_{ND}$ and $Rule_{AA}$. We applied each one of them as a filter in the complete radius 2 right-toggle CA rule set to remove all secret keys that non attending its conditions. The filtered set obtained applying $Rule_{ND}$ has 41556 right-toggle rules and it was named $Subset_{ND}$. The filtered set obtained applying $Rule_{AA}$ was named $Subset_{AA}$ and it has 47263 right-toggle rules. By using the environment implemented based on VLE, we employed them to cipher one hundred 256-bits plaintexts, by calculating 48 consecutive pre-image steps, as performed to the complete rule set. Table 3 shows the results obtained with $Subset_{ND}$ and $Subset_{AA}$ rules (considering all the remaining rules in each set), including mean values obtained with each set. Results of the complete set (65536 rules), named as $Fullset$, are also presented in this table.

Set	Number of Rules	Complete rule sets				500 worst performing rules			
		L_{mean}	F_{mean}	E_{mean}	σ_{mean}	F_{mean}	F_{max}	E_{mean}	E_{min}
$Fullset$	65536	257.903	0.476	0.876	3.83%	24.607	33.212	0.125	0.036
$Subset_{ND}$	41556	257.442	0.361	0.889	3.67%	10.045	16.608	0.839	0.625
$Subset_{AA}$	47263	257.488	0.372	0.889	3.68%	10.479	17.220	0.837	0.575

Table 3. Mean values of the complete rule sets and the 500 worst performing rules.

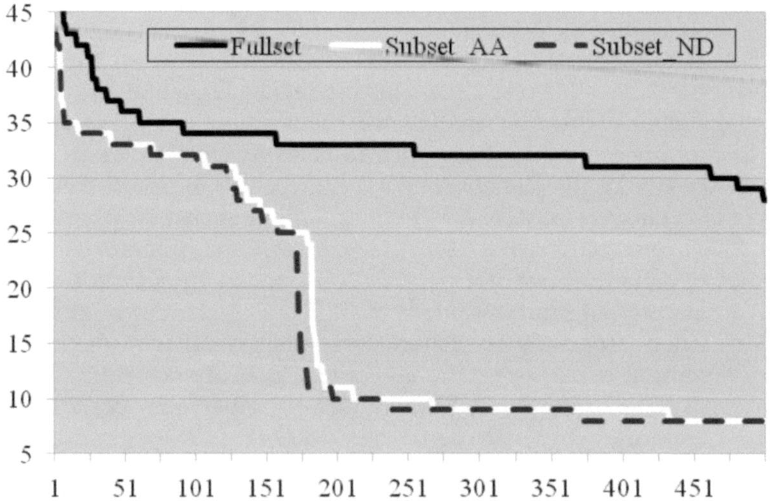

Fig. 1. 500 longest ciphertexts found in each set/subset.

Considering the totality of the rules, $Subset_{ND}$ and $Subset_{AA}$ results are better than those obtained using the entire radius 2 set, but the differences are not so expressive. However, when the worst performing rules are analyzed the advantage of such filters is evidenced. The mean values obtained considered only the 500 worst performing rules in Table 3 (F_{mean}, F_{max},

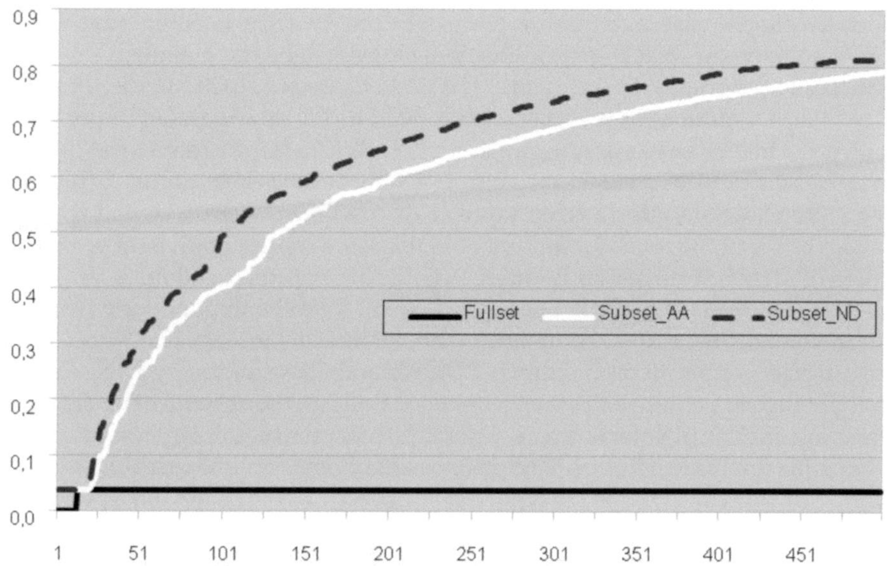

Fig. 2. 500 lowest entropy found in each set/subset.

E_{mean} and E_{min}). The number of fails exhibits a significant decay in both subsets and the longest ciphertexts were also smoothed. But the most expressive results are related to low entropy rules: the mean entropy of the worst rules improved from 0.125 to acceptable values (above 0.8) in both subsets. These results are highlighted in figures 1 and 2. Figure 1 shows the 500 longest ciphertexts while Figure 2 shows the 500 lowest entropy found in each set/subset. Comparing $Subset_{ND}$ and $Subset_{AA}$, the reduction of rules is more severe in $Subset_{ND}$ (41556 against 47263). Besides, it is possible to see that $Subset_{ND}$ returned results slightly better than $Subset_{AA}$, but this improvement does not justify such reduction imposed by $Rule_{ND}$. However, we decided to kept $Rule_{ND}$ as one of the best filters because the generalization of Neighborhood Dominance (ND) parameter from radius 2 to bigger radius is better than Absolute Activity (AA) parameter, as discussed in (Oliveira et al., 2000). Some experiments using radius 3 toggle rules specified using a filter rule based on ND are presented in (Oliveira et al., 2010c). The rule based on ND presented here is better than this previous filter rule which was obtained in preliminary data mining analysis. The tests performed using radius 3 rules returned adequate mean values. Moreover, no rule returns low entropy in any ciphered plaintext (Oliveira et al., 2010c).

6. Conclusions

The variable-length encryption method named VLE is a cryptographic model based on the backward interaction of cellular automata toggle rules. The general idea of this method was proposed in a previous work (Oliveira et al., 2008). This method alternates during the ciphering process the employment of the original reverse algorithm (Wuensche & Lesser, 1992) with a variation inspired in Gutowitz's model (Gutowitz, 1995), which adds extra bits when a pre-image is calculated. The plaintext is encrypted using this method to calculate P consecutive pre-images using a CA toggle rule τ as the secret key. As the number of failures when calculating consecutive pre-images using the reverse algorithm is not fixed, the final ciphertext length is variable. However, in practice, it is expected to obtain ciphertext

length close to original plaintext. Starting from the ciphertext, the recipient needs to apply the transition rule τ forward by P steps and the final lattice will be the plaintext.
We performed three series of experiments. The first one uses a small number of radius 2 and radius 3 rules and a number of pre-image steps fixed in 128 as suggested in previous works. The second experiment uses a variable number of pre-image steps (from 16 to 128) and a more representative set of radius 2 rules: the complete set of all possible radius 2 rules with Z_{left} equal to 1. The third one uses a fixed number of pre-image steps (P equal to 48), pruned based on the results of the second experiment in the same representative set of radius 2 rules. The average of standard deviation found is 3.83%, showing this method is very robust to a differential cryptanalysis-like attack being much lower than the upper bound limit suggested in (Biham & Shamir, 1991): 10%. Comparing with the results presented in (Sen et al., 2002) the superiority of VLE is clear in such criteria: 12%, 7% and 5% returned by DES, AES and CAC respectively, being the last one a CA-based method. Besides, the absence of an ordered pattern when ciphering similar plaintexts was evidenced by the mean entropy found: 0.876. Using VLE we have the guarantee that ciphering is possible even if an unexpected Garden-of-Eden state occurs. However a short length ciphertext depends on the secret key specification. The properly specification of the rules/key was deeper investigated in the present work using all the 65536 radius 2 right-toggle rules. Initially, we investigated specifications based on previous works (Oliveira et al., 2008) and (Wuensche, 2008), which uses static rule parameters Z and S. Our experimental results showed that none of these previous specifications are satisfactory. Thus, in a subsequent phase, we employed an analysis based on several CA static parameters. Therefore, we were able to find two good specifications of rules to be used as valid secret keys. The first specification is based on Neighborhood Dominance parameter while the second is based on Absolute Activity. These specifications had shown to be good to filter the complete set of radius 2 rules.

7. Acknowledgements

GMBO thanks CNPq and FAPEMIG support. The authors thanks to Giordano Ferreira who has participated in the initial steps of this work, specially in the development of the genetic algorithm to perform data mining.

8. References

Benkiniouar, M. & Benmohamed, M. (2004). Cellular Automata for Cryptosystem, In: *Proceedings of IEE Conference Information and Communication Technologies: From Theory to Applications*, 423-424.

Biham, E. & Shamir, A. (1991). Differential Cryptanalysis of DES-like Cryptosystems, *Proc. of Advances in Cryptology (Crypto'90)*. 2-21.

Binder, P. (1994). Parametric Ordering of Complex Systems, *Physics Rev. E.*

de Oliveira, P.P.B.; Bortot & Oliveira, G.M.B. (2006). The best currently known cellular automata rules for density classification and the evolutionary mechanisms that led to them, *Neurocomputing*, Amsterdam, 70:35-43.

Fidelis, M.; Lopes, H. & Freitas, A. (2000). Discovery comprehensible classification rules with a genetic algorithm, *C.Evolutionary Computation, CEC-2000*, USA.

Gutowitz, H. (1995). Cryptography with Dynamical Systems, In: *Cellular Automata and Cooperative Phenomena*, E. Eds: Goles and N. Boccara, 1:237-274, Dordrecht: Kluwer Academic Press.

Kari, J. (1992). Cryptosystem based on reversible cellular automata, Personal communication. *Apud in (Seredynski, Bouvry and Zomaya, 2003).*

Langton, C.G. (1990). Computation at the Edge of Chaos: Phase Transitions and Emergent Computation, *Physica D*, 42:12-37.

Macêdo, H.B.; Lima, M.J.L & Oliveira, G.M.B. (2008). Searching for a Cryptographic Model Based on the Pre-Image Calculus of Cellular Automata, In: *Proceedings of 10th Brazilian Symposium on Neural Networks (SBRN'2008)*, IEEE Computer Society, 153-158.

Nandi, S.; Kar, B., & Chaudhuri, P. (1994). Theory and Applications of CA Automata in Cryptography, In: *IEEE Transactions on Computers*, 43:1346-1357.

Oliveira, G., de Oliveira, P. e Omar, N. (2000). Guidelines for Dynamics-Based Parameterization of One-Dimensional Cellular Automata Rule Spaces, *Complexity*, 6(2):63-71.

Oliveira, G.M.B.; de Oliveira, P. & Omar, N. (2001). Definition and applications of a five-parameter characterization of 1D cellular automata rule space, *Artificial Life*, 7(3):277-301.

Oliveira, G.M.B.; Coelho, A.R. & Monteiro, L.H.A. (2004). Cellular Automata Cryptographic Model Based on Bi-Directional Toggle Rules, In: *International Journal of Modern Physics C*, 15:1061-1068.

Oliveira, G.M.B.; Macêdo, H.B.; Branquinho, A.A.B. & Lima, M.J.L. (2008). A cryptographic model based on the pre-image calculus of cellular automata, In: *Automata-2008: Theory and Applications of Cellular Automata*, ed: A. Adamatzky, R. Alonso-Sanz, A. Lawniczak, G. Juarez Martinez, K. Morita, T. Worsch, Luniver Press, 139-155.

Oliveira, G.M.B.; Martins, L.G.A.; Alt, L.S. & Ferreira, G.B.: (2010a). Investigating a Cellular Automata-Based Cryptographic Model with a Variable-Length Ciphertext, In: *CSC'10 - International Conference on Scientific Computing*, Las Vegas, 2010.

Oliveira, G.M.B.; Martins, L.G.A.; Alt, L.S. & Ferreira, G.B.: (2010b). Exhaustive Evaluation of Radius 2 Toggle Rules for a Variable-Length Cellular Automata Cryptographic Model, In:*International Conference on Cellular Automata for Research and Industry*, 2010, Ascoli Piceno, Lecture Notes in Computer Science (LNCS), 2010, v. 6350. p. 1-10.

Oliveira, G.M.B.; Martins, L.G.A.; Ferreira, G.B. Alt, L.S.: (2010c). Secret Key Specification for a Variable-Length Cryptographic Cellular Automata-Based Model, In: *11th International Conference on Parallel Problem Solving From Nature (PPSN2010)*, 2010, Krakow, Lecture Notes in Computer Science (LNCS), 2010, v. 6239. p. 1 10.

Sen, S.; Shaw, C.; Chowdhuri, D.; Ganguly, N. & Chaudhuri, P. (2002). *Cellular Automata based Cryptosystem (CAC)*, LNCS, 2513: 303-314.

Seredynski, F.; Bouvry, P. & Zomaya, A.Y. (2003). Secret key cryptography with cellular automata, In: *Proceedings of Workshop on Nature Inspired Distributed Computing (IPDPS2003: International Parallel & Distributed Processing Symposium)*, 149-155.

Stallings, W. (2003). *Cryptography and Network Security: Principles and Practice*, ISBN:0-13-091429-0, New Jersey: Prentice Hall.

Tomassini, M. & Perrenoud, M. (1986). Stream Ciphers with One and Two-Dimensional Cellular Automata, In: *Proceedings of Parallel Problem Solving from Nature (PPSN VI)*, LNCS (Springer-Verlag), 1917:722-731.

Wuensche, A. & Lesser, M. (1992). *Global Dynamics of Cellular Automata*, ISBN: 0-201-55740-1, New Mexico: Addison-Wesley.

Wuensche, A. (1998). Classifying Cellular Automata Automatically: Finding gliders, filtering, and relating space-time patterns, attractor basins and the Z parameter, *Complexity*, 4 (3):47-66.

Wuensche, A. (2008). Encryption using cellular automata chain-rules, In: *Automata-2008: Theory and Applications of Cellular Automata*, ed: A. Adamatzky, R. Alonso-Sanz, A. Lawniczak, G. Juarez Martinez, K. Morita, T. Worsch, Luniver Press, 126-138.

Wolfram, S. (1986). Cryptography with cellular automata, In: *Proceedings of International Cryptology Conference (Crypto'85)*, LNCS (Springer-Verlag), 218:429-432.

13

Cryptography in Quantum Cellular Automata

Mohammad Amin Amiri[1], Sattar Mirzakuchaki[2] and Mojdeh Mahdavi[3]
[1,2]*Iran University of Science and Technology*
[3]*Islamic Azad University, Shahr-e-Qods Branch*
Islamic Republic of Iran

1. Introduction

During past several decades, the microelectronics industry has improved the integration, the power consumption, and the speed of integrated circuits by means of reducing the feature size of transistors. But it seems that even by decreasing the transistor sizes, some problems such as power consumption cannot be ignored. QCA which was first introduced by Lent et al. (Lent et al., 1993) represents an emerging technology at the nano technology level.
Utilizing the QCA technology for implementing logic circuits is one of the approaches which in addition to increasing the clock frequency of these circuits to tera-hertz frequencies and decreasing the size of logic circuits to nanoscale, decreases the power consumption of these circuits (Lent et al., 1993; Tougaw & Lent, 1996). QCA cells have quantum dots in which the position of electrons will determine the binary levels of 0 and 1. This is the most noticeable feature of QCA against conventional logic in which logical states are stored by means of voltage levels.
Serpent block cipher was a finalist candidate of Advanced Encryption Standard (AES). This cryptographic algorithm has 32 rounds with an 128-bit block size and a 256-bit key size. This cryptographic algorithm consists of an initial permutation IP, 32 rounds, and a final permutation FP. Each round involves a key mixing operation, a pass through S-boxes, and a linear transformation. In the last round, the linear transformation is replaced by an additional key mixing operation(Anderson et al., 1998).
As an application of QCA technology, we have implemented the Serpent block cipher. Simulation results of this implementation are obtained from QCADesigner v2.0.3 software. QCADesigner is developed by the ATIPS lab at the University of Calgary in Canada. QCADesigner v2.0.3 has different simulation engines. Throughout this paper, the coherence vector simulation engine is used due to its accurate and detailed evaluation of QCA.
The remainder of this chapter is organized as follows. In Section 2, a brief review of QCA is presented. In Section 3, Serpent block cipher and its important modules are discussed. The implementation of the Serpent block cipher by means of the implementation of its modules is presented in Section 4. Section 5 concludes this chapter.

2. Quantum Cellular Automata

Each cell in Quantum Cellular Automata is composed of four quantum dots, as schematically shown in Fig. 1. The quantum dots are schematically shown as open circles. Each cell contains two electrons which are schematically shown as solid dots. The electrons are allowed to jump between the various quantum dots in a cell by the mechanism of quantum mechanical tunneling but they are not permitted to tunnel between two individual cells. The barrier height between each two individual cells is supposed to be high enough to completely block intercellular tunneling. If the electrons are left alone, they will meet the arrangement

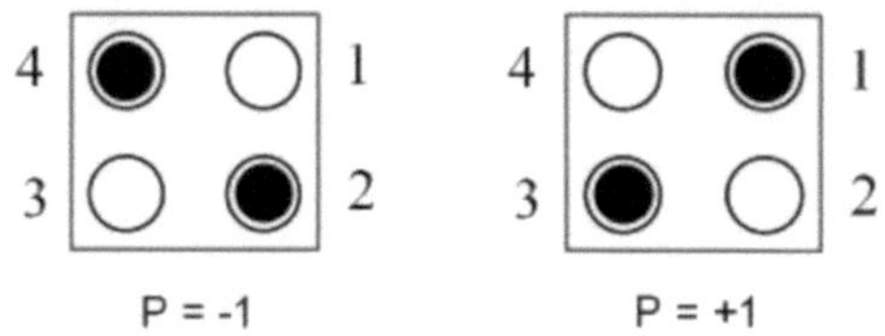

Fig. 1. QCA cell and its ground states

corresponding to the physical ground state of the cell. It is clear that the Coulombic force between electrons will make them occupy different dots. By these concepts, the ground states of a cell will be two basic arrangements with electrons at opposite corners, as shown in Fig. 1. The positions of the electrons are also illustrated in this figure.

Coulombic interaction between electrons in different cells will control their Coupling. Fig. 2

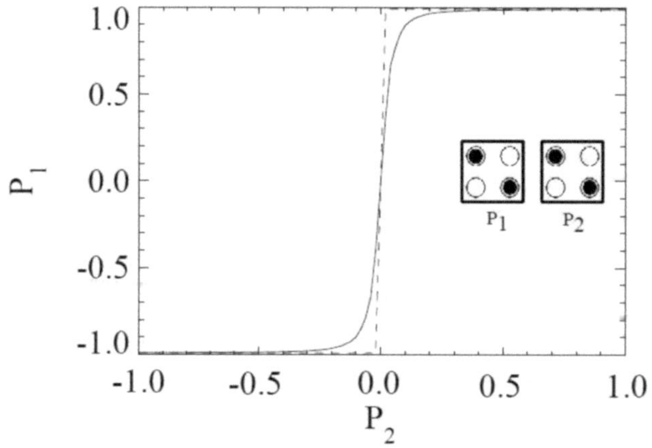

Fig. 2. Coupling of QCA cells

illustrates how one cell is affected by the state of its neighbor cell (Tougaw et al., 1993). This figure shows the two cells where the polarization of cell 1 is affected by the polarization of cell 2. The polarization of cell 2 (P2) is assumed to be fixed at a given value and this polarization will influence the cell 1, thus determining its polarization. The non-linear nature of the cell-cell coupling is a result that can be drawn here. Cell 1 is almost completely polarized in presence of cell 2 which might be partially and not completely polarized (Tougaw & Lent, 1996)(Tougaw et al., 1993). Utilizing the physical interactions between cells, basic Boolean logic functions can be realized. The elementary logic gates in QCA are the Majority gate and the Inverter gate which are illustrated in Fig. 4(a) and Fig. 3, respectively. The Majority gate can be realized by only 5 QCA cells (Tougaw & Lent, 1994). The logic AND function can be implemented by a Majority gate by setting one of its inputs permanently to 0 and the logic OR function can be implemented by a Majority gate by setting one of its inputs permanently to 1. Synchronization of the information flow throughout the QCA circuits and the direction of information flow in these circuits are provided by QCA clocking mechanism. The required power for the

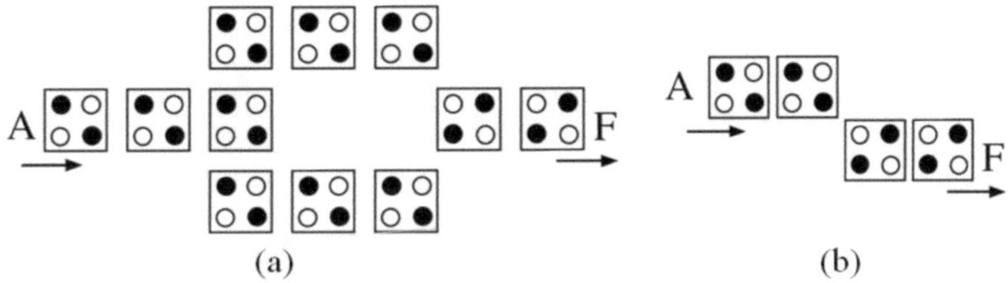

Fig. 3. (a) Redundant inverter gate and (b) Inverter gate

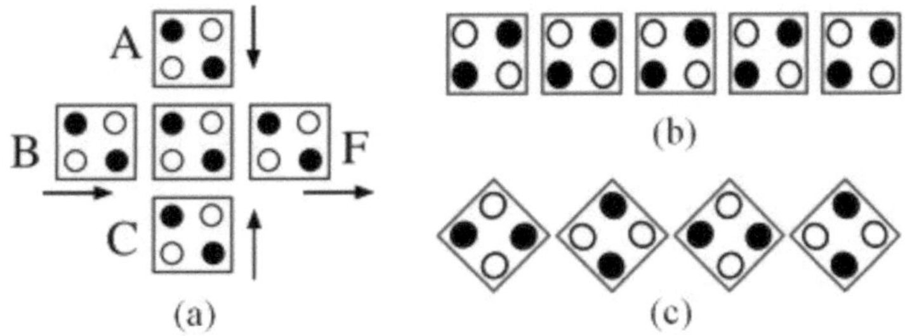

Fig. 4. (a) Majority logic gate, (b) Binary wire, and (c) Inverter chain

operation of QCA circuit is provided by QCA clocking mechanism too. More precisely, the QCA clocking mechanism is used to control the tunneling barrier height in QCA cells. The electrons are trapped in their positions, when the clock is low and they cannot tunnel to other dots, therefore latching the cell (Hold phase). This condition is caused by the intracellular barriers which are held at their maximum height. The cell goes to the null polarization state (Relax phase) when the clock signal is high. This condition is caused by the intracellular barriers which are held at their minimum height. Between these two conditions, the cells are either switching or releasing.

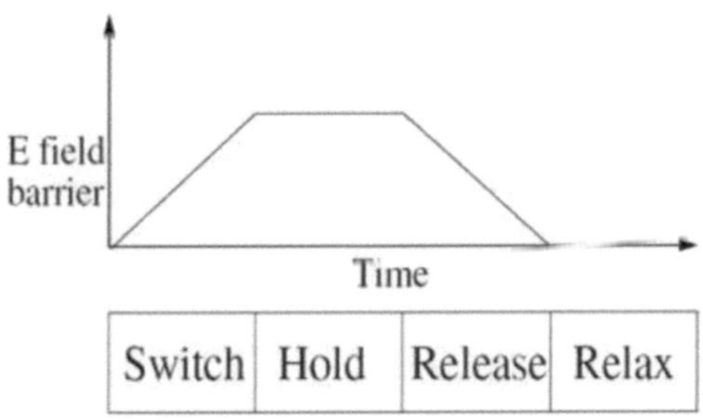

Fig. 5. Barrier hight in four phases of clock

Fig. 5 illustrates the barrier height in four phases of the QCA clock. Each cell in an individual clocking zone is connected to one of the four available phases of the QCA clock which is demonstrated in Fig. 6. Each QCA cell is synchronously latched and unlatched with the changing of the clock signal and therefore the information is distributed throughout the circuits (Hennessy & Lent, 2001)(Amiri et al., 2008)(Kim et al., 2007)(Vankamamidi et al., 2008).

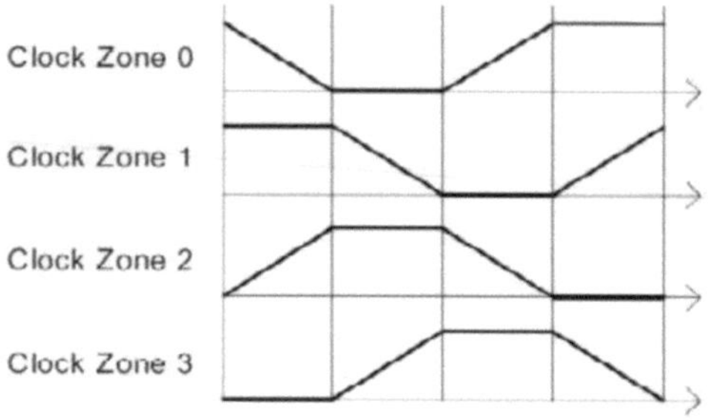

Fig. 6. QCA clock zones

3. Serpent block cipher

Serpent is a 32-round substitution permutation network (SPN) operating on four 32-bit words, thus having a block size of 128 bits (Anderson et al., 1998; 2006). Serpent encrypts a 128-bit plaintext to a 128-bit ciphertext in 32 rounds with 33 subkeys. The user key length is assumed to be variable but in the proposal, it is fixed to be 128, 192 or 256 bits. It should be mentioned that the short keys with less than 256 bits are mapped to 256 bits keys by appending one '1' bit to the MSB end followed by as many '0' bits as required to produce 256 bits. The cipher consists of an initial permutation IP, 32 rounds, and a final permutation FP. Each round involves a key mixing operation, a pass through S-boxes, and a linear transformation. In the last round, the linear transformation is replaced by an additional key mixing operation(Anderson et al., 1998).

3.1 Key mixing

At each round, a 128-bit subkey K_i is exclusively ORed with the current intermediate data B_i.

3.2 The S-boxes

Serpent has 8 individual 4×4 S-Boxes which repeat every 8 round. Every 128-bit input of the S-Box will be divided to 32 blocks of 4-bits and every block will be applied to a 4×4 S-Box. The outputs of these 32 S-Boxes will be concatenated again together to perform a 128-bit block.

3.3 Linear transform

The 128-bit output of S-Box will be divided to four 32-bits and these words are linearly mixed by some shift, rotate and XOR operations. A complete round of Serpent is described as:

$$
\begin{aligned}
&X_0, X_1, X_2, X_3 := S_i(B_i \oplus K_i)\\
&X_0 := X_0 <<< 13\\
&X_2 := X_2 <<< 3\\
&X_1 := X_1 \oplus X_0 \oplus X_2\\
&X_3 := X_3 \oplus X_2 \oplus (X_0 << 3)\\
&X_1 := X_1 <<< 1\\
&X_3 := X_3 <<< 7\\
&X_0 := X_0 \oplus X_1 \oplus X_3\\
&X_2 := X_2 \oplus X_3 \oplus (X_1 << 7)\\
&X_0 := X_0 <<< 5\\
&X_2 := X_2 <<< 22\\
&B_{i+1} := X_0, X_1, X_2, X_3
\end{aligned}
$$

Where $<<<$ means Rotation and $<<$ means Shift. In the last round, this linear transform is replaced by an additional key mixing:
$B_{32} := S_7(B_{31} \oplus K_{31}) \oplus K_{32}$

4. QCA implementation

In this work, each QCA cell is assumed to have the width and length of 18 nm like previous works such as (Cho & Swartzlander, 2007)(Cho & Swartzlander, 2009). The neighbor cells have a center to center distance of 20 nm. Implementation of initial and final permutation which are just bit reordering functions (Anderson et al., 1998), is accomplished by routing of inputs to desired outputs. Key mixing or XOR function is implemented by 3 majority gates. Fig. 7 illustrates the implementation of the key mixing function. This module has two inputs and one output. One of the inputs of this module comes from the round input and the other is the corresponding bit of the round key. This implementation has a latency of two clock periods, a complexity of 68 cells and an area of about 79200 nm^2.

The linear transform function has been first simplified and then it has been implemented.

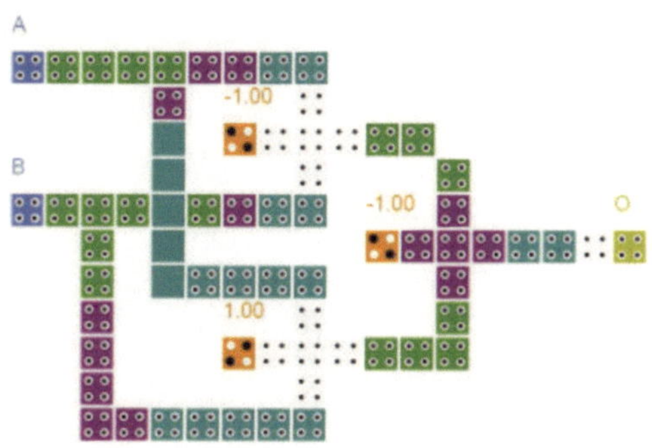

Fig. 7. Key mixing function or XOR

The simplified function was only constructed by XOR gates. As an example, the simplified 33rd and 34th bits of linear transform stage are as follows:

$$LTO(32) = LTI(14) \oplus LTI(33) \oplus LTI(68) \quad (1)$$

$$LTO(33) = LTI(15) \oplus LTI(34) \oplus LTI(69) \quad (2)$$

Fig. 8 illustrates the implementation of the 33rd output of linear transform. As illustrated in this figure, 2 XORs are applied to 3 inputs to perform the output.

This implementation has a latency of three clock periods, a complexity of 143 cells and an area of about 179200 nm^2.

4.1 Design and implementation of S-boxes

Serpent block cipher has 8 individual S-Boxes named S0 to S7. Here, the S0 substitution function is selected among Serpent's S-Boxes to be implemented. Other S-Boxes can be designed and implemented in such a manner. The S0 substitution function is illustrated in Table 1. Input and output values of this S-Box are shown in binary format and they have the length of 4 bits each.

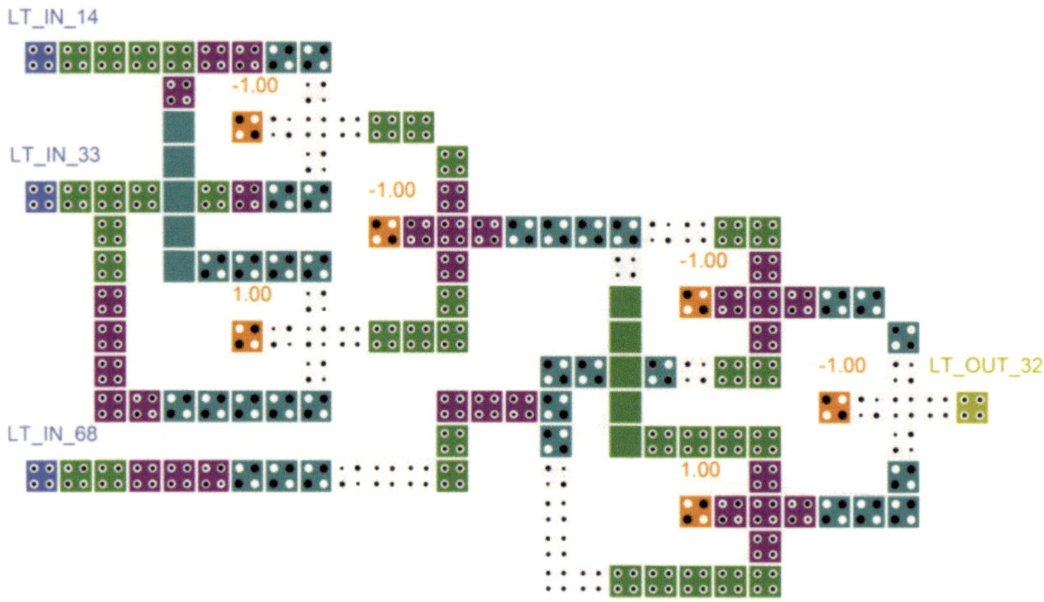

Fig. 8. Linear transform for 33rd output of linear transform

S-Box Input				S-Box Output			
S3	S2	S1	S0	O3	O2	O1	O0
0	0	0	0	0	0	1	1
0	0	0	1	1	0	0	0
0	0	1	0	1	1	1	1
0	0	1	1	0	0	0	1
0	1	0	0	1	0	1	0
0	1	0	1	0	1	1	0
0	1	1	0	0	1	0	1
0	1	1	1	1	0	1	1
1	0	0	0	1	1	1	0
1	0	0	1	1	1	0	1
1	0	1	0	0	1	0	0
1	0	1	1	0	0	1	0
1	1	0	0	0	1	1	1
1	1	0	1	0	0	0	0
1	1	1	0	1	0	0	1
1	1	1	1	1	1	0	0

Table 1. The S0 S-Box of Serpent Block Cipher

4.1.1 LUT-based design

In this method, a Look-Up-Table or memory is used to implement the S-Box. All the output bits of the S-Box *i.e.* O3, O2, O1, and O0 are implemented separately. The O0 design and implementation is discussed here. All the other output bits are implemented in such a manner. Just the memory contents are the differences between the implementation of these

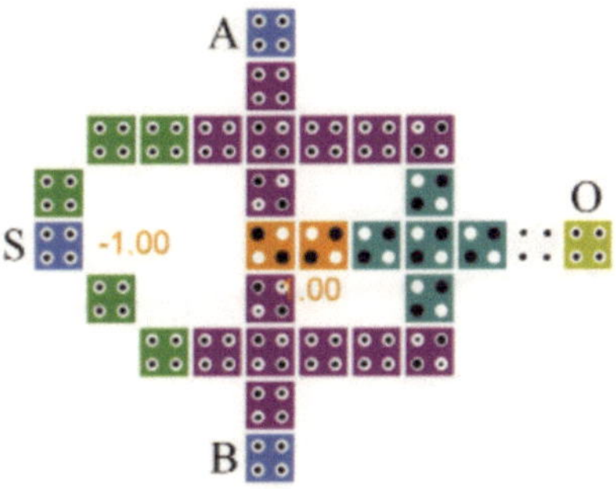

Fig. 9. QCA layout of 2 to 1 multiplexer

output bits. It means that for implementation of each output bit, the corresponding values should be stored in the memory. A 16 to 1 multiplexer is used to design a LUT-Based S-Box. The 16 to 1 multiplexer is composed of fifteen 2 to 1 multiplexers. A 2 to 1 multiplexer is illustrated in Fig. 9.

This novel multiplexer has a complexity of 31 QCA cells. When the "S" input of this multiplexer has the value of '0', the value of the "A" input will appear on the "O" output and when the "S" input has the value of '1', the value of the "B" input will appear on the "O" output.

The input bits of the S-Box are connected to the "S" input of the 16 to 1 multiplexer. The output values of the S-Box are fixed on the Data inputs of the 16 to 1 multiplexer. Using this structure, when the input value is applied to the "S" input of the multiplexer, the corresponding values will appear on the output port of the multiplexer after 10 clock periods of latency. This latency is the result of clocking which is used for data propagation throughout the circuit. It should be mentioned that after 10 clock periods of latency, the output value of the multiplexer will be valid in each clock period.

LUT-Based QCA implementation of the O0 bit of the S0 S-Box is illustrated in Fig. 10. Each output bit of the S0 S-Box is exhaustively simulated. Simulation results of the O0 bit is illustrated in Fig. 12. The results of LUT-Based QCA implementation of the S0 S-Box is discussed in Table 2. It can be seen that the Delay, Complexity and Area of all the output implementations are the same.

4.1.2 Logic-based design

In this method, the logic function of each output is used to implement it. All the output bits of the S0 S-Box *i.e.* O3, O2, O1, and O0 are implemented separately. Design and Implementation of O0 output bit is discussed here. All the other output bits are implemented in such a manner. The following logic functions are extracted from Table 1. Considering any output bit, the implementation of each term of logic function is composed of one, two, or three majority gates which are used as logic AND functions.

$$O3 = \bar{S_2}\bar{S_1}S_0 + \bar{S_3}\bar{S_2}S_1\bar{S_0} + \bar{S_3}S_2\bar{S_1}\bar{S_0} + S_2S_1S_0 + S_3S_2S_1 + S_3\bar{S_2}\bar{S_1} \tag{3}$$

$$O2 = \bar{S_3}S_1\bar{S_0} + \bar{S_3}S_2S_1S_0 + S_3S_2S_1S_0 + S_3\bar{S_1}\bar{S_0} + S_3\bar{S_2}\bar{S_1} + S_3\bar{S_2}\bar{S_0} \tag{4}$$

$$O1 = \bar{S_1}\bar{S_0} + \bar{S_3}S_2S_0 + \bar{S_3}\bar{S_2}\bar{S_0} + S_3\bar{S_2}S_1S_0 \tag{5}$$

$$O0 = \bar{S_3}\bar{S_2}\bar{S_0} + S_3S_2\bar{S_0} + \bar{S_3}S_1 + S_3\bar{S_2}\bar{S_1}S_0 \tag{6}$$

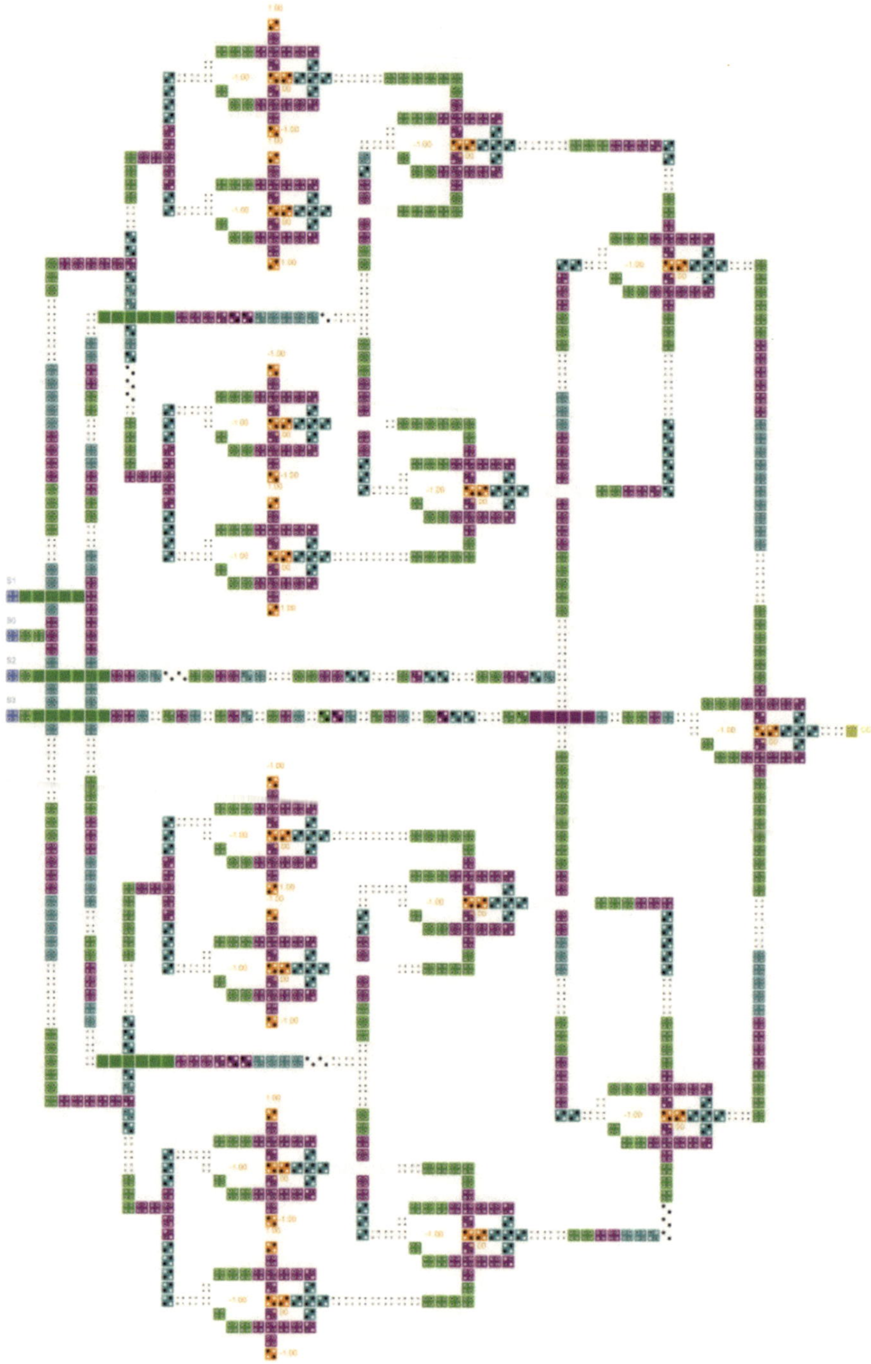

Fig. 10. LUT-Based QCA Implementation of O0 bit of S0 S-Box

Fig. 11. Logic-Based QCA Implementation of O0 bit of S0 S-Box

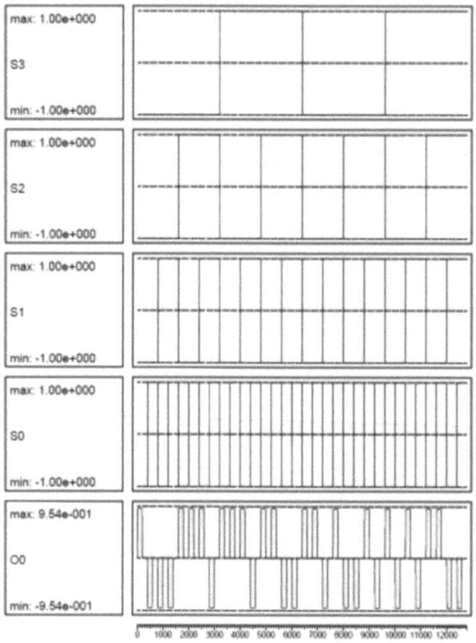

Fig. 12. Simulation Result of LUT-Based S-Box

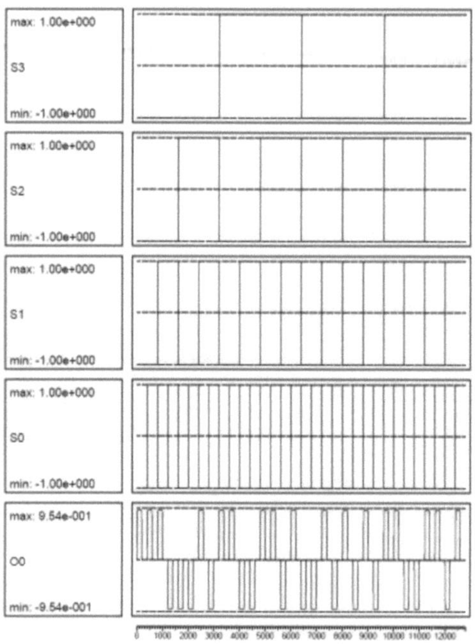

Fig. 13. Simulation Result of Logic-Based S-Box

	O3	O2	O1	O0	S0 S-Box
Complexity(Cells)	1200	1200	1200	1200	4800
Area(μm^2)	2.626	2.626	2.626	2.626	10.504
Delay(Clocks)	10	10	10	10	10

Table 2. Implementation Results of the LUT-Based S0 S-Box

	O3	O2	O1	O0	S0 S-Box
Complexity(Cells)	1204	1205	758	798	3965
Area(μm^2)	1.7236	1.7236	1.1532	1.1532	5.7536
Delay(Clocks)	8	8	6	6	8

Table 3. Implementation Results of the Logic-Based S0 S-Box

One majority gate is used for the terms which contain only two inputs, two majority gates are used for the terms which contain three inputs, and three majority gates are used for the terms which contain four inputs. The output of AND functions are also logically ORed to result the desired output.

Logic-Based QCA implementation of the O0 bit of the S0 S-Box is illustrated in Fig. 11. Each output bit of the S0 S-Box is exhaustively simulated. Simulation results of the output bits are illustrated in Fig. 13. The results of Logic-Based QCA implementation of the S0 S-Box is discussed in Table 3.

The O0 and O1 output values are valid after 6 clock periods of latency and the O2 and O3 output values are valid after 8 clock periods of latency. The maximum Delay among four output bits is considered to be the Delay of Logic-Based S-Box.

5. Conclusion

The implementation of the Serpent block cipher in Quantum Cellular Automata is investigated here. The main modules of this cryptographic algorithm are implemented in this technology and the implementation results are discussed. The two methods of S-Box design, *i.e.* LUT-Based and Logic-Based methods are inspected. The Serpent's S-Boxes are designed and simulated by these two methods. The implementation results show that the Logic-Based method has better advantages than LUT-Based method. Its Delay, Complexity and Area are less than the other method. A novel multiplexer is also introduced. This multiplexer is composed of only 31 QCA cells.

6. References

Lent, C. S.; Tougaw, P. D.; Porod, W. & Bernstein, G. H. (1993). Quantum Cellular Automata. *Nanotechnology*, Vol. 4, No. 1, (1993) page numbers 49-57.

Tougaw, P. D. & Lent, C. S. (1996). Dynamic Behavior of Quantum Cellular Automata. *Journal of Applied Physics*, Vol. 80, No. 8, (Oct. 1996) page numbers 4722-4735.

Anderson, R.; Biham, E. & Knudsen, L. (1998). Serpent: A proposal for the Advanced Encryption Standard, emphNIST AES Proposal, 1998.

Tougaw, P. D.; Lent, C. S. & Porod, W. (1993). Bistable Saturation in Coupled Quantum-dot Cells. emphJournal of Applied Physics, Vol. 74, No. 5, (Sep. 1993) page numbers 3558-3565.

Tougaw, P. D. & Lent, C. S. (1994). Logical Devices Implemented Using Quantum Cellular Automata. emphJournal of Applied Physics, Vol. 75, No. 3, (1994) page numbers 1818-1825.

Hennessy, K. & Lent, C. S. (2001). Clocking of Molecular Quantum-dot Cellular Automata. emphJournal of Vacuum Science and Technology B, Vol. 19, No. 5, (Sep. 2001) page numbers 1752-1755.

Lent, C. S. & Isaksen, B. (2003). Clocked Molecular Quantum-dot Cellular Automata emphIEEE Transaction on Electron Devices, Vol. 50, No. 9, (Sep. 2003).

Amiri, M. A.; Mahdavi, M. & Mirzakuchaki, S. (2008). QCA Implementation of a Mux-Based FPGA CLB, emphProceedings of International Conference On Nanoscience and Nanotechnology, pp. 141-144, Australia, Feb. 2008, Melbourne.

Kim, K.; Wu, K. & Karri, R. (2007). The Robust QCA Adder Designs Using Composable QCA Building Blocks. emphIEEE Transaction on Computer Aided Design of Integrated Circuits and Systems, Vol. 26, No. 1, (2007) page numbers 176-183.

Vankamamidi, V.; Ottavi, M. & Lombardi, F. (2008). Two-Dimensional Schemes for Clocking/Timing of QCA Circuits. emphIEEE Transaction on Computer Aided Design of Integrated Circuits and Systems, Vol. 27, No. 1, (2008) page numbers 34-44.

Anderson, R.; Biham, E. & Knudsen, L. (2006). Smart Card. Research and Applications, Berlin/Heidelberg, 2006, Springer.

Cho, H. & Swartzlander, E. E. (2007). Adder Designs and Analyses for Quantum-Dot Cellular Automata, emphIEEE Transaction on Nanotechnology, Vol. 6, No. 3, (2007) page numbers 374-383.

Cho, H. & Swartzlander, E. E. (2009). Adder and Multiplier Design in Quantum-Dot Cellular Automata. emphIEEE Transaction on Computer, Vol. 58, No. 6, (2009) page numbers 721-727.

14

Research on Multi-Dimensional Cellular Automation Pseudorandom Generator of LFSR Architecture

Yong Wang[1,2], Dawu Gu[2], Junrong Liu[2], Xiuxia Tian[1] and Jing Li[1]
[1]*Shanghai University of Electric Power,*
[2]*Shanghai Jiao Tong University*
China

1. Introduction

Linear feedback shift register (LFSR) is widely used in pseudorandom generator. Chien described an optimized BIST scheme which has a configurable 2-D LFSR structure and presented a synthesis procedure for this test generator. Experimental results show that the hardware overhead is considerably reduced compared with 2-D LFSR generators [1]. Erik H. presents a new test response compaction technique with any Number of Unknowns using a new LFSR Architecture in the test response bits [2].
Cellular automata (CA) are used in modern cryptography. R. Breukelaar research on the way using a genetic algorithm to evolve behavior in multi-dimensional cellular automata [3]. Sheng-Uei Guan proposed a variation of two-dimensional (2-D) cellular automata (CA) variation with asymmetric neighborship for pseudorandom number generation [4]. S. Nandi deals with the theory and application of Cellular Automata (CAI for a class of block ciphers and stream ciphers. Which has been proposed as running key generators in stream ciphers. Both the schemes provide better security against different types of attacks [5].
We research on three-Dimensional CA algorithm and LFSR hardware device pseudorandom g feasibility and efficient generator [6]. In order to find feasibility and efficient of multi-dimensional or multi-rank cellular automata (CA) algorithm with LFSR, we design more ways to test. The experiment result show they also can provide better pseudorandom key stream and pass the FIPS 140-1 standard tests.

2. Multi-dimensional cellular automation definition

2.1 One-dimensional cellular automation definition

A simple one dimensional cellular automation (CA) is an 8-cell array. For examples, when the CA is initialized to 0100 1011, each cell changes its state based on some rule. One possible rule, for example, CA could be defined by the immediate neighborhood of each cell. The cell depends on the current value and the values of its left and its right cells [7]. The CA is assumed to be connected in a circle, so the cell to the left of cell 0 is cell 7,and the cell to the right cell 7 is cell 0.The CA Neighborhood is as follows:101 010 100 001 010 101 011 110.A specific rule for this neighborhood could be:Neighborhood 000 001 010 011 100 101 110 111. New state: 0101 0110.

Rules for this type of CA are identified by converting the new state bits into a decimal number. The new state for the preceding rule is 0101 0110, which in decimal is 86.Applying this rule to the initial CA results in the succeeding CA value becoming 1001 0111.A CA can be used to generate random bits by selecting a rule, a CA size, an initial seed and the cell to provide to the random bit [1]. For example, we choose the 7th cell to produce the random bit. The first 5 step to produce the random bits are 10100 [7].

2.2 Two-dimensional cellular automation definition

A two-dimensional cellular CA offers a better random number generator at the expense of additional complexity. A two-dimensional cellular CA is an array of one-dimensional cellular, where a cell's value is updated by some function of this current neighborhood which consist of the cells above, below, to the right, and to the left of the target cell [1]. A general rule structure is defined as follow:

$$
\begin{gathered}
S_{i,j}(t+1) = Xxor\left[C \times S_{i,j}(t)\right]xor\left[N \times S_{i-1,j}(t)\right] \\
xor\left[W \times S_{i,j-1}(t)\right]xor\left[S \times S_{i+1,j}(t)\right]xor\left[E \times S_{i,j+1}(t)\right] \\
\text{Where } X,C,N,W,S,E \in \{0,1\}
\end{gathered} \tag{1}
$$

If X is 1, this is a nonlinear rule, otherwise, it is a linear rule. C,N,W,S and ,E represent the center, north, west, south, and east cells, respectively. The cells that participate in updating the center cell are determined by values of these five variables. The CA is assumed to be connected in a row circle and column circle as the one-dimensional cellular. A simple two-dimensional 3*3cellular automation is like a double circle array. So the cell to the north of cell [0,0] is cell [2,0],and the cell to the west cell [0,0] is cell [0,2].

If N is 1,then the north cell is used to update the center cell ,The values of all six variables are used to identify each possible rule. If (X,C,N,W,S,E)=(001011), then the rule is defined as Rule 11, because 1011 is decimal 11. the rule looks like this:

$$
\begin{gathered}
S_{i,j}(t+1) = \left[N \times S_{i-1,j}(t)\right] \\
xor\left[S \times S_{i+1,j}(t)\right]xor\left[E \times S_{i,j+1}(t)\right]
\end{gathered} \tag{2}
$$

A random stream is generated by assigning a rule to each cell, initializing the CA to a random state, and running the CA using a center cell to produce the bit stream [1], For example, the CA is initialized to {001;000;010},each cell is assigned Rule 11.The value in the center cell is applied to construct the random stream. The cells are randomly initialized, after four steps, the random-bit stream is .01101 [7].

2.3 Multi-dimensional cellular automation architecture

A three-dimensional cellular CA is a cube of circle two-dimensional cellular. A cell's value is updated by some function of its neighborhood, which consists of the cells above, below, to the right, to the left, to the up and to the down of the target cell. A general rule structure can be defined as follows:

$$S_{i,j,k}(t+1) = Xxor\left[C \times S_{i,j,k}(t)\right]$$

$$xor\left[N \times S_{i-1,j,k}(t)\right]xor\left[W \times S_{i,j-1}(t)\right]$$

$$xor\left[S \times S_{i+1,j}(t)\right]xor\left[E \times S_{i,j+1,k}(t)\right]$$

$$xor\left[NW \times S_{i-1,j-1}(t)\right]xor\left[NE \times S_{i-1,j+1}(t)\right]$$

$$xor\left[SW \times S_{i+1,j-1,k}(t)\right]xor\left[SE \times S_{i+1,j+1,k}(t)\right]$$

$$S_{i,j,k}(t+1) = S_{i,j,k}(t+1)xor\left[U \times S_{i,j,k+1}(t)\right]$$

$$S_{i,j,k}(t+1) = S_{i,j,k}(t+1)xor\left[D \times S_{i,j,k-1}(t)\right] \quad (3)$$

If an element is in the corner near the border, its neighbor can't be found. We can imagine the three-dimensional cellular is a cube of circle connection with beginning element and last element. So we can find every element neighbor in the imaged circle. For example element s[0][0][0] up neighbor is s[2][0][0] and it's left neighbor is s[0][2][0].
A simple three-dimensional 3*3*3 cellular automation is shown as Figure 1:

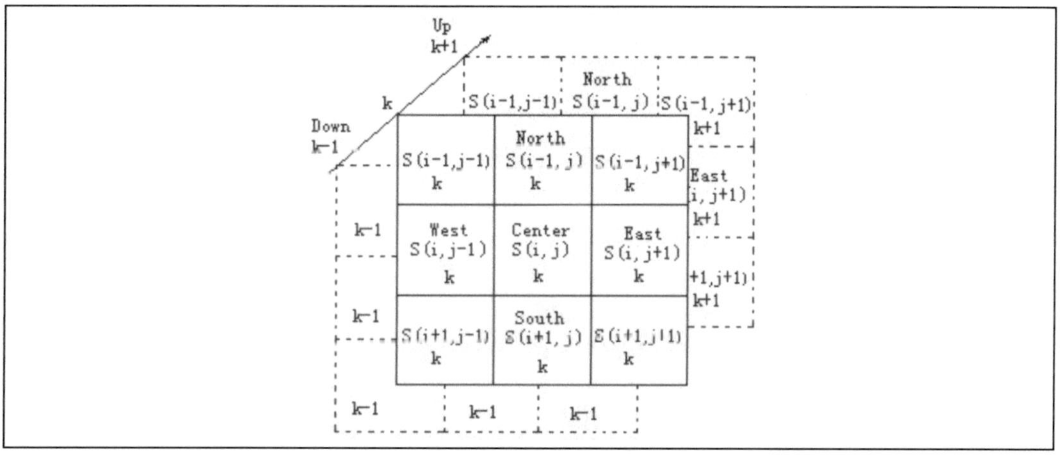

Fig. 1. Three-dimensional cellular automation architecture

Three-dimensional rule array has 0 or 1 variables. We changed the three-dimensional rule array into one-dimensional linear array. For example, element rule[0][0][0] is the first element of linear rule and rule[0][0][1] is the second element of linear rule.
The values of all twenty-seven variables arc applied to identify each possible rule.
If the first rule is equal to binary (110 1001 1011 0100 0101 1001 0100), then the rule is also defined as rule 110839188, because the binary value is decimal 110839188. The first bit of the binary 1 is equal to the element of 3 rule array rule[0][0][0]. When the bit of binary rule is zero, it means the corresponding element don't affect the random stream.

If the second rule is equal to binary (111 1111 1111 1111 1111 1111 1111), then the rule is also made as Rule 134217727, because the binary value is decimal 134217727. The first bit of the binary 1 is equal to the element of 3 rule array rule[0][0][0].

A random stream is generated by assigning a rule to each cell, initializing the CA to a random state, and running the CA using a center cell to produce the bit stream.CA is initialized to three-dimensional 3*3*3 array s[i][j][k]={0}, and the initial data is as follows: s[0][0][0]=1;s[0][2][1]=1; s[1][0][1]=1; s[2][1][1]=1;s[2][2][2]=1;

For example, each cell is assigned the first rule. The value s[1][1][1] in the center cell is used to construct the random stream.

Multi-dimensional cellular automation structure is much complicated than 3-dimesinal cellular automation. For example one 4-dimensional and 3 rank cellular automation is assumed to be two cubes connected with each other. We changed the two cubes into linear array by assigning the first cube's then another cube's element to the array in sequence. The Multi-dimensional cellular automation structure is shown in Figure 2:

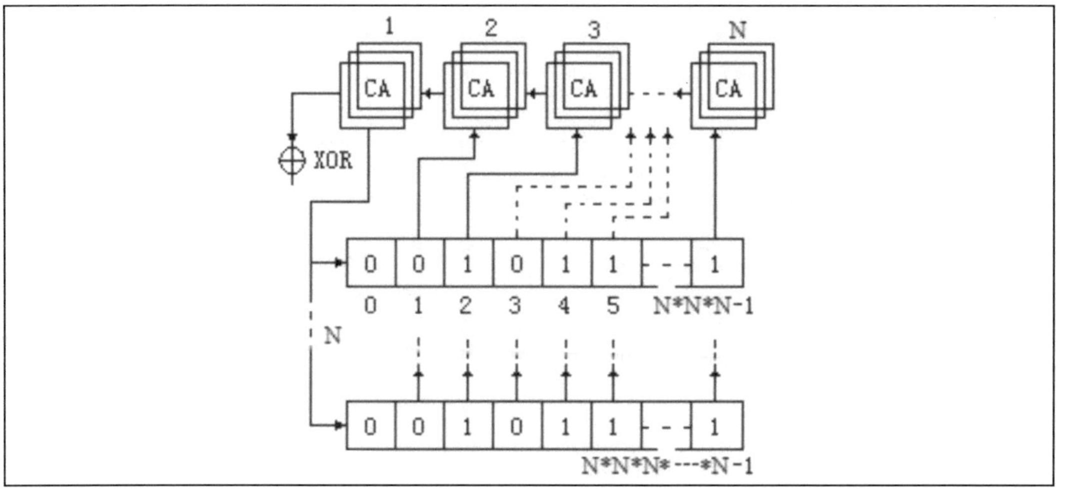

Fig. 2. Multi-dimensional cellular automation architecture

Then by rotating the first cube we can get different sequence. All the cubes is connected with each other, the output terminal will affect with LFSR output bits.

3. Multi-dimensional cellular automation pseudorandom generator of LFSR architecture

3.1 LFSR architecture

The most familiar method is to use a hardware device called a linear feedback shift register (LFSR). Shift register is a very useful, because registers are packed in CPU with very high access speed. This device stores a set of bits. The typical registers are 8-bits and 32-bits registers used in P4 CPU. The bits in register can shift to right by using assembly language instruction. Shift logical right instruction can shift each bit to the right and the leftmost bit is zero. The needed shift register's function is shifting each bits to the right, and the rightmost bit is lost, leftmost bit is replaced with the input bit. Linear feedback shift register (LFSR) choose some bits from the shift register and XOR he input shift in bits. The XOR result is the shift in bits [7].

A general LFSR can be represented by a function of its stored bits and the connections to the shift-in bits. The function is:

$$b_n = c_1 b_1 XOR c_2 b_2 XOR \cdots XOR c_n b_n \tag{4}$$

3.2 Multi-dimensional cellular automation with LFSR architecture

The Multi-dimensional cellular automation LFSR combine the dimensional cellular method and linear feedback shift register (LFSR) to create continues stream bits. The method can be represented by a function of its stored bits and the connections to the shift-in bits from both selected bits and CA random-bit stream. The function is

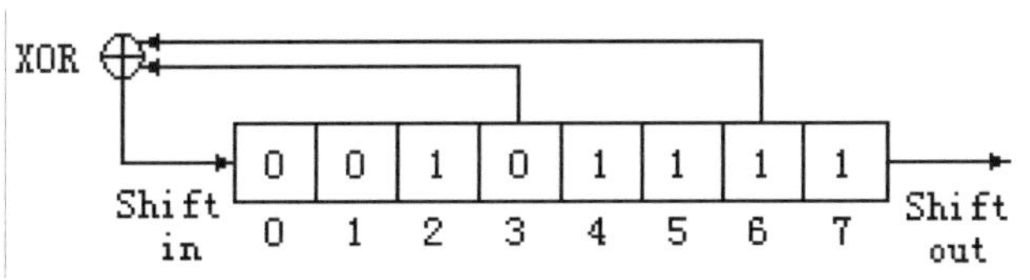

Fig. 3. LFSR hardware device architecture

For example, if 8-bits LFSR is set 0010 1111,in which the shift XOR function among the Shift in bit, cell 3 and cell 6. The LFSR shift procedure includes three steps: the first step is calculating cell 3 and cell 6 by XOR to create shift in bit. The second step is shift bit including shift in bit from left to right [1]. The last step is filling the shift out cell with the cell 7.Then circulate this three steps until the counter is back to 0 [6].

$$b_n = CArbXOR c_1 b_1 XOR c_2 b_2 XOR \cdots XOR c_n b_n \tag{5}$$

CArb stands for cellular automation random bit .Where, if the bit is selected for the XOR operation; otherwise, it is 0. For example the operation of a simple 8-bit LFSR, in which the shift in is the XOR of cells 3 and 6 with s[1][1][1]is shown in Figure 4.

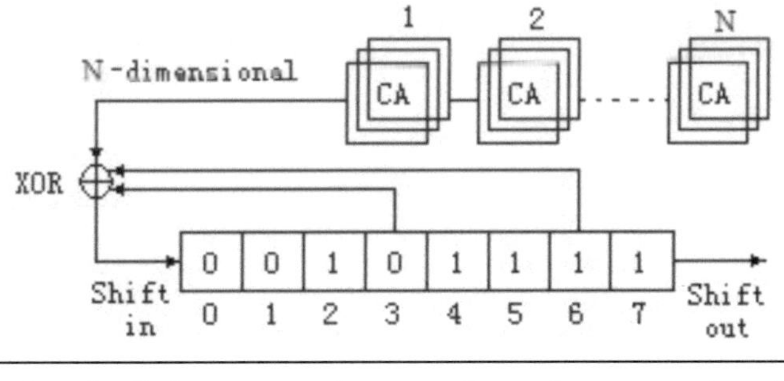

Fig. 4. Multi-dimensional cellular automation pseudorandom generator of LFSR architecture

If 8-bits three-dimensional cellular automation LFSR is set 0010 1111 same as to the CA Rule decimal 110839188, in which the shift XOR function among the Shift in bit, cell 3 and cell 6 with the CA random bit. The procedure is illustrated in Table 2.Then initial data in s[i][j][k] is as CA example.

When loop counter is 20000 times, the 4-dimensional and 3-rank cellular automation LFSR algorithm can create stream bits including 10002 bit zero and 9998 bit one. The result can pass the bit test.

4. Pseudorandom generator program

4.1 Macro definition

```
#define N 3 //rank N=3,4,5,6,7,8,9,10,11,12,13,14
#define RuleInitKey 110839188
#define RuleInitFullKey 134217727
#define E 5
#define Nd N*N*N*N*N
#include<stdio.h>
```

4.2 Variables definition

```
int s[N][N][N]={0},t[N][N][N]={0},i,j,k,count,cx;
int se[Nd]={0},ch,ecx=0,chJudge=N*N*N;//number of N in se array = E dimensional
long low=N*N*N,high=Nd;
int rule[3][3][3]={0},ruleJudge[27]={0};
unsigned long ruleKey=RuleInitKey,ruleKeyTemp=0;
int ic,jc,kc,icc,jcc,kcc;//near i j k
int LFSR[8]={0,0,1,0,1,1,1,1},shiftIN,shiftOUT,loop;
int nsi=0,ssi=0,wsj=0,esj=0,kup=0,kdn=0,x=1;
// Variables definition for mono test
int number1=0,number0=0;
// Variables definition for poker test
int n[16]={0},splitCounter=0,number=0,pokerCounter=0;
double sumNIsquare=0.0,pokerX=0.0;
// Variables definition for run test
int runNum[20000]={0},run[20]={0},runLoop,runCounter=1,run1Counter=0,run0Counter=0;
        FILE *fp;
```

4.3 Initialize the data and rule

```
//----------------init data--------------------------
if((fp=fopen("nn_data.txt","a+"))==NULL)
        printf("Can't open file!\n");
  fprintf(fp,"The %d dimensional array with %d depth\n",E,N);
//init the cube data
s[0][0][0]=1;
s[0][2][1]=1;
s[1][0][1]=1;
s[2][1][1]=1;
s[2][2][2]=1;
 //init the rule:  N dimen rule is  i j k sequecnce  using hex
// 110 100 110 110 100 010 110 010 100 =>69B 4594H=>1 1083 9188 D
 count=26; // [0..26]
```

```
ruleKeyTemp=ruleKey;
for(k=2;k>=0;k--)
        for(i=2;i>=0;i--)
                for(j=2;j>=0;j--)
                {
                        rule[i][j][k]=ruleKeyTemp&1;
                        ruleJudge[count]=rule[i][j][k];
                        count--;
                        ruleKeyTemp=ruleKeyTemp>>1;
                       // printf("rule[%d][%d][%d]=%d\t",i,j,k,rule[i][j][k]);
                }
fprintf(fp,"The rule is %ld\n",ruleKey);
for(count=0;count<27;count++)
        fprintf(fp,"%d ",ruleJudge[count]);
        fprintf(fp,"\n");
                //getchar();
```

4.4 N dimensional with N depth cube Using LFSR

```
for(count=0;count<=20000;count++)
{
// loop three count=20000
        //k i j means every element
        ch=N*N*N;
        for(k=0;k<=N-1;k++)
        {
                for(i=0;i<=N-1;i++)
                {
                        for(j=0;j<=N-1;j++)
                        {
//3 cipher Rule is 00101111(         north      south east kdown kup)=decimal Rule 47
//n Rule is 10101111(self center north  west south east kdown kup)=decimal Rule 175
//-----n dimensional-----------
/*
                                if(i-1<0) nsi=N-1; else nsi=i-1;
                                 if(i+1>N-1) ssi=0;  else ssi=i+1;
//------n dimensional------
                                if(j-1<0) wsj=N-1; else wsj=j-1;
                                        if(j+1>N-1) esj=0;  else esj=j+1;
                                if(k-1<0) kdn=N-1;
                                        else kdn=k-1;
                                if(k+1>N-1) kdn=0;  else kup=k+1
*/
 //----------loop  cube1--------------------
                                cx=0;
                                for(kc=-1;kc<=1;kc++)
                                        for(ic=-1;ic<=1;ic++)
```

```
                                                  for(jc=-1;jc<=1;jc++)
                                                  {
                                                          if(i+ic<0)  icc=N-1;
                                                          else if(i+ic>N-1) icc=0;
                                                             else icc=i+ic;
                                                          if(j+jc<0)  jcc=N-1;
                                                          else if(j+jc>N-1) jcc=0;
                                                             else jcc=j+jc;
                                                          if(k+kc<0)  kcc=N-1;
                                                          else if(k+kc>N-1) kcc=0;
                                                             else kcc=k+kc;
                                                          if(ruleJudge[cx++]==1)
                                                  t[i][j][k]=t[i][j][k]^s[icc][jcc][kcc];
                                                  }
                                                          t[i][j][k]=x^t[i][j][k];
//printf("t[%d][%d][%d]=%d",i,j,k,t[i][j][k]);
                                                  //getchar();
 /*
t[i][j][k]=x^s[i][j][k]^s[nsi][j][k] ^ s[ssi][j][k]^s[i][wsj][k]^s[i][esj][k];
t[i][j][k]=t[i][j][k]^s[nsi][wsj][k]^s[nsi][esj][k]^s[ssi][wsj][k]^s[ssi][esj][k];
t[i][j][k]=t[i][j][k]^s[i][j][kup]^s[nsi][j][kup] ^ s[ssi][j][kup]^s[i][wsj][kup]^s[i][esj][kup];
t[i][j][k]=t[i][j][k]^s[nsi][wsj][kup]^s[nsi][esj][kup]^s[ssi][wsj][kup]^s[ssi][esj][kup];
t[i][j][k]=t[i][j][k]^s[i][j][kdn]^s[nsi][j][kdn] ^ s[ssi][j][kdn]^s[i][wsj][kdn]^s[i][esj][kdn];
t[i][j][k]=t[i][j][k]^s[nsi][wsj][kdn]^s[nsi][esj][kdn]^s[ssi][wsj][kdn]^s[ssi][esj][kdn];
*/
                                    s[i][j][k]=t[i][j][k];
//----------rotate cube-----------
//i<->j  j<->k i<->k
 //s[j][i][k]=s[i][j][k];
                                    s[k][j][i]=s[i][j][k];
                                    s[j][k][i]=s[i][j][k];
//---------------------- expend n dimensional to higher dimensional-----------------
                                    for(ecx=1;ecx<=E-1;ecx++)
                                    {
                                            if (ch>=low && ch<=high)
                                                    se[ch++]=s[i][j][k];
// n dimensional cube xor
//printf("ch=%d\tse[%d]=%d\ts[%d][%d][%d]=%d\n",ch,ch,se[ch],i,j,k,s[i][j][k]);
                                            if(ch%(chJudge/2)==0)
                                            {
                                                    s[i][j][k]=s[i][j][k]^se[ch];
//printf("ch=%d s[%d][%d][%d]=%d\n",ch,i,j,k,s[i][j][k]);
//getchar();//debug
                                            }
                                    }
//------n dimensional-------
```

```
//[j][k]=s[nsi][j][k] ^ s[ssi][j][k];
//printf("\t%d ",t[i][j][k]);
//if(j+1>N-1) esj=0;
//else   esj=j+1;
//t[i][j][k]=t[i][j][k] ^ s[i][esj][k];
//printf("%d ",t[i][j][k]);
 //(k-1<0) kdn=N-1;
//else kdn=k-1;
//t[i][j][k]=t[i][j][k] ^ t[i][j][kdn];
//printf("%d ",t[i][j][k]);
//if(k+1>N-1) kdn=0;
//else kup=k+1;
//t[i][j][k]=t[i][j][k] ^ t[i][j][kup];
//printf("\tt[%d,%d,%d]=%d",i,j,k,t[i][j][k]);
                    if(i==N/2&&j==N/2&&k==N/2)
                    { //LFSR
                         shiftIN=s[N/2][N/2][N/2];
                         shiftIN=shiftIN ^ LFSR[3];
                         shiftIN=shiftIN ^ LFSR[6];
                         shiftOUT=LFSR[7];
                         for(loop=7;loop>=1;loop--)
                              LFSR[loop]=LFSR[loop-1];
                         LFSR[0]=shiftIN;
//printf("\nshiftIN=%d\t shiftOUT=%d\n",shiftIN,shiftOUT);
//getchar();
```

4.5 Mono bit test program

```
//printf("%d \n",shiftOUT);
                         if(shiftOUT==0) number0++;
                         else number1++;
//poker test
                          splitCounter++;
                         if(splitCounter<=4)
number=number | (shiftOUT << (splitCounter-1));// binary bit shift left
                         else
                         {
//printf("number=%d",number);
//getchar();
                              n[number]++;
                              splitCounter=1;
                              number=0;
                    number=number+(shiftOUT << (splitCounter-1));
                         }
//0110111 run test
                         runNum[runCounter++]=shiftOUT;
                    }
```

```
                    }//end of j
//printf("%d ",j);// endline
                }// end of i
        }//end of k
//printf("\tch=%d",ch);
// printf("\t%d",count);
        for(k=0;k<=N-1;k++)
                for(i=0;i<=N-1;i++)
                        for(j=0;j<=N-1;j++)
                        {
                                s[i][j][k]=t[i][j][k];
                                t[i][j][k]=0;
                        }
//printf("\n");
//end of the array
}
fprintf(fp,"\nThe bit test including 0 and 1\n");
fprintf(fp,"bit test:number0=%d number1=%d\n",number0,number1);
```

4.6 Poker test program

```
fprintf(fp,"\nThe pokertest pass  1.03<x<57.4 \n");
for(pokerCounter=0;pokerCounter<=15;pokerCounter++)
{
        fprintf(fp,"n[%d]=%d\n",pokerCounter,n[pokerCounter]);
        sumNIsquare=sumNIsquare+n[pokerCounter]*n[pokerCounter] ;
}
fprintf(fp,"sumNIsquare=%f\n",sumNIsquare);
pokerX=(16.0*sumNIsquare)/5000.0-5000.0;
if(pokerX>1.03 && pokerX<57.4)
        fprintf(fp,"pokerX=%f Passes the Poker Test\n",pokerX);
else
        fprintf(fp,"pokerX=%f Failure the Poker Test\n",pokerX);
```

4.7 Run test program

```
fprintf(fp,"\n The runtest including 0 and 1\n");
for(runLoop=0;runLoop<20000;runLoop++)
if(runNum[runLoop+1]!=runNum[runLoop])
        {
                run[runCounter]++;
                runCounter=1;
        }
        else
                runCounter++;
for(runLoop=1;runLoop<20;runLoop++)
        fprintf(fp,"01 run[%d]=%d\n",runLoop,run[runLoop]);
//------------runTest ------------1
```

```
for(runLoop=1;runLoop<20;runLoop++)
          run[runLoop]=0;
for(runLoop=0;runLoop<20000;runLoop++)

          if(runNum[runLoop]==1)
          {
                    run1Counter++;
                    run0Counter=0;

          }
          else
          {
                    run0Counter++;
                    if(run0Counter==1)
                    {
                              run[run1Counter]++;
                              run1Counter=0;
                    }
          }
for(runLoop=1;runLoop<20;runLoop++)
          fprintf(fp,"1 run[%d]=%d\n",runLoop,run[runLoop]);
//------------runTest--------------- 0
for(runLoop=1;runLoop<20;runLoop++)
          run[runLoop]=0;
for(runLoop=0;runLoop<20000;runLoop++)

          if(runNum[runLoop]==0)
          {
                    run1Counter++;
                    run0Counter=0;
          }
          else
          {
                    run0Counter++;
                    if(run0Counter==1)
                    {
                              run[run1Counter]++;
                              run1Counter=0;
                    }
          }
for(runLoop=1;runLoop<20;runLoop++)
          fprintf(fp,"0 run[%d]=%d\n",runLoop,run[runLoop]);
fprintf(fp,"\n--------------end--------------\n");
return 0;
}
```

5. Pseudorandom bit tests

5.1 LFSR pseudorandom bit test

There are several ways to prove whether the bit stream has the characteristics expected of a random set of bits. The FIPS 140-1 test suite includes tests, which are in the collection of National Institute of Standards and Technology (NIST).The FIPS 140-1 includes three tests: mono test, poker test and runs test. Three tests suite accept 20,000 bits from a random source.

The first test is mono bit test, which verifies that the number of 1's and 0's are almost equal; The process counts the number of 1's: if it is within the range 9654-10,346, then the bit stream passes the mono bit test[1].

We initial LFSR with 0010 1111 set in which the shift XOR function among the Shift in bit, cell 3 and cell 6.The mono test result is:Cycle = 20000;Ones bits Count = 10060;Passes the One bits Count Test (Mono bit test)

The second test is poker test. Passing the mono bit test does not guarantee that a bit stream is truly random. Poker test is another specified test by FIPS 140-1. For the poker test, the 20,000 bits are divided into 4-bit segments. Each 4-bit segment represents a decimal number between 0 and 15. A truly random sequence of bits should result in a random distribution of the numbers 0-15.Let be the number of occurrences of a number . is the number of 4-bit 0110.These values are substituted into:

$$X = \frac{16}{5000}\sum_{i=0}^{15} n^2 - 5000 \tag{6}$$

The poker test is passed if 1.03<X<57.4.The LFSR poker test result is:

Cycle = 20000;The number of occurrences of number from 0 to 15 is as follows set:{275, 317, 316, 314, 313, 315, 314, 315, 314, 316, 313, 314, 318, 316, 315, 315}

X=4.8896 ;1.03<X<57.4, Passes the poker test.

A third randomness test is called the runs test. A run is a consecutive sequence of either 1's or 0's.In a truly random-bit stream, there should be a random distribution so maximal-length runs. If the number of each run falls within the following guidelines, then the sequence passes the test. The required interval is illustrated in Table 1.

Length	Required Interval and Run Test Result					
	1	2	3	4	5	6+
min interval	2267	1079	502	223	90	90
gaps count	2517	1261	630	315	157	158
runs count	2519	1259	630	315	157	158
max interval	2733	1421	748	402	223	223

Table 1. Required interval of runs test

Passes the run gap test [7].

5.2 Pseudorandom bits test of multi- dimensional CA and LFSR algorithm

We initial 3-dimensional cellular automation LFSR. CA is initialized to three-dimensional array

s[i][j][k]={0};s[0][0][0]=1;s[0][2][1]=1;s[1][0][1]=1; s[2][1][1]=1; s[2][2][2]=1;
For example, each cell is assigned rule1:110839188 and rule2: 134217727. LFSR is 0010 1111 set in which the shift XOR function among the Shift in bit, cell 3, cell 6 and s[1][1][1] .The poker test is passed if 1.03<X<57.4.The Multi-dimensional CA LFSR algorithm mono test and poker test result is shown in table 2:

N=3 Rank	Mono Test (Num. of Bit 0)		Poker Test(Value of X)	
	rule1	rule2	rule1	rul2
3	10014	9994	4.37	1.32
4	9957	9969	5.27	7.11
5	9991	9956	13.40	8.33
6	9998	10054	4.50	17.24
7	10085	10096	9.42	9.64
8	10112	9944	14.71	16.14
9	9923	10083	11.97	10.04
10	10042	10010	10.07	8.476
11	10117	10001	19.67	10.25
12	9918	9895	17.72	6.25
13	10014	10077	20.04	15.78
14	10076	10158	10.65	14.72

Table 2. Poker test of three-dimensional and multi-rank CA algorithm

When changed dimensional and rank simultaneously, the algorithm can also pass the poker test as table 3 shows:

poker rank	N=4		N=5		N=6	
	rule1	rule2	rule1	rule2	rule1	rule2
3	12.66	1.75	17.20	1.06	4.58	6.46
4	16.07	18.29	15.20	25.69	5.82	11.37
5	14.59	13.92	18.11	15.97	10.51	10.28
6	10.37	12.85	7.57	13.54	12.45	22.02

Table 3. Poker test of multi-dimensional and multi-rank CA algorithm

All the poker X value is 1.03<X<57.4, passes the poker test. We can't draw other obvious character from the table. It seems that the result isn't apparently changed with the number of dimensional and rank. It implies that it is not necessary to increase the number of dimensional and rank if we want to get stream bit. Maybe a lower dimensional and rank CA is enough.

6. Discussion

According to the random bits test result, Multi-dimensional cellular automation (CA) linear feedback shift register (LFSR) passed three stream bit test. Three tests suite accept 20,000 bits from a random source. The first test is mono bit test, which verifies that the number of 1's and 0's are almost equal, the Multi-dimensional CA LFSR algorithm can create 1 bits and 0 bits, different rank from 3 to 14 of 3-dimensional CA LFSR algorithm can create bit stream. The difference between 0 bit and 1 bits is shown in Figure 5:

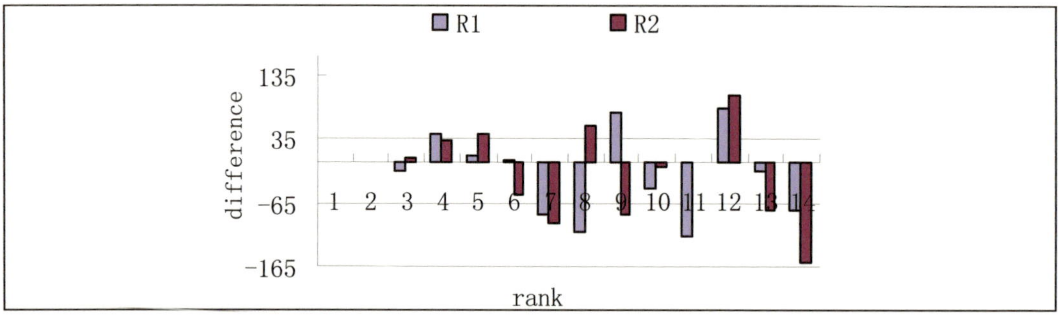

Fig. 5. Bits difference of multi-dimensional and multi-rank CA LFSR algorithm

According the figure, the bits difference can't be decreased by increasing 3-dimensional CA LFSR rank. That's means simple algorithm maybe better than complicated algorithm.
Multi-dimensional CA LFSR algorithm can also pass the poker test. The X value is between 1.03 and 57.4. When 3-dimensional CA LFSR increases its rank from 3 to 14, all the result can pass the poker test. The result is shown in Figure 6:

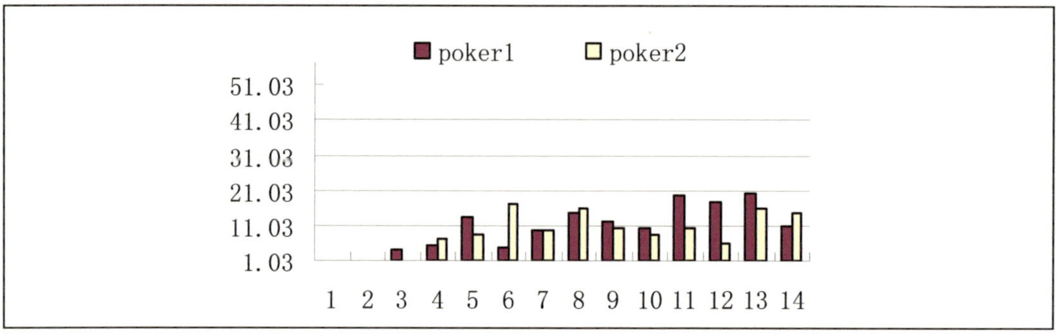

Fig. 6. Poker test of three-dimensional and multi rank CA LFSR algorithm

When increase the dimensional and rank at the same time. The result illustrates the algorithm can also pass the poker test shown in Figure 7:

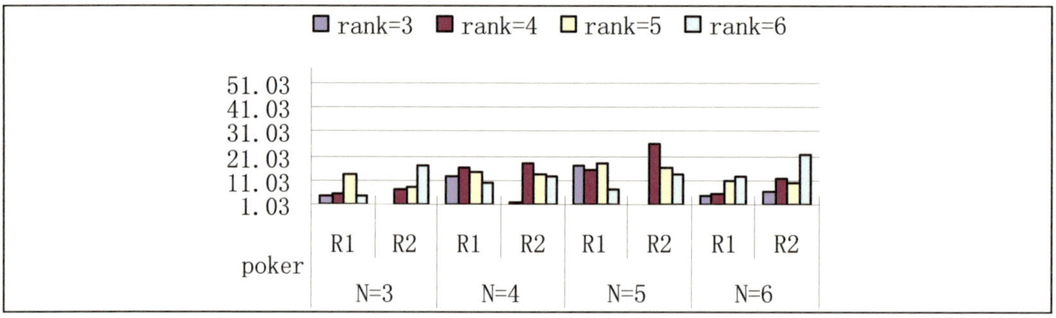

Fig. 7. Poker test of multi-dimensional and multi-rank CA LFSR algorithm

Compared with the Multi-dimensional CA LFSR and 3-dimensional CA LFSR, we can't find the obvious superiority by dimensional or rank increase. The Multi-dimensional CA LFSR algorithm can also pass the runs test, the average 1 bits and 0 bits pass the run and gaps test, the result fills in required interval almost same to the LFSR run gap test. The algorithm result is shown in Figure 8.

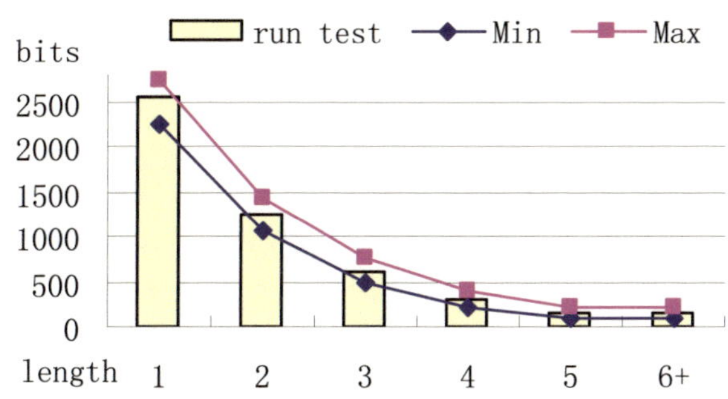

Fig. 8. Run gap test of multi-dimensional CA LFSR algorithm

The Multi-dimensional cellular automation (CA) linear feedback shift register (LFSR) algorithm combined cellular automation method and LFSR method to create random stream bit The design method can pass three FIPS 140-1 standard pseudorandom stream bit test and also can provide better pseudorandom key stream. The results illustrate it is feasible and efficient.

7. Acknowledgment

The paper is supported by the Shanghai Education Commission Innovation Foundation (11YZ192).

8. References

Chien-In & Henry C., Synthesis of configurable linear feedback shifter registers for detecting random-pattern-resistant faults, *ACM ISSS'01*, pp.203-208, Montreal, Quebec, Canada, October 2001. 1-3

Erik H. & Volkerink Subhasish M. Response compaction with any number of unknowns using a new LFSR architecture, *DAC 2005 ACM*, pp.117-122, Anaheim, California, USA. , June 13-17, 2005

Breukelaar R. ; Th. B. & Nutech, S. G. sing a genetic algorithm to evolve behavior in multi dimensional cellular automata, *GECCO' 05*, pp.107-114, Washington, DC, USA , June 25 - 29, 2005

Sheng-Uei G. ; Shu Z. & Marie, T. Q. 2-D CA variation with asymmetric neighborship for pseudorandom number generation", *IEEE Transactions on Computer-aided Design of Integrated Circuits and Systems* , pp. 378-388, March 2004

Nandi, S. ; Kar, B. K. & Chaudhuri, P.P. Theory and applications of cellular automata in cryptography, *IEEE Transactions on Computers*, pp.1346-1357, December 1994, VOL. 43, NO 12

Yong, W. ; Xinming, G. & YuW. Three-dimensional cellular automation LFSR algorithm, *The Sixth International Workshop for Applied PKC*，pp.188-194, Perth, Australia, 3-4, December 2007

Richard J.S. *Classical and Contemporary Cryptology*, The Tsinghua Press, China, July.2005.

15

An Improved PRNG Based on the Hybrid between One- and Two- Dimensional Cellular Automata

Sang-Ho Shin[1] and Kee-Young Yoo[2]
[1]*School of Electronic Engineering and Computer Science, Kyungpook National University Gyengdaejeongmunro 67, Buk-Gu, Daegu, 702-701*
[2]*School of Computer Science and Engineering, Kyungpook National University Gyengdaejeongmunro 67, Buk-Gu, Daegu, 702-701*
South Korea

1. Introduction

Cellular automata (CA) were initiated in the early 1950s to develop complex structures of capable self-reproduction and self-repair. Since then many researchers have taken attend in the study of CA. Initially, CA concept was first introduced by von Neumann von Neumann (1966) for the proposal of modeling biological self-reproduction. His primary interest was to derive a computationally universal cellular space with self-reproduction configurations. Afterward, a new phase of activities was started by Wolfram Wolfram (1983; 1984), who pioneered the investigation of CA as a mathematical model for self-organizing statistical systems. Wolfram was proved that the randomness of the patterns generated by maximum-length CA is significantly better than other widely used methods, such as linear feedback shift registers. The intensive interest in this field can be attributed to the phenomenal growth of the VLSI technology that permits cost-effective realization of the simple structure of local-neighborhood CA Wolfram (1986).
The PRNGs based on CA have been studied for the last decade and a variety of CA PRNGs have been proposed Guan & Tan (Jul. 2004); Guan & Zhang (Feb. 2003); Seredynski et al. (2004); Tan & Guan (2007); Xuelong et al. (Oct. 2005). Recent interest has been focused on the two-dimensional (2-D) CA PRNGs with genetic algorithm Chowdhury et al. (1993); Guan et al. (2004); Quieta & Guan (2005); Tomassini et al. (2000), since, statistically, the point has been established that the quality of randomness of a 2-D CA is significantly better than a 1-D CA.
In this paper, an efficient PRNG based on hybrid between one-dimension (1-D) and two-dimension (2-D) CA is proposed. In the phase of the evolution of 2-D CA cells, the proposed CA PRNG is based on von Neumann neighborhood, in that this method refers to the five cells and new control values (rule decision input value & linear control input value) to decide a rule. In the phase of the evolution of 1-D CA cells, on the other hand, <90, 150> rule combination is used because this rule combination is better than the others Hortensius et al. (1989). In the meantime, the proposed CA PRNG is compared with previous works Guan et al. (2004); Tomassini et al. (2000) to check the quality of randomness. The proposed CA PRNG could generate a good quality of randomness because the proposed CA PRNG is better than

Neighborhood state	111	110	101	100	011	010	001	000	rule number
Next state	0	1	0	1	1	0	1	0	90
Next state	0	0	0	1	1	1	1	0	30
Next state	1	0	0	1	0	1	1	0	150
Next state	1	1	0	0	1	0	1	0	202

Table 1. The examples of the state transition for rules with 2-state, 3-neighborhood

Rule number	Combination Logic gate
$30(= 2^4 + 2^3 + 2^2 + 2^1)$	$s_{i-1}(t) \oplus (s_i(t) \vee s_{i-1}(t))$
$90(= 2^6 + 2^4 + 2^3 + 2^1)$	$s_{i-1}(t) \oplus s_{i+1}(t)$
$150(= 2^7 + 2^4 + 2^2 + 2^1)$	$s_{i-1}(t) \oplus s_i(t) \oplus s_{i+1}(t)$
$202(= 2^7 + 2^6 + 2^3 + 2^1)$	$s_{i-1}(t) \wedge (s_i(t) \oplus s_{i+1}(t))$

where $\oplus$, $\vee$ and $\wedge$ are the Boolean operations XOR, OR and AND, respectively.

Table 2. The combination logic gates correspond with rule numbers

the previous works and passed by the ENT Walker (Oct., 1998) and DIEHARD Marsaglia (1998) test suite.
The rest of this paper is organized as follows. In Section 2, related work is briefly reviewed. The hybrid CA PRNG is proposed in Section 3. Section 4 analyze the proposed CA PRNG. Section 5 shows the experimental results. Section 6 provides a conclusion.

2. The related works

In this section, the concepts of cellular automata will be introduced.

2.1 One-dimension CA

A CA is a dynamical system in which space and time are discrete. A CA consists of an array of cells, each of which can be in one of a finite number of possible states, updated synchronously in discrete time steps, according to a local identical interaction, a rule. The next state of a cell is assumed to depend on itself and on its neighbors. The cells evolve in discrete time steps according to some deterministic rule that depends only on local neighbors.
The next-state function for a three-neighborhood CA cell in one-dimension can be expressed as following equation (1):

$$s_i(t+1) = f(s_{i-1}(t), s_i(t), s_{i+1}(t)) \tag{1}$$

where f denotes the local function realized with a combinational logic, such as AND, OR, XOR, and NOT, i is the position of an individual in the one-dimensional array of the cell, t is the tth time step, $s_i(t)$ is the output state of the ith cell at the tth time step, and $s_i(t+1)$ is the output state of the ith cell at the $(t+1)$th time step.
In a two-state, three-neighborhood CA there can be a total of 2^3 (from 000 to 111) distinct neighborhood configurations. For such a CA there can be a total of $2^{2^3} (= 256)$ distinct mappings from all these neighborhood configurations to the next state. Each mapping is called a rule of CA. If the next-state function of a cell is expressed, then the decimal equivalent of the output is conventionally called the rule number for the cell Wolfram (1986).

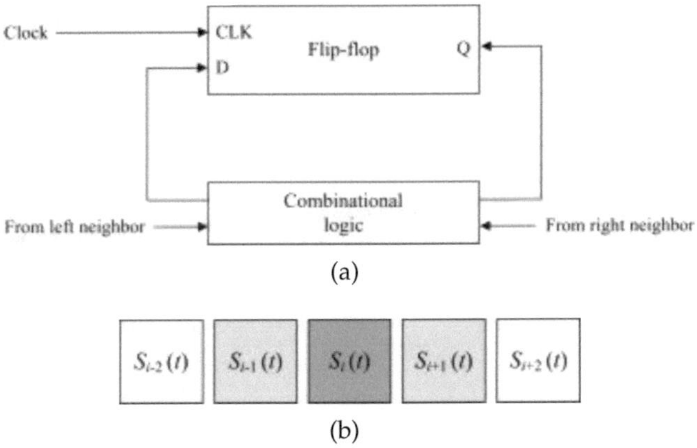

Fig. 1. A CA cell structures: (a) a 2-state, 3-neighborhood CA cell, (b) an example of CA cells with 3-neighborhood in 1-D

Table 1 expresses the state transition for arbitrary rules with 2-state, 3-neighborhood. In Table 1, the top row gives all eight possible states of the three neighboring cells (the left, right neighbor of the *i*th cell, the *i*th cell itself) at the time *t*. The second to fifth rows give the corresponding states of the *i*th cell at time $t+1$ for four CA rules. Table 2 shows that the combination logic gates correspond with rule numbers. In Table 2, rule numbers consist of sum which is converted decimal number of neighborhood states from 111(=MSB) to 000(=LSB). For rule 30, the next state of $111(=2^7)$, $110(=2^6)$, $101(=2^5)$, $100(=2^4)$, $011(=2^3)$, $010(=2^2)$, $001(=2^1)$ and $000(=2^0)$ are 0, 0, 0, 1, 1, 1, 1 and 0, respectively. Hence, $2^7 \times 0 + 2^6 \times 0 + 2^5 \times 0 + 2^4 \times 1 + 2^3 \times 1 + 2^2 \times 1 + 2^1 \times 1 + 2^0 \times 0 = 30$.

A CA is said to be a *Null Boundary CA* (NBCA) if the left (or right) neighbor of the leftmost (or rightmost) terminal cell is connected to the logic 0-state, or a *Periodic Boundary CA* (PBCA) if the extreme cells are adjacent to each other. Figure 2 shows the features of each boundary CA.

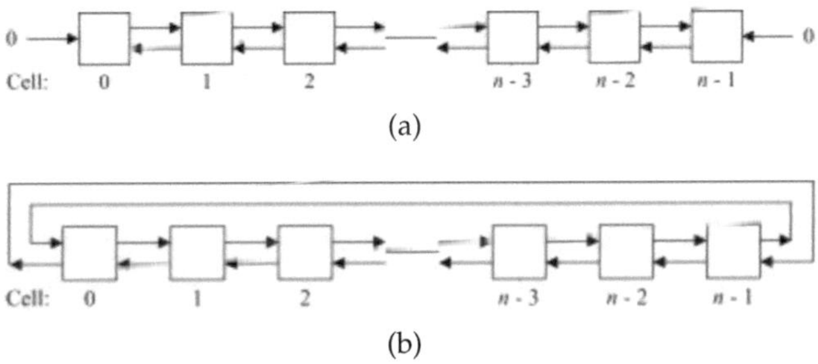

Fig. 2. The features of each boundary CA: (a) Null boundary CA, (b) Periodic boundary CA

2.2 Two-dimension CA

A two-dimension (2-D) CA is a generalization of a 1-D CA, where the cells are arranged in a two-dimensional grid with connections among the neighboring cells. For a 2-D CA, types of cellular neighborhoods are usually considered: five cells, consisting of one cell along with its four immediate non-diagonal neighbors (also known as the von Neumann neighborhood); and nine cells, consisting of one cell along with its eight surrounding neighbors (also known as the Moore neighborhood). In this paper, a type of von Neumann neighborhood is used which considers five-neighborhoods that these consist of *self*, *top*, *bottom*, *left* and *right*.

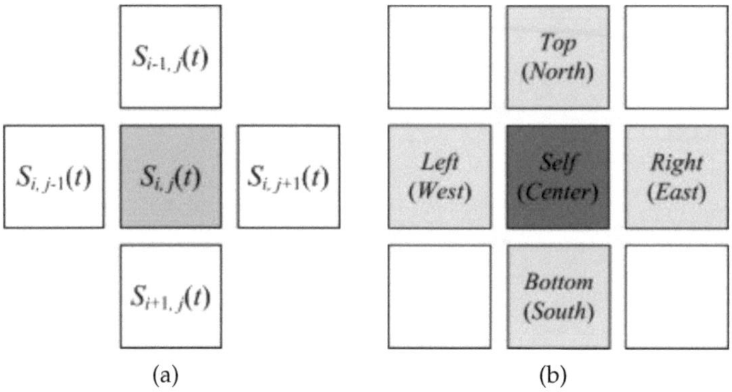

Fig. 3. The geometric representation of the von Neumann neighborhood.

Figure 3 shows the type of von Neumann neighborhood with a five-neighborhood dependency.
The next state $s_{i,j}(t+1)$ of a 2-D CA is given by

$$s_{i,j}(t+1) = f(s_{i-1,j}(t), s_{i,j-1}(t), s_{i,j}(t), s_{i,j+1}(t), s_{i+1,j}(t)). \tag{2}$$

Since f is a Boolean function of five variables, there are $2^5 = 32$ distinct neighborhood configurations. Hence to express a transition rule of a 2-D CA in a manner similar to a 1-D CA, 32-bits are considered which is almost impossible to manage practically.

2.3 The previous works

In this section, previous CA PRNGs are described. Tomassini et al. have been proposed 2-D CA PRNG based on an 8×8 structure Tomassini et al. (2000) and Guan et al. have proposed 2-D CA PRNGs based on asymmetric neighborhood Guan et al. (2004). In the final phase, these PRNGs are constructed by using the evolutional method which is called a genetic algorithm Steeb (2001). A genetic algorithm is an iterative procedure that involves a constant-size population of individuals, each one represented by a finite string of symbols (known as the genome), encoding a possible solution in a given problem space. A genetic algorithm has operators that are a crossover, and mutation and a has fitness function. Iterating this procedure, the genetic algorithm may eventually find an acceptable solution. Hence, a genetic algorithm provides a high randomness quality, but has problems that include high time complexity for the evolution of CA cells.
In Tomassini et al.'s PRNG Tomassini et al. (2000), every cell of the evolving CA assigns a fitness function value and rule number which decides the result of the evolved cell by the fitness function value. Also, to raise the quality of randomness, they used a genetic algorithm. Guan et al.'s PRNGs Guan et al. (2004) are constructed from a asymmetric neighborhood (5×10) CA structure for reducing the number of cells. Similarly, they used a genetic algorithm. To evaluate the randomness quality of the proposed CA PRNG, in this paper, the sequence of the proposed PRNG (PRNS) will be compared with above two CA PRNS.

Cells		XOR logic
0	0	0
0	1	1
1	0	1
1	1	0

Table 3. The result of operation of XOR logic for two cells

3. The proposed hybrid CA PRNG

In this section, the proposed scheme is explained.

3.1 The method of deciding the rules for 1-D & 2-D

First of all, the rule of CA cell for 2-D are considered. A hybrid CA PRNG based on the von Neumann neighborhood method is proposed. The number of rules in this method is 2^{32} because there are 32 distinct neighborhood configurations. In this paper, the XOR logic is considered because the frequencies of occurrence of 0 for the operation of XOR is 2, in four cases given in the Table 2. From this fact, it can be guessed that the binomial distribution for the probability of XOR is $X \sim B(n, \frac{1}{2})$, where n is independent Bernoulli trials. That is, the expected value of the binomial distribution of the frequencies of occurrence of 0 for a XOR is decided by n.

Let $s_{i,j}(t)$ be a state value of the cell at row i, column j, and time t. Its state value at the next step, $s_{i,j}(t+1)$ is then computed as the following equation (3):

$$\begin{aligned} s_{i,j}(t+1) = X \oplus (C \wedge s_{i,j}(t)) \\ \oplus (N \wedge s_{i-1,j}(t)) \oplus (W \wedge s_{i,j-1}(t)) \oplus (E \wedge s_{i,j+1}(t)) \oplus (S \wedge s_{i+1,j}(t)) \end{aligned} \quad (3)$$

where $\oplus$ and $\wedge$ are the Boolean operations XOR and AND, respectively. X, C (center), N (north), S (south), W (west), and E (east) are binary variables (that is, 0 or 1). C, N, S, W, and E denote whether the respective neighboring cell state is taken into account (a value of 1) or not (a value of 0). The binary variable X distinguishes between linear (X = 0) and nonlinear (X = 1) rules. For example, rule 14 (001110), that is, $(X||C||N||W||E||S)$ is represented as follows :

$$s_{i,j}(t+1) = s_{i-1,j}(t) \oplus s_{i,j-1}(t) \oplus s_{i+1,j}(t).$$

Next, the rule of CA cell for 1-D with 2-state, 3-neighborhood is considered. A rule is chosen which is <90, 150> in this paper. The logic of this rules consists of XOR which has $X \sim B(n, \frac{1}{2})$. Moreover, the rule combination of <90, 150> has been proved to have a high randomness quality by Hortensius et al.'s paper Hortensius et al. (1989). Figure 4 shows the structure of rule <90, 150> for a cell in 1-D CA.

The Boundary is considered. Generally, a PBCA is frequently applied, resulting in a circular grid for 1-D case and in a doughnut for the 2-D case. A NBCA can also be used, in which the grid is surrounded by an outer layer of cells of zero. In this paper, a PBCA is chosen to raise the quality of randomness.

3.2 Hybrid between 1-D and 2-D CA PRNG

Figure 4, 5 and 6 show the process & structure of the proposed CA PRNG, respectively. One round consists of four phases. The process step-by-step is summarized as follows.

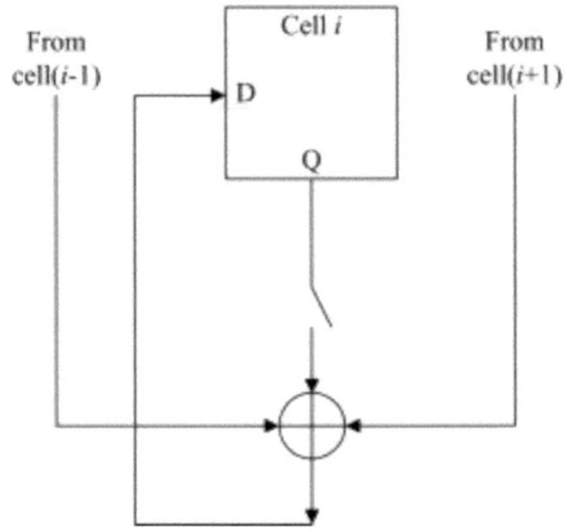

Fig. 4. The structure of rule <90, 150>

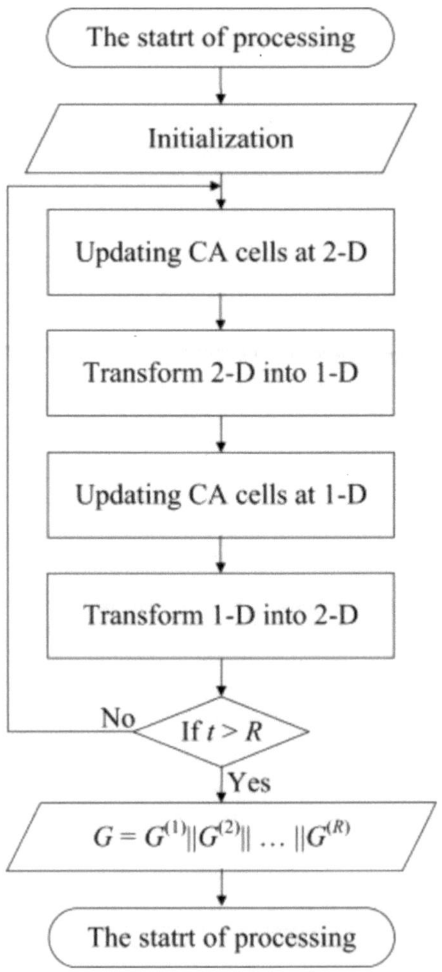

Fig. 5. The process of the proposed CA PRNG

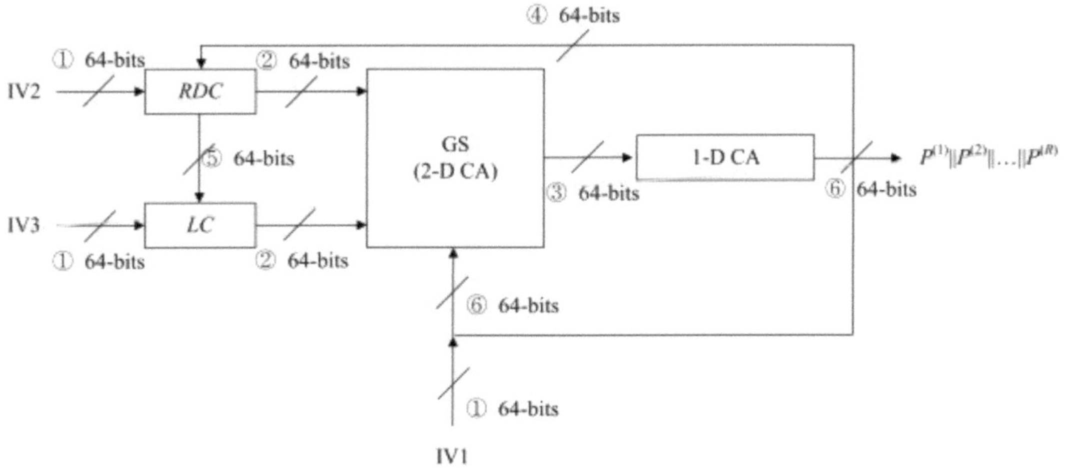

Fig. 6. The structure of the proposed CA PRNG

3.2.1 Initialization

The 192-bit initial seed is randomly generated. The seed, then, divides into three parts, from 0th to 63th (=IV_1), from 64th to 127th (=IV_2) and from 128th to $final$ bit (=IV_3). The initial values IV_1, IV_2, and IV_3 are stored in $GS^{(0)}$ (GS: Global state, consists of the 8×8 2-D CA cells and the first row is from 0th to 7th, the second row is from 8th to 14th, ... , the final row is from 57th to 63th), $RDC^{(0)}$ (rule decision control unit, consists of 64-bit 1-D CA cells) and $LC^{(0)}$ (linear control unit, consists of 8×8 2-D CA cells and the first row is from 0th to 7th, the second row is from 8th to 14th, ... , the final row is from 57th to 63th), respectively.

3.2.2 Updating at 2-D

The rule $r_{i,j}(t)$ is decided by $RDC^{(t)}$ which is decided by self, left 2 bits, and right 2 bits (that is, $s_{i-2}(t)$, $s_{i-1}(t)$, $s_i(t)$, $s_{i+1}(t)$, and $s_{i+2}(t)$ at t-th time step). Then, generate the next state $GS^{(t+1)}$ by $r_{i,j}$, $LC^{(t)}$, and $GS^{(t)}$ and represents the equation (4):

$$GS^{(t+1)} = f(r_{i,j}, LC^{(t)}, GS^{(t)}), \tag{4}$$

where R is a repeating counter for producing PRNS of a demanded cycle length, $0 \le t \le R$, $0 \le i,j \le 7$.

3.2.3 Transform 2-D into 1-D

The generated state $GS^{(t+1)}$ transforms 2-D into 1-D because of applies to the 1-D CA rule <150,90>. The method is that each row in $GS^{(t+1)}$ concatenates 64-bits stream as in the following equation (concatenation is denoted "||") (5):

$$TGS^{(t+1)} = \bigcup_{i=0,j=0}^{7} s_{i,j}(t+1) = s_{0,0}(t+1)||s_{0,1}(t+1)||...||s_{7,7}(t+1), \tag{5}$$

where $s_{i,j}(t+1)$ indicates each cell in $GS^{(t+1)}$ and $TGS^{(t+1)}$ (TGS: Transformed GS) indicates transform 2-D into 1-D in $GS^{(t+1)}$.

$s_{i-1}(t)$	$s_i(t)$	$s_{i+1}(t)$	rule 90	rule 150
0	0	0	0	0
0	0	1	1	1
0	1	0	0	1
0	1	1	1	0
1	0	0	1	1
1	0	1	0	0
1	1	0	1	0
1	1	1	0	1

Table 4. The results of the operation of rule 90 & rule 150 for three cells in 1-D

3.2.4 Updating at 1-D

In order to raise the quality of randomness, the combination <90, 150> is used. This rule provides a high randomness quality Hortensius et al. (1989). This method uses the following equation (6):

$$ATGS^{(t+1)} = f_{<90,150>}(s_{i-1}(t+1),\, s_i(t+1),\, s_{i+1}(t+1)), \tag{6}$$

where $s_i(t+1)$ is cell at $TGS^{(t+1)}$ in 1-D, $ATGS^{(t+1)}$ is applied to the $TGS^{(t+1)}$ by function f based on rule 90 and 150.

3.2.5 Transform 1-D into 2-D

The updated state transforms 1-D into 2-D because of the application of the 2-D rule. The 64-bit streams are divided into each row by modulo 8 as the following equation (7):

$$GS^{(t+1)} = \bigcup_{i=0,j=0}^{7} s_{i,j}(t+1), \tag{7}$$

where $s_{i,j}(t+1) = s_i(t+1)$, i is that values of 0~7, 8~15,..., 57~63 replace 0, 1,..., 7, respectively. And $j = i \pmod 8$, $(0 \leq i \leq 63)$ in 1-D CA state. Then, RDC and LC replace the new values. The method is represented as the following equation.

$$\begin{aligned} LC^{(t+1)} &= RDC^{(t)} \oplus LC^{(t)}, \\ RDC^{(t+1)} &= GS^{(t)} \oplus GS^{(t+1)}_{(updated\,at\,1-DCA)}. \end{aligned} \tag{8}$$

Lastly, t is increased by 1. If t is greater than R, the phase is finished. Otherwise, go back to the beginning of the 2-D phase.

4. Analysis

In this section, the high quality of randomness of the hybrid CA PRNG is proved. The proposed CA PRNG was evolved by rule <90, 150> in 1-D. Abovementioned rule 90 & 150 consist of combinations of XOR logic, that is, $s_{i-1}(t) \oplus s_{i+1}(t)$ & $s_{i-1}(t) \oplus s_i(t) \oplus s_{i+1}(t)$, respectively. The frequencies of occurrence of 0 or 1 for operation of rule 90 or rule 150 is 4, in eight cases in Table 4. Table 4 shows the results of the operation of a rule 90 & a rule 150 for three cells which are $s_{i-1}(t)$, $s_i(t)$ and $s_{i+1}(t)$. Hence, $E(X)$ (expectation value) of the binomial distribution for a rule 90 or a rule 150 is $\frac{n}{2}$, where n is the number of evolutions in

X	$s_{i-1,j}(t)$	$s_{i,j-1}(t)$	$s_{i,j}(t)$	$s_{i,j+1}(t)$	$s_{i+1,j}(t)$	XOR logic
0	0	0	0	0	0	0
0	0	0	0	0	1	1
0	0	0	0	1	0	1
0	0	0	0	1	1	0
	⋮		⋮		⋮	⋮
1	1	1	1	1	0	1
1	1	1	1	1	1	0

Table 5. The results of the rule operation of all case for six cells in 2-D

Test No.	Test Name	The average value		
		Tomassini et al.	Guan et al.	Proposed
1	Entropy (Close to 8.0)	7.99971	7.99983	7.99991
2	Chi-square (Close to 1.0)	0.989412	0.992002	0.999283
3	SCC (Close to 0.0)	0.000227	0.000171	0.000062

Table 6. The average values of ENT test

1-D. Therefore, the meaning of this proposition shows that rule 90 & rule 150 provide a high quality randomness in terms of 1-D CA PRNG.

Next, the rules of CA cell for 2-D are considered. The proposed CA PRNG used von Neumann neighborhood method and evolved by $RDC^{(t)}$ and $LC^{(t)}$ for next state. $RDC^{(t)}$ consists of five cells ($s_{i-1,j}(t)$, $s_{i,j-1}(t)$, $s_{i,j}(t)$, $s_{i,j+1}(t)$ and $s_{i+1,j}(t)$) and combinations of XOR logic. Hence, the rule of 2-D CA cell consists of 1 bit for linear control bit, 5 bits for rule decision control and combinations of XOR logic, and expresses as equation (3). Table 5 shows the results of the rule operation of all case for six cells in 2-D. Meanwhile, a rule 0 and a rule 128 are not consider in the proposed CA PRNG because the occurrence rate of these rules are very few. Hence, $E(X)$ (expectation value) of the binomial distribution for the rule of 2-D CA cell is $\frac{n}{2}$, where n is the number of evolutions in 2-D. Similarly, the meaning of this proposition shows that provide a high quality randomness in terms of 1-D CA PRNG.

5. Experimental results

In this section, the efficiency of the hybrid CA PRNG is analyzed. To analyze, ENT Walker (Oct., 1998) and DIEHARD Marsaglia (1998) test suites are used. ENT test is useful for evaluating pseudorandom number generators for encryption and statistical sampling applications, compression algorithms, and other applications where the information density of a file is of interest Walker (Oct., 1998). ENT test is a collective term for three tests which are the Entropy test, Chi-square test, and Serial correlation coefficient (SCC) test.

The DIEHARD test suite is important because it seems to be the most powerful and difficult test suite to pass. This test consists of 18 different and independent statistical tests. The result of each test is called p-value. Most of the tests return a p-value in DIEHARD, which should be uniform if the input file contains truly independent random bits. For any given test, a smaller p-value means a better result.

The proposed CA PRNG produces a 64-bit output sequence at each round. The DIEHARD test suite requires a minimum of 10 MB of random number sequences Marsaglia (1998).

Test No.	Test Name	The results of tests (Pass or Fail)			
		Shift register	Tomassini et al.	Guan et al.	Proposed
1	Birthday Spacing	Pass	Pass	Pass	Pass
2	Over. 5-Per.	Pass	Fail	Fail	Pass
3	Binary Rank 31×31	Pass	Pass	Pass	Pass
4	Binary Rank 32×32	Fail	Pass	Pass	Pass
5	Binary Rank 6×8	Pass	Pass	Pass	Pass
6	Bitstream	Pass	Pass	Pass	Pass
7	OPSO	Pass	Pass	Pass	Pass
8	OQSO	Pass	Fail	Fail	Pass
9	DNA	Pass	Pass	Pass	Pass
10	Count-The-1's 01	Fail	Fail	Pass	Pass
11	Count-The-1's 02	Fail	Pass	Fail	Pass
12	Parking Lot	Pass	Pass	Pass	Pass
13	Minimum Distance	Pass	Pass	Pass	Pass
14	3DS Spheres	Pass	Pass	Pass	Pass
15	Squeeze	Pass	Pass	Pass	Pass
16	Overlapping Sums	Pass	Pass	Pass	Pass
17	Runs	Fail	Fail	Pass	Pass
18	Craps	Pass	Pass	Pass	Pass

Table 7. The results of DIEHARD test in p-value pass rate $\geq$ 90% for PBCA

Therefore, the proposed PRNG needs $(10^7 \times 8) \div 64$ time steps for the DIEHARD test. On the other hand, the ENT test suite requires fewer numbers, but the test is executed with the same 10 MB sequence for convenience and the next DIEHARD test. A total of 100 experiments are performed for the ENT and DIEHARD test suite. Table 6 and 7 show the average values of ENT test and the results of DIEHARD test. A pass is considered when all the p-values are passed by more than 90% at the 0.05 level. As the results show in Tables, it is obvious that the quality of randomness of the proposed scheme is better than other different scheme. Additionally, we have performed the boundary CA tests for 1-D & 2-D, and the results of these tests show Table 8 & 9. In Table 8, PB and NB indicate PBCA and NBCA, respectively. The randomness quality of the rule 90 & 150 (=<90, 150>) are better than rule 30, 45. Also, The randomness quality of the PBCA is better than the NBCA. Similarly, The randomness quality of the PBCA is better than the NBCA in 2-D.

6. Conclusion

In this paper, an efficient PRNG was proposed based on the hybrid between 1-D and 2-D CA. To better randomness quality, the *RDC* and the *LC* units were used. As a result, the various types of von Neumann neighborhood and $<90, 150>$ rule combination provide few correlation coefficients for each cell in state $GS^{(t)}$ and a high randomness quality by ENT and DIEHARD test suites (average pass rate more than 90% at the 0.05 level).

7. Acknowledgments

We would like to thank the anonymous reviewers for their helpful comments in improving our manuscript. This research was supported by 2nd Brain Korea 21 Project in 2010 and Basic

Test No.	Test Name	The results of tests (Pass or Fail)			
		rule 30(PB)	rule 45(PB)	<90, 150>(PB)	<90, 150>(NB)
1	Birthday Spacing	Pass	Pass	Pass	Pass
2	Over. 5-Per.	Pass	Pass	Pass	Pass
3	Binary Rank 31×31	Pass	Pass	Pass	Pass
4	Binary Rank 32×32	Pass	Pass	Pass	Pass
5	Binary Rank 6×8	Pass	Pass	Pass	Pass
6	Bitstream	Pass	Pass	Pass	Pass
7	OPSO	Fail	Fail	Pass	Pass
8	OQSO	Fail	Fail	Pass	Fail
9	DNA	Pass	Fail	Pass	Fail
10	Count-The-1's 01	Fail	Fail	Pass	Pass
11	Count-The-1's 02	Fail	Fail	Pass	Pass
12	Parking Lot	Pass	Pass	Pass	Pass
13	Minimum Distance	Pass	Pass	Pass	Pass
14	3DS Spheres	Pass	Fail	Pass	Fail
15	Squeeze	Pass	Fail	Pass	Pass
16	Overlapping Sums	Fail	Pass	Pass	Pass
17	Runs	Pass	Fail	Pass	Pass
18	Craps	Pass	Pass	Pass	Pass

Table 8. The results of DIEHARD test in p-value pass rate $\geq$ 90% for rule 90, 150, and<90, 150> with PBCA(PB) & NBCA(NB) in 1-D

Test No.	Test Name	The results of tests (Pass or Fail)			
		U,PB	NU,PB	U,NB	NU, NB
1	Birthday Spacing	Pass	Pass	Pass	Pass
2	Over. 5-Per.	Pass	Pass	Pass	Pass
3	Binary Rank 31×31	Pass	Pass	Pass	Fail
4	Binary Rank 32×32	Pass	Pass	Fail	Fail
5	Binary Rank 6×8	Pass	Pass	Pass	Fail
6	Bitstream	Pass	Pass	Pass	Pass
7	OPSO	Pass	Pass	Pass	Pass
8	OQSO	Pass	Fail	Fail	Fail
9	DNA	Pass	Pass	Fail	Fail
10	Count-The-1's 01	Pass	Pass	Pass	Pass
11	Count-The-1's 02	Pass	Pass	Pass	Pass
12	Parking Lot	Pass	Pass	Pass	Pass
13	Minimum Distance	Pass	Pass	Pass	Pass
14	3DS Spheres	Pass	Fail	Pass	Fail
15	Squeeze	Pass	Pass	Pass	Pass
16	Overlapping Sums	Pass	Pass	Pass	Pass
17	Runs	Pass	Pass	Pass	Pass
18	Craps	Pass	Pass	Pass	Pass

Table 9. The results of DIEHARD test in p-value pass rate $\geq$ 90% for uniform(U) and nonuniform(NU) 2-D CA with PBCA(PB) & NBCA(NB)

Science Research Program through the National Research Foundation of Korea(NRF) funded by the Ministry of Education, Science and Technology (No. 2010-0011968).

8. References

Chowdhury, D. R., Subbarao, P. & Chaudhuri, P. P. (1993). Characterization of Two Dimensional Cellular Automata Using Matrix Algebra, *Information Sciences* 71: 289–314.

Guan, S.-U. & Tan, S. K. (Jul. 2004). Pseudorandom Number Generation With Self-Programmable Cellular Automata, *IEEE Transctions on Computer-Aided Design of Integrated Circuits and Systems* 23(7): 1095–1101.

Guan, S.-U. & Zhang, S. (Feb. 2003). An Evolutionary Approach to the Design of Controllable Cellular Automata Structure for Random Number Generatio, *IEEE Transctions on Evolutionary Computation* 7(1): 23–36.

Guan, S.-U., Zhang, S. & Quieta, M. T. R. (2004). 2-D Variation With Asymmetric Neighborship for Pseudorandom Number Generation, *IEEE Transaction on Computers* 23: 378–388.

Hortensius, P. D., Mcleod, R. D., Pries, W., Miller, D. M. & Card, H. C. (1989). Cellular automata-based pseudorandom number generators for built-in self-test, *IEEE Transaction Computer-Aided Design* 8: 842–859.

Marsaglia, G. (1998). DIEHARD Test suite, *http://www.stat.fsu.edu/pub/diehard* .

Quieta, M. T. R. & Guan, S.-U. (2005). Optimization of 2-D Lattice Cellular Automata for Pseudorandom Number Generation, *International Journal of Modern Physics* 16(3): 479–500.

Seredynski, F., Bouvry, P. & Zomaya, A. Y. (2004). Cellular automata computations and secret key cryptography, *Parallel Computing* 30: 753–766.

Steeb, W.-H. (2001). *The nonlinear workbook: chaos, fractals, cellular automata, neural networks, genetic algorithms, fuzzy logic : with C++, Java, Symbolic C++ and Reduce programs*, World Scientific Publishing Co. Pte. Ltd.

Tan, S. K. & Guan, S.-U. (2007). Evolving cellular automata to generate nonlinear sequences with desirable properties, *Applied Soft Computing* 7: 1131–1134.

Tomassini, M., Sipper, M. & Perrenoud, M. (2000). On the generation of high quality random numbers by two-dimensional cellular automata, *IEEE Transactions on Computers* 49(10): 1146–1151.

von Neumann, J. (1966). *The Theory of Self-Reproducing Automata*, A.W Burks, ed., Univ. of Illinois Press, Urbana and London.

Walker, J. (Oct., 1998). ENT Test suite, *http://www.fourmilab.ch/random/* .

Wolfram, S. (1983). Statistical mechanics of cellular automata, *Reviews of Modern Physics* 55(3): 601–644.

Wolfram, S. (1984). Computation theory of cellular automata, *Communications in Mathematical Physics* 96: 15–57.

Wolfram, S. (1986). *Theory and Applications of Cellular Automata: Including Selected Papers, 1983-1986*, World Scientific.

Xuelong, Z., Qianmu, L., Manwu, X. & Fengyu, L. (Oct. 2005). A Symmetric Cryptography based on Extended Cellular Automata, *Proceeding of 2005 IEEE International Conference on Systems, Man and Cybernetics* 1: 499–503.

16

A Framework of Variant Logic Construction for Cellular Automata

Jeffrey Z.J. Zheng[1], Christian H.H. Zheng[2] and Tosiyasu L. Kunii[3]
[1]*Yunnan University*
[2]*University of Melbourne*
[3]*University of Tokyo*
[1]*P.R. China*
[2]*Australia*
[3]*Japan*

1. Introduction

1.1 Cellular automata

Cellular Automata are regular uniform networks of locally-connected finite-state machines invented by von Neumann (1966) to describe dynamic properties of finite state logic machines. Following the introduction of Conway's Game of Life (Umeo et al., 2008), Wolfram (1986; 1994) applied Boolean algebra to describe the behaviour of Cellular Automata (CA) as a series of dynamic images. His approach used a binary counting sequence to code different rules of behaviour based upon the functions generating the next iteration in the game. Wolfram (2002) identified four classes of transformations within the rules of CA, proclaiming their discovery as "A New Kind of Science", the title of the book. The typical analysis of behaviour in this area of research would begin by choosing a CA operation; by recursively applying the operation to different initial conditions, emergent patterns are identified, creating interesting visuals that are identifiable by behavioural type (Ilachinski, 2001).

After sixty years of research, Cellular Automata are now ubiquitous with non-trivial behaviour; they have been incorporated into mathematical computational models as well as models of natural systems. Cutting edge research using CA include: digital physics and modeling of spatially extended non-linear systems; complex systems, dynamic systems, massive-parallel computing, parallel implementations, language acceptance, and computability; reversibility of computation, system biology, modeling for real phenomena, natural computing, graph-theoretic analysis and logic; chaos and undecidability (Adamatzky, 2008; Schiff, 2007; Wuensche & Lesser, 1992).

Today's scientists rely on computation models as analytical tools for studying reality; using the computational framework provided by packages such as Mathematica and MATLAB to build recursive models that are iterated countless times before emergent behaviour is observed (Wolfram, 2002). Wolfram (1985) and other researchers have systematically applied logical equations to CA in order to systemise such complex dynamics into a science of complexity. Wolfram (1985) summarised twenty questions enquiring into the determination of mathematical properties for CA such as: entropy and Lyapunov exponents, geometric analogue, statistical behaviour, scaling, language complexity, universality and undecidability, irreducibility, & high-level descriptions. All of the questions are excellent from computational viewpoints, but they have not focused on the foundational aspects of the framework. An additional question remains to be answered: What is the governing relationship between the Cellular Automata framework and that of the Classical Logic framework?

1.2 Western and eastern logic traditions

Begining with Aristotle (384-322 B.C.), the foundations of western logic have played a key role in the development of today's global society (Kline, 1972). The modern theory of logic systems comprise of a series of outstanding individuals and their contributions to the theory of logic: G. Leibniz and the introduction of the Binary Number System (1646-1716) [Leibniz (1976); Leibniz et al. (1989)]; G. Boole and the development of Boolean Logic (1854) [Boole (1850/1940/1958)]; G. Cantor and Set Theory (1879); G. Frege and Conceptual Logic (1879) [Dawson (2005); Demopoulos (1995)]; B. Russell and Russell's Paradox (1910) [Russell (1942)]; J. Lukasiewicz and Multiple-Valued Logic (1920); D. Hilbert and Foundations of Geometric Logic (1923 [Hilbert (1899)], K. Gödel and his Incomplete Theorem (1931) [Dawson (2005)], A. Turing and the Turing Machine (1936) [Turing (1936)]; C. Shannon and Switching Theory (1937) [Shannon et al. (1993)]; H. Reichenbach and Probability Logic(1949) [Reichenbach (1949)]; as well as L. Zadeh and Fuzzy Logic (1965) [Zadeh (1965)]. Development of such theorems and mathematical frameworks have enabled western culture to understand the operation of our world as a set of implementable rules. Logic and the development of rules for the expression of logic have provided a language that enabled the construction of today's scientific societies.

In contrast to the binary on-off nature of western logic, oriental culture have been influenced by spiritual traditions of balance and harmony. The theme of balance can be summarized in the I-Ching or 'The Book of Changes', one of the most influential books of classic oriental literature (Chu & Sherrill, 1977; Cooper, 1981; Govinda, 1981, Hook, 1975; Shchutshii, 1979; Whincup, 1986; Wilhelmi, 1979; Wilhemi, 1979). The concept of Yin and Yang forces and the subtle interplay of the two opposing forces yield combinations and permutations of change. Orient philosophy believed that 'the only constant phenomena is change' and such a world view emphasised the dynamic nature of a system; rather than focusing in the individual states of a system (on, off), prominence was instead placed on operations that yield change (on to off, off to on). The structure of thought introduced by the I-Ching allowed change to be systematically documented and analysed. Complex interactions, cyclic behaviour and the interplay of nature at all levels of oriental culture – sociology, literature, medicine, astrology and religion – were able to be described using the tools of dynamic logic provided by the I-Ching; the framework remains a complete philosophy as well as a universal language and has remained unchanged over the past two thousand years (Needham & Wang, 1954-1988).

Leibniz in as early as 1690 realized that the balanced yin-yang structure proposed by Shao Yong (1050) was equivalent to the binary number system (Hook, 1975; Needham & Wang, 1954-1988). However the western scientific community have mostly disregarded the I-Ching; due mainly to cultural and language barriers as well as local superstitions that cloud the essence of the framework. In its ancient form of allegories and metaphors, the I-Ching is unable to satisfy the logician's requirement for completeness, consistence and other such properties. The challenge then is to be able present this philosophy for modern times, in the language of mathematics. Stripped of its colorful language, what insights does this ancient system contain? What are the essential differences between modern binary logic and the I-Ching's dynamic binary structures? The unification of these two schools of thought would bring greater understanding of the world we live in (Whincup, 1986). As the modern formulation of Cellular Automata generates complexity through binary logic whilst the I-Ching analyses complexity though binary logic, the modern language of the I-Ching can be found in the creation of a structural definition of CA.

1.3 Logic and dynamic systems

In the field of mathematical logic, construction of theoretical frameworks focus upon three spatial hierarchies: variables, states and function spaces (Bonnet, 1989; Sikorski, 1960). Boolean algebra and switching theory exploit such properties, using the combinatorial invariance of the framework for implementing new theories and applications (Lee, 1978; Vingron, 2004). Logical operations are restricted to two types of canonical forms namely, the product-of-sums and the sum-of-products approaches. Any complex logic function can be rewritten as these two canonical forms. This is done for reasons of consistency, simplicity and symmetry of structure; as such the use of a truth table enables analysis and the transformation into the canonical representations (Bonnet, 1989).

In the analysis of dynamic systems, it is essential to identify transformation spaces with functional invariance (Dunn, 1988; Paterson, 1992). The Ising model is arguably the simplest binary system that undergoes a nontrivial phase transition (Ilachinski, 2001). In modern physics, this type of model uses a structure linked to phase space representation of a dynamic systems (Griffeath & Moor, 2003). The phase space plays an essential role to describe key properties of any dynamic system, however under classical logic, phase characteristics are difficult to construct. A mechanism for linking low level representations such as variables and states with higher level group properties such as symmetric conditions currently does not exist. This is more a limitation of the language and the operations allowed by the language. Classical logic is based on static combinatorial structures. Permutations, which are intrinsic to phase space, cannot be expressed under such a framework of classical combinatorial logic (Ilachinski, 2001). Cellular Automata frameworks however, are fully dynamic and has been used to describe phase space (Griffeath & Moor, 2003). Inspired by the traditional I-Ching hierarchical structures, new conditions, operations and relationships have been proposed on top of the Classical Logic framework to encorporate the dynamic nature of CA. The additional constructs provide support for CA using framework that is logically consistent and complete (Zheng & Zheng, 2010).

The Zheng & Zheng (2010) proposal builds upon earlier studies of logic systems from a structural viewpoint. Kunii & Takai (1989) applied a n-cell structure for analysis, classification and generation of visual objects using topology and homotopy tools in computer graphics (Kunii, Hioki & Shinagawa, 1993; Kunii & Kunii, 1999; Kunii & Shinagawa, 1992; Kunii & Takahashi, 1993; Kunii, Tsuchida, Arai, Matsuda, Shirahama & Miura, 1993). Zheng & Maeder (1992) proposed a balanced classification on binary images for conjugate classification and transformation of binary images on regular plan lattices in 1990s to visualise different configurations (Zheng, 1994; 1996; Zheng & Leung, 1996; Zheng & Maeder, 1993). All such work used partial constructs of the Zheng & Zheng (2010) framework. The proposed framework supports classical logic, vector permutation and complementary operations. The new construction requires five spatial hierarchies containing $2^{2^n} \times 2^n!$ functional configurations for any n variables. This structure is much larger than classical logic, having three spatial hierarchies supporting 2^{2^n} functions for n variables. Newly defined symmetric properties play an important role in predictions and classifications of possible recursive results. Using such properties, global behaviour can be identified and classified. A disadvantages of the new framework lies in its extreme complexity. It is possible to use parallel computers to do analysis of the configurations contained by $n = 3$ (the space already includes more than 10^7 configurations). It is impossible using today's technology to process the $n = 5$ space due to the extreme growth of structural complexity ($2^{32} \times 32!$ configurations). This chapter describes the variant logic framework proposed by Zheng & Zheng (2010), identifying variant and invariant characteristics of logic under permutations and complementary operations from CA. This allows the definition of a variant space to be introduced into logic. Using an extended truth-valued table, vector permutations and complementary operations can be applied to form a giant structure with equivalent properties in a spatial hierarchy. The framework supports additional operations whithout changing the logic function space. A proposed 2D matrix representation provides additional support to visualise globally symmetric patterns from permutations of generated using the proposed extensions.

2. Truth table in boolean logic

The truth-table plays a vital role in traditional logic construction; It provides a static structure, using Yes | No (1 | 0) to indicate possible conditions from variables, states to any function. The proposed framework includes traditional logic function space and the truth-table representation of the space.

2.1 Basic definitions

$$\begin{aligned} X = X_{N-1}X_{N-2}...X_j...X_1X_0, \quad & Y = Y_{N-1}Y_{N-2}...Y_j...Y_1Y_0 \\ X_j, Y_j \in B_2 = \{0,1\}, 0 \leqslant j < N & \\ f: X \to Y; \quad Y = f(X); \quad X, Y \in B_2^N = \{0,1\}^N & \end{aligned} \tag{1}$$

An example of a transform: the sequence $X = 0001110100, N = 10$ is an input for a function operation f, the output is a sequence of the same length $Y = 1101011001$; $X, Y \in B_2^{10}$.
Definition 2.1 Let $[...X_j...]$ be a n bit structure as a kernel form:

$$\begin{aligned} [...X_j...] = x_{n-1}x_{n-2}...x_i...x_1x_0 = \mathbf{x} \\ 0 \leqslant i < n, 0 \leq j < N, \mathbf{x} \in B_2^n \end{aligned} \tag{2}$$

where $X_j = x_i$ is a corresponding position.

$$Y_j = f([...X_j...]) = f(x_{n-1}x_{n-2}...x_i...x_1x_0) = f(\mathbf{x}) \tag{3}$$

In Boolean logic, n variables in a kernel form correspond to a full truth table with $2^n \times 2^{2^n}$ entries. The I-th meta-state $0 \leq I < 2^n$ has n bit number to occupy the I-th column position, the J-th function $T(J)$ has the J-th row with 2^n bits $0 \leq J < 2^{2^n}$, the function value of the I-th entry is determined by $T(J)_I$. The full table can be represented as follows:
From this type of tables, it is feasible to establish accessing method to look up corresponding table values.
Method 2.1: Process Method of Truth Table:
Input: $\mathbf{x}$: n variables in a $\{0,1\}$ sequence, J: selected function number

$0 \leq I < 2^n$	S_{2^n-1}	...	S_I	...	S_1	S_0
$I_{n-1}...I_i...I_0$	1...1...1	...	$I_{n-1}...I_i...I_0$	...	0...0...1	0...0...0
$0 \leq J < 2^{2^n}$	J_{2^n-1}	...	J_I	...	J_1	J_0
$T(0)$	0	...	0	...	0	0
$T(1)$	0	...	0	...	0	1
$T(2)$	0	...	0	...	1	0
...			...			
$T(J)$	J_{2^n-1}	...	J_I	...	J_1	J_0
...			...			
$T(2^{2^n}-2)$	1	...	1	...	1	0
$T(2^{2^n}-1)$	1	...	1	...	1	1

Table 1. Truth Tables of n-variables

Process: Using the input sequence $\mathbf{x}$, the meta-state number I is to select the I-th column of function $T(J)$

Output: Return $T(J)_I$'s value (1 for true and 0 for false) as output.

3. Cellular automata representations

3.1 Basic representation

Cellular Automata - CA uses a recursive mechanism to represent a given function with a time direction. Dynamic properties of CA can be supported in further expansions. In a one dimensional form of CA, a N length binary sequence is

$$X = X_{N-1}X_{N-2}...X_j...X_1X_0, 0 \leqslant j < N, X_j \in \{0,1\} = B_2$$

For a given function f, the output sequence is defined: $f : X \to Y, Y = f(X)$,

$$Y = Y_{N-1}Y_{N-2}...Y_j...Y_1Y_0, 0 \leqslant j < N, Y_j \in B_2$$

It is feasible to use a moving window with a fixed length n to separate X into a local kernel in length n. The kernel can be presented as

$$[...X_j...] = x_{n-1}...x_i...x_0, x_i \in B_2$$

For a given function f

$$y = f(x_{n-1}...x_i...x_0)$$

It is necessary to assign a certain position i in the kernel for special care to associated with j position of both sequences. All above relations are exactly same as traditional Boolean equation with n variables.

It is possible to distinguish current time and next time sequences, following equations relevant to cellular automata can be identified:

$$y = f(x_{n-1}...x_i...x_0) = f([...X_j...]) = Y_j$$

or $X_j = X_j^{t-1}, Y_j = X_j^t$ i.e.

$$f : X_j^{t-1} \to X_j^t, X_j^{t-1}, X_j^t \in B_2 \tag{4}$$

3.2 Four variation forms

Time direction is a significant property to distinguish a Cellular Automata logic function from a traditional logic function. Considering $f : X_j^{t-1} \rightarrow X_j^t$ for any function of boolean logic system to analyze their variation properties, it is normal to have following proposition.

Proposition 3.1 For any $f : X_j^{t-1} \rightarrow X_j^t$ transformation, four forms of transforming classes are identified: TA: $0 \rightarrow 0$, TB: $0 \rightarrow 1$, TC: $1 \rightarrow 0$, TD: $1 \rightarrow 1$.

Proof: X_j, Y_j are 0-1 variables, only four classes listed are possible. ■

Definition 3.1 Four Transforming forms are corresponding to following sets: TA: Invariant-valued class for 0 value, TB: Variant-valued class for 0 value, TC:Variant-valued class for 1 value, TD: Invariant-valued class for 1 value. Under such definition, following proposition can be established.

Proposition 3.2 Using four classes of transformation, four variant operations are defined.

Type	$X_j \rightarrow Y_j$		Truth	Variant	Invariant	False
TA	0	0	0	0	1	1
TB	0	1	1	1	0	0
TC	1	0	0	1	0	1
TD	1	1	1	0	1	0

Proof: Truth (False) values are determined by $Y_j(\bar{Y}_j)$ and Variant(Invariant) values are determined by {TB, TC} for 1(0) and {TA, TD} for 0(1) respectively.■

4. Permutation invariants

From an accessing viewpoint, many invariant properties can be observed from table operation.

Proposition 4.1 Under sequential mapping in sequential order of Method 2.1, there is $T(J) = J$.

Proof: The relevant output entries of $T(J)$ are mapped to the binary number J having 2^n bits:

$$\begin{aligned} T(J) &= T(S_{2^n-1}(J_{2^n-1}))...T(S_I(J_I))...T(S_0(J_0)) \\ &= T(J)_{2^n-1}...T(J)_I...T(J)_0 = J \in B_2^{2^n} \\ T(J)_I &= T(S_I(J_I)) = J_I \in B_2; 0 \leq I < 2^n, 0 \leq J < 2^{2^n} \end{aligned} \quad (5)$$

■

It is possible to apply permutation operation on the table to generate a transformed table following a certain rule.

Definition 4.1 For any n binary logic variables, let $\Omega(N)$ be a symmetric group with N elements and P be a permutation operator, $P \in \Omega(2^n)$, then for any $J, \exists K, J, K \in B_2^{2^n}, P(T(J)) = K, 0 \leq J, K < 2^{2^n}$, the following permutation can be represented in Truth Table form:

$$
\begin{aligned}
& P : J \to K \\
P(T(J)) &= P(T(S_{2^n-1}(J_{2^n-1})))...P(T(S_I(J_I)))...P(T(S_0(J_0))) \\
&= P(T(J)_{2^n-1})...P(T(J)_I)...P(T(J)_0) \\
&= K_{2^n-1}...K_I...K_0 = K \in B_2^{2^n} \\
P(T(J)_I) &= P(T(S_I(J_I))) = T(S_{P(I)}(J_{P(I)})) \\
&= T(J)_{P(I)} = J_{P(I)} = K_I \in B_2 \\
& 0 \leq I < 2^n, 0 \leq J, K < 2^{2^n}, P \in \Omega(2^n)
\end{aligned} \tag{6}
$$

Proposition 4.2 The Truth Table under permutation operation on 2^n meta states can generate $2^n!$ sequences for 2^{2^n} length of integers.
Proof: For any $P \in \Omega(2^n)$, 2^n are independent, it is composed of $\Omega(2^n)$ elements. ■
For the one-variable condition (ie. $n = 1$) there are only two possible arrangements. The initial sequence is represented as $\mathbf{S} = S_1 S_0 = 10$, and a permutation operation generates the output $P(\mathbf{S}) = S_0 S_1 = 01$. The following shows two groups of results:

Mate-state	**S**	1	0	P(**S**)	0	1
Function	J			P(J)		
0	0	0	0	0	0	0
$\bar{x}$	1	0	1	2	1	0
x	2	1	0	1	0	1
1	3	1	1	3	1	1

For any permutation operation, the function $T(J) = P(T(J))$ is always invariant. The inequality $J \neq K = P(J)$ holds in general.

5. Organisational space

Building upon the three spaces (variables, states, and functions), an additional space of organisation is composed of permutation operations provided by permutation invariance properties defined in the previous section.

5.1 Complementary operation

Definition 5.1 (Complementary Operator) For any binary (0-1) variable $y \in B_2$, let the relevant index $\delta \in B_2$ be a complementary operator:

$$
y^\delta = \begin{cases} \bar{y} & \delta = 0 \\ y & \delta = 1 \end{cases} \tag{7}
$$

Definition 5.2 (Complementary Function Operation) For any n variable function of 2^n meta function vectors $\mathbf{S} = S_{2^n-1}...S_I...S_0$ Let $\Delta = \delta_{2^n-1}...\delta_I...\delta_0, 0 \leq I < 2^n, \delta_I \in B_2, \Delta \in B_2^{2^n}$.
For this type of complementary operations on function,

Δ is :

$$\begin{aligned}
\Delta &: T(J) \rightarrow K; J,K \in B_2^{2^n}, 0 \leq J,K < 2^{2^n} \\
\mathbf{S}^{\Delta} &= S_{2^n-1}^{\delta_{2n-1}} ... S_I^{\delta_I} ... S_0^{\delta_0}, S_I \in B_2^n \\
T(J)^{\Delta} &= T(S_{2^n-1}^{\delta_{2n-1}}(J_{2^n-1}))...T(S_I^{\delta_I}(J_I))...T(S_0^{\delta_0}(J_0)) \\
&= T(J)_{2^n-1}^{\delta_{2n-1}} ... T(J)_I^{\delta_I} ... T(J)_0^{\delta_0} \\
&= K_{2^n-1}...K_I...K_0 = K \in B_2^{2^n} \\
T(J)_I^{\delta_I} &= T(S_I^{\delta_I}(J_I)) = J_I^{\delta_I} = K_I \in B_2 \\
& 0 \leq I < 2^n, 0 \leq J,K < 2^{2^n}, \delta_I \in \Delta
\end{aligned} \tag{8}$$

5.2 Invariant logic functions under permutation and complementary

Definition 5.3 (Permutation and Complementary Operations) For any of the n variables expressed as 2^n meta vectors, Complementary Operations $\Delta \in B_2^{2^n}$ and Permutation Operations $P \in \Omega(2^n)$ are expressed as:

$$\begin{aligned}
(P,\Delta) &: T(J) \rightarrow K; J,K \in B_2^{2^n}, P \in \Omega(2^n), \Delta \in B_2^{2^n} \\
P(T(J)^{\Delta}) &= P(T(S_{2^n-1}^{\delta_{2n-1}}(J_{2^n-1})))...P(T(S_I^{\delta_I}(J_I)))...P(T(S_0^{\delta_0}(J_0))) \\
&= P(T(J)_{2^n-1}^{\delta_{2n-1}})...P(T(J)_I^{\delta_I})...P(T(J)_0^{\delta_0}) \\
&= K_{2^n-1}...K_I...K_0 = K \in B_2^{2^n} \\
P(T(J)_I^{\delta_I}) &= P(T(S_I^{\delta_I}(J_I))) = J_{P(I)}^{\delta_{P(I)}} = K_I \in B_2 \\
& 0 \leq I < 2^n, 0 \leq J,K < 2^{2^n}, P \in \Omega(2^n), \delta_I \in \Delta
\end{aligned} \tag{9}$$

Counting Order	7	6	5	4	3	2	1	0	
S	111	110	101	100	011	010	001	000	Binary counting
0	0	0	0	0	0	0	0	0	a full 0 vector
Δ	1	1	0	0	1	1	0	0	a Δ- vector
$\neg\Delta$	0	0	1	1	0	0	1	1	a not Δ- vector
1	1	1	1	1	1	1	1	1	a full 1 vector
$T(178)$	1	0	1	1	0	0	1	0	initial value
$T(178)^{\mathbf{1}}$	1	0	1	1	0	0	1	0	$T(178)$ Truth
$T(178)^{\neg\Delta}$	0	1	1	1	1	1	1	0	$T(178)$ Δ-Variant
$T(178)^{\mathbf{0}}$	0	1	0	0	1	1	0	1	$T(178)$ False
$T(178)^{\Delta}$	1	0	0	0	0	0	0	1	$T(178)$ Δ-Invariant

Method 5.1: Permutation and Complementary Methods Table $P(T^{\Delta})$:
Input: $\mathbf{x}$: n variables in a binary $\{0,1\}$ sequence, J: is the selected function number, $P \in \Omega(2^n)$ and $\Delta \in B_2^{2^n}$ are Permutation and Complementary operators
Process: Input sequence $\mathbf{x}$ is established, the $P(I)$-th column is selected using the meta-state number I. This represents the I-th column of the function $P(T(J)^{\Delta})$
Output: If $\delta_{P(I)} = 1$, return the value of $T(J)_{P(I)}^{\delta_{P(I)}}$ (1 for true and 0 for false); if $\delta_{P(I)} = 0$, return $\neg T(J)_{P(I)}^{\delta_{P(I)}}$.

5.3 Logic functional spaces

Theorem 5.1 (Logic Function Invariants under Permutation & Complementary Operations) For any logic function, the output of Method 5.1 provides an equivalent output as the original Truth Table under all conditions.

Proof: A J-th row on the permutation and complementary table of $P(T^{\Delta})$ for any $I \in B_2^n, J \in B_2^{2^n}$ is constructed by

$$P(T(J)_I^{\Delta}) = T(J)_{P(I)}^{\delta_{P(I)}} = \begin{cases} \neg T(J)_I & \delta_{P(I)} = 0 \\ T(J)_I & \delta_{P(I)} = 1 \end{cases} \tag{10}$$

After using Method 5.1, the results are shown:

$$P(T(J)_I^{\Delta}) = \begin{cases} \neg\neg T(J)_I = T(J)_I & \delta_{P(I)} = 0 \\ T(J)_I & \delta_{P(I)} = 1 \end{cases} \tag{11}$$

■

Theorem 5.2 (Permutation Group for Meta Function Vector) For 2^n meta function vectors, a total of permutation numbers is $2^n!$.

Theorem 5.3 (Permutation & Complementary Structure) Under permutation and complementary operations, a total of $2^n!2^{2^n}$ permutations can be generated to form a logic functional space for the n variables.

6. Different coding schemes: One and two dimensional representations

The initial step to construct a series of logic functionals. Permutation and complementary differences can be shown in the proposed invariant function structures. Different coding schemes under different symmetric restrictions are established. Four schemes are described, in which one of them is in 1-Dimensional representation and other three schemes are 2-Dimensional representations. For binary sequences in sequential counting order, the scheme is known as the SL (Shao Yong & Leibniz) coding scheme .

6.1 G coding

The General Code (G) is used to map permutation & complementary operations. For any state in the G coding-scheme having 2^n bits,

$$G : (J, \Delta, P) \to K; J, K \in B_2^{2^n}; \Delta \in B_2^{2^n}, P \in \Omega. \tag{12}$$

6.2 W coding

From the G coding-scheme, their bit numbers are separated into two equal parts in the same bits to form a 2D representation. This mapping mechanism can represent a function space as a W coding scheme.

$$\begin{gathered} W : (J, \Delta, P) \to K = \langle J^1 | J^0 \rangle \\ J, K \in B_2^{2^n}; J^1, J^0 \in B_2^{2^{n-1}}; S^1, S^0 \in \mathbf{S}, \Delta \in B_2^{2^n}, P \in \Omega \end{gathered} \tag{13}$$

Under this representation, a given logic functional for the function space is illustrated as a fixed matrix.

$$\{W(J)\}_{J=0}^{2^{2^n}} = \begin{array}{|c|c|c|c|c|}\hline \langle 0|0\rangle & ... & \langle 0|J^0\rangle & ... & \langle 0|2^{2^{n-1}}-1\rangle \\ \hline ... & & ... & & ... \\ \hline \langle J^1|0\rangle & ... & \langle J^1|J^0\rangle & ... & \langle J^1|2^{2^{n-1}}-1\rangle \\ \hline ... & & ... & & ... \\ \hline \langle 2^{2^{n-1}}-1|0\rangle & ... & \langle 2^{2^{n-1}}-1|J^0\rangle & ... & \langle 2^{2^{n-1}}-1|2^{2^{n-1}}-1\rangle \\ \hline \end{array} \tag{14}$$

$0 \leq J^0, J^1 < 2^{2^{n-1}}; 0 \leq J < 2^{2^n}$

In the one-variable condition, there are eight cases in their logic functional spaces as follows:

f	J^{11}, T	W	J^{10}, IV	W	J^{01}, V	W	J^{00}, F	W
0	0	$\langle 0\|0\rangle$	1	$\langle 0\|1\rangle$	2	$\langle 1\|0\rangle$	3	$\langle 1\|1\rangle$
$\bar{x}$	1	$\langle 0\|1\rangle$	0	$\langle 0\|0\rangle$	3	$\langle 1\|1\rangle$	2	$\langle 1\|0\rangle$
x	2	$\langle 1\|0\rangle$	3	$\langle 1\|1\rangle$	0	$\langle 0\|0\rangle$	1	$\langle 0\|1\rangle$
1	3	$\langle 1\|1\rangle$	2	$\langle 1\|0\rangle$	1	$\langle 0\|1\rangle$	0	$\langle 0\|0\rangle$
f	$P(J)^{11}$, T	W	$P(J)^{10}$, IV	W	$P(J)^{01}$, V	W	$P(J)^{00}$, F	W
0	0	$\langle 0\|0\rangle$	1	$\langle 0\|1\rangle$	2	$\langle 1\|0\rangle$	3	$\langle 1\|1\rangle$
$\bar{x}$	2	$\langle 1\|0\rangle$	3	$\langle 1\|1\rangle$	0	$\langle 0\|0\rangle$	1	$\langle 0\|1\rangle$
x	1	$\langle 0\|1\rangle$	0	$\langle 0\|0\rangle$	3	$\langle 1\|1\rangle$	2	$\langle 1\|0\rangle$
1	3	$\langle 1\|1\rangle$	2	$\langle 1\|0\rangle$	1	$\langle 0\|1\rangle$	0	$\langle 0\|0\rangle$

For better visualisation and expression of multiple complementary results, the 1-Dimensional G coding-scheme can be converted into a 2-Dimensional W coding-scheme as an extending matrix. It is convenient to extend different Δ variant matrices into a composed matrix. Four typical Δ variant values: $\{\Delta\} = \{11, 10, 01, 00\} = \begin{array}{|c|c|}\hline 11 & 10 \\ \hline 01 & 00 \\ \hline \end{array}$ corresponding to {Truth, Invariant, Variant, False} matrices respectively. A 2x2 matrix is composed of four block matrices in the order: $\{\Delta\} = \begin{array}{|c|c|}\hline 11 & 10 \\ \hline 01 & 00 \\ \hline \end{array}$.

$$W^{\{\Delta\}} = P(10)^{\{\Delta\}} = \begin{array}{|cc|cc|}\hline \text{Truth} & & & \text{Invariant} \\ & 0\ \bar{x} & \bar{x}\ 0 & \\ & x\ 1 & 1\ x & \\ \hline & x\ 1 & 1\ x & \\ & 0\ \bar{x} & \bar{x}\ 0 & \\ \text{Variant} & & & \text{False} \\ \hline \end{array}$$

$$PW^{\{\Delta\}} = P(01)^{\{\Delta\}} = \begin{array}{|cc|cc|}\hline \text{Truth} & & & \text{Invariant} \\ & 0\ x & x\ 0 & \\ & \bar{x}\ 1 & 1\ \bar{x} & \\ \hline & \bar{x}\ 1 & 1\ \bar{x} & \\ & 0\ x & x\ 0 & \\ \text{Variant} & & & \text{False} \\ \hline \end{array}$$

On each 2x2 matrix, a pair of functions can be identified as follows:

$$0 \cap 1 = 1 \cap 0 = x \cap \bar{x} = \bar{x} \cap x = 0 \tag{15}$$

$$0 \cup 1 = 1 \cup 0 = x \cup \bar{x} = \bar{x} \cup x = 1 \tag{16}$$

(a) $P(10)^{\{\Delta\}}$ composed image matrix (b) $P(01)^{\{\Delta\}}$ composed image matrix

(c) $P(10)^{\{\Delta\}}$ composed number matrix (d) $P(01)^{\{\Delta\}}$ composed number matrix

Fig. 1. One variable variant logic matrices: $P = \{10, 01\}, \{\Delta\} = \{11, 10, 01, 00\}$; (a-b)2x2 base blocks (c-d)2x2 vector blocks

This makes following matrix equations:

$$\begin{pmatrix} 0 & \bar{x} \\ x & 1 \end{pmatrix} \cap \begin{pmatrix} 1 & x \\ \bar{x} & 0 \end{pmatrix} = \ldots = \begin{pmatrix} x & 1 \\ 0 & \bar{x} \end{pmatrix} \cap \begin{pmatrix} \bar{x} & 0 \\ 1 & x \end{pmatrix} = \begin{pmatrix} 0 & 0 \\ 0 & 0 \end{pmatrix} \tag{17}$$

$$\begin{pmatrix} 0 & \bar{x} \\ x & 1 \end{pmatrix} \cup \begin{pmatrix} 1 & x \\ \bar{x} & 0 \end{pmatrix} = \ldots = \begin{pmatrix} x & 1 \\ 0 & \bar{x} \end{pmatrix} \cup \begin{pmatrix} \bar{x} & 0 \\ 1 & x \end{pmatrix} = \begin{pmatrix} 1 & 1 \\ 1 & 1 \end{pmatrix} \tag{18}$$

However this type of complementary properties cannot be directly observed on $W^{\{\Delta\}}$ and $PW^{\{\Delta\}}$ matrices under logic operations.

$$W^{\{\Delta\}} \cap PW^{\{\Delta\}} = \left(\begin{array}{cc|cc} 0 & \bar{x} & \bar{x} & 0 \\ x & 1 & 1 & x \\ \hline x & 1 & 1 & x \\ 0 & \bar{x} & \bar{x} & 0 \end{array}\right) \cap \left(\begin{array}{cc|cc} 0 & x & x & 0 \\ \bar{x} & 1 & 1 & \bar{x} \\ \hline \bar{x} & 1 & 1 & \bar{x} \\ 0 & x & x & 0 \end{array}\right) = \left(\begin{array}{cc|cc} 0 & 0 & 0 & 0 \\ 0 & 1 & 1 & 0 \\ \hline 0 & 1 & 1 & 0 \\ 0 & 0 & 0 & 0 \end{array}\right) \quad (19)$$

$$W^{\{\Delta\}} \cup PW^{\{\Delta\}} = \left(\begin{array}{cc|cc} 0 & \bar{x} & \bar{x} & 0 \\ x & 1 & 1 & x \\ \hline x & 1 & 1 & x \\ 0 & \bar{x} & \bar{x} & 0 \end{array}\right) \cup \left(\begin{array}{cc|cc} 0 & x & x & 0 \\ \bar{x} & 1 & 1 & \bar{x} \\ \hline \bar{x} & 1 & 1 & \bar{x} \\ 0 & x & x & 0 \end{array}\right) = \left(\begin{array}{cc|cc} 0 & 1 & 1 & 0 \\ 1 & 1 & 1 & 1 \\ \hline 1 & 1 & 1 & 1 \\ 0 & 1 & 1 & 0 \end{array}\right) \quad (20)$$

All 8 configurations of one variable conditions for variant logic can be exhaustively listed in two matrices. A total of 8 functional configurations in two groups can be seen in Fig. 1. There are 16 blocks in a comprised matrix in which thin lines separate different recursive images as blocks and each block under a function recursively, thick lines separate four 2x2 blocks and each 2x2 blocks under a set of Δ complementary operations. Four Δ operations apply to four 2x2 blocks respectively and each Δ complementary operation applied to a matrix contained 2x2 block functions. It is convenient to replace corresponding function symbols to recursive images respectively. Fig. 1(a) shows the $W^{\{\Delta\}} = P(10)^{\{\Delta\}}$ matrix; its four sub-blocks use $\{f_0 = 0, f_1 = \bar{x}, f_2 = x, f_3 = 1\}$ for its four operations; in Fig. 1(b) shows the $PW^{\{\Delta\}} = P(01)^{\{\Delta\}}$ matrix; its four sub-blocks use $\{0, x, \bar{x}, 1\}$ functions on each 2x2 block for its four operations: $\{\Delta\} = \{11, 10, 01, 00\}$ respectively to generate truth, variant, invariant and false Δ operations. The four outer corners and inner corners of $P(10)^{\{\Delta\}}$ and $P(01)^{\{\Delta\}}$ composed matrix in Fig. 1 (a) and (b) are one function as four white and four black blocks, $\{\Delta\}$ operations provide both horizontal and vertical reflection effects on two matrices.
From an operational viewpoint, under the same $\{\Delta\}$ operator, $P(01)^{\{\Delta\}}$ and $P(10)^{\{\Delta\}}$ have similar visual effects of rotation 90 degrees each other that can be clearly observed via selected sample images. These structure provide visual mechanism to present all possible configurations of the one variable functional space without repeat exhaustively.

6.3 F coding

Using 2D representation, symmetric condition can be added to arrange meta states into specific order. For each pair of states in W, if they satisfy following condition, then a refined code: F coding scheme is determined.

$$\begin{array}{ccc} J^1 \text{ the } I\text{-th meta state} & \leftrightharpoons & J^0 \text{ the } I\text{-th meta state} \\ \updownarrow & \text{F coding scheme} & \updownarrow \\ X \in S^1 & \rightleftharpoons & \bar{X} \in S^0 \end{array}$$

6.3.1 Pairs of conjugate functions

one special corresponding relationship can be identified as a pair of conjugate functions. For a given function f, its conjugate function $\tilde{f}$ is determined by undertaken following transformation:

$$\{0 \leftrightarrow 1; \cap \leftrightarrow \cup\} \quad (21)$$

all other variables keep invariant, do not transformed into their complementary variables. e.g. $f = x \cap \bar{y}$ and $\tilde{f} = x \cup \bar{y}$; $f = 0$ and $\tilde{f} = 1$ are two typical pairs of conjugate functions.
Under F coding scheme, it is natural to have pairs of conjugate functions distributed on diagonal directions. Such special arrangements are much easier to be observed with complementary symmetric properties via pairs of recursive images.

6.4 C coding

In addition to a pair of states in complementary relationship, further structure is introduced onto F code. When the pair of states in F have the same values in their i-th position, they form a C coding scheme.

$$\begin{array}{cccc} S^1 \text{ the } I\text{-th} & \leftrightharpoons & S^0 \text{ the } I\text{-th} & \text{F coding scheme} \\ \updownarrow & \text{C coding scheme} & \updownarrow & + \text{Four corners} \in \{0, \bar{x}, x, 1\} \\ \forall x_i \in S^1, x_i = 1(0) & \rightleftharpoons & \forall x_i \in S^0, x_i = 0(1) & + \text{General conjugate} \end{array}$$

The C coding scheme, have the strongest symmetric conditions available. Only a relatively small number among the three invariant groups can be identified within this scheme. Under this coding scheme, four corner positions of a matrix are composed of four functions of one variable matrix respectively.

7. Two-variable cases

There are a total of $384 = 24 \times 16$ configurations in functional spaces of two variable configurations. Similar exhaustive mechanism of one variable condition, different configurations of functionals can be illustrated by combining them into a comprised matrix on which satisfy complementary relationships on block matrix condition. Complete arrangements can be assigned as 24 matrices each matrix for a permutation to contain 16 complementary operations to be arranged as 4x4 blocks and each block is linked to a given function. Small sized blocks such as 2x2 are also selected to show special visual configurations. Each block must have complementary relationship with its opposite block on diagonal directions.
In convenient illustration, six groups of examples are selected. Four figures 2-5 contain a logic functional represents 16 logic functions as 4x4 images separated by thin lines. Four functionals are arranged as 2x2 block matrices separated by thick lines in Truth/False, Invariant/Variant properties. Relevant 2x2 block matrices of complementary operations correspond to:

$$\{\Delta\} = \begin{array}{|c|c|} \hline \text{Truth} = 1111 & \text{Invariant} = 1100 \\ \hline \text{Variant} = 0011 & \text{False} = 0000 \\ \hline \end{array}$$

Each matrix contains 16 entries of function images as a 4x4 ($2^2 \times 2^2$) configuration. Each image entry denotes a transformed number and its function number in the form: $\begin{array}{|c|} \langle J^1 | J^0 \rangle \\ J \\ \hline \end{array}$
where $K = \langle J^1 | J^0 \rangle$ is a transformed number and J is the function number. In all four figures, (a)2x2 base block matrices to represent function images and (b)2x2 vector blocks to represent relevant coding schemes respectively.
To show a complete matrix on a functional configuration, two permutation groups of Figures 6-7 are selected. Each figure contain a total of 256 images arranged as 16x16 matrices to

represent 16 block matrices for corresponding complementary operations. Each block matrix has 4x4 images. The 4x4 block matrices contain following $\{\Delta\}$ values respectively:

$\{\Delta\} =$

1111	1110	1101	1100
1011	1010	1001	1000
0111	0110	0101	0100
0011	0010	0001	0000

Each image entry has a corresponding transformed number and its function number respectively.
In Figure 2, the counting order of meta-states has been arranged as W coding (SL code): $P = (3210), \{\Delta\} = \begin{array}{|c|c|}\hline 1111 & 1100 \\ \hline 0011 & 0000 \\ \hline\end{array}$. In this group, only functions 6 & 9 and 0 & 15 can be visualised in complementary symmetric condition in two diagonal directions. Visual symmetric effects of other pairs cannot be easily observed. However under four $\{\Delta\}$ operations generate a composed matrix that has clear horizontal and vertical reflect symmetries. It is directly to use equation to check their complementary properties:

$$\begin{aligned}
&\begin{pmatrix} 0 & 1 & 2 & 3 \\ 4 & 5 & 6 & 7 \\ 8 & 9 & 10 & 11 \\ 12 & 13 & 14 & 15 \end{pmatrix}_{\Delta=1111} \cap \begin{pmatrix} 15 & 14 & 13 & 12 \\ 11 & 10 & 9 & 8 \\ 7 & 6 & 5 & 4 \\ 3 & 2 & 1 & 0 \end{pmatrix}_{\Delta=0000} \\
= &\begin{pmatrix} 3 & 2 & 1 & 0 \\ 7 & 6 & 5 & 4 \\ 11 & 10 & 9 & 8 \\ 15 & 14 & 13 & 12 \end{pmatrix}_{\Delta=1100} \cap \begin{pmatrix} 12 & 13 & 14 & 15 \\ 8 & 9 & 10 & 11 \\ 4 & 5 & 6 & 7 \\ 0 & 1 & 2 & 3 \end{pmatrix}_{\Delta=0011} \\
= &\begin{pmatrix} 0000 & 0000 & 0000 & 0000 \\ 0000 & 0000 & 0000 & 0000 \\ 0000 & 0000 & 0000 & 0000 \\ 0000 & 0000 & 0000 & 0000 \end{pmatrix} = (\ldots f_0 = 0 \ldots)
\end{aligned} \tag{22}$$

$$\begin{aligned}
&\begin{pmatrix} 0 & 1 & 2 & 3 \\ 4 & 5 & 6 & 7 \\ 8 & 9 & 10 & 11 \\ 12 & 13 & 14 & 15 \end{pmatrix}_{\Delta=1111} \cup \begin{pmatrix} 15 & 14 & 13 & 12 \\ 11 & 10 & 9 & 8 \\ 7 & 6 & 5 & 4 \\ 3 & 2 & 1 & 0 \end{pmatrix}_{\Delta=0000} \\
= &\begin{pmatrix} 3 & 2 & 1 & 0 \\ 7 & 6 & 5 & 4 \\ 11 & 10 & 9 & 8 \\ 15 & 14 & 13 & 12 \end{pmatrix}_{\Delta=1100} \cup \begin{pmatrix} 12 & 13 & 14 & 15 \\ 8 & 8 & 10 & 11 \\ 4 & 5 & 6 & 7 \\ 0 & 1 & 2 & 3 \end{pmatrix}_{\Delta=0011} \\
= &\begin{pmatrix} 1111 & 1111 & 1111 & 1111 \\ 1111 & 1111 & 1111 & 1111 \\ 1111 & 1111 & 1111 & 1111 \\ 1111 & 1111 & 1111 & 1111 \end{pmatrix} = (\ldots f_{15} = 1 \ldots)
\end{aligned} \tag{23}$$

In Figure 3, variation the configurations among W coding: $P = (2301), \{\Delta\} = \begin{array}{|c|c|}\hline 1111 & 1100 \\ \hline 0011 & 0000 \\ \hline\end{array}$

$$\begin{pmatrix} 0 & 2 & 1 & 3 \\ 8 & 10 & 9 & 11 \\ 4 & 6 & 5 & 7 \\ 12 & 14 & 13 & 15 \end{pmatrix}_{\Delta=1111} \cap \begin{pmatrix} 15 & 13 & 14 & 12 \\ 7 & 5 & 6 & 4 \\ 11 & 9 & 10 & 8 \\ 3 & 1 & 2 & 0 \end{pmatrix}_{\Delta=0000}$$

$$= \begin{pmatrix} 3 & 1 & 2 & 0 \\ 11 & 9 & 10 & 8 \\ 7 & 5 & 6 & 4 \\ 15 & 13 & 14 & 12 \end{pmatrix}_{\Delta=1100} \cap \begin{pmatrix} 12 & 14 & 13 & 15 \\ 4 & 6 & 5 & 7 \\ 8 & 10 & 9 & 11 \\ 0 & 2 & 1 & 3 \end{pmatrix}_{\Delta=0011} \tag{24}$$

$$= \begin{pmatrix} 0000 & 0000 & 0000 & 0000 \\ 0000 & 0000 & 0000 & 0000 \\ 0000 & 0000 & 0000 & 0000 \\ 0000 & 0000 & 0000 & 0000 \end{pmatrix} = (\ldots f_0 = 0 \ldots)$$

$$\begin{pmatrix} 0 & 2 & 1 & 3 \\ 8 & 10 & 9 & 11 \\ 4 & 6 & 5 & 7 \\ 12 & 14 & 13 & 15 \end{pmatrix}_{\Delta=1111} \cup \begin{pmatrix} 15 & 13 & 14 & 12 \\ 7 & 5 & 6 & 4 \\ 11 & 9 & 10 & 8 \\ 3 & 1 & 2 & 0 \end{pmatrix}_{\Delta=0000}$$

$$= \begin{pmatrix} 3 & 1 & 2 & 0 \\ 11 & 9 & 10 & 8 \\ 7 & 5 & 6 & 4 \\ 15 & 13 & 14 & 12 \end{pmatrix}_{\Delta=1100} \cup \begin{pmatrix} 12 & 14 & 13 & 15 \\ 4 & 6 & 5 & 7 \\ 8 & 10 & 9 & 11 \\ 0 & 2 & 1 & 3 \end{pmatrix}_{\Delta=0011} \tag{25}$$

$$= \begin{pmatrix} 1111 & 1111 & 1111 & 1111 \\ 1111 & 1111 & 1111 & 1111 \\ 1111 & 1111 & 1111 & 1111 \\ 1111 & 1111 & 1111 & 1111 \end{pmatrix} = (\ldots f_{15} = 1 \ldots)$$

This group contains visual symmetric effects in each block similar to Figure 2. Due to different permutation applied, detailed arrangements of each block are significantly different. The composed matrix under $\{\Delta\}$ operations also has horizontal and vertical reflect symmetries.

In Figure 4, the F coding-scheme is selected: under this configuration, $P = (2310), \{\Delta\} = \begin{array}{|c|c|}\hline 1111 & 1100 \\ \hline 0011 & 0000 \\ \hline\end{array}$.

$$\begin{aligned}
&\begin{pmatrix} 0 & 1 & 2 & 3 \\ 8 & 9 & 10 & 11 \\ 4 & 5 & 6 & 7 \\ 12 & 13 & 14 & 15 \end{pmatrix}_{\Delta=1111} \bigcap \begin{pmatrix} 15 & 14 & 13 & 12 \\ 7 & 6 & 5 & 4 \\ 11 & 10 & 9 & 8 \\ 3 & 2 & 1 & 0 \end{pmatrix}_{\Delta=0000} \\
&= \begin{pmatrix} 3 & 2 & 1 & 0 \\ 11 & 10 & 9 & 8 \\ 7 & 6 & 5 & 4 \\ 15 & 14 & 13 & 12 \end{pmatrix}_{\Delta=1100} \bigcap \begin{pmatrix} 12 & 13 & 14 & 15 \\ 4 & 5 & 6 & 7 \\ 8 & 9 & 10 & 11 \\ 0 & 1 & 2 & 3 \end{pmatrix}_{\Delta=0011} \\
&= \begin{pmatrix} 0000 & 0000 & 0000 & 0000 \\ 0000 & 0000 & 0000 & 0000 \\ 0000 & 0000 & 0000 & 0000 \\ 0000 & 0000 & 0000 & 0000 \end{pmatrix} = (\ldots f_0 = 0 \ldots)
\end{aligned} \tag{26}$$

$$\begin{aligned}
&\begin{pmatrix} 0 & 1 & 2 & 3 \\ 8 & 9 & 10 & 11 \\ 4 & 5 & 6 & 7 \\ 12 & 13 & 14 & 15 \end{pmatrix}_{\Delta=1111} \bigcup \begin{pmatrix} 15 & 14 & 13 & 12 \\ 7 & 6 & 5 & 4 \\ 11 & 10 & 9 & 8 \\ 3 & 2 & 1 & 0 \end{pmatrix}_{\Delta=0000} \\
&= \begin{pmatrix} 3 & 2 & 1 & 0 \\ 11 & 10 & 9 & 8 \\ 7 & 6 & 5 & 4 \\ 15 & 14 & 13 & 12 \end{pmatrix}_{\Delta=1100} \bigcup \begin{pmatrix} 12 & 13 & 14 & 15 \\ 4 & 5 & 6 & 7 \\ 8 & 9 & 10 & 11 \\ 0 & 1 & 2 & 3 \end{pmatrix}_{\Delta=0011} \\
&= \begin{pmatrix} 1111 & 1111 & 1111 & 1111 \\ 1111 & 1111 & 1111 & 1111 \\ 1111 & 1111 & 1111 & 1111 \\ 1111 & 1111 & 1111 & 1111 \end{pmatrix} = (\ldots f_{15} = 1 \ldots)
\end{aligned} \tag{27}$$

There are six pairs (0:15, 1:7, 2:11, 4:13, 6:9, 8:14) of complementary functions that can be visually identified in pair conjugate symmetric conditions for each complementary block. The group has four block matrices in which containing the same pairs of configurations. There are horizontal and vertical symmetries too.

In Figure 5, C coding has represented: $P = (0231), \{\Delta\} = \begin{array}{|c|c|}\hline 1111 & 1100 \\ \hline 0011 & 0000 \\ \hline \end{array}$. Checking four blocks under $\cup$ operations:

$$
\begin{pmatrix} 0 & 4 & 1 & 5 \\ 2 & 6 & 3 & 7 \\ 8 & 12 & 9 & 13 \\ 10 & 14 & 11 & 15 \end{pmatrix}_{\Delta=1111} \bigcup \begin{pmatrix} 15 & 11 & 14 & 10 \\ 13 & 9 & 12 & 8 \\ 7 & 3 & 6 & 2 \\ 5 & 1 & 4 & 0 \end{pmatrix}_{\Delta=0000}
$$
$$
= \begin{pmatrix} 5 & 1 & 4 & 0 \\ 7 & 3 & 6 & 2 \\ 13 & 9 & 12 & 8 \\ 15 & 11 & 14 & 10 \end{pmatrix}_{\Delta=1100} \bigcup \begin{pmatrix} 10 & 14 & 11 & 15 \\ 8 & 12 & 9 & 13 \\ 2 & 6 & 3 & 7 \\ 0 & 4 & 1 & 5 \end{pmatrix}_{\Delta=0011} \tag{28}
$$
$$
= \begin{pmatrix} 1111 & 1111 & 1111 & 1111 \\ 1111 & 1111 & 1111 & 1111 \\ 1111 & 1111 & 1111 & 1111 \\ 1111 & 1111 & 1111 & 1111 \end{pmatrix} = (\ldots f_{15} = 1 \ldots)
$$

In addition to six pairs similar to F coding, four corners of the 4x4 image matrix are fixed by the 4 functions (0, 5, 10, 15) in four block matrices. Four functions of each block are $\{f_0 = 0, f_5 = \bar{x}, f_{10} = x, f_{15} = 1\}$. In addition, pairs of horizontal reflection results can be observed via $\{\Delta\} = \{1111, 1100\}$ operations and pairs of vertical reflection results can be observed via $\{\Delta\} = \{1111, 0011\}$ operations. This property makes this coding scheme be the most regular structures among all coding schemes.

In Figure 6, W coding is represented as: $P = (3210), \{\Delta\} =$

1111	1110	1101	1100
1011	1010	1001	1000
0111	0110	0101	0100
0011	0010	0001	0000

.

Four corner blocks are 4 block matrices under {1111, 1100, 0011, 0000} operations contain the same figures in Figure 2. All block matrices have reflection symmetric distributions via horizontal and vertical reflection symmetry distributions. This extending matrix is showing further symmetric properties in this construction, through a lot of image block matrices without clear pairs of local symmetry, a global reflection symmetric matrix can be observed under the complementary operations.

In Figure 7, W coding has represented: $P = (3102), \{\Delta\} =$

1111	1110	1101	1100
1011	1010	1001	1000
0111	0110	0101	0100
0011	0010	0001	0000

.

From a global viewpoint, this configuration has a global horizontal and vertical reflection symmetry in vertical and horizontal directions. From a local viewpoint, this configuration has more local symmetry than Figure 6. Four corners are 4 blocks {1111, 1100, 0011, 0000} are composed of figures to be typical C coding scheme shown in Figure 5. In addition, four inner corners of block matrices {1010, 1001, 0110, 0101} contain a F coding structure. Under a local observation, other 8 block matrices and their relevant functions in each matrix are composed of images without clear pairs of conjugate symmetric properties.

8. Comparison

It is convenient to list numeric parameters to compare for different coding schemes in following table.

Var	State	Function	ExPower	SL	W code	F code	C code
n	2^n	2^{2^n}	$2^n!$	1	$2^{2^n} \cdot 2^n!$	$2^{2^n(1+1/2)} \cdot 2^{n-1}!$	$8 \cdot 2^{n-1}!$
1	2	4	2	1	8	8	8
2	4	16	24	1	384	128	16
3	8	256	40320	1	10321920	98304	192
4	16	2^{16}	16!	1	$2^{16} \cdot 16!$	$2^{24} \cdot 8!$	$8 \cdot 8!$
5	32	2^{32}	32!	1	$2^{32} \cdot 32!$	$2^{48} \cdot 16!$	$8 \cdot 16!$

where we use Var: variable number; State: state number; Function: function number; ExPower: exponent power products; SL: SL coding number; W code: W coding number under vector operations; F code: F coding number under vector operations; C code: C coding number under vector operations in the table respectively.

9. Conclusion

The arrangement of binary function space using a hierarchy of four spaces of classifications can be used to add symmetry and regular structure onto the entire space of binary-functions. This construction has capacities to support vector permutations and complementary operations. For ease of visualization, it is convenient to apply 2D matrix-type representation mechanism that enables symmetric configurations of the system to be analysed via different coding schemes from a local or global viewpoint. Binary functional spaces provide additional optimal information to generate large numbers of potential configurations in order to arrange and organise variant logic spaces. Complementary operations are made further extension easier and visualising in a larger matrix. Sample matrices are shown their configurations in different functionals and complementary operations. From these examples, exhaustive approaches for functional space are illustrated.

From a series of definitions, propositions and theorems, solid foundation of variant logic framework has been constructed. Under selected sample images and operational matrices, a set of typical results are illustrated. This construction can be observed from different viewpoints under symmetric considerations, in addition to detect emerging patterns from each recursively operations, further global transforming patterns can be identified from a functional space viewpoint. Under such expanding mechanism, a beautiful nature of mathematics has appeared. True natural effects are interesting for modern developments.

9.1 Future work

The mechanism can be developed further to establish foundations for logical construction of applications for computational models and structural optimisation requirements. Investigation on different coding schemes within the higher levels of organisation will be described in future work. This new mathematical logic foundation will support further theoretical descriptions to explore dynamic logics using modern mathematical language.

9.2 Acknowledgments

Thanks Mr. J. Wan for generation all sample images and configurations for the paper. Financial support was given by School of Software, Yunnan University.

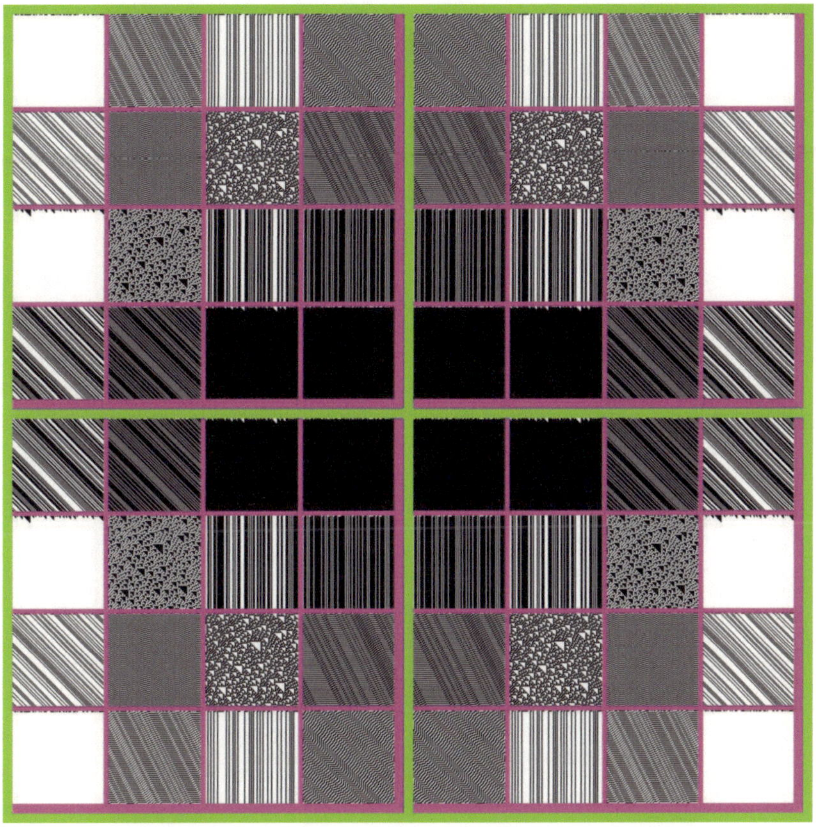

(a)

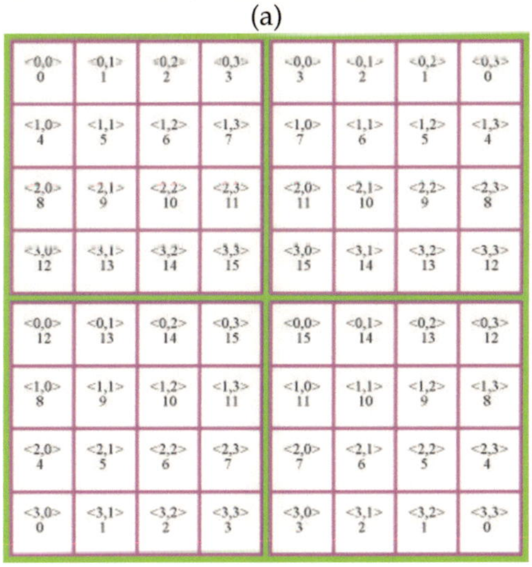

(b)

Fig. 2. W coding (SL code): $P = (3210), P(\Delta) = \{1111, 1100, 0011, 0000\}$; (a)2x2 base blocks (b)2x2 vector blocks

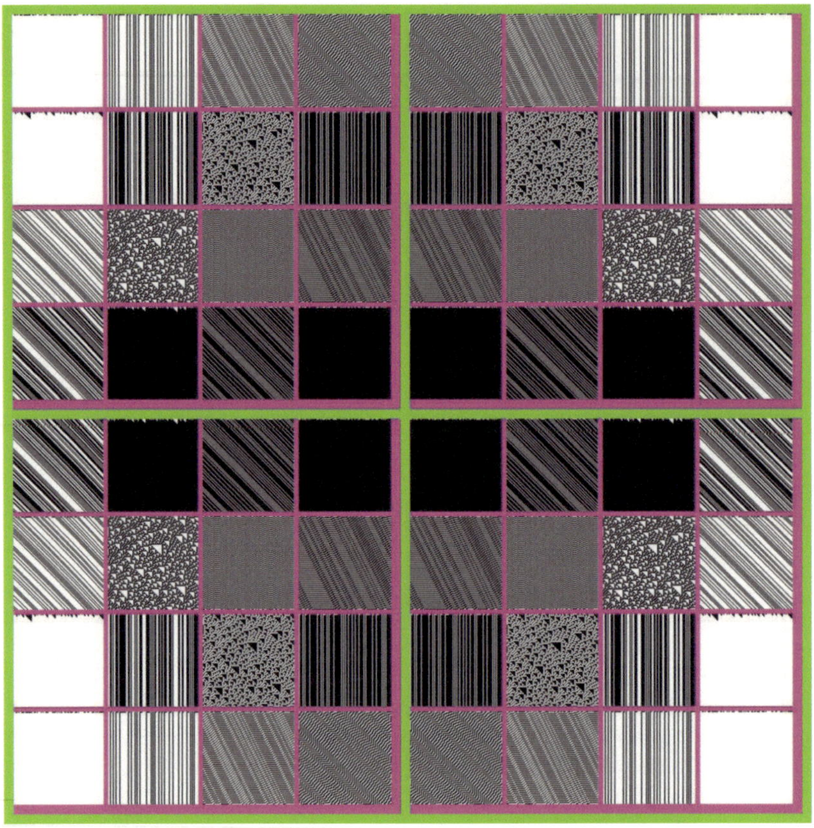

(a)

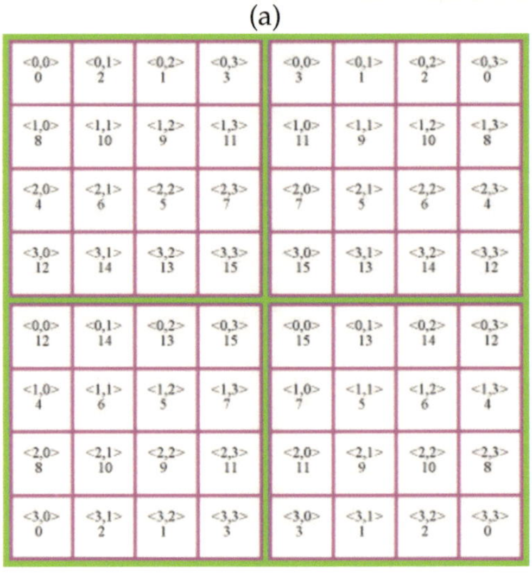

(b)

Fig. 3. W coding: $P = (2301), P(\Delta) = \{1111, 1100, 0011, 0000\}$; (a)2x2 base blocks (b)2x2 vector blocks

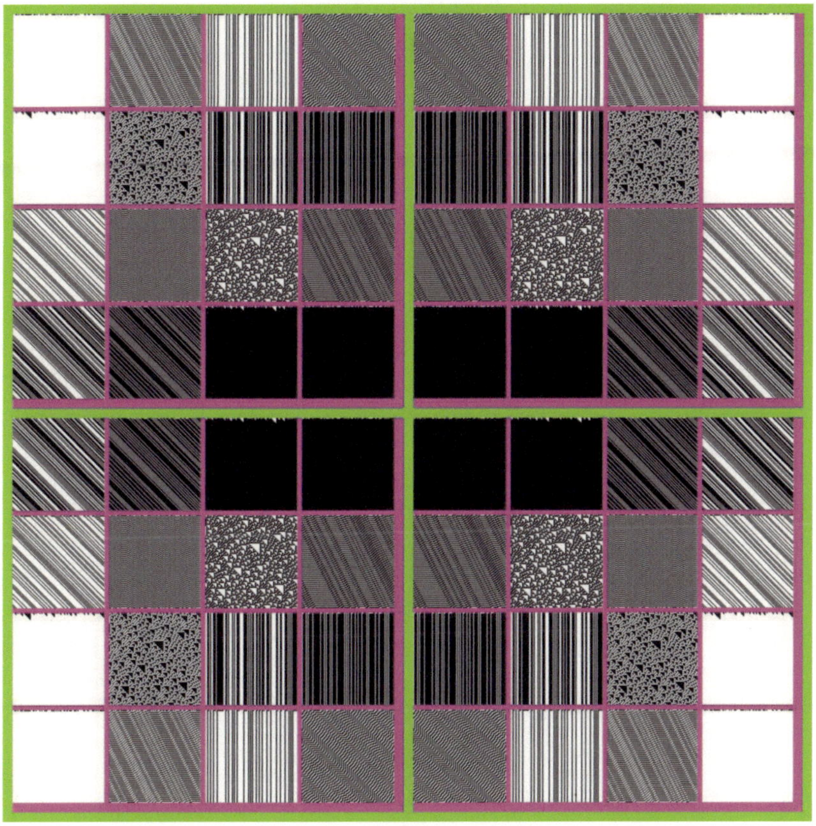

(a)

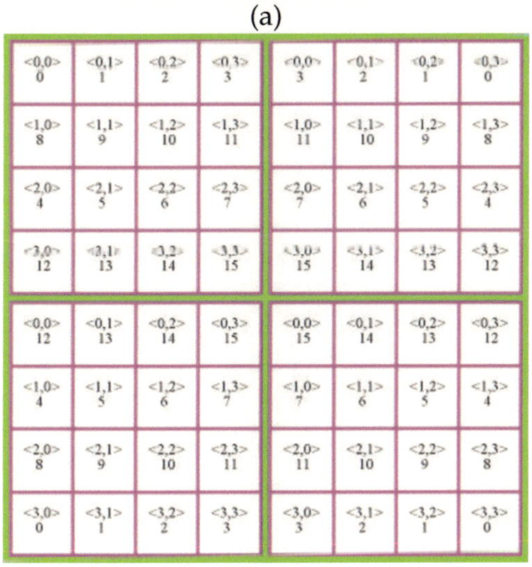

(b)

Fig. 4. F coding: $P = (2310), P(\Delta) = \{1111, 1100, 0011, 0000\}$; (a)2x2 base blocks (b)2x2 vector blocks

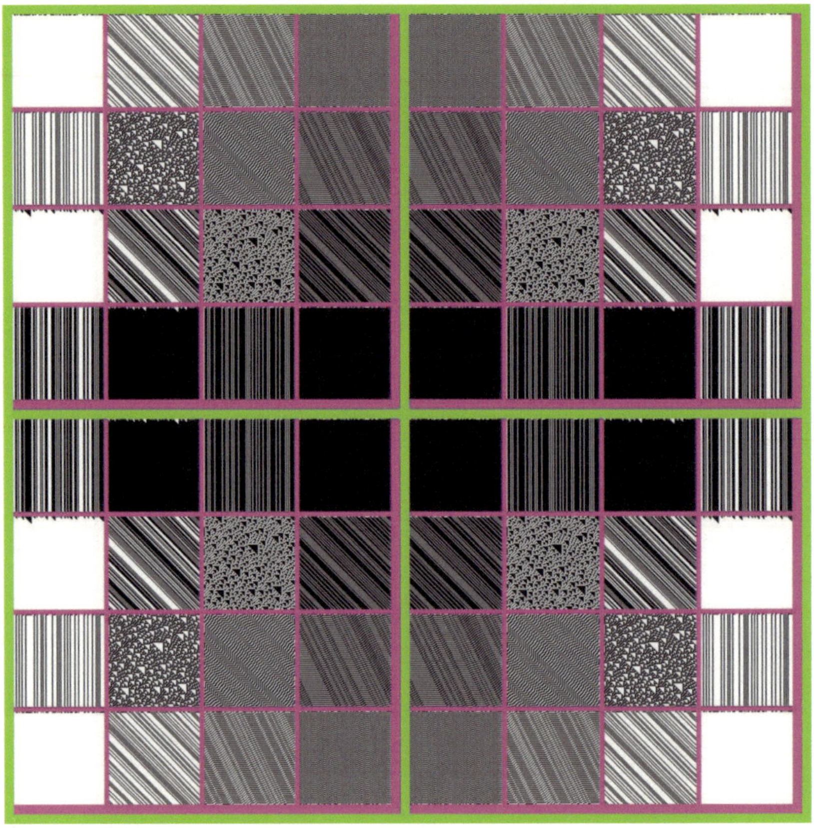

(a)

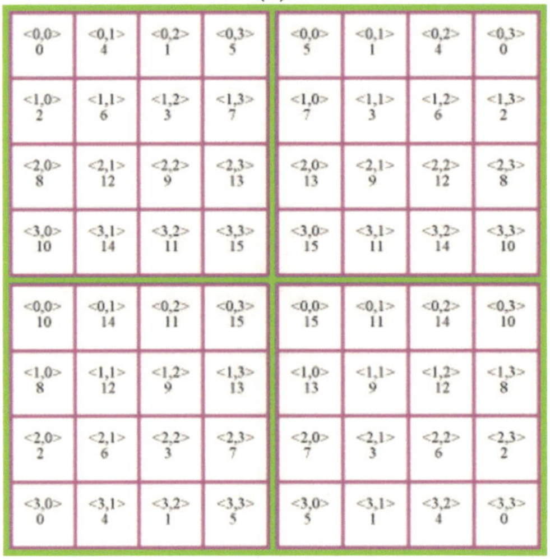

(b)

Fig. 5. C coding: $P = (0231), P(\Delta) = \{1111, 1100, 0011, 0000\}$; (a)2x2 base blocks (b)2x2 vector blocks

(a)

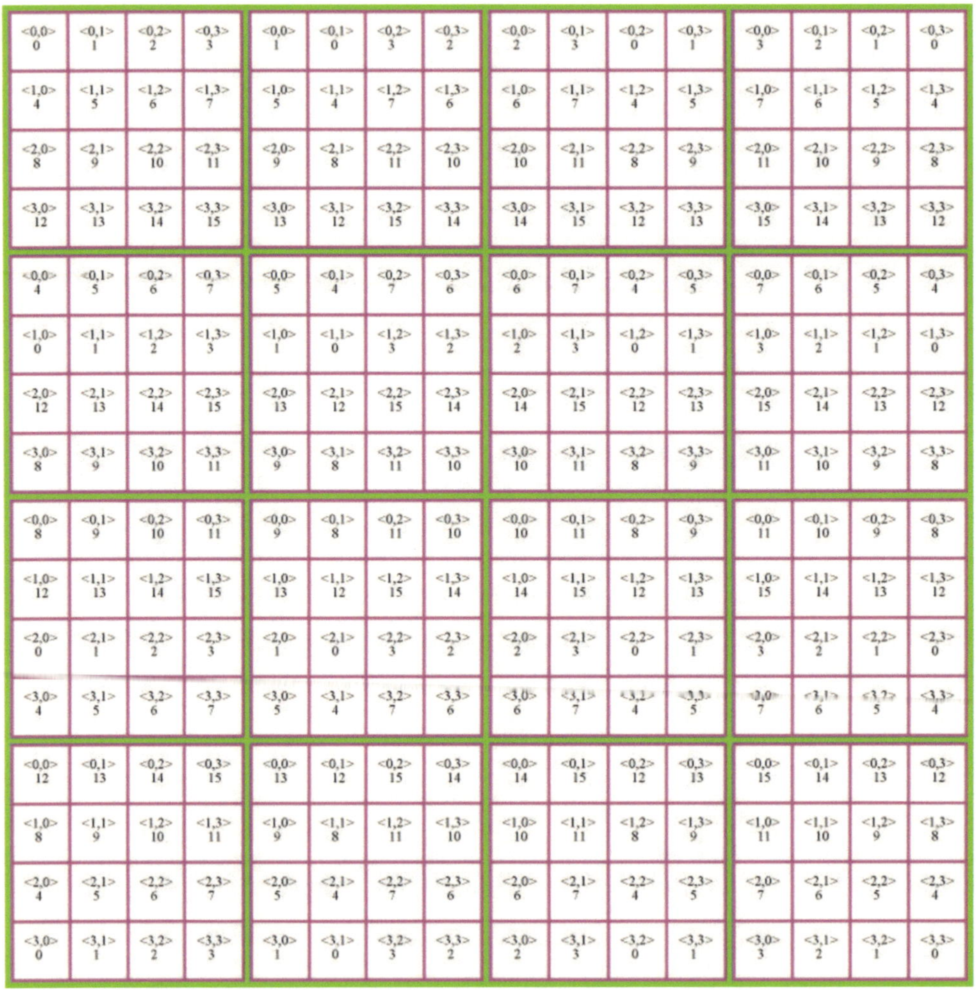

(b)

Fig. 6. W coding: $P = (3210)$,
$P(\Delta) =$
$\{1111, 1110, 1101, 1100, 1011, 1010, 1001, 1000, 0111, 0110, 0101, 0100, 0011, 0010, 0001, 0000\}$;
(a)4x4 base blocks (b)4x4 vector blocks

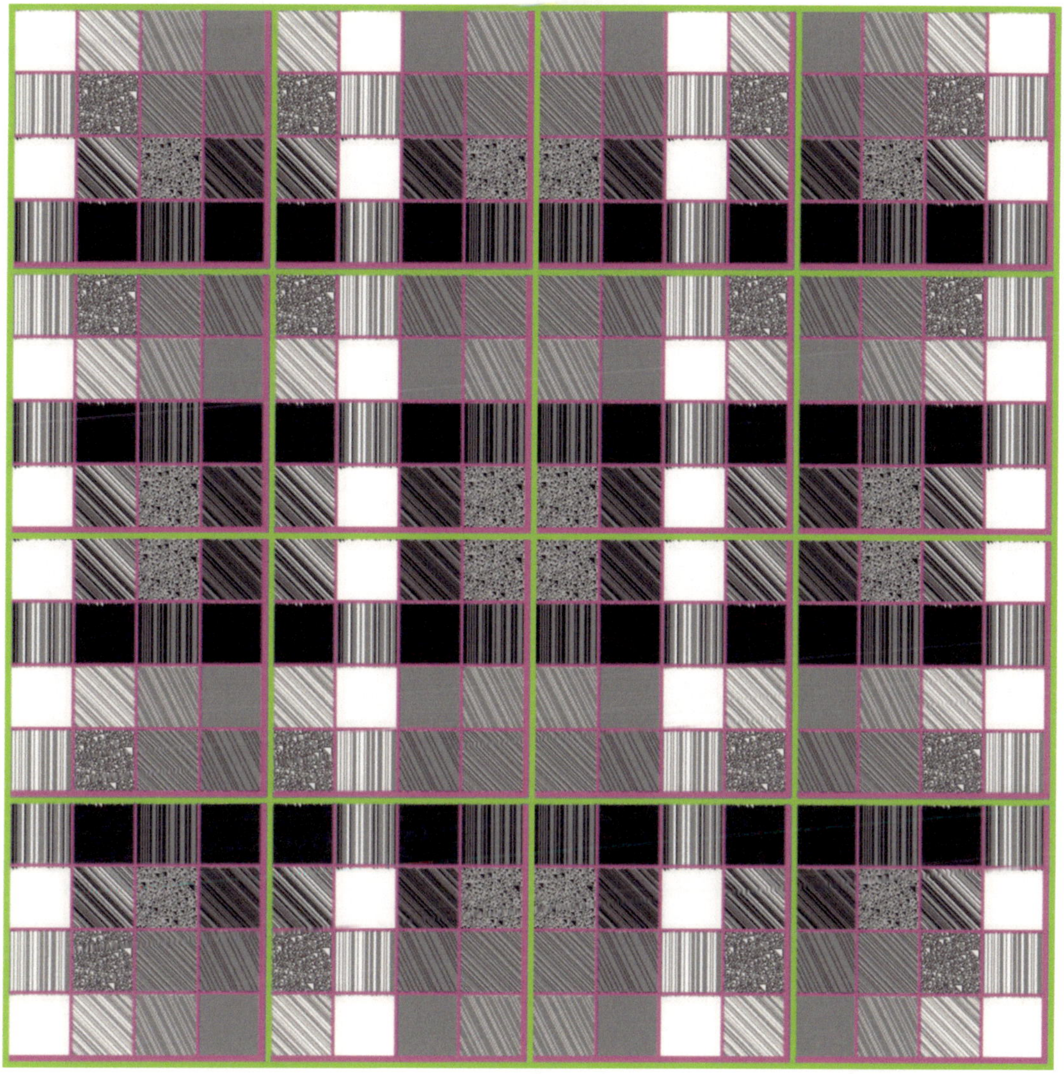

(a)

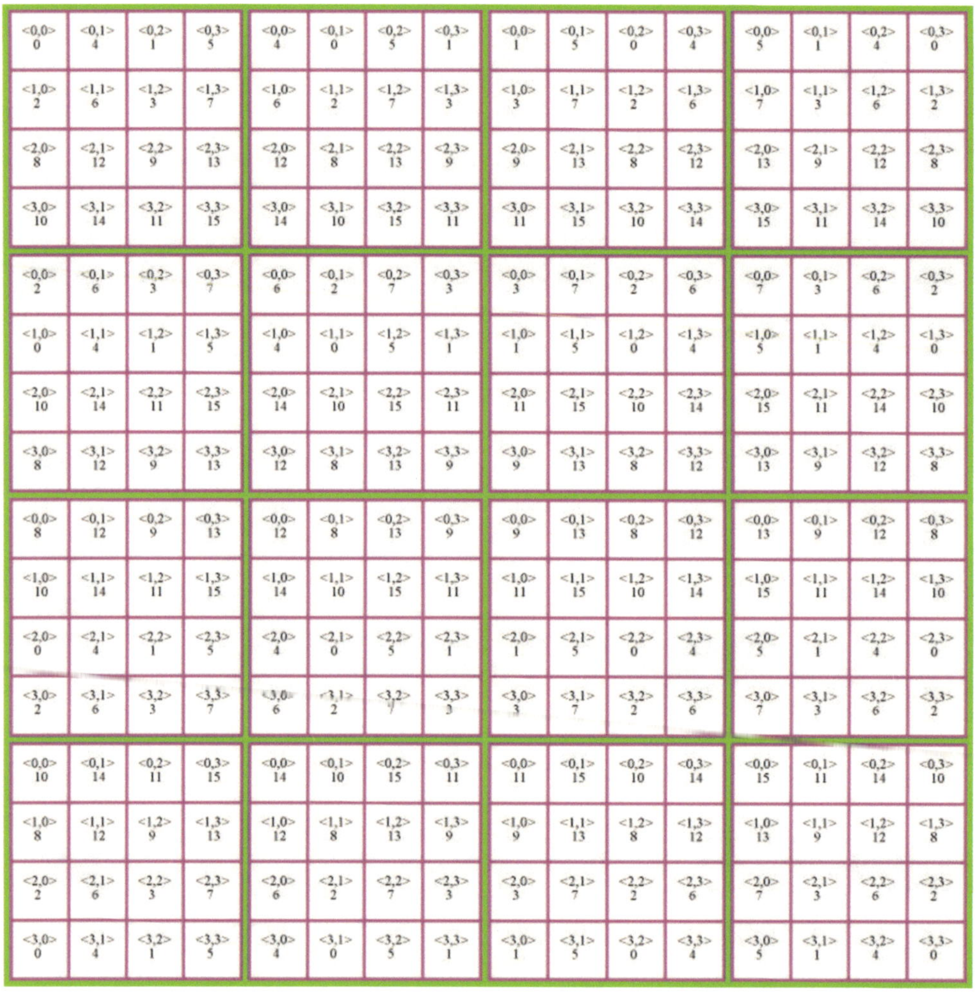

(b)

Fig. 7. W coding: $P = (3102)$,
$P(\Delta) =$
$\{1111, 1110, 1101, 1100, 1011, 1010, 1001, 1000, 0111, 0110, 0101, 0100, 0011, 0010, 0001, 0000\}$;
(a)4x4 base blocks (b)4x4 vector blocks

10. References

Adamatzky, A. (2008). Automata-2008: Theory and applications of cellular automata, *Luniver Press* .

Bonnet, M. (1989). Handbook of boolean algebras, *North Holland* .

Boole, G. (1850/1940/1958). An investigation of the laws of thought, *Dover* .

Chu, W. & Sherrill, W. (1977). An anthology of i ching, *Routledge and Kegan Paul Ltd* .

Cooper, J. (1981). Yin and yang, the taoist harmony of opposites, *The Thetford Press* .

Dawson, J. (2005). Logical dilemmas - the life and work of kurt gödel, *A.K. Peters, Ltd.* .

Demopoulos, W. (1995). Frege's philosophy of mathematics, *Harvard University Press* .

Dunn, P. (1988). The complexity of boolean networks, *Academic Press* .

Govinda, L. (1981). The inner structure of i ching: The book of transformation, *Wheelwright Press* .

Griffeath, D. & Moor, C. (2003). New constructions in cellular automata, *Santa Fe Institute Studies in the Sciences of Complexity* .

Hilbert, D. (1899). Grundlagen der geometrie, *Goettingen* .

Hook, D. (1975). The i ching and mankind, *Routledge and Kegan Paul Ltd* .

Ilachinski, A. (2001). Cellular automata-a discrete universe, *World Scientific* .

Kline, M. (1972). Mathematical thought from ancient to modern times, *Oxford University Press* .

Kunii, T., Hioki, H. & Shinagawa, Y. (1993). Visualizing highly abstract mathematical concepts: a case study in animation of homology groups, *Multimedia Modeling, World Scientific* pp. 3–30.

Kunii, T. & Kunii, H. (1999). A cellular model for information systems on the web - integrating local and global information, *Proceedings of 1999 International Symposium on Database Applications in Non-Traditional Environments, IEEE CS Press* .

Kunii, T. & Shinagawa, Y. (1992). Modern geometric computing for visualization, *Springer Verlag* .

Kunii, T. & Takahashi, S. (1993). Area guide map modeling by manifolds and cw-complexes, *Modeling in Computer Graphics, Springer Verlag* pp. 5–20.

Kunii, T. & Takai, Y. (1989). Cellular self-reproducing automata as a parallel processing model for botanical colony growth pattern simulation, *New Advances in Computer Graphics, Springer Verlag* pp. 7–22.

Kunii, T., Tsuchida, Y., Arai, Y., Matsuda, H., Shirahama, M. & Miura, S. (1993). A model of hands and arms based on manifold mappings, *Communicating with Virtual Worlds, Springer Verlag* pp. 381–398.

Lee, S. (1978). Modern switching theory and digital design, *Prentice-Hall Inc.* .

Leibniz, G. (1976). Philosophical papers and letters, *Springer* .

Leibniz, G., Ariew, R. & Garber, D. (1989). Philosophical essays, *Hackett Publishing* .

Needham, J. & Wang, L. (1954-1988). Science and civilisation in china: History of scientific thought., *Cambridge Press* 2.

Paterson, M. (1992). Boolean function complexity, *Cambridge University Press* .

Reichenbach, H. (1949). The theory of probability, *The University of California Press* .

Russell, B. (1942). Principles of mathematics, *Forgotten Books* .

Schiff, J. (2007). Cellular automata: A discrete view of the world, *Wiley Series in Discrete Mathematics and Optimization* .

Shannon, C., Sloane, N. & Wyner, A. (1993). Claude elwood shannon: Collected papers, *IEEE Press, IEEE Information Theory Society* .

Shchutshii, I. (1979). Researches on the i ching, *Princeton University Press* .

Sikorski, R. (1960). Boolean algebra, *Springer-Verlag* .

Turing, A. (1936). On computable numbers, with an application to the entscheidungs problem, *Proceedings of London Mathematical Society, Ser.2* 42: 230–265.

Umeo, H., Morishita, S. & Nishinari, K. (2008). Cellular automata, *Springer* .

Vingron, S. (2004). Switching theory: Insight through predicate logic, *Springer* .

von Neumann, J. (1966). Theory of self-reproducing automata, *University of Illionois Press* .

Whincup, G. (1986). Rediscovering of i ching, *GreyWhincup* .

Wilhelmi, H. (1979). Chang: Eight lectures on i ching, *Princeton Press* .

Wilhemi, R. (1979). Lectures on the i ching: Constancy and change, *Princeton University Press* .

Wolfram, S. (1985). Twenty problems in the theory of cellular automata, *Physica Scripta* T9: 170–183.

Wolfram, S. (1986). Theory and applications of cellular automata, *World Scientific* .

Wolfram, S. (1994). Cellular automata and complexity, *Addison-Wesley* .

Wolfram, S. (2002). A new kind of science, *Wolfram Media Inc.* . http://www.wolframscience.com/.

Wuensche, A. & Lesser, M. (1992). The global dynamics of cellular automata, *Santa Fe Institute studies in the sciences of complexity: Reference volumes, Addison-Wesley Publishing Company* 1.

Zadeh, L. (1965). Fazzy sets, *Information and Control* 8. 338-357.

Zheng, J. & Zheng, C. (2010). A framework to express variant and invariant functional spaces for binary logic, *Frontiers of Electrical and Electronic Engineering in China, Higher Education Press and Springer* 5(2): 163–172. http://www.springerlink.com/content/91474403127n446u/.

Zheng, Z. (1994). Conjugate transformation of regular plan lattices for binary images, *PhD Thesis, Monash University* .

Zheng, Z. (1996). Conjugate visualisation of global complex behaviour, *Complexity International* 3. http://www.complexity.org.au/ci/vol03/zheng/.

Zheng, Z. & Leung, C. (1996). Visualising global behaviour of 1d cellular automata image sequences in 2d maps, *Physica A* 233: 785–800.

Zheng, Z. & Maeder, A. (1992). The conjugate classification of the kernel form of the hexagonal grid, *Modern Geometric Computing for Visualization. Springer-Verlag* pp. 73–89.

Zheng, Z. & Maeder, A. (1993). The elementary equation of the conjugate transformation for hexagonal grid, *Modeling in Computer Graphics. Springer-Verlag* pp. 21–42.

Part 4

Robotics and Image Processing

17

Using Probabilistic Cellular Automaton for Adaptive Modules Selection in the Human State Problem

Martin Lukac[1], Michitaka Kameyama[2] and Marek Perkowski[3]
[1,2]*Tohoku University*
[3]*Portland State University*
[1,2]*Japan*
[3]*USA*

1. Introduction

The field of the HRI is an important area of research in robotics with wide range of applications and open problems. One of the main reasons for being an attractive research field, is the fact that robots designed to act in environment side by side with humans require highly complex and adaptive interaction mechanisms. This requirement for complex processing is due to the fact that one of the main components of the HRI is the emotional expression. However, emotions are not only present in human communication but also have been found to take part in memory mediation, focus, imagination or complexity reduction (4–7). Because both the human emotional expression and emotional mechanisms are still an open area of research it is not possible to formulate a precise function that would truly model these mechanisms. Thus robots designed for human interaction such as service bots, social robots or simple social agents require a lot of adaptive mechanisms allowing them to at least partially account for the complexity of human communication and adapt quickly to the unpredicted situations arising from hidden emotional human states.

Robots evolving in the social environment cannot always expect explicit feedback. The feedback from a user with respect to a robot can be either explicit (pressing a button, voice command) or indirect; an automated robotic system that extracts the change of user expression, body posture or facial expression can use such information to adapt its behavior. The successful usage of such indirect feedback can be very useful in some robotic applications. However, despite being less invasive, the indirect feedback is more difficult to use because a robotic application might not be always able to determine the proper cause of the human emotional state (the robot might not be able to determine if the patient is unhappy because of wrong service or because of bad internal (personal) state). A good example is a hospital service robot: some patients might not always be able to properly communicate their state explicitly. Thus estimating their internal state or intentions is very important.

To analyze the above introduced problems we propose a so-called *Human State Problem*(HSP). The HSP consist of a robotic application and of a user with some unknown expectations about the robot performance. The robot's behavior is generated with the goal to keep (or bring) the user to a desired target emotional state. The robotic application has only access to the indirect human feedback (emotional state estimation, posture estimation, etc.) to evaluate its performance. The indirect human feedback is unlike classical human feedback - passively captured by robot sensors and without the user's explicit and symbolic feedback. In this manner the robot behavior is seamlessly adapted to user expectations and the user obtains a unique and pleasant experience. Such feedback is considered to be noisy, difficult to analyze and not always represent only the user expectations about the robot's performance. The robot thus cannot analyze fully the environment as well as completely map user preferences (intentions) and must use active emotional-state-mining approach to extract a maximum information from a particular user state to plan its next actions.

In this chapter we first look at the Human State Problem from a probabilistic point of view within the context of the Live-Feeling Communication. As one possible approach to solving the HSP we introduce the Adaptive Functional Module Selection (AFMS) framework of robotics aimed to act in a social context. The AFMS robotic model uses a set of black boxes (computational processes) to map in real-time an input-to-output by quickly selecting the most appropriate computational resources from a pool of available intelligent processing modules. The selection mechanism is based on the indirect user feedback, and in this chapter we provide the initial problem formulation and description of the overall system. We describe a Bayesian Network (BN) example as a method of arbitrating the AFMS mechanism. The BN approach is described as example of real life situations problem solver however, it might not be practically the most efficient approach because the real-life environment does not always posses a hierarchy that could be efficiently exploited in the BN methodology. As an alternative we present a Cellular Automaton (CA) based approach for AFMS mechanism and demonstrate its potential use in such situations where models such as BN cannot be efficiently used.

This chapter is divided as follows. Section 2 introduces the details of the studied problems; the Section 2.1 introduces the details of the HSP and Section 3 introduces the probabilistic formulation of the HSP. Section 4 describes the Adaptive Functional-Modules Selection (AFMS) mechanism (10; 11) and Section 5 presents the AFMS based robotic platform. Section 6 describes the use of Cellular Automaton for behavior arbitration and Section 7 provides a machine learning approach to the HSP using Bayesian Network. Finally Section 8 concludes the chapter and provides discussion on the results and future work.

2. Predicting human intentions from the observations of its emotional expression

2.1 The human state problem framework

The problem framework is shown in Figure 1. A robotic application with a set of sensors and actuators is designed with the goal to keep the user in a *happy* state as long as possible. The mapping from sensors to actuators is done by assigning resources from the *Intelligent Processing Resources* pool by the controller that receives the feedback from the user. The user, observing the output of the robot, changes its state such as from happy to unhappy, or happy to happy, and the change of state is provided as the feedback to the controller.

Let s_{uh} be a user state from a set of all possible observable human emotional states $U = \{u_0, \dots, u_k, \tilde{u}\}$, with $\tilde{u}$ being the target user (set of) state(s), and let c_j be the robot state from the set of all possible robot states $C = \{c_0, \dots, c_p\}$. Each state c is represented by an output that corresponds to the full process of mapping a given input to the output in the state c_j. In the rest of this chapter we use c for an arbitrary robotic state and u for an arbitrary user state. A configuration is given by the state of the user $u \in U$ and the state of the robotic application $C \in \{c_0, \dots, c_j\}$: $\gamma(s_u, s_r)$.

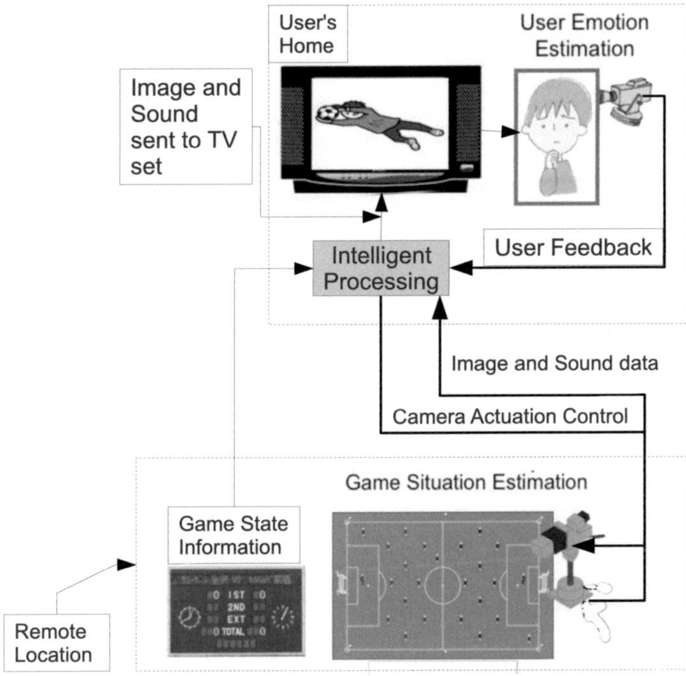

Fig. 1. The Live-feeling communication application. The user sitting in front of the TV has its emotional state passively extracted from a set of sensors on the TV. The emotional state is used to adaptively reconfigure the robotic behavior that controls the actuators of the cameras on the remote location. The decision making is done inside of the box *Intelligent processing* .

In order to make the problem at least partially tractable and allow further investigation, we simplify further the overall framework. We assume the following conditions:

1. The state of the machine c changes the state of the human u immediately
2. If a machine state c does not change the human state u immediately, it is assumed that it will have no effect on later changes on the human state u while the machine remains in the state c
3. For now, the human state as well as the human state change is considered to be only the application related and it is assumed that the desired state is reachable using the robotic application.

The robot changes its state from c_j to c_k using a state change relation $f : (u_l, c_j) \rightarrow (u_m, c_k)$. It is assumed that for each robotic state c there is a corresponding change in human state given by $u_j = (u_i, c)$. But following condition 1, the human state change caused by robot state change is not necessarily observable by the robot.

Figure 2 shows the high level of this framework. On the left is a non-terminal user state: $\bar{u} = U - \tilde{u}$ and on the right side it the user in the target state $\tilde{u}$. The change from an non-terminal state to the desired target state can be triggered by various sequences of robotic states (actions). Formally, from the point of view of the robot architecture the goal is specified by:

$$\{\forall c \in C,\ f|(u,c) \xrightarrow{min_G} (\tilde{u},c)\} \tag{1}$$

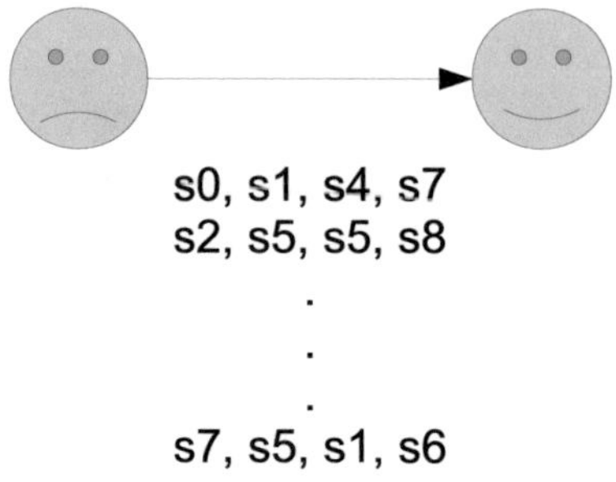

Fig. 2. The problem statement: what is the minimal set of states the robotic controller has to go through to make the user be happy?

This means that we are looking for such a relation f or a set of functions $\hat{f} = \{f_0, \ldots, f_o\}$ that will in a finite number of steps bring the user from an arbitrary state u to the target desired state $\tilde{u}$.

2.2 The human state problem

Definition 1 (The Human State Problem)**.** The problem of finding such a mechanism that would in a particular context of a robotic application successfully estimate human intentions related to the application only from indirect emotional feedback.

Figure 3 shows the concepts and the main components of the HSP setup. The G^t, G^{t+1} represents two consecutive states of the application context - the environment. Similarly, C^t, C^{t+1} represents two consecutive states of the robot and U^t, U^{t+1} represents two consecutive states of the user. The full arrows represent state transitions and the dotted arrows represent inputs to state transition functions. The environment is considered to be

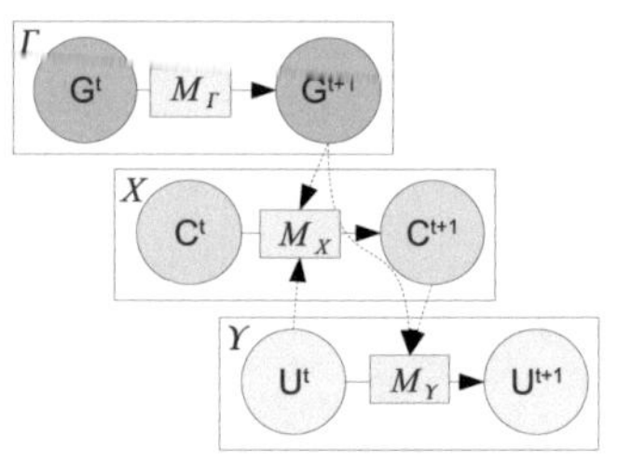

Fig. 3. The HSP context

an autonomous machine - neither the robot neither the user can change how the environment change its states[1]. The change of the environment state triggers a change in the robot state that then triggers the change of the user state. Observe that while the environment is an autonomous machine the robot and the user are both interconnected.

The robotic application used to formulate this model is shown in Figure 1. The robot is represented by the box labeled *Robotic Agent* and its function is to provide the user with a camera configuration most suitable for the user preferences and given a particular state of the environment (live sports event). The user provides feedback in the form of emotional expressions that are used to adaptively change the camera work.

[1] This condition is imposed only in the present application context.

The environment machine Γ represents the live event, The machine Ξ is the robotic agent and the machine Y is the user. For the sake of formalization it is assumed that the user state changes only as the result of the game state and of the machine state.

3. The probabilistic human state problem

The HSP is more realistic when defined using probabilistic approach. This is because beside the states C of the machine both the environment and the user states are incompletely defined and highly noisy. Thus with respect to Figure 3 let $G^i = \{g_0, \ldots, g_k\}$ be the set of the states of the environment (for one particular live event i), $C = \{c_o, \ldots, c_j\}$ the set of all the states of the robot and $U^h = \{u_0, \ldots, u_l\}$ the set of observable user emotional states/expressions (for a particular user and its preferences towards the game i, expressed with exponent h). Let Γ be the autonomous state machine of the environment performing the mapping $M_\Gamma : G^i \rightarrow G^i$ on G. Both the user and the robot are interconnected so that we represent the user by a machine Y performing a mapping $M_Y : G^i \times C \times U^h \rightarrow U^h$ on U and the robot by a machine Ξ performing a mapping $M_\Xi : G^i \times C \times U^h \rightarrow C$ on C.
For any two arbitrary states g_q, g_r of Γ the probability of reaching the state g_r from g_q is given by:

$$p(g_r|g_q) \tag{2}$$

Equation (2) represents the probabilistic autonomous state machine of the environment.
Similarly for any two arbitrary state c_m, c_n of Ξ the probability of reaching c_n from c_m is given by $p(c_n|c_m, u_i, q_r)$ and for u_i, u_j of Y the probability is given by $p(u_j|u_i, c_n, q_r)$.
The two conditional probabilities introduced above can be broken into simpler conditions given by:

$$p(c_n|c_m, u_i, g_r) = p(c_n|c_m) \times p(c_n|u_i) \times p(c_n|g_r) \tag{3}$$

and by

$$p(u_j|u_i, c_n, g_r) = p(u_j|u_i) \times p(u_j|c_n) \times p(u_j|g_r) \tag{4}$$

Equations 2 to 4 represent the formulation of the HSP. The component probabilities $p(c_n|u_i)$, $p(c_n|g_r)$, $p(u_j|c_n)$ and $p(u_j|g_r)$ represent the user preferences while the probability $p(c_n|c_m)$ represent the desired mapping constrained by $p(u_j|u_i)$. In other words, the desired robotic mapping is such that

$$p_{max}(c_n|c_m) \leftrightarrow p_{max}(u_j|u_i), \text{ for some desired } u_j \tag{5}$$

The goal of the robot is thus provide such a mapping that will satisfy the user. This can be written as shown in (6).

$$p(c_n, v|c_m, u_i, g_r) = p(u_j|u_i, c_n, g_r) \approx p(c_n|c_m, u_i, g_r) \tag{6}$$

3.1 Human emotional state data mining

In the previous section we were assuming that condition 3 from Section 2.1 was valid. However in real world applications the user providing feedback to the robotic application might not always express its emotional state only as related to the robot task performance. For instance, the application framework illustrated in Figure 1 can be used for an automated Live-performance TV-set. In such case, the actuators control the camera and the microphone and the sensors accept data from the camera and microphone. The output of the camera and the microphone is transmitted to the user via the TV-set. Thus in a particular sport event, the

user can be angry at the team in question (game quality) or can be unhappy about the viewing angle of the camera (robot performance quality). In both cases the expression can be the same and the robot is required to identify the proper cause of user state.
Our approach to deal with this problem is based on Human-Emotional-State data-mining (HESdm). A user in a given state will show different sensitivity to changed robot's actions depending whether yes or no he/she was displeased with the robot previous behaviors. For instance, assume that the user is watching a sport game, and is dissatisfied; i.e. either the performance of the players is not satisfactory either the viewing angle is not adequate. By following the conditions 1 and 2 from Section 2.1 change in user behavior can be described by two cases:

1. The user will change its state proportionally to the change in robot performance (state). This is the case described by all three conditions 1, 2 and 3 in Section 2.1.
2. The user will not change its state proportionally to the change of robotic behavior, because its emotional state is mainly based on the content of the robot's output rather than on the robot's behavior it self.

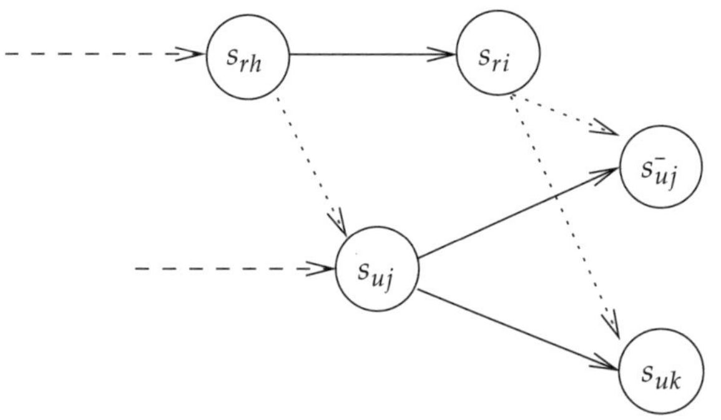

Fig. 4. The human emotional state data mining. The two possible human state changes; the robot changes to a state that either triggers a state of human emotional state or is mostly ignored. This is the trail-and-error approach to determine the relation of user state to the robot's performance.

These two cases are illustrated in Figure 4. The robot is in the state c_h and the human is in the state u_j. It can be seen that we assume that the user-state u_j was generated as the reaction to the robotic state c_h (more or less depending on the content as well). At this point, and depending on the content of the robotic output, the user state is not the desired user state $\tilde{u}_j$. The robot consequently changes the state to c_i to determine the reason of the user state. If the user state is only content related, the resulting user state will be $\bar{u}_j$. The new user state being similar to the previous user state indicates that the user is unhappy because of the content rather than because of the robot performance. In such case the robot can keep the current state until further event either change the user state or particular case of the game will trigger a different robot state. In the opposite case, when the resulting state is u_k, the robot can conclude that the user dissatisfaction is related directly to the robot performance and thus a change in robot actions is required.

4. Adaptive Functional-Modules selection

The Adaptive Functional-Modules Selection (AFMS) (10) was introduced as a mean to provide a mechanism to generate robotic behaviors in real time by recombining component functions.

The AFMS principle is different from the well know behavioral approach to robotics (2) in that in the behavioral approach one deals with monolithic blocks representing behaviors. Instead in the AFMS the monolitic blocks are on the level of functions and each combination of these blocks create a different behavior. The goal of the AFMS mechanism is to provide a lrger repertoire of behaviors while preserving the same amount of computational ressources. Each combination of a set of functions provides a robotic behavior. Using the classical hierarchical robotic paradigm let $P = \{p_\alpha, \ldots, p_\omega\}$ corresponds to a set of functions processing input, $E = \{e_\alpha, \ldots, e_\omega\}$ be a set of functions corresponding to estimation and $A = \{a_\alpha, \ldots, a_\omega\}$ be a group of function controlling the actuation. Also let $B_\Xi = \{b_0, \ldots, b_n\}$ be a set of all possible robot behaviors given by $C \times G$. Let every robot state c_l correspond to a selection of functional modules given by:

$$c_l = p_\alpha \times e_\beta \times a_\delta \tag{7}$$

and the output of the robot to the user is given by a composition of selected functional modules from each group with the current state G:

$$b_j = a_\delta \circ e_\beta \circ p_\alpha(G) \tag{8}$$

resulting in the observable behavior b_j of the robot. Equations 3 and 4 now can be rewritten to a more concise form:

$$p(c_n|c_m, u_i, g_r) = p(c_n|u_i, b_j) = p(c_n|u_i) \times p(c_n|b_j) \tag{9}$$

and

$$p(u_j|u_i, c_n, g_r) = p(u_j|u_i, b_j) = p(u_j|u_i) \times p(u_j|b_j) \tag{10}$$

Note, that unlike the distinct states from C, the behaviors B are not distinct and most of them can be considered equivalent from the point of view of the user. Thus the desired mapping we wish to obtain is given by $p_{max}(c_n|b_j) \leftrightarrow p_{max}(u_j|u_i)$. Because the game states are not completely known and cannot be completely predicted, it is possible to restrict $p(c_n|b_j)$ to $p(b_k|b_j)$ to such set of robotic behaviors that would correspond to unique $C \times G$. This means that for $b_k = b_j$ with $b_k = c_n \times g_q$ and $b_j = c_m \times g_r$, $c_n = c_m$ and $g_q \approx g_r$. In the case when $b_k \neq b_j$, then both $c_n \neq c_m$ and $g_q \neq g_r$. This means that when the robot will estimate that the game states g_r and g_q are similar it will always perform the same camera work. However, from a practical point of view, such restriction could entail that the user will not be able to obtain a maximum satisfaction from the robot performance because the robot will always perform the same camera work for a given group of game states and the user will not be satisfied.
When such generalization cannot be done, in practical application it is the most appropriate to use some sort of machine learning approach because both the user states and the game states are only partially known and cannot be used without a prior learning for making generalizations and predictions.
Before showing the machine learning approach we illustrate the mechanism by which the module selection allows to change robot behavior and how it allows the user to be more or less satisfied with the audio-video data sent to the TV-set.

Example 4.1 (Adaptive Functional-Modules Selection). *The robotic setup shown in Figure 5 shows that the robot has the following functional modules:* player detect (pd), ball detect (bd), position estimator (pe), speed estimator (se), camera movement (cm) *and* camera zooming (cz). *A robotic state C corresponds to a selection of exactly three functional modules; one modules is selected from each column taking input from the previous module (or sensory inputs) and sending its output to the next module or directly to the actuators. In this manner each selection correspond to the assignment of the values to the control variables D,E,A (Figure 5).*

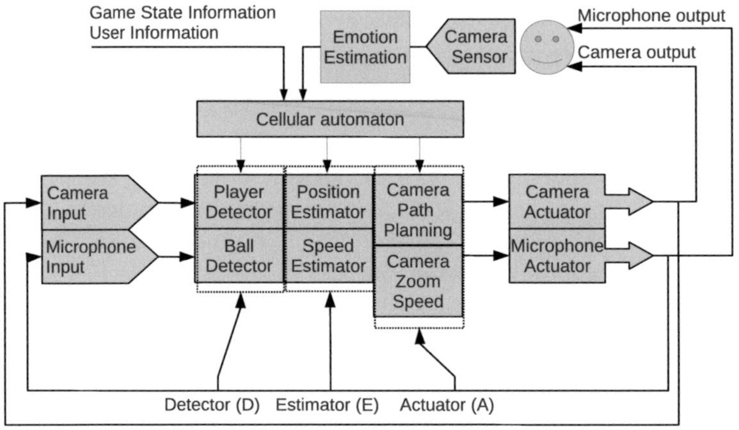

Fig. 5. The Robotic Application schema using the Adaptive Functional-Module Selection Mechanism

Because the generated behaviors are analogous to the reactive behaviors in the model of Arkin (1) or Brooks (2) the output of the robot is content dependent and thus cannot be tested without a proper environmental settings. However the schematic representation of the AFMS architecture shown in Figure 5 is only a simplest example: each real-time behavior controls only one degree of freedom at a time and is represented by a cascade connection of functional modules. It is expected that using AFMS more general methods of computing outputs from each column are available allowing a higher degree of freedom in the selection process.

The AFMS principle is based on biologically-inspired approach to human dealing with infinite complexity using finite amount of resources. In such context the AFMS mechanism provide a mechanism for decision making by switching behaviors not only in the traditional manner - based on the input but also based on feedback and off line learning. As introduced above the presented model is the simplest one. It is not difficult to imagine such AFMS that selects multiple functional modules in each functional column and then propagates the fused result to next column.

Figure 5 shows a feature-based robotic system, that chooses which features should be used to generate the current behavior. Such selection can be altered by allowing the AFMS mechanism representing different algorithms for each of the features. In such case we set of features remains constant in each computation of output from input but the algorithms used are different. Finally, the AFMS can be seen as adaptive mechanism to minimize the internal allocation of resources. For instance, assume that a face is detected on an image. In order to analyze the face in general a set of pattern-templates are used; the selection of the templates is in this case performed by the AFMS in order to minimize the number of patterns that have to be tried on the face.

Thus AFMS can be seen as both, a mechanism for adaptively choosing resources for intelligent processing and as a mechanism of building internal model. The next section illustrates how using a Bayesian Network a module allocation algorithm based on probabilistic reasoning is obtained.

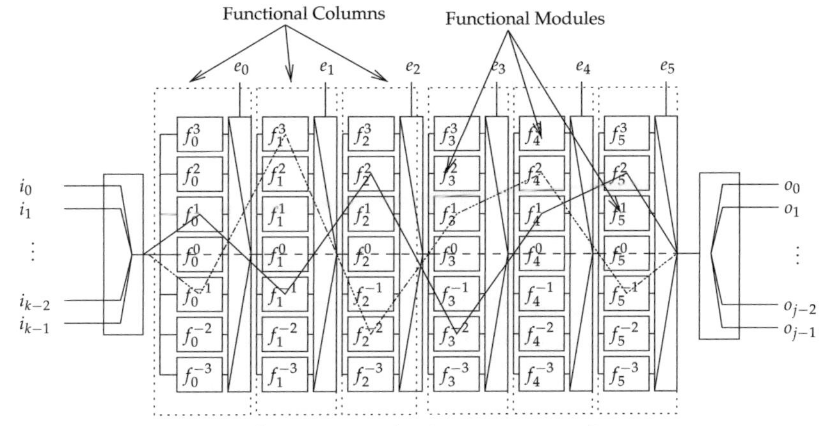

Fig. 6. Example of the behavioral matrix robotic processor architecture

5. The proposed model

To address the above introduced problems we designed a hardware architecture that can in real time generate behavioral layers by adaptively combining functional modules. This hardware architecture designed as the platform for the AFMS mechanism is called the behavioral matrix.

5.1 Behavioral matrix

The principles that this platform is based upon are the following:

- Each behavioral layer can be build in real time by interconnecting a set of pre defined functional blocks (functions).
- Each behavioral layer built in real time is composed from input-activated functions and output-filtered functions.
- Both valid behaviors and invalid ones can be created
- The output from each function in a behavioral layer can be based on current or past input values

The proposed hardware architecture is shown in Figure 6. It is built from functional columns (hardware blocks); each column is built from a set of functions (functional modules), from an output buffer, from an activation module and from an arbitration module (Figure 7). The activation module allows to decide where the data input goes - i.e. which function will generate output. The arbitration module allows to select which functional output will be selected as the output of this column. The set of functional modules can be any type of function: from neural network processor to a Fourier transform or a face detection algorithm. The behavioral arbitration module is represented by a MUX letting only one functional module to propagate its output to the output buffer. The activation module is either a DEMUX (propagating the input only to a single functional module) or is completely ignored and thus allows the input data to be propagated to all functional modules (Figure 6).

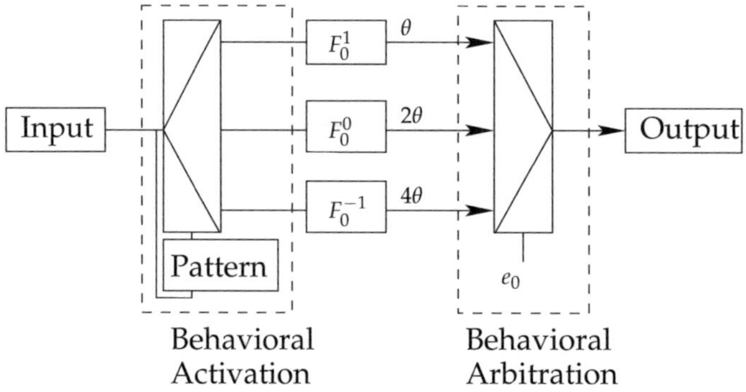

Fig. 7. Example of a functional column with the function activator and the function arbitrator

The output buffer in each functional column allows to be filled with the currently selected functional module output value and thus to propagate sensory input i^t to the output $o^t = f_j(i^t)$. This can be seen in the case when input data reach a functional column and both the activation and arbitration modules are pointing to the same function. The output buffer can also propagate a past input to the output $o^{t-k} = f_j(i^{t-k})$. This is the case when either the arbitration or the activation modules in a functional column point to a different function; the output obtained on the output will be the value last stored in the output buffer.

Observe that using our robotic platform the functionality of each behavioral layer is created automatically in real time by a serial combination of functions. Each function from a column is selected using a control variable $\{e_0, \ldots, e_5\}$ in Figure 6. The output of the last functional column is either propagated to the actuators or can be withheld to be used as a part of the next input. In this manner each functional column can be used as a combinational circuit or as a sequential circuit.

6. Cellular automaton for AFMS

Using the behavioral matrix, the arbitration of behaviors become a a selection of control variables with respect to a particular set of inputs and a feedback.

Because the problem introduced cannot be analyzed from a global point of view, we propose to use an arbitration mechanism based on local rules and feedback. Using local rule based arbitration mechanism we can on one hand build in real time a global representation of the environment based on local rules and on the other hand use computational models requiring less resources. Using a Cellular Automaton (CA) to assign in real time computational resources in the behavioral matrix, saves computational resources (only used functional modules are turned on), uses only local state transition function and as required allows to build a global environment representation. Also and more important, the use of CA for behavior arbitration allow for cyclic sampling of the environment and action generation. The idea behind this approach is the fact that the execution of a task can be done by a sampling through the environment with both various sensors and various actuator actions. This means that a robot with a set of possible actions, can be instructed to solve a particular task by cyclically selecting from a sub-set of these actions and arriving at its goal. The main advantage compared to behavioral robotics for instance is the resource saving; while in standard robotics all resources are computing in parallel at all times, the architecture proposed here allows to selectively activate particular set of computational modules and thus save energy.

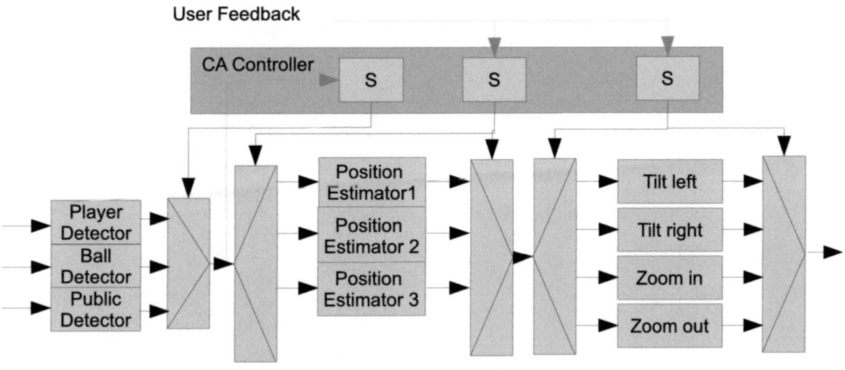

Fig. 8. Example of a behavioral controller based application. The first column represents the detector allowing to detect a player, a ball and the audience, the second column shows three different black-box estimators and the last columns are actuator commands. Observe there is one internal feedback from the first column to the controller as well as the external user feedback allowing to change the output of the robotic application.

Figure 8 shows an example of robotic application using the behavioral matrix with three columns controlled by a three-cell CA. The application that this processor was designed for is the intelligent TV-set. The purposed is to allow the user to change behaviors of cameras and thus allowing the user to fully enjoy for instance a live sport event (Figure 1).
Each functional column has either three or four input functions and thus each of the control cells is considered to use three/four valued logic. The robotic processor has two types of feedback. First, an internal feedback is used to lock the first column; if a given feature is detected the CA will not change the detection module. A change in the detected feature is triggered only by the global robot state change. Second feedback is coming from the user and allows to force the CA to change its state. Thus if both feedbacks are positive the robot will continue to perform the current operation unchanged. In any other case the CA will evolve according to a local rule until both feedbacks are satisfied.
To illustrate the reason of usage of the CA for the real-time behavior arbitration the following example shows how the trail-and error or behavioral arbitration results in minimization of the number of states required to bring user from a non-terminal state to terminal (desired) state.

Example 6.1 (Minimizing path to desired user state). *Let M be a robotic application with a CA controller. The state transition function is specified by the reachability graph shown in Figure 9 and is generated using a three-cell neighborhood CA state transition function f. The two dark squares shows the state transitions of interests. In particular the larger square shows an example situation where the user state and the machine state are respectively given by* (s_{uk}, s_{rj}) *Given this initial configuration the machine proceed in changing its state from* 023 *to* 013 *and so on until the state* 013 *generates the user state* $\tilde{s_u}$ *which is the target user state. Because the goal of the robot is to satisfy the user as quickly as possible or even to keep the user constantly happy, the robot uses local rule optimization to reduce the number of required steps between the* (s_{uk}, s_{rj}) *and the* $(\tilde{s_u}, s_{rj+4})$*. This is shown in Figure 10 where the modified state-transition function partially restructured the reachability graph of the machine M.*
[End of example]

The advantages of the CA based robot arbitration concept introduced in this chapter seem can be summarized by three powerful concepts: the multi-modal-perception (3; 8; 9) decision making, the non-abellian decision making and the sensory noise resistance.

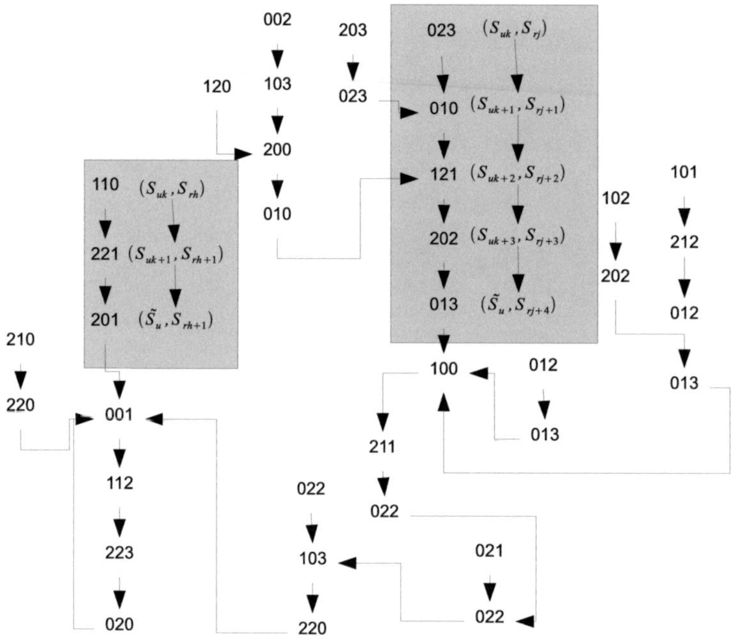

Fig. 9. State reachability graph of machine M.

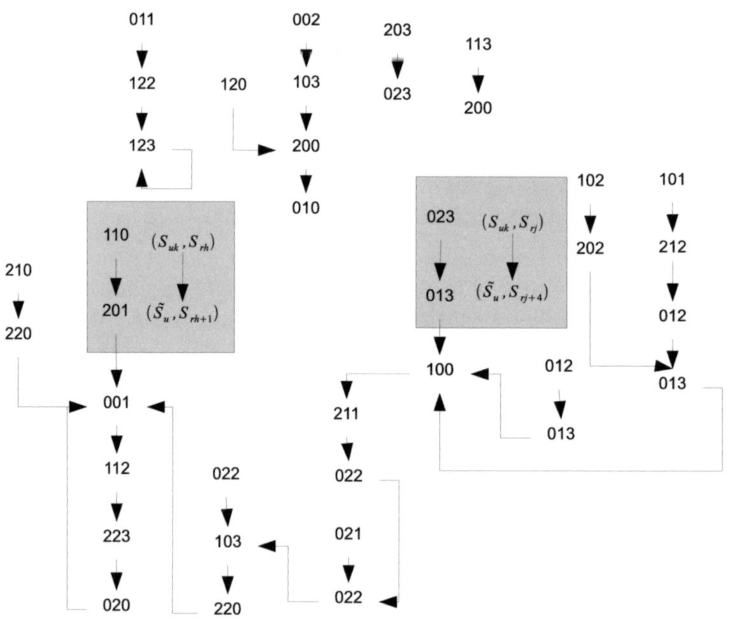

Fig. 10. Two path minimized by changing single rules in the state transition function.

To explain these notions let first assume that the robot has a video camera and a set of image processing algorithms: a set of low level transforms such as Sobel, Hadamard, Haar, HOG (Histogram of Oriented Gradients) as well as a set of high level feature extracting tools such as face detection, face tracking, object detection, shape extraction, color tracking and so on.
The *multi-modal perception* is a well know area in robotics and in general it means that a given decision is made on multiple perception sources and levels. This is illustrated with the approach shown in Figure 8 where various sensor sources can be combined as given by the CA cycle of state change. In this case, using the *Output-per-final-configuration output generation* the output can be generated using the history based approach combining multiple sources of information.
The *non-abellian decision making* is a generalized concept and it means that a sequence of applied behaviors to a given sequence of inputs is not equivalent to the application of another sequence of the same behaviors to the same input sequence. This can be observed from a simple example. Assume a robot is supposed to solve a puzzle consisting in moving blocks around by pushing them. Any action resulting in a block being adjacent directly to the wall does not allow the robot to move that block away from the wall. Such situation can result either from bad planning but also from bad sensory input-sequence evaluation. Because each behavioral layer pursues its own goal and sometimes such goals can lead to mutually exclusive situations, the order of applying of the behavioral layers outputs bears extreme importance. Such choices can allow to explore novel regions or improvise a solution found by mistake.

7. Learning adaptive behavior from training samples

In the previous section we introduced a mechanism of selecting functional modules using Cellular Automaton. However, the design of such automaton might turn out to be difficult. In this section we present a mechanism for selecting functional modules using a statistical method. Notably we show how to use a Bayesian Network for module selection by using symbolic information as inputs to the BN and obtaining outputs a set of user's preferences. The BN is designed so as to generate additional information for the computer which when combined with information from standard image and sound processing will allow a higher degree of control over the automated process. Figure 11 shows the high level schema of the system. Three parallel processes are extracting the ball, the players and the referee(s) by color filtering the raw input image. Each of the players' and the referees' movements are recorded into a sequential memory, where it is used to extract information about their performance in the game (Figure 11: box labeled *Human Behavior Recognition*). At the same time players facial expressions and body gestures are used to determine their emotional state (Figure 11: box labeled *Human Expression Recognition*). This pre-processed information, with the coordinates of all the players, referees and the ball as well as information about user preferences and game information are the inputs to the module M.
Figure 12 shows in more details the inputs and outputs to the module M. In particular it can be seen that the module M contains a Bayesian network and additional computational resources that will together be used to generate the final output. The combined information is shown in Figure 13 on an example containing a schematic of a baseball field with some players on it. Observe that each object (player, referee, ball) has a set of coordinates and a percentage value. The percentage value represents the degree of user's interest in a given object.
To understand this concept assume that the default behavior of the robot is to track the ball with the camera. Such behavior will capture - with appropriate zoom - most of the action

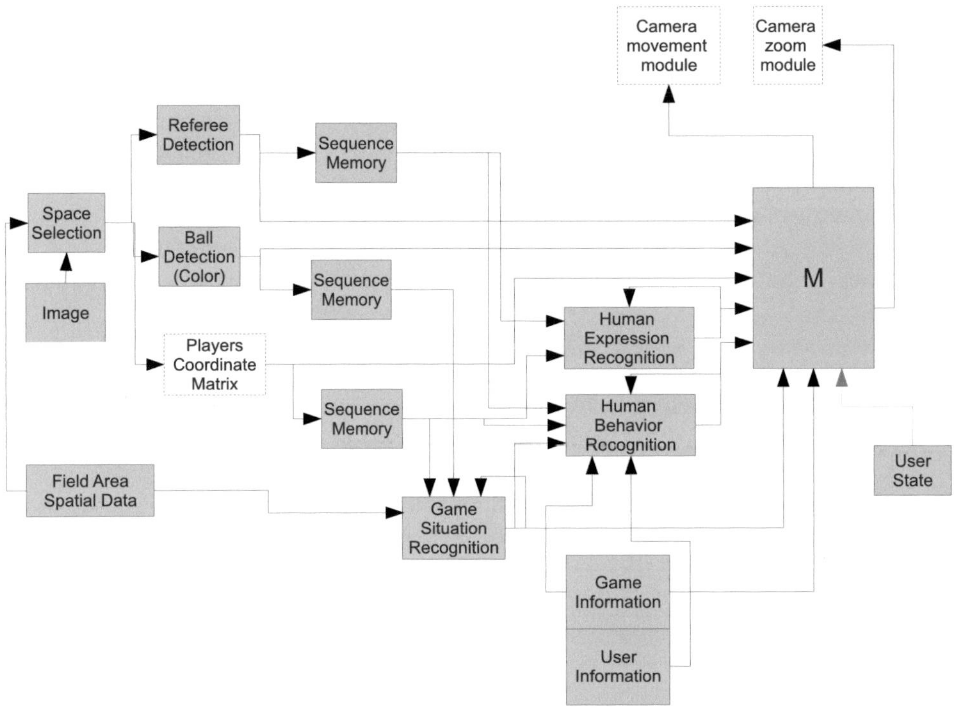

Fig. 11. High level architecture for a Live-Feeling system. Module M represents the processing that is used to provide automated camera and microphone behavior.

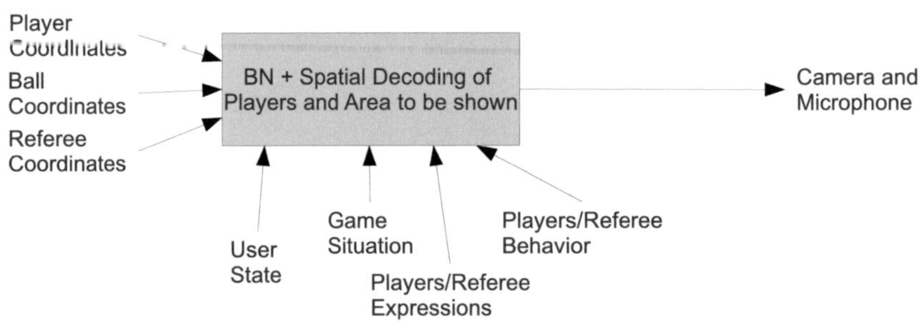

Fig. 12. The inputs and outputs of the module M.

in the game that the user is interested in. However, player's behavior, referee behavior or unusual player's performance can sometimes be more interesting that the center of the game. In such cases it is important to capture such events because an automated system that can detect such highlights of a live event and autonomously show them to the user will provide the user not only with the game elements but also with such scenes that will increase user's happiness.

In order to allow an autonomous system perform such actions, the decision about the content what will be shown to the user as well as about the manner this content is shown must include a prediction about the level of user's interest. In order to do that the following criteria are taken into account:

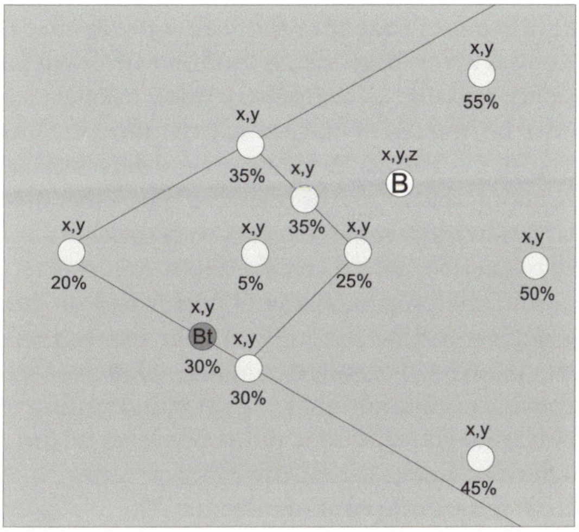

Fig. 13. The complete information generated in the module M.

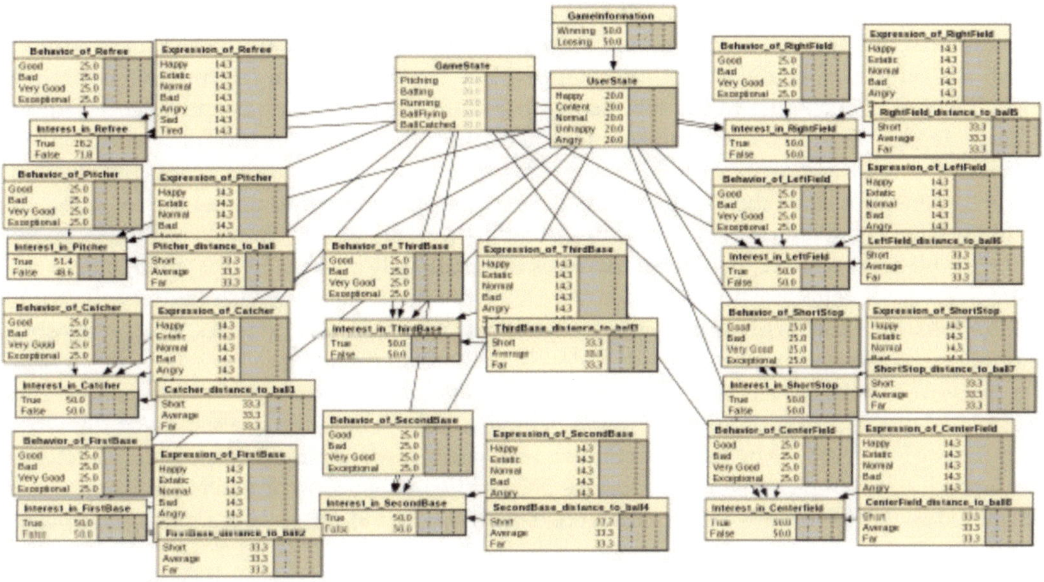

Fig. 14. The complete information generated in the module M.

- Player's emotional behavior: if a player does something unexpected and mostly unrelated to the game performance it increases its chance to be included into the camera image
- Player's professional behavior: if a player performs a directly game related action in an unexpected manner it increases its chance that the camera will focus on him/her.
- Referee's emotional behavior: if the referee performs an action unrelated to the game but with high emotional arousal it increases the chance that the camera will focus on him

An example of system that perform such operation is shown in Figure 14. The BN's inputs are a from preprocessor that has been previously introduced. In particular the BN'sinputs are the players' and referees' emotional expressions, game behavior, the distance between the players' and the ball, the game state and the user's feedback. The goal of the network is to asses the probability of a given player as a modifier of the default robot's behavior. In most of the cases this is only a matter of proper zooming because as already introduced the ball-following behavior will be in most of cases able to capture the most important features of the game. This can be seen in the Figure 13, where every detected object on the game field is given a percentage representing the degree of user interest in that object.

In order to make this evaluation more realistic, one can assume multiple cameras because one camera pointing at a given location with a certain zoom can in general only see a subsets of players. Because the BN and the preprocessing is performed on the current image in most of the cases the interest degree will be the highest near the ball. This is a precondition in our model that represents the overall game dynamics. However in a realistic situation the changes of zoom or of camera orientation that are often interesting are not directly centered centered on the game but rather on different point of views of the given situation or from different location. In such case, images from different cameras can be processed in parallel and evaluated in order to find the best point of interest.

Finally, with respect to the AFMS method described in Section 4, the usage of the BN resides in the resolution of the network outputs. Without the usage of the AFMS mechanism the spatial coordinates and the degrees of interests calculated by the BN can be directly mapped into camera commands using weighted sum or similar linear methods. When used with the AFMS the output of the BN is similarly mapped into the allocation of the functional modules so as the output behaviors of the robot corresponds to the displaying of the objects with the highest degree of interest. This means that according to the output modules selection will vary.

Naturally one can ask: if the BN allows such direct mapping into the camera movements why AFMS is even considered? This can be answered by looking at the example of the BN shown in Figure 14. The architecture of the network is unfortunately a star network which means that there is no advantage of using BN over any other methods, because each nodes will require a large look-up table. This is contrary to the ideal use of the BN network where hierarchy should be used to minimize the size of the look-up table in each node.

The reason for this architecture is the fact that to evaluate the user's interest is based on a multi-level analysis of individual player's behavior a as well on the evaluation of the global properties of the game. The BN from Figure 14 is just a mere example but from it structure it can be deduced that if one would introduce user's interest of group of players in the network, the structure will essentially be not changed. The network will certainly get more complicated but hierarchy will be still lacking.

The machine learning required to allow a proper AFMS mechanism is well known in the case of the Bayesian Network. From a set of samples it is now a standard procedure to generate probabilities and then use these conditionals in the appropriate nodes. In this approach to machine learning the most important is the quality of the data as the learning by itself is done by probabilistic inference. The final result of the computation of the module M is shown in Figure 13 allows by selecting player tracking or ball tracking set of functional modules in order to move the camera to the desired location.

8. Conclusion

We presented a problem of HRI called the *Human State Problem* and showed how it can be partially analyzed and solved using deterministic hardware based approach using a Cellular Automaton as well as probabilistic Bayesian Network. For this we illustrated our robotic processor using a CA for adaptive resources selection and showed by example how it can be used for machine learning of robot behavior by modifying the local state-transition function of the CA in real time. The advantages of this approach are: (1) it is designed to be realized in VLSI leading to low cost and low power consumption, (2) it allows a fast switching of behaviors, (3) it uses multi-valued logic and thus leads to fast realizations of behaviors in hardware. The formalization of the HSP problem allows to at least partially to study the possible solutions and propose some solutions.

The purpose of designing such robotic processor is to allow the robot to deal with noise in real environment as well as with extremely complex situations requiring real-time processing. Examples of such environments are for instance human emotional perception, indirect human feedback or general human-robot interaction. The main problem is that in these environments a single sensory input might not be sufficient and more complex sensor processing and general purpose processing might be required. However the processing must be highly adaptive and should allow variations in both inputs and outputs. Thus the CA controlling the robotic processor by larger or smaller cycles can be used to explore/exploit more or less of the given situation for the purpose of achieving its task. For instance analyzing the input only for object detection and face detection will generate a different output than if the same input is analyzed for face detection, motion tracking and emotional expression. Obtaining different set of features from the input depends on the states of the CA and on how many different states the CA goes through. Thus it is directly related to the size of the cycles and to the states it goes through within these cycles of states.

A common question in this approach is why we propose hardware rather than software implementation? The answer is that it is in hardware where the multi-valued logic can bring power saving and thus is ideal to build small low power behavior based robotic processors. In particular it is interesting for robots that can benefit of having the processing on board as opposed receiving all control commands from a computer through a wireless link. As in general the main power consumption is from actuators, eliminating an active wireless link can save a lot of power. Also, on board implementation eliminates additional devices that a remote computer needs such as hard drive, memory and so on. Thus from a global point of view an on-board implementation is beneficial for both the power saving as well as real time processing. Moreover, the design is meant to be learn-able - both the control logic as well as the functional modules are to be either learned in real time of programmed before the task. Thus such controller can be reused by simple reprogramming for various low power robots.

Finally the future of this work consists in developing the hardware platform and implementing a learning mechanism so that the most desirable robotic behavior can be obtained for various applications. The proposed multi-valued basis for design algorithm is to be extended in more details so that ideally behaviors specified by simple constraints can be designed using standard Logic Synthesis methods. Moreover, to solve some of the problems related to complexity and noisy environment we plan to investigate a different method of machine learning based on probabilistic automaton and probabilistic cellular automaton. This approach, could possibly solve some of the shortcomings of the BN in this application and thus either combining different probabilistic computational models for the module allocation would then provide a feasible result.

9. References

[1] R. C. Arkin. *Behavior-Based Robotics*. The MIT Press, 1998.

[2] R. A. Brooks. Intelligence without reason. In *Proceedings of the 12th IJCAI*, pages 569–595, 1991.

[3] B Chandrasekaran. Multimodal cognitive architectures: Making perception more central to intelligent behavior. In *AAAI national Conference on Artificial Intelligence*, pages 1508–1512, 2006.

[4] A. R. Damasio. *Descarte's Error: Emotion, Reason and the Human Brain*. Picador, 1994.

[5] A. R. Damasio. *Looking for Spinoza*. Picador, 2004.

[6] P. Ekman. Facial expression and emotion. *American Psychologist*, 48(4):384–392, 1993.

[7] P. Ekman. *Basic emotions*, chapter 3. Wiley, New York, 1999.

[8] M. P. Hollier, A. N. Rimell, D. S. Hands, and R. M. Voelcker. Multi-modal perception. *BT Technology Journal*, 17(1):35–46, 1999.

[9] M.H. Luerssen, T.W. Lewis, R.E. Leibbrandt, and D.M. Powers. Adaptive multimodal perception for a virtual museum guide. In *3rd Workshop on Artificial Intelligence Techniques for Ambient Intelligence*, 2008.

[10] M. Lukac, M. Kameyama, and M. Perkowski. Adaptive selection of intelligent processing modules and its applications,. In *The 2010 International Conference on Artificial Intelligence, WORLDCOMP'10*, 2010.

[11] M. Lukac, M. Kameyama, and M. Perkowski. Emotion-aware probabilistic robotics. In *Second International symposium on Aware Robotics, ISAC2010*, 2010.

18

Design of Self-Assembling, Self-Repairing 3D Irregular Cellular Automata

David Huw Jones[1], Richard McWilliam[2] and Alan Purvis[3]
[1]*Imperial College London*
[2,3]*University of Durham*
England

1. Introduction

> The core idea is that nature, imaginative by necessity, has already solved many of the problems we are grappling with. Animals, plants, and microbes are the consummate engineers. They have found what works, what is appropriate, and most important, what lasts here on Earth. This is the real news of biomimicry: After 3.8 billion years of research and development, failures are fossils, and what surrounds us is the secret to survival (Benyus, 1998).

Morphogenesis is a distributed chemical process that is responsible for co-ordinating the self-assembly and self-repair of biological systems. One example of morphogenesis in action is the ability for the human liver to sustain damage to over 75% of its mass and still repair itself.

Another demonstration of the reliability of morphogenesis is evident in the salamander family. Salamanders can regrow the same limbs repeatedly, as well as their tail, jaw, and the lenses and retinas of their eyes. In terms of body mass alone, the salamander can regenerate approximately 60% of itself in the event that it is damaged.

A final, remarkable, demonstration is the self-repair capability of the ascidian (a type of marine filter feeder). They have been reported to regenerate from just partial blood cells to give rise to a fully functional organism (Berrill & Cohen, 1936).

The aim of this research is to apply this robust self-assembly strategy to the design of self-assembling robotics. Here we describe various models for morphogenesis and existing techniques for designing self-assembling robotics. Then we introduce our cellular automata model for morphogenesis and determine the necessary conditions for its robust self-assembly and self-assembly to a pre-defined shape. Finally we demonstrate it co-ordinating the self-assembly of a 55,000 cell virtual robot.

2. Morphogenesis

Imagine an island of cannibals and missionaries. The cannibals can have sex, creating other cannibals in the process. The missionaries cannot have sex but own bicycles; two missionaries convert a cannibal into another missionary. This is the analogy Alan Turing (Turing, 1950) used to describe his "Reaction-Diffusion" model of morphogenesis. On such an island pockets of cannibals surrounded by missionaries are formed (see figure 1).

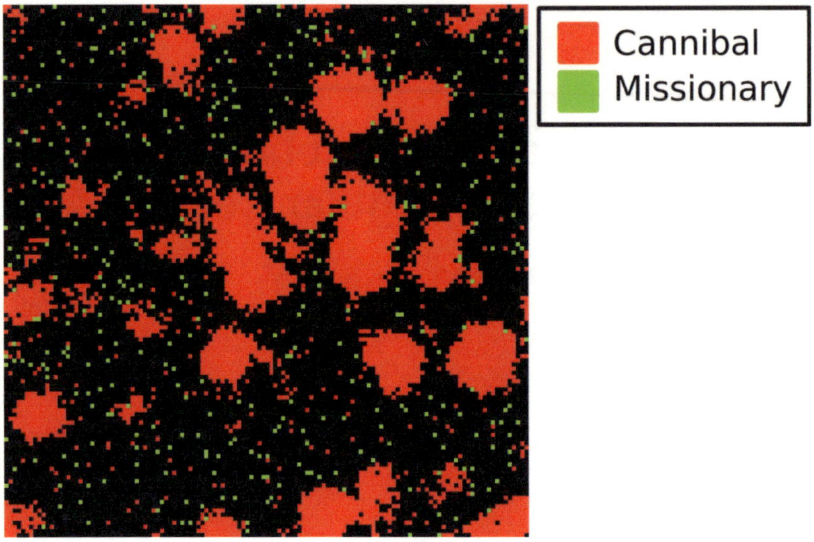

Fig. 1. Clumping of cannibals and missionaries formed by Turing's reaction-diffusion analogy

Turing proposed that the spots of a cheetah, the stripes of a zebra and every other arrangement of cells within living systems could be explained by the diffusion of chemicals he named "morphogens" and their interaction with each other.
To demonstrate this model, let us consider a simple two-morphogen (x_1, x_2) system of cells in one-dimension. [1]

2.1 The resting state

If, for a moment, we consider small perturbations of the concentrations of the morphogens about $\bar{x_e}$, the system's resting state, we can use linear ordinary differential equations (ODEs) (1) to describe their reaction and diffusion.

$$\frac{d\bar{x}}{dt} = \mathbf{A}\bar{x} \tag{1}$$

Where $\mathbf{A} = \begin{bmatrix} a_{11} & a_{12} \\ a_{21} & a_{22} \end{bmatrix}$.
Let λ be an eigenvalue of $\mathbf{A}$. According to Cramer's rule, the system will only have non-trivial solutions if $det(\mathbf{A} - \lambda I) = 0$.

$$det(\mathbf{A} - \lambda I) = a_{11}a_{22} - \lambda(a_{11} + a_{22}) + \lambda^2 - a_{12}a_{21} \tag{2}$$

Let

$$T = a_{11} + a_{22} \tag{3}$$

$$D = a_{11}a_{22} - a_{12}a_{21} \tag{4}$$

[1] Proof derived from Turing's paper (Turing, 1950) and notes from Blowey (Blowey, 2007) and Childress (Childress, 2005).

Therefore $det(\mathbf{A} - \lambda I) = \lambda^2 - T\lambda + D$, its roots are given by:

$$\lambda = \frac{T \pm \sqrt{T^2 - 4D}}{2} \tag{5}$$

For the resting state to be stable (change from $\bar{x}_e$ is opposed), both roots must be negative. Therefore $D \in [0, \frac{T^2}{4}]$ and $T < 0$.

2.2 The transient state

Now let us consider larger permutations of the concentrations of the morphogens, as a result of diffusion of the morphogens between neighbouring cells.
Let each cell be a small cube of side $\triangle$ with the chemicals $\bar{x}$ distributed equally within it. Each cell has an index i from 0 to N and the cells are arranged in a 1 loop such that the neighbours of cell x^N are x^{N-1} and x^0.
Ficke's law states:

> The flow of chemical from one cell to another is proportional to the difference in the chemical concentrations of the two cells, the flow being from the higher to the lower.

The flux, f_j, of morphogen j into cell i, x^i_j, will be:

$$\text{flux } f_1 = k_1 \triangle^2 (x_1^{i-1} - x_1^i) + k_1 \triangle^2 ((x_1^{i+1} - x_1^i) \tag{6}$$
$$= k_1 \triangle^2 (x_1^{i-1} - 2x_1^i + x_1^{i+1}) \tag{7}$$
$$f_2 = k_2 \triangle^2 (x_2^{i-1} - 2x_2^i + x_2^{i+1}) \tag{8}$$

where $\{k_1, k_2\} > 0$ are constants of proportionality. Now

$$\frac{dx^i}{dt} = f(\bar{x}^i) + \mathbf{M}(\bar{x}^{i-1} - 2\bar{x}^i + \bar{x}^{i+1}) \tag{9}$$

where $\mathbf{M} = \begin{bmatrix} \triangle^2 k_1 & 0 \\ 0 & \triangle^2 k_2 \end{bmatrix}$ and $f(\bar{x}^i)$ determines the proportion of $\bar{x}^i$ that remains in cell i.
Note that because the cells form a loop, the system is closed and $\sum_i x^i$ is constant.
If the width, $\triangle$, of each cube tends to 0 we can consider the system continuous. If $s = \triangle .i$ then:

$$\frac{dx(s)}{dt} = f(s) = \mathbf{M}(\bar{x}(s-\triangle) - 2\bar{x}(s) + \bar{x}(s+\triangle)) \tag{10}$$

If we expand each term into its Taylor series through terms in $\triangle^2$ then:

$$\bar{x}(s+\triangle) = \bar{x}(s) + \frac{d\bar{x}(s)}{ds}\triangle + \frac{d^2\bar{x}(s)}{ds^2}\frac{\triangle^2}{2} + \cdots \tag{11}$$
$$\therefore f(s) \simeq \mathbf{M} \triangle^2 \frac{d^2\bar{x}(s)}{ds^2} \tag{12}$$

Let us assume $\triangle \to 0$, the number of cells, $N \to \infty$, $N \triangle \to L$, the circumference of the ring. We want to study the linear stability of the resulting continuous partial differential equation (PDE) in time.

$$\frac{\partial \bar{x}(t,s)}{\partial t} = \mathbf{A}\bar{x}(t,s) + \mathbf{M}\frac{\partial^2 x}{\partial s^2}(s,t) \quad (13)$$

Where $\mathbf{M}$ has been redefined as $\begin{bmatrix} \mu_1 & 0 \\ 0 & \mu_2 \end{bmatrix}$, $\mu_i = k_i \frac{\Delta^4}{2}$. μ_1, μ_2, the diffusion coefficients are finite and positive.

As the cells are in a loop we can look for pattern waves of the form:

$$x = e^{\sigma t + jks} x_0 \quad (14)$$

If for some μ_1, μ_2, k there exists a solution of this form such that $\Re(\sigma)$ is positive, the concentrations of the morphogens within the tissue will form stable patterns.

Using the identity $\frac{d^2}{ds^2} e^{jks} = -k^2 e^{jks}$ and the product rule, the $\frac{\partial^2 \bar{x}}{\partial s^2}$ component of (14) can be found:

$$\frac{d^2 \bar{x}}{ds^2} = -k^2 \bar{x} \quad (15)$$

Substituting (15) into (13) gives:

$$\frac{d\bar{x}}{dt} = \mathbf{A}\bar{x} + M \begin{bmatrix} -k^2 & 0 \\ 0 & -k^2 \end{bmatrix} \bar{x} \quad (16)$$

$$= \left(\mathbf{A} + \begin{bmatrix} \mu_1 k^2 & 0 \\ 0 & \mu_2 k^2 \end{bmatrix} \right) \bar{x} \quad (17)$$

Thus if $\mathbf{B} = \mathbf{A} - \begin{bmatrix} \mu_1 k^2 + \sigma & 0 \\ 0 & \mu_2 k^2 + \sigma \end{bmatrix}$ the pattern wave solutions are determined by the non-trivial solution to $\mathbf{B}\bar{x}_0 = 0$.

Again using Cramer's rule, the determinant of $\mathbf{B}$ must equal 0. Thus:

$$\sigma^2 + \tau\sigma + \psi = 0 \quad (18)$$

where

$$\tau = k^2(\mu_1 + \mu_2) - (a_{11} + a_{22}) \quad (19)$$

$$= k^2(\mu_1 + \mu_2) - T \quad (20)$$

$$\psi = D - \mu_1 k^2 a_{22} - \mu_2 k^2 a_{11} + \mu_1 \mu_2 k^4 \quad (21)$$

Both roots must have negative real components. Thus $\tau < 0$ and $\psi > 0$. For $D < 0$ both $a_{11}a_{22} < 0$ and $a_{12}a_{21} < 0$. For $\psi < 0$,

$$a_{22}\mu_1 + a_{11}\mu_2 > 0 \quad (22)$$

If $a_{11} < 0$ its corresponding entry in the matrix $\mathbf{B}$, $a_{11} - \mu_1 k^2 + \sigma$ is also negative. Thus the chemical, x_1 will decay to the rest state $\bar{x_e}$ in the absence of x_2. Turing called x_1 the inhibitor chemical and x_2 the activator chemical.

2.3 Turing instability inequalities

From (22) and (3) one can deduce that, for the system to form stable patterns $\mu_2 < \mu_1$. Thus the inhibitor chemical must diffuse faster than the activator chemical. Referring back to the "cannibals and missionaries" analogy, the presence of two missionaries in any given square inhibits the progress of the diffusion of the cannibals across the island, however because the inhibitor-missionaries own bicycles they diffuse more rapidly than the activator-cannibals. Equation (21) is a quadratic in k^2, the minimum value of which is:

$$\psi_{min} = D - \frac{(a_{22}\mu_1 + a_{11}\mu_2)^2}{4\mu_1\mu_2} \tag{23}$$

Therefore:

$$a_{22}\mu_1 + a_{11}\mu_2 > 2\sqrt{\mu_1\mu_2 D} \tag{24}$$

2.4 An example reaction-diffusion system

An example two-morphogen system that meets (24), (22), (3) and (4) has the following reaction equations:

$$x_1(\bar{x}) = (16 - x_1x_2)s \tag{25}$$
$$x_2(\bar{x}) = (x_1x_2 - x_2 - 20)s \tag{26}$$

To find the unique equilibrium we set (25) and (26) to zero. Thus $x_{e1} = -4$ and $x_{e2} = 4$. Assuming the system is linear about $\bar{x}_e$ we can differentiate (25) and (26) to form $\mathbf{A}$.

$$\mathbf{A} = \begin{bmatrix} -x_2s & -x_1s \\ x_2s & x_1s - s \end{bmatrix} = s\begin{bmatrix} -4 & 4 \\ 4 & -5 \end{bmatrix} \tag{27}$$

Figure 2 shows the results of this model.

2.5 Experimental evidence for morphogenesis

A two-morphogen system exists in a developing human body, shortly after the creation of the blastula. Two proteins, the BCD protein and the HB-M protein, create a localised determinant centered about the zygote (Griffiths, 1976). Since these proteins have different diffusion rates, and interact with each other, spatial concentration patterns form. Different concentrations activate different genes in the genome of each cell. These gene selections in turn correspond to different types of cell. Thus the beginnings of form and cellular differentiation appear in the developing embryo.

A three-morphogen system exists in the developing fruit fly. The morphogens, bicoid, eve and caudal, are important for patterning the head, thorax and abdominal regions of the embryo (Rosee et al., 1997). Figure 3 shows the concentrations of each morphogen shortly after fertilisation. Figure 4 shows various other morphogenesis patterns that have been sampled during the development of the fruit fly.

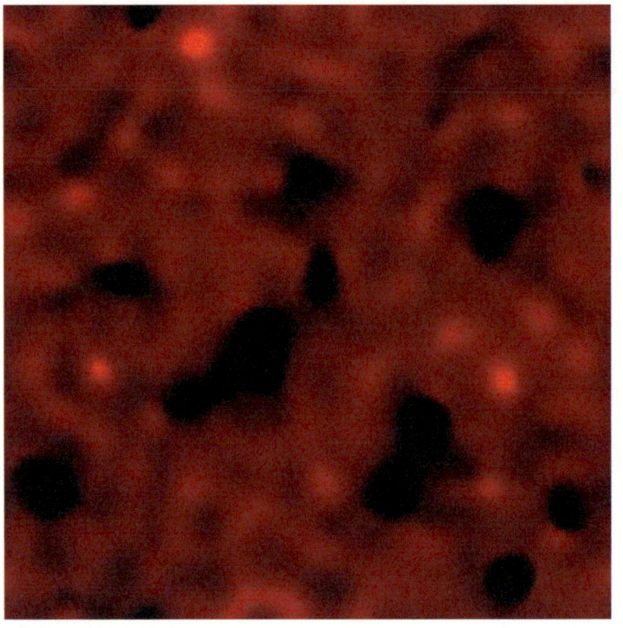

Fig. 2. Example of Turing's reaction-diffusion equations

2.6 A more comprehensive model of the developmental cycle

But experimental results suggests that control of the developmental cycle is not as simple as systems of interacting morphogens. Most tissues have asymmetric distributions of various properties: for example, in a hydra the nerve cell density is much greater in the head than the body. Transplantation experiments (Morgan, 1904) suggest that this polarity affects the decision of where to form structures relative to the tissue.

Further work by the experimental biologist John Gurdon (Gurdon, 1968) suggests that the concentration levels of morphogens within a tissue are typically very small and undetectable by the majority of cells. To ensure each cell in this tissue develops in line with the rest of its surrounding cells, each cell that detects the presence of a signalling protein transmits a chemical signal to its neighbouring cells. This is known as cell-to-cell communication, or the "community effect".

Meinhardt (Meinhardt, 1982) sought to incorporate these theories of development into a more comprehensive model than that proposed by Turing. The following model, one of many he proposed, uses five reaction-diffusion equations to form striped patterns.

$$\frac{\partial g_1}{\partial t} = \frac{c g_1^2}{r s_1} - \alpha g_1 + D_g \frac{\partial^2 g_1}{\partial x^2} + \rho_0 \tag{28}$$

$$\frac{\partial g_2}{\partial t} = \frac{c g_2^2}{r s_2} - \alpha g_2 + D_g \frac{\partial^2 g_2}{\partial x^2} + \rho_0 \tag{29}$$

$$\frac{\partial r}{\partial t} = \frac{c g_1^2}{s_1} + \frac{c g_2^2}{s_2} \tag{30}$$

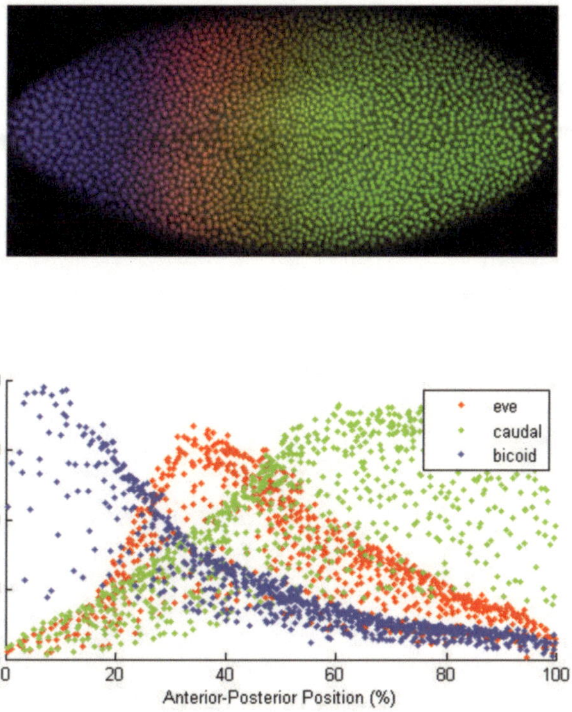

Fig. 3. Anterior-posterior determination in fruit flies. Image courtesy of the FlyEx database (Pisarev et al., 2008)

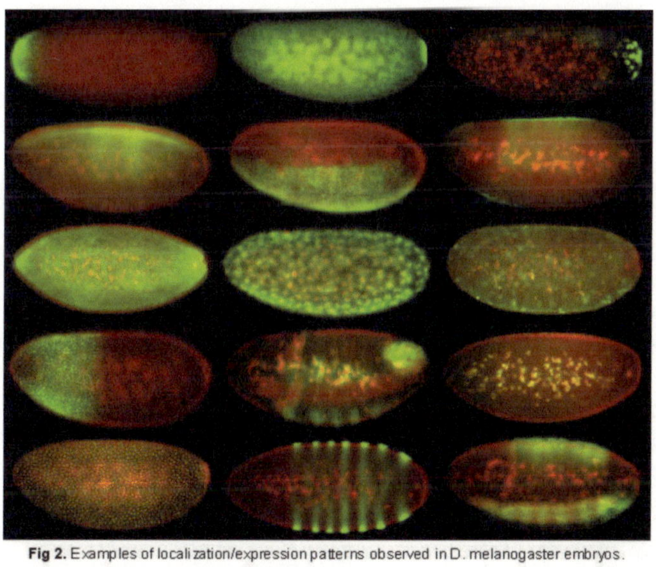

Fig. 4. Morphogenesis patterns in fruit flies
Image courtesy of Dr. Eric Lecuyer, Canadian Institute of Health Research

$$\frac{\partial s_1}{\partial t} = \gamma \frac{g_1 - s_1}{D} {}_s \frac{\partial^2 s_1}{\partial x^2} + \rho_l \tag{31}$$

$$\frac{\partial s_2}{\partial t} = \gamma \frac{g_2 - s_2}{D} {}_s \frac{\partial^2 s_2}{\partial x^2} + \rho_l \tag{32}$$

g_1 and g_2 are short-range activator substances. They form mutually exclusive feedback loops. Each is subject to long-range inhibitor substances, s_1 and s_2. That they are mutually exclusive is ensured by equation (30).

Figure 5 shows a result of the model with different diffusion rates D_g and D_s.

Fig. 5. Example of Meinhardt stripes

3. Morphogenesis for self-assembling robotics

Within the field of robotics, self-assembly describes the spontaneous aggregation of pre-formed cells into well-defined, stable assemblies. This assembly happens without the assistance of any external co-ordinating processes.

The design of large self-assembling systems has been the bailiwick of chaos mathematicians and computational evolutionists for the last ten years because the relationship between locally-interacting cells and the general form of the larger assembly is not well understood. It has, however, been identified as essential to the development of future robotics (Yim et al., 2007).

To complicate matters further, a common assumption is that each pre-formed cell is identical. This means that each cell can take the place of another such that the replacement of damaged cells is trivial. Also the challenge of self-replication is reduced from the procedure of copying the entire system once to that of copying a small cell of the system many times.

There are various existing techniques for the design of self-assembling systems:

Cartesian co-ordinate mapping. One possible way of organising self-assembly is with a co-ordinate system. Each cell works out where it is in the system from the co-ordinates of its neighbours. A map, stored in each cell, that relates each co-ordinate to a particular type of cell is then used to determine what form each cell should take. This is the basis of the embryonics algorithm proposed by Tyrrell (Canham & Tyrrell, 2003).

Hierarchical maps. Murata (Murata et al., 1999) proposed a hierarchical map for the self-assembly of mechanical structures from "fractum", small motorized robots capable of connecting to one another. The assembly program, stored in each cell, contains a description of the neighbourhood of every cell within a simple structure. Cells move randomly until every cell has a correct neighbourhood, at which point every cell freezes. Then another simple structure starts to form about one of the frozen cell. Because repeated simple structures need only be coded once, this algorithm is more efficient than a cartesian co-ordinate mapping.

Ordinary differential equations (ODE). Fleischer (Fleischer & Barr, 1993) studied the effects of biological cell migration, cell hereditary and inter-cellular communications using an ODE model of locally-interacting cells. By using an adaptive euler-solver developed by Barzel (Barzel, 1992), Fleischer was able to design the model to self-assemble into interesting shapes. He concluded that it was difficult to design cells to assemble to specific forms, and went on to suggest the use of evolution as an alternative approach.

Unsupervised evolutionary algorithms. Eggenberger (Eggenberger, 1997) used a multi-cell model to study the effects of genetic lineage and inter-cellular chemical interactions on biological tissue development. A genetic algorithm was used to design the model to converge to interesting patterns. The fitness of each solution was tested against an arbitrary model size and the symmetry of the system about the x-axis.

Supervised evolutionary algorithms. Most recent experiments have relied on supervised evolutionary algorithms for the design of self-assembling systems. For instance, Izumi (Kizotaka et al., 1999) studied supervised genetic algorithms for the self-assembly of Murata's "fractum". Miller (Miller & Banzhaf, 2003) used a 2D array of 256 cells to simulate the inter-cellular chemical interactions of a biological tissue during development. A genetic algorithm was used to design the model to self-assemble to a single pattern (3 vertical stripes) from null or partially corrupt (up to 25%) initial conditions.

Deterministic algorithms for the design of convergent cellular automata (CA). Previous work by the authors (Jones et al., 2008), which this chapter will build upon, has been on the design of convergent cellular automata.

We are going to use a cellular automata model of morphogenesis in order to determine the necessary conditions for robust self-assembly.

4. The conditions for cellular automata convergence

Cellular automata (CA) are dynamic systems in which space and time are discrete. CA consist of a number of identical cells pre-arranged into an array. Each cell can be in one of a number of states. The next state of each cell is determined at discrete time intervals according to the current state of the cell, the current state of neighbouring cells and a next-state rule that is identical for each cell. Let us index each cell with the tuple (i, j), then describe the state of each cell with an integer, $c_{i,j,t}$ and the pattern of the entire array as a matrix, $\mathbf{C}_t$.

If $\mathbf{C}_0$ is the initial pattern of cell states, $f(\mathbf{C}_0)$ is its subsequent pattern after one time step, and $f(f(\mathbf{C}_0))$ or $f^2(\mathbf{C}_0)$ is its pattern at $t = 2$; where f() describes the transition from one iteration to the next. The matrix $\mathbf{C}_t$ is first transcribed into a row-major vector, $\overline{C_t}$ in order for $f()$ to be a linear function of matrix algebra.

Let us define a simple transition function for the next time step:

$$c_{i,j,t+1} = uc_{i,j-1,t} + lc_{i-1,j,t} + rc_{i+1,j,t} + ac_{i,j+1,t} + pc_{i,j,t} + d \tag{33}$$

Where u, l, r, a and p are coefficients of the state of neighbours of each cell, and of the state of the cell itself.

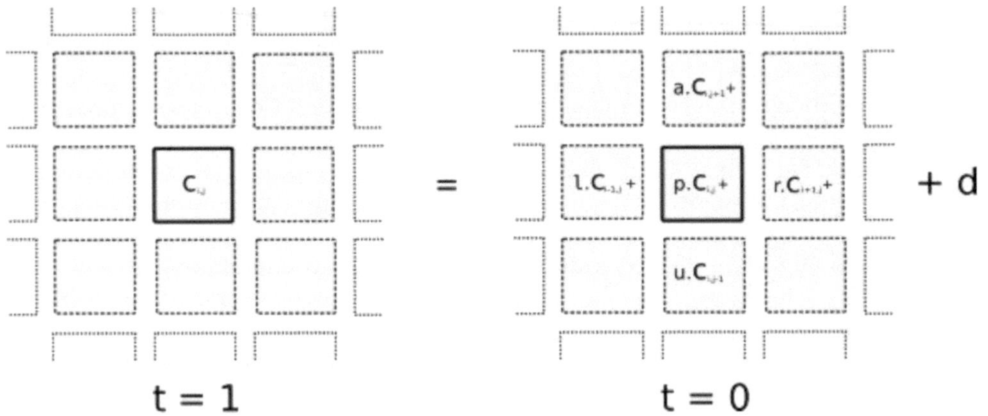

Fig. 6. A simple linear transition function

A transition function for the entire array can be formed from (33) such that $f(C_t) = \mathbf{A}\overline{C_t} + \overline{D}$ where $\overline{D}$ is a constant and the transition matrix (for a three by three CA), $\mathbf{A}$, takes the form:

$$\mathbf{A} = \begin{pmatrix} p & l & 0 & u & 0 & 0 & 0 & 0 & 0 \\ r & p & l & 0 & u & 0 & 0 & 0 & 0 \\ 0 & r & p & 0 & 0 & u & 0 & 0 & 0 \\ a & 0 & 0 & p & l & 0 & u & 0 & 0 \\ 0 & a & 0 & r & p & l & 0 & u & 0 \\ 0 & 0 & a & 0 & r & p & 0 & 0 & u \\ 0 & 0 & 0 & a & 0 & 0 & p & l & 0 \\ 0 & 0 & 0 & 0 & a & 0 & r & p & l \\ 0 & 0 & 0 & 0 & 0 & a & 0 & r & p \end{pmatrix} \tag{34}$$

The spacing of the coefficients a, r, p, l and u within $\mathbf{A}$ depend on the size of the CA.
By the repeated application of $f()$, the transition from $\mathbf{C}_0$ to $\mathbf{C}_n$ (where $n > 1$) becomes:

$$f^2(\overline{C_0}) = \mathbf{A}(\mathbf{A}\overline{C_0} + \overline{D}) + \overline{D} \tag{35}$$

$$f^3(\overline{C_0}) = \mathbf{A}(\mathbf{A}(\mathbf{A}\overline{C_0} + \overline{D}) + \overline{D}) + \overline{D} \tag{36}$$

$$f^3(\overline{C_0}) = \mathbf{A}^3\overline{C_0} + \mathbf{A}^2\overline{D} + \mathbf{A}\overline{D} + \overline{D} \tag{37}$$

This can be expanded to form:

$$f^n(\overline{C_0}) = \mathbf{A}^n\overline{C_0} + \mathbf{A}^{n-1}\overline{D} + \mathbf{A}^{n-2}\overline{D} + ... + \mathbf{A}\overline{D} + \overline{D} \tag{38}$$

Using the geometric series equation this can be simplified to form:

$$f^n(\overline{C_0}) = \mathbf{A}^n\overline{C_0} + (\frac{\mathbf{I} - \mathbf{A}^{n-1}}{\mathbf{I} - \mathbf{A}})\overline{D} \tag{39}$$

Equation (39) determines the pattern the CA forms after n iterations of the transition function (33) have been applied to every cell synchronously.

Given a sufficiently large n in order for the dynamic non-linear system to converge, the final pattern, $\overline{C_n}$, must be independent of the initial pattern, $\overline{C_0}$. Thus no matter what the starting pattern (where $t = 0$ refers to the initial pattern or any pattern that might be the result of system corruption), the pattern of cell states will always return to the same stable pattern.
Thus $\mathbf{A}^n$, the coefficient of $\overline{C_0}$, must equal zero. For this to be so, referring to the coefficients of the states of the cells above, below, left and right and of the cell itself respectively, the following must hold: either l or r must equal zero, either u or a must equal zero, p must equal zero. That is, $\mathbf{A}$ must be an upper-diagonal or lower-diagonal matrix.
Let us now analyse the conditions for convergence of a non-linear transition function, $g()$.

$$g(\overline{C_0}) = \sum_{i=0}^{k} \mathbf{A}_l \overline{C_0} \quad \text{where } A_i = \begin{pmatrix} p_i & l_i & 0 & u_i & 0 & \cdots \\ r_i & p_i & l_i & 0 & u_i & \\ 0 & r_i & p_i & 0 & 0 & \\ a_i & 0 & 0 & p_i & l_i & \\ 0 & a_i & 0 & r_i & p_i & \\ \vdots & & & & & \end{pmatrix} \tag{40}$$

If k is greater than three, expanding $g^n(C_0)$ gives a coefficient of C_0 formed by the multinomial of the transition matrices:

$$(\mathbf{A}_0 + \mathbf{A}_1 + \mathbf{A}_2 + \cdots + \mathbf{A}_m)^n \overline{C_0} \tag{41}$$

The multinomial expansion can be described as:

$$(x_1 + x_2 + \cdots + x_m)^n = \sum\nolimits_{k_0,k_1\cdots,k_m} \binom{n}{k_0, k_1, \cdots, k_m} x_1^{k_0} x_2^{k_1} \cdots x_m^{k_m} \tag{42}$$

Where the summation is taken over all sequences of $k_1, k_2, \cdots, k_m$ such that:

$$\sum_{i=1}^{m} k_l = n \tag{43}$$

And the multinomial coefficient can be expressed as:

$$\binom{n}{k_0, k_1, \cdots, k_m} = \frac{n!}{k_0! k_1! \cdots k_m!} \tag{44}$$

Thus the coefficients of every $\overline{C_0}$ term are constructed from a multinomial coefficient and n members of the set of $\mathbf{A}$ transition matrices:

$$\mathbf{A} = \{\mathbf{A}_0, \mathbf{A}_1, \mathbf{A}_2, \cdots, \mathbf{A}_k\} \tag{45}$$

For every coefficient of $\overline{C_0}$ to be zero, every possible product of n members of $\mathbf{A}$ must be zero. Thus every member of $\mathbf{A}$ must be a lower-diagonal matrix or every member must be an upper-diagonal matrix.
As $g()$ is a sum-of-products function, it can be represented as a two-input one-output logic function. This logic function is best described as a list of rules that form the entries of a look-up table (LUT). Each unique combination of two input-values that is required by the design would form an entry in the LUT.

5. Determining the local rules for a regular CA to converge

Before we can consider the design of self-assembling systems, we need to examine the relationship between the next-state rule each cell obeys and the general form the system converges to. An algorithm is needed to design the next-state rule, $f()$, of a regular CA such that the automata converges to a specific pattern. A technique that works for a limited set of patterns simply assumes the automata has already reached this final pattern, derives the rules each cell must obey in order to stay in the same state then forces every other input combination to a next-state of zero. Figure 7(a) shows a simple example of a pattern to which we would like the automata should converge, figure 7(b) shows the next-state rule, $f()$, that each cell must obey such that the automata converges to this pattern. This example can also use an algebraic next-state rule:

$$c_{i,j,t+1} = 1 - c_{i-1.j.t} - c_{i,j-1,t} \tag{46}$$

Figure 8 shows the automata using equation (46) to converge from null (a) and random (b) initial conditions.

1	0
0	1

(a)

$c_{i-1,j,t}$	$c_{i,j-1,t}$	$c_{i,j,t+1}$
0	0	1
0	1	0
1	0	0
1	1	0

(b)

Fig. 7. A CA pattern and the necessary next-state rule for each cell

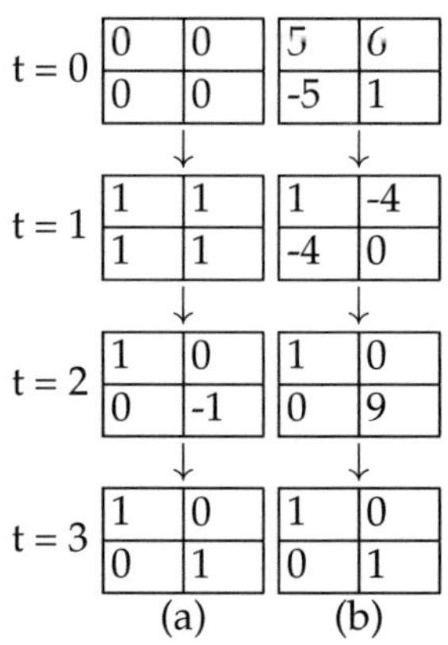

Fig. 8. Example CA convergence from null (a) and random (b) initial conditions

There still exist certain patterns that cannot be generated using this simple deterministic algorithm. This is because the same two input combinations cannot map to different output values. Figure 9(a) shows a pattern that cannot be formed using this approach if the inputs are from above and to the left of each cell.

This is because a portion of this pattern is impossible to form with $f()$ alone because it would require $f(2,2) = 2$ for cell $c_{2,3}$ and $f(2,2) = 1$ for cell $c_{3,3}$, something that is not permissible in a many-to-one mapping.

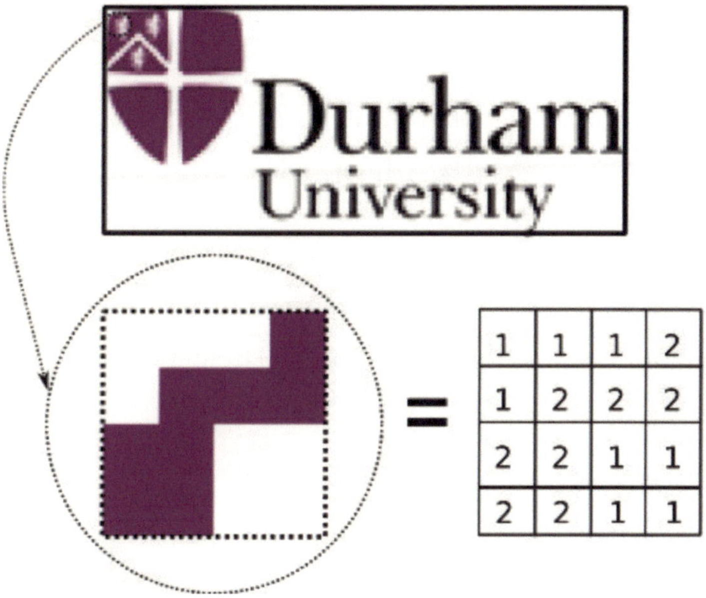

Fig. 9. A pattern for which the design is not trivial

To this end additional computation must be introduced in the form of a many-to-one state-to-output mapping function denoted by $g()$. Figure 10(a) shows an example implementation of how the next state and output of each cell might be calculated. The reader is referred to (Jones et al., 2008) for further information.

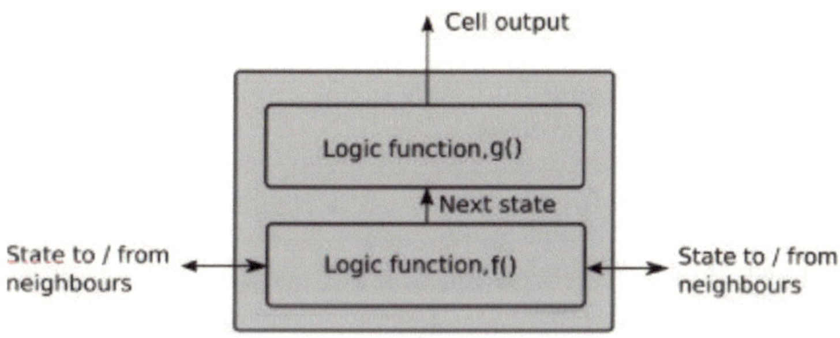

Fig. 10. A possible implementation of $f()$ and $g()$

Thus the pattern of figure 9(b) could be rewritten as figure 11(a). The state of cell $c_{1,2}$ has been replaced with the first available integer that does not form a mapping that contradicts previously determined mappings. Figure 11(b) is the mapping from figure 9(b) to figure 11(a) and figure 12 is the next-state rules each cell must obey.
By introducing as many state values for each output as is necessary, any desired pattern can be generated. However an optimum solution would use as few state values as possible. If the sequence in which cells are assigned a state value starts from the corner furthest from the direction of state-input, a minimum number of state values will be needed. Hence if the inputs are taken from above and to the left of each cell, the first cell to be assigned a value would be the cell in the bottom-right of the array.

(a)

4	4	4	2
1	2	3	2
2	2	1	1
2	2	1	1

(b)

$c_{i,j,t}$	output
1	1
2	2
3	2
4	1
5	1
6	1

Fig. 11. A solution to figure 9(b)

$c_{i-1,j,t}$	$c_{i,j-1,t}$	$c_{i,j,t+1}$
0	0	6
0	4	2
0	5	4
0	6	5
1	0	2
1	1	1
1	2	1
2	1	1
2	2	2
2	3	2
4	2	3
5	1	2
6	0	1

Fig. 12. The ruleset to figure 9(b)

Figure 13 shows the CA converging from null initial conditions. Figure 14 shows the CA converging from random initial conditions.
Implementing the design algorithm using a python script, the derivation for this 120 by 60 cell convergent CA took 180 seconds to complete on a 3.2GHz Intel Xeon processor.

6. Fundamental criteria for convergence of a self-assembling systems

We have so far only considered systems of cells which are pre-arranged into regular arrays. If the state of each cell also includes the position at which a cell should reside relative to other cells, the analysis can be extended to the design of self-assembling systems.
The scheme proposed so far relies on each cell computing its next-state from the current state of two neighbouring cells; the relative location of each neighbour to the cell is common to every cell in the array. Therefore if one cell updates according to the state of cells above and to the left of itself, so does every cell. In a rectangular array of cells, most will have two neighbours upon which they determine their next state from, some will have one neighbour and one will have no neighbours. In effect the desired pattern emerges from this one cell (the origin cell); as shown in figure 15(a). In the case of a partially-assembled CA, or a CA that converges to form an irregular shape, this is not necessarily the case. This is shown in figure 15(b).
A solution is to allow each cell to determine its next-state according to the current state of two neighbouring cells as before, but to determine which two cells (above or below, to the

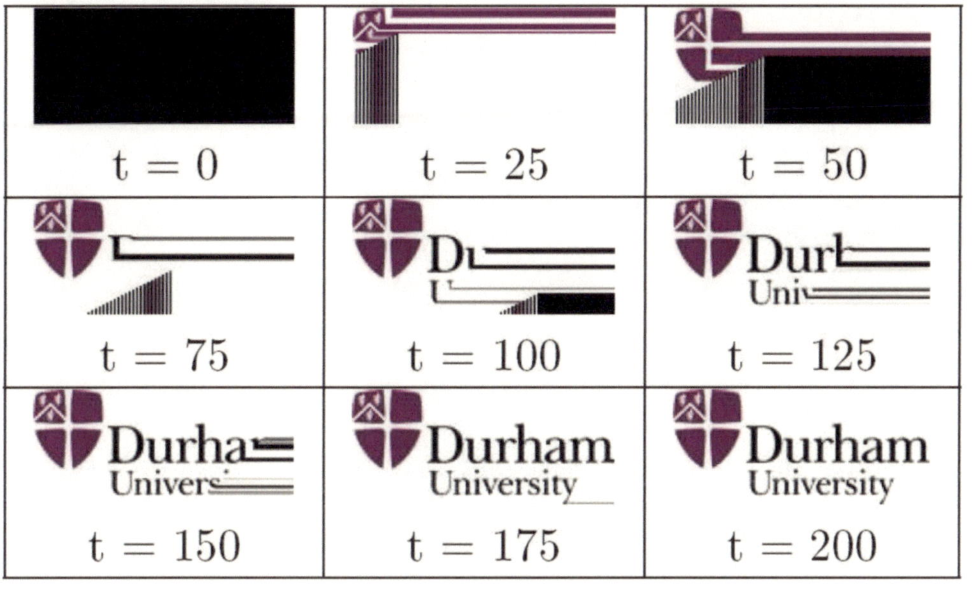

Fig. 13. The convergence of a 120 by 60 CA from null initial conditions

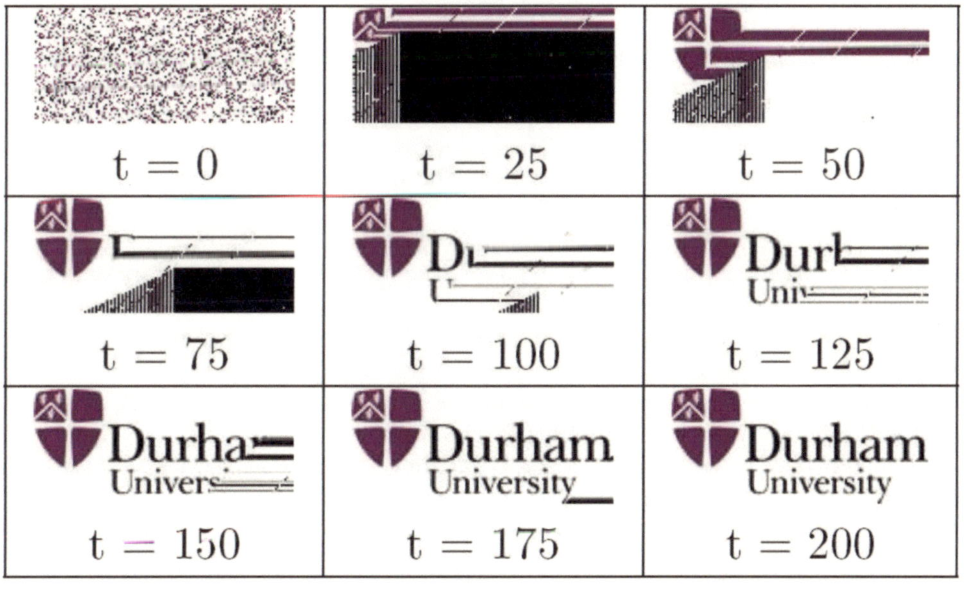

Fig. 14. The convergence of a 120 by 60 CA from corrupt initial conditions

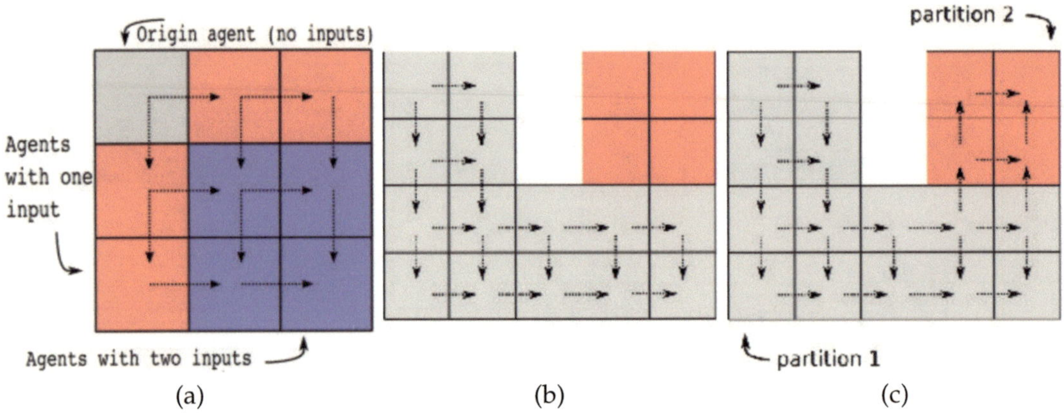

Fig. 15. Inputs combinations, an irregular 2D CA and the flow of state information from the origin cell

left or right) according to its current state. Thus, while one cell may determine its next-state according to cells above and to the left of itself, another might determine its next-state according to cells from below and to the right of itself. This "state to neighbourhood-function" is a many-to-one mapping (see figure 16).

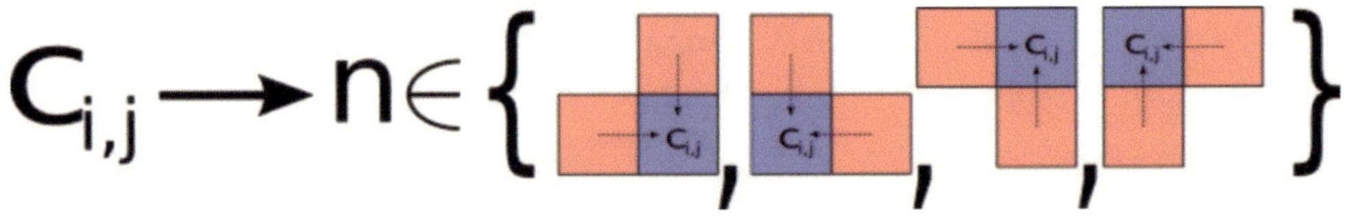

Fig. 16 The state-neighbourhood function mapping

If we divide the CA into partitions with common neighbourhood configurations (as shown in figure 15(c)), where each partition directly or indirectly derives its neighbouring states from the first partition ($P1$) which contains the origin cell, the pattern of this irregular CA effectively emerges from the origin cell. Thus provided $f()$ conforms to the requirements for the automata to converge, a multiple-partition automata with $f()$ as its transition function, will also converge to a steady pattern.

6.1 Determining the local rules for an irregular CA to converge to an arbitrary pattern

The design algorithm for a convergent irregular CA is similar to that for a regular CA. The desired pattern is first divided into partitions of cells with common neighbourhood configurations. This is done so as to maximise the size of each partition. This maximises the number of cells that have two neighbours in their neighbourhood configuration, thus reducing the number of state values needed for the design.

The design algorithm is then applied to each partition in turn. The sequence of partitions is reversed, so the first partition to be solved is the partition furthest from the origin cell. There are now three mappings against which each state-assignment must be tested:

1. The mapping from the current state of its neighbours to the next state of the cell ($g()$).
2. The mapping from the current state of the cell to its output ($h()$).
3. The mapping from the current state of the cell to the relative location of the neighbouring cells to which it transmits this state.

Every mapping created by each state assigned by the design algorithm must first be tested against each mapping previously created by the design algorithm, including those created for cells in different partitions.

6.2 The assembly algorithm

In previous demonstrations the automata has consisted of a pre-assembled array of cells. However the new algorithm makes the self-assembly of the automata possible. If un-used cells fasten themselves to used cells only where that cell is transmitting state-values, the automata will self-assemble from the origin cell until complete. This self-assembly depends on the origin cell already existing.

6.3 Demonstration

Figure 17 shows the five partitions of a 1000 cell 2D system. Figure 18 shows this system self-assembling and converging to the desired stable shape. Figure 19 shows this same system self-healing from a corrupted shape.
Implementing the algorithm of section 6.1 using a python script, the derivation for this 1000 cell self-assembling system took 30 seconds on a 3.2GHz Intel Xeon processor.

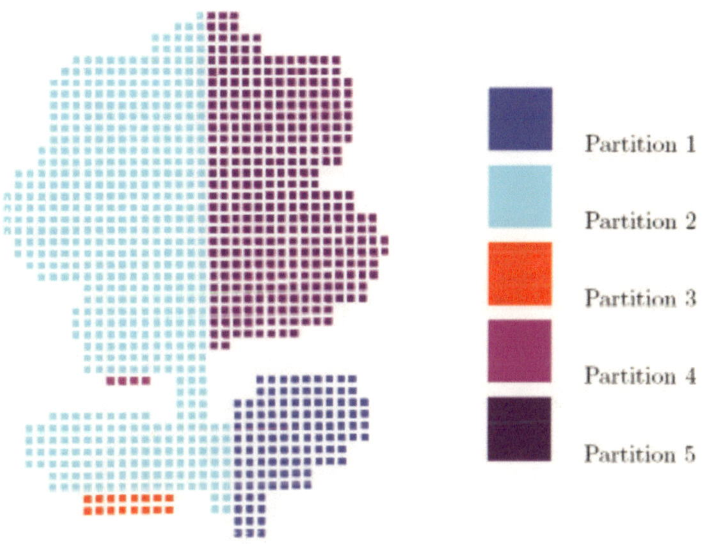

Fig. 17. The partitions of a 2D array of 1000 cells

7. Designing 3D self-assembling systems

To adapt the design algorithm so far presented for the design of 3D systems is straightforward. To expand the analysis presented in section 3 to consider the convergence of 3D automata we must replace the row-major vector representation of the automata with a row-column-major vector. This analysis shows that for a 3D automata to converge each cell must determine its next-state according to the present state of at most three neighbours; one per axis.

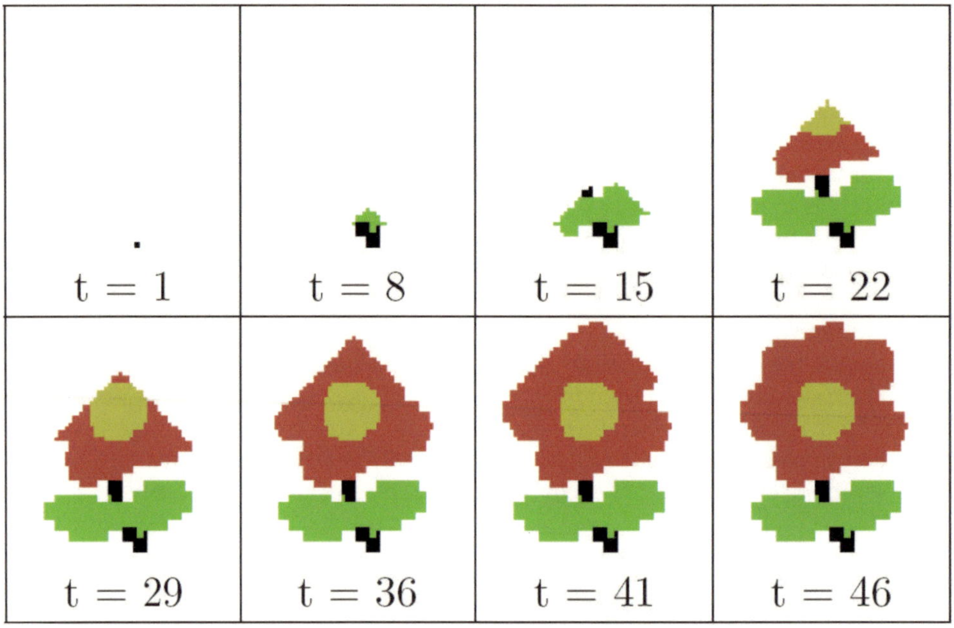

Fig. 18. The array self-assembling and converging from the origin cell

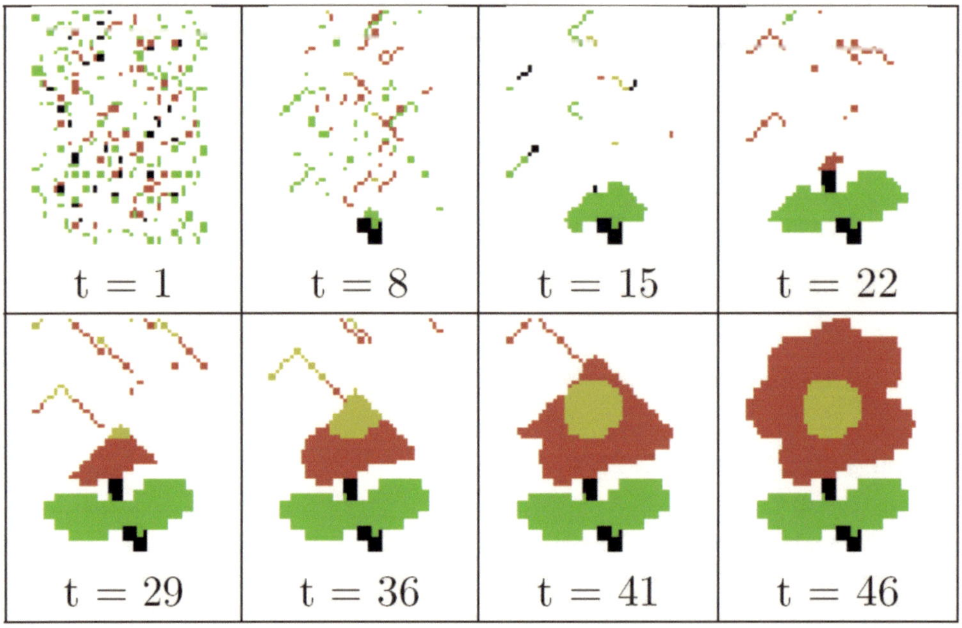

Fig. 19. The array converging from a corrupt pattern

Thus $f()$, the transition function used by each cell to determine its next-state, must be a function of three variables and the design algorithm of section must be adapted to reflect this.
Figure 20 shows the 80 partitions of a 3D irregular system of 55,000 cell. Figure 21 shows this 3D irregular system of identical cells self-assemble into the desired form. Figure 22 shows the same system repair itself after being corrupted.
Implementing the algorithm of section 6.1 using a python script, the derivation for this 55,000 cell 3D self-assembling system took 12 hours on a 3.2GHz Intel Xeon processor.

Fig. 20. The 80 partitions of a 3D robot shape, each colour is a different partition

The design required 31,637 rules and 4692 states. This compares with the 55,000 that would be required for a cartesian design (suitably adapted to cope with irregular shapes). As there is little evidence of hierarchy in the design, a hierarchical map would offer little improvement over a cartesian design. The successes of the adaptive euler-solver and evolutionary algorithms to small self-assembling systems design do not easily scale to larger systems. Their application to the design of a 55,000 cell system would require prohibitive computational resources.

8. Conclusions

During the self-assembly of a system of identical cells, each cell independently determines its state and location within the system based on local interactions with neighbouring cells and an algorithm common to each cell.
Various schemes for this algorithm have been investigated. A co-ordinate scheme; each cell determining its location from the location of its neighbours then using a map to determine where and what type of cell it should be - works for small systems but the size of the map each cell must store is impractical for larger systems. Computational genetic algorithms have been successfully used to create more efficient self-assembling solutions, but only for small simple systems. Thus an alternative is needed for large complicated systems.

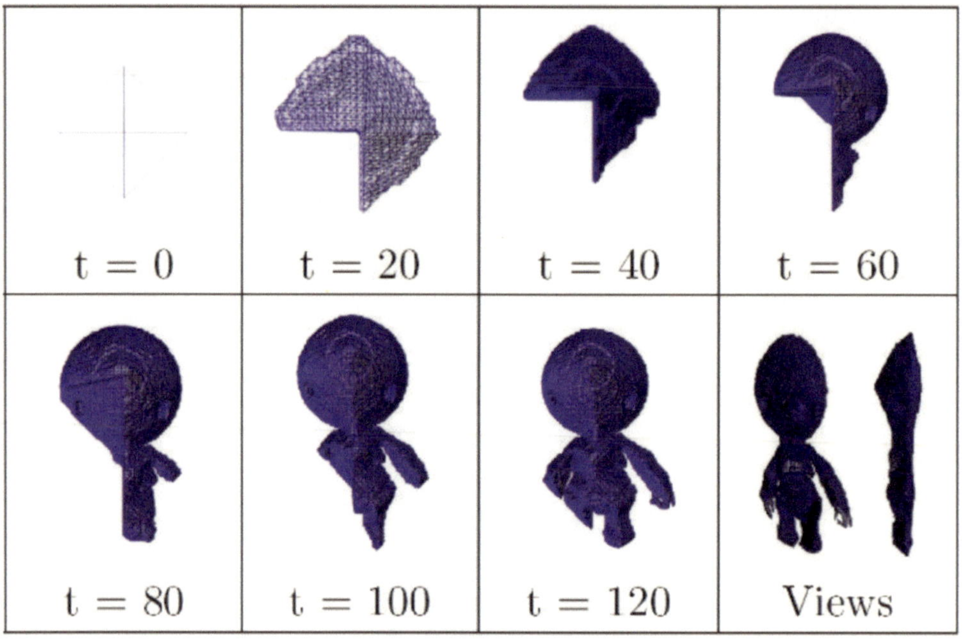

Fig. 21. A 3D system of 55,000 cells self-assembling from the origin cell

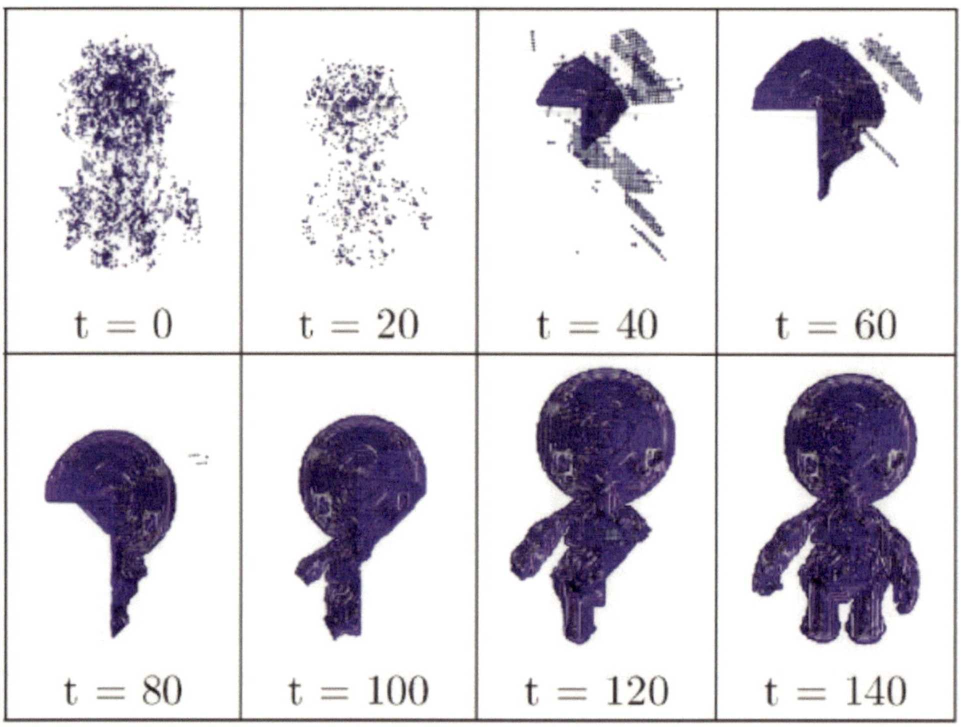

Fig. 22. The same 3D system self-healing from a corrupt shape

In this chapter we have presented a new, deterministic algorithm that can design self-assembling, self-repairing systems in two and three dimensions. The solutions generated by this design algorithm are often more efficient than those based on a co-ordinate scheme and capable of forming larger, more complicated systems than those designed by genetic algorithms.

This research has a broader application potential than just self-assembling robotics. Here we list a few of the fields where morphogenesis-inspired self-assembly may have applications:

Self-assembling micro and nano systems. Attempts to engineer biological, chemical and nano systems to self-assemble to a particular form have been limited by the difficulties of creating specific modules. If overcome, the limited complexity of each module will restrict any attempts to implement complicated self-assembly algorithms. Thus the bio-inspired minimalist strategy presented here may be an appropriate scheme.

Self-assembling micro-electromechanical systems (MEMS). Attempts to engineer MEMS to self-assemble are currently limited by the difficulties of manufacturing the complicated locomotive and inter-module bonding mechanisms. However this field is making progress in the development of small, easy to manufacture components capable of locomotion and gripping. As smaller components become possible, the emphasis on the self-assembly algorithms will be on simple schemes capable of assembling large numbers of components.

Image processing and compression. Images can be encoded as a self-assembling cellular automata described by its next-state rule. Analysis of this rule provides insight into repetition and feature scale within the image. For some images, especially images which contain repeating pattern, this next-state rule is smaller than the image bitmap - providing a means for losslessly compressing an image.

Distributed computing. Computing systems formed from large collections of processing elements are particularly difficult to co-ordinate and write software for. Morphogenesis-inspired software may provide a means of self-organising these systems, be they supercomputers or smart dust.

Plastic electronics. These are electronics that no longer reside on standard FR4 composite PCBs. Instead their components are laid on flexible substrates that are prone to stretching and ripping. One of the few remaining hurdles to the commercialisation of this technology is reliability - billions of plastic radio-frequency identification (RFID) tags cannot be printed if ten percent will fail, nor can large flexible LCD screens be rolled up if the system cannot withstand the stretching of the substrate. Morphogenesis-inspired reliability engineering may be one means of overcoming this hurdle.

Space technology. Since 2002 NASA have been running a series of workshops under the title "Ultra reliability"; this with the goal of increasing systems reliability by an order of magnitude across complex systems, hardware (including aircraft, satellites and launch vehicles) and software (Shapiro, 2006). It is not difficult to see the challenges that standard redundancy techniques will face in long life missions that are vulnerable to cosmic rays.

Heat-resistant processors. Failure rates of electronic systems increase exponentially with temperature, so perhaps morphogenesis-inspired reliability could enable computer processors to run without needing cooling fans.

Multi-agent techniques. A popular technique for modelling complex systems in software, multi-agent systems study the global effects of locally-interacting agents. Where some global effect is required of the system, it is normally very difficult to design appropriate rules of the local behaviour of the agents. We have limited this current research to the domain of a specific type of multi-agent system, cellular automata, but it may prove applicable to the larger domain.

9. Acknowledgements

The authors would like to acknowledge the support of the EPSRC for funding the work presented in this chapter.

10. References

Barzel, R. (1992). A structured approach to physically-based modeling, *Academic Press, Cambridge MA* .

Benyus, J. M. (1998). *Biomimicry: Innovation inspired by nature*, Perennial.

Berrill, N. J. & Cohen, A. (1936). Regeneration in clavellina lepadiformis, *Journal of experimental biology* 13.

Blowey, J. (2007). Lecture notes for course: Mathematical biosciences.

Canham, R. & Tyrrell, A. M. (2003). An embryonic array with improved efficiency and fault tolerance, *Evolvable Hardware 2003* pp. 91–100.

Childress, S. (2005). Case study 2: Turing's model of chemical morphogenesis.

Eggenberger, P. (1997). Evolving morphologies of simulated 3d organisms based on differential gene expression, *Proceedings of the 4th European Conference on Artificial Life* .

Fleischer, K. & Barr, A. (1993). A simulation testbed for the study of multicellular development: multiple mechanisms of morphogenesis, *Artificial life III* .

Griffiths, A. J. F. (1976). *An introduction to genetic analysis*, W. H. Freeman and Company.

Gurdon, J. (1968). Changes in somatic cell nuclei inserted into growing and maturing amphibian oocytes, *J. Embryol. Exp. Morphol.* (20:401-14).

Jones, D. H., McWilliam, R. P. & Purvis, A. (2008). Designing convergent cellular automata, *Biosystems* .

Kizotaka, I., Watanabe, K., Tamura, H. & Ikeda, Y. (1999). Initial configuration dependence in a self-organizing robot, *Artificial life and robotics* .

Meinhardt, H. (1982). *Models of biological pattern formation*, Academic Press, London.

Miller, J. & Banzhaf, W. (2003). Evolving the program for a cell: From french flags to boolean circuits, *On Growth, Form and Computers* .

Morgan, T. H. (1904). An attempt to analyse the phenomena of polarity in tubularia, *Journal of experimental Zoology* 1: 587–591.

Murata, S., Kurokawa, H., Tomita, K. & Kokaji, S. (1999). Self-assembly and self-repair method for a distributed mechanical system, *IEEE Transactions on Robotics and Automation* .

Pisarev A., Poustelnikova E., Samsonova M. & Reinitz J. (2008) FlyEx, the quantitative atlas on segmentation gene expression at cellular resolution. Nucl. Acids Res.; doi: 10.1093/nar/gkn717

Rosee, A. L., Hader, T., Taubert, H., Rivera-Pomar, R. & Jackle, H. (1997). Mechanism and bicoid-dependent control of hairy stripe 7 expression in the posterior region of the drosophila embryo, *The Embryology journal* 16.

Shapiro, A. (2006). Ultra-reliability at nasa, *44th AIAA Aerospace Sciences Meeting and Exhibit* .

Turing, A. (1950). The chemical basis of morphogenesis, *Philos, Trans. Roy. Soc.* Ser. B 237, 37.

Yim, M., Shen, W., Salemi, B., Rus, D., Moll, M., Lipson, H., Klavins, E. & Chirikjian, G. S. (2007). Grand challenges of robotics, *IEEE Robotics and Automation* .

19

Cellular Automata for Medical Image Processing

Sartra Wongthanavasu
Khon Kaen University
Thailand

1. Introduction

Cellular automata (CA) were introduced to provide a formal framework for investigating the behaviour of dynamic complex system in which time and space are discrete. They comprise an array of cells, where each cell can be in one of a finite number of possible states, which is updated synchronously in discrete time steps according to local transition rules (cell rules). A state of a cell at the next time step is determined by its neighboring cell's current state. A substantial numbers of CA activities occurred in the 1970s with the introduction of artificial life. There were a number of distinguished papers and books to date has investigated artificial life (Raghawan, 1993; Langton, 1986, 1992; Pesavento, 1995; Rietman, 1993). Interest in important features of physics was spawned largely by Tommaso Toffoli. Spephen Wolfram was responsible for capturing the wider interest of the physics community with a series of papers in the 1980s, while others were applying CAs to a variety of problems in other fields (Sarkar & Abbasi, 2006; Xiao et al., 2008; Bandini et al., 2001; Mizas et al., 2008). In present, CA are being studied from many widely different angles, and the relationship of these structures to existing problems in being constantly sought and discovered (Reynaga & Amthauer, 2003; Mitchell et al., 1994; Hecker et al., 1999). As the topology of CA, they appear as natural tools for image processing due to their local nature and simple parallel computation implementation. To date, there are a number of papers which generally discuss cellular automata for image processing (Hernandez & Herrmann, 1996; Rosin, 2006; Chen & Horng, 2010; Chen & Lai, 2007; Eslami et al., 2010; Tzionas et al., 1997; Umeo, 2001). In this regard, there were some papers discuss medical image processing using CA model (Cheng et al, 2006; Viher et al, 1998, Ferrari et al., 2004; Chen et al., 2008).
This paper presents a number of cellular automata-based algorithms for medical image processing. It starts by introducing cellular automata fundamentals necessary for understanding the proposed algorithms. Then, a number of cellular automata algorithms for medical image edge detection, noise filtering, spot detection, pectoral muscle identification and segmentation was presented. In this regard, 2-D mammogram images for the breast cancer diagnosis were investigated.

2. Cellular automata

Let I denote the set of integer. A 2-D cellular space is a 4-tuple, (IxI, V, N, f), where IxI is a set of cartesian product of two integer sets, V is a set of cellular states, N is the type of neighborhood, and f is the local transition function from V^n into V. The relevant neighborhood function is a function from IxI into 2^{IxI} defined by g (α) = $\{\alpha+\delta 1, \alpha+\delta 2, \ldots,$

$\alpha+\delta_n\}$, for all $\alpha \in IxI$, where δ_i (i = 1,2,…,n) $\in$ IxI is fixed. The neighborhood state function of a cell α at time t is defined by $h^t(\alpha) = (v^t(\alpha+\delta_1), v^t(\alpha+\delta_2), \ldots, v^t(\alpha+\delta_n))$. For 2-D von Neumann neighborhood, the neighborhood state function of the central cell (α) is defined by: $h^t(\alpha) = (v^t(\alpha+(0,0)), v^t(\alpha+(0,1)), v^t(\alpha+(1,0)), v^t(\alpha+(0,-1)), v^t(\alpha+(-1,0))$, where $v^t(\alpha+(0,0)$ is current state of the central cell, $v^t(\alpha+(0,1)$ ($v^t(\alpha+(0,-1))$ for the north (south) cells, $v^t(\alpha+(1,0)$ ($v^t(\alpha+(-1,0))$ for the east (west) cells.

Now we relate the neighborhood state of a cell α at time t to the cellular state of that cell at time t+1 by $f(h^t(\alpha)) = v^{t+1}(\alpha)$. The function f is referred to as the 2-D CA rule and is usually given in the form of a state table, specifying all possible pairs of the form $(h^t(\alpha), v^{t+1}(\alpha))$. Figure 1 shows 2-D digital image and 2-D CA.

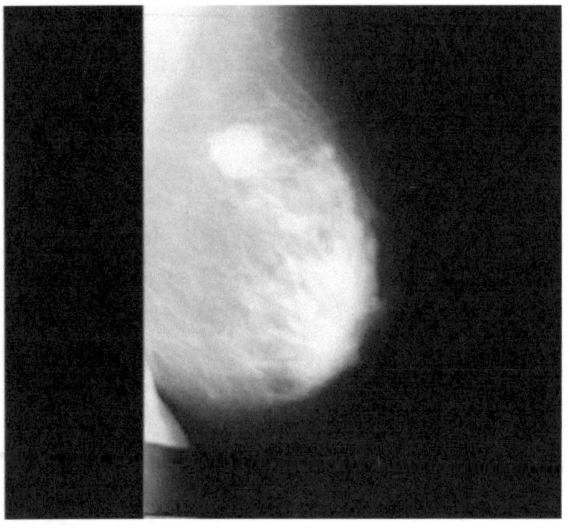

(a) 2-D digital image.

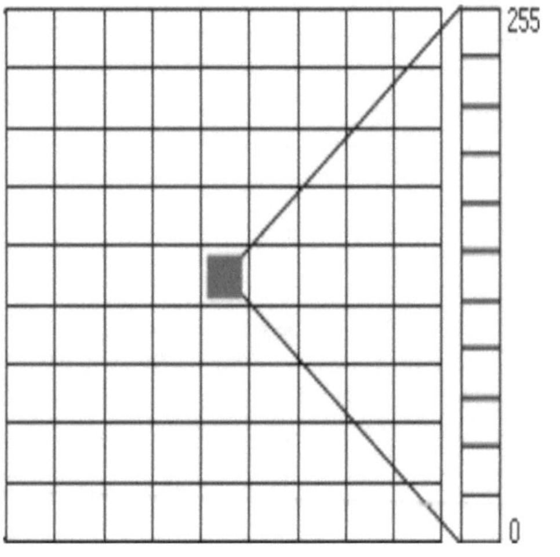

(b) 2-D cellular automata with 256 states.

Fig. 1. A 2-D digital image vs A 2-D CA.

3. Cellular automata for medical image edge detection

As stated previously, cellular automata techniques appear as a natural tool for image processing due to their local nature and simple parallel computing implementation. This section presents one main algorithm and investigates its variation for processing mammogram images. The algorithms will cope with edge detection and noise removal for both binary and grayscale images, while the last one will correspond to hypothesized spots detection for breast cancer analysis. Examples of the application of these cellular automata techniques to real mammogram images will be presented, which together with the results will show the performance characteristics.

The main cellular automata algorithm for k gray levels of digital images is on the basis of a two dimensional cellular automata (IxI, V, N, f) with V = {0, 1, 2, …, k-1}, where k is a number of states, N is the type of neighborhood, while the local transition function f is from V^n into V. The proposed algorithm is shown in (1) below:

$$f((\nu^t(\alpha+\delta_1),\nu^t(\alpha+\delta_2),\ldots,\nu^t(\alpha+\delta_n)) = \begin{cases} E(\alpha), & \text{if } \max_{j=0}^{k-1} N(C_j) = C_{target} \text{ and } sum(\nu^t(C_{target})) > k\text{-}1 \\ B(\alpha), & \text{otherwise} \end{cases} \quad (1)$$

where C_j is the jth class of the pixel values (states) in its neighborhood $(h^t(\alpha))$ for $j = 0, 1, 2,..,m$ and $\nu^t(\alpha+\delta_i) \in C_j$.
$N(C_j)$ is a number of neighbors of α which fall into class C_j.
$sum(\nu^t(C_{target}))$ is summation of $\nu^t(C_{target})$.
C_{target} is the majority class containing maximal number of neighbors.
$\nu^t(C_{target})$ denotes all of $\nu^t(\alpha+\delta_i) \in C_{target}$.
$E(\alpha)$ is the edge pixel value.
$B(\alpha)$ is the background pixel value.
k is a number of states.
For class arrangement, histogram distribution will be utilized to supervise an identification of each class. Automatic class arrangement can be implemented using Otsu algorithm (Otsu, 1979).

3.1 Grayscale images

The objective of the edge detection techniques is to enhance the magnitude of the local differences in gray level values between regions of the images. Over regions which are different, changes must be made to enhance the edges. The proposed variation of (1) which deals with this task is shown in formula (2) for Von Neumann's neighborhood, four classes and 256 gray levels as following:

$$f((\nu^t(\alpha+\delta_1),\nu^t(\alpha+\delta_2),\ldots,\nu^t(\alpha+\delta_5)) = \begin{cases} 255, & \text{if } \max_{j=0}^{3} N(C_j) = C_{target} \text{ and } sum(\nu^t(C_{target})) > 255 \\ 0, & \text{otherwise} \end{cases} \quad (2)$$

where C_j is the jth class of the pixel values in its neighborhood $(h^t(\alpha))$ for $j = 0, 1, 2, 3$ and $\nu^t(\alpha+\delta_i) \in C_j$.
$N(C_j)$ is number of neighbors of α which fall into class C_j.
C_{target} is the majority class containing maximal number of neighbors $(\nu^t(\alpha+\delta_i) \in C_{target})$.
$sum(\nu^t(C_{target}))$ is summation of $\nu^t(C_{target})$.
$\nu^t(C_{target})$ denotes all of $\nu^t(\alpha+\delta_i) \in C_{target}$.
Prior to implementing the formula (2) on a particular image, a class arrangement using histogram information was determined. Figure 2 shows an original mammogram image (a) and its histogram information (b). Results for four classes arrangement and the edge image were shown in Figure 2 (c) and (d), respectively.
It is explicitly shown that the cellular automata algorithm simply provides the promising edge maps shown in Fig. 3(d).

3.2 Binary images

In case of edge detection on binary mammogram, the cellular automata algorithm given in the formula (2) directly enables carrying out to two states efficiently. There is no need to be changed. Figure 3 shows the promising result implementing the algorithm. An Edge result exhibits the superb quality with one pixel wide and edge has no break.

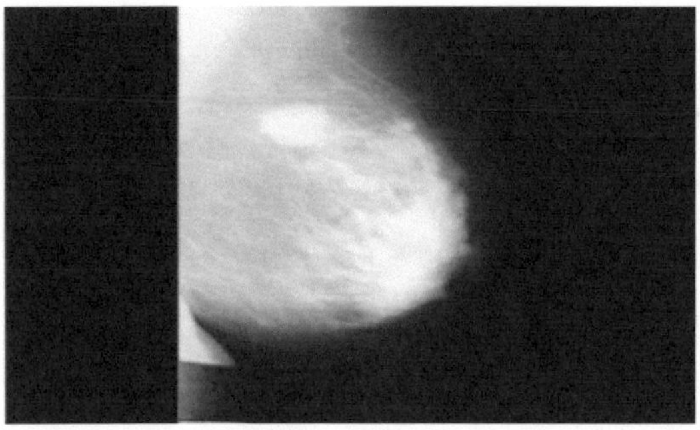

(a) Original mammogram.

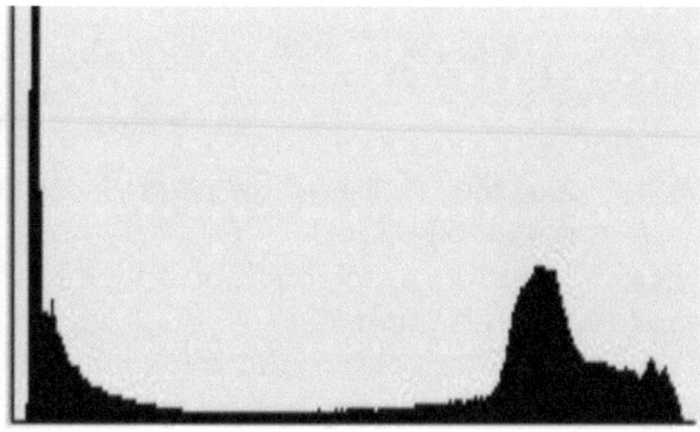

(b) Histogram.

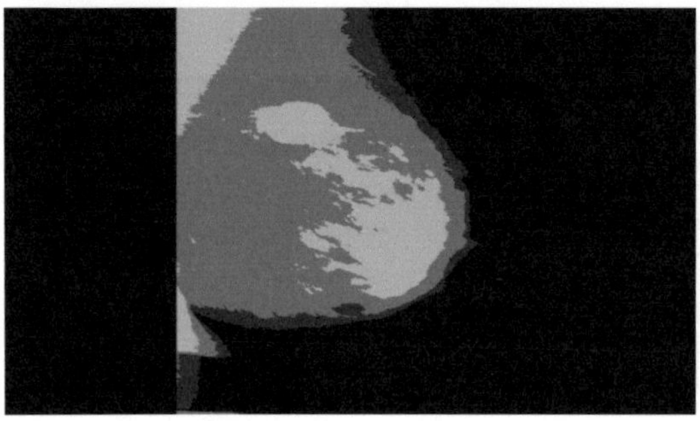

(c) Four class image.

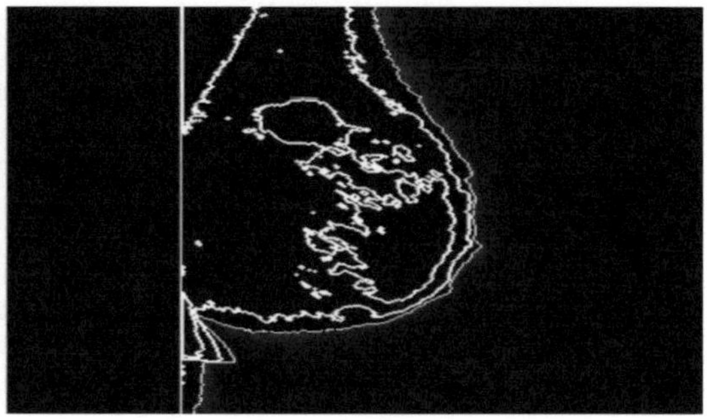

(d) Edge map result.

Fig. 2. (a) Original mammogram, (b) histogram information, (c) four classes of image, and (d) result of edge detection.

(a) Original binary image.

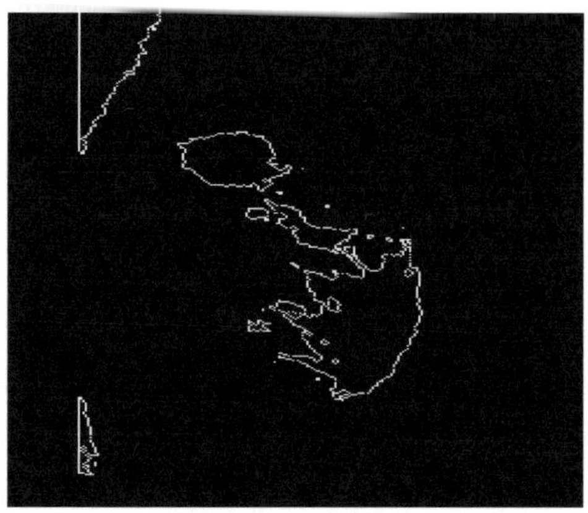

(b) Edge result.

Fig. 3. Edge result as dealing with binary image.

3.3 Noise filtering

The objective of the noise filtering is to reduce the local differences in gray level values between regions of the images. Over regions which are similar, no changes must be made, in order to avoid the destruction of the main characteristics of the image. The proposed variation of cellular automata algorithm given in (1) using von Neumann's neighborhood and two states dealing with this task is shown in formula (3) as follow:

$$f\left(\left(\nu^t(\alpha+\delta_1),\nu^t(\alpha+\delta_2),\ldots,\nu^t(\alpha+\delta_5)\right)\right) = \begin{cases} \max\left(\nu^t\left(C_{target}\right)\right), & \text{if } \max_{j=0}^{3} N(C_j) = C_{target} \\ 0, & \text{otherwise} \end{cases} \quad (3)$$

where C_j is the jth class of the pixel values in its neighborhood $(h^t(\alpha))$ for $j = 0, 1, 2, 3$ and $\nu^t(\alpha+\delta_i) \in C_j$.

$N(C_j)$ is number of neighbors of α which fall into class C_j.

C_{target} is the majority class containing maximal number of neighbors $(\nu^t(\alpha+\delta_i) \in C_{target})$.

$\nu^t(C_{target})$ denotes all of $\nu^t(\alpha+\delta_i) \in C_{target}$.

$\max(\nu^t(C_{target}))$ is the maximal state of $\nu^t(C_{target})$.

Figure 4 shows an original binary mammogram with 2% salt and pepper noise. The noise filtering result obtained by implementing the algorithm (3) using one step of iteration was shown in Figure 4 (b). In this respect, the cellular automata algorithm (3) explicitly provides the promising result.

(a) Noisy binary image. (b) Noise removal.

Fig. 4. Binary image with 2% salt and pepper noise (a) and the image after noise removal (b).

3.4 Spot detection

The objective of the spot detection is to assist the physicians and doctors in locating hypothesized spots for masses in breast cancer. The shape and spread region of spots play a vital role for further steps of analyses and have to be comprehensively taken into account. For this purpose, a set operator is implemented as follow:

$$W = X - Y \quad (4)$$

where X denotes an investigating original image,

Y denotes an edge map resulting from implementing the formula (2), and

W denotes the spot detection image.

The operator (-) represents the subtraction, meaning that it simply carries out the subtraction of pixel values in the same coordinate between two images (sets). By implementing such an operator in an original image (X) shown in Fig. 5(a) with respect to the edge image Y obtained by implementing the formula (2) on grayscale and binary images, the resulting spot detection was shown in Figure 5 (b) and (c), respectively.

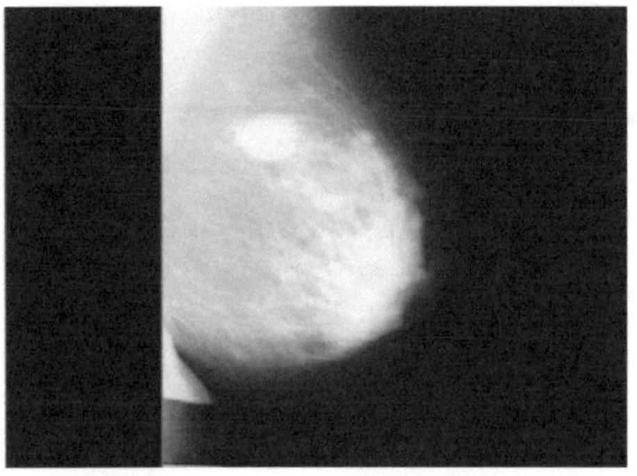

(a) Malignant mammogram

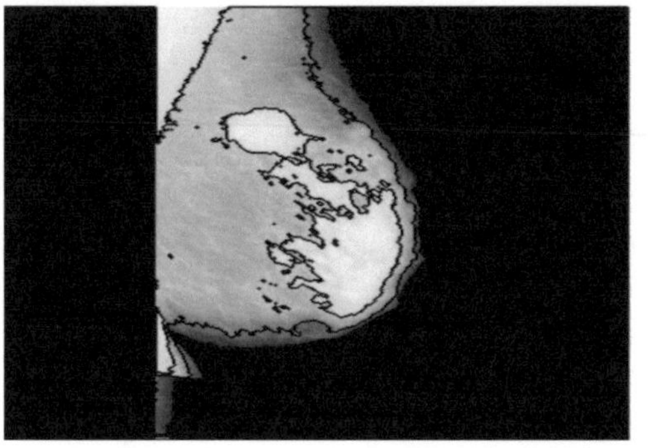

(b) Spot detection using grayscale image.

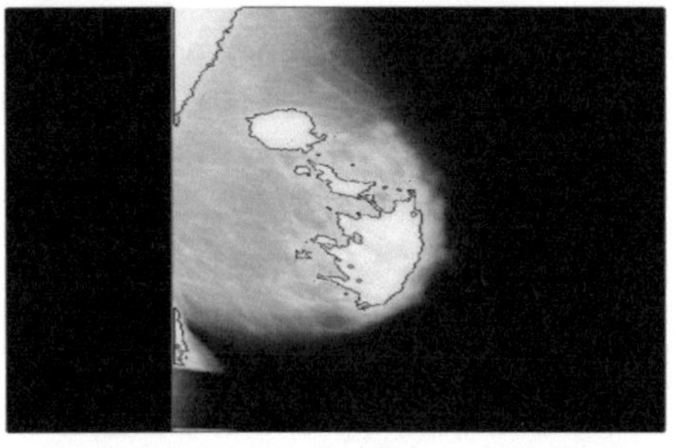

(c) Spot detection using binary image.

Fig. 5. Spot detection due to (2) for binary and grayscale images.

Figure 5. shows mammogram processing with white spot detection: (a) original malignant mass in mammogram, (b) hypothesized mass detection using algorithm (2) for grayscale, and (c) hypothesized mass detection using algorithm (3) for binary image.

4. Cellular automata for identification of the pectorial muscle in mammograms

The pectoral muscle represents a predominant density region in most medio-lateral oblique (MLO) views of mammograms. Its inclusion can affect the results of intensity-based image processing methods. To date, there were some papers has investigated identification of the pectorial muscle in mammograms (Ferrari et al., 2004; Ma et al., 2007). This section presents a new method on the basis of cellular automata model for the identification of the pectoral muscle in MLO mammograms. A dataset of 84 MLO mammograms from the MIAS (Mammographic Image Analysis Society, London, U.K.) database (Suckling et al., 1994) was implemented throughout for evaluation. In this respect, the pectoral muscle edge detected in the mammograms was carried out based upon the percentage of false-positive (FP) and false-negative (FN) pixels determined by comparison between the numbers of pixels enclosed in the regions delimited by the edges identified by a radiologist and by the proposed method.

4.1 Proposed CA-based algorithm

In this section, the method for identification of pectoral muscle in mammogram images were presented. It starts by computing the edge detection by using the formula (2) stated earlier dealing with grayscale images. Then, the result will be segmented by using the rule-based algorithm, leading to the identification of the pectoral muscle. Examples of the application of the proposed method to real mammogram images will be presented, which together with the results will show the performance characteristics.

The proposed cellular automata algorithm for 256 gray levels of digital images are on the basis of a two-dimensional cellular automata (IxI, V, N, f) with V = {0, 1, 2, …, 255}, N is von Neumann type of the neighborhood, while the local transition function f is from V^n into V.

4.1.1 Edge detection

Referred to the formula (2) stated previously, the cellular automata algorithm for this task was revisited as follow:

$$\text{if } ((\nu^t(\alpha+\delta_1), \nu^t(\alpha+\delta_2), \ldots, \nu^t(\alpha+\delta_5)) = 255, \quad \text{if } \max_{j=0}^{3} N(C_j) = C_{target} \text{ and } \text{sum}(\nu^t(C_{target})) > 255$$
$$= 0, \quad \text{otherwise}$$

where C_j is the jth class of the pixel values in its neighborhood $(h^t(\alpha))$ for $j = 0, 1, 2, 3$ and $\nu^t(\alpha+\delta_i) \in C_j$.

$N(C_j)$ is number of neighbors of α which fall into class C_j.

C_{target} is the majority class containing maximal number of neighbors $(\nu^t(\alpha+\delta_i) \in C_{target})$.

$sum(\nu^t(C_{target}))$ is summation of $\nu^t(C_{target})$.

$\nu^t(C_{target})$ denotes all of $v^t(\alpha+\delta_i) \in C_{target}$.

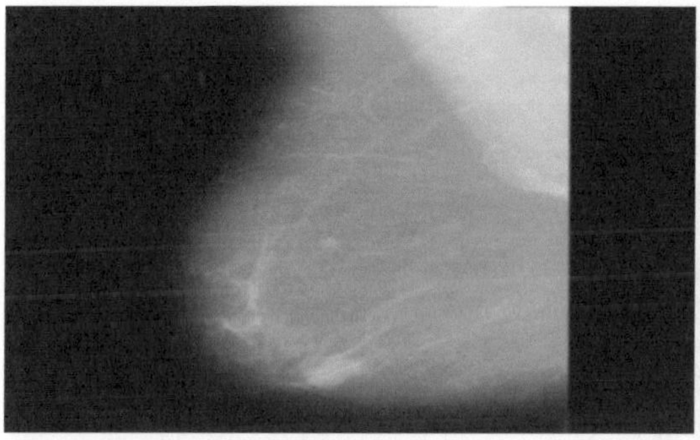

(a) Original image mdb005.

(b) Four class image.

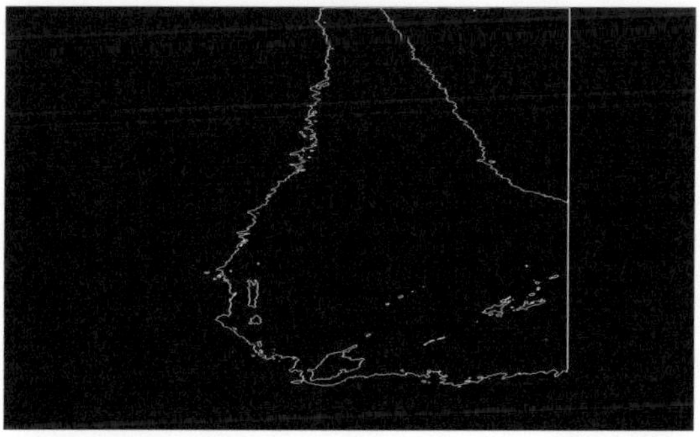

(c) Edged image.

Fig. 6. Results obtained for the image mdb005: (a) Original image, (b) Its four class image, and (c) Edged image obtained by implementing (2).

Prior to implementing the algorithm (2), an original mammogram image of mdb005 (Suckling et al., 1994) was classified into four classes (Cj) due to Otsu algorithm (Otsu, 1979). The results were shown in Figure 6.

4.1.2 Pectoral muscle identification

As already mentioned, the inclusion of pectoral muscle in mammogram can affect the results of intensity-based image processing methods or bias procedures in the detection of breast cancer. The objective of the pectoral muscle identification is to determine the pectoral muscle for the exclusion from the mammograms prior to process in further steps for breast cancer diagnosis. In this regard, the edge resulting image was used in the segmentation algorithm given as follow:

Algorithm: 1 Pectoral muscle identification

Step 1: Removal of unqualified objects.

1. Implement the formula (2) in a mammogram image P, resulting in the image Q.
2. Filter unqualified objects, objects consisting of contiguous edge less than 2,500 pixels, out of the Q resulting in the image R.

Step 2: Identification of pectoral muscle.

1. FOR i:= 1 TO n DO
   Find the area of $ROI_r(i)$.
   { $ROI_r(i)$ is a region of interest *i* inside the image R. ROI_r at region i is the i-th area surrounded by an edge boundary on image R.}
2. Pectoral muscle segmentation:
   2.1 MUSCLE := NIL {empty set}
   2.2 FOR j:=1 TO n DO
   IF ROI_r (j) > max_size AND ROI_r (j) ≤ min_size
   THEN $ROI_r(j)$:= background
   { Set the $ROI_r(j)$ to background when it is not of interest regions. In practical uses in our implementation, max_size = 95,200 pixles, and min_size = 2,500 pixles.}
   ELSE IF min (y, ROI_r (j)) > min_upper
   THEN $ROI_r(j)$:= background
   { min (y,$ROI_r(j)$) denotes minimal value of y for a coordinate (x,y) of any pixels in the region of $ROI_r(j)$. In our implementation, min_upper = 60.}
   { Regions of interest will locate at min(y, $ROI_r(j)$) in which is at the topmost part of the image R. }
   ELSE IF mean (y, ROI_r (j)) > min_y_average
   THEN $ROI_r(j)$:= background
   { mean (y,$ROI_r(j)$) is an average of y for coordinates (x,y) inside the region of $ROI_r(j)$ In our implementation, min_y_average = 350. }
   ELSE IF mean (I, ROI_r (j)) > min_average_intensity
   THEN MUSCLE := MUSCLE $\cup$ $ROI_r(i)$
   { mean (I, $ROI_r(j)$) is an average intensity of all pixels inside the region of $ROI_r(j)$. In our implementation, min_average_intensity = 157. }

The results in implementing the proposed segmentation algorithm on mdb005 and mdb011 were shown in Fig. 7. Fig. 8 shows hand-drawn pectoral muscle edge by radiologist as applied to mdb005, the result obtained by the proposed algorithm, and the pectoral muscle removal according to the proposed algorithm.

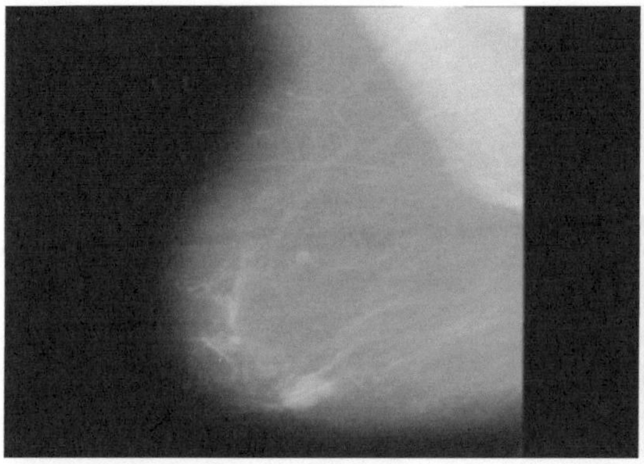

(a) Original image mdb005.

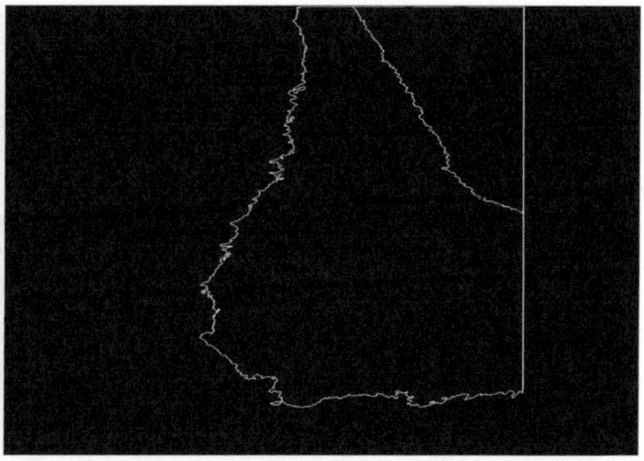

(b) Result obtained by the algorithm 2.

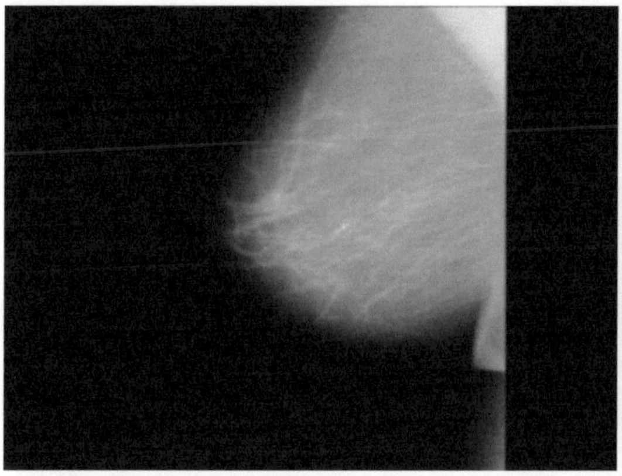

(c) Original image mdb011.

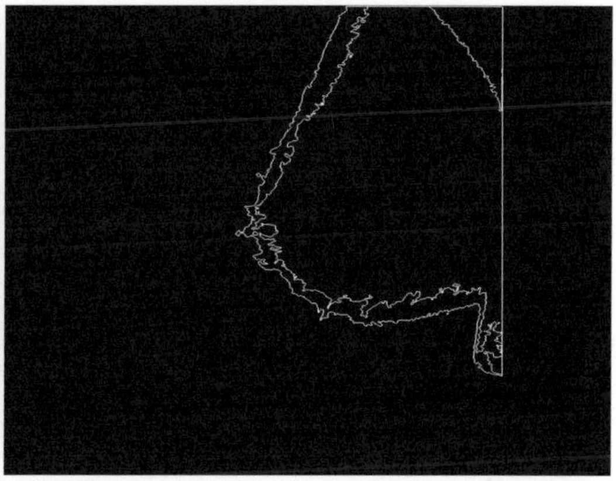

(d) Result obtained by the algorithm 2.

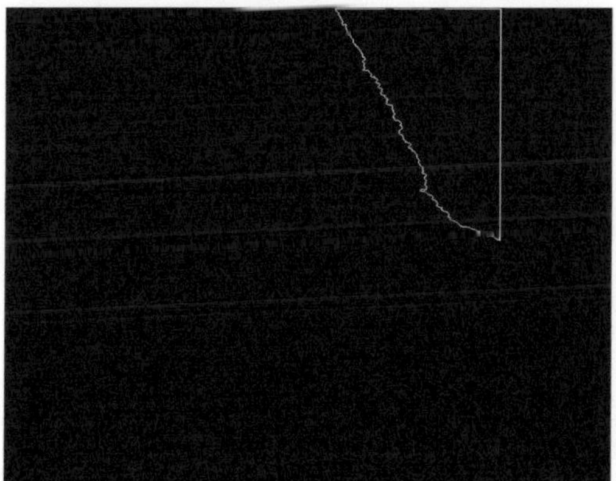

(e) Pectoral muscle identification of mdb005.

(f) Pectoral muscle identification of mdb011.

Fig. 7. Results obtained from proposed algorithm: (a) and (c) are original images mdb005 and mdb011, respectively, (b) and (d) are edge results due to original images (a) and (c), respectively, and (e) and (f) are results obtained from the pectoral muscle identification algorithm due to original images (a) and (c), respectively.

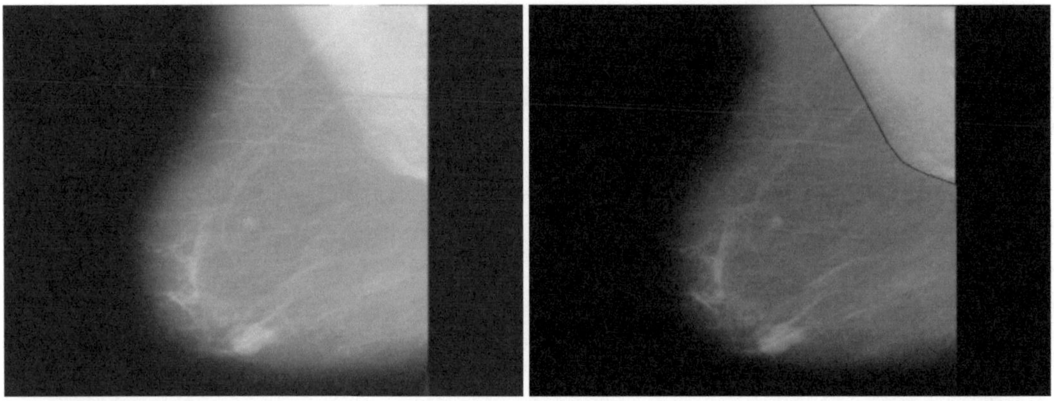

(a) Original image (b) Hand-drawn pectoral muscle edge by radiologist

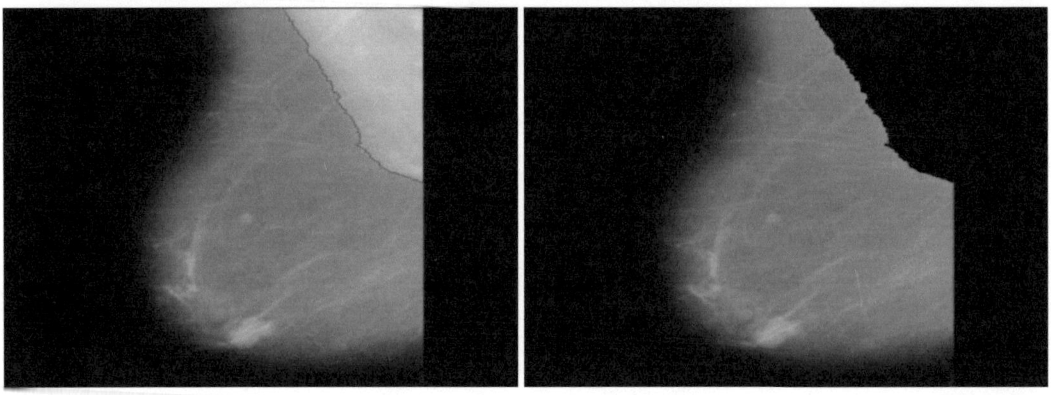

(c) Pectoral muscle edges detected by the algorithm. (d) Pectoral muscle removal using the algorithm.

Fig. 8. Results obtained for the image mdb005: (a) original image, (b) hand-drawn pectoral muscle edge by radiologist superimposed on the original image, (c) pectoral muscle edges detected by the CA-based method superimposed on the original image, and (d) pectoral muscle removal using the CA-based method.

4.2 Performance evaluation and results

For performance evaluation purpose, the total of 84 images, randomly selected from the Mammographic Image Analysis Society, London, U.K. (Suckling et al., 1994), were used in experimentation. The spatial resolution of these images is 200 μm and depth resolution in 8 bit. The images in the database are 1024x1024 pixels in size. The result obtained from the proposed method was evaluated in consultation with radiologists experienced in mammography. Then, the pectoral muscle edges were manually drawn by the author under the supervision of radiologists, without referring to the results of detection by the proposed method. The segmentation results of the proposed method was evaluated based upon the number of false-positive (FP) and false-negative (FN) pixels in the regions demarcated by the manually drawn edges. An FP pixels was defined as a pixel outside the reference region that was included in the pectoral region segmented. An FN pixel was defined as a pixel in the reference region that was not present within the segmented region. Table 1 shows mean and standard deviation values of the FP and FN pixels for the result of the proposed method with 84 images.

CA-based algorithm	Statistics
Analysis of area enclosed	
FP ± σ	1.99±8.19%
FN ± σ	18.89±14.19%
# images with (FP and FN) < 5%	13
# images with 5% <(FP and FN) <10%	15
# images with (FP and FN) > 10%	56

Table 1. Mean and standard deviation values of the FP and FN pixels for the results of CA-based algorithm with 84 images.

Table 1 shows an interesting statistical results that the identification obtained by the CA-based algorithm provides the promising results with minimal FP and FN. In this regard, the proposed CA-based algorithm is one of promising methods in pectoral muscle identification for mammogram processing.

5. Cellular automata for mass segmentation in mammograms

This section investigates algorithms on the basis of cellular automata model for coping with the segmentation of hypothesized masses in mammograms. The 256-states cellular automata algorithms were developed to deal with 256 grayscale mammogram images for determining masses. The proposed cellular automata algorithms investigated here are on the basis of two dimensional CAs (IxI, V, N, f) with V = {0, 1, 2, …, 255}, Von Neumann's neighborhood N, while the local transition function f is from Vn into V. The results will be used for determining mass features in breast cancer diagnosis. An empirical experimentation shows that the proposed cellular automata algorithms provide the superior results.
The proposed segmentation algorithm utilizes a concept of two-types bacteria propagation. The first type confiscates a mass seed, which is an object image, while the second one confiscates the background which is declared by a circle surrounding the mass seed. Both types of bacteria propagate to their neighbors in parallel at each time step depending on its and their neighbor's strengths. A circle surrounding a mass seed shown in Fig. 4 (a) represents the background seed being seized by the other type of bacteria. Both types of bacteria continue propagating in parallel in discrete time steps as stated earlier. In order to reduce the computation time, the proposed algorithm can be stopped anytime earlier so far as the propagation of bacteria taken up the mass seed is consistent. The CA-based segmentation algorithm is given as follow:

Algorithm: 2 CA-based algorithm for mass segmentation
// Identify hypothesized mass seed from a mammogram image P; mark the mass seed
// Identify object seed from a mammogram image P; mark the object seed
// For each cell (pixel) in *P*
  for $\forall p \in P$
  // copy previous state
    $l_p^{t+1} = l_p^t$;

$\theta_p^{t+1} = \theta_p^t$;
// neighbors try to attack current cell
for $\forall q \in N(p)$
if $g(||C_p\text{-}C_q||_2).\theta_q^t > \theta_p^t$ then
$l_p^{t+1} = l_q^t$;
$\theta_p^{t+1} = g(||C_p\text{-}C_q||_2).\theta_q^t$
end if
end for
end for

where P denotes an image, p denotes a pixel.
θ_q^t denotes the strength of a cell $q \in Q$ at time t.
θ_p^t denotes the strength of a p's neighboring cells at time t.
l_p^t, l_p^{t+1} denote the centering cell state of p at time t and $t+1$, respectively.
l_q^t, l_q^{t+1} denote the neighboring cell state of q at time t and $t+1$, respectively.
$N(p)$ denotes neighboring cells of p.
$||C_p\text{-}C_q||_2$ denotes the Euclidian distance between a cell q and a neighboring cell p.
$g(x)$ represents a monotonous decreasing function defined by (2) as following

$$g(x) = 1 - \frac{x}{\max\|C\|_2} \tag{5}$$

In implementing the algorithm 2, the termination condition was satisfied if the configuration of mass seed has not been changed, meaning that their states were steady. This abundantly reduces time complexity in practical implementation. Figure 9 shows the results of implementing the proposed mass segmentation algorithm on the mammogram mdb028. The hypothesized mass seeds, depicted by red shadow, and background seeds, depicted by blue circle, are represented two types of bacteria as shown in In Fig. 8 (a) and (b), respectively. Fig. 8 (c) and (d) show a series of propagating results on the 40 evolution steps and the final result at iteration 72. Fig. 10 shows the results of mass segmentation of mdb005 and mdb092 superimposed on the original mammograms, respectively.

6. Conclusions and discussions

The behavior of cellular automata is fascinating not only from theory but also from applications. They offer the beauty and elegance of results in medical image processing as reported in literature. In this work we have presented a number of uniform cellular automata algorithms for mammogram image processing. Based on empirical experimentation, the proposed algorithms give the promising results when tested on MIAS mammograms. This quite encourages in determining other tasks for the research. In this regard, we have more investigations on applications for mammogram and other medical image processing and hope report in the near future.

7. Acknowledgement

We deeply thank to The Thailand Research Funds (TRF) for financial support of the research project due to RMU5080010.

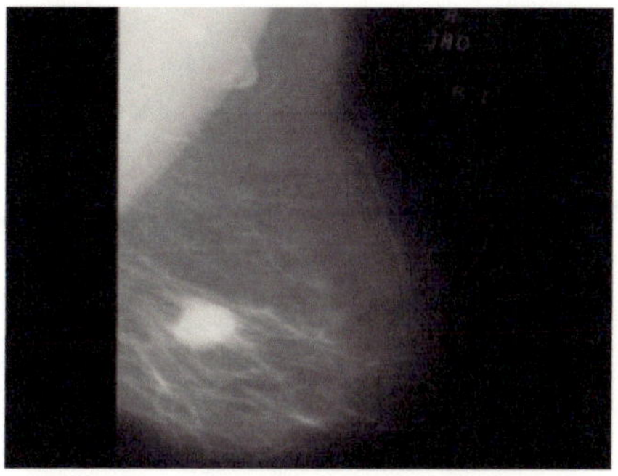

(a) Original image mdb028.

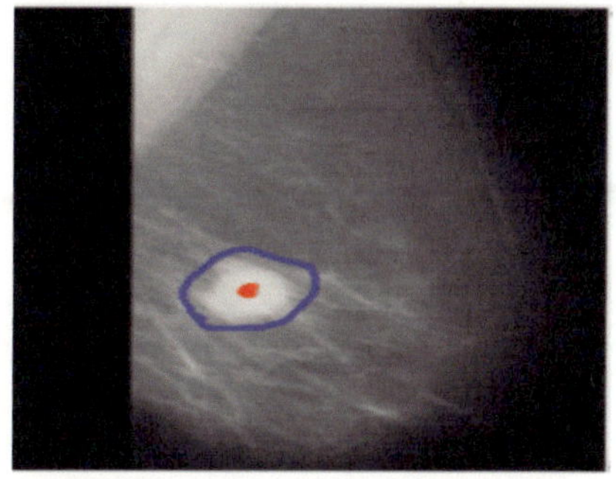

(b) Seeds of object and background.

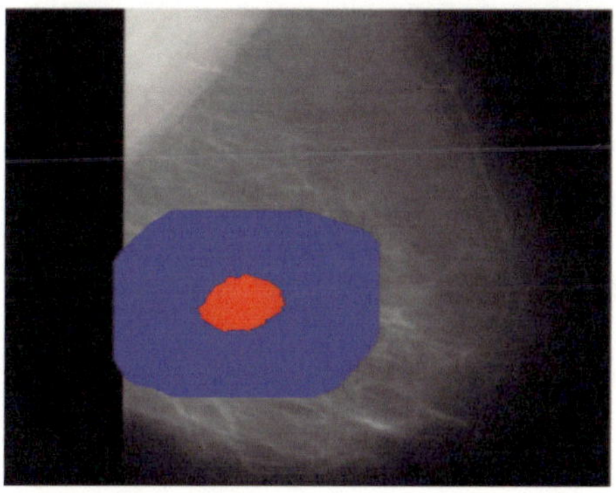

(c) Evolution result at 40 time steps

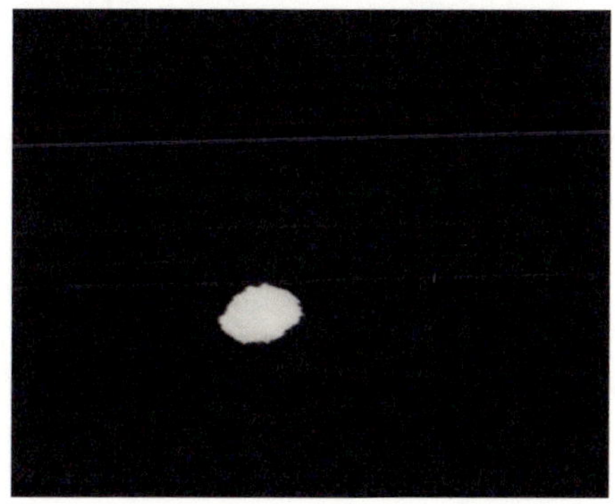

(d) Result at final time steps (72)

Fig. 9. Mass segmentation results obtained from the image mdb028: (a) original image, (b) initial seeds, (c) result after 40 time steps of evolution, and (d) final result at iteration 72.

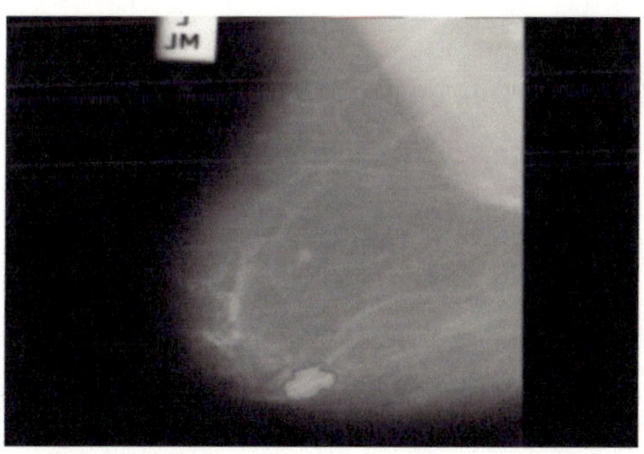

(a) Mass segmentation result of mdb005.

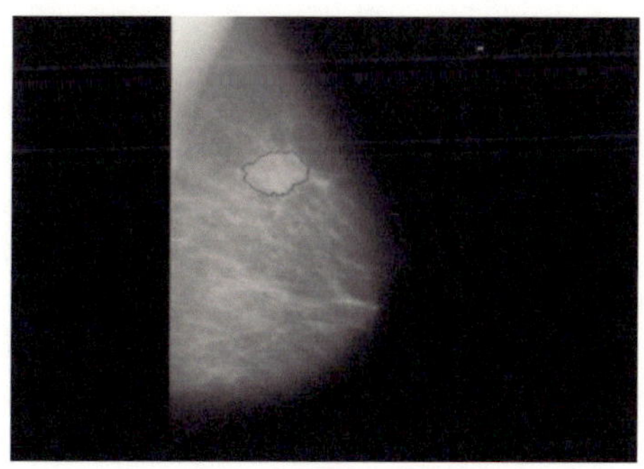

(b) Mass segmentation result of mdb092.

Fig. 10. Mass segmentation obtained from the image mdb005 and mdb092: (a) mass segmentation result of mdb005 superimposed on the original mammogram, and (b) mass segmentation result of mdb092 superimposed on the original mammogram.

8. References

Hernandez, G. & Herrmann, J. (1996). Cellular Automata for Elementary Image Enhancement. *Graphical Models and Image Processing (GMIP),* Vol. 4, No. 58, pp. 82-89.

Wongthanavasu, S. & Lursinsap, C. (2004). A 3-D CA-based Edge Operator for 3-D Images, *Proceedings of ICIP 2004 11th International Conference on Image Processing,* pp. 235-238, ISBN 0-7803-8555-1, Singapore, October 24-27, 2004.

Rosin, P. (2006). Training Cellular Automata for Image Processing. *IEEE Transactions on Image Processing,* Vol. 15, No. 7, pp. 2076-2087.

Cheng, H. D., Shi, X.J., Min, R., Hu, L.M., Cai, X.P. & Du, H.N. (2006). Approaches for Automated Dectection and Classification of Masses in Mammograms. *Pattern Recognition,* Vol. 39, pp. 646-668.

Viher, B., Dobnikar, A. & Zazula, D. (1998). Cellular Automata and Follicle Recognition Problem and Possibilities of Using Cellular Automata for Image Recognition Purposes. *International Journal of Medical Informatics, Vol. 49, pp. 231-241.*

Ferrari, R.J., Rangayyan, R.M., Desautels, J.E., Borges, R.A. & Frere, A.F. (2004). Automatic Identification of the Pectoral Muscle in Mammograms. *IEEE Transactions on Medical Imaging,* Vol. 23, No. 2, pp. 232-245.

Otsu, N. (1979). A Threshold Selection Method from Gray-level Histograms. *IEEE Transactions on Systems Man Cybernetics,* Vol. 9, No. 1, pp. 62-66.

Suckling, J., Parker, J., Dance, D., Astley, S., Hutt, I, Boggis, C., Ricketts, I., Stamatakis, E., Cerneaz, N., Kok, S., Taylor, P., Betal, D. & Savage, J. (1994). The mammographic images analysis society digital mammogram database, Exerpta Medica. *International Congress Series 1069,* pp. 375-378

Ma, F., Slavotinek, J. & Bottema, M.J. (2007). Two graph theory based methods for identifying the pectoral muscle in mammograms. *Pattern Recognition,* Vol. 40, pp. 2598-2598

Wongthanavasu, S. & Tangvoraphongchai, V. (2007). CA-based Algorithms and Its Application in Medical Image Processing. *Proceedings of ICIP 2007 14th International Conference on Image Processing,* pp. III-41-44, ISBN: 1-4244-1437-7, ISSN: 1522-4880, San Antonio, Texas, U.S.A. September 16-19, 2007.

Wongthanavasu, S. & Tangvoraphongchai, V. (2008). Cellular Automata-based Identification of The Pectoral Muscle in Mammograms. *Proceedings of ISBME 2008 3rd International Symposium on Biomedical Engineering,* pp. 294-298, November 10-11, 2008, Bangkok, Thailand, November 10-11, 2008.

Chen, R.J. & Lai, L.L. (2007). Image security system using recursive cellular automata substitution. *Pattern Recognition,* Vol. 40, No. 5, May 2007, pp. 1621-1631

Chen, R.J. & Horng, S.J. (2010). Novel SCAN-CA-based image security system using SCAN and 2-D von Neumann cellular automata. *Signal Processing: Image Communication,* Vol. 25, Issue 6, July 2010, pp. 413-426

Reynaga, R. & Amthauer, E. (2003). Two-dimensional cellular automata of radius one for density classification task, *Pattern Recognition Letters,* Vol. 24, Issue 15, November 2003, pp. 2849-2856

Mitchell, M., Crutchfield, J.P & Hraber, P.T. (1994). Evolving cellular automata to perform computations: mechanisms and impediments. *Physica D: Nonlinear Phenomena,* Vol. 75, Issues 1-3, 1 August 1994, *pp.* 361-391

Wongthanavasu, S. & Sadananda, R. (2003). A CA-based edge operator and its performance evaluation. *Journal of Visual Communication and Image Representation,* Vol. 14, Issue 2, June 2003, pp. 83-96

Rogowska, J. (1999). Overview and Fundamentals of Medical Image Segmentation. *Handbook of Medical Image Processing and Analysis (Second Edition),* pp. 73-90

Hecker, C., Roytenberg, D., Sack, J.R. & Wang, Z. (1999). System development for parallel cellular automata and its applications. *Future Generation Computer Systems,* Vol. 16, Issues 2-3, December 1999, pp. 235-247

Karafyllidis, I. (1999). Acceleration of cellular automata algorithms using genetic algorithms. *Advances in Engineering Software,* Vol. 30, Issue 6, June 1999, pp. 419-437

Sarkar, C. & Abbasi, S.A. (2006). Cellular automata-based forecasting of the impact of accidental fire and toxic dispersion in process industries. *Journal of Hazardous Materials,* Vol. 137, Issue 1, 1 September 2006, pp. 8-30

Xiao, X., Wang, P. & Chou, K.-C. (2008). Predicting protein structural classes with pseudo amino acid composition: An approach using geometric moments of cellular automaton image. *Journal of Theoretical Biology,* Vol. 254, Issue 3, 7 October 2008, pp. 691-696

Eslami, Z., Razzaghi, S.H. & Ahmadabadi, J.Z. (2010). Secret image sharing based on cellular automata and steganography. *Pattern Recognition,* Vol. 43, Issue 1, January 2010, *pp.* 397-404

Tzionas, P., Thanailakis, A. & Tsalides, P. (1997). An efficient algorithm for the largest empty figure problem based on a 2D cellular automaton architecture. *Image and Vision Computing,* Vol. 15, Issue 1, January 1997, pp. 35-45

Umeo, H. (2001). Linear-time recognition of connectivity of binary images on 1-bit inter-cell communication cellular automaton. *Parallel Computing,* Vol. 27, Issue 5, April 2001, pp. 587-599

Bandini, S., Mauri, G. & Serra, R. (2001). Cellular automata: From a theoretical parallel computational model to its application to complex systems. *Parallel Computing,* Vol. 27, Issue 5, April 2001, pp. 539-553

Chen, J.-C., Yeh, C. M. & Tzeng, J.-E. (2008). Pattern differentiation of glandular cancerous cells and normal cells with cellular automata and evolutionary learning. *Expert Systems with Applications,* Vol. 34, Issue 1, January 2008, pp. 337-346

Mizas, C., Sirakoulis, G.C., Mardiris, V., Karafyllidis, I., Glykos, N. & , Sandaltzopoulos R. (2008). Reconstruction of DNA sequences using genetic algorithms and cellular automata: Towards mutation prediction?. *Biosystems,* Vol. 92, Issue 1, April 2008, pp. 61-68

Richards, F.C., Meyer, T.P. & Packard, N.H. (1990). Extracting cellular automaton rules directly from experimental data. Physica D: Nonlinear Phenomena, Vol. 45, Issues 1-3, 2 September 1990, pp. 189-202

Raghavan, R. (1993). Cellular automata in pattern recognition. *Information Sciences,* Vol. 70, Issues 1-2, May 1993, pp. 145-177

Langton, C.G. (1986). Studying artificial life with cellular automata. *Physica D,* Vol. 22, pp. 120-140

Langton, C.G. (1992). Life at the edge of chaos. *Artificial life, Vol. 2, No. 4, pp* 41-91

Pesavento, U. (1995). An implementation of von Neumann's self-reproducing machine. *Artificial Life,* Vol. 2, No. 4, pp. 337-354

Rietman, E. (1993). *Creating Artificial Life : Self-organizatin.* Pensylvania : Windcrest/McGraw-Hill.

20

Accelerating 3D Cellular Automata Computation with GP-GPU in the Context of Integrative Biology

Jonathan Caux[1,2,3,4], Pridi Siregar[4] and David Hill[1,2,3]
[1]*Clermont Université, Université Blaise Pascal, LIMOS, BP-10448, F-63000 Clermont-Ferrand*
[2]*CNRS, UMR 6158, LIMOS, ISIMA, Campus des Cézeaux, BP-10125, F-63173 Aubière*
[3]*ISIMA, Computer Science & Modelling Institute,BP10125, F-63177*
[4]*Integrative Biocomputing, Nouvelles Structures - Place du Granier, 35135 Chantepie*
France

1. Introduction

Integrative biology has a large number of solutions available to simulate multi-scale models: Reaction-Diffusion Equations (Lu et al., 2001), Dissipative particle dynamics (Pivkin et al., 2009) or Finite element method (Sander et al., 2009). But cellular automata can also be used (von Neumann, 1966), this has been shown for instance to simulate a part of an organ behavior (Alarcón et al., 2004) or the depolarization and repolarization of the heart muscle cells which can be seen as an excitable medium (Siregar et al., 1998). In this chapter, we consider 3D cellular automata, consisting in a cube of cells where each cell can be in a specific state. A finite number of states are considered and a cell state evolves over time according to its current state, but also according to the states of the other cells in a defined neighborhood. When we simulate the evolution of an automaton, the future state of each cell is computed simultaneously according to the state of the cube cells at the current simulation time. With basic rules, it is possible to create a simplified model for natural behavior. The most common example is the Game of Life (Gardner, 1970). This model, created in 1970 by John Conway, allows simulating bacteria reproduction on a 2D toric space. In this model, a cell can only have two states: dead or alive, and evolves according to the number of cells alive in the contacting neighborhood (named Moore's neighborhood). But cellular automata can't be reduced to Conway's Game of Life; the interested reader can consult (Wolfram, 2002). For instance, electronic circuits can be simulated with the WireWorld cellular automata (Dewdney, 1990), and in biology, excitable medium, among others models, can also be simulated with cellular automata (Ermentrout & Edelstein-Keshet, 1993).

Even if cellular automata are mostly very simple, large 3D models with an important number of iterations require a very long computing time. Moreover, in integrative biology, computation of cellular automata is often only a part of a more complex problem. Working on larger cubes can therefore improve the result sensitivity, and performing this result faster can speed up the global process.

Our idea was to test cellular automaton implementation on GP-GPU (General Purpose Graphic Processing Unit)[1] (Luebke et al., 2004). This kind of processing unit was first designed to process graphics on a computer, but while the classical CPU computation performances evolution recently began to slow down, the GP-GPU continued to provide very significant speed-up. Ten years ago, developers of high performance computing applications started to port scientific software from CPU to GP-GPU to make the most of it (Trendall & Stewart, 2000). After the initial success, GPU manufacturers started to work on friendlier API for general purpose computation and we are now able to develop directly in languages which are close variants of the C language[2][3]. In the same way, other hardware accelerators like FPGA have been considered to speed up cellular automata computations (Woundeberg, 2006).

The main difficulty lies in the memory manipulation since GP-GPU have various levels of memory with different performances. The GP-GPU global memory which can be accessed by any thread at any time has very important access latency. The shared memory available for each streaming multiprocessor inside a GP-GPU does not have such latency, but this memory is only shared by threads running on the same multiprocessor. In addition, the number of concurrent threads in a streaming multiprocessor is limited. Moreover, memory transfer between the host computer and the GP-GPU device can severely imapir the global speed-up if the computation time is not significant enough in comparison with the data transfer time.

In this chapter, we propose two cellular automata implementations on GP-GPU with different memory usage (Part 3). To understand the benefits of GP-GPU, we compare the results obtained with an Nvidia Tesla C1060 board to a sequential implementation on 2 kinds of CPU (Xeon Core 2 and Nehalem) (Part 4).

2. Accelerate cellular automata computation

2.1 3D Cellular automata

A simple heart model can be created using a cellular automaton. After selecting an appropriate neighborhood (a Moore cubic-shaped neighborhood with a range of one for example), we can simulate the propagation of an electric stimulation with 3 states:

A cell is in an "activated" state over a predefined time interval. In this state, this cell stimulates its neighborhood cells which are in an "inactive" state. This state corresponds to cell depolarization.

A cell is in a "refractory" state for a certain predefined time. It can't be stimulated by an "activated" cell. This state corresponds to cell repolarization.

The rest of the time, a cell is in an "inactive" state.

But this heart model is far from perfect. A critical point is that the number of cells used will directly affect the model accuracy. If the whole heart is represented by a 10^3 cells cube, the accuracy will be low compared to the use of a cube with 100^3 cells. To compare both

---

[1]Four-Dimensional Cellular Automata Acceleration Using GPGPU: http://eric_rollins.home.mindspring.com/gpgpu/index.html. Accession date: 20/01/2010.

[2]What is CUDA ? - Official CUDA web site: http://www.nvidia.co.uk/object/cuda_what_is_uk.html. Accession date: 20/01/2010.

[3]OpenCL Overview - Official OpenCL web site from Khronos : http://www.khronos.org/opencl/. Accession date: 20/01/2010.

possibilities, a ventricle will be represented by a cube of 3^3 cells in the first case whereas in the second case we can use 30^3 cells (27 cells compared to 27000). In the second case the finer grain-size of the 3D ventricle model will lead to a better approximation a real one. Getting a better accuracy cannot be reached only by a growth in cube size. Each time each dimension grows by a factor of 10, the total number of cells grows by a factor of 1000 (1000 cells compared to 1.000.000 cells in the second case with a 100^3 cube). Having more cells implies more computations and this significantly slows down the simulation performances. In addition, even if we assume that a 100^3 cells cube is a good size to represent a heart and that we have enough computing power, it may be interesting to take into account other features in order to have a more realistic model. However, these improvements will increase the computation load. For example, the state corresponding to the cell repolarization ("refractory") can be subdivided into two parts: a first one called the "absolute refractory state", where the cell can't be reactivated by an incoming impulse and a second, called the "relative refractory state" where it can. This small modification will only slightly increase computing load but more complex modifications will likely have wider impact on computing time.
One way or another, if the modeling technique retained is based on cellular automata, increasing the computation speed could be a good way to improve the model representation without damaging the global simulation speed and therefore achieve better accuracy.

2.2 GP-GPU utilization

In order to accelerate the computing time of 3D cellular automata simulation, we have tried a parallelization using a GP-GPU (General Purpose Graphical Processing Unit). GP-GPU is particularly powerful when used to process the same instruction set on an important number of independent data. This approach can be useful for cellular automata evolution if we consider the splitting of the cellular space in sub-cubes. However, neighborhood interactions are going to be a weighty problem for the program. To compute an iteration on a sub-cube, we need a fast access to cells' neighborhood, otherwise the new state of border cells can't be computed. In the next figure, the dark grey sub-cube will need the current state of every black cells present in other sub-cubes to compute the next state (a non-toric cube representation with a Moore cubic-shaped neighborhood with a range of one is used in this figure).

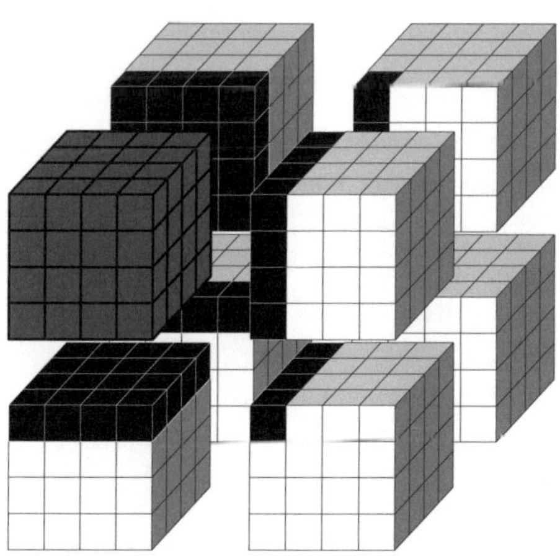

Fig. 1. Example of Moore cubic-shaped neighborhood in red with a range of one.

2.3 Problems induced by the current GP-GPU architectures

To correctly understand the consequences while programming with GP-GPU, it is important to realize that GP-GPU design is quite different from current CPU architectures. While a CPU possesses few cores, each of them allowing the execution of one thread at a time, a GP-GPU possesses a small number of streaming multiprocessors, each of them allowing the parallel execution of numerous instructions in a SIMD approach (Single Instruction Multiple Data). For instance an Nvidia Tesla 10 (see Figure 2), will have 240 vector cores split in 30 streaming multiprocessors (SM) with 8 thread processors (SP Thread Processors) each[4]. Each streaming multiprocessors can run a full warp of 32 threads with the same control flow for different data in two GPU cycle (each SP compute 2 identical operations per GPU cycle because the SM cycle is twice as fast); and since a SM can schedule up to 32 warp at a time, it leads to potentially 1024 threads running concurrently on each of the thirty streaming multiprocessor (potentially 32768 threads running concurrently on the entire card).

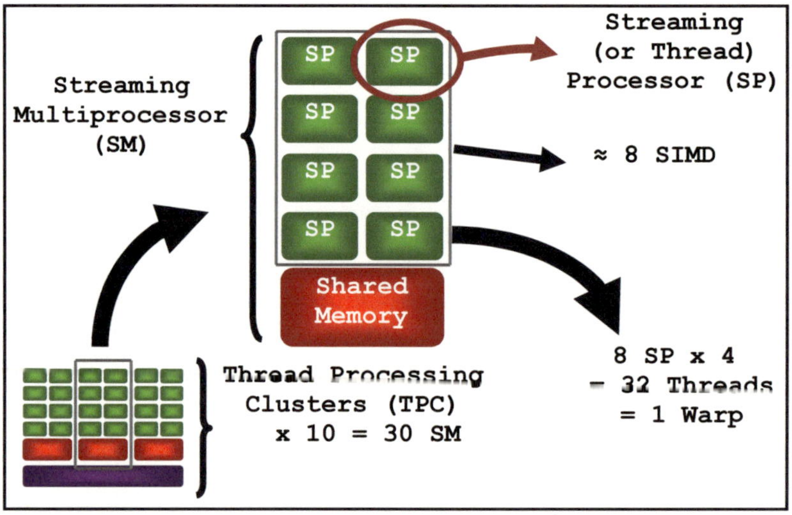

Fig. 2. Simplified architecture of an Nvidia Tesla 10.

With CUDA, all the threads needed to execute a kernel must be grouped in blocks and all these blocks must have the same, limited number of threads. All the threads of a block are executed simultaneously on the same multiprocessors and therefore can make use of its shared memory. To get the best results from GP-GPUs, we have to place data in shared memory. This memory is fast and managed by a streaming multiprocessor. The latency for accessing global memory is very high and we have to limit its access. Thus, dependant threads needing fast communications have to use the shared memory within the same streaming multiprocessor (SM).

When mapping cellular automata to a GP-GPU architecture we will not be able to place all the threads on a single SM, and consequently we will have to communicate using more

[4]CUDA Programming Guide v2.3 - NVIDIA_CUDA_Programming_Guide_2.3.pdf: http://developer.download.nvidia.com/compute/cuda/2_3/toolkit/docs/NVIDIA_CUDA_Programming_Guide_2.3.pdf. Accession date: 20/01/2010.

global memory accesses, implying a significant loss in performance. The difficulty lies in successfully managing memory copy from global to shared memory. Another important consideration is the memory transfer between the host and the GP-GPU which can be very significant if the following ratio: computation duration divided by the transfer duration, is too small.

3. GP-GPU Implementation

3.1 First implementation

The first implementation we tested doesn't use shared memory. Its goal is to use the GP-GPU computation capability to see if we can already obtain a speed-up of the global computation with a basic approach.

To utilize this GP-GPU computation capacity, an elementary thread is used to compute the new state of each cell. The algorithm is then kept simple and an excerpt of the code is presented below.

```
On CPU:
  // Initialize the cell grid.
  int    * matrice, * matriceGPU;

  initGrid( &matrice, size);
  cudaMalloc( ( void ** ) &matriceGPU,
              size * sizeof( int ) );

  // Copy the cell grid from the CPU to the GPU.
  cudaMemcpy(
              matriceGPU,
              matrice,
              size * sizeof( int ),
              cudaMemcpyHostToDevice
            );

  // For each iteration needed:
  for ( i = 0; i < nbIte; ++i )
     // Run the GPU kernel to compute iteration with
     // one thread for each cell.
     nextGeneration<<< nbBlock, nbThread >>>( … );

  //Copy back the cell grid.
  cudaMemcpy(
              matrice,
              matriceGPU,
              size * sizeof( int ),
              cudaMemcpyHostToDevice
            );

On GPU kernel:
  // Compute the global thread index.
  threadIdx = threadIdx.x + blockIdx.x * blockDim.x;

  // Compute the new state of the cell corresponding
  // at this index in function of its neighborhood states.
  […]
```

Code 1. Partial code of the basic algorithm.

In this version, we first copy the cell cube on the GP-GPU. Then, we run the kernel using a thread for each cube cell. Each thread can compute the new state of the cell it handles depending on the neighborhood state. Consequently, at the end of the last thread execution, all the cells are updated for an iteration. When all the iterations have been computed, we transfer the resulting cube back onto the CPU.
This very simple algorithm has two major limiting operations. The first one is the copy of the initial cube from the CPU to the GP-GPU and the resulting cube from GPU to CPU. The second limit of this basic algorithm is almost masked in the previous code: it deals with memory access to the cells and their neighborhood.
For the first point, copying time costs will be very difficult to improve. A solution could be to take advantage of asynchronous memory transfer by dividing computation in multiple parts for example. But this solution would significantly affect the algorithm simplicity and reusability, and moreover it will not allow a significant global speed-up in most cases, particularly when we have a large number of iterations to compute. Furthermore, the greater the number of iterations, the less the copy time costs will be significant in comparison with the computing cost for all iterations.
The second point is related to global memory access. When we perform the Game of Life in three dimensions, it is necessary to know the neighborhood of each cell. This leads to a maximum of 27 cell states if we consider the current cell state. In this first version, all memory access is done in global memory with a very high access latency (between 400 and 600 clock cycles on a Tesla T10 for instance).
If we consider the handling of processing 2 cells at a time, we can notice that 2 neighboring cells share 18 cells in their common neighborhood. Thus we can obtain all their neighborhood with only 36 global memory access instead of 54. And results are even better if we increase the block size to small cubes: a 3^3 cube (27 cells) will need only 125 global memory access (the block including neighboring cells is a 5^3 cube) instead of accessing 729 cells if we consider the handling on a single cell basis (27 x 27). The following implementation tries to take advantage of this possibility.

3.2 Second implementation

To limit at minimum the global memory access, the code hereafter makes use of shared memory between threads of a same CUDA software block. Since the size of a software block is limited, it is impossible to share all the cell information between all the threads needed to handle a large cube. Each software block works on a part of the cube and each thread inside this block works on the generation of the new state of a single cell. Before computing an iteration, data required for a CUDA software block must be loaded from global memory into shared memory. This is done in every software block. When the uploading is done, a synchronization of all the threads of a same block is necessary to ensure that all the data is correctly uploaded in shared memory. After this synchronization, the computing of the new state can be done in function of neighborhood states read in shared memory instead of global memory. The new state obtained for the local cube is written in global memory otherwise it would be lost after the end of the block computation.
In this solution, the aim is the reduction of the global memory access but nothing has been done for the memory transfer between CPU and GP-GPU.
With this approach we still have global memory access to load the shared memory and to update the global memory after an iteration. Even if there is a reduction in terms of global memory access, this approach results in an increase in the total number of memory access

(global and shared) but most of them are shared memory with a final increase in performance.

```
On CPU:
    [...]
    int  neighborSize = [...];
    int  sharedSize   = ( size / nbThread + neighborSize ) *
                        sizeof ( int );
    [...]
    // Run the GPU kernel to compute iteration with
    // one thread for each cell.
    nextGeneration<<< nbBlock, nbThread, sharedSize >>>(...);
    [...]

On GPU kernel:
    // Upload from global memory to shared memory
    int   sharedMatrice[];
    sharedMatrice[ threadIdx.x ]   =   matriceGPU[ ... ];

    __syncthreads();

    // Compute the new state of the cell corresponding at
    // this index in function of its neighborhood states
    // present in shared memory.
    [...]
```

Code 2. Pseudo-code of the shared algorithm.

To maximize the number of cells shared in a same block, the largest block possible has been used. Each block contains 512 threads, allowing the processing of an 8^3 size cube. To limit each thread access to the global memory, the state of each cube cell is loaded in shared memory. This choice implies that all threads handling the cells at the border of the 8^3 cube are not used to compute the next state. To obtain the next iteration state, only the threads processing the inner cube of 6^3 cells are considered.

4. Results

The two algorithms previously presented have been tested on personal computers, the main one using two Intel Nehalem CPUs (at 2.53 GHz) with an NVidia Tesla C1060 board. To compare the benefits of hybrid computing, the CPU only algorithm computes for each cell the new state with a single core (a Core 2 Xeon and a Nehalem Xeon have been considered).

4.1 Memory transfer costs

Figure 3 confirms what has been said previously when explaining the basic algorithm: transfer costs between CPU and GPU are not significant anymore when we compute many iterations. In fact, for a constant cube size, the global simulation duration should be linear with the number of iterations; to this global computing time we naturally add two memory transfer costs for copying the initial cube from the CPU memory to the GPU global memory and for copying back the final result. In Figure 3, with a small 10^3 cube, the impact of this transfer time is important if we have a small number of iterations and becomes insignificant after 400 iterations.

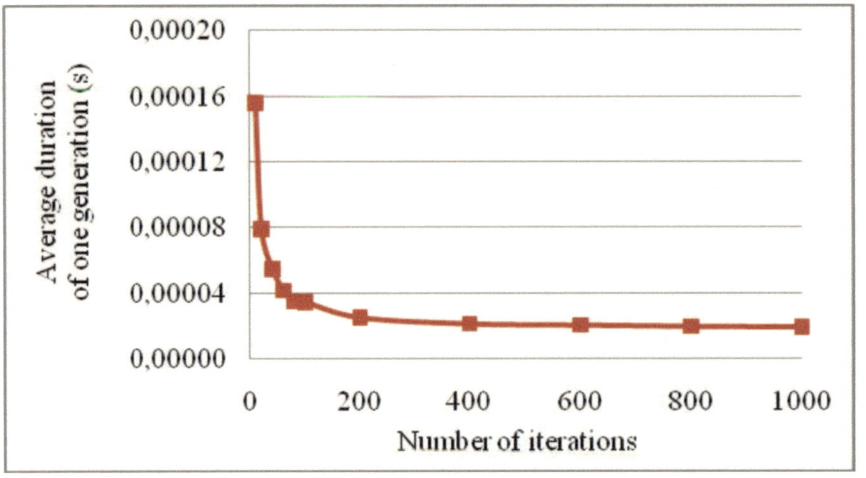

Fig. 3. Average duration (in seconds) of one generation for a cube with 10^3 cells.

The next figure shows the obvious importance of the cube size. For big cubes the transfer time measured became rapidly insignificant even with a small number of iterations. Now that the memory transfer problem has been analyzed, it is possible to start comparing CPU and GPU results.

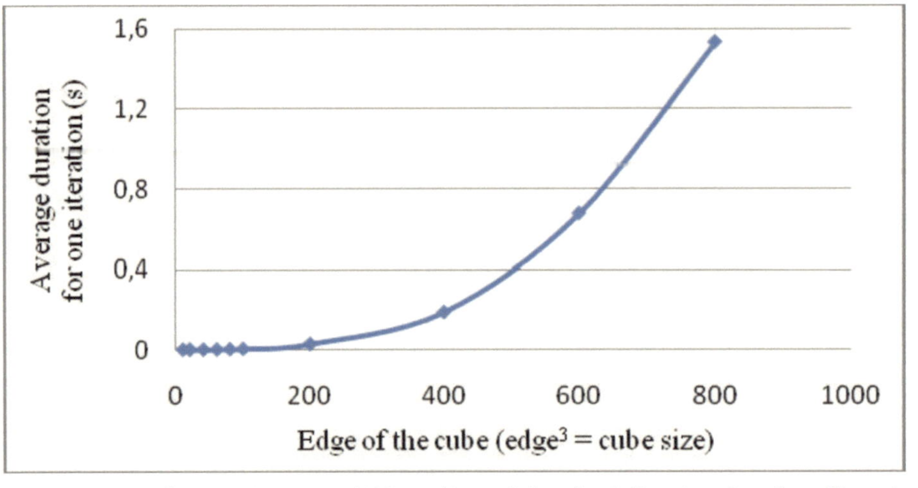

Fig. 4. Average time for one iteration (100 replicates) for the following 3 tasks: allocation of 2 cubes (cube size), copy of a cube from CPU to GPU and copy of the final resulting cube (from GPU to CPU)

4.2 Basic GPU implementation results

The first results deal with the basic implementation which uses only global memory.
Figure 5 shows a comparison between the pure CPU algorithm (Core2 Q9300 at 2.5GHz) and its hybrid implementation with a GP-GPU for a 20^3 cube (Tesla T10 - C1060). We see that the best results are obtained when a significant number of iterations. The performance improvement stops after reaching a threshold.

In Figure 5, we see that the sequential implementation using the CPU is always slower for a 20^3 cube when compared to the GP-GPU implementation.

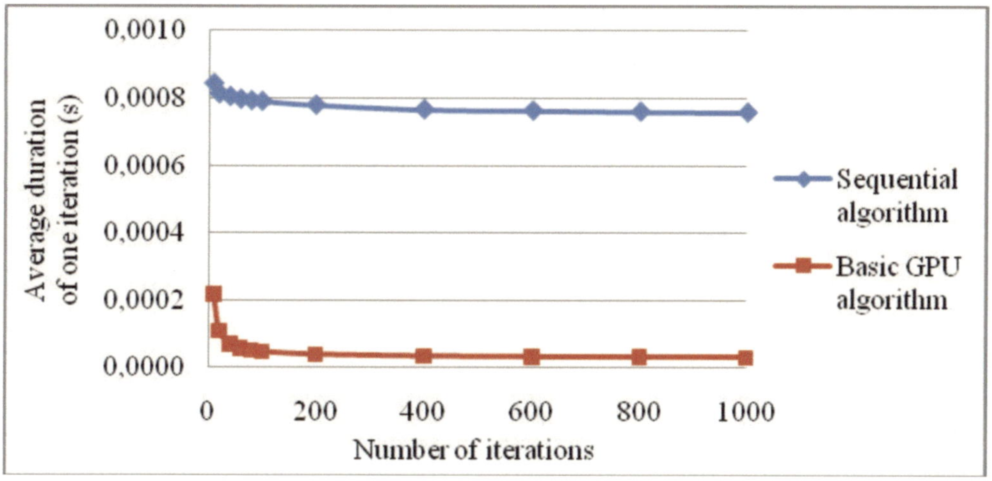

Fig. 5. Average duration of an iteration depending on the number of iterations for a 20^3 cube.

In Figure 6, we notice that when using a GP-GPU, the computing time of an iteration grows slowly with the cube size, whereas the computing time for an iteration according to the cube size shows a polynomial growth if we use the sequential CPU algorithm.

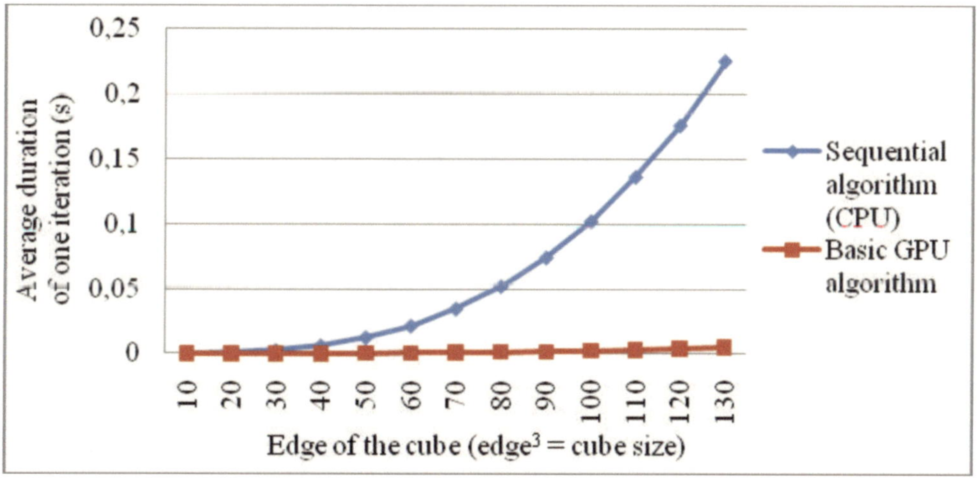

Fig. 6. Average duration of one generation for 1000 iterations depending on the cube size.

Figure 7 presents the speed-up for different cube size depending on the number of iterations. For each cube size we have an upper limit; we also note that the speed-up first increases with cube size and stays approximately at the same level when the cube size reaches 80^3 and over.

This last point can be seen more clearly on Figure 8 which represents the speed-up for 1000 iterations depending on the cube size.

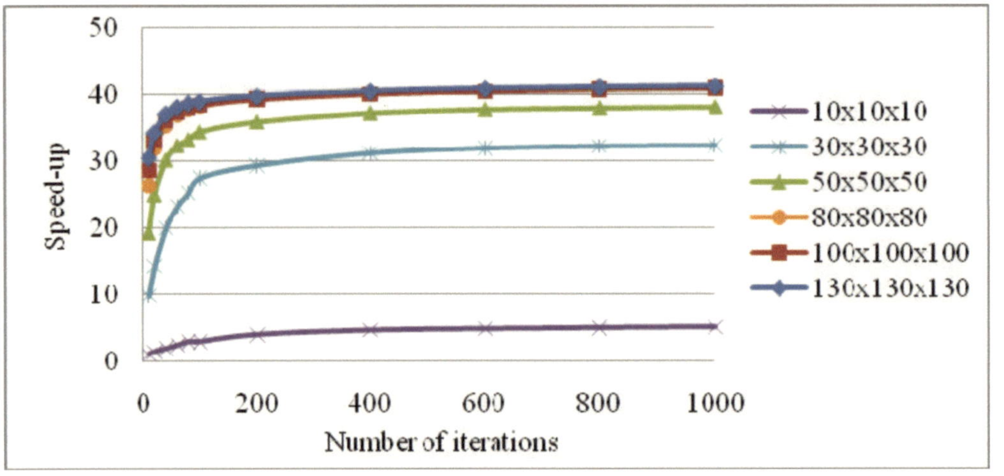

Fig. 7. Basic GPU implementation speed-up compared to a sequential CPU implementation for different cube sizes depending on the number of iteration.

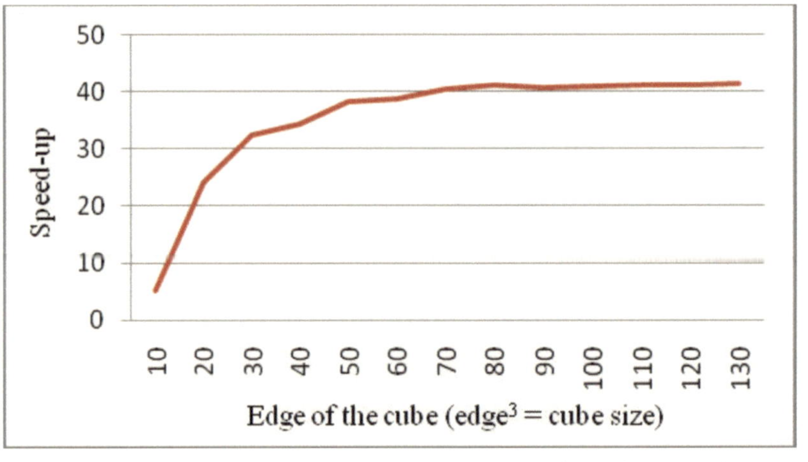

Fig. 8. Speed-up evolution for 1000 iterations depending on the cube sizes (50 measures for each point).

Now that the speed-up trend has been identified, we can discuss speed-up results. If we ignore cube sizes smaller than 80^3, the average speed-up for 1000 iterations is 41x when compared to a single Q9300.

4.3 GPU implementation with shared memory results

The next implementation takes advantage of shared memory between threads of the same streaming multiprocessor to minimize global memory access.

Figure 9 shows the performance increase compared to the first implementation (using a 100^3 cube). It confirms that the two trends are really similar and also that the shared memory algorithm is better than the previous one.

Figure 10 compares the speed-up for 1000 iterations with both implementations. Speed-ups are very similar for small cubes but as expected the shared memory algorithm has better

speed-up for larger cubes (reaching 60x compared to 40x). With this algorithm the upper limit is reached later than with the previous algorithm (see Figure 11).
These results can be generalized for larger cubes. Figure 12 shows speed-up evolution for 1000 iterations comparing the CPU algorithm for two different processors: the previous Core2 Q9300 but also a Nehalem 5500. The first point we can notice is that the speed-up did not slow-down with the increase in cube size (the 800^3 cube size limit will be discussed in conclusion). The second point is that speed-up obtained with the GPU is far better when we compare it with a Q9300 Xeon processor (average speed-up of 62.8x) than in comparison with a Nehalem 5500 processor (average speed-up of 20.5x). This difference shows an impressive advance in CPU performances, at almost the same frequency, particularly if we consider that the Xeon Q9300 was still considered as a very good Intel processor at the beginning of year 2009.

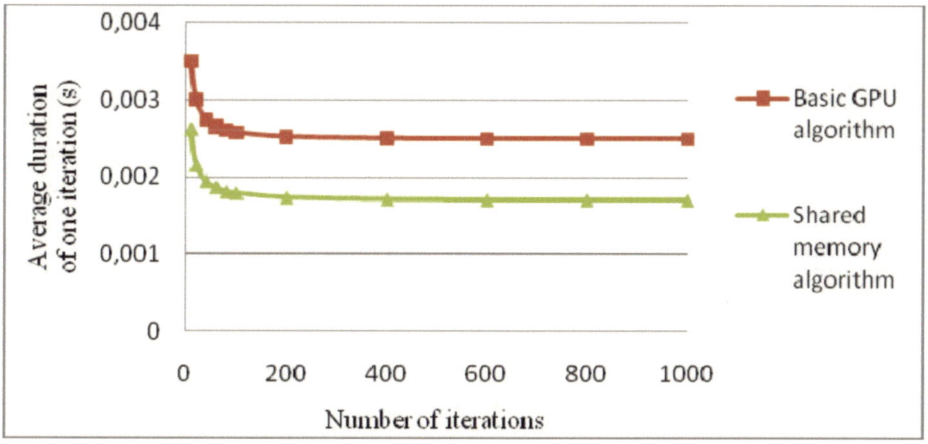

Fig. 9. Average duration of an iteration depending on the number of iterations for a 100^3 cube (50 replicates).

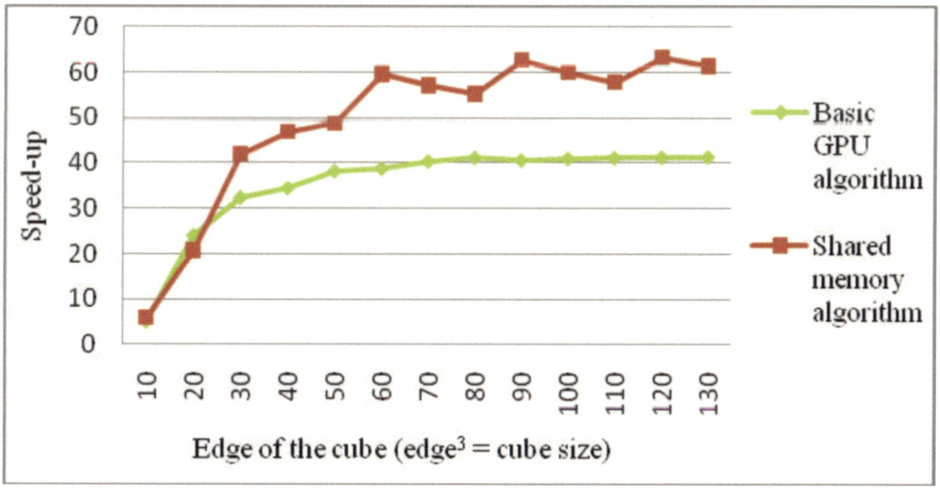

Fig. 10. Comparison of speed-up evolution for 1000 iterations depending on the cube sizes (50 measures for each point).

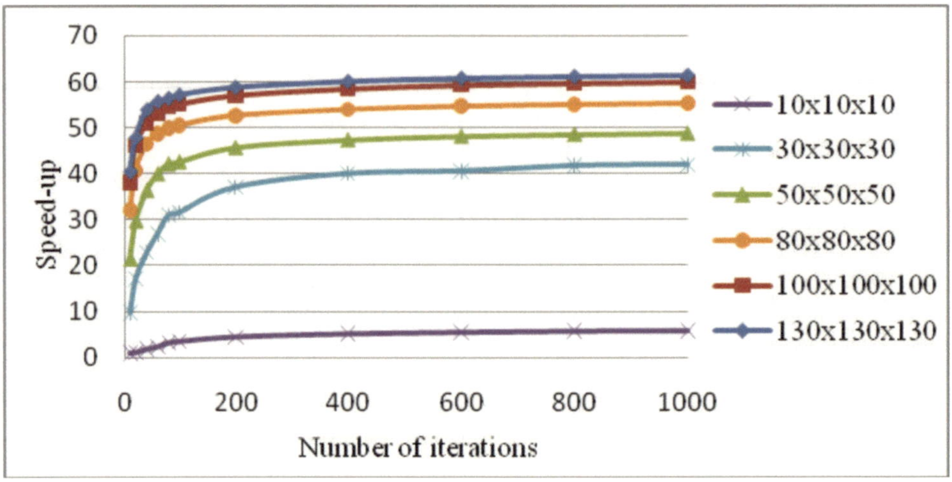

Fig. 11. Shared memory GPU implementation speed-up for different cube sizes depending on the number of iterations.

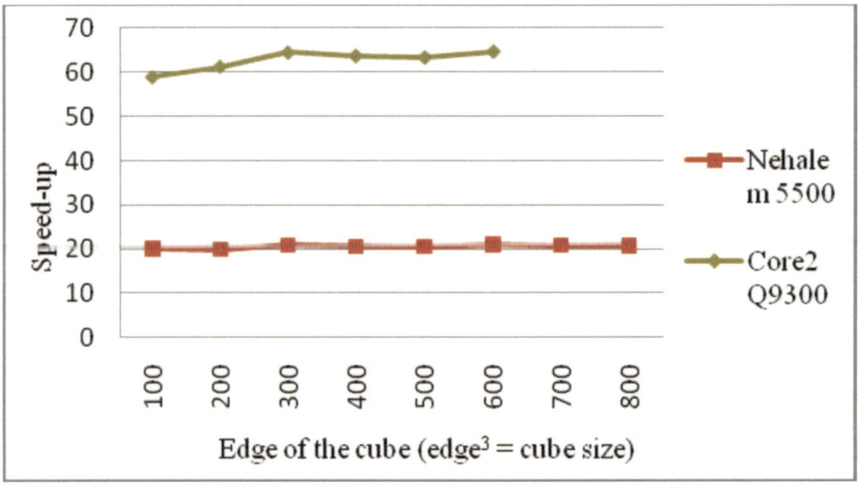

Fig. 12. Speed-up evolution on large cube for 1000 iterations depending on the cube sizes.

5. Future research

In the case of 3D cellular automata, whatever the implementation, basic or more sophisticated, the use of hybrid computing shows interesting speed up. But improving this solution is still possible. Here are some possibilities which it could be interesting to explore.

First, it is possible to have all the threads of a block to work on computing the next status of a cell. Currently, all the threads corresponding to the block border are only used to transfer neighborhood status from global to shared memory. To make them work, it is necessary to make them load multiple cell status from global to shared memory. This solution, which has not been tested yet, does not give any guarantee of speed-up and it probably needs to be tested on different automata configurations.

It would also be interesting to see if using another block size can improve the performance. At the moment a block of 512 threads is used to represent 8^3 cubes. But it could be interesting to test blocks of 256 threads to represent 6^3 cubes.

The second implementation was proposed to improve the memory access of the first version (which used only global memory). The fastest implementation uses mainly shared memory but it still needs to transfer data from the global memory to the shared memory and we think that this transfer could be done faster. In my implementation, each block of threads corresponds to a block of the cube cells. In the example of Figure 13, the 125 threads of a block access 125 cube cells in global memory (the part framed in orange). When each thread accesses the state of a cell, it's clear that the global memory index will not be continuously accessed and with the CUDA architecture, we know that memory access can be done more efficiently by reading continuous data.

A solution could be to reorganize the cube data to allow continuous global memory access for all the threads in a same block. This better memory access, implies that more computation would have to be done on each thread to compute the correct index in the cube but it would be interesting to see if it improves the performance. However this kind of dedicated implementation becomes quite obfuscated and difficult to maintain.

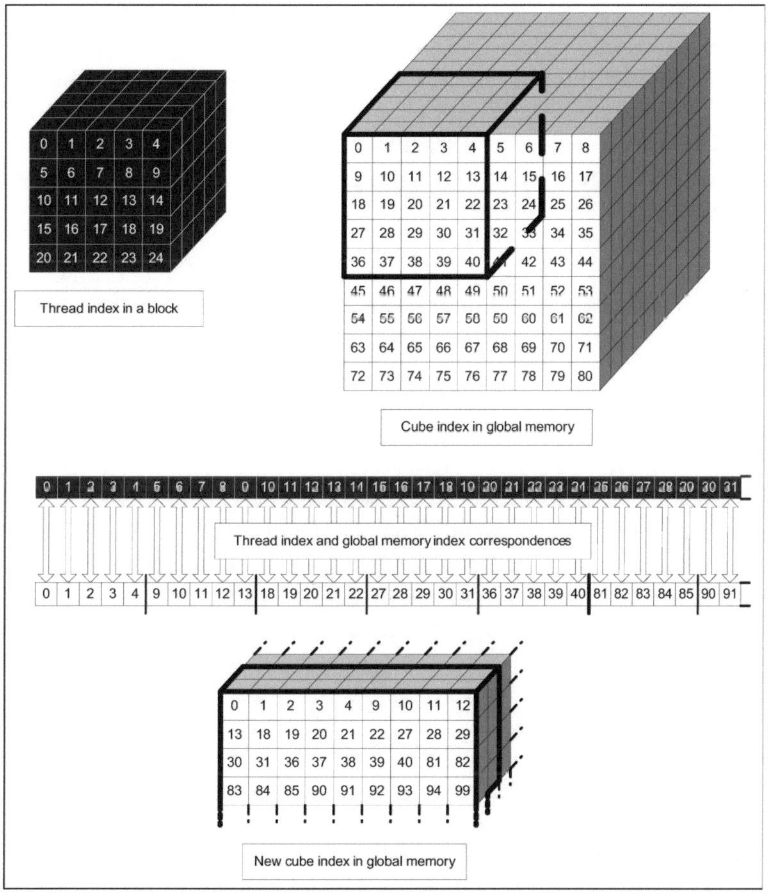

Fig. 13. Improvement of data storage to increase global memory access.

Another solution to improve the results could be to create specific generation algorithm for each cellular automata algorithm by taking advantage of their particularities. For example, in the case of excitable medium, there are generally some important cube parts where no activity is present. It could be possible to locate these parts and therefore avoid doing any computation because these parts won't evolve. But there is an important problem with this solution. It's logically the development cost. If many cellular automata algorithms are used, developing for each one a specific generation algorithm which takes advantage of its particularities could be an enormous task. And even if the number of cellular automata algorithms is limited, specific processing must be fast enough avoid imparing the global computation time. In the previous example, if searching for a large empty cube part takes a longer time than computing a new generation on this part, performance increase can't be guaranteed.

6. Conclusion

We have implemented two cellular automata algorithms on a Tesla C1060 board. The basic principle is the same for both algorithms, a GPU thread is used to compute the new state of a cell. But to compute a new cell state, a thread has to read the states of the 27 neighbouring cells (if we consider a classic Moore neighborhood extended to a 3D automaton). The total number of memory accesses can incur a significant access time when relying on the GP-GPU global memory. A second implementation has been created to minimize the number of global memory accesses by using the fast shared memory present on a GP-GPU streaming multiprocessor. The states of all the cells needed by all the threads running on a same multiprocessor are transferred only once from global memory to shared memory. This is sufficient to compute a significant set of cells in parallel with efficient shared memory accesses.

We have tested both approaches and the results show that we have an interesting speed-up for any cube size when enough iterations are computed. On small cubes, when a little number of iterations is considered, the transfer costs between the host and the GPU make the whole process significantly slower. When large cubes are considered (100^3 and above), the average speed-up for the first implementation compared to a sequential algorithm running on a Xeon Core 2 CPU at 2.5 GHz is around 41x (13x when compared to a Nehalem Xeon at 2.53 GHz). If shared memory is used (second implementation), the speed-up grows to 65x when compared to a Xeon Core 2 CPU (and 20x a Nehalem Xeon).

The results observed show that even with the best CPUs such as Intel Nehalem, we obtain significant speed-ups. However, we have to consider the following limiting points. First, the CPU algorithm used for comparison with the GP-GPU algorithm is a sequential one. Now, most of the computers have multiple cores and taking the best of all of them will significantly increase the regular host performance. This point is not so important in integrative biology because cellular automata are only a part of the whole computation and the computation power of host cores will be used for other computations which have lower speed-ups while computing on the GP-GPU.

The second point is the cube size. We have to take into account the current memory limit for Tesla GP-GPUs (4 GB). To compute a new iteration on a GP-GPU, we use two cubes, one handling the cells current statuses and the other to write the new statuses. A Tesla C1060 has 4GB of global memory, hence the size of the cube can't be too important. Two cubes with 900^3 cells can't be processed on this kind of GPU because it would need more than

5.8GB if 4 bytes are used to store a cell status (1000^3 can be considered if we store cell states on a single byte).

The next GP-GPU architecture (Fermi T20) is very promising, it improves significantly memory access performances with a configurable cache and ECC memory, and it will also be able to address up to 1TB of memory. With this kind of architecture, a cube with 5000^3 cells could be handled on a single GP-GPU board, enabling a fine multi-scale modeling for simulated organs. Grids and clusters of GP-GPUs will soon be considered to simulate interactions between organs (Fan et al., 2004).

7. References

Lu, S.; Michailova, A. P.; Sauverman, J. J.; Cheng, Y., Yu, Z.; Kaiser, T. H.; Li, W. W.; Bank, R. I.; Holst, M. J.; McCammon, J. A.; Hayashi, T.; Hoshijima, M.; Arzberger, P. & McCulloch, A. D. (2009). *Multiscale Modeling in Rodent Ventricular Myocytes*. IEEE Engineering in Medicine and Biology Magazine. March-April 2009; Volume 28 - Number 2; pp. 46-57.

Pivkin, I. V.; Richardson, P. D. & Karniadakis, G. E. (2009). *Effect of Red Blood Cells on Platelet Aggregation*. IEEE Engineering in Medicine and Biology Magazine. March-April 2009; Volume 28 - Number 2; pp. 32-37.

Sander, E. A.; Strylianopoulos, T.; Tranquillo R. T. & Barocas V. H. (2009). *Image-Bases Biomechanics of Collagen-Based Tissus Equivalents*. IEEE Engineering in Medicine and Biology Magazine. May-June 2009; Volume 28 - Number 3; pp. 10-18.

Von Neumann, J. & Burks, A. W. (1966). *The Theory of Self-reproducing Automata*. Univ. of Illinois Press, Urbana, Illinois.

Alarcón, T.; Byrne; H. M. & Maini, P. K. (2004). *Towards whole-organ modelling of tumour growth*. Progress in Biophysics and Molecular Biology 2004, 85; pp. 451-472.

Siregar, P.; Sinteff, J. P.; Julen, N. & Le Beux, P. (1998). *An Interactive 3D Anisotropic Cellular Automata Model of the Heart*. Computers and Biomedical Research, Volume 31, Issue 5, October 1998; pp. 323-347.

Martin Gardner, (October 1970), "Mathematical Games: The fantastic combinations of John Conway's new solitaire game "Life"", Scientific American 223: pp. 120–123.

Wolfram Stephen, A new kind of Science, Wolfram Media, Inc, ISBN 1-57955-008-8, 2002.

A. K. Dewdney. The cellular automata programs that create wireworld, rugworld and other diversions, Computer Recreations, *Scientific American*, Jan: pp. 146-149. 1990.

Ermentrout, G. B. & Edelstein-Keshet, L. (1993). *Cellular automata approaches to biological modelling*. Journal of Theoretival Biology 160, pp. 97–133.

Luebke, D. L.; Harris M.; Krüger J.; Purcell T.; Govindaraju N.; Buck I.; Wooley C. & Lefohn A. *GPGPU : General purpose computation on graphics hardware*. (2004). In SIGGRAPH'04, Proceedings of the SIGRAPH 2004 conference, course notes, New York, NY, USA, ACM Press (2004); p. 33.

Trendall, C. & Stewart A. J. (2000). *General calculations using graphics hardware with application to interactive caustics*. In Rendering Techniques '00 (Proc. Eurographics Rendering Workshop), pp. 287-298. Springer, June 2000.

Woundeberg M. *Using FPGAs to Speed Up Cellular Automata Computations*. (2006). Master's thesis, University of Amsterdam.

Fan, Z.; Qiu, F.; Kaufman, A. & Yoakum-Stover, S. *GPU cluster for high performance computing*. (2004). In SC '04: Proceedings of the 2004 ACM/IEEE conference on Supercomputing, page 47, Washington, DC, USA, 2004. IEEE Computer Society.